D1014722

PSYCHOLOGICAL FOUNDATIONS OF EDUCATION

Harper's Series on Teaching

Harper's Series on Teaching
Under the Editorship of
Ernest E. Bayles

PSYCHOLOGICAL FOUNDATIONS OF EDUCATION

An Introduction to Human Development and Learning

MORRIS L. BIGGE

MAURICE P. HUNT

Fresno State College

HARPER & BROTHERS, PUBLISHERS, NEW YORK

PSYCHOLOGICAL FOUNDATIONS OF EDUCATION

Copyright © 1962 by Morris L. Bigge and Maurice P. Hunt

Printed in the United States of America

*Preliminary version of manuscript published in mimeograph form,
copyright © 1958 by Morris L. Bigge and Maurice P. Hunt*

All rights reserved.
*No part of this book may be used or repro-
duced in any manner whatsoever without
written permission except in the case of
brief quotations embodied in critical articles
and reviews. For information address
Harper & Brothers,
49 East 33rd Street, New York 16, N.Y.*

D-M

Library of Congress catalog card number: 62–10080

CONTENTS

PART III. HOW DO HUMAN BEINGS LEARN?

EDITOR'S FOREWORD

For a quarter-century, and more, there has been a growing need for a textbook in educational psychology, field-theoretical in orientation and definitely focused upon matters essential to teaching. Whether personally inclined toward field theory or not, it seems that any and every professional worker in education, and interested laymen as well, should be highly conversant with the basic tenets of field (or configurational) theory as it relates to human behavior. Otherwise, what justification have they for holding an opinion either for or against it? And, without a well-grounded opinion on this matter, how can they be considered professionally competent or, if laymen, what reasonable basis have they for judging professional competency?

This is a book written by authors who not only demonstrate their knowledge of psychology but who also speak with authority on teaching theory. In fact, one of them is coauthor of a highly respected text in that field.[1] In consequence, while dealing with all conventional topics in educational psychology, this book is centrally focused upon the nature of learning and its meaning for teaching. Moreover, although the authors openly acknowledge their avowal of a broadly configurational point of view, they present throughout a clear, fair, and perceptive treatment of major alternative views, particularly the most active one—psychological connectionism and its modernizations.

The style is lucid, lively, and literary. It is reflectively exploratory and explanatory. It is not polemical; alternative views are presented, together with cogent data and discussions of what those data seem logically to imply. The authors are open and aboveboard on what they recommend, but they are always careful to show the bases for their recommendations and the consequences that they entail. This is an important and needed contribution to the literature on educational psychology.

ERNEST E. BAYLES

[1] Hunt and Metcalf, *Teaching High School Social Studies*, Harper, 1955.

PREFACE

This book is designed for use as a basic text in courses in educational psychology, development and learning, or, as now often entitled, psychological foundations of education. Because of its rather extensive treatment of learning theory, it might also have a place in introductory courses which focus on that aspect of psychology. Instructors of courses in introductory general psychology, especially those who wish to acquaint their students with a systematic development of field psychology, will also find the book useful, at least as a supplementary text.

In a teaching field which already seems crowded with textbooks, the authors of any new entry in the field are obligated to explain how their book makes an original contribution. This volume breaks with tradition in several ways.

First, unlike most books in educational psychology, it is noneclectic in its over-all point of view. The authors feel that the outlook in psychology which they have labeled "cognitive-field" has more to offer teachers than any other outlook. Consequently, they continually point out what the cognitive-field frame of reference means for teaching. However, they stress comparison, and in so doing devote considerable space to the nature and implications of other positions—including several which have been prominent in the historical past and still influence educational practice. They treat with particular detail associationist psychologies; as a case in point, an entire chapter is devoted to the position of B. F. Skinner, which is one of the strongest psychological bases for the development of "teaching machines."

Cognitive-field psychology is systematic, not eclectic. Through use of its constructs, it benefits from the research and thinking which has been conducted under various psychological banners, but applies the results within a cognitive-field frame of reference. Contributions from various lines of study are not arranged as a patchwork or mosaic, but are assimilated into a new system of thinking.

One can argue for or against eclecticism in the field of psychology. At best, eclecticism produces compromises which are not entirely satisfactory to anyone. At worst, it leads to inconsistency and confusion. We are well aware, given the state of the science, that issues in psychology cannot be resolved readily. Nevertheless, in spite of such uncertainty, it seems to the authors usually more productive to work within a systematic position. Systematization in any science usually has led to more discovery than has eclecticism. And we feel that a systematized outlook in psychology provides more effective directives for classroom teachers than any other. The outstanding achievements of Albert Einstein resulted from a systematic approach.

In addition to its noneclectic but comparative treatment, the book contains a great deal more historical analysis than is commonly found in books in psychological foundations. This appears to be the only means by which one can explain and clarify certain points of confusion in contemporary education. The authors have observed classroom practice in a large number of public schools in several states and are convinced that educational practice today is based upon a blend of incompatible psychological assumptions. Only a recounting of how these assumptions arose can reveal why they exist and where they point.

The twentieth century has been called the century of relativism. Certainly, the concepts of relativism have invaded virtually all of the natural and social sciences, as well as literature and the fine arts. So far as the authors have been able to determine, no other available text in educational psychology, development and learning, or psychological foundations of education makes clear what relativism means for psychology. In this book a strong attempt is made to develop a psychology with a consistently relativistic orientation. We hope to dispel some of the confusion that exists concerning the general meaning of relativism.

Although this book is intended for use by college students who may have had no more than one or two courses in general psychology, we have deliberately tried to keep it challenging. We have noted lately that many textbooks have resorted to a kind of "popular-magazine treatment" of their subjects—with a plethora of photographs or drawings and few words of more than two syllables. We think that a typical college student of today does not need to be talked down to. Adult treatment of issues in psychology should appeal not only to undergraduates but to graduate students and practicing teachers as well. We are even presumptuous enough to hope that some professors will find the book stimulating.

The general plan is as follows: After an opening chapter which introduces the field to students, we have included a section (Part I) on the nature of a human being. Although to some degree this section reviews basic facts about the psychological, biological, and sociological nature of man, it is in the main a more advanced treatment than one would find in freshman and sophomore classes in psychology, physiology, and sociology. The first chapter of Part I (Chapter 2 of the text) summarizes several historically prominent theories of man's psychological nature. Ensuing chapters of the section treat man's biological and sociological nature and some questions relating to individual differences.

Part II focuses upon human growth and development. The first chapter of Part II (Chapter 6) provides basic information concerning processes of bodily growth. Chapter 7 presents some contrasting theories concerning psychological development of people. Chapter 8 focuses upon problems of adolescence, treated within a sociopsychological frame of reference. Chapter 9 attempts to cut through the ambiguity surrounding the concepts of needs and developmental tasks and terminates with a definition of needs which harmonizes with a cognitive-field outlook.

Part III discusses learning theory. Chapter 10 sets the historical stage by presenting the theory of mental discipline, Roussellian "natural unfoldment," and pre-nineteenth-century associationism. Chapter 11 presents in broad outline what the authors see as the two major "families" of contemporary learning theory—S-R (stimulus-response) associationism and Gestalt-field psychology. Chapter 12 gives in some detail a specific description of the learning process as offered by each of these two positions. Chapter 13 presents B. F. Skinner's *operant conditioning,* a specific psychology of learning which is a representative specimen of the S-R associationistic family. Chapter 14 presents a relativistic *cognitive-field psychology* as a systematic representative of the Gestalt-field family. Chapters 13 and 14 are quite technical; they should give a reader some taste of carefully stated systematic psychologies of learning. Chapter 15 is a summation of principles of development and learning which are most pertinent to teaching procedures. The problem of transfer of learning is treated in this chapter.

Part IV applies psychological theory to classroom practice. Chapter 16 is an assessment of present-day confusion and inconsistency with respect to the psychological premises of educational practice. The chapter suggests that confusion might be reduced if educators could agree on the primacy of the goal of teaching to all children the "method of intelligence." Chapter 17 offers concrete directives for "understanding-level" teaching and Chapter 18 for "reflection-level" teaching. Chapter 19 shows how recent findings in group dynamics may be brought to bear in a classroom to increase teaching effectiveness. Chapters 17 through 19 are essentially "how-to-do-it" chapters but at no time is practice divorced from theory.

The volume has been thoroughly classroom-tested. It has existed in mimeographed form for several years, and each year students in the authors' classes in development and learning have been asked to write critical reviews. The manuscript figuratively has been "ripped to shreds" by hundreds of students, and many of their suggestions have been incorporated in one way or another.

The authors are indebted to so many people that any attempt to name them all would be futile. They include the authors' own former professors, students—both graduate and undergraduate—and colleagues on the Fresno State College staff who have read parts or all of the manuscript.

We are grateful to Mrs. Mabel Hunt and Mrs. Ada June Bigge for providing the inspiration and cooperation necessary for us to see the manuscript to completion; we are especially indebted to Mrs. Hunt who typed an uncounted number of pages of the manuscript during its early versions and typed the completed manuscript and indexed the volume for publication.

MORRIS L. BIGGE
MAURICE P. HUNT

January, 1962

1
WHAT IS TEACHING?

By posing a provocative question, this introductory chapter is intended to "open up" the field of development and learning. The chapter raises corollary questions such as: If students learn nothing, has teaching occurred? What are some barriers to effective teaching? Is teaching an art or a science? What are some common barriers to good teaching? What role can professional courses in education play in making better teachers?

At first glance, the question posed in the chapter title seems rather silly. It is obvious, many of you can say, what teaching is. Teaching may be poor or good, but nevertheless teaching is—teaching. A teacher selects subject matter to be learned and performs a series of operations whose purpose is to transmit this subject matter to students. These operations include assigning, explaining, requiring various forms of practice, and testing.

Let us go back a moment and re-examine this definition. "Teach" is a transitive verb; to teach someone is to do something to that person. What if a person employed as a teacher goes through the motions we have just described but nothing happens to his students, that is, nothing which is *permanent* or *functional* outside of class? Or suppose students undergo enduring change, but the change which occurs is of an entirely different nature from that intended—something pernicious, perhaps? Then has teaching occurred? Probably most of us would agree that no matter what motions a teacher goes through, teaching does not occur until there are some results to show for it.

1

HOW DO "KEEPING SCHOOL" AND TEACHING DIFFER?

Much of what passes for teaching actually is not. There may be honest disagreement, of course, as to how effective much attempted teaching really is. It is true that most students pass most of their examinations. They do manage to move from grade level to grade level and eventually receive diplomas. In most school subjects most students learn to repeat a considerable amount of information—factual or otherwise. But the question remains—what have they learned which will remain a permanent part of them and be functional in the sense that they will make repeated use of it in situations outside of school? Has enough worth-while learning occurred to warrant the assertion that teachers have taught? Perhaps there is a rather fundamental difference between teaching and merely "keeping school."

How Effective Are Our Schools?

An impressive amount of evidence has accumulated to support the hypothesis that an average student does not learn all that he should in school. There are several ways of getting such evidence. One can test high school seniors to determine what they have acquired during 12 years of schooling in the fundamental skills (language, mathematics), social adjustment, vocational know-how, and civic-social-moral understandings and attitudes. More realistically, one can test persons who received high school diplomas several years before the test to see what they have retained and what they can use in real-life situations. The long-range effect of education is the pay-off; if there is little long-range effect, we may safely assert that schools have failed.

Another way of assessing the impact of schools is to study the mental characteristics of adults generally, all of whom have had at least some schooling. This has been done by a number of sociologists, anthropologists, and psychologists. They have engaged in what we call "studies of culture" or "studies of American civilization." If such studies reveal that an average citizen is ignorant about many important matters, or is confused and inconsistent, then again we may safely assert that schools have not been doing all that we assign them.

The most comprehensive studies of the level of recall, understanding, and ability to transfer learning by high school students were made in the 1930s. If we are to trust the 1960 edition of the *Dictionary of Educational Research*, very few studies of this nature have been made since. The most ambitious of the early studies was the famous Regents' Inquiry of the State of New York. As many as 20,000 students, in New York State and elsewhere, were given a variety of tests in an effort to assess the total impact of school experience. Perhaps the most significant report to emerge from this massive piece of research discusses the effectiveness of the social studies in producing better citizens.[1]

The Regents' Inquiry revealed, among other things, a very high rate of forgetting. Students who took a course in United States history or civics in the eighth grade forgot most of the subject content by the time they entered the eleventh grade, when they commonly repeat the subject. Students possessed very little accurate information—but a considerable amount of wrong information—about current affairs. They revealed appalling ignorance about their home communities. They performed very badly on tests of map reading, chart reading, and finding sources of information.

Change of attitude is a more important outcome of education than the mere acquisition of information. The Regents' Inquiry did reveal that, during four years of high school, students move somewhat in the direction of what might be termed a "liberal, democratic outlook." However, most students tested indicated that they were unwilling to make any kind of personal sacrifice to promote democratic aims and group welfare.

A comprehensive survey of educational testing done during the 1930s is contained in a volume edited by J. Paul Leonard and Alvin C. Eurich.[2] One of the more significant chapters of this book is written by Lavone Hanna and entitled "Development of Social Attitudes by Conventional Education." Hanna cites a number of studies which reveal that schooling at that time had little or no effect on basic social-civic-moral attitudes of students. One researcher, J. Wayne Wrightstone, concluded that social studies courses have so slight an impact on students that they could be eliminated from the curriculum with little or no change in educational outcome.

The findings of the Regents' Inquiry in the field of English are reported in a book by Dora V. Smith. Composition tests revealed scant relation between fluency of expression and ability to use correct English. Other tests showed that high school students are relatively unfamiliar with books written in the twentieth century. For example, from a list of 40 titles of twentieth-century books considered to be good reading for teen-agers, the average high school senior recognized about 6 titles.[3]

The most recent comprehensive study of the learning achievements of high school youth was conducted by a Purdue research staff headed by H. H. Remmers. This study was directed primarily at revealing attitudes.

[1] Howard E. Wilson, *Education for Citizenship*, McGraw-Hill, 1938.

[2] J. Paul Leonard and Alvin C. Eurich, eds., *An Evaluation of Modern Education*, Appleton-Century, 1942.

[3] Dora V. Smith, *Evaluating Instruction in Secondary School English*, National Council of Teachers of English, 1941.

In Remmers' opinion, the most glaring blind spot in the thinking of teen-age youth is in the general area of citizenship. A substantial proportion of his sample appeared to hold beliefs much more appropriate to a police state than to a democracy: 41 percent disagreed with the idea of freedom of the press; 13 percent believed that religious belief and worship should be restricted by law; 13 percent questioned the value of freedom of speech; 34 percent felt that the government should prohibit some people from making public speeches; 26 percent believed that police should be allowed to search a person or his home without a warrant; 15 percent would refuse some criminals the right to have a lawyer; 17 percent said that it is proper for the police to jail people without naming the charges against them.

In numerous other social-civic beliefs high school students in Remmers' sample disagreed with expert opinion. For example, 41 percent felt congressmen are not influenced by letters and telegrams from the public; 41 percent thought that communism and fascism are basically the same; 76 percent felt that the most serious danger to democracy in America comes from communists. A substantial majority of boys think no more women should be permitted in public office.

Perhaps the most significant conclusion which Remmers' data warrant is that there is a great amount of confusion and inconsistency in the thinking of high school students. Individual students frequently contradicted themselves; they demonstrated an incongruous mixture of liberal and conservative beliefs, and, in the case of a minority, a mixture of beliefs compatible with both fascism and communism. Furthermore, in most cases gains in the direction of accuracy, liberalism, and consistency were not conspicuous between the freshman and senior years; in some instances there was actual retrogression. Remmers concludes that ". . . taking a high school civics course apparently produces no significant effects on a student's political discrimination or attitudes. Where any differences appear between those who have taken this course and those who have not, they seem to be in the opposite direction from what we might expect."[4]

As suggested on page 2, another means of evaluating what the schools achieve is to examine the attitudes, values, beliefs, and knowledge of adults, virtually all of whom have had some schooling, and many of whom have completed high school. Hanna, drawing upon studies made by social scientists through the 1930s, concludes that ". . . large numbers of American citizens have neither the understanding, the skill, nor the value pattern necessary for mature participation in a democratic society."[5]

Had the situation improved 20 years later? One of the most careful

[4] H. H. Remmers and D. H. Radler, *The American Teenager*, Bobbs-Merrill, 1957, p. 193.
[5] Leonard and Eurich, *op. cit.*, p. 71.

pieces of public opinion research of the 1950s leads us to wonder just what gains were made. The study was conceived by Elmo Roper and conducted under the auspices of the Fund for the Republic. The field work was done by the American Institute of Public Opinion and the National Opinion Research Center in the summer of 1954. Depth interviewing techniques were employed with a sample of over 6000 adults of both sexes.[6] The main object of the study was to determine how Americans felt about the communist threat, about the threat to civil liberties posed by ardent anti-communists, and about nonconformists in general.

The study revealed that fewer than 1 percent of American adults have any particular concern about either the communist threat or the threat to civil liberties. What people worry about most are personal and family problems—usually problems of a "bread-and-butter" nature. Although apathy was one of the chief traits revealed, it was fairly well matched by ignorance. One-third of the sample could not name a single congressman who had been involved in investigations of communism, in spite of the fact that the late Senator Joseph McCarthy's name had been regularly headlined in the press. As Stouffer points out, George Gallup has found repeatedly that in presidential elections only about half the voters can name either vice-presidential candidate, and that 1 in 10 does not know who is running for president.

The Fund for the Republic study provides more ground for optimism about the effectiveness of education than most of the other studies reported. The more years of education members of the sample had, the better informed and the more tolerant of differences they were. However, the gain in knowledge and tolerance was not sufficiently marked to afford proof as to the actual effectiveness of schools; other factors besides formal education could account for it.

Even if formal education has been more effective during the past decade or so than formerly, it has evidently not been effective enough. Our schools have done relatively well in teaching technical skills and very well in teaching social adjustment. They have contributed little toward understanding and liberalization of attitudes in the social-civic-moral area, particularly where deep-cutting, controversial matters are concerned. We must do much better in the decades ahead.

Can Schools Be Made More Effective?

As we shall see later, the general ineffectiveness of formal education may have a number of causes. Certainly we cannot place all the blame on teachers, school administrators, and school boards. At best, our educa-

[6] For a report of the study, see Samuel A. Stouffer, *Communism, Conformity, and Civil Liberties,* Doubleday, 1955.

tional problems are complex and knotty and will require time to solve. But solve them we must, at least to some degree. The United States— indeed, much of the Western world—is engaged in a competition of deadly earnestness. The question is probably not so much whether the United States and its allies will secure a dominant place for themselves in the world, but whether civilized society or even man himself will survive. The human race faces unprecedented threats. It becomes increasingly clear that life is a race with catastrophe. We do not wish to be melodramatic; we are saying no more than what our most sober and respected social observers have been repeating ever since the beginning of the atomic age.

There may be a variety of approaches to reducing the threats before us. Formal education may be only one of several approaches. Nevertheless, it seems significant to us that our leading competitor, the U.S.S.R., regards the education of its people as its mightiest weapon, to the degree, in fact, that during the 1950s the U.S.S.R. spent twice as large a proportion of its national income on education as did the United States. And irrespective of the variety and comparative effectiveness of the various instruments by which we can serve our national self-interest, as teachers we can do nothing but assume that education is an important instrument and de- serves the fullest possible use. It follows logically that we do not serve our interest by employing man power and natural resources in an enter- prise as vast as our educational system unless we demand and get the maximum return. As a nation we cannot afford to continue indefinitely into the future with a school system which in some areas achieves results as meager as ours now appear to be.

Obviously we need to explore carefully a number of questions related to the one posed in the chapter title. How can we change what we are now doing so that what goes on in a typical classroom will be teaching— genuinely effective teaching? Before we can answer this question, we must answer several others: What kinds of persons shall we select to be our teachers? How shall we educate them? What kinds of classroom situations shall we provide to insure that they do their job properly?

ARE TEACHERS BORN OR MADE?

As all of us look back over our own experiences with teachers, we recall that some teachers were much more effective than others. Some were stimulating—they made us think; they motivated us to productive work. Others were dull—in their classes we achieved only enough to get by and forgot most of that before the next school year began. It seems obvious that a trait essential to teaching is the capacity to arouse students—to involve and excite them, to get thinking going and keep it going. Is this particular trait one which some people are born with, or can it be acquired? There is no easy answer to this question.

Some persons while still children begin showing traits that suggest they can become exciting teachers. Their thinking shows an unorthodox, creative streak, and they exhibit unusual intellectual curiosity; they want to learn about all kinds of things and are probing and prying constantly. Such children also tend to be critical in the sense that they take nothing for granted; they always have to know *why*. How do we explain such persons? In one view heredity is the explanation; in another, early environment. There is no way of settling this controversy since everyone's personality is a product of his interacting with an environment, and no one can say that trait A is inherited and trait B is learned. Heredity may contribute importantly to qualities of personality but, if so, this has not so far been conclusively demonstrated by scientific means.

Our answer to the question of whether good teachers are born or made is that we have little evidence that they are born; therefore, they must be made. There are still some significant issues related to this question. To what extent does good teaching hinge on general personality factors? To what extent does it hinge on the background of knowledge a teacher possesses? To what extent does it hinge on an understanding of technique or method, such as might be learned in professional education courses?

To the extent that good teaching depends on personality, it is somewhat doubtful that a college education can be of much help. The fundamental characteristics of a personality in most cases seem to be fairly well established before college age is reached. There are occasional conspicuous exceptions: some college students literally achieve a transformation of personality. In the course of time, as college professors themselves learn to become better teachers, we may expect more of these transformations.

So far as background knowledge is necessary to good teaching, certainly colleges can play an important role in the making of teachers. It is by no means settled, however, just what kind of background knowledge a teacher most needs. The college work of a prospective teacher is split between (1) general education in the arts and sciences, (2) specialized education in those subjects which the student expects to teach, and (3) professional education, i.e., those courses which treat problems of pedagogy—child psychology and development, social foundations of education, learning theory, curriculum, and methods. Although each of the above subject areas can provide useful insights, there is a group among professors of the arts and sciences who feel that professional education, at least as now conceived, is of little value and should be sharply reduced in quantity. They argue in favor of an extensive liberal arts education for teachers, coupled with heavy concentration in the fields of specialization. However, there are telling arguments in favor of professional courses, which we shall explore in the section to follow. Also, general education courses in the arts and sciences, as now conceived and taught, have been shown to have little impact on students. Myron Lieberman, citing studies of Philip E. Jacob and others, concludes that

> . . . the impact of the liberal arts colleges on the values and intellectual habits of their students is negligible. Regardless of curriculum, location, or reputation, the liberal arts college typically does not produce profound changes in its student body. . . . The conclusions of the Jacob study, as well as of practically every other major study which has tried to assess the impact of the liberal arts college, are not new. They have never been a surprise to persons who believe that the educational claims of liberal arts colleges ought to be evaluated just as rigorously as the educational claims made for the public schools.[7]

WHAT IS THE ROLE OF PROFESSIONAL EDUCATION?

We have all heard certain so-called "teachers" described as persons "who know their subject but who can't put it across." Undoubtedly there are many walking encyclopedias who cannot teach. Erudition per se bears no necessary relationship to the ability to stimulate students to want to learn. Nor does erudition necessarily mean ability to make content meaningful so that students can learn it. We do not mean to imply that erudition is not a nice state of affairs. Competence in one's field of specialization and a wide range of information about man and his problems (the so-called "human condition") seem highly desirable if not absolutely necessary for all teachers. The question we raise here is whether this kind of background is by itself enough.

As suggested earlier, an occasional person develops, usually prior to college, what might be called a "teacher's personality." If he acquires the necessary background information, he may become, with experience, an excellent teacher. Such persons are exceptional. Even one with an excellent personality for teaching is likely to want help in selecting and interpreting background knowledge in the arts and sciences so that it will be relevant to his needs as a teacher. He is almost certain to require help in pulling together and making some kind of sense out of the welter of information coming at him in the wide range of disparate courses which he must take. Courses in educational foundations are designed for this purpose.

A prospective teacher also cannot afford the risk involved in waiting to learn all the ways of a school through experience. There is a great deal of practical knowledge about what schools are like and how one goes about the daily managing of a group of 35 or 40 youngsters. This knowledge is a product of the experience of practicing teachers and administrators and

---

[7] Myron Lieberman, *The Future of Public Education,* University of Chicago Press, 1960, pp. 130–131.

of studies conducted over the years by psychologists and sociologists. Without considerable prior sophistication about what a modern school is like and the kinds of problems teachers regularly encounter, our neophyte teacher would be severely handicapped. Most parents would not want him experimenting on their children because, even though he did them no particular damage, there would be a great deal of waste involved while experience filled in the gaps. Properly designed professional courses can give a new teacher a "head start" because they can acquaint him with the environment of his job.

Readers of this text are concerned primarily with professional foundations courses. The purpose of a sociological or psychological foundations course is to help students pull together, make sense of, and study uses for the numerous fragments of psychology and sociology which have been acquired in freshman and sophomore courses, and, in addition, to supply further background, on a more sophisticated level, in these areas. This book presents basic psychology, slanted to be of maximum usefulness to teachers.

WHAT IS THE ROLE OF A TEACHER IN MODERN AMERICA?

As we have suggested, much that passes for teaching is not teaching because it leaves students unchanged. We have made no attempt to tell why; the reasons should become increasingly clear as this book progresses. In the meantime, readers may begin to get a sense of direction if we examine some possible answers to the question, What is the role of a teacher in modern America? We shall consider two aspects of a teacher's role: his relationship to the culture and his relationship to students. (By culture we mean the "established way of life of a people.")

What Is the Relationship of a Teacher to the Culture?

Probably most persons would agree that one of the chief functions of teaching is to preserve, by transmitting to the young, that part of the culture regarded by most people as good. However, this task by itself makes education a highly conservative force. Teaching which does no more than conserve is appropriate to a static culture, but not to a dynamic, rapidly changing culture such as ours. Hence, teaching in a fast-moving culture must operate in relation to change so as to keep cultural innovations socially beneficial. Although support for these propositions would probably be unanimous, it would be difficult to get agreement on just how the two tasks of cultural conservation and improvement are to be performed.

One type of controversy concerning the school's cultural role centers about the extent of the school's obligation. Obviously, schools are not the only agents transmitting culture and effecting cultural change. Homes, churches, the mass media, and numerous social organizations are all of importance. In spite of the presence of these agencies, the task of the school appears to be growing—and for the reason that our way of life is changing.

Teachers in early American schools felt that they had fulfilled their obligation when they had done a good job of drilling students in the three R's. It was left to the community outside the school to teach children and youth what they needed to know about the practical affairs of everyday living. In a society characterized by agriculture and handicraft industry, much of the nation's economic production was conducted by family units. Children worked alongside parents on farms, in homes, or in shops. Such situations made both simple and natural the transmission to the young not only of vocational and homemaking skills but also of the common attitudes and values of the culture.

It would be hard to overemphasize the function of small communities in the informal, out-of-school education of early America. A century ago most people lived in rural communities—either on a farm, in a village, or in a small town. The people had a face-to-face relationship with each other. They enjoyed what sociologists call a "sense of community." That is, they experienced a close and intimate kind of interaction; they were psychologically near each other. Everyone knew what almost everyone else thought about most matters, and since behavior could scarcely be concealed, most people followed the pattern dictated by local customs and moral beliefs. In such a society, young persons are easily induced to adopt the thought patterns of adults. In fact, they do it naturally, as a matter of course. Moral, social, and political education can be left to agencies other than schools.

Modern technology has led to disintegration of the older sense of community. Communities now exist only as physical entities. The older psychological bonds between people have dropped away. Henry Ford thought his Model T would enable community members to gather together more readily and thus make the sense of community stronger. But Ford and numerous other technological pioneers did their jobs too well. The Model T and other agencies of communication and transportation led people to look and move outward. The Model T went right through small communities to big impersonal cities, and the communities were doomed.

Today, opportunities for children to learn from parents and community are greatly reduced. True, contemporary culture provides vast opportunities for learning. The regular viewing of television provides an education, albeit not exactly the kind most teachers and parents wish. The welter of facts and ideas coming at a young person is enormous in quantity but contains gaps, unbalanced emphases, and contradictions. Values learned often are not those which adults want children and youth to learn. The content of what is learned is unintegrated to the point that young people can hardly help feeling confused and more or less helpless.

Schools today are expected to perform not only the function of schools of a century ago but a multitude of other tasks growing from the fact that much parental and community teaching which once was operative is so no longer. Not only are schools expected to teach what is now taught nowhere else—such as many vocational skills—but they are also expected to help young people evaluate and make sense of the values and information presented them by the mass media and other cultural agencies of instruction.

There are three basic attitudes which a teacher may take regarding his function in preserving and improving the culture. He may envision himself as (1) a cultural architect, (2) a conservator of culture, or (3) a democratic mediator. Let us explore each of these briefly.

1. *A teacher as cultural architect.* A teacher who adopts this view sees himself as an innovator. In his thinking he draws up specifications of an ideal culture and then tries to teach the attitudes, values, and knowledge which will cause new generations to move in the direction he desires. This point of view has been called "social reconstructionism" because a teacher is assumed to be discontented with things as they are and to want to introduce a new cultural design. Since one who sets out to be a cultural leader is likely to push ideas toward which resistance will develop, the temptation to indoctrinate and propagandize is likely to be very strong.

2. *A teacher as conservator of the culture.* A teacher who accepts this role sees himself as preserver of traditional attitudes, values, beliefs, and knowledge. To the best of his ability he discovers what now is and attempts to transmit this, intact, to new generations. He recognizes that accidents of history will induce cultural change and that if these changes contribute to the welfare of people they will be perpetuated. However, he never sees himself as an active agent of cultural change. Teachers in this framework are conservatives. Since unorthodoxy bothers conservatives, they are likely to try to suppress unorthodox thinking on the part of students. Like a social reconstructionist, a conservative teacher also often is found to indoctrinate and propagandize.

However much teachers may be dedicated to it, the role of conservator of culture is probably impossible to perform. With the loss of the old sense of community and the cohesive and relatively consistent value pattern which accompanied it, there is no longer a harmonious structure of attitudes, values, and beliefs to promote. Confronted with a culture filled with confusion and contradictions, which elements is a conservative teacher to select and teach? Teaching today should help students examine as objectively as possible a disjointed culture in the hope that as they live their lives they will be able to work some integration into it. But this is neither a job for an impetuous seeker of change nor one for a conservative who is frightened of change.

3. *A teacher as democratic mediator of issues.*   In contrast to the two extreme positions described above, a teacher may visualize himself as head scientist in a laboratory. The subject matter under investigation is the culture, but the purpose of investigation is neither to change nor to preserve it, but to determine and strengthen its tenability. An attempt is made to uncover contradictions and conflicts in a culture and to determine possible ways of resolving them, or at least preventing them from causing serious trouble. The ultimate hope of such a teacher is that the culture will be progressively refined by a citizenry which has learned the habit of studying problems in a reflective and democratic manner. This kind of teaching fosters social change but helps to keep it orderly and constructive. A teacher who sees himself as a democratic mediator does not discard acts of leadership. Like either a social reconstructionist or a conservator of culture, he holds one idea in preference to another. However, his method of teaching, unlike that of either a social reconstructionist or a conservator of culture, is the method of democracy. In a very real sense, he and his students are building culture together.

What Is the Relationship of a Teacher to His Students?

We may imagine three broad types of relationship between teacher and students: (1) authoritarian, (2) laissez-faire, and (3) democratic. Each type of relationship produces a distinctive situation within a classroom, characterized by more or less predictable results.[8]

1. *The authoritarian teacher.*   An authoritarian teacher exercises firm and centralized control. He directs closely every action of students. He does all the planning for the class, issues all the directions. He tells students what to think and do. In an authoritarian classroom, a teacher regards himself as the sole active agent and considers students passive receivers of instructions and information. In the experiments in group climate conducted by Lippitt and White, it was found that boys in authoritarian groups tended to be apathetic and dependent and showed little capacity for initiating group action. When the leader left the room, they accomplished very little. Although they did not seem to resent authoritarian leadership strongly, they did occasionally show evidences of hostility, as expressed in aggressive acts toward fellow group members.

2. *The laissez-faire teacher.*   A laissez-faire teacher goes to the oppo-

8 See Ralph K. White and Ronald Lippitt, *Autocracy and Democracy, An Experimental Inquiry,* Harper, 1960.

site extreme. He does not really lead at all. He is present, he may answer questions, but essentially he leaves students "on their own." Students decide what they want to do and how they will do it. In the Lippitt-White experiments, boys in the laissez-faire group got along together much better than boys in the authoritarian group; they showed less tendency to direct resentments at fellow students. They did get some work done. However, they acted insecure; for example, they repeatedly asked for help and after the experiment expressed dissatisfaction with their leadership.

3. *The democratic teacher.* A democratic teaching-learning situation may be defined as follows: the teacher plays the role of a democratic group leader. His chief purpose is to lead his students in the study of significant problems in the area in which he is teaching. Such study presupposes interchange of evidence and insights, give-and-take, and respect for each other's ideas. In a democratic classroom the teacher's ideas are subject to criticism just as are the ideas of students. Although the teacher may be an authority on his subject (and, in our opinion, he should be), the situation is arranged so that students are encouraged to think for themselves. A teacher who chooses to play the role of mediator of cultural issues, as described a few pages back, must operate in the democratic manner just described.

In the Lippitt-White experiments, democratic groups evidenced a more friendly and confiding atmosphere than did members of authoritarian groups. Members seemed able to extend mutual recognition to each other —in this respect resembling laissez-faire groups. However, they worked on a higher level of efficiency than did the laissez-faire groups. They showed much less dependence on the leader. They showed more initiative and worked much more effectively in the absence of a leader than did the authoritarian groups.

The traditional relationship between teacher and student has been authoritarian. Until the twentieth century, teachers tended to be despots— often benevolent, but despots nevertheless. During this century, despotism in the classroom has begun to disappear, but when this has happened, laissez faire has frequently taken its place. Or, perhaps more often, teachers have come to alternate between a friendly despotism and situations close to laissez faire. Throughout this book we urge that consistently democratic relations be substituted. There are good reasons: It ill behooves a nation which is straining in democratic directions to maintain in its schoolrooms nondemocratic relationships between teachers and students. Furthermore, evidence now available indicates that students learn more effectively in a democratic than in either an authoritarian or a laissez-faire classroom. Democratic learning situations seem to produce more retention and more transfer. If there were no other reason for democratic relations between teacher and students, the general adoption of such relations would permit taxpayers who support education to get more for their money.

The idea of a democratic school has fallen into ill repute during the past 20 years, for reasons which we cannot explore fully until much later in the book. However, two reasons should be understood immediately: (1) *Laissez-faire situations have often been mistaken for democratic situations* by the woolly-minded. The authors hold no brief whatsoever for laissez-faire classrooms and feel that it is inexcusable for an educator to call an uncontrolled and undirected classroom democratic. (2) The term *democracy* has been perverted. To some, *democratic*, as applied to teaching, has come to mean "easy," "soft," or "undisciplined." The fact is, a democratic group may work at the maximum level which health permits and its manner of operation may be fully as rigorous as that of any scientific investigation, making allowances for the maturity and capabilities of students.

Merely establishing a democratic classroom relationship and giving more weight to the study of cultural beliefs, particularly in the civic-social-moral area, represent moves in the right direction but alone may be ineffective. An average student is not highly motivated to learn in school. Out-of-school learning often comes easily, or if, as when a child learns his native tongue, it is not easy, it still seems "natural." Most out-of-school learning is either a result of social pressures or curiosity working itself out; in either case, a learner keeps at it until he has achieved what the situation appears to demand. Promotion of maximum learning in school probably requires the use of procedures which so far have not been widely adopted. Psychological research has given us some clues to the nature of a special kind of problem-centered instruction which promises much. Part IV of the book develops this approach in considerable detail.

WHAT ARE SOME BARRIERS TO EFFECTIVE TEACHING?

We have suggested, and presented supporting evidence to the effect, that what often passes for teaching is not teaching because students learn little or nothing from it. It may be helpful to prospective teachers to explore some of the reasons why teaching, or professed teaching, is so inadequate. The tools for much more effective teaching are at hand. We now know, because of abundant evidence from research, how the efficiency of classroom teaching can be stepped up. Why do we not put these tools to use? Is it the fault of teachers, of administrators, of school boards, or of society at large?

A teacher encounters at least three types of barriers which may impede his professional performance:

1. *Barriers unique to an individual school or school system.* A school may have no library—possibly because all the spare money was spent on "activity programs." A school may have a tyrannical principal. A teaching staff may be divided into hostile factions. Students may be handicapped because of the low socioeconomic level of their parents. Barriers such as these often can be eliminated over the course of time. Frequently, all that is required to remove them is desire, ingenuity, and patience. Sometimes barriers of this type eliminate themselves.

2. *Barriers imposed by a community.* This type of barrier is usually much more formidable. Barriers in this category arise through interaction of a school with its community. An example is a community-imposed ban on the study of certain subjects. For example, a "patriotic" organization may insist that the study of communism be excluded from classrooms. Or a community may refuse to give its schools adequate financial support, although lack of money probably has much less to do with poor teaching than is generally supposed. Barriers to good teaching imposed by a community are often difficult to remove. They reflect the intellectual atmosphere—or milieu—of the culture, which cannot readily be changed. However, community climate has often been improved through a program of adult education. Principals, school boards, and teachers can lead in establishing "town meeting" types of discussion with laymen, and often agreements that permit better teaching can be reached. Sometimes community-imposed barriers are a result of ignorance concerning what a school is trying to do.

3. *Barriers imposed by attitudes of teachers.* We sometimes wonder whether teachers are not their own worst enemy. Their attitudes probably contribute more to poor teaching than all other barriers combined. Irrespective of school or community situations, almost any teacher probably could be much more effective than he now is. What kinds of attitudes prevent a teacher from achieving maximum effectiveness?

First, he may underestimate the willingness of his school board and principal to permit him to do a good job. Complaints of limitations on academic freedom, overly rigid courses of study, and lack of needed books, maps, and other supplies are seldom exaggerated but fail to recognize that there are sometimes ways of surmounting these obstacles. Perhaps all that is needed is more ingenuity.

Second, teachers frequently underestimate the capacity of their students. When students appear dull and lackadaisical it may be because of dull and lackadaisical teaching. Even average students, from the first grade on up, can accomplish remarkable feats of learning if they are sufficiently motivated, provided with necessary materials, and given proper leadership.

Third, all too often teachers sell themselves short. They underestimate their own ability to do a better job. Many teachers are inadequately educated, a state which can always be remedied. Many feel too insecure in their own knowledge to permit a democratic teaching situation to develop. They are frightened by the prospect of a give-and-take discussion in which they may have to say "I don't know." (A teacher's status should not be jeopardized by his conceding some lack of information, provided he does not have to do it 15 or 20 times in a class period.) Many, perhaps most, teachers are not up to date in the psychology of learning. Renewed study of basic theory may well provide directives to more effective classroom performance.

Admittedly, barriers to effective teaching are often real and not easily overcome. However, the authors have observed first-rate teaching in situations which on the surface appear most difficult. A teacher who has a well-developed sense of direction—a philosophy—implemented by the best knowledge now available about how students learn and about the most effective techniques of group leadership can accomplish much, even in very difficult situations.

WHAT QUESTIONS SHOULD STUDENTS KEEP IN MIND?

Although each chapter of this book poses questions pertaining to its specific subject, we feel that students will be helped in the course if at all times they keep in mind several key questions. One of the most important has already been suggested: What is teaching?

This book is designed to throw light on the following questions:

1. What knowledge do we now have about the original nature of man— principles which hold true irrespective of race, culture, sex, or age?
2. How does a child or youth develop?
3. How does a child or youth learn?
4. What is the relationship between development and learning?
5. How can knowledge of development and learning be related to the teaching-learning process?

If you will look again at the table of contents, you will see that the book is organized into sections, each one of which is devoted to a major question. The only question in the foregoing list that does not have its own section—question 4—is handled in the two sections which treat development and learning.

We should realize that none of these questions is easy to answer. There is probably no single answer to any of them, nor can any answer be claimed as final. Yet possibly, as we appraise competing answers to each question, we can reach agreement that, as of today, one answer is more adequate than its alternatives. Students will do well at the outset to begin thinking about these fundamental questions.

As students, you do not, of course, have a large background either of practical experience or of "book knowledge" to bring to bear on these questions. Nevertheless, you do have some resources on which to draw, even before reading farther in this book. Take, for instance, the question of how children learn. You have been learning all your life and are continuing to do so—let us hope. And all your life you have been associating with others who were also learning, often from you. What seems to be the essential nature of the process we call learning? What happens within you when you learn? Does the same thing happen to everyone? It would probably be helpful to you in this course to take paper and pen now and write a one- or two-page essay on this subject. (You may not find this an easy assignment!) Repeat the assignment near the end of the course and see the difference in your two essays. The authors suggest this assignment whether or not your professor requires it.

As we have already indicated, this book deliberately presents several competing answers to many of the questions raised, so that students will become increasingly sophisticated about the "schools of thought" that exist in psychology today and understand how differently they approach certain matters. The "comparative" treatment employed in this book requires, among other things, that students do considerable thinking for themselves.

It is one thing to talk about independent thought and another actually to achieve it. Thinking for oneself is never easy. It may be easier for you to do a respectable job of independent thought if you are clearly aware of two competing kinds of criteria for judging the answers to questions: the *authoritarian* and the *scientific*. Think about any statement that you consider to be true. Do you regard it as true merely because you read it somewhere or heard some teacher or other "authority" say it or because, after you examined all the available pertinent evidence, it seemed to have more factual support than any alternative statement? If you accept the statement "on faith" because someone told it to you, you have used an authoritarian criterion for judging truth. If you accept it because you have pursued your own careful investigations of it or studied the investigations of others, you are operating within a more scientific framework.

Although we know the distinction between authoritarian and scientific approaches, the road may still not be smooth. In the first place, often we are required to reach conclusions before we have had time to conduct investigation of our own or study critically the investigations made by those who pose as authorities. In such cases we have no choice except to take someone else's word for it. Whose word do we take? In answering questions in psychology, we might turn to the writings of the most prominent psychologists. Unfortunately, prominence does not guarantee reliability. Less well-known persons may be more nearly right.

Again, let us consider the difficulties inherent in scientific tests of truth. To conduct one's own investigation of the facts relating to a particular question may require more time and more knowledge of research methods than most students have. Furthermore, a student may study investigations conducted by purportedly scientific workers in a field and find that two different workers, looking at the same facts, draw different conclusions. In the field of psychology it is common for top-ranking authorities, who have spent lifetimes in research, to disagree.

The only solution to these problems which the writers can suggest may not be very satisfactory to students: Within the limits of the time you have and of the insights of which you are capable, do the best you can. We do not promise that a study of development and learning which cuts deeply enough to be really useful will be easy for anyone. But please remember that this is not the last professional course you will take bearing on this subject. Furthermore, many issues which do not seem clear to students at the end of their initial college experience become clear as they accumulate experience in classrooms.

HOW MAY A COLLEGE STUDENT BEST STUDY CHILDREN?

If, in conjunction with this course, students can arrange a program for the direct study of children, they should learn more about development and learning than otherwise. At some colleges a child-study project is required as part of the course in development and learning or educational psychology. At other colleges it is not required but is optional.

Students might work with an individual child, a small group, or a fairly large group. Opportunities usually are available through community organizations that conduct child or youth programs: Boy or Girl Scouts, YM or YWCA, Camp Fire Girls, 4-H Clubs, city recreation departments, community centers, Sunday schools, nursery schools—the range of possibilities is wide.

The over-all purpose of such study is to learn as much as possible about young persons—both as members of groups and as individuals. Your opportunity to learn something significant will be increased if you can participate actively rather than merely observe, although observation can also be valuable. Since, rather obviously, it is disadvantageous if not impossible to separate theory and practice, direct experience with groups can provide a testing ground for theory. How many of the theoretical propositions suggested in the present text seem borne out in the behavior of the youngsters with whom you work? Is the theory a practical guide to action or is it not? If not, then the theory needs restatement. We should issue a word of warning here: a group or an individual can be so atypical that it fails to illustrate theoretical principles which would be valid in almost all other circumstances. Furthermore, some theories which over the years have proved to be useful guides to action are not easy to test in action because of the complexity of the issues involved. Indeed, in some instances two competing and contradictory theories may seem to work about equally well in explaining behavior and permitting its prediction.[9] Such bothersome situations do not mean that theory is useless; the fact is, without theory all action would be purposeless and blind. When theory does not seem to check out in practice, either the theory needs to be reformulated or our practical tests were in some way invalid.

Study of Overt Behavior vs. Study of Thought Pattern

As we study children, we have to decide which kind, or kinds, of data will be most helpful. What is the relative value of the information we receive from overt behavior as compared to that derived from "mental life"? The former type of data has often been called *behavioral*, whereas the latter has been called *cognitive*. We have a choice, then, between behavioral and cognitive studies.

In behavioral studies we observe and record what children do or their outward characteristics. Does Johnny regularly sass his teacher? Does Mary burst into tears at the slightest provocation? Is Freddy extremely large for his age? Does Marilyn have defective eyesight? All these questions can be answered simply by observing, or by studying medical or other records. In cognitive studies we try to discover how students *think* about situations—their attitudes, values, and beliefs.

It will have occurred to readers by now that behavioral and cognitive approaches do not represent an either-or choice. By watching overt behavior, or finding out about physical or mental abnormalities, one often can *infer* attitudes, values, and beliefs. In fact, the chief kind of evidence available to students of this course who take field-work assignments, as

[9] Even in the "exact" science of physics, situations of this kind have arisen. For many years there were two theories to explain the nature of light—the wave theory and the corpuscular theory. They appeared to be completely contradictory. Yet, in certain experimental situations the data supported the wave theory; in others, they supported the corpuscular theory. Each theory was a useful predictive tool in situations congenial to it.

well as to most practicing teachers, is necessarily behavioral evidence, even though it be gathered for the sole purpose of unearthing facts about children's mental lives.

We raised a question earlier about the relative importance of these two types of information. Clearly, the authors feel, for the purposes of school-teachers or counselors, the data that count most are cognitive. It is more useful to know what a child is thinking than to know what he is doing. Often—indeed, usually—the attitudes, values, or beliefs of children are somewhat different from what they seem on superficial contact. Jerry may bully smaller boys, but this is not the important fact. The important fact is *why*, and we can find out only by "getting inside" Jerry and discovering what makes him "tick." It is his basic attitudes and understandings that we must know about. Otherwise there is little we can do to remedy the situation. Actually, without cognitive facts about Jerry, we do not even know whether a serious attempt to change him should be made.

In the following section we describe a variety of methods by which children can be studied. In seeking physical defects which need correction, it is usually sufficient to study the child only to the point of uncovering the defect. He will then be referred to the proper medical specialist. But when we suggest procedures for behavioral study, they are usually meant to reveal facts from which inferences about the psychological world of a child can be drawn.

Some Methods of Child Study

There are at least six methods of studying children; circumstances determine which can be used to best advantage. The methods are commonly labeled anecdotal, biographical, autobiographical, questionnaire, psychometric, and clinical.

1. *Anecdotal study.* When a student of child or youth behavior notes specific incidents in the life of a child and describes them in writing, he is employing the anecdotal method. Undoubtedly, an accumulation of anecdotes does contribute to an understanding of children, but in the light of present more scientific methods of study the anecdotal method is not given great weight. However, we must remember that any method of child study may provide hypotheses which can be checked out through other methods, and obtaining hypotheses is always a key step in scientific methodology.

2. *Biographical study.* A biography is a life history of a person written by an observer. In a sense, it is simply a systematic anecdotal record. Like an anecdotal record, a biography is a form of behavioral study which may or may not furnish useful cues about the psychological life of a

child. But again, it frequently provides hypotheses which can be tested through other means. Although more time consuming, a biography is probably more useful than an anecdotal record. At least it provides a more complete account of what has happened to a child and how he has responded.

3. *Autobiographical study.* This method requires a child to write his own life story. An autobiography is likely to be more revealing than either of the two records just described. In an autobiography a child can scarcely avoid revealing something about the way he sees things. However, anyone who writes an autobiography may intentionally or unintentionally distort the truth. He is likely to "put his best foot forward." What one writes may be intended as ego defense and bear little relation to what he sees as reality. Even so, autobiographies combined with other means of investigation are usually highly useful.

4. *Questionnaire study.* The investigator devises a list of questions which he feels will reveal significant facts about the child under study. This technique is one of rapid interview in which the child may himself check answers with a pencil, or the investigator may read the questions and note answers. One of the disadvantages of this system is that a questionnaire is completely structured; responses are necessarily confined to specific categories. Often responses of a child in areas which adults have not anticipated throw more light on the child's mental processes than do structured responses. Another disadvantage of questionnaires, applying to autobiographies as well, is that respondents may falsify.

5. *Psychometric study.* This involves use of carefully devised psychological tests. Certain of these tests uncover the psychological world of a child or youth—his attitudes, values, beliefs, and understandings. Others measure intelligence and aptitudes. There are two basic categories of psychological tests—structured and unstructured. *Structured tests* contain questions or problems to be solved which are quite specific. Intelligence tests and attitude scales are examples. *Unstructured tests* confront a subject with ambiguous situations which may be interpreted in various ways. Examples are the Rorschach Inkblot Test and the Thematic Apperception Test. Through these a trained psychologist or psychometrist may uncover a person's innermost patterns of motivation and thinking.

Obviously, beginning students of development and learning cannot make use of the unstructured psychological tests. Successful interpretation of their results requires much special education and experience. But students can use some of the simpler structured tests if an occasion arises where such tests might provide helpful information.

6. *Clinical study.* In this method of study an investigator, using one or a combination of the methods described above, centers his attention on an individual child. Another name for this approach is the *case study*

method. Emphasis is placed upon studying a child as an individual rather than as a good, average, or poor example of what a normal child should be, as described in some books.

The various methods of child study are usually most successful if they combine cross-sectional and longitudinal study. In *cross-sectional study* an investigator learns all he can about children of a given age. In *longitudinal study* he concentrates on changes in children as they live through a period of time. Even in the course of a college semester a group of children may change their thinking in significant ways and thus be suitable subjects for longitudinal study. If a student investigator can stay with his group for an entire school year, he is likely to learn still more from a longitudinal approach. However, because of the shortness of time which a typical student in a course in development and learning has with his group, his major effort will necessarily be confined to cross-sectional study.

For reasons of convenience, a system has been devised for age-grouping children and youth. Students should understand that passage of a child from one age group to another does not mean that an abrupt change in his development has occurred. They should also remember that any single age group will encompass a broad range of bodily and psychological characteristics. The following system of grouping is widely used:

Ages 5 through 8	Kindergarten through Grade 3 (primary—lower elementary grades)
Ages 9 through 12	Grades 4 through 6 (upper elementary grades)
Ages 13 through 15	Grades 7 through 9 (junior high school)
Ages 16 through 18	Grades 10 through 12 (senior high school)

Suggested Procedures and Questions

Our first suggestion is that students who have an opportunity to work with children be "all eyes and ears." Watch and listen. A pocket notebook and pencil are indispensable. Now that tape recorders have become truly portable, students who have the use of one will find it valuable for obtaining verbatim conversations and discussions. Occasionally a camera can be used to advantage. Children and youth do not object to a leader's use of such props, provided explanations are given and nothing is done which would cause embarrassment.

1. *Obtaining physiological data.* Much physiological information can be procured simply by observing. Some data are useful only because they give prospective teachers an idea of what to expect within a given age

group and hence an ability to recognize physiological deviants who may have psychological problems due to their abnormality. Getting a feel for what is normal, or average, also helps a teacher detect correctible defects. To get a notion of the physiological facts of his group, a student can try to answer questions such as the following:

a. How tall is a typical child in the group?
b. How great is the range in height?
c. How heavy is a typical child?
d. How great is the range in weight?
e. How do members of the group compare with standards given on height-weight charts?
f. How much do young people of the age of the group grow in a semester (or in a year)? (Note: You would look rather silly carrying bathroom scales and a tape measure around with you. Most youngsters know their height and weight. Ask them. Or, if they are teen-agers, compare them with yourself.)
g. What ranges in posture can you observe in the group?
h. What athletic or other physical skills are apparent? What is the range in strength, dexterity, quickness, etc.?
i. What evidence is there of defective eyesight and hearing?
j. Do any of the youngsters have a speech defect?
k. Do any of them show symptoms of illness, contagious or otherwise? (Every teacher should be familiar with the overt symptoms of the common childhood diseases. Free or low-cost government manuals are available on these illnesses.)

2. *Obtaining psychological data.* Any of the broad approaches to child study described on pages 20–22 may be used to get information on a child or youth's attitudes, values, beliefs, and understandings. Some of the approaches, such as the questionnaire method or psychometric testing, provide no other kind of information. Others may supply psychological data both indirectly and directly. Behavioral study often warrants inferences about cognitive patterns. However, it is extremely easy to misinterpret overt behavior; often a child pursues some action for reasons entirely different from those which would seem logical to an adult.

Following are some questions an investigator might try to answer about overt behavior. In each case, an affirmative answer might provide the basis for tentative inferences about the psychological state of a child. These are specimen questions; the student should try to formulate others.

a. Do any children in the group seem to isolate themselves from other children deliberately, perhaps refusing to talk?
b. Does one member (or more) of the group seem to be a "natural" leader? If so, what methods does he use?

c. Are any children especially popular with other children? What is their behavior like?

d. Do any children commit aggressive acts—such as hitting or shoving without apparent provocation, "telling other children off," and the like?

e. Are any of the children show-offs?

f. How do members of the group relate to adults? Are they friendly, do they seek attention, are they timid, submissive, bold, aggressive, etc.?

g. Are any members of the group unusually boastful (or self-deprecatory)?

h. Are any of them habitual liars?

i. Are there evidences of discriminatory attitudes toward other ethnic groups?

j. Do any of the children burst into tears upon small provocation?

After answering such questions, there still remains the problem of interpretation. For example, what does it mean if a child cries much more often than seems normal? What does it mean if a child is a show-off? Some of the behaviors which questions such as those above are designed to uncover are what psychologists call "compensatory mechanisms." They are used to offset, or escape from, problems which are difficult to bear. The existence of these behaviors indicates a problem but does not always tell us just what the problem is. Therefore, answering questions like those listed is usually only a starting point. The remainder of this book, plus your class discussions and lectures, should provide material to enable you to make some of the necessary interpretations of child behavior.

BIBLIOGRAPHY

Adler, Mortimer J., and Milton Mayer, *The Revolution in Education*, The University of Chicago Press, 1958.
> Sympathetic criticism of present-day teaching and an attempt to ask the right questions, that is, those questions which might help teachers resolve issues confronting them. The frame of reference is that of a classical scholar but the analysis is impartial. Bibliography covers span from ancient world to 1950s.

Barzun, Jacques, *Teacher in America*, Little, Brown, 1945.
> A treatise on teaching—what is taught and why and how, and what can be done to improve teaching. This stimulating book applies more directly to secondary and higher education than to other levels, but is worth reading by anyone.

Barzun, Jacques, *The House of Intellect*, Harper, 1959.
> Explanation by a noted liberal arts scholar of why intellect makes little

headway. See Chapter 1 for Barzun's definition of intellect and Chapter 4 for his pungent comments on education. A very provocative book.

Bayles, Ernest E., *Democratic Educational Theory*, Harper, 1960.
A book on the philosophy of education which contains much material pertinent to this volume. Students should read at least Chapter 1 at this point in the course.

Cantor, Nathaniel F., *Dynamics of Learning*, Stewart, 1956.
One of the best books available on how to improve the effectiveness of teaching. The first few theoretical chapters require for their understanding a rich background in psychology and sociology. Read later chapters which describe in detail how a teacher may conduct a class.

Ehlers, Henry, and Gordon Lee, eds., *Crucial Issues in Education*, Holt-Dryden, 1959.
An anthology which covers many of the larger issues now confronting educators. Presents a range of contrasting viewpoints.

Highet, Gilbert, *The Art of Teaching*, Knopf, 1950.
A book on methods of teaching by a well-known scholar and teacher. His description of some of the world's great teachers is illuminating because many of them steadily violated the "rules" with which we now equip students in our teachers' colleges. Students should discuss critically Mr. Highet's contention that good teaching is solely an art.

Hunt, Maurice P., and Lawrence E. Metcalf, *Teaching High School Social Studies*, Harper, 1955.
A book devoted entirely, in a sense, to the question, What is teaching? Briefly stated, teaching is inducing others to reflect on important issues. The point of view advocated is applicable at all grade levels from kindergarten to graduate school.

Lieberman, Myron, *The Future of Public Education*, University of Chicago Press, 1960.
A sharp criticism of modern educational practice. Lieberman is a professional educator and thus his criticism, unlike that of the liberal arts scholars, comes from the "inside." See Chapter 1–2 for his statement of the problem. Chapters 5–7, and especially 6, are highly pertinent to this chapter.

Meyer, Agnes E., *Education for a New Morality*, Macmillan, 1957.
A provocative little book with profound implications for what and how we teach. It suggests a philosophy of education which might close the gap in our thinking between science and humanism.

Mussen, Paul H., ed., *Handbook of Research Methods in Child Development*, Wiley, 1960.
A comprehensive and somewhat technical treatment. Each chapter is written by an expert on some aspect of child study.

Rasey, Marie I., *This Is Teaching*, Harper, 1950.
A more-or-less verbatim report of what took place in one university seminar. The principle of teaching illustrated might be used at any age or maturity level. Students can gain much from this book, even though they do not on first reading grasp the thought content which emerged from the seminar.

Rugg, Harold, *The Teacher of Teachers*, Harper, 1952.
Historical and comparative treatment of practices in the education of teachers. Part II deals specifically with foundations courses in schools for teacher education. An extremely rich annotated bibliography at end.

Scott, C. Winfield, and others, eds., *The Great Debate: Our Schools in Crisis*, Prentice-Hall, 1959. (Also in paperback, Spectrum Books.)

A reprinting of articles which criticize the job public schools are doing and articles which defend the schools. A good introduction to recent charges and countercharges.

Woodring, Paul, *A Fourth of a Nation*, McGraw-Hill, 1957.

A book focusing on the debate between proponents of classical and progressive education. Woodring, one of the more responsible critics of modern education, concludes that neither side has the answer.

PART
I

WHAT IS THE NATURE OF HUMAN NATURE?

Since psychology is the study of man, it is appropriate to include near the beginning of any psychology text a summary of what is known, or surmised, about man's basic nature.

However, to prepare such a summary is a task neither easy nor free from risk. We know much less about human beings than we would like to know, especially in connection with certain fundamental issues. For example, is human behavior best explained by "mechanistic" or "nonmechanistic" principles? What is the origin of purpose? Do human beings have instincts? These are only a few of the really difficult questions.

In the following group of chapters, we explain some of the issues and, where evidence seems to warrant, suggest some conclusions. Although intended to apply primarily to persons of the United States, most of the material included applies to any age level, social class, or ethnic group. We begin by considering competing theories concerning the psychological nature of man (Chap. 2). We move next to considerations of the biological nature of man (Chap. 3). Then comes a chapter on the sociological nature of man (Chap. 4). The final chapter in the section (Chap. 5) is on individual differences. We recognize that these subjects cannot be set off one from another, except arbitrarily and for purposes of discussion; however, the organization is convenient and follows lines with which most students are familiar.

2
IS HUMAN NATURE NATURAL?

Before one can think about the nature of developmental and learning processes, he must first consider the question of the basic nature of human beings—the center of these processes. Consideration of the basic nature of man would be quite simple were there but one answer. Unfortunately, but interestingly, there are several distinctly different and mutually opposed answers to this question, each enjoying a good deal of support. As students read this chapter, they should attempt to define their own positions in regard to this crucial problem. Is man naturally evil? Or is he naturally good? Or is his moral nature neutral—neither naturally good nor evil? Also, in relationship to his environment is man naturally active? Or is he naturally reactive? Or is he naturally interactive? If he is active, all his basic characteristics come from within—he is born with them. If he is reactive, his basic characteristics are largely a product of environmental influences. If he is interactive, his basic characteristics result from sizing up his physical and social environment.

To prevent confusion, we must state what we mean by *naturally*. When we refer to a "natural characteristic" we mean a characteristic inherited by all members of a species. We could substitute terms such as *original* or *innate*. Thus, the chapter title is an inquiry as to whether any human traits are innate—products of heredity. The manner in which we use *man* should also be made clear. In this chapter it is used in a generic sense; it applies to all members of the human race collectively. This chapter emphasizes certain possible ways in which all men are alike in personality. Chapter 5 will emphasize ways in which they are different.

WHAT IS MEANT BY THE "NATURE" OF A SPECIES?

It is common to talk about animal nature and human nature and to compare or contrast the two, e.g., "That woman is a tigress when she is aroused," or "Old Joe is more like a sloth than anything else I can think of." What do people usually mean when they refer to the "nature" of an animal or of a man? Apparently, they mean personality as it is defined by psychologists and social scientists.

The personality of a person is that which is habitual about his actions. To possess a personality, an individual must have established a pattern of behavior which is at least to some degree predictable. To illustrate the point, let us apply the concept of personality to some animals below man on the phylogenetic scale. Different animal species seem to vary greatly in their habits. Some are timid and retiring, others are bold and aggressive. Some are more active at night, others are more active in daytime. Some are playful, others are not. Some practice multiple mating, others are monogamous. Some kill other animals for food, others are strict vegetarians. When people use the expression "curious as a cat," they are pointing to a characteristic which has been observed widely in cats, namely, their tendency to explore closets, cupboards, and other out-of-the-way places. Everyone who has had dogs and cats around his house knows that these pets seem to display different interests, temperaments, and food preferences. In short, they have different "personalities." Personality, furthermore, refers to the whole behavioral pattern of an individual—to the totality of its characteristics.

People who have had much experience with animals are also aware that members of a single species vary greatly. One cat may kill birds, another leave them completely alone. One dog may habitually chase cats, another may try to play with them. There doubtless is considerable personality range among members of any animal species. This suggests that personality, even among the lower animals, may, in part, be learned.

Considerable research has accumulated to support the idea of individuality among animals and to cast doubt on the notion that animal behavior is completely instinctive, fixed, and uniform. According to folklore, cats are supposed instinctively to hunt and kill rats. But one researcher, Kuo, found that if he reared cats and rats together they associated quite amicably. He found no instance in which an adult cat injured a rat with which it had been reared. Furthermore, cats reared with rats refused to molest any strange rat of the same general appearance as the rats with which they had been reared.[1]

[1] Zing Y. Kuo, "Genesis of Cat's Responses to the Rat," *Journal of Comparative Psychology*, February, 1931. For a report of more recent research on the extent to which cats and rats can be taught to cooperate, see Loh Seng Tsai, "Peace and Co-operation among Natural Enemies," reported at the St. Louis meeting of the American Association for the Advancement of Science, December 30, 1952.

Many biologists would say that animal behavior is flexible only within limits. The limits may be greater than we had previously supposed, but they seem to be there. The limiting factor is the genetic make-up, the genotype, of the animal. Although cats may learn to love rats, there may be a number of other traits which cats will not, or cannot, exhibit. If such be the case, then we may properly speak of a fundamental animal nature, genetically determined and characteristic of each species, which produces at least some of the habitual actions of the species.

Is There a Natural Man?

Just as most persons have made assumptions concerning a basic animal-nature characteristic of each species, fixed in the sense that it is genetically determined, so they have made similar assumptions about human beings. Most persons, at least in the past, have assumed that a part of human behavior results from the racial inheritance, i.e., certain behavioral tendencies are a product of universal instincts. When most persons talk of "human nature," they are referring to an assumed "natural man."

In discussing "human nature" we are treating issues of fundamental importance to mankind and of fundamental interest to psychologists and educators. We will show in historical perspective the major points of view which have been developed concerning the nature of human nature, beginning with two prescientific theories, one based upon the assumption that man is naturally evil and the other upon the assumption that he is naturally good. We will then move into a consideration of major contemporary scientific theories of human nature which are competing for acceptance among educators, biologists, psychologists, and social scientists. Because of limitations of space, our treatment of this complex subject is necessarily oversimplified, and students are advised to consult the chapter bibliography for additional references.

What Is Instinct?

This discussion frequently uses the term *instinct*. Although it is in disrepute among many psychologists and social scientists, the term has had such wide usage that it seems inadvisable to abandon it completely. By instinct we mean a more or less compulsive kind of behavior which is innate in the biological organism. An instinct theory of human nature holds that human beings must behave in certain ways because they are human beings. These instinctive modes of behavior constitute what might be called "human nature," as contrasted to the instinctive actions of, say, a turtle, which has its own "turtle nature."

An instinct theory of human nature, if it is applied consistently, leads to a "doctrine of universal, unchanging traits." It introduces a definite element of fixity to man's nature, frequently expressed in the precept

"You can't change human nature." A person holding this view might assume that only a few of man's observable traits are instinctive (such as desire for self-preservation) and that the remainder are learned; or he might assume that most human traits have an instinctive basis. In either case, he postulates that man's unchanging instincts drive him to perform certain actions.

Any interpretation of human nature which assumes the existence of instinctive tendencies is likely to carry a corollary assumption, namely, that man is an active agent in relation to his environment. He is seen as a dynamic being whose instincts will not be denied and who will therefore use every available resource to modify his environment in a manner to serve better his instinctual needs. Conversely, man's environment is seen as essentially passive—that which is acted upon. One problem connected with this assumption lies in defining environment: is it the world of non-human animals and objects, or does it include other men? If it includes the latter, then it is difficult to see how environment can be construed as passive. Each individual's environment includes other persons equally dynamic and equally seeking to impose their instinctual impulses on all persons around them. Nevertheless, one can assume, and reasonably if one is an instinct theorist, that each person *seeks* a relationship with his social and physical environment in which he is the active agent, bending to his will all that surrounds him.

IS HUMAN NATURE NATURALLY EVIL?

Historically, many people who have assumed the existence of an instinctive human nature have described human nature in moralistic terms —as either bad or good. According to the notion that human beings are naturally bad, all mankind is thought to be afflicted with evil impulses. This notion may be expressed as the *bad-active principle* of human nature: man is innately bad, and since he is driven to be so instinctively, he tries to maintain an active pose in relation to his environment.

The idea that human nature is instinctively evil is very old. Its origin is unknown and may lie farther back than recorded history. Noss reports the thinking of Hsun-tzu, a Chinese philosopher of the third century B.C., as follows: "The nature of man is evil. . . . Therefore to give rein to man's original nature, to follow man's feelings, inevitably results in strife and rapacity."[2] Hebraic thought during the pre-Christian era also seems to reflect this idea. In Genesis 8:21 we are told, ". . . for the imagination of man's heart is evil from his youth . . ." and in Psalm 51:5, "Behold, I was shapen in iniquity; and in sin did my mother conceive me."

The idea that man has two selves, a higher and a lower, also developed

[2] John B. Noss, *Man's Religions,* Macmillan, 1949, p. 384.

at a relatively early period in human history. The ancient Egyptians, like the members of many nonliterate cultures before them, conceived of human beings as made up of two parts: body and spirit. A number of pre-Christian Greek philosophers made a very definite distinction between body and spirit. They believed that the body was impure, a "prison of the soul," and that, in contrast, the soul was pure. This notion was shared by a number of religious sects of the Persian region. Early dualists, i.e., persons who believed in the twofold nature of body and spirit, tended to think that, when bodily impulses got the upper hand, man's behavior was highly evil, but when the spirit or soul dominated, behavior was much better. However, the ancients—and many of their modern descendants as well—took a rather pessimistic view of man's ability to curb his bodily impulses. The spirit might win, but it would have rough going. Hence, dualists tended to take a dim view of man; most of the time, they felt, he exhibited considerable depravity.

During the Christian era the idea that man is naturally evil has been widely held and has often been part of the formal theology of the churches of the Christian world. Martin Luther said of man that "no spark of spiritual power was left him for the knowledge of truth and the accomplishment of good." John Calvin wrote that man, because of "an hereditary corruption and depravity," is "obnoxious" to God.

The Inherent Evilness Concept in the United States

In the United States, notions about the inherent evilness of man have come down to us most strongly through the Puritan outlook, which put its stamp on much of American thought down to recent times. Of the Puritan outlook, Smith tells us,

> The Puritan ideal was one of extreme personal righteousness, the Puritan consciousness an ever-present sense of the all-pervading and innate character of sin. Emphasis on Augustine's theory of concupiscence and infant damnation made mortification of the flesh one of the central duties of life, and gave to all true Puritans a somber and gloomy character scarcely to be surpassed for miserable self-deprecation except by those early Christian ascetics who had spent their lives in sackcloth and ashes. . . . [The emphasis of Puritanism] on original sin led it to distrust the child: infants are bound by their own innate fault; though they may not have given evidence of their iniquity, they have the seed shut up in them, their whole nature is a sort of seed of sin. . . .[3]

In the American colonies, Jonathan Edwards exemplified the Puritan beliefs. Probably the colonies produced no more effective exponent of the notion that human nature is intrinsically vile. Referring to what he spoke of as "the total depravity and corruption of man's nature," Edwards argued that man is "wholly under the power of sin, and . . . utterly un-

[3] Homer W. Smith, *Man and His Gods,* Little, Brown, 1953, p. 379.

able, without the interposition of sovereign grace . . . to do anything that is truly good," and that "the natural state of the mind of man . . . is corrupt and depraved with a moral depravity, that amounts to and implies their utter undoing." Edwards depicted man as utterly repugnant to God because of his corrupt state and based a series of sermons upon this theme. The most famous was delivered at Enfield, Connecticut, on July 8, 1741, and was entitled "Sinners in the Hands of an Angry God." Edwards that day told his congregation: "Were it not for the sovereign pleasure of God, the earth would not bear you one moment; for you are a burden to it; the creation groans with you. . . . The God that holds you over the pit of hell, much as one holds a spider, or some loathsome insect over the fire, abhors you, and is dreadfully provoked: his wrath towards you burns like fire. . . . You are ten thousand times more abominable in his eyes, than the most hateful venemous serpent in ours."[4]

Although we are much less extreme about it than was Jonathan Edwards, today there is a streak in modern American thought which holds that the human race is a pretty ornery lot, with natural, or instinctive, "cussedness" taking a variety of forms. No longer do we decry pride, as did the early church fathers. But we talk a great deal about such undesirable human traits as selfishness, dishonesty, aggressiveness, laziness, and lust. Many Americans appear to feel that almost everyone is motivated by these tendencies. It is often said that the only thing which keeps most people from stealing or murdering is the fear of being caught. Proponents of beliefs such as these tend to urge the passage of increasingly comprehensive and severe laws to control the moral failings of others. Probably there is no other advanced civilization in the world where people are more interested in trying to curb the immoral impulses of others than in the United States. Likewise, many people feel that it is only through coercion that children do anything productive.

The Problem of Inducing Goodness

If one accepts the notion that human nature is intrinsically bad and that this condition is common to the young as well as the old, then certain conclusions about the rearing of children seem to follow. Obviously steps must be taken by adults to reduce, at least in their outward manifestations, the evil impulses of children. There might be two quite different reasons for this necessity. If one believes that people get to heaven only through good works, then reduction of a child's evil impulses may be the only thing which will save his soul. On the other hand, one may not be concerned with heaven, but only with making possible a decent social life

[4] Clarence H. Faust and Thomas H. Johnson, *Jonathan Edwards: Representative Selections with Introduction, Bibliography, and Notes,* American Book, 1935, pp. 321, 162–164.

here on earth, in which case it is still necessary to eliminate as much as possible lying, selfishness, envy, greed, vanity, and dishonesty in children. In either case, an important object in the life of each person is altering, suppressing, or overriding natural impulses. The good life (either now or in the hereafter) can be had only for those who learn to disobey their instinctive desires. Burtt clearly describes the human task:

> As long as they [i.e., instinctive impulses] are present . . . they obstruct the way to man's fulfillment of his most wonderful potentialities, in virtue of which he can realize with his fellows and with the universe a deep harmony. In order to attain this harmony our natural urges and yearnings must be radically disciplined, and not just satisfied; we need to be transformed into personalities in which they fill a quite different role from that which they fill in their undisciplined form. In short, our very inmost selves need to be, and can be reshaped into something other than they naturally are, and only when thus reshaped can they enter into the true happiness of which man is distinctively capable.[5]

The answer, to many, has been discipline. To achieve inner peace as well as harmony with the universe, one must learn discipline. An adult is expected to discipline himself. A child, however, may need help in the form of advice, exhortation, threats, or corporal punishment. The Puritan attitude toward child rearing has always called for liberal doses of the latter. As Smith puts it, ". . . the child's naturally evil will must, if necessary, be broken by the rod as early in life as possible and its mind from infanthood nourished on the all important themes of personal guilt and duty."[6]

IS HUMAN NATURE NATURALLY GOOD?

If what we have been discussing may be called the bad-active principle of human nature, by the same token the notion that human nature is naturally good may be referred to as the *good-active principle*. Obviously the principles are mutually exclusive. The idea of the innate goodness of man, like that of innate badness, has ancient origins. In the sense that in many primitive cultures man's natural impulses have been worshiped or idolized, the idea of innate goodness appears to date from the prehistoric era. Burtt comments that primitive man generally was not aware of any need to be "remade" or "reborn" in order to fulfill the demands of moral law. "Primitive religion . . . assumes that man's natural desires form the core of his true self; these desires press legitimately for satisfaction, and religion provides one important set of techniques by which their satisfaction can be assured."[7] The chief role of the deities conceived by

5 Edwin A. Burtt, *Types of Religious Philosophy*, Harper, 1951, p. 440.
6 Smith, *op. cit.*, p. 379.
7 Burtt, *op. cit.*, p. 439.

primitive man was to help him satisfy his natural impulses. Hence, sexual orgies, gluttonous banquets, and drunkenness were often a part of religious worship and ceremony. It would be easy, however, to oversimplify this picture. Primitive societies also entertained numerous taboos which had the effect of suppressing or denying an outlet to common impulses. Primitive man was not as uninhibited as modern man sometimes imagines.

When we analyze man's historical period, as from the time of ancient Greece, we encounter two versions of the idea that human nature is intrinsically good. One of these holds that man's natural impulses are good in themselves and that if man lives according to their dictates he automatically will have a good life. This view is commonly associated with the philosophy of humanism. A second version of the idea that man is naturally good holds that, even though human beings (particularly those who call themselves civilized) often display very bad traits indeed, man's hereditary nature is good and needs only to be developed in an environment free from corruption. This version is usually associated with the thinking of Jean Jacques Rousseau (1712–1778), whose major ideas we examine in the pages that follow.

Rousseau and Romantic Naturalism

Jean Jacques Rousseau was a champion of the idea that a child at birth is naturally good; provided the child is not corrupted by society, this goodness will manifest itself. Rousseau's combined philosophy and psychology has been labeled *romantic naturalism*.

There were at least two large themes of the eighteenth century. The classical-rationalist theme emphasized the use of reason in human affairs which later led to a plea for widespread reliance upon scientific methodology. The other theme was essentially sentimental and served as a foundation for the nineteenth-century movement known as *romanticism*. We associate Rousseau with this latter tendency. Rousseau exhibited a sentimental, worshipful attitude toward nature and all things close to nature. "All things are good as they come out of the hands of their Creator, but every thing degenerates in the hands of man."[8] The nature which Rousseau found at the bottom of things was primarily unspoiled human nature—the nature of simple, uncorrupted persons such as peasants, savages, and children.

Rousseau's concept of human nature seems, on the surface, to be quite simple. He is insistent that children are born free of inherited sin. During the very earliest period of his existence, man acquired the necessary instincts to satisfy his biological demands—for food, sex, and sleep. Accord-

[8] Quoted in Robert Ulich, *Three Thousand Years of Educational Wisdom,* Harvard University Press, 1954, p. 383.

ing to Rousseau, man is not, by instinct, reflective; he is, like lower animals, a creature of impulse.

At times Rousseau seems to say that man has a natural impulse to be kindly, sympathetic, outgoing, and democratic. At other times he seems to portray natural man as morally neutral. He speaks of a child as if it is a plant, which, because of its inborn nature, will grow in the direction of perfect adulthood if not deformed by environmental circumstances. This idea carries the implication that not only bodily but also psychological growth is guided by inborn principles. Hence, Rousseau's concept of human nature seems as firmly based in instinctive impulse as was Puritanism, yet it describes the nature of instinctive impulse in almost precisely opposite terms.[9]

Popularization in the Modern World of the Doctrine of Innate Goodness

Space does not permit tracing the development of Roussellian concepts in the nineteenth and twentieth centuries. Friedrich Froebel (1782–1852), a German educational reformer, and Georg Wilhelm Friedrich Hegel (1770–1831), a German philosopher, developed more completely the doctrine that growth is a process of unfolding, according to an innate pattern, toward a predetermined and perfect end. As time passed, the concept of innate goodness of human nature became increasingly influential.

With the development of more liberal types of Protestantism early in the twentieth century and with the concurrent decline in influence of the older Puritanism, more and more people dropped their belief in original sin and the natural depravity of man. Not that they had made a complete about-face. Many accepted the idea that man was morally neutral at birth. Thus, twentieth-century thinking did not promote in positive fashion the notion that man is naturally good or that a child, if reared in a permissive atmosphere, will unfold toward a perfect goodness. However, a school of thought in psychology and education has developed which in certain respects seems to show Roussellian influence.

The development of child study as a field of inquiry sometimes appears to reflect certain Roussellian assumptions. Arnold Gesell, a foremost leader in child study, states that in describing a child it is best to use the analogy of a plant. His description of child development seems to depict progress through a series of psychological stages, each normal in the sense that it is foreordained in the protoplasm of the child at birth. One gets the impression from Gesell and from numerous other child psychologists that

[9] For a good treatment of the Roussellian concept of human nature, see F. C. Green, *Jean Jacques Rousseau; A Critical Study of His Life and Writings,* Cambridge University Press, 1955. Or read Rousseau, particularly *Discourse on Inequality, The New Heloise,* and *Émile.*

children will show naturally good traits if their environment is proper. To some degree, the field of social work seems to have been influenced by a belief in natural goodness. According to most social workers, it is only the adversity of a bad environment that suppresses naturally good inclinations. The idea has carried over into our popular folklore, so that it is rather common nowadays to hear such an expression as "There is no such thing as a bad boy; there are only bad parents."

It is interesting to note shifts in attitude which may occur within a relatively short time. The latter part of the nineteenth century, the Victorian era, was a period of retreat to Puritan morality. Calvinism lay heavy over the land until World War I, when a revolution in American manners and morals began. One researcher, Martha Wolfenstein, became interested in the extent to which official publications of the United States government reflect the changing climate of opinion. She analyzed the *Child Care* bulletins published by the Children's Bureau of the federal government, beginning with the first issue (1914) and continuing through the issue of 1951.[10] She found that, prior to World War I (as in the 1914 edition), the bulletins depicted a child as the possessor of numerous impulses which, if permitted indulgence, were extremely dangerous. That is, the things an infant might want to do naturally were usually regarded as bad. Tabooed activities included anything which might produce sensory pleasure. Hence, parents were advised not to permit a child to masturbate or suck his thumb; and they were to avoid fondling, stroking, and tickling children. Parents, rather than infants, were to determine how much food, how much sleep, and how much of everything infants were to have. Great care was advocated lest an infant be overindulged.

In recent years, the tone of these bulletins has reversed itself. They now say, in effect, "Whatever is pleasurable is good for a child." Further, there even seems to be some worry that a child may not enjoy himself fully enough. As Wolfenstein puts it, "Fun has become not only permissible but required. . . . Where formerly there was felt to be the danger that in seeking fun one might be carried away into the depths of wickedness, today there is a recognizable fear that one may not be able to let go sufficiently, that one may not have enough fun."[11] Hence, a child is to be encouraged to give rather free rein to his impulses, even when the pleasure involved has a strongly sensual element.

The ideological implications seem highly significant. Government bulletins, even when written by so-called "objective scientists," reflect the *Zeitgeist*—the spirit of the times. Perhaps much scientific literature does likewise—whether it deals with the social sciences, psychology, or the

10 See "The Emergence of Fun Morality," *Journal of Social Issues*, Vol. VIII, No. 4, 1951, pp. 15–25.
11 *Ibid.*, p. 22.

natural sciences. In any case, many persons have come to view natural impulses as good in themselves or good in reference to the achievement of some good end, such as "mental health," or "happiness." Even if we do not go to the extremes of some Roussellians in the past, Americans today widely accept the thesis that, if people are to be happy, human nature must be allowed to express itself. Such thinking seems necessarily based on the assumption that there is a human nature, instinctive rather than learned, and that its natural tendencies may be indulged without harm.

The Problem of Inducing Goodness

Theoretically, rearing children should be much simpler in a culture where most people are dedicated to the proposition that human beings are naturally good. There should be very few problems, because parents who are consistent with their belief have only to "let nature take its course." That is, children may be reared permissively. It is only necessary to feed, clothe, doctor, and love them; they will manage the rest.

A person accepting the Roussellian premise would probably believe that children can be left to set their own standards of attainment. They will know "instinctively" what is right for them at their age levels. There is more than a hint of this notion in much of the literature of twentieth-century psychology. For example, we often encounter the idea that the proper attitudes, values, and beliefs for a child are those which are characteristic of his age group. The implication appears to be that children can set their own standards and, if allowed to do so, will set standards appropriate to their own age level. This sounds very much like Rousseau's doctrine of "unfoldment."

Scientific Method and "Bad" and "Good" Concepts of Human Nature

Although both of the outlooks concerning human nature which we have described remain influential, students should realize that they were developed within prescientific modes of thinking. To say that human nature is naturally bad or naturally good is to state a supposedly "self-evident" absolute—not a scientific hypothesis which can be tested through accuracy in interpretation or prediction.

The only way something can be good or bad in a scientifically demonstrable way is for it to be dependably instrumental in the attainment of some agreed-upon goal. For example, it can be shown in many cases that penicillin is "good for" a person who has a bacterial infection; conversely, it can be shown that heavy indulgence in alcohol is "bad for" some persons—it damages the liver. Since almost everyone is agreed that any disease should be avoided, it is proper to use the terms *good* or *bad* in the foregoing examples. All that is meant by *good* and *bad,* as so used, is that something will contribute toward attainment of an end which is desired or help avoid one which is undesired.

On the other hand, it has been argued that there are eternal and universal standards for judging goodness and badness. These standards, if they exist, would be absolutes—truth with a capital "T." Many persons have thought not only that such absolutes exist but also that human beings, or at least a *few,* can ascertain the nature of the absolutes through intuition or revelation. Within this pattern of thinking, if there are innate traits of personality, they might indeed be judged against the absolute principles established by authority. For example, if it could be shown that human beings are naturally dishonest and if there is an absolute principle in the universe to the effect that "dishonesty is bad," then we could say, defensibly, that human beings are a pretty bad lot; they are all, by nature, dishonest. Or if there is some universal, absolute law which decrees that pity is a virtue and if all human beings are endowed with instinctive sympathy for sufferers, as Rousseau thought, we might logically argue that human beings are indeed naturally good.

The same line of reasoning could be applied to the strictly physiological drives. According to most persons who have believed in the natural depravity of human nature, there is some sort of eternal law which decrees that any activity delighting the senses is evil. And believing in this universal principle, they have maintained, with logic, that sensory indulgence of any sort is evidence of depravity. Also, since virtually everyone within their experience has acted as if he enjoyed at least a certain amount of "wine, women, and song," they could logically say that mankind is naturally depraved.

The trouble with using absolutes for judging whether people are naturally good or bad is that absolutes as such cannot be verified by any scientific means. A mystic may claim that he intuitively senses that the taking of life is always wrong, but he has no way of demonstrating this knowledge scientifically. He can cite no experimentation, no observation of fact. He has nothing to cite but his own personal feelings. For this reason, most modern scientific psychologists avoid describing the instinctive nature of man—if they believe he has an instinctive nature—in moralistic terms. This is not to say that psychologists or anyone else can avoid making moral judgments—this we must all do every day of our lives.

Even though modern psychology prefers not to construe human nature as either naturally bad or good, there is reason to believe that Roussellian concepts still have considerable influence. Especially apparent among some psychologists is the idea of natural unfoldment—that people are born with genetic determiners which guide the development of personality.

Not only can it be demonstrated that the whole approach of Puritanism and Roussellianism lacks a scientifically demonstrable basis; we may point also to an accumulation of evidence to the effect that the particular descriptions of human nature fostered by these outlooks are untenable. Puritans tended to take the view that human beings, instinctively, want to do the things which Western society historically has condemned. Rousseau took the view that man in his original state, before society corrupted him, instinctively wants to do what Western society historically has acclaimed. Evidence from modern cultural anthropology denies both outlooks.

One can name any practice which has been upheld as good (except perhaps sexual chastity) and can point to some society in which this practice has represented a dominant behavior pattern. One can name any practice which has been widely condemned and point to a human society in which the practice is prominent. In short, any good or bad trait ever mentioned can be found as a predominant part of the life style of some cultures but not of others. This suggests that there is no race-wide predisposition for either goodness or badness, as these terms traditionally have been defined in Western civilization.

WHAT ARE SOME "SCIENTIFIC" INSTINCT THEORIES OF HUMAN NATURE?

We now come to what may be called the *neutral-active principle* of human nature. At the turn of the twentieth century several instinct theories were developed which had a better claim to scientific status than their earlier counterparts. They could base this claim on the fact that they did little or no moralizing about human nature. They tended to take human nature as it was, so to speak, and to focus on description. Also, their leading propositions appeared susceptible to the test of factual evidence. Instinct psychologies of this sort came to the fore late in the nineteenth century. The eminent American psychologist and philosopher William James (1842–1910) compiled a list of 32 human instincts. This included such innate propensities as imitation, emulation, pugnacity, sympathy, hunting, fear, acquisitiveness, and curiosity.[12] Until about 1925, such instinct theories were widely promoted; however, by the mid-1920s criticism had become so severe that at least in their extreme forms they were abandoned by most psychologists. Of the numerous promoters of instinct theory, we shall examine in very brief and unfortunately oversimplified summaries two important figures, William McDougall and Sigmund Freud.

[12] William James, *The Principles of Psychology*, Holt, 1890, Vol. 1, Chap. 24.

William McDougall (1871–1938)

McDougall was born a Scot, received most of his education in England, and moved to the United States in 1920, where he taught first at Harvard and later at Duke University. He outlined his instinct theory most systematically in *An Introduction to Social Psychology* (1908). This volume passed through approximately twenty-five editions and impressions and was highly influential for a considerable number of years.

McDougall called his system "hormic psychology." Hormic means striving, purposive, or nonmechanical; it derives from the Greek *Hormé*, an approximate synonym for which is "impulse." Hormic psychology assumes that human beings are motivated by an *élan vital* (life force) which is nonmaterial and nonmechanical in its principles of operation—hence, his position is a form of vitalism. (This, of course, is an idea not original with McDougall.) The *élan* provides purposes or goals, which goad an individual into action even when he does not fully understand them. Each specific purpose, or goal, is linked to an instinct or to some combination of instincts.

These instincts are much less specific in a child than in an adult. They are affected by learning; as one grows older the instincts are evoked with considerable consistency in situations appropriate to them. In his 1908 volume McDougall listed a total of 12 instincts, of which he considered 7 to be primary and 5 secondary. Later he extended his list to 13. McDougall's list of instincts includes flight, repulsion, curiosity, pugnacity, self-abasement, self-assertion, parental instinct, instinct of reproduction, sexual jealousy, female coyness, gregariousness, instinct for acquisition, and instinct for construction.[13]

Each instinct has three aspects. The first aspect insures that its owner will see features of his environment in a certain way, e.g., as menacing, and might be called the *perceptual*. The second aspect consists of an *affective* (emotional) response, e.g., the feeling of fear, and might be termed the *emotional*. The third aspect consists of appropriate action, e.g., trying to run away, and might be referred to as the *striving* or *conative* aspect.

Sigmund Freud (1856–1939)

It would be impossible to overestimate the impact of Freud on psychology, or, for that matter, on Western civilization in general. We like Roback's statement concerning Freud:

In psychoanalysis, we have a dynamic psychology with a vengeance. Its originator, Sigmund Freud, whatever we think of his elaborately evolved system, was a genius. . . . Beginning as a physician, engaged at first in neurology

---

[13] William McDougall, *An Introduction to Social Psychology*, Luce, 1923, Chap. 3.

and pediatrics, he found himself in the field of psychiatry, and thence proceeded to revolutionize not only our whole psychological conception but the entire outlook on civilization. There is scarcely a nook or cranny in our humanistic structure but which has been illuminated by the psychoanalytic torch; and the prejudices which Freud has had to surmount in order to spread his gospel have been far more intense than those which Copernicus, Galileo, Kepler, and Darwin had to contend with.[14]

Freud's thinking changed the manner in which mental processes are interpreted, gave us a new vocabulary for labeling mental phenomena, placed sex in a new perspective, and offered a new approach to the treatment of mental illness.

Although containing elements of environmentalism, Freudian psychology is basically an instinct psychology—that is what Roback means by the term *dynamic* in the above quotation. Freud assumed the existence of certain inborn psychological drives which work themselves out as a person grows. Freud did extensive clinical work and felt that his experience with mentally disturbed patients provided scientific support for his interpretation of what is innate in human nature.

Freud divided the mind into three regions—the conscious, the preconscious, and the unconscious. The first is the region of awareness; the second, a region of psychological content which can fairly easily be brought into consciousness when the need arises; the third, a region of deeply buried psychological content which is relatively inaccessible to consciousness. Freud held that much of the content of the unconscious is "repressed" material, i.e., material too distasteful and subject to conflict to be faced openly.

The unconscious, Freud argued, becomes a kind of spring from which well up certain primal—instinctive—impulses. These genetically determined impulses, although seldom understood by a person, direct the formation of his personality. If he fails to handle them properly, they produce illness—either psychological or physiological, or, more often, both.

It has often been noted that Freud spent his formative professional years working with upper-middle- or upper-class Europeans. Furthermore, his clinical work was largely limited not only to these particular social classes but to a particular period in history. We associate Freud's work with the late nineteenth and early twentieth centuries, a period often referred to in the Western world as the Victorian era. During this time middle- and upper-class persons led a return to a rather strict Puritanism. The ideas of John Calvin enjoyed a strong resurgence. Among other things, this meant that most persons of the high social stratum with which Freud worked were both repressed and guilt ridden. Such a group could scarcely be considered representative of the human race in general. Nevertheless,

[14] A. A. Roback, *History of American Psychology*, Library Publishers, 1952, p. 280.

Freud based his conclusions and erected his psychological system on this highly unrepresentative sample of humanity; and here lies one of the important bases for criticism of the Freudian system. What he took to be instinctual impulses might be explained at least to some degree as the learned wants of a particular cultural group during a particular stage of history.

According to Freud, the human personality consists of three major interacting systems, of which the primary is the *id*. The id consists of everything psychological that is present at birth, including the instincts. Instincts stem from somatic excitation, or tension, another name for which is *need;* but they are felt by the person as a *wish*. Although Freud made no attempt to catalog the instincts, he classified them under two main groups, the *life* instincts and the *death* instincts. Life instincts include hunger, thirst, and sex; the form of energy which impels them Freud labeled the *libido*. Of the various instincts encompassed under the libido, Freud considered sex to be the most driving. The life instincts tend to subside as a person ages and the death instincts increase in force—leading to Freud's famous dictum, "The goal of all life is death."

According to Freud, as a child matures he develops a tendency to restrain his id. He learns, so to speak, to clamp a lid on it (or perhaps the idea of the governor on a motor would be more apt). This tendency is what most people refer to when they speak of development of conscience. Freud used the term *superego* for this restraining force. The superego is learned: it grows as a result of threats and punishment and later becomes established in the form of ideas which make an individual to some degree self-governing.

The third major tendency in a developing person is toward the use of reason. Through rational thought processes one tries to work out a decent balance between the demands of the id and of the superego. One attempts to gratify the demands of his id but not to let such gratification get out of hand. This tendency Freud labeled the *ego*. Like the superego, the ego appears to be largely a product of learning. The potentiality is there at birth, as in the case of the superego, but environment determines the extent to which the potentiality is developed. Freudian theory, then, although properly called an instinct theory, also contains a large element of environmentalism. We stress that id, superego, and ego are processes or functions and not substances.

Since we are treating instinct theories, let us return to the id, which, according to Freud, represents the instinctual component of human nature. In the first year of life an infant gains his primary satisfaction from eating. Sex, in the Freudian system, must be construed broadly. Erotic pleasure is gained not merely from stimulation of the sexual organs but also from manipulation, rubbing and stroking, or normal functioning of other bodily organs and areas. Hence feeding, specifically sucking, may be an infant's first source of erotic pleasure, and this early period in life is referred to by Freudian psychologists as the *oral period*.

The oral period ends some time near the close of the first year of life. A new stage appears when erotic pleasure becomes centered in the processes of elimination. Freud referred to this as the *anal period*. According to him, perhaps because he did his major work in the Victorian era, parents typically attempt to toilet-train their children through relatively autocratic methods. Therefore, a child is frustrated in one of his most firmly implanted instinctual drives.

At about the end of the third year a typical child enters the third stage; he discovers that his genitals can be used as a source of direct pleasure. But, in the Freudian system, there is more to this period than mere manipulation of the sexual organs. A child—instinctively—begins to be attracted by the opposite sex. Since the members of the opposite sex whom a child knows best are his parents, a boy is drawn to his mother, a girl to her father. At the same time, a child may develop hostility toward the parent of his own sex. Because of a child's growing interest in direct gratification of the sexual urge, Freud referred to this third stage as the *phallic period*. Freud introduced the term *Oedipal period*, as a description of the growing attachment to the parent of the opposite sex.[15] If a child never outgrows the attachment, he is said to have an Oedipus complex. According to Freudians, people who never fully outgrow the oral or the anal period are oral or anal personality types. In fact, it appears that Freud did not place emphasis on the oral, anal, and phallic periods as divisions of time in a person's life, but rather considered them orientations of personality which could exist any time during a life span.

Objections to Scientific Instinct Theories

We have seen that there are several grounds for criticizing the "moralistic" theories of instinctual human nature described earlier in the chapter. There are likewise grounds for criticizing the more modern, nonmoralistic instinct theories. The chief problem with the so-called "modern" theories is that they are very difficult to support with factual evidence. It is easy to say, for example, that man is instinctively warlike and that for this reason permanent peace among nations is an impossibility. Certainly throughout his history man has fought intermittently. However, there are uncountable instances in which human beings have lived in peace together, for long periods of time. Therefore, one can find just as much evidence to support the opposite idea that man is instinctively peace-loving.

[15] The term is derived from the Greek play by Sophocles, *Oedipus, the King*, in which a son kills his father and marries his mother.

It is very easy to assign instincts to man; in fact, we can make a parlor game out of it. Everyone can come up with his own list. Psychologists of the late nineteenth and early twentieth centuries who claimed numerous rather specific instincts for the human species offered no real evidence to support their theories; nor did they agree among themselves as to what should be included in a listing of instincts. It appears that every behavioral trait which has been listed as instinctive could also be learned.

Contemporary instinct theorists place most of their reliance on two sources of evidence:

1. *Clinical experience.* Clinical psychologists and psychiatrists work with large numbers of patients. Their relationship with patients enables them to uncover much about a patient's inner thoughts. If a pattern is discovered which seems to be present in all patients, the temptation is to describe it as instinctual. The weakness of this kind of evidence is that most or all of the patients of a given clinical psychologist or psychiatrist have a common cultural background and it is always possible that their shared thought patterns are simply an outcome of common experiences—in short, a result of learning.

2. *Evidence from anthropological study.* Cultural anthropologists have tried to identify manners of thinking common to all human cultures. Some psychological traits have been identified which certainly are widespread and possibly exist in every culture. However, it always seems possible to find exceptions—individuals who do not exhibit these traits. Even if we could locate a psychological trait which is expressed universally, we still would not have conclusive evidence that the trait was not learned as a result of some element common to all cultures.

WHICH THEORIES OF PERSONALITY REJECT INSTINCT?

We have treated a series of outlooks, each of which assumes that to some degree human personality is "given." That is, there is something about human nature that is both innate and distinctive, setting man off from other members of the animal kingdom.

There is an opposed school of thought which denies that any of man's psychological traits are hereditary. In other words, what we call human nature is entirely a matter of learning. Man learns to be human as he associates with other human beings; he is born human only in the sense that he comes into the world as a biological organism different in many respects from the organisms of other species. If man is born without innate psychological tendencies, obviously he is *morally neutral*. Moreover, most persons who reject completely the possibility of innate personality construe man as a passive organism who, in his behavior, is entirely dominated by his environment. Thus, the over-all position we are about to describe reflects the *neutral-passive principle* of human nature.

A favorite type of study which persons of this school of thought cite is the study of feral man. A feral child or youth (or man, if one were ever to be found) is a person who through some unusual circumstance has been deprived of human culture. An infant may have been taken and reared by animals, as by wolves, or in solitude in a room or part of a house shut off from human habitation. A considerable number of such cases have been reported.[16]

There is some doubt concerning the authenticity of most accounts concerning feral children. Often they are based upon second- or third-hand reports. Sometimes they are incorporated in the legendry of a culture, as in the Romulus and Remus myth. However, a few such stories seem authentic. In each instance, a child reared outside of human culture lacked all human characteristics except the strictly biological. In fact, a child so reared lacks a definable personality—he appears to be *nothing but a physiological organism*. In the few instances where infants were reared a few years by animals the child acted like the animal with which he lived. His personality was the animal personality. These cases are cited as evidence supporting the notion that human personality and character are a matter of learning rather than of instinct. We should remember, however, that such children cannot talk and we have no adequate means of determining what their "psychological world" is really like.

Another popular type of evidence to support this view are personality studies conducted by cultural anthropologists. Many workers in this field, as well as in psychology and sociology, think there are national character types. (Character, in this instance, should be taken to mean the same as personality.) These character types appear to be a product or function of a culture. Within a particular culture, individuals share enough traits in common so that it might appear to those who study them that personality is instinctive. However, according to anthropologists, a personality type which is common in one culture may not exist at all in another, and personality differences from culture to culture may be relatively extreme.[17] Whereas in one culture a typical individual may be aggressive, in another he may be self-effacing, in a third he may be puritanical and repressed, and in a fourth he may be a libertine.

The notion that man is lacking in instincts, that personality is strictly a learned affair, may be very old; but its period of popularity does not

[16] For a treatment of such reports, see J. A. L. Singh and Robert M. Zingg, *Wolf-Children and Feral Man,* Harper, 1942.

[17] For a classic exposition of this subject, see Ruth Benedict, *Patterns of Culture,* Houghton Mifflin, 1934. She compares the Zuñi, Kwakiutl, and Dobu cultures and their personality types.

extend backward very far in time. We shall present a small part of the history of this idea.

John Locke and *Tabula Rasa*

John Locke (1632–1704) was in large part responsible for popularizing the notion that man not only comes into the world without instinct but also is so constructed as to be a passive receiver of environmental stimuli. According to Locke, the mind of an infant at birth is a *tabula rasa,* an expression which in Latin means literally "scraped tablet." A scraped tablet (meaning a "clean slate" or "blank sheet of paper") is completely free of impressions. It is ready to receive sensory data from the environment and to record it. Locke recognized that a human mind is hardly as simple as a camera; for example, in his theory of "secondary qualities" he held that the mind is capable of experiences which do not duplicate any reality existing outside the experiencer. However, he regarded these secondary qualities as somehow derived from sensory perception. ". . . even the most *abstruse* ideas, how remote soever they may seem from sense, or from any operation of our own minds, are yet only such as the understanding frames to itself, by repeating and joining together ideas that it had either from objects of sense, or from its own operations about them."[18] Hence, we see that in Locke's frame of reference a mind consists either of impressions, or images, which reflect or portray environmental objects; or of impressions derived from these. So in a very real sense a human mind is like a camera, except that it is a very special kind of camera which can make additional, and different, pictures from the pictures it has already taken of the outside environment.

Under the *tabula rasa* concept, man is not regarded as an active dynamic agent, acting upon a passive environment. Now it is the environment which is regarded as dynamic and the individual as passive. The person is shaped by an environment which may not have any more interest in him than it has in a horse, a snake, or a stone. This outlook is an extreme form of environmentalism. It contrasts sharply with theories which assume that human nature has an instinctual basis. It rejects the idea of an active, purposive mind and assumes that mind is essentially a reactant and receptacle.

Twentieth-Century *Tabula Rasa* Theorists

We already have seen how a large group of psychologists and social scientists, about the beginning of the twentieth century, came to accept

---

[18] John Locke, *On the Human Understanding,* in *The Works of John Locke,* Ward, Lock, 1888 (?), p. 110.

a nonmoralistic type of instinct theory and how, after 15 or 20 years, this notion, in turn, came under widespread attack. It should be noted that the supposition that human beings lack instincts was being introduced at the same time that a few instinct theorists were still developing their positions. Even as McDougall tried to clarify and communicate his dynamic psychology, with its intricate pattern of instincts, John B. Watson was attracting attention with a form of behavioristic psychology reminiscent in certain respects of the ideas of John Locke.[19]

Watson, following the experimentation and thinking of Pavlov and Bekhterev, held that virtually all of human behavior can be explained as conditioning. Responses become linked to stimuli as a result of repeated conjunction, and a person's personality represents the sum total of these responses. Watson did not rule out completely the existence of innate patterns of behavior. He saw any supposedly innate behavior as taking the form of mechanical, inborn reflexes. Thus, he accepted the idea of a variety of innate reflexes related to the physiological processes involved in maintaining the body. In addition to organic reflexes such as sucking and breathing, he postulated the existence of innate "love," fear, and anger responses. These inborn reflexes he regarded as essential to organic self-preservation or race preservation. Man was not "given" these reflexes so he could survive; rather, the men able to survive through the ages of history were the ones who happened to have these reflexes.

In spite of his recognition of these survival characteristics of the human organism, Watson evidently thought of human nature as being relatively "open"—that is, without content prior to conditioning by the environment. His view is made clear by the following quotation: "Give me a dozen healthy infants, well-formed, and my own special world to bring them up in, and I'll guarantee to take any one at random and train him to become any kind of specialist I might select—doctor, lawyer, artist, merchant-chief, and, yes beggarman and thief, regardless of his talents, penchants, tendencies, abilities, vocations, and the race of his ancestors."[20]

Watson was without question highly influential in American psychology. The school of thought to which we attach his name—behaviorism—dominated American psychology for a generation or more. We cannot credit Watson or his followers with being the chief agents of the demolition of instinct theory; behavioristic psychologists were themselves not in agreement as to whether instincts exist and, if so, what role they play. But the general tendency of behavioristic psychology was toward environmentalism, toward the idea that the chief content of a human per-

[19] See John B. Watson and William McDougall, *The Battle of Behaviorism*, Norton, 1929.

[20] John B. Watson, *Behaviorism*, rev. ed., Norton, 1930, p. 104.

sonality is learned responses, that an adult is very much what his environment has made him. According to this view, a learner's role is merely to react mechanistically to environmental stimulation.

This over-all point of view, which we refer to here as the modern *tabula rasa* outlook, has influenced an entire generation of sociologists and cultural anthropologists, as well as psychologists. It even has spilled over into the popular mind, so that probably most adults have at least a streak of *tabula rasa* thinking in them.[21]

Those who insist that there is no instinctual basis for human personality have not fully established their case. Just as we have no convincing evidence that there is an instinctual component in human nature, likewise we have no convincing evidence that there is not. One prominent group of psychologists, the neo-Freudians, many of whom are engaged in the practice of psychiatry, are convinced that the human mind is not merely a *tabula rasa*. If we define instinct broadly so as to allow for great flexibility in the way it can manifest itself, including the time in life when it first appears, the case for instincts can be strengthened.

It is possible to by-pass the issue of instinct vs. *tabula rasa*, or the "active" vs. the "passive" conceptions of human nature. Indeed, a popular approach today is to focus on the *interaction* of man and his environment, and to adopt a position which might be stated in its shorthand form as a *neutral-interactive principle* of human nature. The interactive concept, at least as we intend to define interaction, stems from, and in fact is only made possible by, growth of the concept of *relativism*. The idea of relativism has invaded all the sciences and has influenced the thinking of laymen as well. In the section to follow, we set forth this position in brief outline. Much of the rest of the book will contribute toward developing in detail a relativistic neutral-interactive position.

WHAT IS A RELATIVISTIC DEFINITION OF HUMAN NATURE?

A central idea of relativism is that any object derives its qualities not merely from something inside itself but from the total situation, i.e., its surroundings as well as itself. Another way of putting it is that no object has meaning apart from its context. Applying this idea to man, we can understand what a man is like only by studying him as he operates within his environment. Our object of study must be a *unit* which can be stated as "a-discerning-person-in-interaction-with-his-environment."

Since man-environment situations seem capable of endless variation, then human nature is capable of endless variation. A San Franciscan is

[21] For an excellent exposition of the *tabula rasa*, or mechanistic, view of man, see Joseph Wood Krutch, *The Measure of Man*, Bobbs-Merrill, 1954.

likely to have a different nature from a Bostonian. Both San Franciscan and Bostonian are likely to have different natures ten years from now from what they have now. Human nature does not "stay put."

It is necessary at this point to distinguish between *human nature* and *original nature*. Original nature consists of the organic structure and functions possessed at birth. To a large degree it is determined genetically—that is, by heredity—although the interaction of a fetus with its prenatal environment may influence the precise manner in which genetic inheritance manifests itself at the time of birth. Original nature is to a considerable degree fixed; but as soon as this is said, a qualification is necessary: even man's original nature is modified in small ways through interaction. For example, a person may inherit the potential for a certain body structure, but this structure may never be realized because of disease or malnourishment.

In contrast to his original nature, man does not have human nature prior to birth. Human nature is acquired through human fellowship. It is a descriptive term for the attitudes, values, beliefs, and knowledge which accrue through a person's interaction with a social environment. Human nature cannot be defined in terms of specific traits. That is, we cannot say that man is naturally warlike or naturally selfish or naturally gregarious. It is true that most human beings are rather gregarious; but it is just as "natural" to want to "take to the hills" and be alone as it is to want to be with people. With this viewpoint about human nature, we are now prepared to answer the question posed in the chapter title. Human nature is *not* natural if by natural we mean instinctive or innate.

At this point readers may feel inclined to ask how this definition of human nature differs from that of John B. Watson and all other *tabula rasa* theorists. The difference lies in our conception of man as an active, exploring, and purposive creature. To the *tabula rasa* theorist, man's habitual pose is passivity; man waits to act until he is stimulated. On the other hand, the neutral-interactionist position holds that man is fundamentally purposive; he continuously generates wants which he then sets out to satisfy. Notice that, when man is considered neutral-interactive, his neutrality extends only to goodness-badness, not to activity-passivity. Man's wants may or may not be related to basic organic drives, such as hunger, thirst, or sex. When they are not so related, they are still not derived from instincts. Instincts are usually defined as inherited specific patterns of behavior which are common to a species. Human wants are specific so far as individuals are concerned but vary greatly from one individual to another.

Granting that human purpose is highly individualized, are there no common purposes, common motivations, or common thoughts apart from those directly related to satisfaction of organic drives? Are there no general principles governing human behavior? We think it is possible to make some general statements about the psychological functioning of persons in a social environment. A human being has two kinds of "organization," physical and psychological. We do not mean to imply that they are unrelated, or, in fact, that they are anything other than different sides of a coin. But from the standpoint of an individual, it is possible to talk of one's physiology and one's conscious behavior in different terms. Therefore, it is fair to say that we have a physiological or bodily organization and a psychological organization. A prime goal in life is to maintain organization. Many persons do not seek strongly to maintain their bodily organization, otherwise we would have no suicides and no people eating or drinking themselves to death, or in other ways damaging their bodies unnecessarily.

On the other hand, apparently a nearly universal trait of human beings is a desire to preserve their psychological organization. One's psychological organization is one's self, or, as Combs and Snygg call it, one's *perceived self*. Psychological organization consists of interests, attitudes, values, beliefs, and knowledge and their relationship to one another.[22]

We do not merely seek to maintain our psychological organization at a status quo level. We try to improve it so that we will be able to cope with future exigencies. We improve our psychological organization by adapting it to our changing needs; only in this manner may the organization be said to be adequate. One of our major needs is self-enhancement—not merely bodily preservation but also improvement of perceived self. We must engage in self-enhancement in order to maintain self-respect. Combs and Snygg stress the importance of achieving a satisfactory psychological organization. "From birth to death the maintenance of the . . . [perceived] self is the most pressing, the most crucial, if not the only task of existence."[23]

Once a man has achieved a reasonably adequate perceived self, he may resist any change in thought pattern which would jeopardize his present organization. However, when he perceives his mental structure as inadequate, he may actively seek new ideas, and he is therefore capable of change. He may even become a revolutionary. The old saying "You can't change human nature" is rooted in the assumption of instinctive and fixed personality traits. A relativistic psychologist's position is that human nature changes all the time and that the range of man's capacities is doubtless tremendously wider than has been indicated in anything now achieved or even envisioned.

Man probably is the only creature who is aware of himself—who is

---

[22] Arthur W. Combs and Donald Snygg, *Individual Behavior,* rev. ed., Harper, 1959, pp. 129–130.
[23] *Ibid.,* p. 45.

"self-conscious." He can and does think about the state of human existence: what he is, whence he came, and what is his destination. Probably man alone among living creatures speculates about the nature of his dying and fears (or in some cases welcomes) dying long in advance of the occasion. Man is apparently the only creature who can think abstractly and capture abstractions in the form of symbols. Although many lower animals undoubtedly think, in man the power of thought reaches its highest complexity. Man, more than other animals, can direct the course of his life through using his current judgment of a past to structure a future. It is in this power to remold himself and his environment intelligently that hope for future improvement in the human condition lies.

Although man is capable of reflective decisions, we are all too well aware that much of the time he seems irrational and irresponsible. Up to this point in history, only a very small part of his effort has been given to the exercise of intelligence. But if human nature is not fixed, if it is infinitely modifiable, then there is no reason why man should not learn to follow the course of intelligence more of the time than he now does.

BIBLIOGRAPHY

Brinton, Crane, *Ideas and Men*, Prentice-Hall, 1950. (Last half published as a Mentor paperback under the title *The Shaping of the Modern Mind*, 1953.)
  A history of Western thought which contains good background material on subjects such as the traditional Christian view of the nature of man, the Roussellian conception of human nature, and the Lockian view. Brinton's *History of Western Morals* also contains much material pertinent to the good-bad antithesis.
Burtt, Edwin A., *Types of Religious Philosophy*, Harper, 1951.
  A revised edition of an earlier work. Surveys historically, and in terms of contemporary issues, leading religious outlooks concerning the nature of man.
Cantril, Hadley, and Charles H. Bumstead, *Reflections on the Human Venture*, New York University Press, 1960.
  Treatment of major issues in psychology from a relativistic view. Draws evidence largely from insights of novelists, poets, and playwrights. Excellent quotations. A profound book, likely to become a classic.
Dewey, John, *Human Nature and Conduct*, Holt, 1922.
  Dewey's "psychology." It describes human nature in relativistic terms. Difficult but extremely rewarding for superior students.
Fromm, Erich, *The Sane Society*, Rinehart, 1955.
  The most recent major statement of a famous neo-Freudian. The concept of alienation, although defined by different writers differently, runs through the writing of most neo-Freudians.

Hall, Calvin S., and Gardner Lindzey, *Theories of Personality*, Wiley, 1957.
  Description of 12 different "scientific" personality theories, including stimulus-response, Freudian and neo-Freudian, Lewin's, and other relativistic and nonrelativistic theories. Excellent as a reference source.

Kelley, Earl C., and Marie I. Rasey, *Education and the Nature of Man*, Harper, 1952.
  Very readable. See Chapters 3–6 for one of the best available treatments of a relativistic conception of human nature.

Krutch, Joseph Wood, *Human Nature and the Human Condition*, Random, 1959.
  Krutch's attack on relativistic explanations in favor of a belief in an innate human nature. Contrasts with his attack, in an earlier book, *The Measure of Man*, on all mechanistic explanations of human nature.

Murphy, Gardner, *Historical Introduction to Modern Psychology*, Harcourt, Brace, 1949.
  A history of psychological thought treating the positions of Locke and the modern scientific psychologists. Perhaps the most readable of the histories of psychology.

Murphy, Gardner, *Human Potentialities*, Basic Books, 1958.
  An optimistic book which focuses on what man might become. Draws upon a number of sciences, but at times seems more of an inspirational statement than a sober scientific thesis. Murphy presents a field psychology derived from Lewin's which in the main is relativistic.

Parrington, Vernon L., *Main Currents in American Thought*, Harcourt, Brace, 1927.
  An excellent treatment of American Puritanism, focusing on thought patterns (Vol. I). Vol. II, Part II, continues the discussion. Vol. II also explores some aspects of the impact of Rousseau.

Pastore, Nicholas, *The Nature-Nurture Controversy*, King's Crown, 1949. Foreword by Goodwin Watson.
  Description of how a number of distinguished scientists have analyzed this issue. In addition, the book shows how their scientific conclusions may have been influenced by the prevailing social-political outlook of the times. Watson's short foreword is excellent. Students should read at least the essay by Charles Horton Cooley.

Randall, John Herman, *The Making of the Modern Mind*, Houghton Mifflin, 1940.
  Excellent treatment of most of the conceptions of human nature which have been popular historically. See Chapters XIII and XX for "scientific" theories, Chapter XVI for romantic naturalism, and Chapter VII for the Calvinist-Puritan view.

3
WHAT IS MAN'S BIOLOGICAL NATURE?

In the previous chapter we discussed different theories concerning the psychological nature of man. We now undertake to explore certain questions relating to man's biological or "original" nature. Some pertinent questions are: Is a psychological person the same as a biological organism? Is it closely related to a biological organism? Or is it something completely different? A student concerned with the nature of man should in some way incorporate biological man into his total scheme.

In this chapter we turn to another way of looking at man in his most generalized aspects. We describe certain facets of human beings, and of life in general, as a biologist might. It should be realized that, although a substantial amount is known about human biology, there are still many unanswered questions. So far, biologists have asked more questions than they have been able to answer; yet there is no assurance even that the best questions have been formulated.

Psychology is related to biology in the sense that the two subjects represent different ways of looking at the same life process. A biologist is primarily interested in the organic, physiological, or somatic aspects of living creatures; a psychologist is—or should be—primarily interested in the psychological, mentalistic, or motivational aspects. Students in each field need to know the major findings in the other.

Some of the material covered in this chapter reviews the work of freshman or sophomore biology and physiology courses. However, the chapter delves into matters, such as the nature of mind, which students rarely encounter in lower-division college courses. Furthermore, it focuses primarily on a particular school of thought in biology—that commonly labeled *organismic*. Just as there are different views about the psychological nature of man, as we showed in Chapter 2, there are different views about the biological nature of man. We intend to describe some of these views and show how they contrast.

Our treatment of biological questions, like our treatment of psychological—and in Chapter 4 sociological—questions, is philosophical in the sense that it grapples with fundamental questions which have philosophical implications. To a student of biology, there is no question more fundamental than the one posed in the following heading.

WHAT IS LIFE?

Living creatures, including man, seem in much of their functioning to act like complicated, exquisitely constructed mechanisms which obey many of the common laws of chemistry and physics. At the same time, such life processes as assimilation, metabolism, and muscular contraction appear to be under some sort of central control. Life is coordinated. Also, life seems to display a coordination of effort directed toward certain ends, such as preservation and propagation of a species and the maintenance of as much physical comfort as possible. In lower forms of life, plants, sea anemones, and amoebas, for example, a control center is not visible. In higher forms, control appears to be centered in the neuroendocrine system, i.e., brain, nerves, and the regulatory glands. The higher an animal on the phylogenetic scale, the more important the brain, and particularly the cerebrum, as a control center.

But to explain this is not to explain much. How does the control center work? What makes it go? Perhaps there is as yet no scientifically defensible answer. We know that in the higher life forms there is continuous electrical activity in the central nervous system and that the waves, or pulsations, which can be measured, vary greatly depending on the state of the animal—whether it is at rest, asleep, thinking, engaged in physical activity, etc. But to the question of the significance of the apparent autonomous electrical activity of the central nervous system a well-known psychologist, Hebb, tells us, "Not even a tentative answer is available."[1] One of the pioneers and present ranking experts in the measurement of electrical activity of living creatures is E. D. Adrian. He states, "Perhaps the chief impression which will be left by this account [Adrian's discussion of the significance of brain waves] is the complete inability of contemporary science to give a satisfactory picture of any kind of mental activity."[2]

[1] D. O. Hebb, *The Organization of Behavior,* Wiley, 1949, p. xvi.
[2] E. D. Adrian, *The Physical Background of Perception,* Oxford University Press, 1947, p. 1.

Although little can be demonstrated scientifically, one of the favorite subjects of human speculation through the ages has been the basic nature of life, and particularly that aspect of life which we call mind. Out of this speculation several hypotheses have arisen. We discuss three of them on the pages to follow. The first two have ancient origins; the last is largely a product of twentieth-century thought.

Vitalism

According to a majority of vitalists, a living organism may be compared to a living piece of machinery which *in itself* is incapable of experiencing consciousness. It is unable in itself to will, purpose, reflect, imagine, or have aesthetic experience. Like an electronic computer, it requires something of an entirely different and unique order to direct it. A person who defines a physiological organism in this manner must assume the presence of some kind of "life force" which "makes the body go." McDougall's "hormic psychology" (p. 42) is an example of a vitalistic position. The life force, or *élan vital* as it is often called, is nonmaterial, nonmechanical, and nonchemical. To use a simple analogy, the body is an automobile, the life force its driver; or the body is a piano, the life force its player.

To a vitalist, the *élan vital* is mind, or at least one aspect of mind. One theory has been that mind is a substance, or entity, but obviously a substance utterly unlike the material objects of experience.[3] Mind has been regarded as a substance because of its assumed unchanging qualities (compare oxygen, a material substance, which, so long as it remains oxygen, continues to have the same properties). What are the properties of mind substance according to those who think it exists? It is nonmaterial, invisible, indestructible, the same among all men, and possessed of certain powers, all of which come under the general head of thinking. Examples of the powers of mind substance are willing, purposing, reflecting, imagining, and remembering.

Plato usually is regarded as one of the first persons to systematize and popularize the idea that mind is a substance. René Descartes (1596–1650) was probably the next person to do major work with the concept. Descartes asserted that mind is sharply separated from nature, that matter and mind are substances completely different in essence. The essence of mind is *pure thought*. The essence of matter is *extension;* it has length, breadth, and thickness. A human mind uses the body as its instrument, but mind can act independently of brain. Descartes felt, however, that mind resides in the body; he was even so specific as to pinpoint the location: the pineal gland, a tiny organ imbedded in the base of the brain. Descartes's outlook is commonly referred to as "mind-body" dualism.

[3] Most of the discussion in this chapter on the nature of mind is influenced by Charles W. Morris, *Six Theories of Mind,* University of Chicago Press, 1932. Also highly pertinent is Boyd H. Bode, *How We Learn,* Heath, 1940.

Cartesian, i.e., deriving from Descartes, dualism has been a subject of much dispute and criticism. Its critics argue that no dualist has ever provided an adequate explanation of how a nonmaterial substance can act upon a material substance. Furthermore, the evidence of common sense suggests that mental functioning is profoundly affected by physical states; for example, people who are ill, or who have suffered brain damage, think less well than those in a normal physical state. Dualists have never explained how, if mind is a nonmaterial substance independent of matter, it can be so affected.

Many philosophers, and psychologists with a philosophical turn of mind, have tried to retain the idea that mind is a nonmaterial substance, equivalent to soul or spirit, and at the same time eliminate the difficulties arising from trying to explain how a nonmaterial substance can act upon a material one. In short, they have tried to avoid a mind-body dualism, most commonly by simply eliminating one side of the mind-body pair—a person retains mind but assumes that physical matter is such in superficial appearance only. This position assumes that in actuality the physical body, and indeed all material substance, is a *projection* either of the finite minds of individuals or of the infinite mind of God. A leading exponent of the idea that perception of a thing is what gives it existence was an Irish philosopher and bishop, George Berkeley (1685–1753). The notion that mind is the only existent in the universe, and that material substance is an illusion, is associated with a philosophical school of thought known as *absolute idealism* and identified with G. W. F. Hegel.

Another point of view regards mind as a nonmaterial entity but not as a substance in the sense that its properties are fixed. According to this view the properties of mind evolve, and there is no telling what the outcome may be. We see here the influence of the concept of evolution. Although there have been a great many exponents of the idea that mind is an emergent spiritual force, two persons who stated the position sharply were the Frenchman Henri Bergson (1859–1941) and the Italian Giovanni Gentile (1875–1944). Bergson went a long way toward eliminating mind-body dualism by declaring the supremacy of mind. In this respect, we can see in him a Berkeleian influence. However, Bergson talked of the mind's using the body as an instrument and of the separability of mind from body. He also talked of mind as having unity, in contrast to matter, which is divisible. Such ideas are obviously dualistic.

Gentile did not refer to mind as an existent but rather as pure activity from which all that we know as existence springs. Since, according to Gentile, mind is activity or process in an everlasting state of change, and since all material substance is a product of mind-acts, it follows that all material substance is likewise in a state of constant flux. To Gentile, the universe consists basically of acts of thought, that is, acts of mind. Mind has no existence apart from its acts and its actions have no limitations in space and time. Gentile went about as far as one can go in making mind, or spirit, the basis of everything man is aware of and at the same time eliminating any kind of eternal law or governing principle.

All of this may seem to students abstruse and even irrelevant. Nevertheless, we have been dealing with one of the bedrock issues in connection with the question, What is life? Our attitudes toward children, and the way we go about working with them, are likely to be colored by whether we are vitalists or take some other position.

Most contemporary biologists in the United States reject vitalism in favor of one or the other of the two outlooks to be described next. Vitalism has come to be regarded as old-fashioned. However, to be fair we cannot ignore the fact that a number of brilliant scientists have, in despair, given up trying to explain the full range of behavior among animals and men without introducing a mental force separate from, but interacting with, the physical body. The well-known physicist A. S. Eddington has expressed what is essentially a dualistic position (*The Philosophy of Physical Science*, 1939). C. S. Sherrington, a pioneer in neurophysiology, adopted a dualistic outlook (see his *Man on His Nature*, 1951). E. D. Adrian, one of the world's leading authorities on neural electrical phenomena, talks in terms of a mind-brain dualism and says "the addition of mental events . . . seems to rule out a purely physical description of all that happens . . ." and ". . . if it is found that physical mechanisms cannot even explain all that happens in the brain, we shall have to decide when and where *the mind* intervenes."[4] Another neurophysiologist, John C. Eccles, frankly espouses a Cartesian dualism, i.e., the theory of mind-body dualism proposed by René Descartes, and attempts to develop a scientifically respectable theory of how a brain could interact with a life force which is not detectable by any instruments we now have.[5]

Mechanism

Mechanists (also sometimes called materialists) try to explain the whole of life in terms of operation of the laws of physics and chemistry. They assume that living protoplasm is nothing more than a highly complex organization of chemicals and electrical phenomena. They stanchly refuse to accept, as necessary in explaining life, any sort of nonmaterial mental or spiritual force. Behavior, they maintain, is best explained as responses to stimuli from either outside or inside an organism. Wells, Huxley, and Wells compare the mammalian body to a gasoline motor and

[4] Adrian, *op. cit.*, p. 4. (Our italics.)
[5] John C. Eccles, *The Neurophysiological Basis of Mind,* Clarendon, 1953, especially Chap. 6.

go on to say, "Now is this analysis sound? Is a living man fundamentally a machine? That is a question capable of experimental decision. We can measure the amount of food that a man or an animal consumes over a given period of time, and we can measure the energy yielded during the same period. If we burn an equal weight of similar food in a suitable apparatus and find out how much energy its combustion yields, and if this value is equal to the energy yielded by the experimental subject, then evidently the living organism, so far as its energy-output is concerned, is really and precisely a combustion engine."[6] After citing experiments designed to test this proposition, these authors conclude that "man and the animals generally are fundamentally mechanisms, driven by the energy liberated in the oxidation of food."[7] They concede, however, that the machine-like properties of the body do not explain everything. For example, they do not explain growth, reproduction, and consciousness. But the latter phenomena are explainable, they reason, without resorting to a belief in soul, spirit, or mysterious "life force."[8] Huxley in his later writings, such as *Evolution in Action* and certain essays in *Man in the Modern World*, seems to move toward an outlook more like what we describe under our third category, which will follow.

Mechanists have given much attention to the task of explaining mental phenomena in physical terms. The development of electronic computers ("electronic brains") has stimulated attempts to describe what we call mind as a product of a complex system of computation, making use of electrochemical processes. In a provocative paper delivered before the Hixon Symposium in 1948 the late John von Neumann, a brilliant mathematician associated with the Princeton Institute for Advanced Study, explored the question of whether it would be possible to build a computer having the essential attributes of a living organism. Von Neumann states, ". . . some regularities which we observe in the organization of . . . [natural organisms] may be quite instructive in our thinking and planning of . . . [automata, or computers]; and conversely, a good deal of our experience and difficulties with our artificial automata can be to some extent projected on our interpretations of natural organisms."[9] Von Neumann compares an individual neuron with a vacuum tube of a computer. A vacuum tube in a digital computer is a yes-or-no organ; similarly, individual neurons discharge on a yes-or-no basis. Computing machines are capable, he says, of logical calculations and of memory. Von Neumann

[6] H. G. Wells, Julian S. Huxley, and G. P. Wells, *The Science of Life*, Literary Guild, 1934, pp. 29–30.

[7] *Ibid.*, p. 30.

[8] *Ibid.*, pp. 1270–1277.

[9] John von Neumann, "The General and Logical Theory of Automata," in Lloyd A. Jeffress, ed., *Cerebral Mechanisms in Behavior*, Wiley, 1951, p. 2.

also elaborates on the idea that it is theoretically possible to build an artificial automaton which can reproduce itself.[10]

Mechanists have historically favored some sort of reflex-arc theory for explaining behavior. A reflex arc is defined as a circuit which consists of a sense organ, such as an eye, a nerve leading from the sense organ to a central "switching area" (the spinal cord or brain), and a nerve leading outward from the switching area to a muscle or gland. When the sense organ is stimulated, a "message" tours the circuit and produces a response of muscle or gland.

The reflex-arc concept in biology has a long history. Descartes came to conceive of all the lower animals as simple machines. He noted that muscular reactions seemed to follow predictably from stimulation of sense organs and reasoned that there were incoming and outgoing pathways which provided fixed channels for an animal's whole repertory of acts. (As we have seen, Descartes placed man in a different category—man had a soul, or mind.) Pierre Cabanis (1757–1808), a French philosopher and physician, argued that human beings exhibit a level of behavior as mechanical as that of the lower animals. He asserted that stimulus-response connections in man which do not reach the brain but are channeled through the spinal cord show the same reflex quality which Descartes thought he had observed in the behavior of lower animals.[11] The term *reflected movement* (or reflex) was coined in 1736. Boring attributes the first detailed treatment of the subject to the German physiologist, Müller, who published his work on the subject between 1833 and 1840.[12]

It remained for psychologists of the late nineteenth and early twentieth centuries to extend the reflex-arc concept to include all, or virtually all, of human behavior. Reflexes were thought to be either inborn—a part of a person's original biological equipment—or learned. In the latter case, they involved the fixing, or "stamping in," of some new connection between specific afferent (incoming) and efferent (outgoing) nerves. The afferent "messages," it was thought, may be channeled through the spinal cord only, or through both cord and brain. Stimulation of the receptor (sense organ) was held to cause an automatic, predictable, and almost instantaneous response in the effector (reacting muscle or gland). Reflex arcs presumably are illustrated by such phenomena as knee jerk, blinking

[10] Advanced students who wish further to study modern attempts to explain life in physicalist terms may find of interest Norbert Wiener's *Cybernetics*, Wiley, 1948, or W. Ross Ashy's *An Introduction to Cybernetics*, Chapman & Hall, 1956. Also by the same author, *Design for a Brain*, Wiley, 1952. John von Neumann's posthumously published *Computer and the Brain*, Yale University Press, 1958 is also pertinent.

[11] Gardner Murphy, *Historical Introduction to Modern Psychology*, Harcourt, Brace, 1949, pp. 18, 38.

[12] Edwin G. Boring, *A History of Experimental Psychology*, Appleton-Century, 1929, p. 39.

(when an eye is threatened), withdrawal from a painful object, and the like. We associate such a development in biological and in psychological thought with the names of I. P. Pavlov (1849–1936), a Russian biologist, Vladimir Bekhterev (1857–1927), a Russian neuropathologist, and, in this country, Edward L. Thorndike (1874–1949), and John B. Watson (1878–1958).

The reflex-arc concept, particularly in the simple form in which it was held early in the twentieth century, has fallen into disrepute. Since the intent of this section of the chapter is to present positions and to keep pros and cons to a minimum, we shall not describe here specific criticisms which have been leveled against it.

Most modern mechanists take for granted the inadequacy of the original reflex-arc theory and describe behavior in different, but still essentially mechanistic, terms. For example, one well-known psychologist, D. O. Hebb, has constructed a rather elaborate theory which takes into account the criticisms of the reflex-arc concept. Hebb is a mechanist who believes that persons wishing to stay in his camp must be able to account for higher thought processes (such as purposing, valuing, and reflecting) as a product of the electrochemical activity of the body.[13] G. L. Freeman, also a mechanist, likewise develops a highly sophisticated conception of the life process in which he meets many of the traditional objections to a biology based on mechanistic premises. Freeman's mechanistic view is organismic in the sense that he prefers to define a life form as a "system" which operates purposively.[14] It would not be far wrong to say that a majority of biologists and psychologists today place themselves within the mechanistic frame of reference but that there is movement toward a third position, to be described in the next section.

So far we have said nothing about how mechanists define mind. If a person is a pure mechanist, i.e., if he has eliminated every trace of dualism, obviously he must reject the notion that mind is a nonmaterial vital force. If he is true to his materialist principles, he must deny that any kind of nonmaterial force exists; or if he concedes its existence, he must at least hold that such a force is inconsequential.

In what way, then, can a mechanist use the term *mind?* He can use it only if he regards mind as a function—as a manner of behaving and not as a thing in itself. To a mechanist mind is the capacity for learning, i.e., the capacity for building and storing new reflex arcs. Most mechanists, however, avoid use of the term *mind,* since from their point of view, the term often connotes a nonmaterial spiritual force. Most mechanists, we believe, have dispensed with the concept of mind. To them an electronic

13 Hebb, *op. cit.*
14 G. L. Freeman, *The Energetics of Human Behavior,* Cornell University Press, 1948.

computer is analogous to a mammalian brain; and a computer, even though it can solve many problems if the data are fed in correctly, cannot be said to have a mind.

We have asserted that mind to a mechanist can be nothing more than a function—a pattern of behavior resulting from the environmental forces acting upon a living organism. Adherents of the position we are to describe next also regard mind as a function. However, they define the nature and role of mind in a fundamentally different manner.

Organismic Biology

The organismic view is rather popular among biologists of the twentieth century. Those who accept this general frame of reference tend to reject both vitalism and mechanism on the ground that neither provides an adequate explanation of the life process. Organismic biologists object particularly to mechanism, to the tendency of most mechanists to explain the behavior of living creatures in terms of a collection of reflex arcs. Organismic biologists also question vitalism because of its postulation of an unproved life force. A central feature of the organismic outlook is an emphasis on study of life forms by *wholes*, rather than in terms of a collection of response connections. Organismic biologists are interested in how a total creature, or organism, behaves as it interacts with its environment.

It is true that some biologists who call themselves organismic regard life forms as machines. These biologists are likely to adopt a behavioristic psychology, such as Thorndike and Watson expounded (pp. 260–263). But others, and probably the great majority, avoid entirely the machine analogy. One of the originators and most prominent figures of organismic biology was Ludwig von Bertalanffy. He describes three points on which the organismic position diverges from traditional mechanism. These are as follows.

1. *Life is a "system" rather than a collection of cooperating parts.* Or, to state the idea differently, life is characterized by organization—an interdependence of parts and some kind of coordinating agency. Further, a living organism is a "system of systems." That is, a single cell is a system in itself, although it is under the general control of the organ of which it is a part; likewise, a single organ, such as the stomach, is a system but under the general control of the entire organism; a total organism is a system whose behavior is influenced by a still larger system—the "organism-in-its-environment." An analogy of systems within systems might be our solar system. The sun with all its planets behaves as a unit; nevertheless, each planet has its own system of interacting forces, as does each moon or man-made satellite of each planet.

2. *Life is dynamic rather than static.* That is, life is purposive in the sense that it tries to maintain and better itself in its environment. Its fundamental pose is "activity, exploration, movement." Life does not wait for environmental stimuli to impinge upon it and thus excite it to action; action is its normal state. Purposiveness of higher life forms is likely to involve conscious design, growing from unpredictable wants, and not at all times related to physiological drives.

3. *Life is interactive rather than reactive.* Since the fundamental orientation of an organism is toward exploration and manipulation of its environment, it is unlike a slot machine, which is passive until someone pulls the lever. On the other hand, life forms are modified by environment: living is a two-way process in which a life form and its environment exert simultaneous influence upon each other. This viewpoint contrasts with the traditional mechanists' view that life is reactive, that its fundamental pose is waiting, that it acts only after stimulation.[15]

In addition to what Bertalanffy states, it should be noted that organismic biologists have devoted much study to that side of life which we call "psychological"—in contrast to a mechanist's almost exclusive interest in the physical side of life. In one sense the organismic and vitalistic views are alike. Organismic scientists have no objection to studying the physical aspects of life—in fact, they would insist that much which is valuable may be learned only in this way. However, they insist that we can achieve useful definitions of the life process only if we include theories of "central control," i.e., purposiveness, which we can do only through study of the mental as well as the physical characteristics of life forms.

An eminent American biologist, H. S. Jennings, asserts that, with reference to human beings, biologists have two kinds of data to work from: one kind results from observation of how living beings act (outer, or behavioral, data), the other from observation of mental lives (inner, or cognitive, data). It is proper, Jennings says, to label what we can discover through the use of outer data *physical,* and what we can discover through inner data *mental.* Jennings then points out that many biologists and some psychologists have largely ignored the mental aspect of life. He obviously thinks those scientists who have dismissed mind as unimportant, or nonexistent, are misguided. "The universe," says Jennings, "is a system that brings forth life, sensation, emotion, thought." With the development of life, the universe ". . . begins to become conscious of itself, it begins to feel, to think, to have ideas and purposes and ideals."[16]

How do organismic biologists conceive of mind? They regard it as a function, but in a very different way from the mechanists' way. To an

---

[15] See Ludwig von Bertalanffy, *Problems of Life; an Evaluation of Modern Biological Thought,* Wiley, 1952, Chap. 1.

[16] H. S. Jennings, *The Universe and Life,* Yale University Press, 1933, p. 16.

organismic biologist, mind is a function that arises in interactive situations—that is, situations in which experience is incurred. The role of this function is to further an organism's purposes, the shaping and fulfilling of organic need and the creating and fulfilling of nonorganic need.

To be more explicit, mind is the capacity of an organism, in an interactive situation, to see and be guided by meanings. Meaning is the "sign-quality" or "pointing-quality" which objects come to have as a result of an organism's having experienced them. For example, the "sign-quality" of a hot stove soon becomes apparent to a small child; a stove means "Touch me and you will get burned." To extend the illustrations: growling dogs *mean* bite, thunderheads *mean* rain, paddles *mean* spank, the smell of cooking food *means* dinner. A human being probably begins acquiring his first meaning during his prenatal period, long before he can verbalize them. But mind becomes of major effectiveness in the life of a human person only after he is old enough to verbalize meanings and only after he has learned to socialize with others. The foregoing reference to human beings should not be construed to mean that mind, as defined above, is confined to humans. It is evident that all the higher animals may acquire meanings as they interact with their environment. All life forms *may*, although the "mental" experiences of an amoeba must be very different from those of a Harvard professor.

In a single paragraph Morris, drawing mainly from the thinking of John Dewey, sums up a definition of mind which would probably be satisfactory to most organismic biologists:

When the ongoing activity of the organism is blocked there arises a situation with the character which Dewey calls "doubtful" or "tensional." It is in such situations that mind and consciousness make their appearance, serving the purpose of resolving this ambiguity so that the situation can be controlled in the service of the frustrated organic demands or interests. It should be noted that this view does not make thought instrumental to sheer activity but to specific interests. Nor does it specify the limits of such interests—they may range from the need of food to a solution of the problem of mind. The insistence is simply that thought is inseparably linked with the demands of interested behavior, and is instrumental to the satisfaction of such demands.[17]

How do the three major outlooks in biology concerning the nature of central control relate to the various theories of human nature advanced in the previous chapter? All conceptions of human nature which insist that there is a nonmaterial entity involved in human life are "vitalistic." Historically, both Puritans and some Roussellians made this assumption. So did John Locke, although it should be emphasized that Locke's thinking was leading in the direction of mechanism. The twentieth-century *tabula rasa* theorists, such as the Watsonian behaviorists, were highly

[17] Morris, *op. cit.*, pp. 294–295.

mechanistic. However, psychological relativists, as described in the final section of Chapter 2, are virtually certain to prefer an organismic biology.

The remainder of the chapter treats certain aspects of human biology from a basically organismic point of view; however, certain of the facts which we recount would be equally acceptable to a vitalist, mechanist, or organismic biologist.

WHAT IS THE FIELD CONCEPT IN BIOLOGY?

At one time biologists tended to regard living organisms as "collections of parts" capable of being understood only through careful analysis of the structure and functioning of each part. When one looks at life in this way, he conceives of an organism as a mosaic or perhaps as an assembled jigsaw puzzle. Although this atomistic analysis of living creatures still has its uses, it now is supplemented with a concept of the "organism-as-a-whole" in which the organism is seen as a unit or organic entity. We go even further than this by assuming that an organism cannot be fully understood except when it is studied in the context of its environment. Hence, the unit of study is now usually an "organism-in-an-environment."

In biology, the organismic point of view makes use of what many scientists call the *field concept*. The idea of the field first appeared in physics. It has since come to be used in biology, psychology, and the social sciences. The field concept in biology is not identical with the field concept in psychology; the differences will become apparent in later chapters. A simple definition of a field is "a totality of coexisting facts which are conceived of as mutually interdependent. . . ."[18] A characteristic feature of a field is that, because of the interdependence of its elements, it tends to maintain some degree of balance or stability. If the equilibrium of a field of forces is disturbed, counterbalancing forces tend to arise which reinstate equilibrium, although not necessarily the same state of affairs as existed prior to disturbance since the new equilibrium may incorporate factors not previously present.

If a living organism is regarded as a field of forces, an example of disturbance and restoration of a different but useful state of balance would be as follows: A four-legged animal loses a leg. It "compensates" by learning a new gait which permits walking with three legs; further, the muscles of the three remaining legs will grow stronger. To take an example incorporating both animal and environment: a certain species of squirrel, let us say, subsists on a certain kind of pine seed. But a disease kills the pines in the area. The squirrels learn to substitute a different kind of nut

[18] Kurt Lewin, "Behavior and Development as a Function of the Total Situation," in Leonard Carmichael, ed., *Manual of Child Psychology*, 2nd ed., Wiley, 1954. Lewin's formulation is derived from a statement by Albert Einstein, p. 919.

and, although less well nourished, continue to exist in depleted numbers. A new equilibrium has appeared.

There is nothing in nature guaranteeing that new equilibria necessarily will be better for a particular form of life; sometimes a change in a field destroys a life form (as happened to the dinosaurs). But when a field of forces includes life forms or is confined to a single life form, reorganization of the field usually will be influenced by the attempts of the life form to preserve and better its conditions of living.

The field concept also includes the notion that a total field has qualities unlike those of any single element of the field. In physics, the nature of elements in chemical combination illustrates this. A compound is, on its own level, one kind of field. Water is an example of a chemical compound. Consider how different are the qualities of water from either of its components—hydrogen and oxygen—taken singly. Conversely, all the components of a field take their qualities, while a part of the field, from their location and role in the field. If a field changes, the properties of its constituent parts change.

Biologists for some time have been aware that animals have "electrical systems." These are characterized by differences in potential and by resulting flow of electrical current. The flow of electrical current produces electromagnetic fields. There is good reason to believe that there is a continuous reciprocal relationship between these electrical phenomena and metabolic processes. That is, changes in metabolism are associated with changes in electrical phenomena; but it is impossible to say that one is the "cause" of the other. They are both aspects of the same underlying life process.

Thus, the term *electrometabolic field* has come into use in biology. A total organism can be regarded as a field of forces but it consists also of a number of subfields, each overlapping and continuously interacting with the others. The nature of the smaller fields is not well understood; undoubtedly each organ, and each cell in an organ, exhibits field characteristics. (We are saying here what Bertalanffy says when he asserts that a living creature consists of "systems within systems.")

Of what significance is all this for teachers? In studying a child or youth, it seems wise to take into consideration as much of the "field" as one can encompass. Insofar as possible, that part of his environment which affects his biological functioning must be seen in its entirety. How well is he nourished? What pattern of rest and activity does he follow? What kind of medical attention does he receive? In what ways have his more pressing organic drives been satisfied, redirected, or frustrated? After the environment has been considered, it then seems wise to interpret specific physiological traits in their relationship to a total organism. For example, Johnny's tooth cavities may be partialy a result of genetic inheritance, partially a result of his mother's illness while he was a fetus, and partially a result of a general bodily malaise produced by emotional upset or other factors.

Although the organismic approach may present enormous complexities, it is also probably a pretty good safeguard against some of the oversimplification of the atomistic, piecemeal approach. If we understand the organismic principle, and apply it, we never cease looking for relevant factors in a web which we recognize at the outset as being very complex.

IN WHAT WAY IS LIFE PURPOSIVE?

Central to the organismic view is the idea that life is purposive. This is an easy statement to make, but knotty problems appear when we try to become more specific.

One level of purpose appears to be simply the maintenance of normalcy. As Dashiell puts it, "Through all animal life an outstanding characteristic runs—the tendency of the organism to maintain its normalcy against internal or external disrupting agencies."[19] This characteristic often is referred to as *homeostasis,* a term popularized by Walter Cannon earlier in the century.[20] A good example is the way a person fights disease —often successfully without aid of medicine. Other examples are the ways in which wounds heal, broken bones knit, or a kidney increases its functioning to compensate for loss of its twin. Some animals seem to have developed homeostasis more fully than man: they can "regenerate" lost tails or legs. Homeostasis produces kinds of behavior which appear purposive; it makes a creature appear to be trying to regulate itself in terms of a goal—survival.

As formerly defined, homeostasis is the process by which a disturbed organism eliminates the disturbance and returns to its former state. Defined in this way, the concept is too static to explain much that we now know. C. A. Mace has developed some extensions of the original theory which seem helpful. He has suggested that what is maintained or restored in homeostasis is not so much an internal state of an organism—although to a degree this happens—but also a satisfactory relation of the organism and its environment. Also, a specific equilibrium is rarely maintained; it is better to refer to the attainment of "new equilibria" than to "restoration of equilibrium."[21]

[19] Quoted in Arthur W. Combs and Donald Snygg, *Individual Behavior,* rev. ed., Harper, 1959, p. 41.

[20] See Walter Cannon, *The Wisdom of the Body,* Norton, 1932, for many excellent examples of homeostasis at work.

[21] C. A. Mace, "Homeostasis, Needs and Values," *British Journal of Psychology,* August, 1953, p. 3.

Students will note at this point that homeostatic theory ties in very closely with the general statement of field theory a few pages back.

The Role of Organic Drives

An organic drive is a tendency to act in fulfillment of an organic need. That is, when a physiological need appears it produces a state of tension which is uncomfortable; to relieve discomfort and thus restore a state of normalcy an organism engages in appropriate behavior—the manifestation of drive. Since organic needs are never completely satisfied (unless an organism is dead) *some level of tension is normal to life.* In short, a field is never relaxed but only at times relatively so.

A moment's thought is all that is required for us to identify several organic needs common not only to man but to most other members of the animal kingdom. These needs have become embedded in the biological organism through long evolutionary processes; they are indispensable, in the sense that their satisfaction contributes to well-being and survival.

1. The need for food and drink. The role of this need in permitting continued metabolism and maintenance of chemical balances is obvious.
2. The need for regular elimination of waste products from the organism.
3. The need for satisfactory rest-activity rhythms. A certain amount of rest is needed to permit repair of fatigued tissue. Apparently activity, varying in amount and kind according to the organism, also plays an important role in promoting physical well-being.
4. The need for protection of the physical organism from threats of the physical environment—from poisons, extremes of noise, and various physical dangers.
5. The need for a modicum of physical comfort. Generally speaking, animals avoid discomfort and seek comfort. Discomfort may come from a variety of causes—extremes of hot and cold, extremes of light, disease, insect pests, and the like.
6. The need for sexual release, which is not always so specific as to require for its satisfaction the mating act. Sexual need seems unrelated to desire to procreate, which, among humans, is a culturally derived need with no discernible organic roots.

Although organic needs are relatively specific in that we can describe the processes involved and understand fairly well the drive-reducing behavior which leads most directly to satisfaction, the kinds of behavior human beings have devised to satisfy organic need are immense in number and highly complex. This is also true to some degree of the higher animals. Man, because of his capacity to think, symbolize, and hand on his ideas from one generation to another, is the culture-building animal par excellence. Human culture may in many ways become far removed from the task of organic-need satisfaction. In fact, man among all the earth's creatures seems to have been the only one to invent the notion that some organic needs are evil and ought to be denied.

In a study of man, therefore, we must make a sharp distinction between what organic need demands and what human desire wills. For example, a person may *feel* as his strongest need a fast of thirty days or a whip-lashing. Lest modern Americans scorn too much the religious ascetics who have deliberately practiced "mortifying the flesh," they should remember that in numerous ways they punish their physical organisms, perhaps not so painfully but in ways even more damaging. (West coast smog is perhaps more damaging to the physical organism than any forms of penitence yet devised.)

Psychological and Organic Needs

In the final section of Chapter 2, we pointed out that our most pressing psychological need is maintenance of the perceived self. This means, approximately, keeping one's psychological person in a state which permits self-respect, security, self-expression, etc. Students should note that this is a psychological and not an organic need. As a matter of fact, it is often necessary for persons to deny organic needs in order to achieve satisfaction of psychological needs. And in many persons psychological needs become far more pressing than the organic; in an extreme case one might even get in a position where he can serve his psychological needs best only by committing suicide.

To return to the question with which this section was headed: life is purposive on different levels. It is purposive on a level where what happens seems fairly automatic, as in the case of the internal homeostatic processes of digestion, assimilation, respiration, and the like. It is purposive on the level of the organic drives of which human beings are consciously aware. It is purposive on a level which we might call psychological need, wish, or desire. The latter may be unrelated to organic need and does not necessarily contribute to either physical health or survival.

How many teachers use the understandings which we have sought to communicate in this section? Young persons basically have the same organic needs as adults. Thus, if teachers understand the nature of organic drives, they will understand children better. Any school program which takes advantage of the impulses of young people resulting from organic needs stands a better chance of success, in the sense that motivation of students to do hard and original work will be higher. However, psychological needs, which are highly individualistic and often have to be revealed and stimulated through skilled teaching, can provide even stronger motivation than that arising from organic drives.

WHAT SHOULD TEACHERS KNOW ABOUT GENETICS?

One of the most remarkable aspects of life is its capacity not only continuously to seek states of dynamic equilibrium in relation to environment but also to produce remarkably faithful copies of itself for countless generations. Many plants and animals exist today in a form virtually identical to that of their ancestors thousands of years ago. Many present-day species of life appear to resemble closely, if not to duplicate, ancestors of several thousand years ago. Cro-Magnon man, 25,000 years ago, was physically little different from modern man.

The Carriers of Heredity

Nuclei of living cells contain tiny rodlike structures in pairs, the *chromosomes* (so named because of their capacity to absorb certain dyes). The two sets appear upon examination to be identical or nearly so. Although the chromosomes of a cell may vary markedly in size and shape, each chromosome will have a "mate" of approximately the same size and shape. Where reproduction is sexual, one set represents the inheritance from the father, the other set the inheritance from the mother. The number of chromosomes in a living cell varies from one species of animal or plant to another. In human beings there are 23 pairs.

Chromosomes carry what Schrödinger has called a "code script."[22] This code script somehow directs the development of the organism from the time the egg is fertilized to the adult state and in major ways governs the biological functioning of the organism throughout life.

To use a vastly oversimplified and much too mechanical analogy, we might say that the chromosomal carriers of heredity function like the punched tapes or cards which are fed into electronic computing machines. They cause a machine to run through a series of predictable steps. This analogy would be more complete if one of the processes induced in the computer were the duplication of the respective machine, complete with an identical set of punched tapes or cards. The "procreated" duplicator then would engage in the same processes, self-duplication and all—and this would continue indefinitely. For the analogy to be perfect, the reproduction of a computer would require the functions of two parent computers, "male" and "female," each of which would contribute to the off-

[22] For one of the most provocative treatments of this subject, see Erwin Schrödinger, *What Is Life?* Cambridge University Press, 1955. See especially Chap. 2–5. Schrödinger's discussion of the nature of genes is now obsolete, but most of his thesis remains valid.

spring a set of its own punched tapes or cards, which would work jointly in directing the offspring's functioning.

Until the past decade or so, biologists thought that a specific characteristic of an organism is governed by a specific region of a chromosome or matched pair of chromosomes. This region was referred to as a *gene*. Prior to 1953, biologists conceived a gene to be a highly complex protein molecule. However, gene theory has in late years undergone a revolution. First, it was discovered that the chemical carrier of hereditary traits is not protein but a chemical, desoxyribonucleic acid—DNA for short. Chromosomes consist mainly of molecules of this chemical. DNA has the unique capacity for reproducing itself whenever its environment contains the necessary chemical raw materials. In some fashion it "gathers in" from its chemical environment the same kinds of atoms contained in DNA and arranges them in the form of a usually perfect replica, which in turn repeats the process.[23]

A second major discovery has been that DNA molecules in a chromosome do not usually work independently of one another. They tend to work in teams, in the sense that the functioning of one affects the functioning of others. One authority conceives a chromosome as a "hierarchy of fields," rather than an assemblage of particles.[24] The gene concept is still useful but it now seems best to think of a gene as a function of a region of a chromosome rather than as a specific particle.

As we have seen, chromosomes occur in body cells in matched pairs; apparently their functions—genes—also occur in matched pairs, one of each pair being associated with one chromosome, its mate with the matched chromosome. When we say that a hereditary characteristic, like skin color, is governed by a gene group, we really mean a pair of gene groups. However, it is common for one member of a gene pair or gene group pair to be recessive; that is, when paired with a dominant gene or gene group it fails to make its characteristic evident in the resulting body structure. Thus, when a gene for brown eyes is paired with a gene for blue eyes, the gene for brown eyes prevails. For a person to have blue eyes he must carry two recessive genes for blue.

Eye color is one of a few characteristics in human beings apparently governed by a single gene pair. Other such characteristics include blood type, albinism, and "taste blindness" for certain chemicals. In these cases, if we know the genetic history of a man and woman for a few generations

---

[23] For a remarkably lucid short explanation of DNA theory, see George Beadle, "The Chemical Basis of Modern Genetics," *Proceedings,* Plant Science Seminar, Camden, N.J., 1960. See also George Beadle, "Physiologic Aspects of Genetics," *Annual Review of Physiology,* 1960. Dr. Beadle is now Chancellor of the University of Chicago.

[24] See Edmund S. Sinnott, L. C. Dunn, and Theodosius Dobzhansky, *Principles of Genetics,* McGraw-Hill, 1958, p. 387.

past, we can predict with considerable accuracy the proportion of their children likely to exhibit a given trait. This type of inheritance follows Mendelian principles, i.e., the principles of heredity formulated by Gregor Mendel (1822–1884). Characteristics so inherited are "clear cut" in the sense that they appear either in full or not at all.

Much more common among human beings are inherited characteristics which are the result of blending, i.e., the interplay of gene teams. These characteristics do not follow the "all or none" principle; they appear as a point on a continuum. Good examples among humans are stature, skin color, and predisposition to certain diseases. It is very hard to predict the outcome of blending; for example, even if we knew the skin colors of a baby's ancestors for several generations, it would still not be safe to predict the baby's color before his birth.

Of course, one is never safe predicting how any kind of hereditary trait will appear in an adult offspring because of the ways in which environmental factors seemingly can influence physical traits. This question is sufficiently important to be explored in more detail.

The pattern of genes of an organism is referred to as that organism's *genotype*, its internal chromosomal structure. The genotype governs what an organism can become in a given environment and also determines the hereditary characteristics which an organism can transmit to its offspring (although, where reproduction is sexual, the genotype of the offspring is of course a product of the genotype of both father and mother).

The external appearance of an organism is called its *phenotype*. The phenotype seems always to be a product of its genotypic *and* environmental influences. Phenotypes may vary considerably even when genotypes remain the same. For example, when persons of Asiatic extraction move to the United States, their children (if reared in this country) tend to be larger than the parents, and their grandchildren larger still. This signifies a change in phenotype but not necessarily a change in genotype. Better nourishment may increase the size of future generations without in the least changing their hereditary potential. Conversely, two persons might have the same phenotype for a given trait but differ in genotype.

Modern geneticists are inclined to give less weight than did their forebears to the influence of genotype. Certainly, genetic inheritance counts for a good deal in determining the kind of adult a person will become, but the fact is, we do not know the exact role genotype plays in determining phenotype. Scientists used to debate what they called the nature-nurture issue. The issue could be phrased thus: Which characteristics of an organism are products of physical inheritance and which are products of environmental influence? Modern scientists have virtually abandoned debate on this issue; many say that since we have no adequate means of ascertaining the facts, continuing such a debate is futile.

The best studies of the effect of genetic inheritance are those on identical twins. Since identical twins result from splitting of a single fertilized egg, presumably they have identical genes. What is determined by heredity should therefore appear in exactly the same form in the two twins, subject, of course, to such environmental modification as may have occurred. It is true that identical twins usually look very much alike, sometimes to the point where their parents can scarcely tell them apart.

According to one study, the IQ difference of identical twins who have been reared together is 3.1 points; that of fraternal twins reared together, 8.5 points. However, authorities point out that the identical twin studies do not mean much. Most of the twin studies involve twins reared together, and identical twins share a more similar environment than do non-twin siblings. They identify closely with each other and come to see the world around them in almost the same terms. They normally share the same diet and medical care.

The most valid type of study with respect to the nature-nurture controversy is that of identical twins who were separated in infancy and reared out of contact with each other and in dissimilar environments. Under these conditions, twins tend to be less alike; for example, the average difference in IQ score is double that of identical twins reared together. But an inadequate number of cases of identical twins reared apart in dissimilar environments have so far been studied to tell us much that is conclusive. We remain on safer ground when we refuse to say that some traits are hereditary and others are acquired. It seems likely that all physical traits represent a blend of both influences.[25]

Are Personality Traits Inherited?

This question has an easy answer: No evidence! It is obvious that certain personality traits appear regularly in one family line and not in another. A considerable proportion of the members of a family may be unusually energetic or unusually lazy; unusually excitable or unusually phlegmatic; unusually quick-tempered or unusually slow to anger; unusually amorous or unusually cold; and so on.

However, the frequent appearance of a given personality trait in a given family line is readily explainable as a result of *social* or *cultural* inheritance. John Jr. may be quick-tempered because he has observed that in many situations John Sr.'s equally quick temper gets desired results. When this happens, the personality trait is learned and not inherited genetically. So far as we know, *all* personality traits are learned. However, we have no conclusive evidence that this is true; if we ever learn

25 *Ibid.*, p. 30.

how to conduct meaningful studies, we may find that some personality traits have a genetic basis.

Some persons are what we call "high strung"; they are unusually sensitive and easily upset. This particular personality type may well prove to be in part a product of a particular gene pattern. But we do not know this is the case.

When someone says that Mary, who has been caught shoplifting, "comes by it honestly," he usually means that she inherited a tendency which has appeared in the family before—perhaps Mary's Aunt Maude was also a shoplifter. To impute such behavior to inheritance is to go far beyond the evidence. This way of thinking is a part of our "folklore biology" just as some of the notions about psychology described in Chapter 2 are "folklore psychology."

The wisest stand for a teacher to take is that physical inheritance is rarely of any crucial importance. That is, as teachers we can get few clues as how to handle a child or youth from knowledge of his genetic make-up, even if we have such knowledge. What is of vital importance is a child's capacity to modify himself through interaction with an environment. All but the hopelessly defective have this capacity.

Race and Genetics

Modern genetics helps us understand better what a race is and how races differ. Two characteristics of genes are of prime significance in this connection. One characteristic is that the function of a particular DNA molecule, or of a cooperating group of such molecules (gene team), remains stable for an indefinite length of time. Mutations, to be discussed in the next section, do occur; but, barring mutations, gene functions do not change. Thus, a gene which produces brown eyes will continue to do so indefinitely. Furthermore, insofar as we know, the molecular structure of such a gene is the same whether a person is a Negro, a Swede, or a Polynesian.

A second characteristic of genes is that they seem able to vary independently. At first thought, this statement may seem to contradict the earlier assertion that most physical traits are products of gene teams and that a chromosome may be better understood as a "field of forces" with highly complex lines of interaction. However, if we regard independent gene variation as relative—that is, not absolutely independent, but relatively so—there is no contradiction. As a result of this second aspect of genes, genes which produce tall stature may occur in persons who carry genes for black or white skin, narrow or broad nose, blond or dark hair, blue or brown eyes. Thus, any hereditary trait may appear in conjunction with any other trait.

These two genetic principles give meaning to the following definition of race: "Races are populations which differ in the relative commonness of some of their genes."[26] Thus, in a particular race a given trait, such as tallness, may occur more often than in another race. A particular shade of skin may be more common in one race than in another. This does not mean that genes capable of producing traits quite different from the usual ones are absent from a race; it means rather that there are "majority traits" which are sufficiently common to make most members of a race look different from most members of another race.

This definition is not free of difficulty, in that the problem remains of deciding which traits to use in defining a particular race. If we use only one characteristic, such as skin color, and assume that everyone with a black skin belongs to a "black race," we must include peoples who differ markedly from one another in other characteristics (e.g., Asian Indians, Melanesians, and Africans). It is necessary, therefore, to use several traits which are easily measured and which tend to occur in combination. Anthropologists have used skin color, hair color and texture, eye color, head shape, and stature. Classificatory schemes used at present usually propose three primary races, or racial stocks: Caucasoid, Negroid, and Mongoloid. Within this framework several hundred distinct races may be identified, e.g., Nordic, Alpine, Mediterranean, Armenoid, Hindi, and so on. Since the bases now commonly used for classifying people racially are arbitrary, and since racial mixing apparently has occurred since the first development of distinctive races, we can only conclude that the concept of race is not very meaningful. In Dunn and Dobzhansky's words, "When we say that two populations are racially different we are not saying very much."[27]

There may be vast differences *culturally* between races, but this is a matter of learning and not a product of biological difference. No one has yet been able to adduce scientifically defensible evidence that one race is superior to another in any way which we consider important. Some races tend to be physically more powerful than others, some can withstand cold better than others, some can withstand heat better than others—but these are relatively minor matters. There is no evidence that any race has a superior capacity for intelligent behavior or a monopoly on morality.

Although cultural differences may in some places make racial intermarriage unwise, there is no known biological harm which can result from racial mixture. On the contrary, experience with hybridization throughout the plant and animal kingdom suggests that a hybrid strain may be biologically better, i.e., stronger and more vigorous, than the parent varieties. Many social scientists feel that ultimately widespread racial intermar-

[26] L. C. Dunn and Theodosius Dobzhansky, *Heredity, Race, and Society,* New American Library, 1952, p. 114.
[27] *Ibid.,* p. 125.

riage not only will occur but will be the only final solution to the problem of racial prejudice.

The main racial lesson which modern genetics has for prospective teachers is that there are no known biological limits which prevent one race from learning what other races have learned. Cultural limitations may be quite serious and may require generations to overcome.

Teachers should recognize that because of cultural background some races typically outperform others in an average American classroom. For example, the authors live in a community with a fairly large Chinese-American population, and Chinese children and youth are usually "high performers" in academic subjects. A cultural tradition of prizing scholarship, which extends backward thousands of years, undoubtedly explains the Chinese performance.

HOW DO SPECIES EVOLVE?

In the previous section we stressed the permanence of species. But it is obvious that species change. Plant and animal breeders, in seeking new varieties, deliberately induce or take advantage of genetic change. Permanent change in an organism results only from genetic change, i.e., a change in the functioning of the genes. Insofar as is known, there are only two ways in which this can occur: (1) sexual recombination of hereditary units, as when we crossbreed two different strains or varieties and get a new type of organism; and (2) mutation, or internal change, of the chromosomal DNA.

Just how mutations occur is still a matter of speculation. Beadle suggests that when a DNA molecule creates a copy of itself it sometimes makes a mistake. As a result, the new molecule has a different atomic arrangement from that of its parent. Beadle compares mutations to typographical errors, of which there are four basic types: (1) extra letters inserted; (2) letters omitted; (3) letters substituted; and (4) letters transposed. The new faulty molecule, with its added, missing, or rearranged atoms, goes on duplicating itself in its new form with its normal precision. What causes a DNA molecule to make a mistake? We know of at least two causes: one is high energy radiation, the other the action of various chemicals which an organism ingests from its environment.[28]

Errors in replication, i.e., DNA reproduction, would accumulate steadily in a species and thus make species-stability impossible, except that they tend to be self-destructive. Present species are already highly selected, i.e., relatively perfect in relation to environment. Since present species represent a high order of development, in terms of potential for survival, almost all new mutations are harmful. New mutant strains of a species

[28] Beadle, *Proceedings, op. cit.*

usually have a poor survival potential and die out—unless human beings intervene to provide a type of environment which will permit survival.

It would be in exceptionally rare instances that both sets of a gene pair would mutate at the same time in exactly the same way. Hence, in almost all cases, mutations affect only one gene of a gene pair. The mutation may produce a recessive or dominant character, although the former is much more common. Since mutations are so often recessive, a new characteristic may not appear immediately in the offspring of a mutated parent. Until enough descendants have been produced so that they can inbreed, a new trait is unlikely to appear as a detectable change in bodily characteristics. Undoubtedly, because of taboos on incest and on the marriage of cousins, many damaging mutations in human beings never have become apparent in phenotypes.

The Mechanism of Evolution

The changes induced by mutation are usually small. However, occasionally they are quite large, as when, apparently as a result of a single mutation, a strain of mice known as the "varitint waddler" appeared.[29] Evolution operates when changes appear giving a species, or a strain, some advantage or disadvantage which is significant in the struggle for survival. The crucial period in the life of a member of a species, with respect to the survival of the species, is the period through the age of reproduction. For example, if individuals of a particular species tend to remain fertile through the age of, say, seven years, then any mutation which enhances their chances of survival, or increases their fertility, during the first seven years will have survival value for the species. Some types of insects exist in their adult, reproductive form for only a few hours before they die. However, because of their ability to survive in large numbers just long enough to breed, they represent highly viable species. In human beings, any mutation which increases survival or enhances fertility through about the first 40 or 45 years of life would tend to have survival value for the species.

Natural selection is the name given to the process by which, through the failure of their carriers to survive, some mutated genes are lost; and by which, because of their relatively higher survival value, other mutated genes form the basis of a new and flourishing strain or species. In nature, it is often the case that several species compete for scarce food or scarce habitat. Successful species tend to multiply until their numbers create a food or space shortage or create other problems. Evidently, therefore, a life form often may exist in a rather delicate state of balance with hostile

[29] John L. Fuller and W. Robert Thompson, *Behavior Genetics,* Wiley, 1960, pp. 19–20.

environmental influences. If a mutation gives its bearers only a slight advantage over the rest, then over the long run the new strain will prevail; just as, conversely, an adverse mutation which confers only a slight disadvantage will in time make its bearers extinct.

Natural selection may operate in a highly competitive situation; there may be so many of a species in relation to food supply that only the strongest or craftiest survive. It is easy to draw unwarranted conclusions from this fact. And wrong conclusions have indeed been drawn. Many persons have assumed that competition is the natural state of animals in nature. This is the so-called "law of the jungle"—the stronger devour the weaker; the weaker devour those weaker still; and so on.

Biological studies of the twentieth century have led to a rather drastic modification of this point of view. It is now common opinion among biologists that ability of the members of a species, or of different species, to cooperate may have much more "survival value" than competition of one individual against another. Wolves hunting in packs find this to be a successful means of procuring food. Crows and ravens find that more food can be had if sentinels are placed to warn of impending danger. Prairie dogs survive better in cooperative colonies.[30] Human beings likewise furnish an excellent example of the survival value of cooperation. Except in occasional isolated instances, human life outside societies governed by a large measure of internal cooperation is unknown.

Evolution and Man

It is now generally accepted by biologists that human beings are a product of natural selection and also that they represent the "pinnacle" of the evolutionary process because of their superior adaptability. Beadle, in the reference cited, hypothesizes that all physical substance started as hydrogen and is still evolving. From hydrogen the more complex elements developed. The next step was the combination of elements into molecules. From simple molecules evolved more complex ones until finally the first life appeared. Beadle suggests that life began as single DNA molecules. At this point we approach the virus level of existence: a virus is a bundle of DNA molecules with a protective protein coating. From viruses the next step was to cells; then to multicellular organisms and finally man.

Has man ceased changing biologically? There is no reason to believe so. However, biological evolution has ceased to be very important, at least for the time being. With the appearance of a culture-creating organism, evolution can operate in another realm—that of ideas. Julian Huxley calls this stage in the evolutionary process the *psychosocial*. In this stage

[30] See the provocative discussion of animal cooperation in Ashley Montagu, *The Direction of Human Development,* Harper, 1955, pp. 17–58. For a fuller treatment of the same subject, see W. C. Allee, *The Social Life of Animals,* Beacon, 1958.

changes in ideas take the place of genetic change. New ideas enable man to adapt to a changing environment. Ideas themselves undergo a process comparable to natural selection: those with survival value tend to persist and those which reduce the potential for survival are lost.

This does not mean that ideas, because they survive, are necessarily good; we undoubtedly harbor many very ancient ideas which have the effect of reducing human well-being. Such ideas can survive if they do not markedly reduce the birth rate.

Even though human life flourishes without need for further biological change, nevertheless man cannot escape biological change. Dobzhansky states that human sperm and ova contain mutations at the rate of one in every 10,000 to 250,000 cells produced. This does not seem like a very high rate of mutation. However, Dobzhansky suggests that the mutation rate has probably increased in recent years and may increase still more in the future. Industrialization not only increases the level of radiation to which everyone is subjected but also necessitates human contact with mutation-producing chemicals. Since natural selection no longer operates in man, there is a risk that the human race will accumulate a large stock of harmful mutations.

As a specific example, Dobzhansky points out that as we eliminate infectious diseases we protect genes for susceptibility. If natural selection were operating, many persons carrying the genes for susceptibility would die young and thus the genes would be destroyed. Conceivably, through preserving mutants for susceptibility, the level of susceptibility could become so high that if our artificial means of controlling the disease were to break down we would be disastrously vulnerable.[31]

Of what significance for teachers is our treatment of genetic change? Its significance is certainly not so obvious as is the case with some other aspects of human biology. Our hope is that prospective teachers will be impressed with the idea that man is a piece of "unfinished business," both biologically and culturally. We hope to show that human life is not static in any of its aspects, that its only stable feature is change itself. Such an idea should be of significance in helping teachers find a sense of direction.

Another idea of possible significance is simply that man does not have all of his biological problems solved. In spite of the tremendous strides he has made in conquering disease, he dare not forget that evolution works inexorably but not necessarily in his favor. At the same time, we know enough about the nature of genetic change to be able to control the spread of harmful mutations.

[31] Theodosius Dobzhansky, "The Present Evolution of Man," *Scientific American*, September, 1960.

BIBLIOGRAPHY

Beach, Frank A., and others, eds., *The Neuropsychology of Lashley*, McGraw-Hill, 1960.
  A collection of Lashley's representative papers, showing the range of his work. Of interest in connection with this chapter because Lashley's work is considered by many to abolish decisively the tenability of a traditionally mechanistic biology and psychology. See the introduction by Edwin G. Boring.
Dunn, L. C., and Theodosius Dobzhansky, *Heredity, Race, and Society*, New American Library, 1952.
  A popularly written but authoritative treatment by two experts in the field.
Hebb, Donald O., *The Organization of Behavior; a Neuropsychological Theory*, Wiley, 1949.
  Presentation of a highly sophisticated mechanism which avoids some of the more serious criticisms of this position.
Huxley, Julian, *Evolution in Action*, Harper, 1953.
  One of the best treatments of how evolution works and its implications for mankind. Huxley also discusses his conception of man's biological nature.
Jennings, Herbert Spencer, *The Biological Basis of Human Nature*, Norton, 1930.
  A pioneering work that continues to raise many of the right questions. Although the book is obsolete in some respects, see Chapter IX on "Biological Fallacies and Human Affairs." A very useful counteractive to folklore biology which still exists.
Jennings, Herbert Spencer, *The Universe and Life*, Oxford University Press, 1933.
  Opinion of one of the most eminent of American biologists as to the role of biology. He is bound by neither vitalism nor mechanism, and speculates on what biology might tell us about many of the crucial issues of life. He is an optimist—life will advance to ever greater heights.
Knobloch, Irving W., *Readings in Biological Science*, Appleton-Century-Crofts, 1948.
  An excellent selection of readings covering all major topics of the field.
Krutch, Joseph Wood, *The Measure of Man*, Bobbs-Merrill, 1953.
  An extraordinarily stimulating book on issues between mechanistic and non-mechanistic approaches in biology, psychology, and sociology, by a noted humanistic scholar and writer.
Montagu, M. F. Ashley, *The Direction of Human Development; Biological and Social Bases*, Harper, 1955.
  A book bearing on the question of what man's original nature is and how that nature is influenced to assume a socially functional form. Highly readable, considering the subject matter involved.
Schrödinger, Erwin, *What Is Life?*, Cambridge University Press, 1955.
  Treatment of some fundamental issues in biology by a world-renowned physicist. This book is a "must" for any student who seriously wishes to understand the biological side of life. Note, however, that modern DNA

theory carries us farther than Schrödinger's now outdated discussion of the nature of genes.

Sinnott, Edmund Ware, *Cell and Psyche; the Biology of Purpose,* University of North Carolina Press, 1950.

The philosophical implications of observed levels of organization in living forms, by a biologist with more than twenty years' research experience. Man is his main interest. Much of his thinking is in line with a relativistic psychology. Highly recommended reading.

Wheeler, Leonard R., *Vitalism: Its History and Validity,* Witherby, 1939.

An invaluable work for those interested in historical and comparative biology. It is unfortunate that we apparently do not have an up-to-date version of this book which would present a relativistic concept of organism as a real alternative to mechanism and vitalism. Wheeler is leading in this direction, however; see Part III.

Young, Clarence Whitford, and others, *The Human Organism and the World of Life,* Harper, 1951.

A general treatment of human biology with an added section on "The World of Life." A very useful reference source.

4

WHAT IS MAN'S
SOCIOLOGICAL NATURE?

The emphasis of a book on psychological foundations of education is on the psychological nature of man, particularly the processes by which man develops and learns. But to set the stage for such study it is essential to view man in some of his other dimensions. In Chapter 3 we discussed some of the relevant biological aspects of human organisms. In this chapter we turn to some sociological—or cultural—aspects of man. Although to some degree we take into consideration all human culture, our focus is upon culture in the United States with special reference to the culture of children and youth.

Social or *cultural* refers to man's operations within group relationships. The culture or social heritage of a community provides the enveloping elements—matrix—within which children emerge as persons and achieve development and learning throughout their lives. Thus, a cultural heritage is distinctively different from a biological heritage in that it is acquired, not genetically, but through learning. This chapter, therefore, describes some of the common social learnings of American children and youth and some of the educational problems produced by these learnings.

Students should approach the chapter with such questions as these in mind: What role does culture play in human life? Does our culture produce "well-adjusted" people? What kind of adjustment do we want to promote in school? What role do social classes play in American life, particularly in public education? What are some of the more troublesome contradictions in American culture? In what ways does our culture confuse children and youth? What should teachers do about cultural contradictions and confusions?

WHAT IS THE ROLE OF CULTURE?

Discussion of cultural influences on man should be preceded by a careful definition of culture. One widely accepted definition is that of Kroeber and Kluckhohn: "Culture consists in patterned ways of thinking, feeling, and reacting, acquired and transmitted mainly by symbols, constituting the distinctive achievements of human groups, including their embodiment in artifacts; the essential core of culture consists of traditional [i.e., historically derived and selected] ideas and especially their attached values."[1] Note that, according to Kroeber and Kluckhohn, the essential core of culture is ideas, i.e., patterns of thought. In this book culture will refer primarily to attitudes, values, beliefs, and knowledge which are somewhat stable and widely shared.

We may distinguish between general, or national, culture patterns and subcultures. A subculture is a pattern of learned traits distinctive to a specific group which is smaller than, but a part of, the general culture. A geographic region, an ethnic group, a social class, or an age grouping may form the basis of a subculture. Boston Irish, Chicago slum dwellers, the Hollywood community, and Texans have all constituted subcultures. The long-range tendency in the United States is for subcultures based upon ethnic group, region, and social class to become more and more like the national culture and eventually to lose their identity.

Socialization—A Paramount Goal of Development

Socialization is the process by which a person develops from a mere biological organism, as at birth, to an adequate adult human person. Socialization means learning the ways of a culture. No one is regarded as fully grown, in a psychological sense, until he learns to display a measure of the prevailing adult attitudes, values, beliefs, and knowledge of the subculture to which he belongs.

Socialization requires moving through a series of age-related subcultures. At any given time in the life of a growing child or youth we may refer to the dominant thought patterns of his age mates as his *peer culture*. This statement should be qualified with the observation that until a child is old enough to become a member of a neighborhood play group, or a nursery school group, he has no true peer culture. During the first two or

[1] A. L. Kroeber and C. Kluckhohn, "The Concept of Culture: A Critical Review of Definitions," *Papers of the Peabody Museum,* Harvard University, Vol. XLI, 1950.

three years of life the only culture he knows is that part of the adult culture which his parents and adult relatives see fit to teach him, or the peer culture which older siblings transmit.

The nature of peer culture changes continuously as children grow older. For any given age level, the peer culture changes with the passage of time: this change is very conspicuous, for example, in the case of teen-age jargon and teen-age clothing, eating, and dating habits. Adults rarely understand child and youth peer culture. They see the surface of it, but with childish wisdom youngsters realize that it saves trouble to keep a part of the peer culture hidden from adult view.

What Is the Relationship of a Person and His Culture?

Each one of us is a personality, based upon the cultural elements with which we have had contact. The content of each individual personality is limited by his culture. Without the existence of a surrounding culture, it is unlikely that a person would show human characteristics other than those biological features which belong distinctively to *Homo sapiens*.

The limitation of persons by their cultures does not necessarily imply the validity of Locke's *tabula rasa*—neutral-passive—concept of man. Human beings give every appearance of being dynamic, in the sense that they are interactive, exploring, and purposive. To a degree, each person actively selects those elements of the culture that get incorporated into his own personality. Selection is not always guided by verbalized purposes and often does not seem to be very rational; nevertheless, it appears that no one uncritically adopts for himself the total culture which surrounds him. However, each person in some way adjusts to his culture. What is the nature of the process commonly called adjustment?

IS "GOOD ADJUSTMENT" A PRIMARY GOAL OF SOCIALIZATION?

Except to say that socialization requires "growing into" adult culture, we have not so far discussed the general goals of socialization. However, certain lines of growth might be considered more important than others. In recent years much has been written about adjustment as one highly desirable goal of development. Our problem in this section is to determine what adjustment means, and whether, as usually defined, it is indeed an aim of primary importance.

How May Adjustment Be Defined?

Often, when persons use the term *adjustment* they are referring to social adjustment. Social adjustment is something like learning how to "win friends and influence people" or developing a "pleasing" personality. It involves achievement of the kinds of social skills which enable one to be liked by a wide range of persons, to like them in turn, to mingle easily with them, and to work smoothly with them. However, when social psychologists use the term *adjustment* they mean something more than simply learning to be a jolly good fellow.

Adjustment as "Fitting In"

In the literature of psychology there are at least two distinct definitions of adjustment. One appears to be much more widely than the other; it equates adjustment with fitting into, or adapting to, an environment. This definition implies a passive human nature, or at least one which is capable of learning passive acceptance of things as they are. According to this definition, an adjusted person learns what the status quo is and then bends his personality and character to harmonize with it. A well-adjusted person, in this sense, is just the opposite of a social rebel. This definition of adjustment harmonizes with the Lockian neutral-passive concept of human nature.

According to this view of adjustment, the farther a person can go toward satisfied acceptance of his culture, the better adjusted he is. Adjustment is equated with reduction of tension and achievement of calm. Of course, if one carried this conception through to its logical conclusion—perfect equilibrium with one's environment—the result might not be satisfactory to everyone, because ". . . when a living system passes . . . to a state of thermo-dynamical equilibrium, death takes place."[2]

Adjustment as Achieving Personal Effectiveness

Another, but less popular, definition of adjustment assumes a more active and creative role for people. Adjustment is construed to mean, not passive fitting into an environment, but active reordering of environment to bring it more in accord with the purposes of the person concerned. Implicit in this definition is the idea of two-way giving: environment is modified, but in the process the persons also undergo modification. This is the interactionist position.

This definition has some very provocative ramifications. It suggests, among other things, that happiness, if we define happiness as a relatively continuous state of contentment, is not a primary goal of adjustment. The primary goal of adjustment is effective reworking of both one's environment and oneself so as to achieve goals which are regarded as important. A person may be a lifelong social rebel, and frustrated much of the time,

[2] F. S. C. Northrop, *The Logic of the Sciences and the Humanities*, Macmillan, 1948, p. 158.

but, if he is able to operate effectively in remaking his world so it will be more in accord with his heart's desire, he can be considered adjusted.

For a person to be effective, it is obviously necessary that he be able to "fit in" sufficiently to maintain persuasive communication with others. This may require considerable conformity in some areas of life, or at least *seeming* conformity. Anyone who is such a deviant that people quit taking him seriously has ceased being effective. To show adjustment, a person must remain within the culture—he cannot become an outsider looking in.

Also, although an adjusted person may exhibit a number of neurotic tendencies, he ceases being adjusted whenever he lets his neuroses get him completely down. Many of the world's great creative thinkers have shown symptoms of mental ill health, but they still managed to get their work done: they were effective.

The foregoing definition of adjustment departs so far from the customary concept, "conforming to," that it might be better to use a different terminology, such as "dynamic adaptation." However one chooses to define adjustment, students should be aware that one's preferred definition of this term, like that of many other terms, is influenced by his basic psychological and philosophical orientation. A person who is committed to a neutral-passive conception of human nature, and the mechanistic stimulus-response psychology which accompanies it, is likely to prefer to think of adjustment as fitting into or conforming. A person who is committed to a neutral-interactive view of human nature, and the relativistic field psychology which accompanies it, is equally likely to prefer to regard adjustment as "achieving personal effectiveness" through dynamic adaptation.

Whichever definition is accepted, to treat problems of adjustment concretely one must consider the specific cultural elements to which it is related—folkways, mores, institutions, and laws.

Folkways, Mores, Institutions, and Laws

Adjustment cannot adequately be understood without a consideration of social controls. Social controls are institutionalized forms of social pressure exerted by a culture to insure that individuals within the culture conform sufficiently to cultural standards to perpetuate its style of living. Social controls are "security measures" employed by a culture in its self-defense. They result in cultural stability, except where controls are used to perpetuate contradictions or other cultural weakness: in these cases the maintenance of controls may produce cultural disorganization.

Folkways, according to one group of authors, are *"typical or habitual beliefs, attitudes, and styles of conduct observed within a group or com-*

munity."[3] In other words, folkways are accepted ways of acting. Violation of a folkway may cause a person to be teased, shunned, or even punished, depending upon how seriously people take the folkway in question. Consequently, folkways tend to be self-perpetuating, although it is obvious that within the course of a single generation many folkways change. In this country, fifty years ago it was considered highly improper if a man failed to take off his hat in an elevator when a lady was present, or to give up his seat to a woman in a crowded public conveyance. Now, if a man wears a hat at all, he is unlikely to take it off as a sign of respect to females; nor is he expected to give up a seat to a lady unless she is obviously much older and weaker than he.

Folkways may be classified according to their life span. When a folkway persists for more than a generation and attains some degree of formal recognition, it is a *custom*. On the other hand, some folkways are quite transitory, in which case they are *fashions*. Fashions observed by a relatively small segment of the population are *fads*. Fads which involve extreme and irrational forms of behavior are *crazes*. "Russian roulette" and a game played by teen-agers with automobiles called "chicken" are examples of crazes.[4]

Folkways are sometimes considered essential for group survival. Such morally toned folkways evolve into *mores*. Violation of mores is considered shocking and unforgivable. Like the less binding folkways, mores change in the course of time. They are likely to change more slowly than folkways, and change is usually accompanied by emotional distress on the part of many persons, and often severe conflict.

A good illustration of how mores in the United States change is found in our attitudes toward modesty of dress. In the late nineteenth and early twentieth century modesty in dress was one of our more binding mores. Public exposure of any part of the body except the extremities was shocking to most persons. Today, near nudity is customary not only among night club performers but among suburban housewives in the summertime as they do lawn work and go shopping. A growing number of public beaches are permitting women to wear bikini bathing suits and men the scantiest of trunks. It is easily possible that within a few decades nude bathing at public pools and beaches will be permissible, as it is now at some Scandinavian beaches.

A cultural change of this type is very upsetting to many persons. They have come to see the principle of modesty as a moral absolute and feel that any revision of it is a sign of the collapse of civilization. Consequently they protest the change violently and attempt to restore earlier standards.

[3] George A. Lundberg, Clarence C. Schrag, and Otto N. Larsen, *Sociology,* rev. ed., Harper, 1958, pp. 290–291.
[4] *Ibid.,* pp. 293–294.

However, when a long-range trend in mores becomes firmly established, it is rarely reversed. Probably the reason is that most of our common mores are related to a central core of value and institutional structures in the culture, and when this core changes it carries the mores along with it. Industrialization, the rise of science, the modernization of religion, and emergence of relativism in many areas of thinking work altogether to color our attitudes about modesty in dress and most other matters.

Institutions are relatively stable and formalized ways of performing some function essential to social life. Often, institutions serve the purpose of transmitting, enforcing, and perpetuating mores. Examples which come readily to mind are the economic system, government, church, and family. Like folkways and mores, institutions tend to evolve over time. The family is a much different institution today from what it was a century ago.

Laws are codified mores and institutions. They are formally enacted or proclaimed by an authority. Violation of laws may lead to formally prescribed punishment. Often laws are passed in areas where there is no widespread agreement as to what the mores are; in such cases, law becomes virtually unenforceable. Also, mores and institutions may change without corresponding change in the laws originally designed to enforce them. Many "wide open" towns have laws which strictly forbid gambling, prostitution, and racy night club shows. The fact that these are legally forbidden gives them added appeal to many persons.

As we have seen, adjustment may be defined in more than one way. It may refer to social adjustment, i.e., learning to get along smoothly with people. It may refer to conformity to existing folkways, mores, institutions, and laws. Or it may refer to effective interaction with the cultural elements of social control with the intent of modifying these elements. In the section to follow, we discuss the emphasis which our culture places upon social adjustment.

The Present Cult of Social Adjustment

Some persons consider the teaching of social adjustment the chief task of a kindergarten and an important function of any public school. By the time children have reached the middle elementary years they are expected to show considerable social skill. This does not mean that they will have ceased to quarrel and fight, but they will have learned to manage organized group games and play together fairly well much of the time. Also, even though they do not show consistent adherence to them, children by then are supposed to know the common rules of courtesy.

It usually is expected that youth will show a relapse in social adjustment during the teen years. This apparent decline is more conspicuous in relations between youth and adults than between youth and their peers. By the middle teen years an average youth has mastered a complex set of social skills, including a complicated etiquette.

Because of the seeming crudeness and impoliteness which so frequently is present in the relations of youth to each other, mastery of social skills may not appear evident to adults. However, much of the crudeness is a form of play-acting; it is part of an elaborate teen-age game and is not to be taken too seriously. However impolite he may seem, almost every middle-class youth knows that in the United States one of the primary cultural demands is to know "how to get along with others."

In the heading of this section we used the term *cult*. A cult, in the sense intended here, is a social practice which is regarded with virtually religious veneration. It is clear to sociologists that the twentieth century has seen a great upsurge in emphasis upon social adjustment, as first defined. There are a few rather obvious reasons why. Industrialization and urbanization force us to live and work in close proximity to others, and even more important, they demand cooperative group effort in almost every area of life. If people are to live and work together and engage in many forms of collective endeavor, they must be able to avoid social friction. An ant colony would not survive if the ants fell to quarreling; the human situation, like it or not, has become rather analogous.

We may anticipate that teachers will continue to be expected to encourage children and youth to work together with a minimum of rudeness and argumentation. This, however, is not the same as saying that study of human relations will force exclusion of other concerns from the curriculum. Nor is it the same as saying that children and youth should be encouraged to agree with one another in passive fashion. Social peace does not require agreement of opinion; it requires, rather, the learning of civility during discussion.

In the following discussion of conformism it will be evident to readers that we agree at least in part with those writers who deplore the present apparent level of conformism. But in arguing for a social climate which is more tolerant of unorthodox ideas and behavior we are not arguing against social adjustment, provided social adjustment means a capacity for productive group thinking.

Adjustment as Conformity

With respect to teaching conformity to the folkways and mores, adults usually begin with young children and work assiduously at this educational task until the children are grown. As soon as a child is old enough to talk, they indoctrinate him in certain cultural norms. For example, they teach the "evils" of lying, stealing, fighting, immodesty, sexual experimenting, and using "dirty language." Later they teach him the "evils" of atheism, free love, and socialism. However, the particular folkways and mores which are taught the young depend upon the subculture of which they are a part. As we shall see later in the chapter, "lower-class" parents are much less strict, much less likely to insist upon conformity to traditional "middle-class" folkways and mores.

By the teen years, most youth have learned pretty well the cultural expectations of their particular social class. Lower-class youth may have learned that it is not a serious offense to the mores of their group to carouse, use risqué language, and engage in premarital sex relations. Middle-class youth will have learned that it is against the mores of their group to do any of these things. If skeptics remain unconvinced about the effectiveness on a verbal level of moral instruction among middle-class youth, they may turn to several well-documented studies. Hollingshead found that middle-class youth generally expressed moral opinions much like those of their parents.[5] Havighurst and Taba found that in a fairly typical middle-class-oriented midwestern community, a sample of 16-year-old boys and girls expressed allegiance to traditional middle-class mores such as chastity, responsibility, honesty, self-reliance, thrift, and good manners.[6] The extensive studies of teen-age opinion conducted by Purdue University under the direction of H. H. Remmers and staff reveal essentially the same thing. In one of the Purdue studies a large number of teen-agers were asked to indicate, in order of badness, the 16 "worst things that a person could do." The three worst, in order of seriousness, were killing or murdering, using or selling narcotics, and sexual misbehaving. Less offensive to the youth, but still listed among the 16 worst behaviors, were stealing, cheating, lying, being cruel, drinking alcoholic beverages, swearing, being irreligious, and smoking.[7]

We may conclude that at the present time we are being highly effective in our culture in teaching assent, or at least open verbal assent, to conventional middle-class values to middle-class children and youth. More than most parents think, youngsters seem to accept the values which parents have hoped to inculcate. However, there is reason to believe that there are many exceptions. Youth go through many phases, including alternating periods of conservatism and liberalism.

The conclusions just stated do not tell the whole story. Some of the studies cited, as well as others not cited, indicate that there may be a wide gulf between what young persons say they believe and the convictions they reflect on an action level. That is, when asked what he believes, a young person is likely to express allegiance to traditional folkways and

---

[5] August B. Hollingshead, *Elmtown's Youth: The Impact of Social Classes on Adolescents,* Wiley, 1949.

[6] Robert J. Havighurst and Hilda Taba, *Adolescent Character and Personality,* Wiley, 1949.

[7] H. H. Remmers and D. H. Radler, *The American Teenager,* Bobbs-Merrill, 1957, p. 162.

mores. At the same time, in his behavior (and especially his behavior when adults are not present) he may flagrantly violate these same folkways and mores. In the area of sex, for example, it appears that even middle-class youth with the most impeccable upbringing are fairly likely to transgress the mores before they have reached the age of 25.

Furthermore, most of the studies show the presence of much confusion and conflict among children and youth. In other words, although youth may transgress the traditional mores, they do not do so without generating high anxiety levels.

Students should understand that the foregoing paragraphs are not in any sense to be taken as condemnatory. If children and youth often appear confused and inconsistent it is because their culture contains confused and inconsistent elements. Apparently, since the period of World War I, we have been undergoing a fairly rapid transition with respect to many of our more fundamental values. Such periods of cultural transition always produce conflicts in people because people retain a loyalty to the old at the same time that they are attracted to the new. Furthermore, in a time of cultural transition adults are perhaps even more likely than youth to exhibit inconsistent and troubled thought patterns.

The answer to confusion, inconsistency, and conflict probably does not lie in pressing for adjustment of a conforming type. Rather, it seems to lie in the kind of adjustment which leads to personal productivity through interaction with culture. To achieve a more interactive adjustment may require that we attach more value than in the past to the right—and even the obligation—to dissent.

What Groups Carry Folkways, Customs, and Mores to the Young?

We must recognize that, as the writers to whom we referred above suggest, many pressures operate to make critical examination of the culture difficult. It is time now for us to examine more specifically some of the specific carriers of culture, i.e., groupings or institutions which have direct contact with children and youth and tend to impose the attitudes, values, beliefs, and knowledge of the culture.

What are the agencies which carry a culture to the young? Of first importance are *primary* or *face-to-face* groups. A primary group is relatively small, so that all members of the group are well acquainted with one another. Frequency and duration of contact also are characteristic. Although common interest and affection do not necessarily characterize any group which is small enough to permit intimate face-to-face relations, if a group is to have maximum impact upon its individual members there must be some degree of common purpose and mutual affection. The extreme penalty a primary group can impose on its members is expulsion or avoidance. Two most important primary groups are families and peer groups.

The Family

The most important primary group in the life of a small child is his family. The greater part of what most young children believe and know comes from their parents, siblings, or other relatives with whom they have close contact. Throughout the life of a young person, family influences continue to be a major force in determining which folkways and mores he will accept. This is true because of the persistence of family influence. In comparison with family membership, friends, teachers, playmates, and other associates are temporary. Because of its nature, a family is also more cohesive—and hence its values are more binding on individuals—than other groups.

The foregoing assertions require some qualifications. In the life of most young persons family associations assume more importance at certain times than at others. As we shall see in discussing the impact of peer groups, a young person "grows away" from his family as he becomes enmeshed in peer relationships. The growing away continues through the teen years until a young person finally feels it necessary to assert his independence of family. The break with family is largely on the surface and enables a young person to demonstrate his independence and his adulthood to himself and his peers. Once this demonstration is complete, he is likely to accept a renewal of parental influence—often to the point where a newly married person may prefer "going home to mother" than accommodating his ways to those of his mate.

At all ages, influence of family associations on the young appears to be less strong than it once was. The influence of parent on child is strongest in a family which functions as an economic unit—the "rural type" of family described in Chapter 1. Influence is weakened proportionately as family members lose common goals. Modern urban families are less cohesive than were their nineteenth-century counterparts. Working wives, adult clubs and other nighttime activities which infest suburbia, long hours away from home of suburban fathers who commute, and the frequency with which adults from divergent subcultures marry in a mobile, fluid society—all contribute to the reduction of family influence on children and youth. The rising incidence of divorce also contributes to the looseness of family structure.

Peer Groups

The first peer groups in the life of a child are neighborhood play groups. Informal groupings of children of roughly the same age, they form more or less spontaneously, and membership is largely determined by physical proximity. Most children become members of such groups by the age of 4 or 5.

Before a child is very old he becomes involved with other primary groups composed of peers. Examples are his Sunday school class, his nursery school or kindergarten class, and a little later Brownies or Cubs. These groups may become as influential as neighborhood play groups; their impact depends in large part on the opportunities they are given for free interaction. If they are kept formal, the influence of children on each other is minimized. Whether socialization, in its desirable sense, is fostered by these various primary groupings depends entirely on the nature of each group.

The play groups of early childhood turn into the gangs and cliques of middle childhood and adolescence. As children and youth identify ever more closely with their peer groups, competition in loyalties develops, and, as we have seen, loyalty to parental thought patterns is likely to give way somewhat to loyalty to the culture of the peer group.

We have noted that the ultimate end of socialization is mastery of the adult culture. This does not normally occur until a person is grown. Even though a child eventually "grows into" the adult culture, his affiliation with peer groups may temporarily lead him *away from*, rather than toward, acceptance of the approved adult culture.

A child may find it difficult to learn from adults what certain features of the adult culture are. For example, his parents will likely neglect to tell him the common adult attitudes and knowledge concerning sex. In such a situation, he usually turns to his peers for information. But the version of adult culture that comes to him through his peers is almost certain to be highly garbled and incomplete.

In addition, childhood peer cultures tend to develop their own distinctive ideas about most aspects of life. A group of 8-year-olds will develop a genuine subculture. A group of 12-year-olds will do likewise, but their subculture will be distinctively different from that of 8-year-olds. To illustrate more clearly what we mean by a peer culture: a group of 8-year-olds may come to value tormenting animals. In contrast, their parents may value kindness to animals and be quite shocked to see dogs and cats of the neighborhood with tin cans tied to their tails.

As a child grows older, he comes under the influence of numerous other groups: organizations associated with churches and lodges, social welfare agencies, Boy Scouts and Girl Scouts, 4-H clubs, YMCAs and YWCAs, and various in-class and out-of-class groupings at school. Any of these may function as primary groups and be of great consequence in a youth's life.

Secondary groupings may also function to some extent as carriers of culture. A secondary group is a group characterized by larger numbers of persons, disparity of ends, little empathy among members, little close knowledge of other members, and operation of more or less formal controls. Except for the cliques to which he belongs, and perhaps certain classes and clubs, a school is likely to remain a secondary group to a child or youth. Lundberg, Schrag, and Larsen list some sample relationships of a secondary group as "announcer-listener," "performer-spectator," "officer-subordinate," and "author-reader."[8] Secondary groups rarely mold their members to the extent that primary groups do.

Mass Media as Agents of Cultural Transmission

Generally speaking, primary groups are the most potent force for the transmission of a culture. However, other nongroup agencies are of great importance. The impact of TV and motion pictures on children has not yet been assessed adequately. It is logical to believe that these media do have impact; they are constantly before children and youth, and TV and motion picture shows are subjected to time-tested attention-getting formulas.

Much has been written about the influence of reading materials, particularly comic strips and comic magazines. Since a considerable amount of cartoon material prepared for the young treats serious, nonhumorous themes, including themes of horror, the term *comic* is no longer descriptive. It seems more accurate now simply to speak of cartoon strips and magazines. One well-known psychiatrist has published a controversial book attacking horror cartoons.[9]

There can be little question but that the cartoon strips reflect attitudes and values. That is, what the cartoonists think is good tends to be reflected in the personalities and behavior of the leading character or characters in the cartoon. Some attempt has been made to analyze the values stressed in cartoon strips.[10] Some strips and books appear to glorify power, taking the law into one's own hands, using force to settle disputes, and brutality. Others just as clearly tend to uphold more democratic and humane values.

The over-all content of the mass media of communication is highly complex, but there is reason to believe that, to a large degree, it is fairly conservative. That is, taking the mass media as a whole, the predominant content reflects traditional values. However, our traditional values contain many inconsistencies. For example, at the same time that we have elevated peace as a primary value and insisted that our way of life is

[8] Lundberg, Schrag, and Larsen, *op. cit.*, p. 411.

[9] Frederic Wertham, *Seduction of the Innocent*, Rinehart, 1954. For a well-balanced critique of Dr. Wertham's position, see Robert Warshow, "Paul, the Horror Comics, and Dr. Wertham," reprinted in *Mass Culture*, Free Press, 1957, pp. 199–211.

[10] For a good example of such studies, see Lyle W. Shannon, "The Opinions of Little Orphan Annie and Her Friends," reprinted in *Mass Culture*, pp. 212–217.

basically Christian, we have practiced cruelty and violence (witness violence on the frontier, violence between labor and management, race riots in the Southeast, the rate of violent crime, and our many wars). If one combines the fact of inconsistency with the fact that mass media at times promote values which are historically unorthodox in the American culture such as glorification of sex, he can only conclude that the total impact of these media on children and youth is disintegrative. That is, the mass media tend to thrust on children attitudes, values, and beliefs which have no consistent or sensible pattern but are characterized by inconsistency and confusion. Just as competing allegiances toward family and peer group produce conflict in a child, so may inharmonious values pressed upon him by the mass media.

HOW DOES SUBCULTURE MEMBERSHIP AFFECT THE TASK OF SOCIALIZATION?

A subculture is a grouping within the broad national culture which differs in distinctive ways from other groups. A subculture shows some traits of the common culture, but in addition some unique traits. One type of subculture is based upon social stratification. Membership in a social class profoundly affects the outcome of the process of socialization. In certain important respects, lower-class people are very much unlike middle-class people. Or a subculture may be based on nationality. Recent immigrants from, say, Germany exhibit different cultural traits from old-line Americans. A subculture also may be related to the region in which a person lives. Appalachian hill people are very much unlike residents of Boston. Let us turn first to the influences of our class system.

Stratification in the United States

Sociologists have long recognized that we live in a stratified society. Stratification may take one of two forms: *caste* or *class*. A caste is a social stratum which is sharply defined and fixed in the sense that its members do not move from it. To move from one caste to another is a violation of the mores. A class system is less rigid. In some countries, notably in the United States, it is so flexible that, within limits, persons move rather freely from one level to another. A flexible class structure of our type is known as an *open class system*.

Different schemes are available for classifying persons on a social scale. One method of determining a person's class is to ask him if he belongs to the upper, middle, working, or lower class. Sociologists use the term *lower* to embrace the working class, but when people are asked where they belong they prefer to identify themselves with the *working* rather than the lower class—to many persons "lower" has a stigma attached. Although self-classification is useful for certain purposes, people tend to place themselves at levels other than where their fellows in the community place them. Thus, a certain proportion of business executives rate themselves as working class and a rather large proportion of lower-class persons rate themselves as middle class.

A generally more useful system is that of determining what people of a given community regard as symbols of high, medium, and low status. Which aspects of a person's life style function as status symbols depends upon the community and the time in history. In contemporary United States, occupation, source of income, home type, home location, speech habits, dress, manners, number and make of automobiles owned, knowledgeableness about the fine arts, and ancestry are all status-determining items. Once these items are isolated and the proper weighting is assigned to each, a sociological investigator can develop a numerical rating scale which will indicate how each person stands in his status-conferring possessions and habits. This is essentially the system used by W. Lloyd Warner and his associates.

Note that we did not include amount of income in our list of items. We could have done this, but amount of income is a rather poor index of status. A junk dealer may make $100,000 a year but his occupation classifies him; if he happens also to be an immigrant who has not yet learned how to display status symbols correctly, he may be a virtual "nobody." On the other hand, a resident of a southern city who is descended from one of the more prominent ante-bellum planters and who retains all the social graces associated with aristocracy does not need much money to rate high socially.

We shall describe first the six-class system devised by Warner and then indicate some needed modifications and qualifications.

1. *Upper-upper class.* This group consists of the "old rich"—persons whose families have been prominent for at least two or three generations and have established themselves as an aristocracy. Upper-uppers obviously constitute but a tiny fragment of our population and are completely absent in many communities.

2. *Lower-upper class.* These are the *nouveaux riches*—persons whose wealth has been acquired recently. They lack family tradition and are less "cultivated" than members of the upper-upper class. In most of the communities studied, the two upper groups constitute from 1 to 3 percent of the population.

3. *Upper-middle class.* In this category are successful business and professional people who have not acquired enough wealth and prestige to be regarded as upper. The growing hoard of technological and managerial personnel in corporations and government (engineers, scientists, junior executives) belong in this group, as do most attorneys, physicians, den-

tists, and independent businessmen. In some studies, however, physicians appear to be regarded as upper class.

4. *Lower-middle class.* Usually placed in this group are white-collar workers who are reasonably secure economically but who have less money and prestige than those in group 3. Clerical workers of all sorts, sales persons, civil service workers—most are classifiable in group 4. The two middle-class groups embrace an increasingly large proportion of the American population. In 1956, for the first time, the number of white-collar workers in the United States exceeded the number of blue-collar workers.

5. *Upper-lower class.* Occupationally, these are skilled laborers. They differ from middle-class categories in that they work for wages rather than salaries and wear "work clothes" to work. In many instances upper-lowers possess more complicated skills than an average middle-class worker and they may also earn considerably more money. Upper-lowers are now moving in large numbers to new suburban areas and the distinction between them and lower-middle-class persons becomes more and more blurred.

6. *Lower-lower class.* This category is comprised mainly of unskilled and semiskilled persons who tend to live in urban depressed areas or farm labor camps and to be at the bottom of the income scale. The term *lower*, in connection with categories 5 and 6, is not meant in any derogatory sense; as sociologists use the term it is morally neutral. As a matter of fact, many lower-class persons, including some lower-lowers, make a serious attempt to follow middle-class folkways and mores.

Obviously the American class system is not as neat as the above classification makes it appear. There is a rapidly growing category, best be called "middle-middle," perhaps, which is not provided for in Warner's scheme. It includes middle-income people who wear business clothes to work, receive salaries, fees, or commissions, and are obviously of higher status than the traditional "poor but respectable bank clerk." In our wealthier states teachers, to cite one example, have become middle-middle. Furthermore, there is no cutoff point where a person ceases being lower class and becomes middle; millions of persons fall between Warner's categories. What we are dealing with is essentially a continuum and not a series of sharply defined groupings.

Within any of the schemes which social scientists use for classifying people, thousands of persons are unclassifiable. The six-point scale we have described fits urban much better than rural people. Many persons gain high prestige for reasons too special to include in a scale meant for general application. Intellectuals, entertainers, artists, writers, scholars, airline pilots, military career men, players of professional sports, politicians, diplomats, and college students are examples of persons who do not fit readily into any of the foregoing six categories. Where could a sociologist place a popular singer of lower-class origin, little education, and uncouth ways who owns half a dozen expensive automobiles and other material symbols of high status?

How Are Children Affected by Class?

We shall discuss in this section some of the class-induced problems of children and youth with which teachers must be concerned. Deliberately omitted is a consideration of the problems of upper-class children; teachers see so few of these children in a public school that they pose no serious problem. The most common interclass problems emerge from the clash of lower- and middle-class subcultures. This clash is most sharp when lower-class children and youth from environments which middle-class persons regard as disreputable come into contact with "respectable" middle-class folkways and mores. Let us see precisely what some of these cultural differences are.

Typically—but with many exceptions—lower-class parents, and particularly those of the lower-lower class, do not expect or demand the kind of behavior from their children that is usually expected from middle-class children. Lower-class child-rearing practice alternates permissiveness with occasional corporal punishment. Lower-class children are not toilet-trained or weaned as young as are middle-class children. In fact, lower-class children are pretty much allowed to set their own schedules in these matters. Lower-class children and youth also frequently are permitted to set their own schedules for feeding and rest. Lower-class parents are likely to permit their children to fight as a means of relieving aggressive impulses. Demands for personal cleanliness and grooming are not usually as stringent as among the middle class. The foregoing characteristics of lower-class child rearing are more conspicuous among the lower-lowers than among the upper-lowers, although they are much more conspicuous among the latter than among the middle class.

As lower-class children grow older, cultural demands of home and neighborhood continue in much the same pattern. In general, a lower-class child is subjected to much less pressure to achieve than is a middle-class child. Adults in his environment do not expect him to make high marks at school, to manage money carefully, or to behave according to middle-class standards. A lower-class teen-ager has wide latitude with respect to sexual behavior, drinking, smoking, gambling, and the use of uninhibited language.

Qualification is needed at this point. The foregoing assertions obviously do not apply to the "respectable," i.e., middle-class-oriented, segment of the lower class. Furthermore, although middle-class youth publicly proclaim for themselves rather puritanical moral standards (see results of the Purdue and other studies cited elsewhere in this chapter), on the level of *private belief and action* they tend to be less circumspect. Probably because of less close police surveillance, middle-class youth *get caught* less often than lower-class youth.

In contrast to the environment of a lower-class child or youth, the environment of a middle-class child or youth is relatively demanding. His parents or other adult relatives watch him closely. He is implored to keep clean, to use respectable language, to avoid fights, to stay in his own yard, and to refrain from sexual experimentation. He is toilet-trained and weaned early and kept on a fairly rigid schedule of feeding and resting. The word he hears most often is "Don't." In fact, typical middle-class parents spend a good deal of their time badgering their children.

After studying children reared in both lower- and middle-class environments, Allison Davis concluded that middle-class children of preschool age show more symptoms of nervous tension than do those of the lower class.[11] A nervous child is not necessarily a poorly adjusted child; if readers will recall our previous discussion of adjustment, they will perhaps agree that a child with a relatively high level of tension is more likely to be a "doer" than is a persistently relaxed child. However, contemporary American culture is so complex that it is difficult to assess adequately its impact at the various social-class levels. The usual intent of a middle-class parent is not to make an independent, productive thinker of his child but rather a conformist. Thus it may be that much middle-class tension is an outcome of attempts to conform and has nothing to do with creativity.

In any case, once school age is reached, the pressures on a lower-class child become much greater. If his home and neighborhood environment remain somewhat permissive and tension-reducing, his school environment is just the opposite. Teachers, school administrators, and counselors are drawn primarily from the lower-middle or middle-middle class and school board members from the upper-middle class. Thus American public schools tend to reflect middle-class attitudes and values. To a lower-class child or youth, then, a public school seems an alien environment. It is opposed to all that he has been taught is natural and approves much he has been taught is "putting on airs" or "being uppity." It is rather remarkable that so many lower-class children and youth do accommodate themselves sufficiently to public school to remain there.

Middle-class children usually find it farily easy to cope with school. At home they have been pressured into accepting, at least on a surface

[11] W. Allison Davis and Robert Havighurst, *The Father of the Man,* Houghton Mifflin, 1947, pp. 10, 24–26. Also relevant is W. Allison Davis, *Social Class Influences on Learning,* Harvard University Press, 1952.

level, the traditional middle-class values. Since the school environment promotes identical attitudes and values for middle-class children, it seems "homey," if not in every way satisfying. Thus, school per se does not pose special blocks and frustrations for a middle-class child. Teachers observe that middle-class youth do better academically, are quieter, fight less, and in other ways fit better into the school environment.

If the impact of schooling is omitted from the picture, socialization for a lower-class child or youth is probably just as easy as for a middle-class young person. Each has to "grow into" his class-related subculture. If it were not for the special but not uncommon lower-class situations of economic deprivation, broken homes, and alcoholism, lower-class culture would probably be friendlier to the young of all ages because it would be less taxing.

The Impact of Regional Cultural Differences

Regional cultural differences today are much less pronounced than at any time in our historical past. Mass media of communication and entertainment impose a set of common attitudes and values on people everywhere. A Bostonian blue-blood, a North Dakota farmer, a Texas cattleman, a San Francisco beatnik, and an Appalachian hillbilly each, to some degree, is affected by mass culture. The gradual erasure of regional cultural differences is accelerated further by the extraordinary mobility of the American population. In 1958 more than 11,000,000 of the 175,000,000 residents of the United States moved from one county to another, and about one-half of this number moved to a different state. An average American moves to a different state twice during his lifetime.[12] Furthermore, there is no reason to suppose that the present rate of mobility will not continue to increase. Some sections of the country are highly urbanized, others are not. The east coast region, the more industrialized sections of the north central states, and the Pacific coast region are highly urbanized. Certain sections of the southeastern coastal plain are in the process of becoming so. Conversely, for the most part, the Appalachian highland region, the great plains, and the western desert regions remain strikingly rural.

Because of differences in opportunities for educational attainments, people in rural areas are less likely to be "advanced" culturally than middle-class urban dwellers. Opportunities to read and keep abreast of current affairs, leisure time for cultivated pursuits, and presence of a generally stimulating intellectual atmosphere are not as readily available to rural folk. Rural children are just as bright as others but their over-all range of information appears more limited. However, because of their

[12] Myron Lieberman, *The Future of Public Education,* University of Chicago Press, 1960, p. 36.

more serious attitudes toward school work—except among migrant or semimigrant farm labor groups—their academic performance in school may equal or exceed that of urban children.

Regional cultural differences also may be affected by the length of time areas have been settled. However, this type of influence can probably not be separated from that provided by the type of persons who did the initial settling. In this connection, sociologists, like script writers for western TV shows and movies, have noted the rather conspicuous differences between "easterners" and "westerners." It appears that easterners continue to be more formal, more conservative, more attached to family traditions, and more concerned with social status and associated rituals, than westerners. There is something about western living that gives it a more "loosely structured" quality. Too, a westerner is a more restless type. However, these differences seem doomed to extinction; the steady migration of population from east to west may have the effect of diluting and gradually canceling out traditional western cultural traits. Or, conversely, western traits may spread to the East.

Space permits mention of only one more type of regional difference. The segregation controversy has highlighted regional differences in attitude toward minority ethnic groups. In the Southeast, prejudice among whites is directed primarily against Negroes, and the highest level of racial prejudice is probably in this region. However, we are prone to forget that whites the country over, and particularly those of northern European descent, tend to harbor prejudice against all minorities. In the western states, much of this prejudice is directed against Indians, although Mexicans also come in for a share. At one time whites of the Pacific coast discriminated strongly against persons of Asiatic descent; however, this particular type of discrimination appears to be waning rapidly. In regions where recent immigrants from Europe have settled, considerable prejudice exists toward them. This usually takes the form of hostility directed by "old Americans" of northern European descent against immigrants from southern Europe.

Of what concern are regional cultural differences to teachers? One reason for concern is obvious: in many parts of the United States a teacher can expect that some students in his classes will have migrated from an area with a subculture very different from his own. For example, teachers in industrial cities must recognize and learn to cope with the subculture of rural people who flow continuously toward the cities. Cultural differences are especially conspicuous where southern Negroes have migrated in large numbers to northern or west coast cities. Likewise, teachers in areas receiving a large influx of people from other parts of the country must learn to establish effective interaction with children of these people. This problem is particularly noticeable in Florida and on the west coast

—areas which are now major recipients of migrations from other parts of the country.

Much patience is required for two diverse cultures to achieve a successful accommodation to each other. Through the process of cultural diffusion —an outcome of interaction—each group acquires some of the attitudes, values, beliefs, and knowledge of the other. Thus, a teacher in California, as he makes his young Oklahomans more like the standard California types, will himself inescapably "take on" some of the traits of Oklahomans. However, all this takes time. A teacher whose background is middle-class suburbia will find that he cannot move children of a radically different subculture very far in a year's time. In fact, they will not move very far in a lifetime. The fusing of cultures usually requires generations.

Of What Consequence Are Cultural Differences Based on Ethnic-Group Membership?

When America was originally settled, national groups tended to congregate in specific localities: English Puritans in New England, Dutch in New York, English Episcopalians in the middle colonies, French in the New Orleans and Great Lakes regions, and Spanish in the Southwest. Later waves of immigration also had their focal points of destination. However, the operation of the "melting pot" principle has to a large degree reduced cultural differences based upon national origin. Boston Irish, Cincinnati Germans, Minnesota Swedes, and California Japanese have to a degree been homogenized by the mass media and by ever closer contacts with other cultural groups.

Nevertheless, in understanding his students, a teacher may find it essential to take national origin into account. In this connection problems of children of first-generation immigrants are particularly significant. If a child's parents were born and reared in a non-American culture, the child is fairly likely to have conflicts of greater than normal severity. He is caught between two sets of cultural pressures. His parents thrust at him one distinctive set of attitudes, values, and beliefs; the surrounding American culture thrusts at him another distinctive, and contrasting, set.

A frequent incompatibility between old-world and new-world cultures lies in the differences in roles of the sexes. A child of immigrant parents probably lives in a home where the father is dominant—in every sense, the head of the family. But this same child frequently will visit in homes of the modern American pattern where no one is "boss." Further, in the modern American home the husband assumes many of the chores reserved in Europe and Asia for the wife; he may cook, wash dishes, and clean the house, while his wife mows the lawn. It is easy to understand how a child of first-generation immigrants may become confused. He is torn between loyalty to his parents and their old-world ways and loyalty to the American culture, of which he hopes to become a full-fledged member.

However, a child or youth of immigrant parents actually is in a situation not unlike that of any American child or youth who is caught "between generations." Parents, and more particularly grandparents, often are committed to cultural values different from those of the child and youth peer culture, and also from those of the young adult peer culture which is emerging.[13] If children and youth of immigrant parents have a rougher time of it than those of native ancestry it is only a difference in degree: the problems are similar.

WHAT ARE SOME OBSTACLES TO SATISFACTORY SOCIALIZATION?

Socialization involves the acquisition of a mass of complex learnings. Under even the best of circumstances, we must expect children to make many mistakes. For a typical child, socialization is probably much easier in cultures simpler than ours. In agrarian civilizations, where most persons live on farms or in small rural villages and the rate of change is slow, people develop a "sense of community." In a small community everybody knows everybody else; furthermore, everybody knows how everybody else thinks about most issues in life, and the way people think changes very slowly. This gives different generations a feeling of closeness: grandparents, parents, and children may all live under one roof in relative harmony. Under such conditions children are assimilated into the culture rather smoothly. It is little wonder that a century ago a youth seemed much more mature at age 15 than he does today. But times have changed. Socialization is no longer so easy.

How Have Changed Living Conditions Made Socialization More Difficult?

Industrialization brought vast cities and amazing technological innovations. As people from far-flung subcultures were thrown together in cities, they realized, for the first time, that there were ways of looking at things different from their own. They found that there were alternatives in belief of which they had never dreamed. Although adults moving to the city might remain for the rest of their lives in "the same old rut," their children were almost certain to be attracted by new and unsettling ideas.

The rise of modern transportation and communication speeded the destruction of the old sense of community. As soon as people became free

---

[13] For an interesting discussion of the problems of youth who have parents and grandparents belonging to a fundamentalist religious faith, see Hollingshead, *op. cit.*, Chaps. 10, 12.

to move long distances quickly and relatively cheaply, a new element of spacial mobility was introduced into the culture. A person born in the Bronx might move to Texas, where his participation in community life very probably would be inharmonious. Development of telephone, radio, motion pictures, television, and a highly diversified press contributed to the mingling of heterogeneous ideas. As the complexity of ideas and beliefs with which a person was confronted multiplied, so did his confusion. Culture became increasingly fragmented, as did the personalities of most people. Thus, socialization became more and more complicated and difficult, requiring a longer period of years and promising less satisfying results than formerly.

At first glance, the ideas of the foregoing paragraph may seem to contradict the comments earlier in the chapter about the "homogenization" of culture brought about by the mass media and increased physical mobility of our population. However, there need be no contradiction. The development of cultural sameness, i.e., groups within a society becoming more and more alike, can proceed side by side with development of inconsistency and confusion. The outcome is that almost everyone—eventually—is inconsistent and confused *about the same matters.*

What Are Some Persistent Aspects of American Culture Which Impede Socialization?

In addition to the impact of industrialization and urbanization, there are several other features of our culture with which the young encounter special difficulty. We have selected three such features for comment: double standards, contradictions, and "closed areas" of culture.

1. *Double standards.* By a double standard, we mean existence of two sets of rules of conduct, each applying to a different category of persons. Students have long been familiar with the double standard relating to sex. Men are permitted and expected to follow a moral code different from that of women. A sex-based double standard applies likewise to teenagers and even to younger children. Provided everyone understands just which rules apply to each sex, a sex-based double standard is workable. However, if the rules keep shifting, much confusion can result.

With the passage of time, the double standard governing the two sexes seems to be eroding. Women and girls are now permitted many of the freedoms once reserved for men and boys. Girls, particularly teen-agers, may be confused because they do not know just how much freedom they will be allowed to exercise. Boys may suffer confusion and conflict as a result of not being certain of what kind of behavior to expect from girls. Is a girl who makes "passes" at boys "nice," since according to the historical rule it is the boy who is supposed to make the passes?

Perhaps more confusing to the young than our sex-related double standard is our age-related double standard. We have certain rules for children and other quite different rules for adults. Unlike many other peoples, Americans feel it desirable to protect their young from knowledge of numerous aspects of adult life.

For example, we make strenuous attempts to keep children innocent about the facts of sexual love, birth, death, suffering, dishonesty, criminal behavior, certain language usages, and many other things about which it is thought improper for children to know.

Then, sometime during his late teens or early 20s, a person is supposed to know all about these things. Hence, for all young persons who follow the cultural expectations, coming to maturity in our culture is a *jumplike* process. Of course, children and youth do learn, *sub rosa*, many of the banned facts, although often a highly distorted version of them.

Our culture may be contrasted to cultures in which no child-adult double standard exists. Many cultures have few or no activities which simultaneously are banned for children but proper for adults.[14] Therefore children experience most elements of their culture from the earliest age. At first they may not understand much of what they see, but they come to understand it rapidly and in step-by-step fashion. Where children are free to witness childbirth there can be no equivocation about the source of babies. There is one point in the life of a youth in a culture like the foregoing where socialization may be jumplike: when he undergoes an initiation ritual at adolescence, and after the ritual is regarded as an adult. However, it may remain the case that he understands all about the adult culture by the time he is old enough for the initiation ritual.

The absence of a child-adult double standard has two psychological advantages for a child or youth: (1) he is required to do a minimum of *relearning* during socialization and (2) he does not find himself confronted rather suddenly with an unmanageable burden of new learning in areas which were previously taboo to him. The more marked a child-adult double standard, the more likely a child is to feel confusion, insecurity, and conflict.

2. *Contradictions in attitudes, values, and beliefs.* As we have seen, the greater the number of contradictions in a culture, the more confusing is the socialization process. Contradictions tend to produce conflict. For example, if a culture harbors two opposed sets of beliefs about race relations, people gravitate toward one set or the other and form opposing groups. Arguments and even riots or armed conflict may follow. Conflict on this level is *interpersonal* (that is, between individuals or groups).

Interpersonal conflict, however, tends to become internalized in many

[14] A good case study is the Samoan culture as it existed at the time Margaret Mead made her famous studies there. See Mead's *Coming of Age in Samoa,* Morrow, 1928.

persons; they are "at war with themselves." Having accepted two inharmonious outlooks they find it impossible to act in accordance with
either without feelings of guilt. Conflict on this level may be called *intrapersonal.* There appears to be much intrapersonal conflict in the area of
race relations, but innumerable other areas of culture also produce conflict
within an individual. All of the so-called "closed areas" (treated in the
next section) are conflict producing.

Social scientists are inclined to think that Americans feel more conflict
than the people of most other cultures. A partial explanation lies in our
history. Of all nations, ours probably comes nearest to being a true melting pot of diverse cultures. In many areas of life divergent outlooks of the
numerous national, religious, and ethnic groups which settled this country
have clashed. Although the diverse cultural strands of our early history
are now rapidly blending and merging, we can still identify some hetero-
geneity of belief attributed to them.

Another factor producing cultural contradictions and hence conflict is
the rapidity of social change. American civilization is one of the most
dynamic in the world. Each new generation adopts changed attitudes,
values, and beliefs about most areas of life. This has the effect of separating the different generations; parents disagree with grandparents and
children with parents. Such disagreements may begin as interpersonal
conflict but almost invariably become internalized and end as intrapersonal discord. For example, a grandmother may feel that women should
not smoke, her daughter may feel that moderate smoking by adult women
is proper and the teen-age granddaughter may feel that it is perfectly all
right for a 16-year-old girl to smoke. However, everyone concerned is
likely to have mixed feelings. The teen-ager especially, at one and the
same time, may try to be loyal to her mother's values and to those of her
peer group—with ensuing conflict.

3. *Closed areas.* In most cultures there are certain areas of interest
which are partially or largely closed to reflective thought. In these areas
people tend to react in accordance with deeply rooted prejudices. Instead
of thinking, they act blindly, stubbornly, and irrationally. The specific
areas of interest which are "closed" vary from culture to culture and from
time to time. In the United States, those now partially or largely closed to
reflective thought include religion, morality, sex, race and minority-group
relations, social class, nationalism and patriotism, and certain aspects of
foreign policy, economics, and politics. An area which is closed to one
person may not be to another. For an area of culture to merit the label
closed, it is only necessary that it be closed or partially closed to a considerable number of persons.

An area of culture becomes closed whenever thinking in that area comes
to be dominated by a relatively inflexible ideology. When people are

dominated by such inflexibility, attempts to discuss issues in the area rationally and calmly lead to the erection of "ego defenses" by all those who feel strongly about them. Another way of putting it is to say that personality becomes rigid. Rigidity in this case is a form of defense; it is a barrier erected to prevent the jeopardizing of cherished beliefs.

However, people do change their outlooks concerning closed areas. They may "loosen up"—that is, become receptive to evidence which will lead them to change their ideas; or they may "tighten up," becoming less receptive than before. Shortly after World Wars I and II, Americans tended to become extremely rigid and dogmatic in connection with foreign economic ideologies, especially Russian communism. They went through a period when rational thought on this subject was virtually impossible. Then they began to loosen up, to become more flexible. By the middle 1950s it became possible, for the first time since 1947 or 1948, to discuss communism on a somewhat reflective level. But, as of the 1960s, many people seem to be "closing down" again in the area of communism.

Some social scientists feel that, as time passes, most if not all of the closed areas in American culture will gradually open. It is true that on most "touchy" subjects Americans in general seem somewhat more open-minded now than half a century ago. In some areas of thought the relaxation has been quite remarkable. For example, 50 years ago religion was a tightly closed area; now discussion of religion on a factual and reflective level is frequently possible.

It is hardly surprising that our sharpest intrapersonal conflicts occur in the closed areas. Conflicts in areas of belief such as social status, politics, religion, economics, race, and sex are not only common but often sufficiently intense to cause severe emotional disturbance. In a closed area every problem is likely to be troublesome because of the difficulty of examining it. In areas open to free reflection, on the other hand, conflicts are frankly faced and resolved—if not easily, at least without intolerable tension.

BIBLIOGRAPHY

Brown, Francis J., *Educational Sociology*, Prentice-Hall, 1954.
   A textbook designed for use in college courses in educational sociology. Contains much content pertinent to this chapter. See particularly the first 10 chapters.
Davis, Elmer, *But We Were Born Free*, Bobbs-Merrill, 1954. (Permabook paperback, 1955.)
   On the threats posed by blind conformism and the erosion of the democratic idea. Excellent.

Hollingshead, August, *Elmtown's Youth*, Wiley, 1949.
A study of the impact of social class on adolescents in a midwestern town. Reveals much about the American social structure as it affects both the young and the old.

Hunt, Maurice P., and Lawrence E. Metcalf, *Teaching High School Social Studies*, Harper, 1955.
Cited in Chapter 1 bibliography. Chapters pertinent here are 11–16, on the closed areas of culture.

Lerner, Max, *America as a Civilization*, Simon and Schuster, 1957.
A major work devoted to explaining numerous facets of our culture. Students should give first attention to Chapters VIII, IX, and X. Chapters VII and XI are also highly pertinent.

Mercer, Blaine E., and Edwin R. Carr, *Education and the Social Order*, Rinehart, 1957.
Excellent readings on the sociological aspect of life in Parts II, III, IV, and V.

Mettzer, Bernard N., and others, *Education in Society: Readings*, Crowell, 1958.
Particularly pertinent readings in Parts 2 and 3.

Petersen, William, ed., *American Social Patterns*, Doubleday, 1956. (Available in Anchor paperback.)
Studies of race relations, popular heroes, voting, union democracy, and government bureaucracy.

Rose, Arnold, *The Negro in America*, Harper, 1948.
A condensation of Gunnar Myrdal's *An American Dilemma*. One of the most comprehensive and penetrating studies of Negro-white relations in the United States. Excellent.

Rosenberg, Bernard, and David Manning White, eds., *Mass Culture*, Free Press, 1957.
A large selection, somewhat spotty in quality, of essays and articles on the impact of the mass arts on Americans. In Part 1 the two editors take contrasting positions as to the long-range effects of the popular communication media.

Smith, T. V., and Eduard C. Lindeman, *The Democratic Way of Life*, New American Library, Mentor paperback, 1951.
One of the best available statements of what democracy has come to mean to most Americans. All teachers and prospective teachers should be familiar with the thesis of this book.

Stanley, William O., and others, *Social Foundations of Education*, Dryden, 1956.
A rich collection of readings. One of the best is that by Margaret Mead, pp. 27 ff.

Warner, W. Lloyd, *The Living and the Dead*, Yale University Press, 1959.
The final volume of the famous Yankee City series, which reports an anthropological-sociological investigation of Newburyport, Mass. The volume treats political life, communal ceremonies, holidays, myths, and rituals and their meanings and symbolism.

Whyte, William H., Jr., *The Organization Man*, Simon and Schuster, 1956. (Also in Anchor paperback, 1956.)
An excellent book which has had wide impact. What kind of person is required to staff modern corporations, government agencies, schools, and other organizations? Don't miss the appendix, "How to Cheat on Personality Tests."

5

HOW DO PEOPLE DIFFER FROM EACH OTHER?

In addition to understanding some of the common aspects of man's psychological, biological, and sociological nature, it is important for teachers to understand the ways individuals differ from each other. For differ they do, and tremendously. After saying this, we must remember that if everyone were completely unique in every aspect it would be most difficult for people to work together in groups or for teachers to teach groups of children and youth. Human beings of a given culture are more alike than they are different and, as indicated in the previous chapter, there appear to be forces at work in the American culture which induce ever greater similarity among individuals. In spite of our similarities, we must take individual differences seriously into account.

In the United States we attempt to educate all the children of all the people through the twelfth grade. For social reasons, we try to keep children moving along through school so that most of those of a given age will be concentrated at a single grade level, e.g., most 8-year-olds will be in the third grade. Whether this is the best possible practice may be debatable, but nevertheless we do it and must prepare teachers as best we can to cope with the situation.

Because of our practice of promoting pupils according to age rather than achievement or ability, a teacher can expect to find a wide range of difference among students in his classroom. A typical four-year comprehensive high school will enroll freshmen with measured IQs from 60 to 125 or higher, reading levels from the third to beyond the twelfth grade, and arithmetic levels from fourth to fourteenth grade. Although spreads of personality, interests, and attitudes cannot be stated so readily, we can assume that the span of differences here is equally great. In a large unselected population there is a continuous variation from a very low to a very high manifestation of traits. However, the wider the deviation from the average of any trait, the fewer are the individuals in which that degree of the trait is manifested.

Before we examine current concepts regarding individual differences, we may profitably survey some of the ideas which have appeared historically. As in the other areas we have explored, in our ideas concerning individual differences past influences are always with us.

WHAT ATTITUDES HAVE BEEN HELD HISTORICALLY CONCERNING INDIVIDUAL DIFFERENCES?

Attitudes in regard to individual differences date back to and before the time of the ancient Greek philosophers. Aristotle tended to divide people into two kinds: those with and those without "deliberative faculty." He taught that men who lack the deliberative faculty are by nature slaves. He thought that inferior persons have enough ability to follow directions given by others but not enough to direct their own lives. They differ from lower animals in that, rather than being driven by instinct, they do engage in reason, but only passively. Thus, Aristotle believed that, although natural slaves are men and not brutes, they differ in kind, not merely degree, from those men who are naturally free. Consequently, he considered use of slaves similar to use of domesticated animals.

Ancient aristocrats, represented by Aristotle, denied anything like natural equality of men and justified the institution of slavery in terms of natural inequality. As free men were distinguished from slaves, so education was distinguished from training. It apparently never occurred to an ancient aristocratic thinker that a manual worker of any kind should, for any reason, study subjects such as poetry and music. Workers were trained to master a specific job and their education stopped. Adler and Mayer state the role of education in the ancient world, as conceived by the aristocratic class: "Education, liberal in purpose and character, is for free men, for citizenship, leisure, and lofty pursuits. Slaves, serfs, manual workers, and even skilled artisans are trained, much as animals are trained."[1]

The idea of a natural aristocracy, that is, a group superior because of its biological inheritance, continued to be accepted without much question down to the eighteenth century. In fact, in colonial America the sharp

[1] Mortimer J. Adler and Milton Mayer, *The Revolution in Education*, University of Chicago Press, 1958, p. 72.

class structure reflected the widespread belief that people differ naturally, ranging all the way from those who are fit only to rule to those who are fit only to serve. Certainly such colonial leaders as Alexander Hamilton and the Adamses believed in a natural aristocracy. Although Thomas Jefferson personally may have believed that all men are born potentially equal, as his statement in the Declaration of Independence seems to imply, he was clearly aware of the social fact of inequality. In a letter written in 1814 he stated, "The mass of our citizens may be divided into two classes —the laboring and the learned. . . . At the discharging of the pupils from the elementary schools the two classes separate—those destined for labor will engage in the business of agriculture, or enter into apprenticeship to such handicraft art as may be their choice; their companions, destined to the pursuits of science, will proceed to the College."[2]

Growing Ideas of Natural Equality

If readers will recall the various theories of man's psychological nature, as presented in Chapter 2, they will realize that, well before the eighteenth century ended, lines of thought running counter to the idea of natural inequality had appeared. In a large sense Western religions—Judaism and Christianity—contained a strong element of equalitarianism. If all men are equal in the sight of God, then may it not also be true that under the right social conditions they would be equal in the sight of man?

John Locke's seventeenth-century *tabula rasa* theory supported the idea of natural equality. If mind at birth is a clean slate, environment evidently plays a crucial role. Although one might assume that some clean slates are better than others, one can just as easily assume that a slate is a slate and all that is important is the writing on it. This is precisely what John B. Watson, a twentieth-century follower of the *tabula rasa* idea, did (see p. 49).

Faculty psychology was explicitly developed by Christian Wolff in the eighteenth century. It emphasized that individual differences are developed and that people are born virtually equal. The central thesis of faculty psychology is that each person has a single unitary mind; this mind has several specific faculties, such as memory, will, and reason; and the strengths of these faculties depend upon the degree to which they are exercised. Within this pattern of thinking individual differences might be construed as the result of different amounts of exercise of the various faculties of the mind. (Faculty psychology is developed in considerable detail in Chapter 10.)

A curious pseudo science, designed for the purpose of measuring individual differences, arose in connection with faculty psychology. This was

2 *Ibid.,* p. 3.

phrenology. Phrenologists felt it reasonable to assume a relationship between the development of one's faculties and the contour of one's skull. Early in the nineteenth century, E. G. Gall listed 27 powers of the mind. He then attempted to link them with 27 regions of the brain. He assumed that development of a specific function depends on development of the corresponding brain area. Such cerebral development was thought to exert pressure on the skull, pressing it outward in the form of bumps.

Phrenologists thus thought they could measure the relative development of a person's faculties by feeling his skull. "Bump feeling" was taken very seriously by some of our most prominent early American educators. Horace Mann, secretary of the Massachusetts State Board of Education from 1837 to 1848 and a leading figure in American education, was enthusiastic over the "science" of phrenology. Even now the modern testing movement, with its tendency to think of each personality as consisting of a mosaic of abilities, talents, and traits, sometimes is referred to as "bump feeling gone statistical."

In spite of such developments as phrenology, professional psychologists of the nineteenth century were little concerned with individual differences. The introspectionist Wilhelm M. Wundt (1832–1920), who established the world's first experimental psychology laboratory at Leipzig in 1879, was not interested in particular human beings. He arrived at his generalized man in a manner fairly satisfactory to himself, but the process gave him little, if any, insight into what a particular person would do in a specific situation. Science, as he saw it, was concerned with abstract generalizations, not with specific cases. To him individual differences were but exceptions which proved the rule. Any particular person, because of his special constitution, might not fit exactly the conditions prescribed by the general rule. However, he was confident that generalized man, like gravity or any other generic concept, when completely formulated, would account for each individual case. Hence, he saw little purpose in studying the unique nature of individuals.

Growing Interest in Individuals

Some educators of Wundt's period or slightly earlier were transitional figures in that they were beginning to show an interest in individual children as such. These pioneering thinkers used "the individual" sometimes to mean human nature in general, other times to mean an individual child or youth. They began to observe individual children and youth, but usually continued to think of them as representatives of children and youth in general. Yet their growing interest in individual children and youth eventually led toward study of individual differences.

The scientific movement in child study and education in the early 1900s specifically focused attention on individual differences among school children and youth. Edward L. Thorndike in 1906 stated, "The practical consequence of the fact of individual differences is that every general law of teaching has to be applied with consideration of the particular person in question. Every stimulus must be given not to men or to children in general, but to a particular individual or group characterized by certain peculiarities."[3]

At about the same time, John B. Watson was writing about human behavior and learning in such a way as to imply that all healthy normal people are essentially equal *at birth*. However, like Thorndike, he was aware of great differences among them and attributed these to differences in environment. In recent years so much emphasis has been placed on individual differences that many people tend to assume that each child, in every respect, is completely unique. This represents as great an extreme on the side of individualism as is represented on the side of "sameness" by those who regard all persons as essentially alike.

WHAT ARE THE SOURCES AND NATURE OF INDIVIDUAL DIFFERENCES?

Traditionally, the two basic sources of individual differences have been considered to be heredity and environment. Although it is true that heredity and environment do influence human traits, they also influence each other and human traits cannot be separated into those which depend entirely upon heredity and those which depend completely upon environment (see pp. 73–74 for a discussion of the futility of the nature-nurture controversy). For any individual, presence or absence of a certain type of hereditary structure can provide or limit opportunity for development, but it cannot insure that a certain kind of behavior will or will not be manifested. A person's genes help provide and limit opportunity but do not determine what will be made of that opportunity.

Although all traits manifested by human beings are to some degree a product of interaction of genetic and environmental factors, for all practical purposes certain physical characteristics, such as blood type, may be attributed to heredity, and certain behavioral traits, such as customs and language, to environment. Other traits, stature and skin color, for example, are strongly affected by both genetic and environmental factors.[4]

Genetic endowment is probably more similar among the races of man than most biologists and psychologists thought two or three decades ago. It is interesting to know, however, that, except for identical twins, every human being on earth is probably genetically unique. The number of

---

[3] Edward L. Thorndike, *Principles of Teaching*, Seiler, 1906, p. 83.
[4] John L. Fuller and W. Robert Thompson, *Behavior Genetics*, Wiley, 1960, p. 2.

possible gene combinations is such that a single human pair can produce 20^{24} different types of children—more than the total number of human beings who have ever existed.[5] Nevertheless, what we must remember is that, among people considered normal, the *range* of genetic variation is not very great.

Environmental influences begin interacting with hereditary factors even before a child is born. Congenital influences (those entering the picture during the gestation period) should be differentiated from genetic influences (those exercised by the nature of a germ plasm). Since an embryo or fetus, through osmosis, receives nourishment from the blood stream of its mother, any conditions which alter the chemical composition of the mother's blood may have some effect upon development of the fetus or embryo. When embryos have suffered drastic changes in physical environment, including changes in temperature and nutrition, they sometimes have grown into monstrosities. Many psychologists are convinced that the very event of birth has at least some influence upon the characteristics of an individual. Birth also brings with it a sudden and drastic change in environment. There is a marked change in posture and external temperature. New functions such as breathing and eating must be established.

Some factors of postnatal environment which influence development of a child are the economic and social status of his family, the attitudes he senses in his parents and other adults, his position in the family, and his relationships with his siblings. School environment, too, is important, particularly during a child's early years. Each child, on his level of comprehension, sizes up his environment so as to contribute to his frame of mind and attitude toward learning. Pupil-teacher and pupil-pupil relationships have much to do with the structure of the personalities involved in a school situation.

As we continue our exploration we should bear in mind that differences, particularly those which result largely from environmental influence, remain relative to one's situation throughout his lifetime. Although there is a high degree of continuity in the traits of a given person, they do change. No child carries within him a rigidly fixed degree of introversion, temper, generosity, mechanical interest, musical ability, or any other characteristic.

Differences Imposed by Specific Cultural Forces

Most of the cultural forces discussed in Chapter 4 may have bearing on individual differences. The impact of family and peer group is probably of greatest importance. A child or youth may appear as a deviate to teachers because he is in some respects very much like his parents or

[5] *Ibid.,* p. 15.

friends. For example, if he steals school property, it is possible that this kind of thievery is a culture trait of his peer group or family, or both.

Several of the more conspicuous kinds of individual differences are related to social-class membership. Achievement in school, particularly in academic areas, tends to correlate closely with social-class membership; middle-class children or youth tend to outperform lower-class children or youth. The same is true of achievement on intelligence tests and other tests of academic aptitude. This should not be taken to mean that the genetic endowment of lower-class persons necessarily decrees inferior performance. There is little question that most of the tests used to measure academic aptitude reflect a "culture bias," i.e., they discriminate unfairly against lower-class children.

Kenneth Eells, a well-known contemporary psychologist, found that by changing tests so that verbal skills played a less important role in determining ability, and by changing problems to insure their being familiar to lower-class children, he could greatly reduce the differences in test scores between middle- and lower-class children.[6] However, many psychologists do not agree with Eells' position. His conclusion that the chief difference in performance between children of various social strata results from differences in verbal skills has been challenged by other experts, including F. T. Tyler.[7]

If, as Eells suggests, differences in test performance and achievement in school between lower- and middle-class children are largely attributable to differences in verbal skill, then genetic endowment may have little to do with differences in performance. A middle-class child usually has vastly greater opportunity to learn verbal skills than does a lower-class child.

Race, nationality, and ethnic-group membership also help furnish an explanation for some of the individual differences which teachers observe in children. With respect to academic achievement, children from an ethnic group which has a tradition of scholarship will, on the average, achieve at a higher level than others. Personality differences may also be tied to ethnic-group membership.

Race may contribute to individual differences in the sense that a particular race may be culturally different from other races. This cultural difference may be a result of national origin, or differences in educational opportunity, or other factors. In any case, a teacher sometimes finds that those of his students who are members of minority races are different in significant ways from the rest.

Some major difficulties are encountered when we attempt to measure

[6] Kenneth Eells and others, *Intelligence and Cultural Differences,* University of Chicago Press, 1951.

[7] F. T. Tyler, "Comments on the Correlational Analysis Reported in Intelligence and Cultural Differences," *Journal of Educational Psychology,* May, 1953.

and explain racial and nationality differences. First, with such admixtures of peoples as now exist it is virtually impossible to isolate representatives of pure races. Second, because of prejudices within some cultures, people who are labeled as members of a minority race often have not experienced the environmental situations common to the majority. Generally, discriminatory practices of a majority group tend to limit opportunities of a minority group. Third, psychological tests usually have been standardized on specific populations of the nation where they are developed and their scores are thus relatively meaningless when the tests are given to other racial or national groups.

Careful study of individual differences in relation to race and nationality discloses wide variation in specific traits within any "race" or "nationality," overlapping of racial and nationality groups measuring similarly on any trait, and lack of any one pattern of traits characteristic of a racial or nationality group. Although societies commonly attribute certain stereotyped psychological traits to each racial and nationality group, careful scientific study of differences does not support these generalizations.

After discussing the foregoing hereditary and cultural factors which produce individual differences, we must make clear that probably no single factor can be isolated as the determiner of any specific aspect of personality. Personality traits appear to be products of a totality of interacting personal and environmental influences.

Sexual Differences

On a variety of types of tests, boys and girls show significant differences from each other. For example, boys are superior in reaction time, speed of tapping, muscular strength, dexterity with tools, skill with numbers, and comprehension of spatial relations. Girls excel in speed of word association, quick adaptations, shift of attention, finger dexterity, color discrimination, and verbal memory. These differences appear early in life and tend to increase with age. (Why are little girls in the first and second grades generally considered to be "ahead" of boys of the same age?) On Bernreuter's Personality Inventory, boys indicate more extraversion, dominance, and self-sufficiency, and fewer evidences of neurotic inclinations than do girls. On the Allport-Vernon Study of Values, men register higher in verbal commitment to theoretical, economic, and political values and women to aesthetic, social, and religious values.[8]

The value of some of these tests is open to question, chiefly for the reason that they might seem to suggest "instinctive" differences between

[8] E. G. Boring, H. S. Langfeld, and H. P. Weld, *Foundations of Psychology*, Wiley, 1948, p. 430.

sexes. Anthropological research has shown that, if one looks at the human race as a whole, no such differences can be proved or disproved. Even if it could be proved that "instinctive" differences, such as are indicated in the foregoing studies, exist, such differences would not be of major importance to teachers.

What is of great importance to a teacher is an understanding of the sex roles which our culture and its major subcultures create. Most members of each sex from a rather early age try to follow the roles specified for them. Some do not succeed, and as a result we have "tomboys" and "sissies." But most do succeed fairly well.

What are some of the more important aspects of these roles? Any attempt to describe male and female roles in our culture is complicated by the fact that they have changed rather drastically within the past one-third of a century. Some of the historical features of male-female roles are so deeply seated, however, that they remain highly influential even if not consistently practiced.

Boys are supposed to be boys, which has meant rough and tough, aggressive, bold, inquisitive, and uninhibited. The plea of adults to little boys is "Act like men," which usually means "Don't cry when you get hurt," "Don't run away from a fight," "Be independent." Girls are supposed to be girls, which means dainty, gentle, obedient, cautious, and circumspect. When we enjoin girls to "act like ladies" we mean such things as "Keep clean and neat," "Don't think or talk about sex," "Don't cause adults any trouble."

Change has been in the direction of confusing and even reversing the traditional sex roles. We no longer expect women to be as retiring, obedient, and modest as we once did. We no longer expect men to be as stalwart, unemotional, and independent as we once did. As pointed out in Chapter 4, the sex-related double standard is eroding.[9]

Teachers need to realize that changing sex roles confuse children and youth, as well as adults. Boys often no longer know what to expect from girls and girls no longer know what to expect from boys. Both are likely to feel conflict. Teachers can be of real service by helping boys and girls understand what is happening. Frequently a person who feels conflict is helped if he can see how cultural change tends to produce conflict in individuals.

HOW ARE INDIVIDUAL DIFFERENCES MEASURED?

Individual differences of students are customarily measured by use of copyrighted standardized psychological tests. Such tests are designed to

[9] For one of the best treatments of sex roles in American culture, see Margaret Mead, *Male and Female,* Morrow, 1949.

gain a comprehensive picture of some aspect of students. Thus, they are quite different in purpose and structure from teacher-made tests. Tests have been devised to measure various kinds of differences. However, intelligence or ability tests continue to hold a prominent position in most comprehensive testing programs.

A psychological test is an instrument so constructed as to achieve an objective and standardized measure of a sample of a person's behavior. When a psychologist or psychometrist sets out to measure the vocabulary of a child or youth, he observes that person's performance with only a limited number of words. He carefully selects these words with the goal of having them typify the total vocabulary of the child. Thus, testing discovers in short order what less systematic observation of a child's daily life can unearth only in a much longer period of time. Tests are a quick and relatively objective method of systematically observing a child in a variety of situations. Since standardized tests judge all children by the same standards and hence supposedly eliminate the influence of personal biases, these tests appear to be more "scientific" than are personal observations and interviews.

What Will Standardized Tests Not Do?

Teachers use systematic testing to the best advantage when they are acquainted with tests to the point of knowing what and what not to expect of them. Thus, it is essential that the purposes and limitations of each test be known. A teacher who realizes that standardized tests are possibly—but not necessarily—the most accurate method yet devised of estimating the nature of certain human characteristics will be able to benefit his students and himself through the use of standardized test scores. On the other hand, one who blindly becomes a test enthusiast probably will do more harm than good with tests. Although some tests are valuable for more than one purpose, each type of test has its unique function. A test which is very good for one purpose may provide useless or even misleading information when used for a purpose for which it was not devised.

Below are listed some limitations of standardized tests which should be recognized.

1. Tests do not reveal universal human abilities the natures of which are sharply defined and well understood.
2. Results of one standardized test, regardless of its excellence, do not alone provide a sound basis for counseling and guidance.
3. Intelligence tests do not measure a faculty which, although differing in degree, is essentially the same in all human beings.

4. Intelligence tests which measure academic aptitude do not necessarily measure capacity for intelligent behavior in life.
5. Although bright students usually remain bright adults and dull students usually remain dull, a person will not necessarily continue to score at a certain level merely because he did so on one occasion.
6. Tests never have been devised which exactly measure any general ability, capacity, aptitude, or other trait.

What Knowledge of Statistics Must a Teacher Have?

A psychological test is usually accompanied by a formula for deriving its score. To score a multiple-choice test accurately the formula often specifies that the grader count the number of items right and subtract some fraction of the number wrong. The fraction of the number wrong to be subtracted is the reciprocal of a number one less than the number of choices on each question. (The reciprocal of 3 is $\frac{1}{3}$.) A true-false test with two possible answers for each question should be scored by taking the number right less the number wrong. A selection test with four possible answers for each question should be scored by taking the number right less one-third the number wrong. Statistically, when this procedure is followed those students who know no correct answers probably will score zero. A student will receive a positive score to the degree that he has accurate hunches or insights into the correct answers for the questions.

Some knowledge of statistics seems necessary in order to interpret test scores accurately. A few fundamental statistical concepts are described below.

AVERAGE. The average, or arithmetic mean, is the score most representative of an entire group tested. It is found by dividing the sum of all the scores by the number of scores. If four students measure IQs of 70, 90, 95, and 113, the mean is 92. This is found by adding the scores and dividing their sum by 4. An average score provides a means of comparing an individual child's score with that of members of his group. It also may be used in comparing scores of various groups.

STANDARD DEVIATION. Some measure other than average must be used to determine just how far above or below the average the score of a child or youth falls. Two groups may show the same averages on the same test and yet have a great difference in variability. Variability means the extent to which scores are spread or scattered. The measure of variability most commonly used and encountered is standard deviation, indicated by the symbol SD or σ (sigma).

Let us assume two hypothetical groups of 35 children each. Each group measures a mean or average IQ of 100, but the groups are so composed that there is a great difference in their variability. The variability of the two groups is shown in Fig. 1. Respective sigmas are 15+ and 28+.

Here we see that it is the comparative σ scores or standard deviations which indicate the relative variability of the groups. A standard deviation is obtained by taking the square root of the average of the squared deviations. Steps in this process are:

1. Find the deviation of each person's score from the mean.
2. Square each of these deviations.
3. Find the sum of these squared deviations.
4. Divide this sum by the number of scores in the group.
5. Find the square root of this average. This is σ or SD.

If the scores on a test constitute a normal distribution, about two-thirds (68 percent) of the scores will fall within one SD above and below the mean, 95 percent of the scores will fall within two SDs above and below the mean, and three SDs above and below the mean will include almost all of the scores. Fig. 3 (p. 135) shows a normal distribution curve.

The use of standard deviation is valuable in that it enables the measure

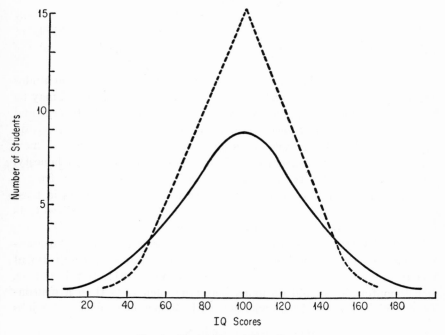

Fig. 1. Variability of Two Groups.

of a particular trait to be divided into approximately six equal parts. The spread in the trait being measured is about the same from the mean to one SD above or below the mean as it is from 2 SD to 3 SD above or below the mean. Note that standard deviations equate the degrees of the trait being measured, not the number of people scoring any particular score. On a normal curve as we move farther away from the average, or mean, the amount of change in each succeeding given numerical fraction of the group becomes greater.

PERCENTILE.   A percentile is that point in a distribution below which a given percentage of the cases occurs. When we divide the scores made by a large group of children on a given test into 100 equal parts, each part is called a percentile. When a student scores at the 85th percentile, his score is equal or superior to 85 percent of those taking the test. The amounts of ability represented by each percentile are not equal; in fact, when the distribution of scores is normal there is about the same amount of difference in the measured trait between the 98th and 99th percentile as between the 50th and 60th.

What Kinds of Traits May Be Measured with Psychological Tests?

The physiques, personalities, interests, intelligence, aptitudes, and achievements of children may be measured with varying degrees of accuracy. Organic traits are measured quite readily. The other kinds of traits are less tangible and consequently more difficult to evaluate mathematically.

Personality is especially hard to measure because in this area attitudes and behavior tend to vary with the situation. For example, a child may be introverted in a classroom but extraverted at a ball game. Hartshorne and May, in their studies of deceit,[10] found honesty to be specific to certain situations. Even without such studies, any student of culture would know that most Americans learn to turn such personality traits as honesty, truthfulness, and charity on and off as convenient, like water from a faucet. Even so, there is enough continuity of personality traits in most persons to give the tests some predictive value. Several standardized tests in this field have been used extensively with useful results.

Personality tests are controversial in the sense that they measure adjustment and the test writers, some critics feel, assume that adjustment is conformity to the cultural status quo (see pp. 89–91). If this is true, then a conformist should do much better on such tests than a nonconformist. Since these tests are widely used in screening applicants for jobs

[10] Hugh Hartshorne, Mark A. May, and others, *Testing the Knowledge of Right and Wrong*, Religious Education Association, 1927.

in corporations, one critic of such tests included in his book a section entitled "How to Cheat on Personality Tests."[11]

Such tests may be valuable in spotting personality deviations of such serious nature that special counseling or psychiatric referral is desirable. But one should guard against using scores of these tests as a weapon to suppress the creativity of "odd balls," who may sometime produce great works of art or achieve spectacular breakthroughs in science.

As in the case of personality traits, interests of a given individual vary according to time and place and great caution must be observed in interpreting interest tests. Without further evidence, a test score showing high interest in one area and low interest in another probably should not be given too great weight in vocational counseling. Many persons have found great contentment in a vocation which at one time in their life had no appeal.

Intelligence and aptitude are closely related. Both are measured through sampling achievement in certain areas. Intelligence is ability to learn or capacity to form insights. It is measured by finding out how much a person knows and can do. Thus, intelligence tests are designed to find how much a person knows about certain matters and how well he can solve certain types of problems. On the basis of a person's performance, we infer his "mental age," from which an IQ score can be derived.

Aptitude is ability to learn in specific areas, such as music, mechanics, clerical tasks, and relatively abstract academic subjects. It is usually measured by how well a person can perform certain tasks directly or indirectly related to high performance in the area. Relatively high ability to succeed in the tasks required by the test is assumed to indicate relatively high aptitude in the area to which the task is relevant.

Achievement tests are designed, as a rule, to measure how much a student has learned in one or more of the standard school subjects—reading, composition, arithmetic, social studies, science, foreign language, and the like. One of the authors recently undertook the study of a large number of achievement tests in widespread use. He found the available tests to be very spotty in character, with weaknesses of the following nature.

1. English mechanics tests stress too heavily pure mechanics, such as comma placement, in contrast to ability to recognize whether a sentence or paragraph is, in the main, a good sentence or paragraph.
2. Reading tests properly include tests of comprehension, but almost never do they include items which would reveal the most important comprehension skill of all—"ability to read between the lines."
3. Arithmetic tests focus almost exclusively on mechanics, and but rarely

[11] See William H. Whyte, Jr., *The Organization Man*, Doubleday Anchor, 1957, appendix.

attempt to reveal a student's understanding of mathematical concepts or number theory.

4. Tests in social studies focus on fact learning—the names of people, dates, and places. For the most part the items deal with trivial matters. The tests, with rare exceptions, do not attempt to discover a student's understanding of critical issues confronting twentieth-century civilization.

5. Literature tests ignore important works of fiction, drama, and poetry of the past 20 years, and some ignore all works of the twentieth century.

6. Science tests are frequently obsolete, and in addition emphasize terminology far too much. Virtually without exception, science tests appear to ignore completely the question of what the scientific outlook is.

Children deviate the farthest from the average in specialized abilities and traits as contrasted with their more general abilities. Thorndike noted that variability is greater in traits peculiar to man than in those peculiar to animals and in acquired traits as contrasted with original traits. Binet observed that the higher (the greater degree of abstraction required) and more complex the process, the more it varies from individual to individual.

Studies of abnormal persons provide examples of how extreme variation of traits may be found in a single individual. People have been observed who were so deficient in general intelligence that it was necessary to confine them in institutions for the feeble-minded, but who, at the same time, were strikingly gifted in some specific trait such as artistic ability, mechanical aptitude, arithmetic ability, ability to memorize, or musical talent. These often are spoken of as idiot-savants. On a less extreme level, often people who are mediocre in most respects are phenomenally good in one area of activity.

Verbal or linguistic ability is the one area in which people are not found highly proficient when they measure below average in general intelligence. In our culture verbal ability and general intelligence correlate highly. In fact, one of the best measures of academic or school aptitude is a vocabulary test. The *coefficient of correlation* of verbal ability or vocabulary and academic aptitude or intelligence is about .50. This means that there is a fair degree of correspondence between the two sets of measures—verbal scores and intelligence scores.

Coefficients of correlation vary from a perfect positive (+1.00) through 0.00 to a perfect negative (−1.00). Numerical description of a correlation enables one to realize the degree of relationship that exists. The degree or size of a correlation refers not to positiveness as opposed to negativeness but to the distance from zero (whether positive or negative). A positive correlation between verbal aptitude and intelligence means that persons who tend to score high in verbal aptitude also tend to score high in intelligence. A negative correlation would exist if persons who scored high on one scored low on the other.

A zero correlation signifies that there is no relationship between the scores different persons get on the two tests which are being evaluated against each other. A correlation of .50 means that there is a fairly strong, but only a fairly strong, positive relationship between scores. Actually it means that scores on one test can be predicted from scores on the other test 13 percent better than they could if there were no correlation at all, that is, if prediction had to be based upon pure chance. The formula for finding *efficiency of prediction* in percentage is $100 \ (1 - \sqrt{1 - r^2})$ where r represents the coefficient of correlation.

WHAT IS INTELLIGENCE?

Considerable controversy and confusion have surrounded the use of the term *intelligence*. Our purpose in this section is to cut through some of the uncertainty by describing, in comparative fashion, the major positions which have been taken with respect to a number of the issues surrounding intelligence.

Nature of Intelligence

In the literature relating to intelligence, we find implied a distinction between the *nature* of intelligence and the *origin* of intelligence. The nature of intelligence is how intelligence works in situations calling for it. It is the process, working itself out. For purposes of analysis issues relating to the process can be discussed independently of issues relating to the origin of intelligence, although obviously the two cannot be regarded as unrelated.

INTELLIGENCE AS CAPACITY TO LEARN. Psychologists have advanced numerous competing theories of the nature of intelligence. Alfred Binet (1857–1911), a French psychologist who in 1905 designed the first widely used test of mental ability, gave little attention to a theoretical definition of intelligence. To him, intelligence was unitary in the sense that each person had a certain amount which could be used for any purpose; it was a general ability to learn. If a person did better in one field of activity than in another, it was due, not to any fundamental variation in intelligence relative to the two fields, but to factors such as learning, interest, and motivation. To illustrate: a person who learns to play a musical instrument brilliantly does not have a different kind of intelligence from that of a brilliant engineer, chef, actor, or seamstress. Rather, he chooses to direct his talents toward music because a combination of environmental factors impels him in this direction.

Although their formulations were different, most other early twentieth-century psychologists likewise held the view that intelligence is a general capacity or potential for learning and can be directed along any line which interest dictates. Lewis Terman (1877–1956), an American psychologist, saw intelligence as ability to do abstract thinking, an ability which can be directed toward repairing an automobile motor just as well as toward solving a problem in quantum mechanics. William Stern (1871–1938), a German professor, regarded intelligence as adaptability to new problems and conditions of life. To him, solving a problem involving marital discord was as good an example of the functioning of intelligence as devising original algebraic formulations.

The concept of intelligence, as unitary or general, finally came under considerable criticism. Charles E. Spearman (1863–1945), an English psychologist, thought that two factors contributed to every intelligent act: g, a general factor operative in all situations, and s, a specific factor operative only in situations where that specific factor is involved. Thus, he thought that a person's capacity to act in any situation depends both upon his general capacity and upon the special capacity involved in that particular act. To illustrate: a person might have a fairly mediocre general intelligence but a very high order of special capacity in, say, music.

To split intelligence still further, the American psychologist Edward L. Thorndike (1874–1949) divided intelligence into three kinds, mechanical, social, and abstract. He thought that each kind of intelligence is manifested by the quality of response which a person can make to stimuli in whichever of the three areas is involved. A person might have a high order of mechanical intelligence without a corresponding level of social or abstract intelligence. In this case he would be highly competent in working with, say, motors but might be ineffective in working with other persons or solving problems in higher mathematics. Similarly, a person might be extremely adept in persuading others, in which case he might perform brilliantly as a salesman; but he might be incapable of changing a tire or passing first-year economics.

All of these early definitions of the nature of intelligence assumed that, whether intelligence is unitary or composed of two, three, or more somewhat independent factors, it is basically a capacity—a learning potential. This capacity, whatever its origin, was assumed by early twentieth-century psychologists to be relatively fixed once a person reached adulthood. Further, virtually all of the early workers in the area of intelligence were adherents to some degree of a stimulus-response (mechanistic, reflex-arc) psychology. This means that they construed the nature of intelligence as capacity to form new responses to stimuli in rapid and accurate manner in situations which so permit.

INTELLIGENCE AS ABILITY TO ACT WITH FORESIGHT. When we think of intelligence as the ability to act with foresight, we are not contradicting the notion that intelligence is a capacity; we are making different assumptions about the nature of this capacity. When one acts with foresight, he "looks ahead"; he tries to anticipate the consequences of acting in a particular way. He makes forecasts regarding the outcome of alternative lines of action. These forecasts are based upon experience. They are made possible by the fact that experience has equipped the person with a number of functional generalizations (rules or principles), which are invoked as needed to predict the consequences of present action. For example, if experience has taught that although rattlesnake bites are not usually fatal they do make one very ill, a person will behave very cautiously in rattlesnake country so as to avoid getting bitten.

When intelligence is defined in such manner, the quality or level of intelligence hinges in part on the number and accuracy of rules which a person has learned and also on his ability to invoke these rules, flexibly and imaginatively, in situations which call for them. Seldom does a rule learned from past experience fit a new situation precisely. Thus, ability to recognize what is appropriate to a situation and to take proper action is, from the point of view here stated, an indication of intelligence. We cannot divorce intelligence from what we usually call originality or creativity.

When two situations seem alike superficially, then, intelligent persons characteristically discern differences that would escape the less intelligent. They do not slur over fine distinctions whenever such distinctions are relevant to solving the problem at hand. They are able to test their hunches and hypotheses intellectually so that in their overt behavior they appear to do a minimum of fumbling in difficult situations; they choose the correct act almost instantly. (But not in every kind of situation—Einstein required many years to develop and perfect the theory of relativity.)

The foregoing view of intelligence rejects the notion that intelligence is fixed. With an increase in age and experience, a person may show increased flexibility and imagination of behavior. Furthermore, a person's gain in intelligence may not be equated with a gain in age: it may be much faster in rate, or much slower; and adults may continue to gain in intelligence as long as they live. On the other hand, for certain individuals intelligence may appear to be relatively fixed—these are persons who, for various reasons, cease growing intellectually. The point is, we cannot say such persons cease growing because of innate limitations.

Advocates of the view that intelligence is capacity to act with accurate foresight are not likely to take a stand with respect to the old argument of whether intelligence is unitary or a composite of special capacities. Evidence which would settle this issue does not seem to exist. Furthermore, as time goes on, the issue seems increasingly unimportant. A view consistent with organismic biology and field psychology would be that, whether intelligence is characterized either by generalized or specialized capacities, these capacities are interdependent and interact continuously.

Whereas this second over-all position concerning the nature of intelligence harmonizes well with a relativistic, field psychology, it does not harmonize with the notion that intelligence is based upon the capacity to form and retain new connections in the nervous system. Although this second position does assume that intelligence is related to capacity to learn, it defines learning in a very different manner. Some of the issues involved must wait for a later chapter for full development.

Sources of Intelligence

We now turn to a second category of issues. Where does intelligence come from? What causes one person to act with high intelligence and another with low? Again, we present three positions which may be taken on this matter.

INTELLIGENCE AS GENETIC ENDOWMENT. According to this position, intelligence bears a one-to-one relation to the quality of genes which determine the structure and functioning of the organic-neural-endocrine system. Intelligence is a function of the way an organism is put together. In other words, intelligence hinges on physical structure. From this point of view, intelligence is relatively fixed in each individual; a person can function only to a certain point of efficiency in the neural connections he can form —he can do no more. To expect additional achievement would be like expecting the runner of a 4-minute mile to increase his speed so that he was running the mile in, respectively, $3\frac{1}{2}$ minutes, 3 minutes, $2\frac{1}{2}$ minutes, etc. The limits of an organism permit only so much of a given kind of achievement and no more.

Obviously, this outlook harmonizes well with a psychology which emphasizes physiology as a determiner of what can be achieved. In American psychology, connectionism and behaviorism are most in tune with this view of intelligence. A brief survey of the history of the intelligence testing movement bears this statement out. During the early 1900s, psychologists tended to define intelligence mechanistically as the capacity to establish new S-R bonds, form new connections in the nervous system, or form new habits. These psychologists assumed intelligence to be dependent upon the number and variety of potential neural pathways and the speed with which these pathways could be activated.

The two traits crucial to intelligence—complexity and modifiability of the nervous system—supposedly were transmitted from parents to offspring. Thus, connectionistic psychologists reasoned that intelligence, like other physical traits, is determined by physical inheritance and that its level is constant for each individual just as the color of his eyes and skin is constant. Even though most professional psychologists have abandoned this point of view, it persists in the thinking of many public school teachers, counselors, and administrators.

INTELLIGENCE AS A PRODUCT OF LEARNING. An opposite point of view holds that all people except those who are obviously defective have the same potential at birth. The intelligence they achieve stems from opportunities for learning which they have had. Since the potential of each person is very high, few persons ever come close to reaching maximum biological potential. It should be obvious to readers that this outlook is consistent with Locke's *tabula rasa* idea and with one version of early nineteenth-century behaviorism, e.g., the ideas of John Watson (see p. 49).

Every environmentalist necessarily—if he is consistent—accepts the notion that intelligence is, at least in large measure, learned. This is a comforting belief for persons who are required to work with seemingly retarded people. It provides a source of never ending optimism. To a considerable extent welfare workers, sociologists, and some public school teachers find the extreme environmentalist point of view satisfying.

Some of the studies of changes of IQ in individuals give support to the hypothesis that intelligence is learned rather than inborn. A number of these studies are cited in a following section. However, other research rather strongly supports the notion that one's potential intelligence is a matter of genetic endowment and is therefore relatively fixed. Actually, research provides us with no conclusive data to back either of the extreme positions we have just described.

INTELLIGENCE AS A FUNCTION OF INTERACTION. A third position concerning the origin of intelligence harmonizes well with a relativistic, field psychology and also with the data provided so far by test results. This position assumes that intelligence is capacity to act with foresight, i.e., to assess accurately the consequences of a proposed action, and then goes on to by-pass completely the issue of whether intelligence is inherited or learned. This third position considers the latter argument to be as fruitless as arguments over any other aspect of the nature-nurture controversy.

Intelligence, in this view, is a product of the interaction of a human self and its perceived environment. That is, in assessing the basis of intelligence one assumes that both poles—person or self and psychological environment—are important *but that it is impossible to assess the relative importance of either pole.* Further, in the interactive process the *quality of perception* is of crucial importance. A person may have a physical organism of excellent quality, but his perceptions (interpretations of environment) may, because of previous learnings, be extremely faulty. Conversely, a person may have a mediocre physical organism, but, because of previous learnings, his perceptions may be first rate. Since there is no known way at present of determining the relative importance of physical structure or learning as a source of intelligence, we may relegate this argument to the same limbo as the argument over how many angels can dance on the head of a pin.

One qualification is necessary: perception hinges in part on the efficiency of sensory organs and other physical structures. If the goal is to pounce on a field mouse, then a high-flying eagle can behave more intelligently than a man; not only does his position vis-à-vis the mouse confer an advantage, but he can *see* more acutely. Obviously, poor eyesight, deafness, "taste blindness," and other sensory defects reduce the capacity for dependable perception. On the other hand, man as well as other creatures can often go far in compensating for impaired sensory capacity, e.g., consider Helen Keller.

This interactionist position appears similar to that taken by Combs.[12] After pointing out that certain physical conditions, such as mongolism, microcephalia, cretinism, etc., as well as certain injury- or disease-induced defects of the central nervous system or sensory organs, may reduce the capacity to make accurate perceptions, Combs goes on to say that in most persons the quality of perception hinges on the kinds of experiences one has had. He cites factors such as opportunity for exposure to a rich environment, the length of time a person has had to improve perceptions, a person's goals and values, the cultural milieu in which he is placed, his concept of self, and his feeling of threat.

The two latter points need to be enlarged upon. A person is unlikely to behave any more intelligently than he thinks he can. If I am convinced that I am stupid with respect to certain tasks, my conviction will limit my capacity for perception in connection with these tasks. All teachers have known students who had persuaded themselves that they could not learn arithmetic, the parts of speech, or spelling. Once convinced, they found it quite impossible to learn these things. On the other hand, overconfidence as to what one can learn can lead to equally serious inaccuracies of perception.

---

[12] Arthur W. Combs, "Intelligence from a Perceptual Point of View," *Journal of Abnormal and Social Psychology*, July, 1952. For a more recent statement, see Arthur W. Combs and Donald Snygg, *Individual Behavoir*, rev. ed., Harper, 1959, Chap. 11.

A sense of threat also limits capacity for accurate perception. People are inclined, when they feel threat, to restrict their perception to the source of threat; they become aware of nothing else. For example, a man may reach a state where he can think of nothing but a disliked employer. Obviously, his capacity to think in balanced fashion is greatly reduced. In addition to the "tunnel vision" effect mentioned above, threat tends to make persons defensive and rigid concerning their present pattern of attitudes, values, and beliefs. That is, threat produces "closed-mindedness." In either case, capacity for intelligent action is reduced.

To summarize and restate the position, intelligence is a product of the *interaction of a person and his perceived, i.e., psychological, environment.* We can attribute no particular portion of intelligence to heredity and no particular portion to environment.[13]

WHAT IS THE INTELLIGENCE TESTING MOVEMENT?

We have touched upon some of the figures prominent earlier in the century in the study of intelligence. Binet will be long remembered as the pioneer. He developed his first tests as a means of identifying academically promising children in the schools of Paris. The few tests available at that time measured only special aptitudes; Binet wanted tests that would survey broadly a child's capacity for academic learning. He developed thirty tests of tasks which he deemed related to academic success or failure.

The use of intelligence tests received its first big impetus during World War I. In the interests of efficiency, group tests, the famous Army Alpha and Beta, were developed. (The Binet test is administered by a trained practitioner to one person at a time.) Persons who scored extremely low on the tests were rejected from the service and those who were retained were, if lucky, assigned duties in accordance with test scores.

During the 1920s some of the shortcomings of early intelligence tests were brought to light. The constancy of the IQ was seriously challenged and standardized tests were found to overemphasize verbal skills and to confer an unfair advantage on persons with middle-class language skills and thought habits. Consequently, although World War II provided another major stimulus to the testing movement, the term *intelligence* tended to be taboo in military circles. Military general classification tests (not

[13] Some scholars make a distinction between intelligence and wisdom or discernment. So distinguished, intelligence is *capacity* to form insights, and wisdom or discernment is *possession* of tested or dependable insights. However, a broader definition of intelligence to cover not only that capacity which a person has as a result of innate ability but also his learned ability seems more practicable for a basic text in development and learning. See Ernest E. Bayles, *Democratic Educational Theory,* Harper, 1960, p. 101.

recognized as intelligence tests) and tests of special abilities and aptitudes were designed to give quick measures of abilities and aptitudes. There was little concern for the *source* of these traits. Note that a distinction was made between ability and aptitude. An ability was defined as capacity to do something, such as fly an airplane. Abilities are already achieved. An aptitude was defined as capacity to learn—one's potential in a particular field. For example, a person may not know how to fly yet, but he may indicate, through test results, a high aptitude for flight instruction. No assumptions were made in these tests as to whether aptitudes are primarily a matter of inheritance or of learning.

There are now on the market a number of group intelligence tests designed to be administered to entire classrooms of youngsters at one time. These can be scored by a teacher or, if machine scoring is available, by machine. As we discuss the inadequacies of intelligence tests in a later section, remember that group tests are more subject to criticism than are individual tests, although both types can be criticized—as much on the basis of how they are used as on the basis of inherent defects in the tests.

The two best-known and most widely used individual tests today are the Wechsler Intelligence Scale for Children (WISC) and the Stanford-Binet Intelligence Test (SBIT). The latter is a revision, performed at Stanford University, of the earlier Binet scales. The Stanford-Binet seeks to find the general intelligence of a child by means of a many-sided survey of his mentality. Some of the tests are nonverbal, which makes it possible to administer them to any person who can understand spoken directions.

HOW IS INTELLIGENCE MEASURED?

There is evidence that tests available at present measure something that, under certain circumstances, is useful in predicting certain future behaviors. In order to make any use at all of these tests, teachers must understand some concepts employed by the test makers.

The Concept of Mental Age

Intelligence is measured in terms of either mental age (MA), intelligence quotient (IQ), or percentile. Mental age, introduced by Binet in 1908, is a year-month notation which supposedly represents an absolute level of capacity. *Absolute*, as used here, is an antonym of *relative*. It means that a mental age is not determined by a relationship of other units. Rather than stating a relationship—as the IQ and the percentile do—MA states a maximum level of achievement. A scored MA of 9 years, 6 months, means that the person being measured can perform a group of tasks which can be performed by an average 9½-year-old.

Mental age has no relationship to chronological age (CA). It is determined entirely by a subject's performance on a test and by a table of norms found by testing a large number of children of each age. An MA of 10 means the same regardless of the chronological age of a subject. Even though a 4-year-old with an MA of 6 probably does not act the same way in a given situation as a 6-year-old with an MA of 6, test scores would not indicate any difference between them.

The Concept of Intelligence Quotient

Intelligence quotient represents the relationship of mental age to chronological age. The use of mental age implemented placement of pupils in grade levels adapted to them, but it gave no help in anticipating the level upon which children would be learning three or four years later. Four students, at present measuring the same mental age, might be far apart in their school work four years from now. Suppose that student A is 6 years old, B is 8, C is 10, and D is 12, and all four measure a mental age of 8 years and so are placed in the same class. Four years hence, provided their motivation and opportunity remained constant, A's mental age would be 13.3, B's would be 12, C's would be 11.2, and D's would be 10.7.

For the testing process to be serviceable something new was necessary. This was the intelligence quotient—IQ. By definition, IQ equals mental age divided by chronological age and multiplied by 100—$IQ = MA/CA \times 100$. Then, through transposing, one may derive the formula $MA = CA \times IQ/100$. Teachers have greater use for the latter formula. Its application indicates that a 12-year-old with an IQ of 80 is capable of working at approximately a 9½-year level; his MA is 9.6.

The principal advantage of the use of IQ as contrasted with a statement of a retardation or acceleration of so many months in mental age is that it makes it possible to compare relative degrees of measured intelligence of children and youth of different ages. An IQ of 100 means normal or average capacity for performance regardless of a child's age. IQs of 90 or 110, for children of any age, indicate comparable degrees of retardation or acceleration.

Wechsler recently has developed the concept *deviation IQ*, which is slightly different, but perhaps more functional, than the earlier meaning of IQ.[14] Within Wechsler's system, each person tested is assigned an IQ which, at his age, represents his intelligence rating as related to the abilities of other people his own age. IQs obtained by successive retests with the WISC automatically give the subject's relative position in the chronological age group to which he belongs at each time of testing.

[14] David Wechsler, *Wechsler Intelligence Scale for Children*, Psychological Corporation, 1949, pp. 3–4.

Deviation IQ is the amount by which a subject deviates above or below the average performance of individuals of his own age group. An IQ of 100 on the WISC is set as the mean score for each age, and the standard deviation is set equal to 15 IQ points. When any standardized IQ test is given to a cross section of a large number of children, it can be assumed that the mean IQ will be approximately 100 and the standard deviation of the IQ will be approximately 15 or 16. Wechsler, however, has developed his tests and norms in such a way that the SD is definitely 15.

When the intelligence of a large number of children representing a cross section of Americans is measured by means of the WISC, certain general results may be anticipated. The middle 68 percent (one σ each side of the mean) will measure IQs between 85 and 115; 95 percent (between —2σ and +2σ) will score IQs between 70 and 130. Practically all children (between —3σ and +3σ) will score IQs between 55 and 145 (see Fig. 2).

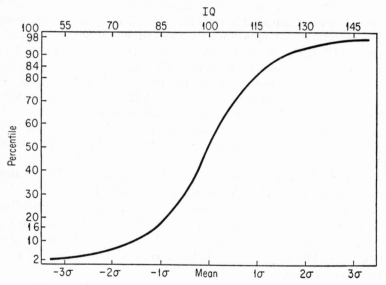

Fig. 2.　Relation of WISC IQs and SDs with Percentile Ranks.

The Concept of Percentile

A *percentile* means the percentage of people whose scores fall below that point on a curve. Thus, when a person scores in the 90th percentile on a test, it means that 90 percent of the people being tested have scores below or equal to that score. Hence, percentile scores are in terms of people, not test items. Table 1 means that 90 percent of people measure an IQ of 119 or below on the WISC.

TABLE 1. Relations of IQ on WISC to Percentile Rank

Percentile Rank	Equivalent IQ
99	135+
97	128
95	125
90	119
80	113
75	110
70	108
60	104
50	100
40	96
30	92
20	87
10	81
5	75
3	72
1	65

Some Facts About the Distribution of IQs

When an IQ test is given to a large number of children representing a cross section of a population, the scores will tend to fall into a normal distribution or bell curve. It will be recalled that about 68 percent will lie within one standard deviation above and below 100, 95 percent will lie within two standard deviations above and below the mean, and three standard deviations above and below the mean will include almost all of the scores.

A normal distribution curve indicates that, although there are some extremes in measured intelligence, most children are pretty much alike. However, our growing tendency to have an increased number of children

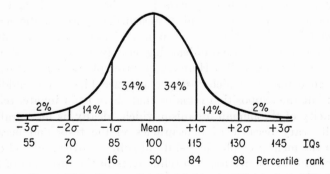

FIG. 3. Normal Distribution Curve with Standard Deviations, WISC IQs, and Percentile Ranks.

in school for an increased number of years has meant greater spread in IQ of students in most classes. Schools now contain virtually the whole child population representing the entire range of human differences as measured by IQ tests. In a typical school class, the mental ages of children cover a range of about six years. The upper 50 percent of pupils in a grade are capable of about the same quality of learning as are the lower 50 percent of those in the next higher grade.

HOW USEFUL ARE INTELLIGENCE TESTS?

If we understand clearly what can and cannot be done with intelligence test scores, they can serve as a useful adjunct to other kinds of information about individual differences.

Probably the greatest fault of present test results lies in the more or less confused assumptions of both test makers and test users as to the nature and source of intelligence. We have already indicated that intelligence testing gained its impetus in a period when connectionistic psychology was in vogue. Intelligence was defined as capacity to make new responses and this capacity was regarded as rooted in the physiological make-up of the organism and hence as largely hereditary. This conception of intelligence seems virtually impossible to prove and can be judged only on the basis of the long-range consequences of accepting it. Enough studies have been completed which show marked variability of IQ in a single individual to force even connectionists to modify their thinking—if not about the nature and origin of intelligence, at least about what available tests can measure.

Some qualifications have been introduced during the past 25 years or so: (1) It is perhaps impossible to devise a test which will separate what is innate in capacity from what is learned. However, this qualification usually leads to the supposition that further refinement of tests will reduce the learning component that appears in results, thus making tests approach ever more closely the ideal of measuring "pure intelligence." (2) Tests commonly used in schools tend to measure, more than anything else, capacity for an academic kind of learning, closely associated with middle-class values and verbal skills. Here again, attempts at refinement lead to reducing the extent to which test performance hinges on middle-class verbosity; but the supposition remains that there is an innate, relatively fixed, capacity of the human organism which, ideally, is measurable. (3) Test results vary because of inaccuracies in the tests and because of changes in the mental or physical state of subjects over a period of time. This criticism leads to attempts to refine tests in the direction of greater validity and to control better the conditions under which tests are given. Again, the assumption is that mental capacity of a relatively innate and fixed nature exists.

None of these qualifications markedly reduces confusion over the use of intelligence tests. The modifications in thinking about tests still fail to cut loose from the assumption that intelligence is a given quantity, which, if only we could learn how, could be measured in its "pure" or "absolute" state. In contrast, such modern *tabula rasa* theorists as still exist would perhaps deny the validity of intelligence test results altogether except as a possible measure of pure learning.

If one accepts the interpretation of intelligence preferred by relativistic, field psychologists, he is forced at once to abandon all attempts to measure either innate capacity per se or learning per se. A person with this psychological orientation will cease being concerned with the sources of intelligent behavior as such. Instead he will focus on trying to measure how effectively people engage in the process of intelligent behavior—or, simply stated, how well people can test ideas so as to achieve desired consequences. Such a change in emphasis might lead teachers to consider student achievement on certain types of teacher-made tests, intelligent student behavior, and discerning student statements during discussions possibly as valid measures of intelligence as existing IQ tests.

In order to show the basis for certain persistent criticisms of the all-too-common assumption that intelligent tests measure a fixed, innate capacity, we review some of the studies which show how, in some instances, measured IQ fluctuates.

The Variability of IQ Scores

In 1935 a study was conducted to see how a group of children would perform on various intelligence tests.[15] During a period of one month, 14 different intelligence tests were administered to 149 children in the high sixth and low seventh grades. There was found to be no correlation between the order of taking the tests and the results obtained. No child showed an IQ variation of fewer than 21 points. The average variation was about 42 points; i.e., the average child scored 42 points lower in IQ on one test than he did on some other tests in the 14. One child showed a spread of 84 points between his lowest and his highest IQ scores.

Other studies have been made to determine how specific children would score on the same or similar IQ tests over a period of time within which their psychological environments were significantly changed. These studies seem to indicate that, whatever it is that an IQ test measures, it can be raised, or lowered, through a marked change in environment. We shall give one example of each of three different kinds of studies which have contributed to a knowledge of the effects of changes in environment upon IQ scores.

[15] P. L. Boynton and Rosa F. Parsons, *Pupil Analyses in the Peabody Demonstration School,* Bulletin V24, No. 9, George Peabody College for Teachers, 1935.

1. *A study of identical twins reared in different kinds of environments.* Newman, Freeman, and Holzinger in 1937 reported a complete case study of 19 pairs of identical twins reared apart.[16] They found that, whereas the average IQ difference of the identical twins reared together was 5.9 points, it was 8.2 for the twins reared apart.

2. *A study of two groups that, on the average, had the same hereditary potentialities but different environmental influences.* Burks in California[17] studied a group of adopted children placed in foster homes during the first year of their lives and a control group of "own children" matched with the adopted children in regard to age and sex of children and locality and occupational level of homes. She estimated the average IQ of the adopted children at the time of adoption to be approximately 100. When tested from ages 5 to 14 they averaged IQs of 107.4. However, the mean IQ of the control group of "own children" was 115.1. This seems to be evidence that a "superior" home can promote a considerable increase in a child's tested intelligence quotient.

3. *A study of a group of children measured before and after experiencing a decidedly changed environment.* Several studies were pursued in the child study laboratory of the University of Iowa during the late 1930s which are pertinent to the problem of constancy of IQs. Wellman has reported these studies.[18] One was an investigation of the effect on IQ of a child's attending the University of Iowa Nursery School; 228 children with an average age of 40 months and a mean IQ of 117.3 in the fall measured a mean IQ of 124.3 in the spring. The following fall they measured a mean IQ of 123.9; this grew to a mean IQ of 127.7 in the spring. Thus, in a 20-month period, average measured IQs were raised 10.4 points.

Experiments with twins, siblings, and children in foster homes seem to indicate that children living in privileged environments test higher in intelligence than do children in less privileged environments. Children moved from unfavorable to more favorable environments tend to measure higher in intelligence than their twins who remain in the more unfavorable environments. Stoddard in 1943 wrote: "It can be predicted with some confidence that when homes and schools give the child what he truly needs, at all ages from the first year upward, there will be a radical revision in the norms and standards of mental tests."[19]

An article published in 1961 reported data on intelligence score variability as dramatic as any the authors have seen.[20] Mr. Mayer begins by

[16] Leona E. Tyler, *The Psychology of Human Differences,* Appleton-Century-Crofts, 1956, p. 532.

[17] *Ibid.,* p. 513.

[18] *Ibid.,* p. 543.

[19] George D. Stoddard, *The Meaning of Intelligence,* Macmillan, 1943, p. 392.

[20] Martin Mayer, "The Good Slum Schools," *Harper's Magazine,* April, 1961, pp. 47 ff.

reviewing studies demonstrating what is commonly called the "culture bias" of intelligence tests used at present. For example, in large American metropolitan areas the average IQ of school children in a wealthy suburb is about 120, while school children in the worst slums average about 85. New York City, among others, is making a determined effort to "build a fire" under slum youngsters in order to improve academic performance and increase the proportion who graduate and go on to college.

In Manhattanville Junior High School 43, a few spectacular results have been observed. One boy leaped from a measured IQ of 97 on entrance to 139 before high school graduation. Another who started with an IQ of 74 ended with a scholarship to New York University. Another started with an IQ of 99 and finished in the top 15 percent on the College Entrance Board's examination and with a full scholarship to Amherst.

How Can We Make the Best Use of Intelligence Test Scores?

In the authors' judgment, we are on the safest ground by beginning with the assumptions implicit in a relativistic, field psychology. We begin by assuming that *no available "intelligence" tests measure completely satisfactorily what a field psychologist means by intelligence.* Opinions may vary as to what present IQ tests measure, but the burden of evidence suggests that they measure a certain kind of academic capacity—that which we commonly associate with success in a college preparatory curriculum in a school dominated by traditional middle-class culture. Further, the scholastic potential which these tests do measure is highly unlikely to "stay put" and, in some cases, will vary over a wide range. By establishing the right sort of learning environment, it seems well established that IQ scores for given individuals can be raised markedly. Since a capacity is itself regarded as a function of person-environment interaction, we cease thinking of anyone as having a fixed capacity, or potential, along academic lines or any other.

BIBLIOGRAPHY

Anastasi, Anne, *Differential Psychology*, 3rd ed., Macmillan, 1958.
    An excellent introduction to major concepts which pertain to individual and group differences. Sources and nature of differences and their measurement are treated in detail. Chapters 13 and 14 on genius and sex differences are particularly interesting.
Cronbach, Lee J., *Essentials of Psychological Testing*, 2nd ed., Harper, 1960.
    A standard text on psychological and educational testing of ability and per-

sonality. Emphasizes general principles of psychological testing. Provides lists of tests.

Eells, Kenneth, and others, *Intelligence and Cultural Differences*, University of Chicago Press, 1951.
"A study of cultural learning and problem solving." The validity of standardized intelligence tests as a measure of intelligence of children from widely varying cultural backgrounds is examined.

Fullagar, William A., and others, *Readings in Educational Psychology*, 1956.
Six excellent articles on the nature and meaning of differences in mental ability (pp. 158–224). These articles cover the gifted and the mentally retarded as well as the "normal."

Fuller, John L., and W. Robert Thompson, *Behavior Genetics*, Wiley, 1960.
Consideration of the nature of intelligence, personality, temperament, and the evidence relating to their inheritance (Chaps. 7 and 8). Treatments of the relation of heredity to individual differences (Chap. 10).

Gordon, Ira J., *The Teacher as a Guidance Worker*, Harper, 1956.
Treatment of the major aspects of pupil guidance by classroom teachers. Emphasizes biological and social factors and interpersonal relations.

Mead, Margaret, *Male and Female*, Morrow, 1949.
Analysis of sex roles and behavior in primitive societies and modern America, providing a foundation for understanding the emerging pattern of sex relationships in contemporary America.

National Society for the Study of Education, *Intelligence: Its Nature and Nurture, Part I, Comparative and Critical Exposition*, Public School Publishing Company, 1940.
A rather technical symposium by psychologists on the nature and development of intelligence. It considers the meaning, deviations, physiology, and significant factors of intelligence.

Stroud, J. B., "The Intelligence Test in School Use: Some Persistent Issues," *Journal of Educational Psychology*, February, 1957, pp. 77–86.
Survey of the historical development of intelligence tests presenting several basic persistent issues in regard to testing.

Tyler, Leona E., *The Psychology of Human Differences*, Appleton-Century-Crofts, 1956.
An analysis of quantitative studies of individual differences. The author appraises sex, race, nationality, and class, as well as individual differences in intelligence, school achievement, vocational aptitude, personality, interest and attitudes, and perception.

Vernon, Philip E., "Education and the Psychology of Individual Differences," *Harvard Educational Review*, Spring, 1958, pp. 91–103.
An analysis of practices and proposals current in England and the United States designed to deal with student differences in intellectual ability.

Wellman, Beth L., and Edna L. Pegram, "Binet IQ Changes of Orphanage Preschool Children: a Reanalysis," *Journal of Genetic Psychology*, December, 1944, pp. 239–263.
A reanalysis of the data collected in 1938 by Miss Wellman and three others on their experiment in raising IQs of orphans through environmental stimulation. This article substantiates the earlier conclusions.

PART II

HOW DO HUMAN BEINGS DEVELOP?

Part II deals with the development of the individual from the time of conception to the late teens. Note that the authors regard growth processes as essentially the same at all age levels. Psychological development is construed as a matter of learning through interaction with an environment. Physical growth is thought to follow the same basic principles, irrespective of age. In both cases, the pattern fluctuates somewhat from one age level to another. In the case of physical growth, such variation stems from genetic endowment; in the case of psychological development, the culture tends to produce a culture-related pattern. Adolescence, for example, has its genetically induced physical side, but psychological characteristics of adolescence appear to be largely culture-related.

Chapter by chapter treatment is as follows: Chapter 6 treats physical growth. Chapter 7 discusses certain aspects of psychological development, and, like previous chapters, shows students some possible contrasting points of view which might be held about the nature of development. Chapter 8 focuses upon development during a particular period in life which, in our culture, produces more than its share of problems—adolescence. Chapter 9 treats the subject of needs and developmental tasks, again in comparative fashion.

6
WHAT IS THE NATURE OF BODILY GROWTH?

This chapter is devoted to description of growth processes as seen through the eyes of a biologist or physiologist. It treats "principles" of bodily development and its progress in human organisms from conception through the teen years.

Whatever the precise nature of an individual's outlook in regard to psychological development, he must take into consideration man's known biological growth processes. Biological processes may be considered by some to be the materials of a more basic science with which all psychological principles and concepts must agree; however, this is not necessarily true. A psychologist may consider his subjects to be primarily psychological persons in psychological environments as contrasted with biological organisms in physical environments. A biological organism, then, in a sense becomes an aspect of a psychological environment as well as that of a psychological person.

WHAT IS KNOWN ABOUT PRENATAL DEVELOPMENT?

The life of a human being does not begin with birth. This truism would not need to be stated were it not for the fact that prenatal existence is now commonly assigned much more importance than it was a few years ago. It is well established that certain abnormalities which may appear in a child, and which once were believed to be a consequence of faulty heredity, are caused by unfavorable conditions in the uterine environment of an embryo or fetus. However, the extent to which fetal life and

143

the experience of birth affect the later psychological and biological make-up of a person remains highly controversial.

The study of prenatal life in human beings involves serious difficulties. For one thing, an embryo or fetus cannot be removed from its natural environment without killing it. Our moral standards do not permit deliberate destruction, even for the most laudable scientific purposes, of prenatal human life. One exception is that laws of most states permit destruction of an embryo or fetus when this is necessary to save the life of a mother.

Most of our knowledge of embryonic development has come from study of embryos suffering natural death or embryos destroyed in order to save the lives of mothers. Enough such study has been possible to provide a fairly detailed record of the biological development of embryos. Fetuses become available for study as a result of abortions or premature natural births. In addition, fetuses may be studied indirectly. Stethoscopes, cardiographs, galvanometers, and X ray have been used to study fetal heartbeat, position, and activity. Reports of mothers concerning movement of fetuses are also helpful.

It is customary to divide the human prenatal period into three parts: (1) a germinal period, which lasts one or two weeks; (2) an embryonic period, which extends from the second to about the eighth week; and (3) a fetal period, which continues from the eighth week to birth. The average human gestation period (term of pregnancy) usually is given as 280 days, but as anyone who has had experience in the matter knows, babies rarely arrive exactly "on time." It is exceedingly rare that a fetus carried less than 180 days lives; and 334 days is the longest period of gestation known that resulted in a live birth.

The Germinal Period

A fertilized ovum divides and subdivides many times, forming a tiny blob of cells. This globular mass then forms an outer layer and a separated inner cluster of cells. The outer cells develop into a placenta and embryonic sac; some of the inner, into an embryo. While this is occurring, the fertilized ovum has been unattached and free moving. When it reaches the uterus wall, it implants itself there and becomes dependent upon the mother for nourishment and oxygen.

The Embryonic Period

Beginning with the second week of life an embryo rapidly loses its egglike appearance. It begins to elongate like a tiny tadpole and differentiation of parts soon becomes evident. The cell mass first develops three layers, which grow unequally with a folding in and out of various parts.

Each layer gives rise to separate groups of organs. Embryonic development is in many respects quite similar in all vertebrates. Embryonic vertebrate development also shows certain similarities to the developmental sequences of most of the animal kingdom. For example, at the beginning of the fourth week, an embryo shows a segmented structure, characteristic of many creatures relatively low on the evolutionary scale, such as earthworms. Another embryonic structure of interest is a rod of tissue called the notochord—an organ which is found in some primordial creatures in place of a jointed backbone. An embryo also develops fishlike gill pouches and a tail. Later, the fetus will be covered with a dense growth of hair. Biologists for a long time have said that, in the case of most living creatures, including man, "ontogeny repeats phylogeny." This *recapitulation theory* was developed by the great German biologist Ernest Haeckel (1834–1919). Simply stated, it means that individual development recapitulates, or follows the same steps as, the evolutionary development of life forms in general. This theory no longer is regarded as strictly true; but biologists do tend to accept the idea that ontogeny (the development of an individual) does reveal patterns of ancestral structure and thus can shed light on the nature of evolution.

The Fetal Period

By the eighth week, an embryo is as much as two inches long and weighs two-thirds of an ounce. By this time it has become distinctively human in appearance, except for its short tail. When human characteristics appear, we call the growing organism a fetus. The fetal period is characterized by further growth of parts that emerged during the embryonic period and by full functional development of many organs. Near the beginning of the fetal period there occurs a rapid increase in body length followed by a lessening rate of growth. Proportions change, the head becoming smaller and the arms and legs longer in relation to the trunk, so that a fetus becomes more and more "babylike" in appearance. Detectable heartbeat usually appears during the fourth month. The mother also begins to feel movement about this time. Before the end of the gestation period a fetus is able to squirm and kick in a fashion which may prove quite disconcerting to the prospective mother.

Eventually, after the ninth month, a fetus is sufficiently developed to be able to cease its parasitic ways and begin an independent existence. Of a fetus at this time one group of writers says, "In all the rest of his life there will never be such a sudden and complete change of locale. No other journey will ever start from such profound seclusion. . . . At a given moment on the final day of uterine existence there will be a sharp and sudden signal that the term is over. The placenta and umbilical cord can no longer supply sufficient food and oxygen. Escape, as it were, becomes imperative."[1]

Prenatal Influences

Until quite recently in the history of the human race prenatal development was shrouded in mystery. It was but natural that many superstitions should arise about the way a mother could influence her unborn child. It has been believed that if the mother were severely frightened, by, say, a grizzly bear, the child would be "marked" with an inborn fear of bears; that if a woman ate strawberries during pregnancy, her offspring might come into the world adorned with strawberry birthmarks; that if a pregnant woman listened frequently to Beethoven symphonies, her child would inevitably be a lover of fine music. Martin and Stendler cite the case of a father who became convinced that he was to blame for his child's being born with a missing arm because he had always driven a horse and buggy with one arm with the result that one arm was weaker than the other.[2]

Facts do not seem to bear out the actuality of this type of prenatal influence. An embryo or fetus is connected to its mother only by an umbilical cord. Nervous systems of mother and fetus are in no way connected. The blood stream of mother and fetus do not mix; they are separated by a semipermeable membrane. Mother can transmit to fetus only the chemical substances which can be carried in a blood stream—oxygen, nutrients, hormones, antibodies, and the like.

This is not to say that the psychological state of a pregnant woman has no effect on a fetus or that a child after birth will never show the effects of the mother's psychological state while pregnant. A mother's emotional state apparently can affect fetal behavior and subsequent development. During emotional states, such as anxiety, fear, or rage, a mother liberates into the blood stream acetylcholine, epinephrine, various hormones, and possibly other chemicals about which little is understood. In short, emotional states produce chemical changes in a mother's blood. The chemicals are absorbed into the fetal blood stream and apparently act as irritants.

Sontag, working in the Fels Research Institute in Yellow Springs, Ohio, studied fetal reactions to chemical changes in mothers' blood. Fetuses became hyperactive as a result of mothers' emotional states. Furthermore, babies of emotionally upset mothers weighed less at birth than babies of calm mothers; they tended too to be hyperactive and irritable, to cry more, sleep less well, have more frequent bowel movements, and spit up more often. Sontag says that such a baby is to all intents and purposes

[1] Arnold Sundgaard, *The Miracle of Growth*, University of Illinois Press, 1950, p. 21.
[2] William E. Martin and Celia Burns Stendler, *Child Development*, Harcourt, Brace, 1953, p. 115.

a neurotic infant when he is born.[3] Since a mother who is emotionally upset during pregnancy often continues to be upset after the birth of her child, it is difficult to distinguish effects of the prenatal environment from those of the later neurotic environment; hence, long-term congenital effects on a person born to a neurotic mother are hard to assess.

Mussen and Conger report several studies which attempted to show the relationship between a mother's attitude toward pregnancy and the mental health of her baby. Some of them made an attempt to discover the cause of favorable or unfavorable attitudes. These studies, like Sontag's, suggest that a mother with a negative attitude toward pregnancy (who is usually also an emotionally upset mother) is more likely to have a "problem baby" than a mother who has a positive (accepting) attitude.[4]

Many factors may be involved in determining a woman's attitude toward pregnancy. The socioeconomic condition of the family, her desire (or lack of desire) for another child, her general health (including mental health), and her attitudes toward sex and childbirth—all seem to be possible factors. The latter appears significant, in that a woman who is sexually responsive, who accepts fully and gladly her biological role, also (other things being equal) is likely to accept happily the role of motherhood.

As a result of the physical condition of a mother while pregnant, various kinds of injuries, including those with permanent effects, may occur to a fetus. Malnourished women are likely to produce sickly babies. Since drugs may be absorbed into a fetus' own blood stream, the use of drugs by a pregnant woman may have an adverse effect on a fetus. Certain diseases of a mother may affect the fetus adversely. Since placental membranes seem to constitute a rather effective barrier against bacteria and viruses which may be in a mother's blood stream, a fetus usually does not contract contagious or infectious diseases of its mother. (As an exception to this, syphilis spirochetes have been found in the blood stream of fetuses taken from syphilitic mothers.)

However, a disease of a mother, by upsetting her blood chemistry, may have a deleterious effect on the fetus even though the latter does not contract the disease. For example, rubella (German measles) contracted by a mother during the first three or four months of pregnancy may produce deaf-mutism, cardiac lesions, cataracts, or various forms of mental deficiency. Prenatal development follows a kind of timetable. If an organ is not permitted to develop properly at its "appointed" time, it will not do

[3] See L. W. Sontag, "Maternal Anxiety During Pregnancy and Fetal Behavior," in *Physical and Behavioral Growth*. Report of the 26th Ross Pediatric Research Conference, San Francisco, October, 1957. Reprinted by Ross Laboratories, Columbus, Ohio, 1958.

[4] Paul H. Mussen and John J. Conger, *Child Development and Personality*, Harper, 1956, pp. 67–70.

so later. But an organ's failure to develop, provided the harmful condition passes, will not affect the development of later organs. Thus, if it is known at what time during a pregnancy a mother experienced disease or other condition harmful to a fetus, to some degree it can be predicted what part or function of the baby will be impaired.

HOW DOES A NEWBORN BABY GROW AND BEHAVE?

If a visitor from Mars, familiar only with adult human beings, were to see for the first time a newborn babe, he might fail to recognize the species to which it belonged. A human infant comes into the world more or less red and wrinkled and, by adult standards, vastly out of proportion. His senses function poorly or not at all. His movements are generally uncoordinated, but he can yell loudly enough, and he soon learns to suck from his mother's breast. To strangers he is homely—like a robin fledgling or a newborn rat—but to his mother (and sometimes even to his father) he is the most beautiful thing in the world.

Let us observe in more detail what a newborn infant (often called a *neonate*) is like. His average weight is 7.5 pounds and his average length is 19.5 inches. However, weight may range from 3 to 16 pounds, and length from 17 to 21 inches. Boy infants are normally slightly larger than girls. A neonate's head comprises almost a fourth of his body length; by comparison, the head of an adult is only one-seventh the length of his body. An infant's face is broad and short, his nose flat. His cranial region bulges. Arms, legs, and trunk seem small. His shoulders are narrow, but his abdomen protrudes like that of a middle-aged business executive. His neck is extremely short. Sometimes a growth of downy hair covers parts of his body, but this soon disappears.

Because of needs imposed by rapid growth and incessant motion, an infant generates and uses energy much faster than does an adult. He also eats more often and consumes each day a greater proportion of his body weight in food. Compared with an adult's 70, his pulse averages 130 to 150 beats a minute. Compared with 18 for an adult, his respiration averages from 40 to 45. His body temperature is slightly higher and more variable than that of an adult.

What a newborn infant can do—besides breathe, cry, feed, burp, and eliminate—has long interested investigators. As noted above, his sensory capacity is weak. Although his eyes are sensitive to light, he cannot coordinate their movements; he appears cross-eyed one moment, "cock-eyed" the next. He can detect loud noises, but full hearing capacity comes only after tubes and middle ear become free of amniotic fluid. Most day-old infants react positively to sweet or salty tastes, negatively to bitter or sour tastes. Of all the senses, the sense of touch seems most highly developed; but skin sensitivity is more pronounced in the upper part of the body and for several days is poorly developed in the lower trunk and legs.

A neonate does not differentiate his body or its parts from the rest of his environment. This means he cannot use his own bodily resources very well. His arm and leg movements appear to be random and uncoordinated. However, at birth an infant may possess a limited number of more or less "set" responses. It has been customary to label these responses *reflexes*. We all are familiar with the fact that an infant seems to "know how" to breathe, cough, sneeze, and digest food. Other such responses are less familiar to an average adult. For example, some writers report that if we stroke the sole of a neonate's foot he will fan his toes (Babinski's reflex). If we put a neonate's hands on a horizontal bar, he will grasp the bar (Darwinian reflex). Almost all newborn infants can support their weight in this fashion, but after the first month this ability declines rapidly. Some writers also report that if an infant is placed on his back on a table, and the table is struck a forcible blow, he will thrust out his arms with an arclike motion as if trying to embrace something (Moro reflex).

The question of the extent to which an infant possesses innate, or inborn, reflexes—in fact, the "reflex arc" concept itself—is highly controversial. Lashley, for example, was most skeptical concerning existence of innate reflexes (at least, as the term *reflex* is customarily defined).[5]

Anyone watching a young infant is likely to marvel at his almost ceaseless activity. In fact, movement is often so rapid and varied that it is difficult for an observer to follow. Even while asleep (and he sleeps an average of 17 or 18 hours a day) an infant is likely to be moving. To an adult most of this movement seems random or purposeless. However, it is reasonable to assume that much of an infant's apparently random movement really is purposive. An infant may move to satisfy a physiological need for motion, or he may move in order to learn. Actions that seem random and uncoordinated may be interpreted as attempts to experience his environment (including himself). Arm motion may be related to a desire to find out what an arm is and what can be done with it. Nodding or shaking the head (seemingly without purpose) may be related simply to an infant's desire to "get the feel" of himself, to find out what he can do. The point we wish to make is that even in a neonate probably much more behavior than has been supposed is related to purpose.

WHAT IS THE SIGNIFICANCE OF PROLONGED HUMAN INFANCY?

To parents, who usually would prefer that time pass more slowly, an infant seems to move into childhood and a child into adolescence with almost terrifying speed. An adult imagines that he can almost see a baby

[5] K. S. Lashley, *Brain Mechanisms and Intelligence,* University of Chicago Press, 1929.

grow before his very eyes. Actually, a human being requires more years and a greater proportion of his life span to reach adulthood than does any other animal. Huxley points out that the period from birth to the first onset of sexual maturity comprises nearly one-fourth of the normal span of a human being's life. In lower animals this same period comprises from one-eighth to one-twelfth of the normal life span.[6]

Not only is bodily maturation a lengthier process in man than in other animals, but also the capacity for complex learning is much slower to develop. Although we seldom take time to reflect about its significance, most of us realize that we can teach a puppy tricks, or housebreak him, much more easily than we can a human child of the same age. We are less aware that a chimpanzee "child" can be taught numerous actions much more readily, and at an earlier age, than a human child. For example, a young chimpanzee can learn to skip, to be obedient and cooperative, to kiss, to open and shut doors, to eat skillfully with a spoon, to drink from a glass, and to indicate a need to go to the toilet, all at ages considerably younger than a human child can learn these same things.[7]

What is the significance of this prolongation of human infancy? Apparently in some way greater prolongation of infancy is related to the greater *potential* possessed by human beings. We know that an adult human being has a much greater capacity for learning (whether of the manipulation of things or of symbols) than does any of the lower animals. Furthermore, throughout the animal kingdom there seems to be a rough correlation between the length of time it takes the young of a species to become adult and the apparent intelligence, or capacity to learn, of an adult. Thus, next to man, the primates (apes) have the most extended period of infancy and childhood; and, next to man, they also are the most intelligent. Recent research, however, indicates that dolphins could probably learn as rapidly and as much as apes if they were land-going creatures and had the advantage of legs, feet, arms, and hands.

Prolongation of infancy may be related to lack of specific instincts. The "lower" a species on the phylogenetic scale, the greater the amount of "inborn knowledge," or instinctive behavior, with which the young appear to be equipped.[8] Absence of instincts, when coupled with high capacity for learning, confers a great advantage. It permits a highly flexible type of

6 Julian Huxley, *Man in the Modern World,* New American Library, 1948, p. 15.
7 W. N. and L. A. Kellogg, *The Ape and the Child,* Whittlesey, 1933, pp. 315–316.
8 There is some danger in this generalization, and it must be pointed out that considerable evidence has accumulated to suggest that animal behavior, particularly on the vertebrate level, is much less dependent upon specific instincts than was once supposed. For example, Kuo and others have demonstrated that members of the cat family apparently have no instinctive desire to kill other animals. See the highly interesting discussion of "animal culture" in Ashley Montagu, *The Direction of Human Development,* Harper, 1955, pp. 33–42.

behavior. Hence, a prolonged period of infancy in a species is a mark of superiority, rather than of inferiority. A prolonged period of postnatal care becomes a prolonged period of learning—during which the young assimilate the culture of the adult group into which they are born. As Huxley puts it, a long period of infancy and childhood ". . . is a necessary condition for the evolution and proper utilization of rational thought. If men and women were, like mice, confronted with the problems of adult life and parenthood after a few weeks, or even, like whales, after a couple of years, they could never acquire the skills of body and mind that they now absorb from and contribute to the social heritage of the species."[9]

WHAT ARE SOME CHARACTERISTICS OF THE PHYSICAL GROWTH AND DEVELOPMENT PROCESS?

We next turn to an examination of how a child, as a biological organism, matures. Our story carries us from childhood to the late teens. We consider such aspects of biological growth as the development of skeleton and muscles, brain and nervous system, internal organs, and total functioning.

The organic growth process is not haphazard. As we have seen in connection with a developing embryo and fetus, one step follows another in a generally predictable fashion. What force, what cause, operates to push (or pull) growth in this way? At our present stage of knowledge, this question is largely unanswerable. The only answers we can give must to a degree be stated in the language of analogy and metaphor. We can say that growth of an organism is "directed" or "organized" by the electrometabolic "field" of that organism, which in turn is a function of the organism's genes.[10] We can say that growth of regions and organs of an organism is "directed" by the subfield associated with that region or organ (with each subfield more or less under the "direction" of the "master field" of the total organism). We can say that the carriers of heredity, the genes, somehow "tell" the electrometabolic field how it must manage. When we talk this way we are not really explaining very much. Furthermore, the most detailed descriptions, with their mathematical treatment of chemical reactions, electrical potentials, and the like, actually tell little more.

It is possible partially to describe the over-all growth process in terms of a few broad principles. Although the statement of these principles leaves much unanswered, knowledge of them does help us understand

---

[9] Huxley, *op. cit.*, p. 15.

[10] You may want to review the material in Chapter 3 on electrometabolic fields and gene functions.

growth better. Principles which are commonly enumerated include the following:

1. *The principle of developmental direction.* Growth, both in physical structure and in functioning, tends to proceed along head-to-foot (cephalocaudal) and center-to-periphery (proximodistal) gradients. Thus, the head reaches adult size first, the legs last, and internal organs like the heart reach full capacity to function (but not necessarily their full size) before the extremities do. This principle may be observed most readily in the development of embryo and fetus, but it also appears to be generally true during childhood.

2. *The principle of continuity.* Bodily growth proceeds in continuous fashion. It is not reversible and never stops—except when a child is affected with disease or severe malnutrition. However, somatic (bodily) growth does not always proceed at the same rate; it may spurt or slow down. For example, typically the periods from birth to 2 years and from 11 to 15 years are times of very rapid growth; the years from 3 through 10 and from 16 through 18 show relatively slow growth.

3. *The principle of developmental sequence.* As a general rule, steps of physical growth follow one another in a somewhat uniform and predictable order. That is, almost all children lose certain baby teeth first, certain others last; almost all reach puberty before they attain full physical stature. All children do not operate according to the same timetable, but the sequence of events tends to be predictable. However, we must be willing to grant exceptions, e.g., some babies are born with several perfectly formed teeth.

4. *The principle of maturation, or readiness.* Most accomplishments of a child require a certain level of skeletal-muscular-neurological development (or a certain level of organization of the electrometabolic field). When this level of development has been reached, we say that a child biologically is "ready" to perform a certain task. Although he may not perform it even when he is ready, he cannot perform it before that time. Thus, a child of 6 months appears to be unable to control his bladder, no matter how he may try. Nor can a child of 6 months learn to walk. It remains a controversial matter whether attempts to induce a child to perform a task before physiological readiness have any effect in speeding up the rate of growth toward readiness. Some psychologists feel that, within limits, if a child can be brought to feel a strong desire to learn a new task the physiological development required will appear sooner than otherwise.

5. *The principle of individual growth patterns.* Although developmental direction and sequence (in a physiological sense) are roughly the same for all children, individual children differ greatly with respect to their own time schedules. One baby is able to pick up a ball much sooner

than another; one child loses his first incisors earlier than another. Furthermore, the old beliefs that a "slow grower" will catch up by spurting later on and that a given child will grow faster in some respects than in others seem highly questionable. A child who grows fast in one physical feature is likely to grow fast in all features; and he is likely to continue growing fast until his full growth is reached. The converse is true for a slow grower.

How may we use these principles? It seems clear that an understanding of principles of organic growth will help a teacher, counselor, or group leader better to understand children. For example, a physical education teacher who grasps the principle of readiness and some of the facts concerning developmental sequence will not try to teach games or any type of physical performance beyond the capacity of the children with whom he is working. Furthermore, he will recognize that in groupings based on chronological age there will be considerable range in somatic age; thus, in a group of 10-year-olds some will be physically 8, others physically 12 (and there will be similar variation in mental age).

We cannot stress the foregoing point too strongly. The statistical tables in the section to follow show average height and weight of children of different ages. Unless a student understands limitations in the use of averages, such tables are likely to be misleading. In a given group of children, not a single one may be average in height and weight, yet all may be quite normal. An average is almost always fictitious when applied to an individual case. Nevertheless, statements regarding averages remain useful for giving some idea of what to anticipate. Children who depart in extreme ways from the average for their age group deserve careful study to determine whether there is indeed anything about them which needs to be remedied.

WHAT IS THE COURSE OF BODILY DEVELOPMENT DURING THE SCHOOL YEARS?

The Kindergarten and Primary Years (Ages 5–8)

By the time a child has reached the age of 5, he has come a long way. He has arrived at a state of physiological development making possible rather complex learnings, including those which can best be fostered in a school environment.

After the extremely rapid physical growth of the first two or three years of life, a child settles down to a steady but decelerating rate of development until the preadolescent period. The unspectacular but steady progress of physical growth from age 5 through 8 is indicated in Table 2. During this period, ossification of cartilage proceeds at an even rate, mak-

TABLE 2.   Average Heights and Weights (Ages 5–8)

| | Average Boy | | Average Girl | |
Age	Height (in inches)	Weight (in pounds)	Height (in inches)	Weight (in pounds)
5	43.8	42.8	43.2	41.4
6	46.3	48.3	45.6	46.5
7	49.6	54.1	48.1	52.2
8	52.0	60.1	50.4	58.1

SOURCE: Adapted from George M. Wheatley and Grace T. Hallock, *Health Observation of School Children,* McGraw-Hill, 1951, pp. 54–57.

ing the skeleton more rigid and the joints less flexible. A child of 5 to 8, however, still has a much more flexible and less easily damaged skeleton than does an adult. By the end of the primary grades he has made a good start toward acquiring a permanent set of teeth; a typical child by this time has 12.

His internal organs have kept pace generally with his bodily growth. His stomach soon will have a capacity almost two-thirds that of an adult —although it seems like much more! However, between the ages of 4 and 10, one's heart is smaller in relation to one's body size than at any other time in life, the lag being greatest at age 7. Lung capacity also remains smaller in relation to body size than it will be in adulthood.

By the early school years, a child's body proportions have come to be much better (judged by adult standards) than during infancy. His head by now is about one-sixth his body length. His face is larger in relation to the rest of his head. His legs are longer in relation to arms and trunk. His muscles, which grew at about the same rate as the rest of him until age 4, now are developing more rapidly. From now on they will represent a steadily increasing proportion of total body weight. But a kindergarten and primary child is highly susceptible to muscular fatigue. He tires much more rapidly than an adult; he also recovers more rapidly.

His brain and nervous system have already undergone their period of greatest growth. By the age of 2, sensorimotor equipment is relatively complete. By the age of 6, 90 percent of adult brain weight has been achieved. This does not mean, of course, that a 6-year-old is 90 percent as intelligent as an adult. It does mean that he has achieved an organic capacity for learning highly complex and closely coordinated motor activity.

By the age of 6, most children have developed a variety of physical skills. They climb with agility, often to the great but usually needless alarm of adults. They can hop, skip, jump, and gallop. They can bounce a ball and play catch. They can ride a child-size bicycle and roller-skate. Furthermore, by the end of the primary period the average child will have learned to do these things with a measure of grace, in contrast to the awkwardness with which he attempted them at age 4 or 5.

The picture we have drawn is of a fictitious average child. It must be remembered that in the various aspects of actual physiological development some children may be as much as two years ahead, and others two years behind, their age group. Whereas one 6-year-old may be able to throw and catch a ball with considerable dexterity, another may be largely unable to do so. Differences in size and strength are marked. Boys of this age differ little from girls in size, weight, coordination, and physical strength. By the end of the primary period, however, an average girl is at least a year ahead of an average boy in bone development.

The Upper Elementary School Years (Ages 9–12)

Although growth is steady during this period, it is proportionately less rapid than during the kindergarten and primary years. This represents a middle period of childhood when physiological change is not marked. Table 3 demonstrates the truth of this statement, so far as outward physical growth is concerned.

TABLE 3.   Average Heights and Weights (Ages 9–12)

| Age | Average Boy | | Average Girl | |
	Height (in inches)	Weight (in pounds)	Height (in inches)	Weight (in pounds)
9	53.3	66.0	52.3	63.8
10	55.2	71.9	54.6	70.3
11	56.8	77.6	57.0	78.8
12	58.9	84.4	59.6	87.6

SOURCE: Adapted from George M. Wheatley and Grace T. Hallock, *Health Observation of School Children*, McGraw-Hill, 1951, pp. 54–57.

The growth trends established in the primary grades continue. That is, legs continue to grow at a rate exceeding that of trunk length, body continues to grow at a rate exceeding that of head, bones continue hardening, additional cartilage ossifies, new permanent teeth are acquired (an average 11-year-old has 20 of the 32 permanent teeth which he will eventually have), internal organs grow larger and more stable in their functioning. Faces mature somewhat during this period but remain relatively round in contour; noses remain small and foreheads convex. Gains are made in musculature, but physical stamina is still "childish" in the sense that muscular fatigue appears more rapidly than in healthy adults. Brain and nervous system reach virtual physiological maturity by the end of the elementary years.

Improvement in coordination and capacity to learn physical skills is steady. During this age period a child is likely to learn to ride a bike "no hands," to walk on top of a narrow fence, and to play ball with dexterity.

Note that by the age of 11, girls have overtaken boys in both stature and weight. An average girl of this age has entered the phase of rapid growth which immediately precedes puberty. The prepubertal growth spurt will be more fully described in the following section.

The Junior High School Years (Ages 13–15)

Much more than in the few years preceding, junior high school years are marked by rapid and conspicuous physiological changes. One of these is a resurgence of rapid growth, reminiscent of the infant growth rate. The preadolescent growth period is sometimes called the "pubescent spurt" because of its apparent close association with sexual maturing. The pubescent spurt typically occurs in girls between the ages of 10 and 13, with the greatest annual weight gain, 12½ pounds, occurring in the latter year. The growth spurt in boys is typically about two years later, between 12 and 14, with the greatest average weight gain, almost 15 pounds, occurring in the latter year. It is only during the ages 10 to 13 that an average girl is taller and heavier than an average boy of the same age (see Table 3). Every junior high school teacher is aware of the fact that during these years boys seem small and childish in appearance—little changed from the late elementary years—but girls have moved far in the direction of physiological maturity.

TABLE 4.   Average Heights and Weights (Ages 13–15)

Age	Average Boy		Average Girl	
	Height (in inches)	Weight (in pounds)	Height (in inches)	Weight (in pounds)
13	61.0	93.0	61.8	99.1
14	64.0	107.6	62.8	108.4
15	66.1	120.1	63.4	113.5

SOURCE: Adapted from George M. Wheatley and Grace T. Hallock, *Health Observation of School Children*, McGraw-Hill, 1951, pp. 54–57.

Marked changes in dimensions accompany the preadolescent growth spurt. Legs are the first part of the body to show conspicuous growth. This is followed by broadening of pelvis and change in hip contour in girls and broadening of shoulders and increase in chest cavity in boys. Faces assume the ovalness of adulthood, and noses and chins become more prominent. By the end of the pubescent growth spurt, hands and feet have reached adult size; and this, combined with the natural awkwardness of the period, makes a youth seem all hands and feet.

Visceral growth is largely completed by the end of the pubescent spurt. However, the heart does not reach its full size until several years later. Muscle weight continues to gain in relation to total weight through the junior high school years, but the major gain in musculature does not occur until the senior high school period. Boys gain slightly in physical endurance; girls gain similarly until about the age of 13, when they reach a plateau.

Organs showing the most noticeable development during the junior high school age are the sex organs, although quite a number of boys and an occasional girl do not mature sexually until after 14. For a majority of youth the most important feature of the junior high age level is sexual "coming of age." This is characterized by glandular development and hormone production, which are not externally visible, and by the appearance of the so-called primary and secondary sexual characteristics. Primary sexual characteristics are the maturing genital organs. Secondary sexual characteristics include pubic and axillary hair and sex-related body contour. Secondary sexual characteristics unique to girls are development of breasts and menstruation. Those singularly characteristic of boys are voice change and development and coloration of facial hair. These changes are accompanied by full development of the sex drive in males and its partial development in girls. In the American culture, according to Kinsey, the sex drive of females in many cases does not appear to reach its fullest development until a decade or more later—perhaps not until the age of 30.[11] However, anthropological studies suggest that the later development of the sex urge among females is probably a culturally imposed trait; American parents typically make greater efforts to inhibit girls than boys.

The Senior High School Years (Ages 16–18)

This period is characterized by virtual completion of physiological maturation. Table 5 shows the reduced rate of growth in size during this period. A slight gain in stature may occur following the age of 18 and up

TABLE 5. Average Heights and Weights (Ages 16–18)

| | Average Boy | | Average Girl | |
Age	Height (in inches)	Weight (in pounds)	Height (in inches)	Weight (in pounds)
16	67.6	129.7	63.9	117
17	68.4	136.2	64.0	119.1
18	68.7	139	64.0	119.9

SOURCE: Adapted from George M. Wheatley and Grace T. Hallock, *Health Observation of School Children*, McGraw-Hill, 1951, pp. 54–57.

[11] Alfred C. Kinsey and others, *Sexual Behavior in the Human Female*, Saunders, 1953, p. 549.

to 20. Mature adults in the United States appear to be becoming relatively larger. Boys today are from 6 to 8 percent taller than were boys of similar age a half-century ago.

By age 18, youth have gained proportions characteristic of adulthood. The head is now about one-seventh of total body length; legs are one-half body length. Since infancy, the head has doubled in length, legs have increased by five times, and the trunk has tripled. One notable characteristic of this period is increased musculature of boys. By the age of 16, muscle weight has reaced over 44 percent of total body weight—the adult proportion. Physical strength doubles between ages 11 and 16.

Stamina among males increases rapidly during the late teen years. However, capacity for sustained physical output appears to remain less than that of a well-conditioned male in his 20s and 30s. (Tenzing was 38 when, with Hillary, he conquered Mount Everest.) In the United States, girls do not progress in this respect. After reaching a peak of endurance at about 13, females decline in physical endurance; between the ages of 17 and 20, a typical female has the physical endurance of a girl of 6 or 8. Cultural factors undoubtedly account for this; girls become rather sedentary during the late teens. Because of a belief that boys do not prefer girls with muscles, feminine "softness" is cultivated in our society. In many other countries, including those of western Europe and the Soviet Union, teen-age girls, with few exceptions, engage in fairly strenuous sports and calisthenics. In these countries differences in stamina and physical strength between the sexes are not great.

BIBLIOGRAPHY

Breckenridge, Marian E., and E. Lee Vincent, *Child Development*, Saunders, 1960.
>   The fourth edition of a popular text which surveys in considerable detail both physical growth and mental development from infancy through adolescence. The authors are highly eclectic in their approach. Chapter 7 focuses on physical growth.

Carmichael, Leonard, ed., *Manual of Child Psychology*, 2nd ed., Wiley, 1954.
>   Nineteen articles on a variety of subjects relating to development. Chapter 4 is one of the best short treatments of physical growth available. This large book is a standard reference in its field.

Gesell, Arnold, and Frances L. Ilg, *The First Five Years of Life; A Guide to the Study of the Preschool Child*, Harper, 1940.
>   Detailed description of the physiological and behavioral characteristics of infants and small children, by the director of the Clinic of Child Development at the Yale University School of Medicine and a colleague. The as-

sumption that a child unfolds both physically and mentally according to an innate growth plan runs through all of Gesell's writing.

Gesell, Arnold, and Frances L. Ilg, *The Child from Five to Ten*, Harper, 1946.
A rich fund of information about the physical and behavioral characteristics of 5- to 10-year-olds. Gesell's book treating the years from 10 to 16 is cited at the end of Chapter 8.

Jenkins, Gladys Garner, and others, *These Are Your Children*, expanded ed., Scott, Foresman, 1953.
A simply written and concise portrayal of physical and behavioral characteristics of children from infancy to age 14. Many pictures.

Lane, Howard A., and Mary L. Beauchamp, *Understanding Human Development*, Prentice-Hall, 1959.
A lucent book, written in a personal and literary style. Discussions of physical and mental development are woven together. References are excellent.

Lee, J. Murray, and Doris May Lee, *The Child and His Development*, Appleton-Century-Crofts, 1958.
A treatment which is largely noneclectic and conforms to the psychology of Combs and Snygg (Harper, 1959). This book is highly readable and contains most of the psychological concepts stressed in the present volume. It is steadily pertinent to Chapters 6 and 7 and most other chapters. Its Chapter 3 deals specifically with physical development.

Martin, William E., and Celia Burns Stendler, *Child Development*, Harcourt, Brace, 1953.
Treatment of both physical and psychological development. Makes much use of the findings of cultural anthropologists.

Martin, William E., and Celia Burns Stendler, *Readings in Child Development*, Harcourt, Brace, 1954.
An excellent selection of readings which cover numerous phases of development, both physical and psychological.

Merry, Frieda K., and R. V. Merry, *The First Two Decades of Life*, 2nd ed., Harper, 1958.
A well-done book on general development. Chapter 1 treats techniques of studying children. Later chapters treat bodily structure and functions and the development of personality.

Mussen, Paul H., and John J. Conger, *Child Development and Personality*, Harper, 1956.
A general treatment of development from birth through adolescence, written from an eclectic point of view. See especially Chapters 2–4, 7, 8, 10, and 13.

7

WHAT IS THE NATURE OF PSYCHOLOGICAL DEVELOPMENT?

Psychological development is closely related to physiological growth. *Growth* and *development* sometimes are used as synonyms; however, each has a special connotation. *Growth* more often is used to describe biological changes in an organism as it moves from conception to adulthood. Chapter 6 is devoted to description of this aspect of human life. *Psychological development,* somewhat in contrast, means the psychological changes which parallel biological growth. This concept encompasses the expansion of abilities of individuals to learn through their perceptions, to achieve judgments based upon their experience, and to think for themselves in imaginative, creative, and exploratory manner. Whereas the end of biological growth is a mature biological organism, the product of psychological development is an adequate human self or person.

The nature of psychological development hinges directly upon the nature of human beings. In Chapter 2, we saw that one might assume the psychological nature of persons to be *good, bad,* or *neutral* in innate moral nature and *active, reactive,* or *interactive* in relationship to their environment. Each outlook has definite implications for human psychological development. Do people develop through active unfoldment of natural badness or goodness in a relatively passive environment? Or do they passively develop through reaction to their respective environments?

Or is development a matter neither of active unfoldment nor of passive nurture, but rather of person-environment interaction? The latter position is the one introduced in the last part of Chapter 2.

If children are basically *active,* psychological reality comes from within them. Environments merely serve as locations for their natural unfolding. If they are basically *passive* or *reactive,* reality is centered in environment. If they are *interactive,* reality is person-environment centered; *it consists of what one makes of what comes to him.* These three mutually opposed assumptions in regard to human development are illustrated by three models in Fig. 4.

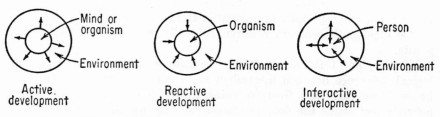

FIG. 4.   Models of Mutually Opposed Assumptions in Regard to Nature of Psychological Development.

Everything a teacher does is colored by the psychological theory of human development he holds. Although he may never have examined it, every teacher has such a theory. His psychology may be nothing more than folklore—traditional customs or beliefs. It may go no further than saying, "You can't change human nature," "People are instinctively religious," or "Spare the rod and spoil the child." Yet these are all theoretical statements, and their acceptance calls for particular kinds of action in relation to other persons. If one thinks the converse of each, then an entirely different kind of action is needed.

A teacher need not base his thinking on folklore; he may be quite aware of all of the more important theories developed by professional psychologists, and his psychological theory may be quite sophisticated. It is the latter state of affairs that professional psychologists interested in the education of teachers are trying to achieve. Teachers who are well grounded in scientific psychology (in contrast to "folklore psychology") have a basis for making decisions which are much more likely to lead to useful results in classrooms.

Often, theories of development held by modern man (including some educators) are inconsistent hodgepodges of bits and pieces from several influential theories which historically have appeared throughout the ages.

A step in resolution of conflicting ideas is a study of the major approaches to human development, always with the aim of resolving their basic issues.[1]

IS A CHILD A MINIATURE ADULT?

The assumption that a child is a miniature adult leaves little place for a concept such as psychological development. Although this position no longer is advocated in teacher education programs of colleges, it is so deeply ingrained in our American culture that its vestiges will appear in school situations for a long time to come. This view toward children enjoyed great popularity in earlier centuries. It was imported from Europe and was especially prominent in the New England colonies. Prior to the eighteenth century, children generally were trained to act like adults.

New England Calvinists saw no reason for suggesting a basic psychological difference between themselves and their children. A father, when he awakened early on a frosty morning, called his sons *once*. If he did not hear six feet strike the floor in unison, he went upstairs with his buggy whip which always stood in a threatening pose in the corner of the dining room. Members of a pious Puritan family attended Sunday church services from 10:00 until 2:00, and their children "behaved" in church. When they returned home from church, they ate a simple meal which had been prepared the day before, then spent the afternoon quietly reading the Bible and in meditation and prayer. It was not too difficult for a tired farmer and his wife to do so, and their children did likewise. Children and youth were regarded as miniature, although irresponsible, adults.

The Puritan concept of original sin (discussed in Chapter 2) influenced parents to be as rigid and strict with their children as they were with themselves. A child was to be broken by the rod and impressed with his personal guilt and religious duty. Puritan parents took life seriously; therefore, they tended to frown upon the frivolity and play of children. Laws and rules were as exacting for children as they were for adults. A prominent Boston Puritan minister in 1641 recommended the following law: "Rebellious children, whether they continue in riott or drunkenesse, after due correction from their parents, or whether they curse or smite their parents, to be put to death."[2]

---

[1] Development and learning are closely related. Chapters 10–15 describe the various outlooks toward learning which are practiced or advocated in today's schools. Table 6 on p. 231 of Chapter 10 should be used in studying this chapter on psychological development.

[2] Freeman Butts and Lawrence Cremin, *A History of Education in American Culture,* Holt, 1953, p. 67. As taken from *The Hutchinson Papers,* publications of the Prince Society, Albany, 1865, Vol. II, p. 198.

Cotton Mather, in *A Family Well Ordered,* set forth obedience, fear, discipline, and absolute authority as crucial characteristics of teaching methods of parents and teachers. Puritan ministers reasoned that sinners should be terrified—and so should erring children. Thus, feelings of guilt and fear systematically were instilled into children. Since a child had a mind which was essentially the same as he would have as an adult, his schoolmaster was expected to discipline that mind in the same manner in which an adult mind was disciplined. Hence, the schoolmaster inculcated in a child's mind the discipline and facts which as an adult he would need to have. "Disciplines" were in the form of arbitrarily predetermined subject matter, and their learning was primarily a matter of rote memory.

As previously mentioned, today there are vestiges, at least in some of our schools, of the "miniature adult" pattern of thinking about children. Many examples may be cited. Teachers may expect children in school to maintain the supposed continuous stillness of adults over a prolonged period of time. Adults may be unduly disturbed at children's frankness of speech, awkwardness in movement, and assumed faulty reasoning. Subject matter may be selected and organized wholly by adults and given to children in a way in which adults would be expected to take and absorb it. Students may be assigned meaningless and aimless lessons accompanied by the "explanation" that they will be glad to have the content of those lessons in mind when they grow into adulthood. Or, not realizing the immaturity and inexperience of their children, teachers may impose upon them an unreasonable adult task.

Those who react against the miniature adult approach note that a child is not only biologically different from an adult but also psychologically different. Not only is a child's skeletal structure differently proportioned, but his nervous system and his hormonal and biochemical organization are unlike those of a grown person. A child's psychological difference means that, although he is related ultimately to the adult into which he later develops, his development requires a good deal of active experiencing and changing as well as his merely growing larger.

DOES A CHILD DEVELOP THROUGH NATURAL UNFOLDMENT OF INSTINCTS, ABILITIES, AND TALENTS?

Opposition to the "little adult" theory of development led to the formation of its extreme opposite—that of saltatory development. (*Saltatory* is derived from the Latin adjective *saltatorius,* meaning "dancing" or "leaping.") *Saltatory development* means development through jumps or stages rather than by gradual, orderly progression. This theory may be presented by summarizing the ideas of three men who have led in promulgating it—Rousseau, Hall, and Gesell. Rousseau's writings appeared in the latter half of the eighteenth century (see Chapter 2). Hall was most active during the last quarter of the nineteenth and the first quarter of the twentieth centuries (see pp. 165–166). Gesell is a contemporary scientist who only recently has retired from the Yale faculty.

Jean Jacques Rousseau's *Émile* was written in 1762. It is Rousseau's account of his rearing and educating a fictitious urban boy in France. His central thesis is that a child should be permitted to develop according to nature. Since nature, to Rousseau, was a rational universal nature, he had a worshipful attitude toward it. He was convinced that a child, were it not prevented by societal influences, would grow, like a plant, to perfect adulthood. Rousseau assumed that a child in his development retraces the racial development of mankind. Just as man, in many centuries, has advanced from a state of nature to a highly organized society, so a child begins his life in a state of nature and in 20 years or so becomes a social individual.

Rousseau taught that there are four distinct stages through which a child grows, and a child is a unique being in each stage. Thus, his education should be according to the respective racial period of his development. First, from birth to 5 years, a child is a healthy little animal. He should be treated as such and be left alone to grow according to primeval nature (instinct). At 5, he passes into the savage stage. This is evidenced by his proclivity to climb trees, go camping, pull the wings from grasshoppers, and catch animals and dismember them alive. During this second stage, which lasts until he is 12, a boy should be out with nature. His development should be not from positive instruction but a result of experiences achieved through sensory and motor activities.

The period from 12 to 15 is the age of reason. The reasoning ability now unfolds and should be permitted to operate in a natural, unrestricted manner. Finally, at 15 to 20, the boy has reached puberty. He becomes aware of other persons. Socialization, a sort of necessary evil, occurs.

In keeping with his basic theory of saltatory development, Rousseau taught that children should never be treated as miniature adults. A child should not be scolded or whipped but permitted to suffer the natural results of his own acts. So that he may be permitted to develop naturally, there should be unrestricted opportunity for expression of natural impulses, instincts, and feelings.

Modern Roussellians are called *romantic naturalists*—romantic in that they see the natural unfolding process as a highly creative one. Romantic naturalists place primary emphasis upon *basic needs* and their unfoldment. When carried through to its logical implications, romantic naturalism focuses education of a child upon a predestined future. Nature supposedly has *enfolded* into a child certain talents, ideas, and purposes, and these *unfold* as he moves into his future.

Consequently, children are assumed to be naturally creative, and since creativity is an inherent characteristic, it supposedly unfolds best in a permissive atmosphere. Thus Roussellian romantic naturalism, when applied to classroom situations, became "Progressive Education." Emphasis was upon self-activity in a child-centered school, i.e., a first-grade teacher waited to teach reading to a boy until the boy realized his "need."

G. Stanley Hall (1846–1924) and other eminent psychologists of the early twentieth century were influenced by the theory of biological evolution; they expanded the idea of saltatory development. Hall was the father of adolescent psychology. His was the first doctor of philosophy degree in psychology granted by an American university. He later was head of the psychology department of Johns Hopkins and from there went to be president of Clark University. He was one of the leaders in developing the field of educational psychology in American colleges and universities. Hall did much to dignify the *recapitulation theory* in educational circles. His development of the psychological implication of the recapitulation theory emerged from his profound interest in the theory of evolution and his understanding of physiological psychology.

According to the recapitulation theory, man, in his embryological development, passes through the different stages of biological evolution of the animal kingdom. Hall taught that this evolutionary process continues after birth. Thus, the recapitulation theory was extended to include the psychological process of child development.

The recapitulation theory, applied to child development, meant that a child or youth, in his growth processes, follows the evolutionary development of the human race. The natural stages of an individual's development were assumed to run parallel to the stages of growth of human civilization. Hall used the term *genetic psychology* to cover that area of study which might have been called evolutionary psychology. In a sense, his work on child development was *Roussellianism gone biological*. Quotations from one of his books in regard to the sharp difference between preadolescence and adolescence will give an idea of his approach to the study of child development.

Everything, in short, suggests that this period (ages 8 to 12) may represent in the individual what was once for a very protracted and relatively stationary period an age of maturity in the remote ancestors of our race, when the young of our species, who were perhaps pygmoid, shifted for themselves independently of further parental aid. . . .

Adolescence is a new birth, for the higher and more completely human traits are now born. The qualities of body and soul that now emerge are far newer.

The child comes from and harks back to a remoter past; the adolescent is neo-atavistic, and in him the later acquisitions of the race slowly become pre-potent. Development is less gradual and more saltatory, suggestive of some ancient period of storm and stress when old moorings were broken and a higher level attained.[3]

Hall regarded play as evidence of racial recapitulation. When a child played he was repeating racial history. When a child brought into his play the actions of a cave man, he released actions which were vital to the species ages ago. Successive steps in development of play corresponded to successive cultural stages of man. Fig. 5 lists the evolutionary cultural stages and their corresponding play stages in children, as Hall saw them.

Cultural Stages	Play Stages
Primitive life	Climbing, swinging, babbling
Savage life	Chasing, hiding, hunting
Nomadic life	Wandering, gay life, fighting
Tribal life	The above plus team games
Early civilization	Imitations of adult occupations

FIG. 5.   Cultural Stages and Corresponding Play Stages.

Dr. Arnold Gesell has devoted his professional life to a study of growth and development of children and youth and has made many valuable contributions. His method of study has been to observe, photograph, and measure children and youth of a certain age group and to describe the average of those age groups as representative of them.

It is Gesell's conviction that the task of science is to make reality about children and youth more intelligible, and that the *growth plan* of children and youth comprises one reality. Development in accord with this growth plan is a series of progressions. "As with a plant, so with a child. His mind grows by natural stages. A child creeps before he walks, sits before he stands, cries before he laughs, babbles before he talks, draws a circle before he draws a square, lies before he tells the truth, and is selfish before he is altruistic. Such sequences are part of the order of Nature. . . . Every child, therefore, has a unique pattern of growth, but that pattern is a variant of a basic ground plan."[4]

His studies, Gesell reports, confirm that higher psychological manifestations of child life are "profoundly subject to laws of development." Thus, he feels that laws of development apply to emotions, morals, and personality as well as to such physical reactions as walking and stair climbing. He states that, although nothing is inherited fully formed, the basic pattern for development is decreed by hereditary law.

[3] G. Stanley Hall, *Youth, Its Education, Regimen, and Hygiene*, Appleton, 1907, pp. 1–6.

[4] Arnold Gesell, *Studies in Child Development*, Harper, 1948, p. 8.

No one doubts that Dr. Gesell has accumulated evidence germane to his assertions in regard to biological and psychological maturation of behaviors of children. However, his basic assumptions which set the stage for the conclusions derived from his research can be seriously questioned. That biological maturation brings successive organic changes in the body of a child and youth is universally accepted. But we may ask two crucial questions: (1) Are organic changes a series of progressions through stages? and (2) Is there basis for asserting that a developing self—psychological development—makes the same kind of changes as does a biological organism?

IS A CHILD A PASSIVE ORGANISM WHOSE DEVELOPMENT DEPENDS UPON CONDITIONING BY ITS ENVIRONMENT?

Rousseau, Hall, and Gesell in their theories of development implied that the basic pattern of a child's development comes from the plan or design of nature. This "nativistic" pattern of thinking assumes that each child comes equipped with a constant human nature which is the ultimate source of the pattern and steps of his development. The gravity-like nature of development is assumed to be a working out of pre-existent natural law.

In contrast with the thinking of these men, we can assume that human psychological characteristics arise not through unfoldment from within but only through the influence of an external physical, sociological, or personal environment. This is the contention of adherents of the next two positions in regard to human development. Whereas they differ sharply from one another in regard to the nature of person-environment relationships, they are alike in their opposition to theories of natural unfoldment or psychological recapitulation.

The *S-R* (stimulus-response) *associationistic* concept of development, too, is based upon the assumption of fixed natural law. However, it has been formulated as a more "scientific" position in contrast to nativistic ideas. In contrast to the emphasis of nativistic outlooks, development is asserted to be not *child-* but *environment-centered*. Whereas theories of natural unfoldment or recapitulation imply that a child's development is an *active* process, S-R associationisms are built upon the assumption that any child fundamentally is *passively reactive*. This means that development is a process of forming responses to environmental stimulation. In the process, environment provides the stimulation and thus determines what responses are to be made.

According to S-R associationists, a child manifests his development through tendencies and habits which are observable by others. These tendencies and habits, supposedly, are formed through two processes. Through the hereditary process, raw materials appear in the form of innate mechanistic responses. Learning is the process in which environment acts upon inherited characteristics. Since innate responses are comparatively few, mechanistic learning—environmental conditioning—is central in child development. (An S-R associationistic description of learning is expanded in Chapters 11 through 13.)

Development is explained by S-R associationists as involving primarily the formation of mechanical connections of some sort between stimuli and responses. Everything a child does, whether it is thought or action, is explained in terms of responses *following* stimuli or stimuli *following* responses. Stimuli are features of the environment which act on an organism to cause it to respond. Responses are reactions of an organism to stimulation. The approach of S-R associationisms may be diagramed as in Fig. 6.

$$\text{Stimulus or situation acting on an organism} \left\{ \begin{array}{c} \xrightarrow{\hspace{2cm}} \\ \text{A lapse of time} \\ \xleftarrow{\hspace{2cm}} \end{array} \right\} \text{Response or behavior of the organism}$$

FIG. 6.   The Approach of S-R Associationism.

Superficially, S-R associationism may appear to provide an adequate description of human development. Children often have been so habituated to responding to indoctrination and propaganda that they seem passively conditioned; and they carry this habit into adult life. Evidence of this is the way a gullible public reacts passively to advertising and propaganda of all kinds. However, this does not necessarily mean that human beings, by nature, are passive mechanisms. Rather, it may indicate that people have been treated as if they were passive so long and so constantly that they feel they *are* that way.

IS A CHILD A PERSON WHO DEVELOPS THROUGH INTERACTION WITH HIS PSYCHOLOGICAL ENVIRONMENT?

The key concepts in the above heading are *person, interaction,* and *psychological environment.* In exploring this fourth alternative outlook in regard to human development we should be mindful that each concept has its special significance. Furthermore, each concept has arisen as a more effectual expression to be used in place of less adequate concepts of the opposing outlooks toward development. Advocates of an interactionist approach, in thinking about psychological development of people, prefer the terms *person* to *organism; interaction* to *action* or *reaction;* and *psy-*

chological environment to *physical* or *biological environment*. Such preference is not merely a whim; there is a conviction that the concepts *person, interaction,* and *psychological environment* are highly advantageous for teachers in describing developmental processes.

In the latter pages of Chapter 2 we identified the position represented by supporters of this outlook as *interactionism* or *relativism*. When one attacks problems of development and learning within a relativistic frame of reference, he needs a systematic psychology which harmonizes with his relativistic outlook. This is *cognitive-field* psychology, described in detail in Chapter 14; only its developmental aspects are treated here.

The central idea of relativism is that an object derives its qualities, not as a thing in itself, but through its relationships with other objects.[5] Applied to human psychology, this means that a person derives his qualities or characteristics through his *interactive* relationships with his psychological environment. The task of cognitive-field psychology is to provide adequate ideological tools for describing person-environmental relationships of persons. The aspects of a psychological *field* or *life space* are the tools of cognitive-field psychology.

What Is a Life Space?

Life space is a term which describes a person's total psychological situation. It includes a psychological person and his environment. So construed, this psychological concept represents all of the factors giving rise to an individual's behavior at a stated time. The time may vary in length, but strictly speaking, a life space has a *duration of a moment*. Thus, as a child develops, he lives through a series of life spaces. Each life space of a moment contains a person and his psychological environment of that moment. In developing this concept we draw heavily from the works of Kurt Lewin and his students.

A life space usually is represented by related geometric figures. However, it is important to keep in mind that the essence of life space is its functional nature; it represents, not physical entities, but functional relationships. It constitutes an instrument whereby one may be objective in studying child development by being, to some degree, subjective. A teacher may think, "What would I be thinking if I were a student and were acting that way?" or "If I were in his situation why would I be acting the way he is?" A life space is, uniquely, a psychological phenomenon. All psychological events—acting, thinking, learning, hoping, dreaming—are functions, not of isolated properties of an individual or his environment, but of mutual relations of a totality of coexisting facts which constitute a life space. Life space is a technical term for a psychological situation.

[5] Relativism is discussed in detail in Chapter 11, pp. 271–274.

From a cognitive-field point of view, development is centered in the total psychological situation, which includes a person and his psychological environment considered *simultaneously*. A psychological situation is a functional interpretation and patterning of physical, social, and conceptual facts insofar as, and in the manner that, they involve the person under consideration.

In terms of a psychological situation, development is a function of both a person and his environment. Thus, actual behavior, in every case, depends upon a person's individual characteristics and the momentary structure of his environment. This means that people with a cognitive-field emphasis in studying development do not center the process in either a child or his environment. Rather they think that development is defined most usefully as a situational process within which a person interacts with his environment.

How is life space related to development? Psychological development, relativistically defined, is the process whereby a psychological person emerges and grows. It is that procedure whereby man, a biological organism, lives in a human society and becomes a human, a cultural being. Whereas, from the viewpoint of biology, man is construed as a physical organism, psychologically he is a dynamic person who emerges in a social environment. Thus, psychological development has no necessary one-to-one relationship to physical or biological behavior. A child's becoming larger is biological growth and his being moved from a theater to his home while he is sleeping constitutes physical movement, but neither represents psychological development. Psychological development of a child cannot be ascertained merely through direct observation; it must be inferred through study of his total situation. And the total life situation is a *life space* or a *psychological field*. To summarize: the key concepts of a psychological situation or life space are environment, person, and the relationship between them—*simultaneous mutual interaction* (SMI).

What Is a Child's Psychological Environment?

A child's psychological environment consists of everything around him which has any meaning for him. Thus, it contains everything that a person can do anything about. In the same sense that psychological development is distinctly different from physical or biological development, a psychological environment is distinctly different from a physical environment. Whereas the physical environments of a group of students in a classroom are relatively the same, each of their psychological environments is unique.

Let us visit Miss Smith's classroom of sixth-grade students at Carbondale Elementary School. At 10:30 Tuesday morning what is happening in the room? Miss Smith is holding reading class. What are Alice, Frank, Helen, and John doing? Alice is so absorbed with her teacher and school work that she is oblivious to everything else about her including the other children. Frank is listening halfheartedly to the teacher but is concerned primarily with the other children in the room. Helen is a social butterfly; she wants the attention of most of the children in the classroom. She does give attention to the teacher from time to time, but right now she is concerned with other things. John's body is in the classroom but "psychologically" John is riding a shiny new tractor which is being operated in the field adjoining the school.

This classroom is illustrated in Fig. 7. Each small circle represents a

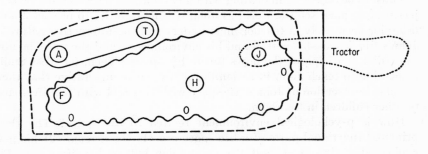

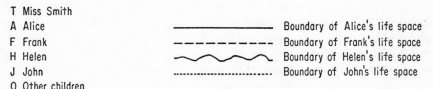

T Miss Smith
A Alice
F Frank
H Helen
J John
O Other children

————————— Boundary of Alice's life space
————————— Boundary of Frank's life space
∿∿∿∿∿∿∿∿∿ Boundary of Helen's life space
·············· Boundary of John's life space

FIG. 7.   Life Spaces Involved in a Classroom.

person and has his initial on it. Each person has his respective environment, indicated by a larger figure which includes the person. Each person and his respective psychological environment constitute a life space.

How does psychological environment differ from physical and social environment? The physical environment of an object or person includes everything surrounding that object or person as seen by an unbiased observer. Likewise, social environment consists of the generalized social milieu or atmosphere around a person. It is the attitudes, values, and beliefs of the community, region, or nation. Although physical and social environment furnish a setting for the psychological environments of individuals in a group, they are distinctly different from the psychological environment of any one member of the group. We may never consider a child's physical or social environment as it appears to others to be his psychological environment. A psychological environment is what a person "makes of" his own physical and social environment.

A psychological environment, strictly speaking, is a momentary situation, involving a specific person. Such an environment and the person involved are constantly changing as the person actively lives in relationship to that environment. What *appears to an observer* to constitute John's environment may include many elements not actually in John's psychological environment, and the observed environment may exclude some elements which, for John, psychologically are in it. For her to understand John, the teacher must study John in *his* own environment (John's psychological environment), not *the* physical environment.

Thus, to be objective in dealing with a child a teacher also must be subjective. She must see the world as John sees it. In order to predict John's behavior accurately, a teacher must understand the interactive nature of John's life space—his person and his environment—and she must be able to predict (anticipate) the boy's future life spaces. Then, for Miss Smith to be able to teach John in a significant way, it is imperative that there be some intersection of John's life space with hers and with the life spaces of other children in the room.

How is psychological environment related to life space? The three principal functional parts of a life space are (1) the person, (2) his psychological environment, and (3) the foreign hull of his life space. The "foreign hull" of a person's life space is that part of his physical and social environment not included in his psychological environment. It has physical but not psychological reality. In Figs. 7 and 8, practically everything within the four walls of the classroom, as well as much more, is included within either John's life space or his foreign hull. John's life space, drawn alone, would appear as in Fig. 8.

Although a series of momentary environments of a person usually are more or less similar, there is nothing fixed or static about them. As one develops, he lives through a series of life spaces, each with its own environment and to some degree different from the one which preceded it. However, there is a continuity of life spaces. In a reasonably normal person, a new life space and its environment is not completely different from the one of the moment before.

Since succeeding nonpsychological physical and social environments—foreign hulls—are outside psychological environments, they can have no immediate effect upon a person's intelligent behavior. However, through interaction with the environment, parts of a present for-

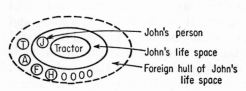

FIG. 8.   John's Life Space.

eign hull are transformed into goals, barriers, and other psychological factors of future life spaces. They then are no longer a part of the foreign hull. Factors thus transformed become parts of subsequent psychological environments. What a moment before constituted only a part of the foreign hull may at the succeeding moment be a central part of the person or his psychological environment.

How Does a Child's Self or Person Develop?

Cognitive-field psychologists place one's *self* or *person* at the center of his psychological field. A self or person is that body or configuration of matters with which one becomes identified and to which he gives his allegiance. So defined, it is not a fixed quantity or static thing. It is *achieved,* as contrasted with being inherently possessed.

One's person grows so that soon the central feature of his social and personal motivation becomes the maintenance and betterment of the welfare of that self. A child, to a greater extent than an adult, is a dynamic unity. When he cries, he cries all over; when he is hungry, all of him is hungry; and when he is frightened, he is startled completely. Consequently, he perceives his self only as he distinguishes it from his environment and various aspects of it from one another. The rather sharp distinction between one's person and his psychological environment is something which only grows in an individual's thinking, as the "I" or "self" is gradually formed.

How does a child construct his self? His awareness of his self is manifested in at least four different ways: (1) he comes to feel responsible for his acts, priding himself on his achievements and blaming himself for his failures; (2) his self, being embodied in values and goals, is realized in his transactions with other people; (3) as he evaluates his conduct over and against an ideal, an ideal self emerges (people often identify this ideal self with "conscience"); and (4) his self grows to a prominent place in his memories of a past and his anticipations of a future.

Learning to concentrate entails learning to separate out—or structure —certain parts of one's self and his psychological environment, the two central aspects of his life space. Through this differentiating process, a self grows to be a most important functional region in a psychological field. Under normal conditions an individual self is likely to involve his strongest motives. When a child uses the terms *I, me, mine, you, yours, he,* or *she, him,* or *her, his* or *hers*—a self is emerging. Such concepts arise only as a person interacts with other individuals and groups of people. Through this interactive process each person acquires such achievements as language, conceptual thinking, and moral, social, and religious predispositions and insights.

Man is born a very complex biological organism in a social environment. Through actively living in a human environment he develops as a person or self. The normal process of development produces self-involvement with objects, people, groups, and social organizations in a physical and social environment. In a negative sense, a human organism growing up in complete isolation probably would not develop a self-concept or appear to others as a personality. It seems reasonable to assume that he would have no basis for distinguishing between right and wrong, he would have no developed aesthetic sense, and he would have no language or symbols and would thus be incapable of abstract thinking. Only by living in a human world and having a biological organism of unique type does he emerge a psychological person or self.

A person adjusts to his social and physical environment by identifying himself with the activities or concerns that comprise it. Thus, *self, person,* and *interest* are names for the same psychological phenomenon. The content of self is taken to consist of one's cherished ideals and interests. The kind and amount of interest actively taken in affairs is a measure of the quality of one's selfhood or person. To say that a child is interested or "concerned" is a brief way of saying that he is engaging interactively his person and his psychological world. In its widest possible sense, a child's self is the total configuration of all that he calls or thinks of as *his*. This can include his body, his speech, his thoughts, his clothes, his home, his parents, his grandparents, his brothers and sisters, his reputation in various groups, his personal property, and his attitudes toward all these and the institutions for their realization.

How many selves does an individual have? In a sense, he has as many different selves as there are distinct groups for whose opinion he has any concern. Thus, Jimmy Jones at home is one self, in school another, on a date another, and on a football field still another. Every normal person maintains a variety of interests or values in different situations and so might be said to have a corresponding number of selves. Although there is a different self in each successive life space of an individual, we can anticipate a continuity of selves of such nature that, in case of conflict, a deeper continuous self pushes the others aside and claims the "right of way." Consequently, each person, if reasonably "normal," is a basic self made up of his major allegiances and commitments, among which there is some degree of harmony and continuity. Usually the psychological structure of a person is relatively constant over a long period of time, particularly as he advances in chronological age.

Many persons do not have harmonious commitments. Fractured selves are especially evident in recent times and offer one explanation for the present rate of mental illness. A major goal of education is to help people resolve reflectively conflicts produced by incompatible commitments—and thus to help them establish integrated selves.

Are selves always in the process of making? Insofar as one knows, a baby does not make sharp distinctions between his body, his environment, and the aspects of each. His life space is quite simple and undifferentiated. As a child lives and grows he extends his world of understanding in an attempt to have it encompass more and more of the world about him as he sees it—his world of effect, or psychological environment. In turn, the resultant extension and differentiation of his life space leads to an enlargement of his psychological environment. It is in this dynamic process that essentially different facts acquire their psychological reality. Selfhood, except as it has encased itself in a shell of routine, always is in the process of making. Any self, in process, is capable of including a number of inconsistent selves or unharmonized dispositions.

Were this not true, with man as intelligent as he is, life would be quite drab. Impulsive action in a child means he is ripe for discovery of a more inclusive and richer self which is possible but as yet unrealized. A self is in the making constantly as one develops new insights, or changes old ones, and forms new habits.

Teachers should bear in mind that a far-reaching change in structure of a self or person can occur through his developing a significant educational insight. Acquiring a new educational insight can be as significant and far reaching as falling in love, becoming converted, or realizing a great change in physical and social environment.

How Does One Develop Through Person-Environment Interaction?

Interaction is a concept which best characterizes the functional nature of a life space or psychological situation of a child or youth. The "reality" with which a person interacts consists of what he *makes* of the things that come to him through his senses or any other sources available to him. The meaning of any object arises from one's interpretation of the relationship between the object and one's self. When one interacts with an object or activity, *he sizes it up*. When a child sees a tiger as a kitty, psychologically it is a kitty; and a kitty, which adults call a tiger, is a part of the child's psychological environment.

Learning may be defined as the process by which one changes or develops new insights or understandings and is the very essence of the human developmental process. One develops psychologically through gaining an increased understanding of himself and his psychological environment. He achieves this understanding by a combination of three fundamental, complementary processes—*differentiation, generalization,* and *restructurization.*

DIFFERENTIATION. Differentiation means learning to discern more, and more specific, aspects of oneself and his environment. What once were "kitties" come to be "leopards," "tigers," "lions," and "cats." What once was "toast" comes to be "bread," "crackers," "donuts," and "toast." What once was "baby" comes to be "doll," "me," "my arms," or "my legs," and later, "student," "member of club," "ball player," and "lady-killer."

GENERALIZATION. Although, in common usage, generalization is the opposite of differentiation, psychologically they are complementary. Generalization is the process whereby one groups a number of particular objects or functions under a single heading. "Development" and "learning" are examples of generalized concepts. A student of professional education, through differentiation of various instances of learning, may develop a generalized concept, learning, to cover any learning in any situation. A child, through differentiation and generalization, may divide the physical world into vegetable, animal, and mineral.

RESTRUCTURIZATION. Restructurization means making more sense or better sense of oneself and his world. One changes the way he sees the relationships of the various facets of his life space and he grows to have a better idea of what leads to what. Thus, he restructures his life space. In short, if development is normal, a person becomes an increasingly better thinker. Within this process of restructuring, differentiation and generalization constantly are occurring.

How Are the Developmental Processes Manifested?

A developmental process is basically perceptual in nature. It may take the form of one's changing his *motivation* and *group identification,* his *bodily coordination,* his *time perspective,* or his *differentiation of reality from irreality.*

CHANGE IN MOTIVATION AND GROUP IDENTIFICATION. A child's change in motivation arises through his seeing regions or factors of his life space in a new light. To a 14-year-old boy, a girl, once "something to pull the hair of," comes to be a thing to be quite gently cuddled. A change in motivation is very closely related to changes in group identification. To a large degree it is the groups to which one belongs that are the source of his ideology and consequently of his motivation. One's person emerges through his becoming a member of a group and it develops as he changes his group allegiances. An adolescent's conformity to his peer group standards is a striking example of this developmental process.

CHANGE IN BODILY COORDINATION. A more noticeable evidence of a child or youth's development is his change in control of his bodily muscular system—his bodily coordination. A small child gradually learns to handle himself quite well. Then comes the adolescent growth spurt (see Chapter 6). This entails such great changes in bodily size and proportions that a youth must almost start all over again in learning to control his musculature. This process ultimately becomes refined into development of the fine coordination of complex skills.

CHANGE IN TIME PERSPECTIVE. During development, an enlargement of time perspective occurs. A small child lives very much in the present. His time perspective includes only an immediate past and an immediate future. As age increases, time perspective tends to expand. More and more, remote future and past events influence present behavior. These time-binding events occupy such a central part of many adult life spaces that it often is assumed that a past and a future actually exist psychologically in their own right. Careful thought, however, will bring the realization that the only past with which a person can deal is *what he thinks happened in the past*. Likewise the only future which can influence a person *now* is his anticipation of a future which he thinks may, or is going to, eventuate.

A child's present life situation contains traces, or "memories," of past incidents and anticipations of future ones; but all of these are in his present situation or life space. The "past" can be of present significance only through operation of factors in the present which are identified as "past." That which persists from prior experience so that it is "past" in the present is *trace*.

When a second child has appeared in a family sometime in the past, the important factor, now, as far as the first child is concerned, is not whether his mother rejected him but whether he interpreted the situation as one of rejection and carried the rejection into his present life space.

Anticipation of a future also occurs in the present; it is how one envisions the future—not what will actually happen then—that counts in the present. If a child is good in school on Monday so that he will get a star on Friday, whether or not he actually receives a star on Friday has nothing to do with his being good on Monday. His *anticipation* of the star is his motivation for his goodness on Monday. Recognition of the "presentness" of past and future in no way depreciates them; it places them in a psychological frame of reference—growth of time perspective is in terms of trace and anticipations which are functional parts of a present life space.

DIFFERENTIATION OF REALITY FROM IRREALITY. Irreality, as used in cognitive-field psychology, refers to wishing, dreaming, imagining, and kindred processes. Normal development carries with it an increased differentiation in the reality-irreality dimension of one's life space. A young child does not distinguish clearly wishes from facts, hopes from expectations, or imaginative objects or events from facts. To a young child nurtured upon concepts such as Santa Claus and Satan, these are among the most real things in the world. Although in adults wishful thinking is very common, they generally are better able to distinguish between daydreams, wishes, and reality.

To a large degree a person's intelligence is dependent upon the degree of his changes in motivation, bodily coordination, time perspective, and differentiation of reality from irreality. As a child develops by means of these processes, he learns increasingly to understand and control his environment. However, teachers have no reason to fear that a student will

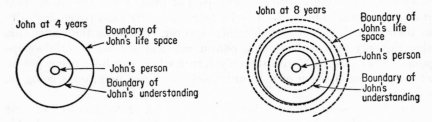

FIG. 9.   John's Understanding of His Life Space at Ages 4 and 8.

soon acquire complete understanding and will see no further need to learn. Once a student launches a serious study of his environment, his life space begins to expand. As his understanding expands to encompass his life space, so does his life space dilate to such a degree that his motivation for study actually multiples. This is illustrated graphically in Fig. 9.

What Determines the Direction of Psychological Development?

Objects and events are not neutral to a child; they have an immediate psychological effect on his behavior. Psychologically, the nature of things and events is determined by their appearance and functional possibilities. Lewinian psychologists identify the imperative or challenging facts of an environment as its *valences*. For a particular child, psychological facts may include dogs, cats, rooms, chairs, knives, friends, things that fall down, things that turn over, things that start and go, things that take one places, things that go up and down, places where one is safe from danger, and places where food is available. These things and events attract a child to play, sit, eat, ride, climb, hide, and manipulate. It is in connection with these psychological functions that valences or attractions of objects and activities derive their strengths. Valences are the aspects of an environment which make it attractive or repulsive.

The valence of an object or activity usually arises from the object's being a means of satisfying a need. Thus, the valences of factors of one's environment determine the direction of his psychological development or movement. It is a person's interaction with his environment that gives a thing valence. The valence of an environmental object and the needs of a child are correlative. The particular objects or activities which bear valences, and the strengths of their valences, are quite different for a baby, a kindergartner, an adolescent, and an adult. A child's insistence on independence in some activity indicates that that activity has taken on a definite valence and that a part of the child's goals has become the enhancement of his "self." A child of 3 trying to jump down a step may refuse help. The step, to him, has a definite valence. Unless he reaches certain results by his own effort, he will not be content. This is evidence of emergence of a self—of his psychological development.

By means of experimentation readers may observe how, through a person's ego or self involvement, valences of his activities arise along with corresponding personal needs. The experiment may involve any activity of such nature that the subject can set goals of differing degrees. The activity might be high-jumping, distance swimming, or making a chain of paper clips. Ask the subject where he thinks he will achieve, and place his goal at that level. (Permit the subject to compete with himself and provide his own motivation; do not say, "How far do you think you can go?") The subject's goal is the cross-bar placed at a certain level on the standards, the spot to which he hopes to swim, or the number of clips he will assemble in five seconds. As the subject makes tries and sets new goals, a relationship will develop between what he achieves in one trial—his *level of achievement*—and where he sets his next goal—his *level of aspiration*. He will set his goal at a point which he thinks he might achieve but is not certain that he will. If he falls far short he will lower his goal. If he reaches his goal he will raise it the next time.

A person, if left to decide for himself, will set his goal at a point which he thinks he probably, but not surely, can reach. Since there is a possibility of failure, accomplishment of the goal will give him a sense of success; for success to be success there must be a possibility of failure. When left to choose between several goals a person will prefer the goal which is more difficult to reach, provided he anticipates a possibility of reaching it and it is not identical with other goals easier to reach. Everything else being equal, a child will prefer a toy which is slightly more difficult to reach. If, however, he is permitted to choose between tools with which to get the toy, he will prefer that tool which is in easier reach. The law of parsimony—least action—holds for psychological means but not for psychological ends. A professor walks to the campus to give himself exercise, but when he heads for the campus he cuts every corner along the way. Is he naturally lazy?

SUMMARY

Each of four conflicting approaches to the study of human development continues to have a large number of advocates in our American schools. Each may be identified through use of a descriptive statement: (1) A child is a miniature adult who does not develop psychologically; he merely grows bigger. (2) A child is a naturally enfolded pattern of instincts, abilities, and talents which serially unfold as he actively develops by jumps through sharply delineated stages (saltatory development). (3) A child is a passive organism which develops according to the way it is nurtured and conditioned (S-R associationist approach). (4) A child is a dynamically purposive—intelligent—person who develops through interacting with his psychological environment (cognitive-field approach) (see Chapter 14 for further expansion of this approach to development and learning).

When thinking is focused upon some distinct period in the development of persons, an outlook in regard to psychological development is more readily explained and understood. Chapter 8 is devoted to an interpretation and expansion of the meaning of adolescence within a cognitive-field frame of reference.

BIBLIOGRAPHY

Combs, Arthur W., and Donald Snygg, *Individual Behavior*, rev. ed., Harper, 1959.
A perceptual approach to psychology which supports the SMI position on psychological development. Study centers upon perceived selves and their needs, goals, and purposes.
Gesell, Arnold, *Studies in Child Development*, Harper, 1948.
A description of general characteristics and conditions of child development, in a biological-psychological frame of reference.
Kuenzli, Alfred E., *The Phenomenological Problem*, Harper, 1959.
A collection of technical papers clarifying the phenomenological—perceptual—approach in modern psychology which harmonizes with the SMI outlook on psychological development.
Lewin, Kurt, *A Dynamic Theory of Personality*, translated by Adams and Zener, McGraw-Hill, 1935.
A collection of articles which Lewin had written prior to 1935 and a new

survey chapter. This book shows Lewin's earlier thinking as his topological and vector psychology was emerging.

Lewin, Kurt, *Field Theory in Social Science,* Harper, 1951.
A collection of Kurt Lewin's papers. The first three and last chapters develop guiding principles and constructs of *field* psychology. The remaining six chapters demonstrate application of *field* psychological principles to study of learning, development and regression, ecology, group dynamics, and social psychology.

Lindzey, Gardner, ed., *Assessment of Human Motives,* Rinehart, 1958.
The thoughts of nine distinguished psychologists in regard to human motivation. Chapter 1 by the editor summarizes various outlooks on motivation and is highly relevant to psychological development.

Montagu, M. F. Ashley, *The Direction of Human Development,* Harper, 1955.
A book describing how biological man becomes socialized. Montagu's basic thesis is that people naturally are cooperative, not competitive. "The fundamental social nature of all living things has its origin in the reproductive relationship between parents and offspring" (p. 12).

Piaget, Jean, *The Child's Conception of the World,* Harcourt, Brace, 1929.
A report of Piaget's observations and clinical study of children. More recent studies of this eminent Swiss psychologist concern the origin and development of intelligence and children's conceptions of morality, reality, space, physical causality, number, and geometry.

Russell, David H., *Children's Thinking,* Ginn, 1956.
A psychological interpretation of backgrounds, materials, processes, and techniques for improvement of children's thinking based upon extensive research findings.

Sherif, Muzafer, and Carolyn W. Sherif, *An Outline of Social Psychology,* Harper, 1956.
A social psychology text focusing on social behavior that is an outcome of the way individuals perceive situations.

Stone, L. Joseph, and Joseph Church, *Childhood and Adolescence,* Random, 1957.
A translation of facts and ideas from psychological, zoological, medical, psychiatric, and sociological sources into a common language for eclectic study of growing persons. A key notion is that persons shift from a biological to a psychological level of functioning.

8
WHAT IS ADOLESCENCE?

Adolescence is the developmental period during which growing persons make a transition from childhood to adulthood. Naturally, it is of great concern to high school teachers. However, teachers of all grade levels can benefit from a knowledge of this period of human development. When they are interpreted broadly, principles of development manifested by any age group will apply to all age levels. Furthermore, all elementary teachers help children develop understandings and appreciations which they carry with them into adolescence, and teachers in the upper elementary grades deal with some students actually entering adolescence.

People in Western society generally recognize adolescence as a time of striking change. Adolescents often are considered problems to themselves as well as a source of perplexity and irritation to adults. Adolescence is such a familiar concept among those dealing with development of children and youth that it may be described by a common set of physiological and sociological characteristics. The early part of this chapter describes them. Later sections will treat more precise psychological meanings of this period.

WHAT ARE SOME GENERAL PHYSIOLOGICAL AND SOCIOLOGICAL CHARACTERISTICS OF ADOLESCENCE?

Adolescence denotes a more or less unique period. In Western cultures, this period has been institutionalized into one of several years' duration when individuals no longer are children but are still too immature to be treated as adults. It begins when young people enter pubescence and continues until they are sexually mature and have reached their maximum growth in height and in mental ability as measured by intelligence tests. Chronologically, adolescence covers roughly the years from 12 to the early 20s, but as Chapter 6 pointed out, girls physiologically are about two years ahead of boys at the onset. During adolescence, youth are expected to attain physical, mental, and emotional maturity and to make some major effort in the direction of vocational and civic responsibility. The one word which best characterizes adolescence is *change*. The change is physiological, sociological, and psychological.

What Are the Physiological Changes of Adolescence?

Some of the material to follow repeats what was said in Chapter 6. However, inclusion of the more detailed discussion here of the physiology of adolescence seems necessary if the chapter is to be complete.

One's body is the façade with which he faces his world. Although physiological changes, in themselves, may not account adequately for the psychological changes of adolescence, they are of sufficient importance to merit careful consideration. Some physiological changes of adolescence are characteristic only of this period. Other changes happen at other periods as well. Changes of the latter type include decrease in pulse rate, rise in blood pressure, increase in total respiratory volume, and diminution of basal metabolism. Physiological changes which uniquely characterize adolescence fall into three categories: sexual changes, changes in skeletal dimensions, and changes in body chemistry.

SEXUAL CHANGES OF ADOLESCENCE. Maturation of sex organs and development of sex power are the most impressive physiological characteristics of adolescence. *Pubescence* and *puberty* describe the period and process within which sexual maturity is achieved. We should take careful note of their respective meanings. Pubescence is an approximately two-year period of physiological change which characterizes the biological onset of adolescence and culminates in a person's reaching puberty. Pubescence is marked by maturation of primary and secondary sex characteristics, related changes in glandular balances and body proportions, and a spurt in physical growth. Puberty is the point in biological development when marked indicators of sexual maturity appear. Puberty in girls is indicated by their first menstruation. In boys, the indicator is the presence of live sperm cells in seminal discharges. However, since sperm cells cannot be detected by unaided eyes, and boys' genitals are so obvious, mere growth of boys' genitals often is considered an indication of puberty. For girls the average age of puberty is slightly under 13 and for boys it ranges from $13\frac{1}{2}$ to $14\frac{1}{2}$. However, the range in reaching puberty is at least from 9 to 17 in girls and from 11 to 18 in boys.

PRIMARY SEX CHARACTERISTICS. Those features of an organism which are most immediately associated with procreation and reproduction are called primary sex characteristics. In boys they are penis and testes; in girls, ovaries, fallopian tubes, uterus, and vagina. As puberty is approached, genitals of both sexes make rapid growth and development. In boys this growth is quite apparent and is indicative of approaching manhood. Girls' sexual organs grow in parallel fashion but, since theirs are not so obvious, menstruation, a secondary sex characteristic, is usually considered the indicator of puberty. Anthropologists are acquiring more and more evidence that a period of some months usually elapses between a girl's first menstruation and her attainment of the capacity to become a mother. Nevertheless tradition persists, and people commonly connect the first menstrual period with the advent of female fertility.

SECONDARY SEX CHARACTERISTICS. Girls and boys manifest other sex characteristics commonly labeled *secondary*. A change in girls' figures occur: breasts develop and the pelvis widens. Girls also acquire fatty deposits in breasts and on hips, and hair appears in pubic regions and under arms. Boys, too, develop pubic and axillary hair but in addition to this they have their own secondary sexual characteristics. They rapidly develop hair on limbs and trunk, hairlines of their heads develop a wedge shape, facial whiskers become pigmented, and voices drop in pitch. Boys also broaden through the shoulders and acquire larger chest cavities. A normally proportioned girl takes on an hourglass shape while a normal boy becomes the shape of a carrot.

CHANGES IN SKELETAL DIMENSIONS. Sexual changes of adolescence are accompanied by noticeable modification of body height, weight, and proportions. Both boys and girls manifest a pubescent growth spurt about six months before the advent of puberty. However, the spurt in girls averages about one to two years ahead of that in boys.

The rate and span of changes in growth during adolescence are far from uniform. However, growth curves plotted from averages of different ages of the two sexes tend to obliterate individual spurts and abatements of growth. When one finds the average heights and weights of successive age groups, they form a pattern of gradual increase. However, studies of the increments of growth of individuals show that each has a period of sharp acceleration during pubescence. Some adolescents have been known to grow 6 or 7 inches in height and to gain 20 to 30 pounds in a single year. Since youth reach pubescent growth spurts at varying ages, growth changes tend to compensate for one another. When they are handled statistically, the astounding changes in individuals are concealed.

Not only does a person reach his pubescent growth spurt at his own particular time, but different organs and different parts of the body grow and develop at different speeds and their curves of growth take different forms. Growth of organic systems and other physiological dimensions may lag behind or overtake growth in stature. A very tall boy of 15 may appear to be a man and still have relatively undeveloped genitals.

CHANGES IN BODY CHEMISTRY. In addition to glands like the liver and sweat glands which have ducts to carry away their secretions, a human body also has ductless glands, or endocrines, which secrete hormones directly into the circulatory system. Special changes in size and function of some endocrines are an important aspect of the physiology of adolescence. The endocrines most closely related to physiological changes of adolescence are thymus glands, pituitary glands, and gonads, i.e., testes and ovaries.

The thymus gland, the "gland of childhood," is located in the upper breast and is associated with the changes of pubescence. In the years just prior to adolescence this gland diminishes in size and activity. This is part of a shift of glandular balance which begins at 9 or 10 in girls and 11 or 12 in boys. The shift takes several years to run its course. The anterior branch of the pituitary gland at the base of the brain also plays an important part in change of glandular balance. It becomes more and more active in the period just preceding puberty, and its function is related to the rapid growth spurt of adolescence. Secretions of various endocrines or ductless glands interact; thus, the anterior pituitary probably tends to energize some other glands. Normal physiological growth and development depend in part upon properly timed actions of pituitary and gonadal hormones.

Before the onset of puberty, secretions of the anterior pituitary gland stimulate growth of gonads. Female gonads produce, in addition to ova, or egg cells, the female sex hormone, estrogen. Male gonads produce, in addition to sperm cells, the male sex hormone, androgen. Estrogen influences growth of female sex organs and development of girls' secondary sex characteristics and contributes to sex drive. Androgen seems to speed growth of male sex organs, initiates and regulates development of secondary sex characteristics, and stimulates boys' sex drive. There is a difference in gonadal glandular activity of an adolescent male and of an adolescent female. However, the activities are not utterly dissimilar. Both androgen and estrogen are found in both sexes, but androgen is more highly developed and more active in males and estrogen in females.

What Is the Sociological Significance of Adolescence?

In discussions of adolescence quite often the development of primary and secondary sex characteristics receives major attention. However, biological development of human beings is always paralleled by sociological development. The radical changes in an adolescent's body are accompanied by equally significant changes in his relationships with groups with which he is identified. Changes in social attitudes parallel changes in physical structure. An adolescent, looking forward to and interesting himself in responsibilities of adult life, stands in sharp contrast to his earlier circumscribed, self-centered personality which existed when his mental horizons were relatively low and his bodily strength was limited.

Adolescence is not by nature a period of storm and stress, as Margaret Mead's studies of Samoan youth so well demonstrate.[1] The values of adults in Western culture lead it to be one. Western culture patterns (except those of Scandinavia and perhaps a few other European countries) are such that adolescents tend to find themselves in social environments full of continuing restrictions and frustrations for which they are inadequately prepared and commonly have no satisfactory solution. Although parents and other grownups have definite ideas about how the transition from childhood to adulthood should proceed, usually these ideas seem rather nonsensical to adolescents, who must accomplish the change.

In light of the fact that adolescents consider dealings with their own age group signally important, the transition to adulthood can be very painful and difficult. Adolescents must find their place in a society which is composed not only of their own peers but also adults to whom they, as citizens, job holders, members of society, parents, and voters must adjust. They must learn to be socially acceptable, to accommodate themselves to folkways, customs, and mores of their group. Furthermore, regardless of how much adult patterns of thinking and acting are out of tune with adolescent peer group ideals and values, adolescents are expected to adjust to those patterns.

PEER GROUP RELATIONSHIPS. In modern society informally organized groups, cliques, or gangs become especially widespread and important during adolescence. People of all ages draw in large measure upon their fellows for their thoughts, emotions, and modes of behavior. But as youth move into adolescence, peer groups become even more important to them. Whereas, during middle childhood, peer group influence supplements that of home and school, during adolescence it takes priority over, and may even supplant, influence of these institutions. Informal groups of adolescent age mates often become the very center of a youth's experience with personal identity and stability.

Adolescents will stake almost everything to win and hold approval of their age mates. Frequently they are well aware of the great importance of age mate groups in their lives. In 1955 Rosen found that, for the group

---

[1] Margaret Mead, *Coming of Age in Samoa*, Morrow, 1928.

of youngsters he studied, peer groups tended to be more important than adults in influencing choices. He stated that, in cases where parent and peer groups had conflicting attitudes in regard to issues examined in the study, adolescents more often agreed with their peers than with their parents.[2]

Groups with which adolescents identify themselves influence almost everything they do. Peer groups influence speech, moral values, clothing habits, and modes of eating. Some by-products of group interaction are special catchwords, nicknames, jargon, and ambitions. Group approval is so alluring to adolescents that they become virtual slaves to peer group customs and seem bound by certain peer group standards, ideals, and attitudes. This is true in a negative as well as a positive sense. If members of an adolescent's peer group frown upon his earlier ideals, he too will belittle them. For the time being, peer groups become dominant reference groups which, to a considerable degree, regulate attitudes, interests, activities, and aspirations. Consequently, within a peer group-centered setting, parents and adults may become annoyances in many aspects of living which are vitally important to youth of adolescent age.

Identification with peer groups is not all a bed of roses. Since an American adolescent usually identifies with more than one group, he is subjected to conflicting loyalties. His roles are different in the various groups and not all are equally attractive. Yet, while he is with each group he must show unstinted enthusiasm. A group of Future Farmers—a peer group—attend an agricultural field day. The events are directed by adults, many of whom smoke freely throughout the day. However, the Future Farmers act as if they and cigarettes are perfect strangers. The same boys away from school in a car together probably smoke cigarettes, almost to a man. Furthermore, those same boys will manifest three different languages depending upon whether, at the moment, they are Future Farmers, Sunday school students, or pals "draggin' the main" on Saturday night.

RELATIONS WITH ADULT SOCIETY.   An adolescent not only must accept an altered body and the necessity of adjusting to new motor and sensory patterns but must adapt himself to a world of people and situations in which he must play a new and different role. Although, at least on a superficial level, he tends to feel competent to make these adjustments, his family is not so sure of his ability. Thus, there are many possibilities for conflict and misunderstanding.

Adolescents assert desire for independence more aggressively than ever before, but economically and vocationally they are not yet able to escape from dependence on their homes. Consequently, many adolescents in

[2] B. C. Rosen, "Conflicting Group Membership: A Study of Parent-Peer Group Cross-Pressures," *American Sociological Review,* April, 1955, p. 160.

present-day society regard themselves as rather useless and resent conditions which make them that way. If society offered them adequate opportunities to participate in productive endeavors, it is rather doubtful that they would turn to a "hot rod" type of activity for their basic satisfactions.

Adult-adolescent conflict is a common phenomenon in Western societies, where, to a large degree, expediency determines patterns of thought and behavior. This situation gives rise to many inconsistencies and contradictions in adult society making it doubly difficult for an adolescent to understand and adjust. When practices and values sanctioned by adults of a family and those sanctioned by an adolescent's peer groups point in opposite directions, conflict is certain to arise. In such situations, youth, in an attempt to maintain some degree of stability, gravitate back toward one another and their peer groups. Adult-adolescent conflict then becomes conflict between the family group and the adolescent peer group. The amount of difficulty adolescents encounter in relating themselves to their peer and adult groups largely determines the degree to which the adolescent period is characterized by storm and stress.

GROWING INTO ADULTHOOD.   Adolescents frequently continue to think of themselves as children beyond the time when it is most effective for them to do so or the time which is justified by their biological development. Their resulting behavior leads adult associates to wonder why they do not "grow up and act their age." Only rarely is an adolescent suddenly conscious that he is "grown up." He lacks the evidence of some crowning event, like the rites which initiate boys and girls into adulthood in certain primitive cultures. Even changes in the way others treat him are so gradual that he is scarcely aware of them and would have great difficulty expressing them in words. In societies where transition into adulthood is gradual and relatively easy, as in some primitive cultures, there is little need for a youth to be conscious of his participation in developing a new role for himself.

Margaret Mead has described the developmental patterns of the mountain-dwelling Arapesh of New Guinea,[3] among whom transition from childhood to adulthood is easy. Both men and women are affectionate, trusting, and unaggressive. They consider bearing children and growing food the principal ends of life. The total community is the group to which all Arapesh feel they belong. Children refer to all adults by the same terms they use in speaking of their fathers and mothers. After an initiation which involves much ceremony but little hardship, boys gradually take over adult economic and social responsibilities.

[3] See Margaret Mead, *Growing Up in New Guinea*. This book is the second in the trilogy *From the South Seas*, Morrow, 1939.

At the age of 7 or 8 years a girl is betrothed to a boy several years her elder. She thereupon goes to live with his family. Some years later she, too, goes through initiation ceremonies, but her life goes on as before. Her future parents-in-law are quite as indulgent as her own parents. During their adolescent years, both she and her betrothed are members of the same family and community groups. Thus, there are no sudden shifts from one group to another, and the transition from childhood to married life is very gradual. Here is an example of how in some primitive societies a young person settles with little fanfare into his appropriate adult role shortly after puberty. In addition to performing adult social and economic duties, he functions sexually as an adult. In societies such as this the passage from childhood to adulthood is so smooth that it goes unrecognized as a special period. Adolescence, as defined in Western societies, is not a world-wide phenomenon.

Adolescence, then, is a cultural invention. In many primitive societies, where the transition is not so smooth, quite often there is a ceremonial adolescence of relatively short duration. This usually takes the form of puberty rites or initiation ceremonies and is timed to occur near the onset of sexual maturity. Such rites have been observed among various primitive peoples in many parts of the world. Apparently, such peoples recognize the onset of adolescence as the time to initiate boys and girls, often with bizarre and impressive ceremonies. Initiation rites include filing the teeth of adolescents, isolating them for a period of time, or in various ways mutilating their genitals. In males this consists of circumcision or subincision; in females, clitoridectomy or laceration of hymen or vaginal walls. At the conclusion of his puberty rites a young person assumes the role of full adulthood. He enters into all adult activities of the group as a full-fledged member. These activities include marriage, preparation of puberty rites for other youth, and sharing in previously withheld secrets of the tribe.

In that initiation ceremonies dramatize achievement of adult status, primitive groups may handle the problem of adolescence better than do "civilized" societies. Today, in modern civilization some vestiges of primitive initiatory ceremonies remain. Initiations are used to bring boys and girls into formal membership in various political, religious, and social organizations. However, such activities usually are not central to acquiring manhood or womanhood.

Some primitive societies stretch adolescence over a considerable period of time. Up to the time of adolescence, both sexes of Tchambuli youth remain with groups of women and smaller children. Men spend most of their time by themselves planning ceremonials. When boys reach the age of 9 or 10, they are eased out of the warm protective groups of adult women and children. However, they are not yet welcome to join men's groups. Men consider them mere boys who are not fit to be trusted with ceremonial property and secrets. Consequently, for three or four years, youth have the status neither of children nor of men. The strain accompanying this situation is considerable and probably has much to do with creation of easily hurt feelings, which Tchambuli men manifest.

In complex modern society, as in the Tchambuli society, transition from childhood to adulthood tends to be greatly prolonged. During this period fulfillment of adult desires, in most instances, must be delayed. Youth no longer are considered children and are not consistently accepted and treated as men and women. While adults who surround an adolescent still look upon him as a child to be petted and loved, or directed and commanded, the youth may have developed new powers, new interests, and a new sense of his personality. At one moment he feels himself being treated as a man and tries to act like one. At the next moment he may be forced again to act the part of a child.

Why Is Development of Heterosexuality a Problem?

Heterosexual literally means *other-sexual.* Heterosexuality involves various relationships between the two sexes. Although a growing child develops a gradually increasing interest in the opposite sex, prior to adolescence his dominant social interest is with children of his own sex. This interest continues into adolescence but is paralleled by rising heterosexual interests and activities. Ordinarily many of a person's childhood acquaintances and friendships extend over into the adolescent period. However, these must be restructured to harmonize with his new adolescent role, within which events are seen differently. The socioeconomic status of his family and his friends becomes much more important to him than it was when he was a child. Even more important, his motivations become heavily sex tinged. He becomes very much involved in learning all he can about members of the opposite sex. His answers usually come from inadequate, limited, and faulty sources. Consequently, a typical adolescent in the United States avidly seeks knowledge in regard to sex but is in the unfortunate position of not having available adequate sources of such information.

SOCIAL MOTIVES AND SEXUALITY. Adolescent boys and girls in modern society are preoccupied with social activities and experimentation. Often high schools serve as social laboratories. In the same sense that a group of people do not eat, sleep, and talk in just any way, adolescents do not choose just anybody as a steady boy or girl friend, and do not socialize with him or her in completely random manner. As the social structure of a society becomes more highly developed, acquired tastes and motives become more numerous and complex, and perhaps more inhibiting or coercing. This is particularly true for persons belonging to the middle and upper strata of a highly developed society. Many of an adolescent's ways of expressing his tastes and motives stem from social standards of his particular group. Thus, in his sexual relationships, as in others, he feels a need to "keep up with the Joneses."

FROM HOMOSEXUALITY TO HETEROSEXUALITY.   In itself, bodily and sexual maturation during adolescence has dramatic effects. Long before boys and girls reach adolescence, they have discovered that there is an anatomical difference between the sexes. They also have developed much curiosity with regard to sex and reproduction. However, generally speaking, it is only at the start of his pubescent period that a youth begins really to feel pressures of his organic sexual drives. Changes in his body and physical desires alter the way he sees everything which is related to him, but naturally they bring greatest modifications in his relationships with the opposite sex.

Studies have shown that less than one-third of sixth-graders voluntarily choose companions of the opposite sex. But by the twelfth grade almost two-thirds are doing this. As adolescence is approached, there is a shift in composition of social groups from childhood gangs of one sex to adolescent groups composed of both sexes. Individual youth parallel this social change by shifting their center of interest from a chum of the same sex to a boy friend or girl friend of the opposite sex.

SEX-LINKED PROBLEMS OF ADOLESCENTS.   Since an adolescent's interest in the other sex is so new and so strong and he has so little accurate understanding of his own sexual nature and that of the opposite sex, he is likely to blunder a good deal in his sexual life. The wide individual variation in rates of sexual maturation often make an adolescent feel out of step and contribute further to the botching of heterosexual affairs.

A late-maturing boy or an early-maturing girl especially is a problem to himself. To a high degree, an adolescent's physique represents his image of himself. Any atypical change, especially if it is relatively sudden, can be quite disconcerting. Although at the beginning of their teens girls are generally taller than boys, some girls reach the adolescent growth spurt earlier than most and are likely to be highly sensitive in regard to their heights and other bodily proportions which accompany this growth. It is rather common for tall junior high girls to develop hunched postures in an attempt to hide their atypical stature. Other girls are equally sensitive because of retarded physical development.

Adolescent girls not only disapprove of their own body's showing unusual growth or underdevelopment; they also spurn "mannish" physical characteristics in themselves or their female peers. Consequently, they often try to hide "male characteristics" such as unusual tallness, large hands, large feet, pigmented facial hair, hairiness of arms and legs, heaviness of the lower jaw, massiveness of body build, or underdeveloped breasts.

Whereas girls are worried when they seem to mature too rapidly, boys become apprehensive that their manliness may not be appearing rapidly enough. To an adolescent boy his body changes may seem excruciatingly slow. He is concerned frequently over the rate of growth of his genitals and body hair. At least 29 out of 93 adolescent boys studied at the University of California, at some time during an eight-year period, were disturbed over their physical characteristics. Greatest concern was about lack of body size, particularly height. It is significant, however, that only four of the seven boys so concerned were actually in the shortest 15 percent of the group of 29.[4]

Adolescent boys tend to stigmatize boys who exhibit feminine physical characteristics. Such traits include fat around the hips, scanty and colorless pubic hair, narrow shoulders, and fatty nipples. Some boys, at the onset of pubescence, show these traits and are anxious for them to be replaced by adult characteristics as soon as possible.

Sex-linked problems during early adolescence are quite different from those of late adolescence. Problems of early adolescence involve matters such as physical build and proportions, bashfulness, being teased by elders, and accomplishment of a first "date." In late adolescence sex-linked interests center in regular dating, selecting a mate, courtship, marriage, and participating in family life.

Since early-adolescent girls are more mature than boys of the same age, they tend to develop heterosexual interests one or two years sooner than boys. In the seventh and eighth grades boys often find themselves almost literally being dragged toward heterosexual relationships which they do not welcome. During this period girls are prone to make overtures toward boys to the point that so-called "dominant" males find their roles reversed. One of the authors vividly recalls sponsoring a party of 13-year-olds in a junior high school where he taught. Wistful females would wait in the ballroom or dance with one another while the boys were either roughhousing or consuming soft drinks.

Sexual Activity of Adolescents

By the time a primitive youth's sex drive ripens, his culture permits him to begin earning a living and to marry. In contrast, the economies,

4 See Herbert R. Stolz and Lois M. Stolz, "Adolescent Problems Related to Somatic Variation," in Nelson B. Henry, ed., *Adolescence,* Forty-third Yearbook of the National Society for the Study of Education, University of Chicago Press, 1944, pp. 85–87.

customs, and even laws of most industrialized societies make it virtually impossible for a 14- or 15-year-old boy and a 13-year-old girl to enter economic pursuits which would enable them to support a family. Even though organically there is little, if any, difference between pubescent youth of a primitive society and those of civilized society, most adolescents of civilized society are still in school preparing themselves for "the future." For them economic independence still is only a dream. Furthermore, whereas many primitive societies sanction sexual mating of youth before or at least by the time of puberty, American society attempts to ban any sexual relations until after marriage. This is six or more years after sexual maturity has been reached.

The Kinsey and other studies indicate that a large percentage of boys and many girls are active sexually in some way even prior to adolescence, and that premarital sexual relations are not uncommon in the United States. This means that there is a wide discrepancy between sanctioned, professed, and discussed sexual relations of youth and their actual behavior. A possibly harmful result of this condition is development of guilt feelings which may hamper adult heterosexual adjustment.

The Confused American Teen-Ager

Obstacles to satisfactory socialization are likely to appear in their most conspicuous form during the teen years. By this time adults expect socialization to have been substantially accomplished. If it is not, glaring inadequacies appear. Various studies have been made of the state of American teen-age minds. We have already mentioned the studies conducted at Purdue University under the direction of H. H. Remmers. A representative sampling of about 7,000 high school students were given a variety of attitude and information tests; in addition, some 2,000 students wrote letters in which they described their problems and revealed their attitudes on many matters.[5]

One conclusion to be drawn from the Purdue studies is that American youth do, after a fashion, become socialized but to a culture which in itself does not make as much sense as it should. That is to say, as youth acquire the attitudes of the adult world they do so in a way that seems to an impartial observer to be senseless, irrational, and contradictory.

For example, a sizable minority—and on some issues a substantial majority—of the sample seemed to hold attitudes more appropriate to citizens of a police state than of a democracy. Large numbers of the youth studied favored more police surveillance, more censorship, the general use of wire tapping and third-degree police methods, and the denial of free speech and the right to employ an attorney to certain categories of

[5] H. H. Remmers and D. H. Radler, *The American Teenager*, Bobbs-Merrill, 1957.

persons. The Purdue researchers felt that they uncovered evidence to support Riesman's contention that Americans are becoming increasingly "other directed"—which, in a moral sense, means more expedient.

The studies also furnished empirical evidence to support the contention that there is much inconsistency, confusion, and irrationality in the "closed areas" (see Chapter 4, pp. 107–108). In the area of religion, students exhibited a confused combination of piety and doubt. However, high school seniors appeared to hold more orthodox views about religion than did freshmen; for example, a larger proportion of seniors rejected the theory of evolution.

In the area of sex, much ambivalence and confusion was shown by the sample. A considerable proportion of teen-agers indicated that they were ashamed of their bodies and their natural functions. Although most of those who dated said that they petted on occasion, they confessed at the same time that they felt strong feelings of guilt about petting. When asked to list, in rank order, some of the "worst things which a person can do," a typical member of the Purdue sample rated "sexual misbehaving" as a more serious offense than stealing, cheating, lying, and being cruel to others.

Evidence produced by the Purdue researchers suggested that at least 10 percent of high school youth have serious emotional disorders, and that a considerably larger number, although not seriously ill, definitely need help in solving their emotional problems.

Evidently our public schools are not doing the job that is needed. Much more attention should be given to helping young people achieve well-integrated, sensible value systems. Young people come to school already in possession of a large quantity of cultural learning. Qualitatively, what they bring is appallingly inadequate. This suggests that *one of the most important functions of our schools is to help youngsters make sense out of what they have already learned.*

To this point in the chapter we have been surveying and analyzing physiological and sociological data pertinent to adolescence. Little attempt has been made to develop psychological explanations of the phenomena we have studied. Knowledge of physiological and sociological characteristics of adolescence provides basic information for treating adolescence psychologically.

WHAT IS THE PSYCHOLOGICAL MEANING OF ADOLESCENCE?

Cognitive-field psychology, an interpersonal, social psychology, provides an effective structural vehicle for the study of adolescence. Since its focal point is "individuals in relationship to groups," it is a social psychology. When we refer to it as interpersonal, we mean that the inter-relationships of persons are very important. Neither development of persons nor development of groups receives exclusive emphasis. Rather, the two processes are considered complementary. Just as groups cannot develop without persons, persons cannot develop independently of groups. The nature of persons is influenced greatly by the nature of groups with which they identify. Likewise, the nature of groups is influenced by the nature of interpersonal relations within them.

A growing number of psychologists and educators are becoming convinced that interpersonal, social factors of adolescence are as important as physiological factors, or even more so. Since the key factors of inter-personal, social situations are persons, field psychologists place psychological persons at the center of the psychological scene. Interest of field psychologists centers upon the process whereby nonpsychological factors are transformed into psychological worlds—or life spaces—of individuals. Consequently the pivotal question regarding adolescence becomes "What does adolescence mean to and for persons growing through it?"

Within cognitive-field psychology, *psychological person* is a broader concept than *biological organism*. There is a critical difference between ideas of a passive organism *in* a physical and social environment and those of an interactive person *and* his psychological environment. A person is considered interactive; he is purposively reaching out and perceiving his environment in line with his purposes at that particular time. Within the life space of an interactive person, his organism is an aspect of his environment with which he deals and simultaneously is closely identified with his self or person.

A psychologist working within a mechanistic frame of reference concentrates upon observing adolescents behaving. He studies causal relationships which can be observed and measured. He looks for such things as the correlation between different ages and speeds of growth and the position in sequence of appearance of secondary sex characteristics. Contrariwise, one who operates within an *interactive* pattern feels a necessity to *think his way* into the life spaces of adolescents—to see things as they see them. He concerns himself with formulating hypotheses as to why adolescence often is a period of storm and stress and testing these hypotheses in light of adolescents' apparently purposive actions.

From a cognitive-field point of view, psychological development is neither physical development alone nor physical development plus other factors. It is the process whereby a person with a unique organism emerges and grows through interaction with his physical and social environment. In this process organism simultaneously is environmental as well as personal. In the sense that a person identifies himself with it, it is personal. In the sense that it is something with which a person must learn to live, it is environmental.[6]

How Is the Adolescent Transition an Interactive Process?

Cognitive-field psychologists make a sharp distinction between psychological adolescence and physical pubescence. To them the social-psychological aspect of adolescence is its major feature. They recognize that changes in behavior which are supposed to characterize the adolescent period seem at first sight to provide excellent support for a biological view, and that adolescence is related to sexual hormones and to certain periods of bodily growth. However they note that, even though biological development as such is relatively the same in different societies, recent anthropological and sociological studies indicate that behavior typical of adolescent ages differs from culture to culture. Consequently, there is little value in attempting to describe generalized adolescent behavior patterns.

When we view adolescent experience as an interactive process, we emphasize the relationships between persons and groups during the adolescent age of individual youth in their respective social situations. The patterns of person-group relationships vary greatly from society to society.

The American social scene with its "adolescent difficulties" is a state of affairs within which children and adults constitute clearly defined groups, but they are separated by an extended adolescence within which group memberships are somewhat unstable. Whether, and the degree to which, youngsters display "adolescent behavior" depends upon the incidence of social-psychological conditions of conflict.

If special efforts were made early and gradually to provide increasingly mature experiences and to introduce children to their larger environment, much of what is commonly considered adolescent behavior would probably never occur. Continuity of the life spaces of children, youth, and adults would persist to the point that any semblance of "stages" would be obliterated. Growth into adulthood would be marked by its continuity; there would be no vestige of saltatory development.

Children accomplish their psychological development into adulthood through experiencing at least five kinds of changes: (1) shifts in group belongingness or identification, (2) conflicts in motivation, (3) intensification of self-awareness, (4) perplexity in regard to bodily appearance and functions, and (5) modifications of time and reality perspectives.[7]

---

[6] See Chapter 14, p. 352–353.
[7] See Kurt Lewin, *Field Theory in Social Science,* Harper, 1951, pp. 137–141.

SHIFTS IN GROUP BELONGINGNESS OR IDENTIFICATION. A social group is a dynamic whole based on the interdependence of its members. It is composed of two or more people who bear explicit psychological relationship to one another. Often people in a group are similar, but not always; it is their interdependence that makes them a group. Members of a family group—husband, wife, and children of, say, ages 9 months, 2 years, and 10 years—are less similar to each other than is a man to another man or a baby to another baby. High school boys of different racial and national background often weld themselves into a group on the basis of a feeling of similarity, which constitutes their measuring stick for group belongingness. Note that it is *feeling* of similarity, not similarity in itself, which makes a group. A youth's identifying himself with a social group means that he and other members of that group form dynamic interrelations.

Any change in belongingness from one group to another is of great importance. A shift from a child group to an adult group makes possible certain activities which previously were forbidden but now are socially permitted. It also brings to the forefront certain taboos which exist for adults but do not apply to children in the same culture. A child does not smoke cigarettes or drink beer, and most adults do. In turn, a child, when he feels like crying, may do so; an adult, according to his group standards, may cry rarely, if ever.

An adolescent may not wish to belong to a children's group any longer and at the same time realize that he is not really accepted in an adult group. The inverse condition also may exist: he may want to continue his identification with a children's group and at the same time feel himself being "pushed" into adult status. In either case he has a position similar to that of what sociologists call a *marginal* man.

A marginal man is one who stands at the boundary between two groups. He is halfway between both and a full-fledged member of neither. Thus, he is uncertain about belonging to either group and is ill at ease with both. An example of a marginal man is a second-generation immigrant who no longer is fully identified with the nationality of his parents but at the same time is not fully accepted as an "American." Characteristic symptoms of behavior of a marginal man are emotional instability and exaggerated sensitivity. To some extent, this symptomatic behavior can be found in most adolescents.

At the same time that a youth finds identity with a new group, he also experiences some degree of perplexity. His status with his peers in a group is contingent upon his conformity or nonconformity, and often he is not sure of what constitutes conformity. The shift from a children's group to an adult group entails a movement to a more or less unknown position. The degree of its being unknown depends upon the habits of the particular culture involved. Psychologically, a child's growing into adulthood is comparable to a person's moving to a new town. He does not know just what he is going to find there.

A child entering adolescence or an adolescent entering adulthood stands on shaky ground, never sure he is doing the "right" thing. The adolescent no longer wishes to belong to a group which he now recognizes as less privileged than a group of adults, but at the same time he knows he is not fully accepted by adults as one of them. Thus, he tends to be oversensitive, he easily shifts from one extreme to another, and he is particularly cognizant of shortcomings of his younger companions who are still "children."

CONFLICTS IN MOTIVATION. In modern Western society there is a more or less permanent conflict between various attitudes, values, ideologies, and styles of living of children and adults. Adolescents are caught midway in this conflict. Consequently, they experience great difficulty in defining their roles. In turn, uncertainty of their roles creates ambiguity in their motivations. They do not know when they should behave and be treated as adults and when they should continue as children. When they desire to behave like adults, they lack understanding of the adult world they are entering. Particularly if youth have been excluded from surrounding adult worlds, they are in the dark concerning them.

They have little idea of consequences of various kinds of adult behavior. Thus, broadening of life spaces to include both childhood and adult roles brings with it ambiguous situations which they often are ill equipped to handle. These conflicts and inadequacies in motivation lead adults to feel that adolescents manifest inadequate appreciation of values, emotional instabilities, tendencies to take extreme positions, and, from time to time, undue shyness and aggressiveness.

Adolescents' tasks are magnified by the basic nature of the society within which they find themselves. What they learn from books, as well as adult precepts about what they should accomplish, is laden with contradictions. A youth is urged to develop the habit of doing free reading at home; simultaneously he goes home from school loaded with busywork to be done. A boy is told that honesty always is the best policy, then hires out part-time and sees the "tricks of the trade." In experiences like these, adolescents find a great variety of conflicting religious, political, economic, and occupational values being fostered within the groups with which they identify themselves. These conflicting principles often become personalized as individual conflicts in motivation.

Because of their unstable position in regard to values, adolescents are likely to be ready to follow anyone who will offer a definite pattern of values which gives "all the answers." This is one explanation of why adolescents are particularly susceptible to conversion to absolutistic systems of thinking, which enable them to structure their fields, i.e., make sense of their personal-environmental relationships, in a rigid manner and thereby resolve their conflicts.

In a life space, everything is interrelated. Instability of a psychological environment leads in some respects to greater instability of the other major region of a life space—the person. Regions of a life space are functional areas, objects, or activities which have some meaning to the person who is involved. Both major regions—the person and his environment—include subregions. The very fact that a person in adolescence is moving from one region of his life space (A) to a new region in a subsequent life space (B) and consequently is cut loose from region A before he is established in region B puts him in an unstable position. The pattern of his person-environmental relationships is different, and he is never sure of what he is going to do next. An adolescent obtains his first full-time employment. In his job relationship everything is changed. Old habits or insights, to some unknown degree, are now inadequate for the changed situation.

The relative difference in degree of cognitive differentiation of life spaces of adolescents and adults causes adults to feel that adolescents often go to extremes. *Differentiation* refers to the functional separation of a life space into regions and subregions; subregions become regions differentiated into more subregions. Although any child's development naturally leads to experiencing previously unknown subregions in his life space, a period of transition, such as adolescence, is characterized by a more than usual impact of the emergence of subregions. However, in a new situation with its emergent subregions, the subregions are differentially structured but little, and what differentiation does exist is not as yet firm. This means that changes come relatively easily in life spaces of adolescents. Since an adolescent's life space tends to have comparatively little clear-cut differentiation into subregions, what appears to an adult to be a major shift covering many steps of restructurization may, to an adolescent, involve only one step of change. In addition, the boundaries of the subregions of an adolescent's life space are less rigid than those of an adult's life space. This makes restructurization less difficult; an adolescent is less "set in his ways."

INTENSIFICATION OF SELF-AWARENESS.   Self-awareness involves who and what a person is and what he does about it. From birth, a self is in constant process of emergence and development. However, one's awareness of himself is sharpened as he becomes more cognizant of groups with which he associates. Personalization and socialization are complementary processes. A group, although different from the persons of which it is constituted, is dependent upon those persons for its very existence. In turn, a human organism without association with any social group probably would continue merely as a biological organism; no self or person would emerge.

An adolescent is very much aware of himself. At times he experiences agonies of self-consciousness as he attempts to come to terms with a new constellation of meanings. Some evidences of adolescents' intensification of self-awareness are proneness to religious conversion, sense of futility of it all, idealism, rebellion, and cynicism. An adult might view a sloppily dressed adolescent and conclude that the youth does not care about anything. However, should he gain the complete confidence of that same adolescent, he would probably find him deeply concerned with many things, but most of all with the enhancement of a self of which he is very much aware but does not understand.

PERPLEXITY IN REGARD TO BODILY APPEARANCE AND FUNCTIONS.   Although physiological change in itself is not enough to account for the turmoil of an adolescent, his changing body with its new potential for feeling and behaving is a significant part of his life space. Body constitutes a region which is particularly close and important to an adolescent. Although people sometimes speak of their bodies and themselves as if they were identical, psychologically their bodies also are parts of their environments and are treated as such. A youth structures his body into a region of his life space in the same way that he perceives other parts of his environment. His psychological body is that which he *makes of* his biological body.

Just prior to adolescence, a child generally knows his body quite well. He knows what he can expect from it and how it will act under given circumstances. Then come the glandular and primary sexual changes of pubescence with accompanying secondary sexual changes. The individual becomes somewhat disturbed by his own body. The strange new bodily experiences cause this part of his life space, which is so close and vital to him, to become enigmatic and unknown.

The kind of perplexity arising from a change in an old environment which had been stabilized is quite different from that experienced when one enters a new environment that has never been structured. It may be compared to the feeling of a midwesterner who, arrived in California, has the experience of standing on firm earth and suddenly having it move under him.

In the case of his body, an adolescent experiences unknown and unreliable changes in regions which previously were well known and reliably staked out. Such change tends to shake his faith in the stability of the psychological ground upon which he stands, and perhaps even undermines his confidence in the world he lives in. Since one's body is a region of his life space which is very important and central for him, doubts in regard to its stability are crucial. However, as pointed out earlier, some cultures—including our own—require much more, and more difficult, restructurization of the life space of adolescents than do others.

MODIFICATIONS OF TIME AND REALITY PERSPECTIVES. Adolescence is a period of particularly deep changes in respect to time perspectives and of sharper distinctions of "reality" from "irreality." Man's "time-binding" ability is one of his most unique features. It grows from birth to adulthood, but at adolescence there is a definite expansion of its scope, paralleling that of physical growth. Whereas children consider days, weeks, or months in their goals, adolescents consider years. As one develops, more memories of a "past" and anticipations of a "future" figure in the motivation for present behavior.

One's view of the future includes his expectations, fears, and hopes. These involve a scope of time. Furthermore, one's fears and hopes and imaginations are characteristic of an "irreality" level of his life space. However, they are a part of a present life space and they influence present "reality" behavior. A child tends to make no sharp distinction between reality and irreality. In a sense, since a very young child cannot distinguish between the reality of things and the irreality of his imagination, he cannot tell a lie. However, by the time he reaches adulthood such a distinction is fairly well developed.

An adolescent, being a "marginal man" in this regard too, fluctuates between making the sharper distinctions of adults and the quite fluid differentiation of late childhood. Even though he wanted to, he would encounter great difficulty in trying to make himself believe in Santa Claus. However, this does not mean that adolescents, or adults, completely cease attributing reality to figments of the imagination. Expansion of a person's time perspective and his discrimination of reality from irreality cannot adequately be described bimodally as either-or situations; rather they are a continuum of relationships.

For a child, ideal goals and real goals for a distant future are not sharply distinguished; the future has a fluid indefinite character. An adolescent makes a more definite differentiation in regard to time perspective. He usually feels the need to structure his time perspective in such a way that his ideal goals or values and the realities of life are both taken into account in developing realistic ambitions and expectations. Thus, he is likely to distinguish between what he dreams of or wishes for and what he really expects. Vague "irreality" ideas are replaced by more or less real decisions in regard to preparation for future occupations and positions. He wants to grow up, but modern American society won't let him.

BIBLIOGRAPHY

Cole, Luella, *Psychology of Adolescence*, 5th ed., Rinehart, 1959.
   A comprehensive treatment of all aspects of adolescent development. Contains many illustrative case studies and anecdotes. Applies adolescent psychology to teaching.
Garrison, Karl C., *Psychology of Adolescence*, 5th ed., Prentice-Hall, 1956.
   A standard text for adolescent psychology. Adolescence is portrayed with a biological and social emphasis. Youth are pictured as personalities growing and developing according to their genetic constitutions and environmental factors.
Gesell, Arnold, Frances L. Ilg, and Louise B. Ames, *Youth: The Years from Ten to Sixteen*, Harper, 1956.
   A report based upon study of a selected group of adolescents. This book traces development of behavior of each age group from 10 to 16 and interprets the patterns and trends of successive stages.
Henry, Nelson B., ed., *Adolescence*, The Forty-third Yearbook of the National Society for the Study of Education, Department of Education, University of Chicago Press, 1944.
   A balance of views on adolescents which covers their physical and physiological changes, development of physical and mental abilities, and socialization.
Jersild, Arthur T., *The Psychology of Adolescence*, Macmillan, 1957.
   An attempt to integrate an "objective," a developmental, and a personal approach to the study of adolescence. Focuses upon the adolescent as a person and his discovery and acceptance of himself.
Lewin, Kurt, "Field Theory and Experiment in Social Psychology: Concepts and Method," *American Journal of Sociology*, May, 1939, pp. 868–896. (Also *Field Theory in Social Science*, Harper, 1951, Chap. VI.)
   Discussion of the problem of adolescence and the social group concept provides examples of how it is necessary to represent the dynamics of a total situation to explain social behavior.
Loomis, Mary Jane, *The Preadolescent; Three Major Concerns*, Appleton-Century-Crofts, 1959.
   Points of focus of the personal-social development of preadolescents: aspiring to greater independence, striving for sexual identification, and anticipating junior high school living.
Mead, Margaret, *Coming of Age in Samoa*, Blue Ribbon Books, 1928.
   A psychological study of the youth of Samoa. Comparison of Samoan youth with youth in "civilized" societies permits some deductions about "natural" behaviors.
Seidman, Jerome M., ed., *The Adolescent—A Book of Readings*, rev. ed., Holt, Rinehart and Winston, 1960.
   A broad selection of excellent outside readings by specialists in adolescent psychology. Includes adolescent transition, growth and development, peer group relations, multiple-group membership, interests and attitudes, and problems.

A Study of Adolescent Boys, conducted by Survey Research Center, Institute for Social Research, University of Michigan, for the National Council, Boy Scouts of America, University of Michigan and Boy Scouts of America, 1956. A report of a national survey of 14- to 16-year old boys. It analyzes dominant needs, problems, and concerns; kinds and amount of leisure-time activities; group membership and relationships; and sources of motivation of the boys.

9

WHAT ARE "NEEDS" AND "DEVELOPMENTAL TASKS" OF CHILDREN AND YOUTH?

Children achieve much of their development through their experiences in school. For teachers to make their maximum contribution, they must have a basis for determining the nature of desirable school experiences. It is generally assumed that educational experiences will be designed to foster the *needs* or achieve the *developmental tasks* of students.

The term *needs* holds a prominent place in the minds and vocabularies of a great many American educators. Whenever problems involving educational objectives, curriculum, pupil growth, or learning are treated, the word *needs* usually appears, especially when these problems are approached from a motivational or developmental point of view.

As its use has expanded, the concept of needs has come to be increasingly ambiguous. On one hand it has meant the basic needs of a child himself which must be met if he is to develop adequately. Emphasis upon needs in this sense entails a child-centered approach to the study of development; and development is considered a process of natural unfoldment of innate patterns of behavior and characteristics. In its extreme form, this use of the concept leads to educational anarchy—no government or order—and overindulgence of children.

On the other hand, needs may mean deficiencies in children which society feels must be corrected for the health of society. When needs are considered only societal, a teacher is likely to become a despot, even though a benevolent one. Such interpretation results in authoritarian situations where adult goals are imposed upon children.

Needs sometimes are centered intermittently in individual organisms and in society. Cole and Bruce ably present needs from such a biosocial approach.[1]

Some educational leaders, who have struggled with definitions such as these, have come to the conclusion that a more advantageous concept should be developed to replace that of needs. Consequently, an alternative concept, *developmental tasks*, has emerged in current educational literature. This concept was designed to occupy a middle ground between the two opposite theories of development and learning: ". . . the theory of freedom—that the child will develop best if left as free as possible, and the theory of restraint—that the child must learn to become a worthy responsible adult through restraints imposed by society. A developmental task is midway between an individual need and a societal demand."[2]

The concept of developmental tasks strikes a compromise between the theory of "basic needs," or natural unfoldment through instinct, and the theory of societal determination of children's needs. It is supposed to represent both opposing approaches in such a way as to close the gap between them. However, in practice the developmental-tasks emphasis has tended toward a teacher- or society-centered school. The way adults have listed developmental tasks implies that the tasks hold true for *all* children and youth. Since the developmental-tasks concept has been concerned primarily with curricular matters, it, alone, has had no direct implications for teaching procedure. These tasks are systems of behavior which can be "taught" in more or less authoritarian fashion, as can the subject matter of a traditional curriculum.

Now, what should be our standards for determination of desirable student experiences or behaviors? Should standards be in terms of needs as traditionally defined (either child- or adult-centered), in terms of developmental tasks, or in some still different terms? There is a fourth alternative, to be explored later in the chapter—the cognitive-field alternative, which does not discard but redefines needs.

WHAT ARE NEEDS?

Child psychologists and educators, in attempting to arrive at a psychological foundation for educational programs, have assumed that there

---

[1] See Lawrence E. Cole and William F. Bruce, *Educational Psychology*, World Book, 1958, pp. 231–247.
[2] Robert G. Havighurst, *Human Development and Education*, Longmans, Green, 1953, p. 332.

is some objective means of determining "needs" of children and youth. Once these needs have been determined, they have become the basis for selection of experiences and kinds of subject matter to be included in a curriculum. In a "needs curriculum," needs and objectives of education have been virtually synonymous. Often the primary objective of education is said to be "to meet the needs of children." It is essential, therefore, that teachers clearly understand the possible meanings and inadequacies of the term.

Although school personnel and psychologists generally agree that needs somehow are associated with motivation and goal-seeking behavior, there is a lack of accord in regard to the source and nature of needs. This perplexity arises from the fact that needs cannot be observed directly; they are theoretical explanations for observed behavior and must be inferred from watching children and youth in various situations.

People who make great use of the term *needs* often overlook the fact that need is a hypothetical construct. Murray says, " 'Need' is therefore a hypothetical concept.... It is a resultant of forces, one need succeeds another. . . . Thus, we may loosely use the term 'need' to refer to an organic potentiality or readiness to respond in a certain way under given conditions. In this sense a need is a latent attribute of an organism. More strictly, it is a noun which stands for the fact that a certain trend is apt to recur."[3]

When need is considered as something other than a hypothetical construct, there is a tendency for users to accept validity of the concept as self-evident and make no attempt at careful definition. *Needs*, so used, conceals existing differences in its definition. Attempts are made to explain pertinent psychological phenomena by classifying them as various kinds of needs, as if this provided an adequate explanation.

WHERE ARE NEEDS CENTERED?

The varied and sometimes ambiguous use of *needs* has permitted the term to appear extensively in treating the problem of development from several conflicting points of view, as we have indicated. If a child is regarded as an unfolding organism or mind going through a series of stages each with its own unique needs, his needs are deemed child-centered. If he is seen as a passive organism, his needs are assumed to be environment- or adult-centered. When a child is studied as a psychological person in a life space, as in cognitive-field psychology, needs become situation- or child-environment-centered.

[3] Henry A. Murray, *Explorations in Personality,* Oxford University Press, 1938, pp. 60–61.

Are Needs Child-Centered?

Needs have been defined by Mursell as "permanent trends of human nature which underlie human behavior from birth to death under all circumstances and in all kinds of societies."[4] Needs defined in this way are child-centered. Persons who accept this frame of reference reason that the constant pressure of basic needs gives general direction to all human purposes, even though there is great variety in the outcomes which ensue.

When this outlook is translated into a theory of education, needs, i.e., inherited structural, physiological, and psychological drives, become the basis of statements of objectives. There is assumed to be much therapeutic and educational value in the untrammeled expression of native impulses arising from basic needs. School experiences are selected and organized according to needs of the students—for example, needs for love, security, belongingness, etc. Children's interests are assumed to be the most valid indications of their needs.

With this approach some adults are wary of correcting children for fear they will inhibit expression of some basic need and cause a permanent trauma in personality. Therefore, they believe, children should be allowed to unfold according to nature even though this may lead to their dancing on the dining-room table or destroying a neighbor's fence. Of course, there are much less extreme positions which a believer in inborn needs may take, and the total permissiveness suggested above is practiced by very few teachers. However, the over-all outlook is essentially that of Roussellian romantic naturalism.

Are Needs Environment- or Adult-Centered?

Again, needs might be interpreted to mean largely necessities of which children are unaware. Educators may think that children have a broad need for preparing for adult life and that only adults are in a position to analyze and understand this need. Thus, adults should identify the most pressing societal needs and see to it that children are educated to be able to meet them. Granted that needs of children and youth should be the basis for their education, adults alone are best able to determine their nature and to specify the order in which they are introduced.

In many primitive societies, practices which deform and distort bodies of children and youth are regarded by adults as necessary if children are to develop as prescribed by the society. These practices have included flattening babies' heads, stretching lips and ears, circling necks with coils of metal, binding feet, and piercing ears. Similarly, various societies have

4 James L. Mursell, *Psychology for Modern Education,* Norton, 1952, p. 48.

rigidly channeled patterns of elimination, sleeping, eating, and breathing. Although contemporary "civilized" societies perpetuate only a minimum of physical distortion of the bodies of children and youth, it may be contended that psychological distortion is still rampant. Children may be forced to conform to behavior patterns which for some reason have gained respectability within a society but which make little contribution to happy, adequate living. The strict sex-linked mores of many "civilized" societies may be cited as an example. Some of the coercive elements of American culture are discussed in detail in Chapter 4.

Are Needs Situation- or Child-Environment-Centered?

If needs are situation-centered, they are not centered in a child or in his environment, either concurrently or recurrently, but in a child-environment interactive situation. Interaction is the key idea in explanation of situation- or child-environment-centered needs. Interaction is the process by which a person in relation to his culture develops goals and seeks to use himself and the culture in such way as to achieve these goals.

In the latter part of this chapter, we expand the definition of needs as child-environment- or situation-centered. To the authors, this manner of defining needs has advantages over the others. But first let us examine some listings of child- and environment-centered needs and of developmental tasks which supposedly are an improvement over the original ideas of needs.

WHAT ARE SOME POPULAR FORMULATIONS OF NEEDS?

In recent years many different lists of needs have been formulated and classified. Indeed, we seem to be pushed toward the conclusion that needs are infinite in number and greatly varied in expression, and that perhaps no single list of needs will suffice. A representative list is that presented by Daniel A. Prescott. He interprets "need" to mean that which children require for the promotion of their mental health and for the development of normally adjusted personalities.

Prescott's method of arriving at these needs was to ask himself, "Just what is a child or young person trying to accomplish by each item of *observed* behavior?" He made a broad survey of human nature in action and attempted to understand and explain the spectacle. He does not attempt to set up a rigid framework of concepts into which all behavior must be fitted; rather, he emphasizes that behavior has a unity which transcends its arising out of mutually exclusive categories of drives. Thus, he thinks that various needs do not operate independently of each other.

He also states that needs are related to culture and vary from one culture to another.

Prescott lists three major categories of needs of developing children: physiological needs, social or status needs, and ego or integrative needs.

I. Physiological needs—needs that spring primarily out of structure and dynamic biochemical equilibria.
   A. Essential materials and conditions
      1. air
      2. appropriate food and liquids
      3. adequate clothing and shelter
      4. regular and adequate bodily elimination
      5. avoidance of poisons and debilitative substances
   B. Rhythm of activity and rest
      1. muscular activity
      2. affectively vivid experience
      3. habits of sufficient and conscious relaxation
   C. Sexual activity
II. Social or status needs—describe relationship that it is essential to establish with other persons in our culture.
   A. Affection
   B. Belonging
   C. Likeness to others
III. Ego or integrative needs—needs for organization and symbolization of experience so that the individual may discover and adequately play his role in life.
   A. Contact with reality
   B. Harmony with reality
   C. Progressive symbolization
      1. organize experience
      2. establish logical arrangement of ideas
      3. arrive at general concepts
      4. development of language—verbal and postural
   D. Increasing self-direction
   E. A fair balance between success and failure
   F. Attainment of selfhood or individuality.[5]

Lawrence K. Frank developed a somewhat similar list of "The Fundamental Needs of Children." A child needs

1. To be protected from unnecessary pain, deprivation, and exploitation.
2. To be accepted as an unique individual.
3. To be allowed to grow at his own rate.
4. Emotional satisfaction in feeding during infancy.
5. Constant reassurance during toilet training.
6. Extra affection when the new baby arrives.
7. Help in regulating his emotional responses.
8. Help in accepting his or her own sex.
9. Help in learning how to behave toward persons and things.

[5] Daniel Alfred Prescott, *Emotion and the Educative Process*, American Council on Education, 1938, pp. 114–125.

10. Help in accepting authority.
11. The affectionate personal interest of an adult in order to create a constructive ideal of self.
12. Wisely administered regulation or direction.
13. Education that does not arouse hostility and aggression.
14. A clear-cut definition of a situation and of the appropriate conduct.
15. The warmth of mothering at home and in school.
16. Help in meeting life tasks.[6]

Frank sees fundamental needs of children as being also fundamental needs of society. He emphasizes that the fundamental needs of a child are not his organic requirements but the psychological needs he develops during socialization and culturization as his personality emerges. Frank thinks that people working with children should study and understand child growth and development in order to discover a child's needs as a basis for his education and nurture.

In any culture it is quite difficult to separate physical from psychological needs. Thus, it seems more reasonable to think of both as forming a continuum. Since means and ends are so much a part of one another, the meaning of any need is found in the means for satisfying it. For example, need for food is generally accepted as a biological need; yet, because of cultural or societal attitudes toward food and its ingestion, it is also a psychological need. To some Oriental peoples, even though they were starving, cheese would not be food. A plate of roasted grasshoppers, a delicacy in some cultures, would not be food to most people in the United States.

Since "needs" denote organic or psychological necessities or social expectations, perhaps the term is not adequate for what we are attempting to describe. A need is organic, social, or psychological. What seems to be called for is a term meaning a bio-socio-psychological developmental unit.

WHAT ARE DEVELOPMENTAL TASKS?

The concept of developmental tasks was developed by Robert J. Havighurst, working with the University of Chicago Committee on Human Development. A developmental task covers a combination of a personally felt need and a societal demand—both of which were previously included in conflicting definitions of needs—and is midway between the two. Note that this term arose as a *compromise* between two supposedly less adequate concepts, both of them expressed by the term *needs*. Being rooted partially in innate needs and partially in the demands of a culture, it represents a functional recognition that children live in a

[6] Lawrence K. Frank, "The Fundamental Needs of Children," *Mental Hygiene,* July, 1938, pp. 353–379.

social world. However, it does not necessarily imply interaction between a child and his social environment. Rather, advocates of the developmental-tasks concept see tasks centered partially in the organism, partially in the social environment, and partially in personal relationships.

Havighurst explains that a developmental task arises at, or about, a certain period in the life of a person. Successful achievement of a task opens the way to happiness and success with later tasks; failure leads to disapproval by society, unhappiness in the individual, and difficulty with later tasks.[7]

Developmental tasks are criteria for behavior which represent satisfactory growth within a culture. There are assumed to be biological, psychological, and sociological bases for determining which tasks are essential for a particular stage of development. The developmental tasks of a child of a certain age have a direct bearing upon the instructional tasks of teachers dealing with that age. Thus, developmental tasks should influence the role of a school in helping children and youth to form mature patterns of behavior for their respective ages.

From birth until death, according to Havighurst, there are developmental tasks—certain learnings or adjustments—which each person must achieve to make normal progress in growth and development. Two developmental tasks of childhood in our society are learning to read in the lower grades and learning to practice the social graces considered appropriate to one's stage of development.

The concept of developmental tasks seems to offer greatest usefulness when it is applied to the adolescent years. A typical youth needs to make rather large changes in outlook and life style within a few years, often without adequate sense of direction. According to Havighurst, the developmental tasks of adolescents are

1. Achieving new and more mature relations with age mates of both sexes.
2. Achieving a masculine or feminine social role.
3. Accepting one's physique and using one's body effectively.
4. Achieving emotional independence of parents and other adults.
5. Achieving assurance of economic independence.
6. Selecting and preparing for an occupation.
7. Preparation for marriage and family life.
8. Developing intellectual skills and concepts necessary for civic competence.
9. Desiring and achieving socially responsible behavior.
10. Acquiring a set of values and an ethical system as a guide to behavior.[8]

These developmental tasks manifest certain common characteristics: they are necessary learnings of great variety, opportunity to achieve them

---

[7] Robert J. Havighurst, *Human Development and Education,* Longmans, Green, 1953, p. 2.

[8] *Ibid.,* pp. 111–158. (Each of these tasks is elaborated in the book.)

occurs only during restricted time intervals, they are common to all youth, and they define areas of concern to adolescents.

Havighurst sees the prototype of a developmental task as a purely biological formation of organs in the embryo. In developing this idea he quotes from Erik Erikson:

> In this development each organ has its time of origin and this time factor is as important as the place of origin. If the eye, for example, does not arise at the appointed time . . . it will never be able to express itself fully, since the moment for the rapid outgrowth of some other part will have arrived, and this will tend to dominate the less active region, and suppress the belated tendency for eye expression. . . . The organ which misses its time of ascendancy is doomed not only as an individual, it endangers at the same time the whole hierarchy of organs. . . . Through developmental arrest one or more organs may become disproportionately small; this upsets functional harmony and produces a defective person.[9]

Accordingly, Havighurst thinks that "These purely biological developmental tasks of the body illustrate the essentials of the bio-socio-psychological tasks with which we are concerned. If the task is not achieved at the proper time it will not be achieved well, and failure in this task will cause partial or complete failure in the achievement of other tasks yet to come."[10] Just as there is a unique time and place for development of the various organs in a human fetus, so there are equally crucial times for certain aspects of personality development in the first years of life. For example, there is a time to change from liquid to solid foods, a time to become interested in one's genitals, and a time to learn bowel control.

When schools reflect the implications of the developmental-tasks concept, they must provide situations in which students can accomplish their tasks satisfactorily to themselves and to society. Mastery of the tasks of each period is the prerequisite for mastery of the tasks of the succeeding period. Failure to achieve the tasks of childhood supposedly means that later social adjustments will be inadequate and the cause of unhappiness. Advocates of the developmental-tasks concept think that, once they understand the stages of development through which children pass and the tasks germane to each stage, they can build a system of education which will nurture emotional, social, and intellectual growth and adjustment of each child.

Developmental tasks result from maturational changes in children's bodies, pressure of cultural processes of society acting upon individuals, and desires, aspirations, and values of emerging personalities. Walking is an example of a task arising mainly through physical maturation. Learning to participate in a society as a responsible citizen is a task

[9] Erik Erikson, *Childhood and Society,* Norton, 1950, pp. 61–62.
[10] Havighurst, *op. cit.,* p. 3.

resulting primarily from societal pressures. The level of a person's physical maturity is a vital factor in determining his dominant motivation and the order of his developmental tasks. Adequate development of each child necessitates his working at many tasks not found in a conventional school curriculum. More than half of Havighurst's list of tasks ordinarily are not included in classroom subjects, yet they are essential to adequate development of children and thus should be a concern of schools. All curriculum changes, Havighurst assumes, should proceed from the common premise that only to the extent that a curriculum conforms to the developmental tasks of children can it foster mental health of those children.

Some proponents of the developmental-tasks concept think of the forming of a critical outlook and the process of critical thinking as important developmental tasks of adolescence. The implication seems to be that children should be left uncritical until adolescence or later and then be taught to become critical. This point of view overlooks the fact that children generally are thoughtful and reflective—interactive—each on his own level, from the time of birth (and, for all we know, from even earlier). Hence, although youth are urged to learn to think for themselves at the adolescent stage, a stamp of approval is placed upon traditional teacher-centered procedures in dealing with children up to the age when they are supposedly capable of critical thinking.

The concept of developmental tasks encompasses aspects of bio-socio-psychological development, but in a rather mechanistic, authoritarian fashion. The tasks are teacher- or society-determined steps through which schools are expected to take students at proper times. The concept is beneficial in consideration of objectives of education. However, its implications for educational methodology and teacher-student relationships may be seriously challenged.

HOW MAY NEEDS BE DEFINED MORE ADEQUATELY?

The term *needs* does not have to be superseded or discarded; it can be redefined in such a way that its use will be less ambiguous and more effective. Cognitive-field psychologists have attempted to do just this. Kurt Lewin conceived of need as a nucleus around which other psychological concepts are clustered; it has ". . . somewhat the connotation of a demand for something regarded by the person as more or less essential for himself."[11] A need is equal to a psychological tension which is manifested in goal-seeking behavior; thus, each person is aware of needs even though he may be unable fully to verbalize them. Since needs arise from the

[11] Robert W. Leeper, *Lewin's Topological and Vector Psychology,* University of Oregon, 1943, p. 212.

interaction of a person and his psychological environment, they are as individualized and unique as the numerous interactive situations through which a person lives.

No one with a cognitive-field point of view would attempt to list the basic needs which all human beings now are, always have been, and always will be attempting to satisfy. Such a listing would have to be broad enough to cover motivations of all people in all cultures during all times. Although, within a culture, some degree of commonality of needs exists, it is not usually in the area of common cultural needs that a teacher faces his crucial problems in dealing with children.

The One Basic Need

Should we attempt to define one basic need which would encompass all other varied human needs, it would be stated as a need "for the maintenance and enhancement of the self."[12] Specific needs arising in the course of maintenance and enhancement of a self take many forms. As a child grows, his needs constantly change in kind and intensity. Crises in development are periods of unusually rapid or marked changes in needs. The changing constellation of one's needs parallels the changing organization of his behavior.

In earlier chapters we discussed the biological "wisdom of the body." We have seen that a biological organism, through homeostatic processes, seems to attempt to maintain its normal organization against all external and internal disrupting agencies. Speaking now in psychological terms, persons likewise exhibit the tendency to preserve and enhance their psychological selves as they see or experience them. It is in connection with protection of the "I" or "me"—psychological self—that psychological needs arise.

There is some degree of similarity between the various lists of universal needs which have been compiled and the psychological needs of any one person, but we cannot assume anything like a one-to-one relationship between the two. Furthermore, while it is true that a need, as ascertained by a specialist, may be a real need although it is not felt at all by the person involved—as in the case of certain physiological needs—for a need to be a psychological need the person must feel it as such. A crucial function of teaching is helping students sense their needs and verbalize them. We emphasize that the nature of a person's psychological needs is very often unclear to him; he feels unrest or anxiety but does not know why. In such instances a person can do something to satisfy his need only after he clearly formulates its nature. As a motivational device, a teacher may

12 See Arthur W. Combs and Donald Snygg, *Individual Behavior,* rev. ed., Harper, 1959, p. 58.

deliberately promote a feeling of tension in students. This idea is elaborated in Chapter 18.

Teachers with a cognitive-field orientation, instead of using needs as a starting point for education, should educate people to discover, define, and realize their own needs. As defined by a cognitive-field psychologist, psychological needs are not activated or aroused either by internal changes within an organism or by stimulus events in the environment of an organism. Consequently, they cannot be determined from a study of individuals alone or from a study of environments alone, but only from a study of individuals as they interact with their environments.

Psychological Ecology

In recent years, a group of field psychologists, in studying the relationships of children to their school environments, have developed a fertile concept: psychological ecology.[13] Ecology, biologically defined, means the interrelations between organisms and their environments. Psychological ecology involves the task of determining the physical-biological-social world with which a person seems to be surrounded and of understanding the way in which aspects of this world are transformed into a psychological environment.

A teacher, to teach adequately, ought to know about actual life conditions of *individual* pupils in his classroom and about the specific *behavior settings* that influence actions of each of them. "A behavior setting is a discriminable part of the whole physical and social milieu of community that has within it certain generally seen possibilities for human action."[14] This means that a behavior setting is any part of an environment that is generally perceived, by the people of a community, as appropriate for particular kinds of behavior.

Every behavior setting has two sides. On the one side there is always a set of environmental raw materials for behavior. These may be physical or social or both. On the other side of a setting there is always the set of possibilities for action that are seen by the generality of persons living in the community as "what you do there," as "fitting," or "appropriate." . . . A complete psychological ecology of the classroom must describe both the environmental raw materials and the generally seen things-to-do of this setting in different communities and cultures. . . . Behavior settings are coercive. Every adult who has yelled at a ball game, bowed his head at church, ridden all day on a train, or listened at a concert knows this to be true. So does every child who has sat tight in his assigned seat in his classroom. With frequent and important exceptions, in any behavior setting different persons do like things in similar ways.[15]

[13] Herbert F. Wright *et al.,* "Toward a Psychological Ecology of the Classroom," in William E. Martin and Celia Burns Stendler, eds., *Readings in Child Development,* Harcourt, Brace, 1954, pp. 428–436.

[14] *Ibid.,* p. 429.

[15] *Ibid.,* pp. 429–430.

A behavior setting provides and limits opportunity for persons within it to do various things.

> . . . It has to be recognized, however, that there is no binding dynamical relationship between behavior setting and human action. In any setting anything *can* happen—as a teacher facing a classroom full of children knows well. For, at bottom, what the person does in a behavior setting, the classroom or any other, depends upon his own goals and paths or obstacles; upon his own needs and abilities. It depends, in all, upon the forces in quite another zone of influence than the world of behavior settings. This other world is the naturally occurring life space, the relevant context of everyday behavior, which we have called the *psychological habitat* of the person. This world includes conditions in both the person and the environment, the environmental part of it lies between the person and the raw physical and social materials, together with the generally seen things to do, of the behavior setting. The coercive effect of a setting upon behavior, then, is indirect. It stems only from the fact that every setting tends to bring about certain psychological habitats rather than others.[16]

Needs, Situationally Defined

The concept *psychological ecology* harmonizes with the *situational* approach of cognitive-field psychology to the problem of human needs. A human life may be considered to consist of a series of distinguishable person-environment transactions. Neither objective physical factors nor objective social factors in the environment have a one-to-one psychological relation to a child. Thus, there is no known way that a child can experience the absolute nature of things in themselves. What one experiences is *that which he makes* of what comes to him as he pursues his various goals.

It is in connection with personal goals that needs enter the scene. A need is a state of a person which, when it exists in relation to a goal, induces behavior toward that goal. The state of a person in itself does not cause behavior; part of the environment—a perplexity or a goal—also must be operative before a psychological situation can exist. When a person is perplexed, he feels it necessary to do something but has no good idea what to do; he has a need even though he has not yet formulated a goal in relation to the need.

A person's living in a world entails his living in a series of situations. *In,* as used here, has a distinctly different meaning from *in* when used in regard to beans in a can or money in a purse. It is more like the meaning of a bee in a swarm. A person is *in* a situation and the situation is *in* the person. Interaction is taking place between the two—the person and what at that time constitutes his psychological environment.

In a psychological situation needs and goals, although not identical, are closely interrelated. A child's behavior may be described either as his

[16] *Ibid.,* p. 430.

trying to reach his environment-centered goals or as his trying to satisfy his person-centered needs. Goals and needs are in no sense mutually exclusive. Goal achievement and need satisfaction are accomplished through the same process of intelligent action.

A situational study of the origin of needs and their effect on conduct is more important, more complex, and perhaps more difficult to understand than ordinarily has been assumed to be the case. A field or situational use of the concept *needs* is sufficiently important to justify development of some specialized technical ideas to aid us in identifying and understanding the factors and relationships involved. A cognitive-field psychologist is convinced that problems concerning origin of motives cannot be solved adequately by studying only the physiological or physical origins of needs. Needs cannot be ascertained and identified through mere observation of facial expressions, startle reactions, visceral changes, and electrochemical responses. Neither can they be found simply by observing gross behavior of children.

What Are Sources of Needs?

The question of how needs arise in the long-range history and in the momentary situations of a person is basic in the psychology of children and youth. New needs, or, more correctly, changed needs, may result from a great variety of circumstances. A child, seeing that his friend thinks highly of certain actions, comes to value them himself. A high school freshman's attendance at a class party significantly changes his needs in regard to his social manners. Behavior in a specific situation usually stems from a combination of several needs, a "derived need." During his lifetime a person's needs constantly change in intensity and degree of differentiation. Nevertheless, many of his needs and other features of his successive life spaces remain the same over long periods of time, e.g., a boy's liking for fried chicken. This latter tendency is called a "continuity of life spaces." However, there are periods of crisis in development when quick and striking changes in needs occur, even in those needs for which a high level of continuity had been established.

NEEDS AND THE CULTURE. Cognitive-field psychologists regard traditional separations of organism from environment, individual from society, and a personality from his culture as false or at least misleading in their consequences. They place great emphasis upon individuality, but they also consider it a truism that individual needs are closely related to social influences. The culture in which a child grows affects, but does not determine, practically every one of his needs. Needs of a growing child are changed and new needs induced through influence of the social groups with which he identifies himself. His needs also are influenced by ideologies of groups to which he would like to belong and of those from which he desires to be set apart.

Thus, throughout a situational approach to needs, it is recognized that without a culture or society a human being probably would be devoid of personality and of psychological needs. The matrix of each personality and its needs consists of the customs, beliefs, attitudes, values, and habits of the group within which a child grows. The form which needs take, however, depends upon how individuals interact with the institutionalized behaviors of a culture.

NEEDS AND VALUES.   A child's person-centered needs and abilities parallel his environment-centered goals and valences. To speak of needs as centered in person and goals and valences as centered in environment does not mean that they are *located* in these respective places. They are located in a situation or life space—both person and environment. Centeredness means closer identity with one than with the other. Valence is an "imperative environmental fact." It is a property of a region—functional part —of one's life space which psychologically draws the person toward it or impels him away from it. Valences, contrasted with needs, which are person-focused, are focused in environment. When a boy has a strong need for a bicycle, the valence of a bicycle is high. *Valence* and *value* are similar concepts.

Although needs and valences contrast in being focused respectively in person and environment, they are very closely related. The valence of a certain object or activity depends partly upon its nature and partly upon the state of the relevant needs of the person at the time. Any statement regarding change of needs can be expressed by a statement about certain positive and negative valences. An increase in the intensity of need (for instance, the need for recreation) leads to an increase in the positive valence of certain activities (going to the movies or reading a book) and to an increase in the negative valence of certain other activities (doing hard work).

NEEDS AND TENSION.   "A need corresponds to a tension system of the inner-personal region of a life space."[17] The inner-personal region of a life space consists of matters which are most vital to the person. His cognitive (knowing) and manipulative (doing) abilities functionally are located between his needs and his environment. These abilities are used in development of understandings of, and relationships to, the person's environment.[18]

Psychological needs do not arise within an organism or from an environ-

17 Kurt Lewin, *Principles of Topological Psychology*, McGraw-Hill, 1936, p. 218.
18 See Chapter 14, pp. 356–360.

ment, but only through one's interaction with his environment. Through perception and manipulation of environment, a person delineates tasks for himself—he develops tensions and needs. The intensity of tensions corresponds to the degree of needs. Changing of goals or removal of barriers to a goal, as well as reaching a goal, can bring release of a tension. Whereas a task not completed perpetuates a state of tension, satisfaction of a need is accompanied by a release of tension.

Some interesting studies have been made of the tension involved when a person is interrupted in the course of tasks rather than being permitted to complete them. Results of the studies show the *Zeigarnik effect*—superior recall of uncompleted tasks.[19] Miss Zeigarnik performed the pioneer study at the University of Berlin in 1927. Since then several similar studies have confirmed her findings.

Zeigarnik gave each of 138 people a series of 20 simple tasks such as molding an animal from clay. Each person was permitted to finish half the tasks. On each of the remaining half of the tasks he was "accidentally" interrupted before the task could be completed. The task was left unfinished and he went to the next. When the twentieth task had been attempted each person was asked to recall all of the tasks.

Eighty percent of the subjects recalled more uncompleted tasks, 12 percent recalled more completed tasks, and 8 percent recalled both kinds equally. This finding indicates that greater tension in regard to a task remains when a person has not completed it. On the whole 1.6 as many uncompleted as completed tasks were recalled. This suggests that a teacher who tries to "complete" a class lesson each day is violating a fundamental psychological principle.

A person tries to achieve an equilibrium of tensions within his life space. However, a system cannot come to equilibrium in a state of tension. If a psychological person were completely devoid of tension, his biological organism would be in a state of thermodynamic equilibrium—a biological definition of death.

A need leads not only to actual physical locomotion toward a goal but also to thinking about this type of activity. In psychological locomotion, a person selects alternatives, examines possibilities, develops goals, tries routes to goals, and experiences successes and frustrations. The intention to carry out a certain action is somewhat equivalent to the creation of a need. As long as a particular need is not satisfied there is a strong tendency toward action in the direction of the goal.

A need may be satisfied either by reaching the desired goal or by reaching a substitute goal. Any changes of goals depend largely upon the interdependence of needs. A general psychological assumption is that when a

[19] See W. C. H. Prentice, "The Interruption of Tasks," *Psychological Review*, November, 1944, pp. 329–340.

need exists in relation to a certain goal, a corresponding force causes movement toward that goal. Conversely, when no need exists in relation to an object or activity, there is nothing to direct movement in this direction. When a child finds himself in what seems to be a strict obedience situation, because he is not involved, he has no needs; in this situation, he shows little tendency to resume an activity if it is interrupted.

Needs commonly emerge in relation to one's psychological future or past. If the effects of the needs of an individual's psychological *future* are particularly great, we speak of him as an unrealistic person, a daydreamer. Some extreme forms of the relation of needs to the structure of a psychological past are rationalization, repression, and lying. These commonly are called defense mechanisms, psychological devices which individuals use in defense and support of their selves or persons. Rationalization is a process whereby a person, by cognitive distortion, develops acceptable reasons for his questionable acts. He may have traded his two-year-old car for a new one because it was "cheaper" than putting new tires on the old car.

Evidence of repression is inability to recall an unpleasant or highly emotional experience. One's needs are served through his inability to remember certain events. Lying, on the part of a young child, often seems to mean an actual change in his psychological past to bring it in harmony with his present needs. Young children, however, do not make sharp distinctions between levels of reality and irreality; a child's lying, observed by an adult, often is not lying as the child sees it.

There are other interesting examples of how the cognitive structure of a life space is influenced by needs. Murray found that faces of other people appear more malicious to children already in a state of fear than normally.[20] McDonald found that pictures without definite meanings will be seen according to the mood of the child.[21] Carter and Schooler found that if selected samples of rich and poor children were asked to estimate the size of coins from memory, poor children rather consistently overestimated whereas rich children did not.[22] The investigators regarded this finding as evidence that, because of their needs, poor children experienced coins in exaggerated fashion, compared with children for whom money did not have such pressing importance.

Within a situational approach to needs it is beneficial to have in mind a few broad categories of needs which children and youth in American

[20] Henry A. Murray, *Explorations in Personality,* Oxford University Press, 1938.
[21] William Stern and Jean MacDonald, "Cloud Pictures: A New Method of Testing Imagination," *Character and Personality,* Vol. 8, 1937, pp. 132–147.
[22] L. F. Carter and K. Schooler, "Value, Need, and Other Factors in Perception," *Psychological Review,* July, 1949, pp. 200–207.

society probably will develop. Lee J. Cronbach, a professor of educational psychology at the University of Illinois, thinks that almost all problems of school children relate to needs for affection, for adult approval, for peer approval, for independence, and for self-respect.[23] These needs grow out of attempts to maintain and enhance the self; they become a reality only as a person interacts with his psychological environment.

BIBLIOGRAPHY

Barker, Roger G., and Herbert F. Wright, *Midwest and Its Children, The Psychological Ecology of an American Town*, Row, Peterson, 1956.
A report of research conducted in a midwestern town. Describes ecological methods for psychological study of interpersonal, social living. Human behavior is studied in a psychological habitat. Interactions are recorded.

Bode, Boyd H., *Progressive Education at the Crossroads*, Newson, 1938.
Discussion of "The Concept of Need," still timely (Chap. IV). Other chapters support an interaction frame of reference for "needs."

Fullagar, William A., and others, *Readings for Educational Psychology*, Crowell, 1956.
An explanation of the developmental-tasks concept and of needs, by experts in these fields—the first by Robert J. Havighurst, Chapter 14; the second by Lawrence K. Frank, Chapter 15.

Havighurst, Robert J., *Human Development and Education*, Longmans, Green, 1953.
An overview of developmental tasks of childhood, adolescence, and adulthood. It explains the meaning of the developmental-tasks concept for education and describes success and failure in developmental tasks of middle childhood and adolescence.

Lewin, Kurt, *Field Theory in Social Science*, Harper, 1951.
Situational treatment of needs within a field frame of reference (pp. 273–297). Needs arise through a relation between a person and his psychological environment. Kinds of needs, changes in needs, and possibilities of satisfying them also are discussed.

Montagu, M. F. Ashley, *The Direction of Human Development*, Harper, 1955.
A development of the thesis that under cultural conditions no basic need can function as a purely physiological one, and that cultural patterns and values are intimately associated with needs (Chaps. 6 and 7).

Murray, Henry A., *Explorations in Personality*, Oxford University Press, 1938.
A classic, giving one of the more adequate earlier treatments of the concept *need* (pp. 54–129). Need is seen as a hypothetical process and a dynamic concept.

[23] See Lee J. Cronbach, *Educational Psychology*, Harcourt, Brace, 1954, pp. 100–112.

Prescott, Daniel Alfred, *Emotion and the Education Process,* American Council on Education, 1938.

> Explanation of the thesis that the structure of an organism, the processes of society, and the nature of a person's experiences give rise to a series of needs which are the basis of our adjustment problems. See Chapter VI.

Raths, Louis E., "Teacher Training and Emotional Needs," *Journal of Educational Sociology,* March, 1951, pp. 369–380.

> An excellent survey of the development of the needs concept in relation to curriculum problems. Four other articles in this issue also center on needs.

Raths, Louis, and Lawrence E. Metcalf, "An Instrument for Identifying Some Needs of Children," *Educational Research Bulletin,* October 17, 1945, pp. 169–177, 196.

> A theory of needs implying that human behavior is purposive and that all needs are socially derived. Presentation of the Wishing Well, a needs inventory to measure eight postulated felt needs—to belong, to achieve, for economic security, to be free from fear, for love and affection, to be free from guilt, to share in decisions, and to understand their world.

Tryon, Caroline, and Jesse W. Lilienthal, III, *Fostering Mental Health in Our Schools,* 1950 Yearbook, Association for Supervision and Curriculum Development, National Education Association, 1950.

> Chapter 6, "Developmental Tasks: I. The Concept and Its Importance"—discussion of the meaning of the concept and summary of the developmental tasks of five stages of development. Chapter 7, "Developmental Tasks: II. Discussion of Specific Tasks and Implications"—an expansion of the meaning of the tasks listed in Chapter 6.

Wright, Herbert F., and others, "Toward a Psychological Ecology of the Classroom," in William E. Martin and Celia Burns Stendler, *Readings in Child Development,* Harcourt, Brace, 1954.

> One of the best introductions to psychological ecology—its meaning and its purpose (pp. 428–436). This book of readings also contains many other articles of great interest to a student in development and learning.

PART III

HOW DO HUMAN BEINGS LEARN?

Although, as indicated in the previous section, psychological maturing occurs as a result of learning, we have not as yet focused our discussion on learning per se. It is the purpose of Part III to treat explicitly the learning process.

Because historical theories of learning which are no longer held by professional psychologists continue to influence teaching, Chapter 10 presents the more prominent of the *historical* positions and shows their implications for school practice. Chapter 11 introduces what the authors see as the two major competing "families" of learning theory of the twentieth century. This chapter offers background by explaining how the families arose and how they relate to the outlooks of mechanism and relativism in psychology. Chapter 12 focuses on the specific explanation of learning which each family offers.

Chapters 13 and 14 are about representative systematic versions of the two families of psychological theory. B. F. Skinner's *operant conditioning* is chosen to represent mechanistic neobehaviorism. His position is the subject of Chapter 13. A relativistic cognitive-field psychology is the subject of Chapter 14. The basic structure of this position was developed by the late Kurt Lewin. In these chapters, we use terminology and phraseology characteristic of the positions. Since both chapters are fairly technical, they will bear rereading, probably more than once.

Chapter 15 summarizes some of the learning principles which are fairly well agreed upon, irrespective of the school of thought to which one belongs.

10

WHAT EARLY THEORIES OF LEARNING ARE REFLECTED IN CURRENT SCHOOL PRACTICES?

The purpose of a course in psychological foundations of education is to aid students in critical evaluation of competing psychological theories (of both the folklore and scientific types) and in thinking about their applications to classroom practice. This statement may be refined further by saying that the purpose of such a course is to help students think about *issues* in psychology and their implications for classroom practice.

Psychology is not a field of study characterized by a body of theory which is internally consistent and accepted by all psychologists. Rather, it is a field characterized by the presence of several "schools of thought." These may in some instances supplement one another, but at other times they are in open disagreement. Psychologist X, who is both scholarly and sincere, may find himself opposed to virtually every crucial idea of psychologist Y, who is equally scholarly and sincere. Disagreement among psychologists may be frustrating to students in psychology courses. On the other hand, in the fact of disagreement lies one of the challenges of such study. Only to the degree that a student of psychology is willing to think for himself can he emerge from his studies with something worthwhile. Some consolation may be had in the fact that similar disagreement exists in the physical sciences.

Quite often in our scientific age we erroneously think of *theory* as something indefinite or unusable, which existed prior to scientific method and evidence. Consequently, although we might not object to using the term in a description of the historical development of modern concepts of learning, we would expect the word *fact,* rather than *theory,* to be used in describing the current scene. After all, are we not now on ground solid enough for the term *theory* to be discarded?

Theory cannot be abolished. Any distinction between theoretical and established knowledge, and the action which stems from such knowledge, is faulty. Action, whether a part of teaching or any other activity in life, either is linked with theory or is blind and purposeless. Consequently, any purposeful action is governed by theory. Everyone who teaches or professes to teach has a theory of learning. A teacher may be able to describe his theory in explicit terms or he may not—in which case we can usually deduce from his actions the theory which he is not yet able to verbalize. The important question is not whether a teacher has a theory of learning but rather how tenable is his theory.

A teacher who does not make use of a systematic body of theory in his day-by-day decisions is behaving blindly. No long-range purpose or plan, no rationale, is observable in his teaching. A teacher without a strong theoretical orientation inescapably makes little more than busywork assignments. True, many teachers operate this way and use only a "bag of tricks" without theoretical orientation. However, this muddled kind of teaching undoubtedly is responsible for many of the adverse criticisms of public education which we hear today.

Unfortunately, some teachers who are theoretically oriented have never developed their psychology beyond the stage of folklore. It may go no farther than such cultural beliefs as "You can't change human nature," "People are instinctively religious," "There has never been a bad boy—only bad parents," and "Spare the rod and spoil the child." Folklore though they be, these are all theoretical statements, and their acceptance calls for particular kinds of action. If, in each case, one should believe the opposite, an entirely different kind of action should follow.

It is possible for a teacher to be aware of the most important theories developed by professional psychologists, in which case his own psychological theory is likely to be quite sophisticated. The latter state of affairs is what professional psychologists interested in education of teachers are trying to induce. Teachers who are well grounded in scientific psychology (in contrast to "folklore psychology") have a basis for making decisions in the classroom which will produce highly fruitful results.

Man shares with other mammals primary organic drives such as hunger, thirst, sex, cravings for oxygen, warmth, and rest, and possibly primary aversions such as fear and rage. But in some way human beings seem to transcend these drives. In large measure, this transcendence is centered in the human capacity to deal with a complex past, present, and future world so as to develop abstractions or generalizations which organize mazes of particulars into sensible patterns. Perhaps a desire to perceive, understand, and imagine is just as much a part of human nature as are the specific organic drives (see pp. 50–53).

There apparently is no group of human beings that has not developed some devices for enriching its contacts with the world about it. People have attempted to derive satisfactions from understanding and manipulating the world as well as through merely touching, smelling, and tasting it. Contrasted with capacities of less advanced animals, man's potential for becoming human lies largely in his capacity for extension of experience to a world of symbolism.

Animals seem to derive satisfaction from using the abilities they have. Likewise man derives satisfaction from using his natural and acquired abilities. Thus, the very process of abstract learning can become satisfying to man. In his social, aesthetic, economic, religious, and political life he shows some tendency to explore. Stated figuratively, man likes to "roll ideas around on his tongue" or "sniff at them" to discover what they will do. Not all people develop sophisticated ideological outlooks. However, rarely if ever are there groups of people who subsist solely on a vegetative level with no imaginative or mentalistic endeavors. Even the most primitive Indians had some symbolistic folklore.

Not only has man wanted to learn, but often his curiosity has impelled him to try to learn *how* he learns. Since ancient times, at least some members of every civilized society have developed, and to some degree tested, ideas about the nature of the learning process. Since the seventeenth century, more or less systematic theories of learning have emerged periodically to challenge existing theories. Typically, a new theory of learning is not translated into school practice until 25 to 75 years have elapsed. Then, as a new theory eventually comes to affect school policy, it usually does not displace its predecessors; it merely competes with them. Thus, as new theories have been introduced they have been added to the old and the educational scene has become more and more muddled. Probably most teachers, from time to time, have adopted conflicting features from a variety of learning theories without realizing that they are basically contradictory in nature and cannot harmonize with each other.

WHY IS CLASSROOM LEARNING A PROBLEM?

In most life situations learning is not much of a problem. A "lay" person takes it for granted that we learn from experience and lets it go at that; he sees nothing problematical about learning. Throughout human history people have learned, and in most cases without troubling themselves as to the nature of the process. Parents taught children and master workmen taught apprentices. Children and apprentices both learned, and those who taught felt little need for a grasp of learning theory. Teaching was done by telling and showing how, complimenting the learner when he did well and scolding or punishing him when he did poorly. A teacher simply taught the way he had been taught when he was a youth.

When schools were developed as a special environment to facilitate learning, teaching ceased to be so simple a matter. The subjects taught in school were different from the things learned as a part of routine life in a tribe or society. Mastering school subjects, whether the three R's, foreign languages, geometry, history, or something else, appeared to children as an entirely different sort of learning task from the tasks taken for granted in everyday life. Often their relevance to the problems of daily living seemed unclear. Such subjects, whose immediate usefulness is not obvious, strike a learner as quite different from the crafts and skills needed to carry on day-by-day social, economic, and political life.

Ever since education became formalized in schools, teachers have been aware that learning in school is often highly inefficient. Material to be learned may be presented to students innumerable times without noticeable results. Many students appear uninterested. Many become rebellious and make serious trouble for teachers. Consequently, classrooms often have seemed like battlegrounds in which teachers and students made war against each other.

Such a state may come to be taken for granted by teachers, students, and parents. They may all consider it "natural" that youngsters dislike school and try to resist school learning. They may assume that it is simply one of the unpleasant facts of life that many children will learn very little in school. From the colonial period through the nineteenth century, most people in America probably made these assumptions.

However, as soon as the professions of psychology and education developed, it was inevitable that professionals would begin asking questions. When teaching moved from mother's knee to a formalized environment designed to promote learning, it was inescapable that a small group of persons would arise to begin speculating about whether schools were getting the best possible results. Professional psychologists and educators, who were inclined to be critical of school practices, found that development of more or less systematic schools of thought in psychology offered a handy tool for crystallization of their thinking. Each of these schools of thought contained, explicitly or implicitly, a theory of learning. A given theory of learning implies a set of classroom practices. Hence, a theory of learning could function as an analytical tool; its exponents could use it to judge the quality of a particular classroom situation.

WHAT ARE SOME TYPES OF LEARNING THEORY REFLECTED IN SCHOOL PRACTICE?

In this section we present a thumbnail sketch of the major lines along which learning theory has developed. In the remainder of this and succeeding chapters we develop each of these lines of thought in considerable detail.

Learning theory is a distinct area within theoretical psychology. At present, psychologists who are dedicated to a study of learning are concentrating upon developing systematic theories supported by experimentation. Experimental and theoretical literature on learning has grown to an almost forbidding mass. Ernest R. Hilgard is perhaps the ranking authority on comparative learning theory. Students of educational psychology should find it interesting to dip into Hilgard's book,[1] which treats in some detail eight learning theories which have currency in the United States. Hilgard discusses only those which are currently acceptable to some professional psychologists. Still other theories of learning are assumed by certain groups of nonpsychologically trained professors and public school personnel. Of the various theories extant, we touch upon five which seem to be most relevant to contemporary issues in education.

The present chapter is devoted to three conceptions of the learning process which emerged prior to the twentieth century but continue to have great influence in today's schools: (1) *mental discipline*, (2) *natural unfoldment*, and (3) *apperception*. These three theories have one characteristic in common: all were developed as nonexperimental psychologies of learning. That is, their basic orientation is philosophical or speculative. Each may be identified with a particular philosophical system and a corresponding school of psychology. The method used to develop these three conceptions of learning was introspective and subjective; philosopher-psychologists who evolved these ideas tried to analyze their own thought processes and then describe in general terms what they thought they found.

Chapters 11 through 14 treat two contemporary types of learning theory which make extensive use of experimental evidence. These are (4) *mechanistic stimulus-response associationisms*, and (5) *nonmechanistic Gestalt-field theories*.

Through study of these five theories of learning and their historical development, prospective teachers should gain insight into the harmonies and conflicts that prevail in present educational theory. Through this insight, they should move toward developing adequate theories of their own. Before attempting to formulate his own learning theory, one would

---

[1] Ernest R. Hilgard, *Theories of Learning*, Appleton-Century-Crofts, 1956.

do well to examine carefully and critically the prevalent theories which have been developed by "experts." Furthermore, in order to understand the teaching climate of present-day schools it is important to develop some comprehension of learning theories which have emerged in the past and still have prominent places in modern education even though they are no longer among the theories advocated by present-day theoretical psychologists.

Table 6 is a categorization and summarization of the better-known theories of learning. Note that each is linked to a basic conception of human nature, as indicated in the second column. Since mental discipline is reflected in two quite different psychological outlooks—faculty psychology and classicism—sections 1 and 2 both are devoted to it. Entries 5, 6, and 7—S-R bond, conditioning, and reinforcement—are encompassed by the more generalized concept *S-R associationism*. Entries 8 and 9—goal insight and cognitive-field theory—are Gestalt-field theories. As students pursue study of learning and teaching, they should find it helpful to refer frequently to this table.

WHAT IS MENTAL DISCIPLINE?

According to the doctrine of mental discipline, education is a process of disciplining or training minds. Proponents of the doctrine believe that in this process mental faculties are strengthened through exercise. Just as exercising an arm develops the biceps, exercise of mental faculties makes them more powerful. Choice of learning materials is of some importance but always is secondary to the nature of minds which supposedly undergo the disciplinary process. People are thought to be composed of two kinds of basic substances or realities—mental and physical. That which is disciplined or trained is *mind substance*.

Mental discipline has roots which extend to antiquity. Its manifestations continue to be quite evident in present-day school practices. The theory was somewhat dormant during the first half of the twentieth century. However, the "Sputnik age" has led to its revival and revitalization.[2]

What Is Mind Substance?

As pointed out in Chapter 3 under the heading of "Vitalism," mental reality often is called *mind substance* and usually is assigned the dominant position in a mind-body dualism. The mind substance theory means that mind is just as real as anything physical. It has a nature of its own and operates in its own distinctive fashion. Physical substance—rocks, buildings, plants, and animals—is characterized by extension; it has length,

---

[2] See Walter B. Kolesnik, *Mental Discipline in Modern Education,* University of Wisconsin Press, 1958.

TABLE 6. Representative Theories of Learning

Theory of Learning	Assumption Concerning Basic Nature of Man	Representative Psychology or Outlook	Basis of Transfer	Key Persons	Contemporary Exponents
1. Mental discipline	bad-active (mind substance)	faculty psychology	exercised faculties, transfer automatic	St. Augustine John Calvin J. Edwards	many Hebraic-Christian fundamentalists
2. Mental discipline	neutral-active (mind substance)	classical-tradition	cultivated intellect	Plato Aristotle	R. E. Brennan M. J. Adler
3. Natural unfoldment	good-active (natural)	romantic naturalism	recapitulation, no transfer	J. J. Rousseau F. Froebel	extreme progressivists
4. Apperception	neutral-passive (mental)	structuralism	apperceptive mass	J. F. Herbart W. M. Wundt E. B. Titchener	many teachers, supervisors, and administrators
5. S-R Bond	neutral-passive (physical or mental)	connectionism	identical elements	E. L. Thorndike	J. M. Stephens A. I. Gates
6. Conditioning	neutral-passive (physical)	behaviorism	conditioned response	J. B. Watson	B. F. Skinner E. R. Guthrie
7. Reinforcement	neutral-passive (organism)	reinforcement	equivalence of stimuli and responses	C. L. Hull	K. W. Spence
8. Goal insight	natural-active or neutral-interactive	Gestalt psychology	transposition of insights	M. Wertheimer K. Koffka	W. Köhler E. E. Bayles
9. Cognitive-field	neutral-interactive (psychological)	field psychology, or relativism	continuity of life spaces, experience, or insight	Kurt Lewin E. C. Tolman J. S. Bruner	R. G. Barker A. W. Combs H. F. Wright

breadth, thickness, and mass. Mind substance, on the other hand, is not extended; it has no length, no breadth, no thickness, and no mass, but it is as real as anything can be. In a sense, man is considered a mental and physical whole. However, body and mind supposedly are of such nature as to be mutually exclusive of one another; they have no common characteristic.

How did primitive man acquire the idea that he had a substantive mind? We do not know, but it is plausible to suppose that dreaming was partially responsible. Picture warrior A and warrior B lying down together after a hard day's hunting and a heavy feast. Warrior A has eaten too much and as a result is unable to sleep. Having been more moderate in his eating, warrior B sleeps all night but his sleep includes an adventurous dream. Upon awakening in the morning, warrior B relates the experience of finding and stalking game during the night. Warrior A expresses disbelief and insists that warrior B has been on the ground beside him all night. But warrior B is equally insistent that he spent the night hunting and describes his dream so convincingly that both men decide that there must be *two* warrior B's. One slept on the ground throughout the night; the other must have come from within the first and carried on his escapades *unhampered by bodily form*. Thus could have been born something like a modern concept of mind substance.

The mind substance concept has been with us so long and is so deeply embedded in present-day cultures that quite often it is assumed to be a self-evident truth. However, the concept of a mental substance with its own unique characteristics is one which man has developed gradually through the ages. It has grown through the experiences of primitive and early civilized man and has been handed down, often uncritically, from generation to generation. The familiar has come to appear self-evident.

A defensible mind substance theory must take mind out of space completely. As long as one attributes to mind some characteristics of matter, even though they are very thin and elusive, he implies that mind is of essentially the same nature as matter. Thus, in understanding a mind-substance theory of learning it is necessary to make a sharp distinction between mind and matter. We must remind ourselves that, if a mind is nonspatial, it cannot be located in the brain or anywhere else; and that, to date, man has devised no way of determining the way in which spatial and nonspatial entities influence one another.

If one adheres to a mind-substance theory, he must see all learning as a process of developing or training minds. Learning becomes a process of inner development within which various powers such as imagination, memory, will, and thought are cultivated. Education becomes a process of mental discipline.

How Did the Mental Discipline Theory of Learning Develop?

Plato believed that mental training or discipline in mathematics and philosophy was the best preparation for participation in the conduct of public affairs. Once trained, by having his faculties developed, a philosopher-king was ready to solve problems of all kinds. Aristotle described at least five different faculties, the greatest and the one unique to man being that of reason. According to Aristotle, faculties which man had in common with lower animals were the vegetative, appetitive, sensory, and locomotive.

At the close of the Middle Ages, *Renaissance humanism* was an endeavor of man to gain more understanding of God, the universe, and himself. Humanism meant that man, rather than the Scriptures, was to be the starting point in satisfying man's urge toward individual development. To gain understanding of the ideal nature of man, humanistic scholars turned to the classics of ancient Greece and Rome. The resulting classicism of the Renaissance was developed on the assumption that a person's direction of growth is to be provided from within, not by yielding to the behest of every chance impulse, but by following principles which an individual himself formulates for guidance of his conduct. Thus, learning was regarded as a process of firm self-discipline; it consisted of harmonious development of all of one's inherent powers so that no one faculty was over-developed at the expense of the others.

Within humanism, the Socratic method was popular as a teaching procedure. A teacher's function was to help students recognize what already was in their minds. Environmental influence was considered of little consequence. "The Socratic method implies that the teacher has no knowledge, or at least professes to impart no information; instead, he seeks to draw the information from his students by means of skillfully directed questions. The method is predicated on the principle that knowledge is inborn but we cannot recall it without expert help."[3]

In the history of education, the nineteenth century could be characterized as the century of mental discipline. Rooted in European traditions of idealistic and rationalistic philosophy, the ideal of mental discipline had some currency in the early part of the century and it gained great popularity in the middle and later decades. A Yale faculty report of 1828 established mental discipline as the supreme aim of education. Study of the classics and mathematics was considered the best means of achieving it. A prominent English scholar, Matthew Arnold, wrote in 1867, "It is vital and formative knowledge to know the most powerful manifestations

[3] George F. Kneller, *Existentialism and Education,* Philosophical Library, 1958, p. 134.

of the human spirit's activity, for the knowledge of them greatly feeds and quickens our own activity; and they are very imperfectly known without knowing ancient Greece and Rome."[4]

Mental discipline placed little stress upon the acquisition of useful knowledge and information as such. Rather, it emphasized the training of mental faculties and the cultivation of intellectual powers apart from any specific application to practical problems. Since mental discipline was especially popular in liberal arts colleges, it was advocated for the college preparatory curriculums of academies and high schools.

REASSERTION OF CLASSICISM IN THE TWENTIETH CENTURY. Traditionally, humanists have been more interested in perfecting the minds of a few superior individuals than in elevating mankind as a whole, although this is not true today of all who call themselves humanists. Some twentieth-century humanists are attempting to repudiate the intellectual leadership of natural and social scientists in the affairs of life and to revert to the precepts of traditional philosophers as represented by Plato, Aristotle, and the medieval scholastics. These modern humanists believe we should make a sharp distinction between man and the world of nature. Man, being a rational animal, supposedly has certain unique universal and eternal qualities which separate him from the lower forms of nature. His education should center upon cultivation of his unique rational faculty. Some leading twentieth-century classical humanists are Robert M. Hutchins, Mortimer J. Adler, and Mark Van Doren.

AN EXAMPLE OF MENTAL DISCIPLINE. A brief history of the teaching of Latin and Greek illustrates development of mental discipline as a theory of learning. Throughout the Middle Ages, Latin served a practical purpose. It was the language of scholars throughout the Western world and the vehicle of instruction in schools. Thus it was a living, growing, changing language which today we would call a "tool subject." During the Renaissance, Latin continued to be the language of communication, particularly of those ideas considered the best that had been thought by man. To keep up with the thinking of his times, a scholar had to be able to read and use Latin and Greek.

After the Renaissance, modern languages gradually came into more general use. English, German, and French rose to prominence and assumed the role previously played by Latin and Greek. By the end of the sixteenth century, the practical value of the classical languages was beginning to wane. Supporters of these languages, however, made a determined fight to preserve them. No longer needed for basic communication, Latin

---

[4] Matthew Arnold, *School Inquiry*, Vol. 6, 1867, p. 593.

and Greek came to be heralded as the best subject matter for mental discipline. Throughout most of the nineteenth century the doctrine of the disciplinary value of these languages was generally accepted in American educational circles. Since, according to the classicists, disciplinary values are intangible and not susceptible to statistical treatment, evaluation of them supposedly was limited to analysis of opinions of recognized authorities on educational matters.

During the early years of the twentieth century when learning theories opposed to mental discipline—apperception, connectionism, and behaviorism—were on the upsurge in educational circles, Greek practically dropped out of the educational picture and Latin suffered a great decline.

However, by the middle of the twentieth century a resurgence of the classical tradition was apparent. With it came its earlier associate, mental discipline, and the teaching of Latin began to be expanded again. A mid-twentieth-century plea for a return to classicism and faculty psychology is expressed in a quotation from an article by Dr. Koerner, Executive Secretary of the Council for Basic Education: ". . . many of us will persist in our notion that the most promising way we have yet found of preparing people to teach is to furnish their minds generously with the best that has been thought and said in the principal fields of man's intellectual activity; to allow them to gain a mastery of, and a delight in, at least one of these fields; to develop in them the power and the habit of thought; and in the process, to awaken their moral faculty and to discipline their will, that they may by example do the same for their students."[5]

What Forms May Mental Discipline Take?

The theory of mental discipline has at least two versions—classicism and faculty psychology. Each is an outgrowth of different cultural traditions. Classicism stems from ancient Greece. It operated on the assumption that the mind of man is an active agent in relation to its environment and also that man is morally neutral at birth.

The psychology known as "faculty psychology" more often is associated with the bad-active principle of human nature than with the earlier Greek neutral-active principle. As is pointed out in Chapter 2, with the spread of Hebraic-Christian religion, the notion became popular that human beings are born intrinsically bad. Because of differences in underlying assumptions concerning the basic nature of man, we find a difference between the kinds of education prescribed by classicists and by faculty psychologists. Let us examine this difference in more detail.

[5] James D. Koerner, "Merely Training in Pedagogy," *NEA Journal*, April, 1959, p. 18.

MENTAL DISCIPLINE WITHIN THE CLASSICAL TRADITION. Within the classical tradition a human mind is assumed to be of such nature that, with adequate cultivation, it can know the world as it really is. Man, being a rational animal, is free within limits to act as he chooses in the light of what he understands. Man, instead of being a creature of instinct, enjoys a complex and delicate faculty of apprehension whose basic aspect is reason. This capacity resides in every normal human individual. It enables human beings to gain understanding of their needs and their environment, to direct their action in accordance with their understanding, and to communicate this understanding to other members of their group. Thus, it is assumed that a mind is of such nature that, if its faculties have been properly exercised and it has an opportunity, it will educe truth; it will develop outward manifestations of its innate potential.

Within the classicist frame of reference, knowledge assumes the character of a fixed body of true principles which are to be handed down as a heritage of the race. These principles have been discovered by the great thinkers of human history and have been set down in the great books. Hence, a classicist takes the content of the school curriculum from philosophical and literary classics. To him, not only training the faculties, but also studying the eternal truths contained in certain books is important.

Furthermore, since every mind has the same faculties and since in everybody a particular faculty profits by the same kind of training, the school curriculum should be the same for everybody. All that is necessary on the part of a teacher is to adjust the difficulty and the speed of work to the capacities of students.

FACULTY PSYCHOLOGY. Although faculty psychology had been implicit in the classical tradition and in virtually every early scheme of education proposed, it did not appear as an explicit, formalized psychological doctrine until the eighteenth century. Christian Wolff, a German philosopher, is credited with its development. His version was described in his *Rational Psychology*, published in 1734. Wolff's thesis was that the mind, although unitary, has different faculties which are distinct. The mind at times enters into particular activities in much the same way that the whole body at different times takes part in widely different acts. According to Wolff, the basic general faculties are knowing, feeling, and willing. The knowing faculty is divided into several others, which include perception, imagination, memory, and pure reason. The reasoning faculty is the ability to draw distinctions and form judgments.

The belief in a willing faculty is an outgrowth of the notion that human nature may be described in terms of the bad-active principle. If human nature is intrinsically evil, then a strongly developed will is necessary to harness inherent evilness. Without will, a person would be unable to function in human society. Will, in the sense in which it is employed here, refers to ability to implement, or put into effective practice, a decision which has been made. A strongly developed will enables a person to "see a decision through" even though such action violates natural, i.e., evil, impulses. Hence, if one chooses to emancipate himself from his natural impulses, a well-developed will is necessary for success; he must make himself do that which he does not want to do. Faculty psychologists have held that if a person pursues any type of unpleasant work long enough his will is strengthened.

Under faculty psychology, the task of a teacher is to find the kind of mental exercises that will train the various faculties most efficiently. Emphasis is not on acquiring knowledge, but rather on strengthening faculties. A consistent faculty psychologist would not be especially interested in teaching "great truths" or the "heritage of the past" or any other type of subject matter except insofar as it is a good medium for exercising the faculties.

The special attention given by faculty psychology to development of the will has led to the notion that school work is better for a child if it is distasteful. When faculty psychology is a dominant influence in a school, teachers deliberately keep their assignments both difficult and dull and use force if necessary to insure that students complete them. Use of severe punishment, including ridicule and sometimes even whipping, is likely to be found in such a school.

THE WEDDING OF CLASSICISM AND FACULTY PSYCHOLOGY.   Faculty psychology, as developed by Wolff and his followers, was at first a challenge to classicism. Logically, faculty psychologists should consider one subject as good as another for exercising a particular faculty; also, knowledge retained by a student was considered much less important than the disciplining effect of learning it. But these conclusions negate the classicists' insistence on the virtues of certain subjects and on learning and retaining the great truths which human experience has unveiled.

However, a rather easy compromise soon became apparent. If it could be established that the best subjects for training the faculties were the classics, then the classical curriculum could be defended. This argument gained strength, and by the late nineteenth century most secondary schools and colleges offered a curriculum limited mainly to the classical liberal arts. These subjects were regarded as valuable for a twofold reason: they were excellent tools for mind training and they incorporated the great truths of human experience.

A curriculum based on traditional philosophy and the liberal arts may not seem very practical to most persons today. However, mental disciplinarians deliberately made a distinction between knowledge of immediate usefulness and practicality, and essential matters grounded in eternal standards of truth, goodness, and beauty. Mental disciplinarians are convinced that knowledge of immediate practical value is of little importance. They hold that only the abstract principles of "pure theory" can free the human mind and promote man's distinctively human capacity for reason.

This emphasis is understandable. Most adherents of mental discipline are mind-body dualists who feel that mind is much the more important member of the partnership. Identification of education with development of mind tends to disparage other aspects of human activity. Thus we are told that "Education, as a whole, can never be a 'science' in the strict sense of the term. It is part of the 'humanities.' "[6]

Scientific Attempts to Evaluate Mental Discipline

Mental discipline proponents generally have held that learning theory, curriculum construction, teaching methods, and educational practices cannot be evaluated scientifically; they are derived philosophically and hence can only be evaluated philosophically. However, by the early twentieth century an imposing array of psychologists and educators had become entranced by the potentiality of scientific processes, particularly objective and statistical procedures as exemplified in such fields as physics and chemistry.

Whereas on the one hand mental disciplinarians insisted that science could not be applied in such a human enterprise as education, on the other hand scientifically oriented educators and psychologists insisted that science could and must be used in education. Increasingly, scientific-minded persons came to view exponents of mental discipline as conservatives or reactionaries who opposed progress in education.

When the classical curriculum first took form, it represented the point of view of liberals of the time and reflected a desire for progress. Its adherents were sufficiently open-minded to permit changes. However, by the beginning of the twentieth century the classical curriculum had come under such sharp attack that its proponents were placed on the defensive. The more defensive they became, the more rigid and dogmatic their thinking seemed to be. They pleaded for a return to a rigid Renaissance ideal, forgetting that the Renaissance ideal itself was an example of change and growth.

Almost to the end of the 1890s public high schools in the United States were loyal to the classical liberal tradition with its psychology of mental discipline. The famous Committee of Ten on Secondary School Studies upheld a doctrine of mental discipline throughout its 1890 report.

[6] Robert Ulich, *Professional Education as a Humane Study*, Macmillan, 1956, pp. 112–113.

In the early 1900s Thorndike and Woodworth, in a newer tradition of empirical psychology, performed experiments at Columbia University to test the validity of mental discipline as a psychology of learning. Their basic conclusion was that the idea of mental discipline is scientifically untenable. Their experiments showed that drill or training in performing certain tasks did not strengthen the "so-called" faculties for performing such tasks. Training in estimating the lengths of short lines resulted in no significant improvement in estimating the lengths of longer lines. Development of neatness in one area of activity showed no or very little improvement of students' neatness in other areas; students' arithmetic papers may be noticeably improved in neatness with no parallel improvement in neatness of language and spelling papers.[7]

Furthermore, Thorndike noted that the results of his experimentation, if corroborated by similar experiments, would prove that the amount of *general* improvement—mental discipline—due to any subject is small and that differences in improvement as a result of different subjects also are small. Thus the values of subjects must be decided largely by the special learnings which they provide. The languages (or any other liberal arts subjects) have no claims to pre-eminence. The order of influence, if any, of subjects upon growth of intellect was, first, arithmetic and bookkeeping; second, physical science; third, algebra and geometry; fourth, Latin and French; fifth, physical training; sixth, social science; seventh, history, music, shop, Spanish, English, drawing, and business; and eighth, dramatics, dramatic art, cooking, sewing, stenography, and biological sciences. Thus the so-called disciplinary subjects appear at all levels interwoven with supposedly nondisciplinary subjects. Thorndike reported in the *Journal of Educational Psychology:*

> If our inquiry had been carried out by a psychologist from Mars, who knew nothing of theories of mental discipline, and simply tried to answer the question, "What are the amounts of influence of sex, race, age, amounts of ability, and studies taken, upon the gain made during the year in power to think, or intellect, or whatever our stock intelligence tests measure?" he might even dismiss "studies taken" with the comment, "The differences are so small and the unreliabilities are relatively so large that this factor seems unimportant." The one causal factor which he would be sure was at work would be the intellect already existent. Those who have the most to begin with gain the most during the year. Whatever studies they take will seem to produce large gains in intellect.[8]

Thorndike was convinced that the principal reason why good thinkers seemed to have been made good thinkers by certain subjects which they

[7] See Edward L. Thorndike and R. S. Woodworth, "The Influence of Improvement in One Mental Function Upon the Efficiency of Other Functions," *Psychological Review,* 1901, Vol. 8, May, pp. 247–261; July, pp. 384–395; November, pp. 553–564.

[8] Edward L. Thorndike, "Mental Discipline in High School Studies," *Journal of Educational Psychology,* February, 1924, No. 2, p. 95.

had pursued is that good students tend to take the subjects which people generally identify with good thinking. Good students gain more than do poor students from the study of *any* subject. When good thinkers study Latin and Greek, these subjects seem to cultivate good thinking. However, "If the abler pupils should all study Physical Education and Dramatic Arts, these subjects would seem to make good thinkers."[9]

In 1914 Thorndike disposed of inborn faculties with two sentences: "[There is] the opinion that attention, memory, reasoning, choice and the like are mystical powers given to man as his birthright which weigh the dice in favor of thinking or doing one thing rather than another. . . . This opinion is vanishing from the world of expert thought and no more need to be said about it than that it is false and would be useless to human welfare if true."[10]

In 1944 Alexander Wesman made a study following up Thorndike's mental discipline studies. High school students were tested at beginning and end of an academic year with a series of general intelligence and achievement tests. Gains on the tests during the year were observed for students taking differing course patterns to see whether some patterns of courses contributed more to intelligence than did others. Wesman's study revealed no superiority of any one school subject over any of the others studied; there was no superior transfer to intelligence for any one of the achievement areas measured. Apparently no scientific basis exists for asserting that one high school subject contributes more to students' intelligence than does another.[11]

WHAT IS LEARNING THROUGH UNFOLDMENT?

We come now to the second major position to be treated in this chapter, often called "learning through unfoldment." This outlook on the nature of learning stems logically from the theory that man is naturally good and at the same time active in relation to his environment. As is pointed out in Chapter 2, early development of this point of view is usually associated with Rousseau. Later, the Swiss educational reformer Pestalozzi (1746–1827) and the German philosopher, educator, and founder of the kinder-garten movement, Friedrich Froebel (1782–1852), used this outlook as a basis for their pedagogical thinking. The over-all philosophical framework of the natural-unfoldment position often is labeled *romantic naturalism*.

Since Rousseau's views on human nature are elaborated in Chapter 2, we provide little more here than a brief review. Rousseau's position was

[9] *Ibid.*, pp. 96–98.

[10] Edward L. Thorndike, *Educational Psychology*, Teachers College, Columbia University, 1914, p. 73.

[11] Alexander Wesman, "A Study of Transfer of Training from High School Subjects to Intelligence," *Teachers College Record*, October, 1944, pp. 391–393.

that everything in nature is basically good. Since mans' hereditary nature is good, it need only be permitted to develop in a natural environment free from corruption. Rousseau qualified his interpretation of human nature as an active, self-directing agent by conceding that a bad social environment could make bad human beings; to him social conditions are not natural. His rejection of environmentalism is thus not complete. However, his constant emphasis is on natural, active self-determination.

Rousseau urged teachers to permit students to live close to nature so that they might indulge freely in their natural impulses, instincts, and feelings. He emphasized that in rural areas children need practically no schooling or tutoring. An example which he gave related to the learning of speech. A country boy, he said, ordinarily did not need instruction in speech. He called to his parents and playmates from considerable distances and thus practiced making himself heard; consequently, without tutoring, he developed an adequate power of speech. It was only the city boy, growing up in close quarters with no opportunity to exercise his voice in a natural way, who had need for speech instruction. Thus, he recommended that in teaching city boys teachers should, insofar as possible, adopt the method through which country boys learn.

Since, according to the good-active definition of human nature, a child grows by unfolding that which nature has enfolded within him, devotees of this position tend to place great emphasis on the study of child growth and development and to minimize the study of learning. When they do allude to learning, they seem to assume or imply that it, too, is nothing more than a process of growth and development. Learning is equated with maturation. It is something which teachers need to do little about; it "just happens naturally."

Learning, in the usual sense of the term, generally is conceived as some form of imposition of ideas or standards upon a person or organism. Within romantic naturalism there is little need for this kind of learning. Instead, a child learns through the promptings of his own interests. There should be no coercion or prescription. A mind and its growth may be considered analogous to an egg in the process of hatching. Its growth is a natural operation which, without imposition from any outside source, carries its own momentum.

Since romantic naturalists depreciate the value of learning as such, they give a prominent place to the concept of needs. Needs are considered child-centered, as contrasted with environment- or situation-centered. As an organism or mind naturally unfolds through a series of stages, each stage is assumed to have its unique needs. Such child-centered needs have much in common with instincts; they supposedly are innate determining tendencies or permanent trends of human nature which underlie behavior from birth to death under all circumstances in all kinds of societies. In Chapter 9 the concept *child-centered needs* is discussed in some detail.

WHAT IS THE BACKGROUND OF APPERCEPTION?

The third major outlook toward learning which we describe—apperception—is far more complicated than faculty psychology or learning as unfoldment. Apperception is idea-centered. An idea is apperceived when it appears in consciousness and is assimilated to other conscious ideas. Thus, apperception is a process of associating new ideas with old ones.

Adherents of both mental discipline and natural unfoldment assume or imply the existence of an inborn human nature, some aspects of which are common to all men. Although, in their treatment of learning, supporters of both theories sharply differ from one another, they agree that the "furniture of minds" is innate. Whereas romantic naturalists in their emphasis upon natural unfoldment expound instinctive natural development of persons, mental disciplinarians often agree that knowledge is inborn but insist that students need expert help to enable them to recall it.

Apperception, in contrast to both mental discipline and natural unfoldment, is a dynamic mental *associationism* based upon the fundamental premise that there are no innate ideas; everything a person knows comes to him from outside himself. This means that mind is wholly a matter of content—it is a compound of elemental impressions bound together by association, and it is formed when subject matter is presented from without and makes certain associations or connections with prior content.

What Is Associationist Psychology?

Scientific learning theories fall into two major categories: associationisms and field or cognitive theories. An *associationism* is any general theory within which it is assumed that learning starts with irreducible elements and the process of learning consists of combinations of these. We supposedly connect ideas or actions in memory or thought simply because they were connected in our early experience with them. To study human beings in a framework of associationism, the method must be analytic or reductionistic; learnings must be reduced to their component successive parts. Modern associationisms include apperception, S-R bond, conditioning, and reinforcement theories. Basic elements associated may be mental, physical, or a combination of both. Within apperception, the elements are mental and constitute the structure of minds. "The 'furniture' of the mind *is* the mind. Mind is wholly a matter of 'contents.' "[12] In his metaphysics, Herbart posited a unitary mind or soul for each person

---

[12] See John Dewey, *Democracy and Education*, Macmillan, 1922, p. 82.

which is part of ultimate reality and consequently exists prior to experience. However, psychologically the concrete character of a mind, according to Herbart, consists of an arrangement of ideas which are very much like the electrons of modern physics—they make up the object which contains them. A mind is an aggregate or group of contents resulting from a person's having certain ideas presented to him.

How Did Associationism Develop?

Plato and other ancient philosophers thought that learning really consisted of remembering ideas with which a learner had been familiar before his birth; it was development of innate ideas from within. His student Aristotle perpetuated Plato's mental disciplinary psychology of learning. However, in his psychology, he recognized a role of the senses. The senses performed a subordinate function; they "tipped off" the faculties of the mind.

The thinking underlying modern associationism goes back to Aristotle, who observed that recollection of an item of knowledge was facilitated by a person's associating that item or idea with another when he learned it. He maintained that three kinds of connections—associations—would aid or strengthen memory: contiguity of one idea with another, similarity of ideas, and contrast of ideas.[13] Contiguity means being together. If a child is told about Eskimos and igloos at the same time, future mention of "Eskimo" will help him recall "igloo." "A tiger is a big kitty" uses the principle of similarity. If a person learns that pleasure is the opposite of pain, mention of "pain" will aid him in thinking of "pleasure."

JOHN LOCKE—A SENSE EMPIRICIST. In the seventeenth century John Locke (1632–1704) challenged the whole notion of innate faculties or ideas and with it the conception of learning as development of innate potentialities or faculties. Locke observed that he could find no common human nature at all. Realizing that he could find no ideas common to all people in any one society or to people in different societies, he developed his *tabula rasa* theory of the human mind. *Tabula rasa*—blank tablet— means that there are no innate ideas. Locke was convinced that, not only was a mind empty at birth, but also any ideas which a person holds must have come to him originally through his senses. See Chapter 2, p. 48.

Locke's theory that all of a person's ideas must come to him through his senses is called *empiricism*. His empiricism was directly opposed to the earlier *rationalism* of Plato and Descartes. Whereas these two scholars considered *reason* the source of knowledge, Locke insisted that knowledge

[13] John S. Brubacher, *A History of the Problems of Education*, McGraw-Hill, 1947, p. 143.

was derived from *experience*. In his view perception is synonymous with learning and is a product of experience. A mind is insulated from the world of objects. That which is perceived is only an idea of an object.

For Locke, ideas were the units of a mind, and *associations* consisted of combinations of ideas. Ideas were either simple or complex. One of the operations of a mind was thought to be a compounding of complex ideas from simple ones. This notion of mental combination and analysis was a beginning of the "mental chemistry" which later characterized *apperception*.

To allow for associations within a mind, Locke recognized an "internal sense." He realized that, if a mind were only a passive receptacle of sense impressions (which basically he thought it to be), the impressions would accumulate in a disorderly manner. Consequently, he gave mind a means for dealing with passive impressions once they were in. To mind was attributed the ability to compare impressions, to generalize them, and to discriminate between them. This meant that it could associate ideas through contiguity, similarity, and contrast.

Locke's writings spearheaded a shift in the conception of education from mental discipline to habit formation. *Tabula rasa* theory implied that the original nature of man was neither good nor bad, nor active. Instead it was morally neutral and psychologically passive. Thus a mind was the product of life experiences. Locke's thinking opened the way for psychologists to place their emphasis upon environmental nurture rather than hereditary nature. In school, this meant that teachers were to be the architects and builders of minds of children. They were to develop a systematic instructional program, a science of teaching centered in procedures which might be used to form proper habits in students. Teaching became a matter of training the senses as opposed to training the faculties.

Locke's work constituted a turning point in professional thinking about *learning*. Up to the seventeenth century, most psychological thinking consisted of restatements and reinterpretations of the psychology of antiquity —classicism. This trend continued into the seventeenth and eighteenth centuries, but alongside it, Locke, preceded by Hobbes and followed by Hartley, spearheaded associatism—a new line of thought in regard to learning.

DAVID HARTLEY—FOUNDER OF ASSOCIATIONISM. David Hartley (1705– 1757) is credited with systematizing and organizing the various threads of thought of Hobbes, Locke, and others into a formal doctrine of associationism. Hartley, a physician, was an early mechanist. He reduced ideas to sensations, and sensations to nerve vibrations. His laws of association were contiguity and repetition; associated ideas are ideas which have been in a mind together, preferably repeatedly.

Empiricist, associationistic thinking, which had been launched by Hobbes, Locke, and Hartley, was pursued by David Hume, James Mill, John Stuart Mill, and Herbart. These thinkers attacked traditional problems such as: What is mind? How does a mind develop its complex array of ideas? What are the laws of memory? They found a new kind of answer in elementalism or atomism, and associationism. They asserted that a mind is built from sense experiences. Simple ideas, through association, coalesce into complex ideas. In this process, associations conform to certain laws such as contiguity, similarity, contrast, and repetition.

Early British and French associationists had assumed that linkages or associations are passive in nature. Herbart replaced this passivity with *dynamic* ideas. We should remember that, in Herbart's *apperception*, ideas, not persons, are dynamic. Persons are *containers* within which laws of mental chemistry operate.

WHAT IS APPERCEPTION?

Johann Friedrich Herbart (1776–1841) developed the first modern systematic psychology of learning to harmonize with a *tabula rasa* theory of mind. Herbart was an eminent German philosopher and a skilled teacher. From 1809 to 1833 he succeeded Immanuel Kant in the world's most distinguished chair of philosophy, at Königsberg, Germany. His speculative thinking developed from his dealing with problems of education. To him, morality was the supreme objective of education; he wanted to make children good. Thus he developed a psychology to achieve this goal. His influence on twentieth-century American education has been great. Although Herbartian pedagogy was developed in the first half of the nineteenth century, it was not until the 1880s that four young Americans—Charles De Garmo, Frank McMurry, Charles A. McMurry, and Charles C. Van Liew—studied at the University of Jena and returned to the United States to spread Herbartian doctrine with religious fervor. "Like a tidal wave, interest in this elaborate system swept over American teachers and students of education during the nineties."[14] The National Herbart Society was organized in 1895. In 1902 it was renamed the National Society for the Study of Education, and today it is a prominent professional organization. However, the purpose of the NSSE now is to promote scholarly study of issues in education, rather than to promulgate the ideas of Herbart.

From the early years of the twentieth century to the time its tenets were seriously challenged by behaviorism and connectionism, Herbartianism dominated teacher education institutions of the United States. Thus,

[14] Frederick Eby and C. F. Arrowood, *The Development of Modern Education,* Prentice-Hall, 1934, p. 786.

if one is to comprehend the psychological atmosphere of today's schools, it is essential that he understand the development, principles, and implications of the theory of apperception. Today, one seldom meets an avowed Herbartian; however, much of what takes place in our public schools carries with it the implicit assumption that neutral and passive minds of children are being filled. Although apperceptive teaching seldom is advocated systematically in teacher-education institutions, much actual teaching continues to follow a pattern in harmony with the theory of apperception.

Herbart perpetuated a mind-body dualism which was prevalent in his time. This was a psychophysical parallelism within which the psychic aspect—mind—played the major role, particularly in the learning process. Psychophysical parallelism is a theory of mind and body according to which, for every variation in conscious or mental process, there is a concomitant, parallel neurological or body process. Yet there is no causal relation between body and mind; a person's mind does not affect his body, nor his body his mind.

Through the use of *presentations, apperception,* and *apperceptive mass* Herbart expanded the concept of mind's neutral passivity into a systematic theory of learning and teaching. He thought minds had no innate natural faculties or talents whatsoever either for receiving or for producing ideas. In them lay not even remote dispositions toward perception, thought, willing, or action. He regarded minds as nothing more than battlegrounds and storehouses of ideas. Ideas, he thought, had an active quality. They could lead "a life of their own" in minds which were completely passive. A mind was an aggregate, not of faculties, but of ideas or mental states.

Herbart's ambition was to build a science of human minds which would parallel the physical and biological sciences. He thought of psychology as "mental chemistry." Thus he felt that the chief role of psychology was to study the various blendings and amalgamations of ideas or mental states in minds. Discovery of the principles by which ideas combine and recombine like chemical elements was Herbart's object in psychological investigation.

Although Herbart felt that his psychology was scientific, probably most experimental psychologists today would not agree; he rejected experimentation and the use of physiological data, both of which have been cornerstones of twentieth-century behavioristic psychology. To him, observation and thought were the proper methods for psychological inquiry. Furthermore, the observation he had in mind was self-observation, or introspection. By looking into his own mind, Herbart thought that its "chemistry" could be observed and described. He felt it proper that a science like physics was experimental, but equally appropriate that psychology be metaphysical and introspective.

What Are Mental States?

Herbart used the German term *Vorstellungen* to name the mental elements which he deemed the constituent parts of a mind. *Vorstellungen* may be translated to mean presentations, mental states, ideas, concepts, or notions. *Presentations* is the English term most often used in connection with Herbartian thought. However, when apperception theory was brought to the United States and subjected to further development, the term *mental states* superseded *presentations*. In this country Herbartianism often has been called a "psychology of mental states."

According to Herbartian psychologists, a mental state is a nonspatial, mental reality which is experienced at firsthand. Mental states have three forms—sense impressions, images or copies of previous sense impressions, and affective elements of pleasure and pain. Mental states furnish the only source of mental activity. Feeling and willing accompany them but are not their source or cause. Feeling and willing are derived, not original, states. A person's stock of mental states at any given time is his "apperceptive mass."

How Does Apperception Work?

Mind is an aggregate of mental states. Until a first presentation occurs, there is nothing whatever present in a mind; it is completely inert and passive. Mental states, the active structure of mind, become associated to produce experience. New things are learned only as they are related to what is already in an apperceptive mass. Addition of new presentations to the old produces various types of mental processes.

The particular combination of ideas which is predominant at any given time determines what will hold a person's attention at that time. Within Herbart's system of mental chemistry every presentation—mental state—has a quality which gives it an affinity for certain other presentations and an aversion for others; ideas either attract or repel one another. Whereas ideas of *book* and *school* would have an affinity and attract each other, ideas of *book* and *fishing rod* probably would have a repugnancy and repel each other.

A Herbartian regards a mind as a battleground of contending ideas. Each idea in the mind of a person has once been in the center of his consciousness and it strives to return. It seeks self-preservation. It tries to conserve itself and to enter into relations with other ideas. Having once held the center of consciousness and subsequently lost it, each presentation, like a deposed king, keeps trying to occupy the throne once again. Compatible ideas may operate as teams, helping each other to remain in a conscious mind. When two ideas are incompatible, however, one is likely to be submerged.

To Herbartians, all perception is *apperception;* it is a process of relating new ideas—presentations—to the store of old mental states. A mind is like an iceberg in that most of it is submerged below the level of consciousness. Memories stored in the subconscious enable one to interpret experience of the moment. Without a background of experience, any new sensation would mean almost nothing at all. In picturing a mind, Herbart introduced the idea of threshold of consciousness. Objects occupying consciousness are constantly changing. At any moment, several ideas may occupy the consciousness. One will be at the focus of attention, some will be sinking below the threshold, and others will be striving to rise into consciousness. In Fig. 10, mental state (b) is at the center of consciousness; (a) and (c) are only slightly above the threshold and in the margin of consciousness.

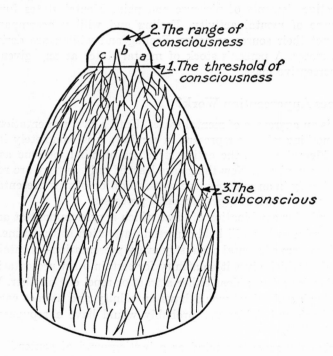

FIG. 10.   Herbart's Scheme of Psychology. An adaptation from Frederick Eby, *The Development of Modern Education,* Prentice-Hall, 1952, p. 481.

The subconscious aspect of mind contains the store of dynamic perceptions and images that have been accumulated during all past experiences of an individual. Any of these are ready to spring back into consciousness whenever a propitious opportunity occurs. The content of consciousness at any moment is the result of an interplay of many ideas. Apperception is a process not only of becoming consciously aware of an idea but also of assimilating it into a totality of conscious ideas.

Within the apperceptive process Herbart saw the principles of frequency and association in operation. The principle of frequency holds that the more often an idea or concept has been brought into consciousness, the easier becomes its return. The principle of association holds that, when a number of presentations or ideas associate or form a mass, the combined powers of the mass determine the ideas which will enter consciousness.

Herbart recognized three levels or stages of learning. First is the stage of predominately sense activity. This is followed by the stage of memory; this second stage is characterized by exact reproductions of previously formed ideas. The third and highest level is that of conceptual thinking, or understanding. Understanding occurs when the common, or shared, attributes of a series of ideas are seen. It involves generalization—deriving rules, principles, or laws from a study of specifics.

What Does Apperception Mean for Teaching?

According to apperception, right thinking will produce right action; volition or willing has its roots in thought. If a teacher builds up the right sequence of ideas, the right conduct follows. Hence, the real work of instruction is implantation not only of knowledge but also of inner discipline or will by means of presented ideas. Psychologically, students are made by the world of ideas which is presented to them from without.

Since, in apperception, there is no substantive mind to be developed, it could no longer be said that learning was a matter of developing or training a mind; rather learning has to do with the formation of an apperceptive mass. Thus the task of education is to cause present appropriate experiences to combine with a background. The problem of education is to select the right materials for forming the backgrounds or apperceptive masses of students. The concept of apperceptive mass implied that teachers must start with the experiences which pupils already have had and enlarge and enrich these experiences.

To Herbartians, the art of teaching consists of bringing to the attention of students those ideas which a teacher would like to have dominate their lives. Through controlling experiences of children, an instructor builds up masses of ideas which develop by assimilation of new ideas to them. Thus, by manipulating ideas he constructs a student's "circle of thought." The goal is a comprehensive circle of thought closely connected or integrated in all its parts. A teacher is the architect and builder of the minds, and hence the characters, of his students.

According to Herbart, at no time should a teacher enter into debate with his students on any matter. "Cases may arise when the impetuosity of the pupil challenges the teacher to a kind of combat. Rather than accept such a challenge, he will usually find it sufficient at first to reprove calmly, to look on quietly, to wait until fatigue sets in."[15]

What Are the Herbartian Five Steps in Learning?

Herbart and his followers have been convinced that the learning process proceeds through an ordered series of steps which a teacher should understand and follow. Effective teaching requires that, regardless of obstacles, the proper succession of steps be followed. Herbart listed four steps—clearness, association, system, and method—expanded to five by American Herbartians. Clearness became (1) preparation and (2) presentation; association became (3) comparison and abstraction; system became (4) generalization; and method became (5) application. Use of these steps came to be regarded as the general method to be followed in all teaching. The steps may be demonstrated by the following example, which involves teaching students the generalization that any object will float in liquid or in air if it weighs less than an equal volume of the air or liquid in which it is suspended.

1. *Preparation.*   To bring into consciousness relevant ideas, the teacher reminds students of certain experiences they have had with floating objects. The students will recall the floating of boats, balloons, bubbles, and the like.

2. *Presentation.*   The teacher presents new facts about floating, perhaps through means of demonstrations. For example, he might demonstrate how oil floats on water, or how a steel ball will float on mercury.

3. *Comparison and abstraction.*   If the teacher has performed the first two steps properly, students will see that the new facts have similarities with those already known. Hence, in the students' consciousness, the new and old ideas associate. They are welded together because of their natural affinity for each other. Furthermore, students at this point should see the nature of the common elements which give the two sets of facts their mutual attractiveness. Sorting out this common element is what is meant by abstraction.

4. *Generalization.*   In this step, students attempt to name the common elements of the two sets of facts as a principle or generalization. They arrive at the principle of flotation—the stated objective of instruction.

5. *Application.*   The newly learned principle then is used to explain further facts or solve problems relating to flotation. This is done through

[15] John Frederick Herbart, *Outlines of Educational Doctrine*, Macmillan, 1904, p. 165.

assigned tasks or problems. The teacher might ask students to explain why boats can be made successfully from steel. Or he might give them a problem which requires them to determine whether a certain object would float in a certain medium. For example, he might ask, "Given a freight barge of specified weight and displacement, how much weight could be placed in it without causing it to sink?"

What Was the Herbartian Doctrine of Interest?

The importance of student interest held a prominent place in the theory of apperception. Present-day policy of "making subject matter interesting" probably has an important root in apperception. Whereas a follower of faculty psychology saw no point in interest—even saw it as a deterrent to developing will power—a Herbartian gave it a central place in his system.

Since, to a Herbartian, formation of mind was wholly a matter of presenting the proper educational materials, the task of a teacher was to select the proper subject matter and arrange its presentation on the basis of the current store of ideas in the student's mind. If the new material involved ideas with a natural affinity for those already present, the student would feel interest.

Interest meant "the natural bend or inclination of the mind to find satisfaction in a subject when it is properly presented."[16] Interest was an active power residing in the contents of the mind. It depended upon the nature of the apperceptive mass and determined what ideas were to receive attention. A person thinks, feels, and wills in accordance with his dominant presentations. To develop "many sidedness of interests" one must acquire a large apperceptive mass. Herbart listed six classes of interests under two major categories, those awakened by the phenomena of nature apart from man and those involving the direct study of human affairs. He then assumed a sort of affinity between the historical development of the race and the stages of mental development of children. He was convinced that the history and great literature of the world, when properly selected and arranged, would make a strong appeal to the interests and understanding of children at their successive periods of growth.

How May Apperception Be Evaluated?

Ideas developed by Herbartians continue to permeate today's schools. However, some of the terms used to express these ideas have been abandoned or redefined. Some key Herbartian terms were *interest, apperception, apperceptive mass, circle of thought, concentration, correlation, culture epochs, sympathy,* and *formal steps in instruction.* Aspects of

[16] Charles A. McMurray, *The Elements of General Method,* Macmillan, 1903, p. 85.

these ideas can still be found in textbooks on curriculum and methodology.

Since it was the approach to teaching stressed most in a great many of our teacher education institutions from about 1900 to 1920, apperception remains influential even today. Large numbers of persons now teaching or holding administrative posts in schools received their first professional education in normal schools or teachers' colleges still strongly under the influence of Herbartianism. And many teachers of teachers are fundamentally Herbartian in their approach to educational problems.

One area in which Herbartian influence is still frequently seen is that of lesson plans. In the Herbartian system, actual teaching was always preceded by construction of a formal lesson plan, built around the "five steps." Teachers followed these plans, more or less rigidly, on the assumption that the thinking of students could be made to conform to the formal steps. Today, many professors in teachers' colleges still insist that there is a fixed order of steps for teaching and learning. They require their students to write lesson plans in which the material to be taught is arranged according to these steps, and in supervising student teachers they insist that lesson plans be followed.

Why Has Herbartianism Ceased to Be a Moving Force in Education?

Even educators who are Herbartian generally no longer think of themselves as such. Herbartian psychology and the teaching to which it led fell under major criticism early in the present century. Its critics saw several flaws in it. One was the assumption about human nature which guided Herbart. The assumption of passive human nature implicit in Herbartian psychology leaves too much to be explained. Herbart recognized that people do think in an active fashion, but he refused to recognize any source or basis for active reflection. Ideas, not the person, carried the burden of thought. How ideas, or mental states, could be active and alive, carrying on a vigorous life of their own within a mind which was essentially passive, simply was not understandable to many people. Herbart's psychology and philosophy could be defended only in terms of the psychophysical parallelism which we mentioned earlier. This philosophical position, never very popular with philosophers, fell increasingly into disrepute.

More important perhaps than criticisms based on the abstruse features of Herbart's philosophy and psychology are criticisms of the teaching practices to which they led. Herbartianism seems to commit teachers to a program of indoctrination. Its approach to teaching requires teachers to determine precisely what their pupils are to be taught. Each lesson plan includes the answers as well as the questions. Students arrive at these answers through a largely mechanical process which is completely dominated by the teacher. Education is conceived as a process similar to filling a storage container. If learning is the mechanical process which Herbart and Herbartians described, how does reflective, creative thinking enter the educational scene?

Within Herbartianism, a teacher might teach for understanding, but not for reflection (see Chapters 17 and 18). In commenting upon Herbartianism, John Dewey felt constrained to say, ". . . It takes . . . everything educational into account save its essence—vital energy seeking opportunity for effective exercise."[17] Since Herbartian theory at no time suggests that a child is interactive with his environment, inescapably, when applied in the classroom, it gives students little or no chance for active participation, including independent thinking.

A third criticism of Herbartianism is theoretical, but nevertheless vitally important. Explanations of the apperceptive process seem to have no adequate treatment of how the first ideas enter a mind so that apperception—perception upon perception—can take effect. How does the first idea tie up with an old one?

What Contributions Has Herbartianism Made to Education?

Modern Herbartianism has some weaknesses; nevertheless it has made important contributions to education. Greatest of all has been its attack upon the doctrine of mental discipline and faculty psychology. Further, it emphasized a psychological approach to teaching and learning, which implied a need for sound methods of teaching based upon knowledge of man and his mental functions. It directed attention to a need for adequate teachers and an enriched curriculum. Preparation of teachers was made an important business. It made "interest" a significant idea. It emphasized the importance of a background of experience in the process of perception.

Furthermore, Herbart, in developing a scientific if not experimental psychology, pointed the way for the later experimental scientific movement in psychology named *structuralism*. Structuralism was developed in the nineteenth century by Wundt in Germany and Titchener in the United States. Its subject matter was the content of consciousness. Consciousness, however, was studied by introspection. Structuralism was highly important in that it helped pave the way for modern psychologies which focus on mental processes and at the same time are experimental in the best scientific sense.

Although apperception preceded behaviorism and connectionism on the psychological and educational scenes, a strong case may be made for its

17 John Dewey, *op. cit.* (1916 ed.), p. 84.

superiority over the later physicalistic psychologies that challenged it. Contemporary Gestalt-field theories, including cognitive-field theory, have deeper roots in Herbartian apperception than in behaviorism, reinforcement, or connectionism—the S-R associationisms. Chapters 11–14 will help a reader evaluate the validity of this statement.

BIBLIOGRAPHY

Bode, Boyd H., *How We Learn*, Heath, 1940.
   A discussion of four distinct theories of mind—mind substance, mental states, behaviorism, and pragmatism. Excellent for historical background as well as for description of the outlooks.
Brubacher, John S., *A History of the Problems of Education*, McGraw-Hill, 1947.
   One of the best overviews of outlooks on learning. Chapter V, "Philosophies of Education," provides theoretical background for learning theory. Chapter VI, "Educational Psychology," summarizes mental discipline, apperception, behaviorism, and Gestalt psychology.
Dewey, John, *Democracy and Education*, Macmillan, 1916. (Also in paperback, 1961 edition.)
   Incisive, enlightening statements concerning natural unfoldment, apperception, and mental (formal) discipline. Pp. 130–138 are devoted to Roussellian natural development; 65–68 to Froebelian unfoldment; 70–79 to mental discipline; and 81–84 to Herbartian apperception.
Eby, Frederick, *The Development of Modern Education*, Prentice-Hall, 1952.
   An excellent account of Herbart and Herbartian education (Chap. 18). Chapter 19 is equally good on Froebel and his system of education through self-activity.
Foxley, Barbara, *Émile*, Dutton, 1911, in the "Everyman's Library."
   A complete translation of Rousseau's *Émile*. It is Rousseau's account of his rearing and educating a fictitious boy born to eighteenth-century city dwellers.
Herbart, John Frederick, *Outlaws of Educational Doctrine*, Macmillan, 1904.
   The best source in English for Herbart's views upon education. It gives Herbart's psychological orientation, then follows with practical advice for instruction.
Kolesnik, Walter B., *Mental Discipline in Modern Education*, University of Wisconsin Press, 1958.
   Reviews of the historical background and recent evidence on mental discipline. The author traces the changes in the meaning of mental discipline and attempts to give a dispassionate overview of the subject. He sees the viewpoints of the Harvard Committee on General Education, of Robert M. Hutchins, and of John Dewey as three approaches to mental discipline.
McMurry, Charles A., *The Elements of General Method, Based on the Principles of Herbart*, Macmillan, 1903.
   A textbook for teachers presenting Herbartian apperception, with its

American modifications, by an early-twentieth-century leader in American education.

Ulich, Robert, *History of Educational Thought,* American Book, 1950.
Educational thought followed through lives and thoughts of great thinkers. Separate chapters are devoted to Rousseau, Froebel, Herbart, etc.

11

WHAT ARE THE TWO MAJOR FAMILIES OF CONTEMPORARY LEARNING THEORY?

The two most prominent families of contemporary learning theory are *stimulus-response associationisms* and *Gestalt-field* theories. These have been in process of development throughout the twentieth century and have roots which extend back into earlier centuries. Their immediate forerunners were mental discipline and apperception. In a sense, both families were protests against inadequacies and inconsistencies of earlier psychological systems.

This chapter and the one to follow describe comparatively these two major families of psychological theory. This chapter develops "background thinking" which underpins the positions of the two families in regard to learning. It traces how they developed historically, their philosophical implications, and their chief assumptions about the role of psychology. It then shows how adherents of the two families differ in their interpretations of perceptive and motivational processes. Chapter 12 focuses specifically on the more technical aspects of learning theory associated with each family.

During the 1920s and 1930s, teachers' colleges moved away from Herbartianism as such. This is not to say that Herbartian ideas were completely dead. They were then, and are today, accepted and practiced by many teachers. However, before the twentieth century had been under way long, a new form of associationism had become popular. This was a nonmentalistic, or physiological, associationism. Its chief exponents during the first third of the century were John B. Watson (1878–1958) and Edward L. Thorndike (1874–1949). Watson's psychology was known as behaviorism. Thorndike's was called connectionism, but it too, in the broadest sense of the term, was "behavioristic." Although the psychological systems of Thorndike and Watson no longer are advocated in their original form, many contemporary psychologists have a sufficiently similar orientation properly to be termed "neobehaviorists."[1] The psychological theories supported by these persons may be identified as stimulus-response associationisms (usually shortening stimulus-response to S-R). If readers wish to refer to Table 6 (p. 231), they will find that items 5, 6, and 7 refer to the S-R associationisms.

The second major family of contemporary learning theories originated in Germany. In 1912 a German psychologist-philosopher, Max Wertheimer, presented a body of theory which came to be known as Gestalt psychology.

Gestalt is a German noun for which there is no English word equivalent, so the term was carried over into English psychological literature. The nearest English translation of *Gestalt* is "configuration." Various other persons who had been thinking along similar lines contributed to this new school of thought. As Gestalt psychology evolved, other names such as *field, phenomenological,* and *organismic psychology* became associated with it. In this book, we refer to related theories which originated from Gestalt psychology as Gestalt-field or cognitive-field psychology. Gestalt-field psychology was introduced into the United States in the middle 1920s. It has gathered a large number of exponents and now can be considered the leading rival of S-R associationism. However, a great many psychologists are eclectic in the sense that they borrow elements from both schools of thought and identify themselves with neither.

Students should be aware of the fact that within each of the two families of psychological theory there is considerable diversity. For example, in the S-R family, followers of Clark Hull and B. F. Skinner would be in disagreement on many points. Likewise, in the Gestalt-field family, followers of Kurt Lewin differ considerably in outlook from followers of Kurt Koffka or G. W. Hartmann. The situation in psychology is somewhat like that in politics; many persons gravitate toward one or the other of our two political parties, but in spite of some common interests, both Democrats and Republicans exhibit a wide range of views. In final

---

[1] *Neo* is a word element meaning "new," "recent," or "modified." When used as a prefix, it refers to a school of thought which is derived from an earlier school of thought but refined in various ways.

analysis, however, S-R associationists have certain key ideas in common, just as do the Gestalt-field psychologists. It is proper to consider each category as a definite grouping which can be discussed in terms of the ideas common to its members.

If students are aware that in spite of variance within each family the two families differ sharply, they will understand the ensuing chapters on learning better. To fundamental issues in psychology the two families provide answers which are often quite incompatible. In dealing with the following questions, a person oriented toward S-R associationism is likely to give a significantly different answer from that given by a Gestalt-field theorist. What is intelligence? What happens when we remember and when we forget? What is perception? What is motivation? What is thinking? What is the role of practice in learning? How does learning transfer to other situations? These and many other questions are controversial in the sense that psychologists with different leanings will offer diverse answers.

Before a student adopts the orientation of one family of psychology or the other, he should recognize that objections may be made to any position one takes in psychology and to any currently available theory of learning. However, although the evidence is not clear enough to warrant dogmatic assertions about learning, he may emerge with the feeling that the ideas central to one family of psychological theory are more tenable and have fewer disadvantages than the ideas central to the other.

Although all modern psychologists, irrespective of their orientation, generally accept the methods and results of experimentation, there is wide divergence in interpretation of experimental results and equally wide divergence on how a given interpretation should be applied in solution of a concrete learning problem. These differences appear to stem from disagreement over the fundamental nature of man, the relationship of man to his environment, and the nature of perception and motivation. In spite of disclaimers by some psychologists, it also appears impossible to detach a number of issues in psychology from related issues in philosophy. A psychologist's philosophical leaning may not only determine the kinds of experiments he conducts but also influence the conclusions he draws from experimentation.

WHAT ARE THE ORIGINS OF S-R ASSOCIATIONISM?

We observe in Chapter 10 that early associationists were interested primarily in mental phenomena; their concern was the association of ideas in minds. As noted at the beginning of Chapter 11, modern associationism is rooted in a different kind of interest—the physiology of bodies.

Nineteenth-century forerunners of modern experimental psychology tended to be philosophical dualists; they considered men to consist of minds and bodies, each genuinely real. There was a good deal of speculation in regard to the nature of the relationship of minds and bodies, but seldom denial of the reality of either. In the transition period between Herbart (1776–1841) and Watson (1878–1958) much vacillation took place between emphasis upon the workings of biological organisms and the functions of minds.

During the first half of the nineteenth century, experimental psychology got its start within experimental physiology. The physiologists Bell and Müller became occupied with testing the workings of the nervous system in seeing and hearing. Thus they became psychologists even though they did not call themselves such.

Wilhelm Wundt (1832–1920) was trained in medicine. He turned from medicine to physiology and from physiology to psychology. In 1879 he established the first psychological laboratory of modern history. His method was introspection; he and his students observed the workings of their respective minds. Students from various parts of the world went to Wundt's laboratory at Leipzig to study introspection. But many became psychological heretics; they turned to study of observable behavior of other persons and animals.

Interest in bodily functioning became apparent among many psychologists late in the nineteenth century. This group of "physiological psychologists" argued that psychology could become a true science only if it switched its focus to bodily processes. In a century which placed ever increasing emphasis upon experimental science, introspection came more and more to appear a highly unreliable procedure. A person could reflect upon the workings of his own mind, but what did this prove? Scientists were ceasing to be concerned with any kind of evidence which was not "publicly verifiable"—that is, subject to public observation and tests. Thus they began to focus their attention on objects or events which could be observed with the "five senses" and studied in the same manner by any number of trained investigators and lead to uniform conclusions.

To a growing number of psychologists, the only logical alternative to the method of introspection was to focus on observable forms of behavior. Such behavior includes not only bodily movement as seen by an observer watching a subject but also the internal physical processes related to overt bodily behavior. Why adrenalin is secreted and how long it takes a person to react to a pinprick are equally proper to a physiological psychologist. Both can be measured objectively, described in terms of definite mechanical sequences or quantities, and reported statistically. Before the twentieth century was very far along, a large number of psychologists had come to feel that psychology, in time, could be made as "scientific" as physics.

We shall name only a few of the persons who contributed to the development of physiological psychology. Marshall Hall (1790–1857) did pioneering work on the neural basis of reflex behavior. Pierre Flourens (1794–1867) demonstrated that different parts of the nervous system have different functions and he took important steps toward identifying the function of each part. Flourens also proposed that conclusions drawn from animal experimentation should be equally applicable to man. This notion gained wide acceptance and greatly simplified the work of experimental psychologists: after all, it is much cheaper and more convenient to experiment with rats than with human beings.

Some of the most notable animal experiments of the late nineteenth and early twentieth centuries were conducted by the Russian physiologist Ivan Petrovich Pavlov (1849–1936). Pavlov put food before a hungry dog and sounded a bell or tuning fork. He found that, if this procedure was repeated enough times, the sound alone would cause the dog to salivate. As we shall see, Pavlov's work was extremely influential, and nowhere more so than among the growing group of S-R associationists in the United States. Thorndike's animal experiments, making use of chicks, dogs, and cats, were possibly even more comprehensive than Pavlov's and, over the long run, more influential in the United States. His famous "laws of learning" were derived mainly from his interpretation of how cats behave when placed in a cage from which they do not know how to escape—until they learn. Since Thorndike was a dominant figure in psychology for almost half a century, we describe some of his ideas in detail.

Thorndike's Connectionism

Thorndike was an eclectic in the sense that he retained in his thinking certain elements of Herbartian "idea associationism." At the same time, he was strongly influenced by the new physiological psychology. In his writings he talks of both physical and mental units. He assumed that there are both physical and mental events, and that learning is a process of linking the two in various combinations. A mental unit was something sensed or perceived; a physical unit was a stimulus or a response. Specifically, he saw learning as a process of connecting a mental with a physical unit, a physical with a mental unit, a mental with a mental unit, or a physical with a physical unit.

Thorndike's theory of learning is called S-R bond theory or *connectionism*. It assumes that, through conditioning, specific responses come to be linked with specific stimuli. These links, bonds, or connections are products of a biological change in a nervous system. Thorndike thought that the chief way in which S-R connections were formed was through random trial and error (or selecting and connecting). It is probably because of Thorndike's influence that the term *trial and error* became popularized and found its way into the vocabularies of many Americans.

In a typical trial-and-error experiment, Thorndike would place a cat in a cage which could be opened from inside only by striking a latch or button. The cat would claw, bite, and scurry wildly about until it accidentally touched the release and was freed. The experiment would be repeated and the animal would behave the same except that over the course of a number of successive "trials" the total time required by the cat to get out would decrease. Eventually the cat would learn to escape immediately without random activity. Thorndike inferred from the timed behavior of his cats that learning was a process of "stamping in" connections in the nervous system and had nothing to do with insight or "catching on."

Thorndike formulated a number of laws of learning and classified them as either primary or secondary. We describe here only his three primary laws:

1. *The law of exercise or repetition.*   According to this law, the more times a stimulus-induced response is repeated, the longer it will be retained. As Thorndike put it, "Other things being equal, *exercise strengthens the bond between situation and response.*"[2] Conversely, a bond is weakened through failure to exercise it.

2. *The law of effect.*   The law of effect states the famous pleasure-pain principle so frequently associated with Thorndike's name. A response is strengthened if it is followed by pleasure and weakened if followed by displeasure. Or, in Thorndike's words, ". . . a modifiable connection being made . . . between an S and an R and being accompanied or followed by a satisfying state of affairs man responds, other things being equal, by an increase in the strength of that connection. To a connection similar, save that an *annoying* state of affairs goes with or follows it, man responds, other things being equal, by a decrease in the strength of the connection."[3]

3. *The law of readiness.*   Thorndike termed the neuron (or neurons) and the synapse (or synapses) involved in establishment of a specific bond or connection a *conduction unit.* He assumed that, because of the structure of a nervous system, in a given situation certain conduction units are more predisposed to conduct than others. And *"for a conduction unit ready to conduct to do so is satisfying, and for it not to do so is annoying."*[4]

In his later writings Thorndike disavowed his law of exercise or repetition and one-half—the annoyance aspect—of his law of effect. But he seemed not to have had the courage of his convictions. Through implica-

[2] Edward L. Thorndike, *Education,* Macmillan, 1912, p. 95 (italics in original).

[3] Edward L. Thorndike, *Educational Psychology,* Teachers College, Columbia University, 1913, Vol. 1, p. 172 (italics in original).

[4] *Ibid.,* p. 127 (italics in original).

tion, he continued to emphasize repetition in learning. His law of effect shifted its emphasis to pleasure, but the pain aspect was not completely discarded.

Students will readily see that Thorndike's laws of learning are closely related and may operate together. For example, if an organism is ready to respond, then response is pleasurable and this fact in itself will tend to fix the response. Students will also see that the laws appear to be exceedingly mechanical. Furthermore, they seem to leave no room for any sort of thought or insight, and they do not appear to require the assumption of any kind of purposiveness of man or lower animals.

The psychological concept *purposiveness* has no direct relationship to the problem of cosmic or teleological purpose. Within a purposive psychology, as contrasted with a mechanistic one, we assume that each animal or person, whatever his developmental level, is seeking some end or purpose and that we can predict his behavior most accurately when we anticipate what it is he is trying to accomplish.

Watson's Behaviorism

Watson felt much more strongly than Thorndike the need to base psychology exclusively on the concepts of physics and chemistry. To his way of thinking, mind and all kinds of mentalistic concepts were not only unsusceptible of scientific inquiry but also irrelevant to the real task of psychology. Watson drew heavily upon Pavlov's work and became convinced that learning was as Pavlov described it, namely, a process of building conditioned reflexes through the substitution of one stimulus for another.

Watson and other "pure behaviorists" came to reject certain of Thorndike's ideas because it seemed impossible to exclude mind and mind-related concepts from them. We have already mentioned that Thorndike talked of "mental units." The pure behaviorists were also bothered by Thorndike's concepts of satisfaction and annoyance. These seemed to behaviorists to be mentalistic concepts and better disregarded in a truly scientific psychology. In the tradition of the earlier physiological psychologists, Watson confined his study to only those aspects of animal life which are sufficiently overt to make possible highly objective observation and measurement.

One of Thorndike's secondary laws of learning, however, seemed very promising to the Watsonians. This was the "law of associative shifting," and it became the keystone for the behavioristic movement of the 1920s.

According to this law, we may *"get any response of which a learner is capable associated with any situation to which he is sensitive."*[5] In other

[5] *Ibid.,* p. 15 (italics in original).

words, any response which is possible can be linked with any stimulus. An animal's "purposes or thoughts" have nothing to do with such learning. In fact, purpose and mentalistic thought supposedly are concepts outside the realm of scientific psychology. We may illustrate this law by using an example involving the training of an animal. Suppose we wish to train a dog to sit up at the verbal command "Sit." It is only necessary to induce the dog to sit up repeatedly by dangling a piece of meat or other food above him at the same time the verbal command is issued. Once this procedure has been repeated enough times, the dog should respond properly—without error—whenever the command is given. In this example, as long as the same "adequate stimulus" is used throughout the experiment, it would not matter if the command were replaced by any other accompanying stimulus to which a dog is sensitive—a light, a bell, snapping the fingers, whistling. Furthermore, by using the same basic procedure, it should be possible to teach a dog to perform any other act of which it is capable—standing on its front legs, rolling over, playing dead, etc. This supposed principle of learning, fundamental to behaviorism, is the principle of stimulus substitution.

Behaviorists defined a living organism as a self-maintaining mechanism. They assumed that the essence of a human machine is a system of receptors (sense organs), conductors (neurons), switching organs (brain and spinal cord), and effectors (muscles) attached to levers (bones)— plus, of course, fueling and controlling organs such as stomach and glands. When an organism is defined in such mechanistic terms, mentalistic concepts can be entirely eliminated. Not only can they be dropped out of the picture but they actually begin to seem rather fanciful. (Can one imagine a *machine* having "tender sentiments" or "soaring on the imagination"?) Among behaviorists, there developed an attitude toward the earlier mentalistic psychologists similar to that of a modern physician toward a primitive witch doctor.

The position of a Watsonian behaviorist can be illustrated amusingly in a morning conversation. Ordinarily, a conventional greeting would go as follows: "Good morning, how are you?" "I'm fine, and yourself?" "Just fine." But such a greeting implies introspection. Each person is "looking into himself" in order to decide what kind of shape he is in. Presumably (according to a behaviorist) this is scientifically impossible; instead the two persons would need to inspect each other. The proper salutation of a behaviorist would be, "Good morning, you appear to be fine; how am I?"

The Neobehaviorists

There is a large group of American psychologists today who assume that life can be explained in essentially mechanistic terms but who have adopted positions somewhat different from that of the Watsonian behaviorists. It might be said that Watsonian behaviorism, in its pure form, is all but dead. Probably the best term to apply to contemporary S-R associationists is *neobehaviorists*.

Contemporary S-R associationists do not place nearly as much emphasis upon the operation of brain and nervous system as did their predecessors. Of course, Watson himself had felt that the precise nature of neural mechanisms was largely irrelevant to learning; but Watson's followers, as well as Thorndike, had exhibited a strong interest in neural physiology and the physical mechanics of S-R linkages. Interests of neobehaviorists lie in analyses of behavior per se rather than in the neural mechanism behind it. They are still concerned with how S's and R's become linked but they are not greatly concerned with the precise operation of the physiological mechanism which lies between.

Neobehaviorists differ from the original behaviorists in another respect. In their experimentation, they have tended to focus attention upon response modification as well as stimulus substitution. Response modification refers to the fate of responses that have already been made—whether they will be strengthened or weakened by subsequent events. In this connection, continual reference is made in the literature of neobehaviorism to *conditioning*. Conditioning means strengthening of a response. It is achieved by stimulus substitution, i.e., accompanying an adequate stimulus by a new stimulus, or by response strengthening or modification, i.e., following a response with a stimulus which strengthens it. The two kinds of conditioning are explained in Chapter 12.

Since Thorndike's concept of learning as a process of "stamping in" a response which was originally accidental is a form of response modification, one might say that many neobehaviorists have returned to Thorndike's conception of learning. However, most neobehaviorists are better systematizers than Thorndike. This is, they are more consistent, largely by virtue of their building systems, which do not at any point require an assumption of conscious behavior. Thorndike tried to be highly mechanical, but the neobehaviorists have developed psychological theories which are more consistently mechanical than Thorndike's.

Another feature of neobehaviorism is its attempt to explain behavior which appears purposive. Purposiveness has always bothered psychologists who are behavioristically oriented because they have felt that purpose is difficult to explain without slipping into a mind-body dualism. However, what seems purposive must be explained in some way. Neobehaviorists tend to develop mechanical explanations for apparent purposiveness. Purposiveness is regarded as a product of a pattern of stimulation, in which certain stimuli are more potent than the rest and thus lead an organism in one way rather than another. Much purposiveness would be interpreted as "drive reduction," that is, a relieving reaction to the stimulation induced by organic drives such as hunger or sex. Neobehaviorists remain careful to explain apparent purposiveness in a way which does not require the assumption of conscious behavior or intelligent experience.

We shall mention but one more difference between the contemporary neobehaviorists and old-line pure behaviorists. Historically, behaviorism was "atomistic" in the sense that it focused on the *elements* of a situation. Attempts were made to identify specific stimuli and to describe the behavior of an organism as a product of numerous discrete and isolable reactions. Today, S-R theorists talk in terms of "stimulus situations," i.e., complex configurations of stimulation, and of "molar behavior," i.e., the coordinated behavior of a whole organism.

Well-known contemporary neobehaviorists include Edwin R. Guthrie, B. F. Skinner, K. W. Spence, and D. O. Hebb. All these psychologists and their followers are greatly interested in the psychology of learning. However, at one extreme Spence feels that in its present stage of development psychology has little to offer schools, and at the other extreme Skinner represents his psychology as the means of placing education on an efficient basis.[6] Since Skinner's views are representative and extraordinarily clean-cut, Chapter 13 is devoted to an exposition of a Skinnerian psychology of learning.

WHAT ARE THE ORIGINS OF GESTALT-FIELD PSYCHOLOGY?

As noted earlier in the chapter, the position of Gestalt psychology was formally stated first by the German philosopher-psychologist Max Wertheimer (1880–1943) in 1912. The central idea of Wertheimer's point of view is expressed in the German word *Gestalt,* which, as we have seen, means an organized pattern or configuration, or, more simply, an organized *whole* in contrast to a collection of parts. The notion that a thing cannot be understood by study of its constituent parts, but only by study of it as a totality, is probably very old. Gardner Murphy suggests that it can be found in the literature of pre-Socratic Greece.[7] Various Greek writers proposed that the universe could best be understood through "laws of arrangement" or "principles of order," rather than through study of its basic building blocks, the elements. In contrast, other Greek writers were "atomists," i.e., they sought the key to understanding through a

[6] See Donald K. Adams *et al., Learning Theory, Personality Theory and Clinical Research,* Wiley, 1954, p. 2.

[7] Gardner Murphy, *Historical Introduction to Modern Psychology,* Harcourt, Brace, 1949, p. 284.

study of individual elements. Just as the former might be called the originators of the Gestalt idea, so might the latter be called the originators of the atomistic idea—which characterized early behaviorism.

Among the nineteenth-century forerunners of Wertheimer we should include Ernst Mach (1838–1916), likewise a German. Although Mach held that the worlds of physics and psychology are essentially the same, he also argued that psychology must take into account those sensations which do not correspond to the physical reality before the viewer. These "nonphysical" sensations are sensations of *relationship*. For example, a person may see three dots on a sheet of paper and think of them as the points of a triangle. There is nothing in individual dots to suggest this; it is their configuration that prompts the relationship.

In the 1890s, following Mach, Christian von Ehrenfels (1859–1932) pursued the same ideas. He stated that, in all perception, qualities appear which represent more than the physical items sensed. A perceiver tends to confer on the physical objects of perception a form, configuration, or meaning. He tries to organize or integrate what he sees. A school of thought began to form along the lines explored by these two men, and a new term came into use—*Gestaltqualitat*, which means approximately "the quality conferred by a pattern."

Wertheimer and his followers went still farther and formulated a series of "laws" of perception—*Prägnanz, similarity, proximity, closure, good continuation,* and *membership character*. According to the basic *law of Prägnanz*, if a perceptual field is disorganized when a person first experiences it, he imposes order on the field in a predictable way. The "predictable way" follows the other five subordinate laws. *Similarity* means that similar items (dots, for instance) tend to form groups in perception. *Proximity* means that perceptual groups are favored according to the nearness of their respective parts.

Closure means that closed areas are more stable than unclosed ones. Draw a 340° arc and ask a viewer what you have drawn. He very likely will say "a circle." This is an example of closure; to achieve closure is satisfying. Closure is an alternative to Thorndike's law of effect. *Good continuation* is closely related to closure. It means that, in perception, one tends to continue straight lines as straight lines and curves as curves.

According to the law of *membership character,* a single part of a whole does not have fixed characteristics; it gets its characteristics from the context in which it appears. As Gardner Murphy puts it, "The Gestaltist insists that the attributes or aspects of the component parts, insofar as they can be defined, are defined by their relations to the system as a whole in which they are functioning."[8] For example, a patch of color in a paint-

8 *Ibid.,* p. 288.

ing derives its quality from its context—the surrounding picture pattern —rather than from anything inherent in itself.

In perception, organization of a field tends to be as simple and clear as the given conditions allow. A viewer imposes an organization characterized by stability, simplicity, regularity, and symmetry. He groups individual items in a field so they will have pattern. He relates similar items required for completeness, and if present patterns are meaningful he tries to maintain them into the future. Imposing a "good" Gestalt, as happens when the foregoing events occur, is a *psychological* task. It does not necessarily involve any change in the physical environment. Rather, it represents a change in how a viewer *sees* his physical environment. However, problem solving often does require a person to manipulate his physical environment in order to make the various elements fall into proper place for a solution.

Two of Wertheimer's German followers, Wolfgang Köhler (1887———) and Kurt Koffka (1886–1941), were mainly responsible for publicizing Gestalt psychology and establishing it in the United States. Köhler is famous, among other things, for his celebrated study of the learning process in chimpanzees (*The Mentality of Apes,* 1925). He set out to test Thorndike's hypothesis that learning is a matter of trial and error in which correct responses are gradually stamped in. Köhler observed that, in addition to learning which might appear accidental, his apes displayed a type of learning which appeared insightful. Hence, Köhler concluded that Thorndike's laws of learning were inadequate. Koffka's book *Growth of the Mind* (1924) contained a detailed criticism of trial-and-error learning as conceived by Thorndike. Koffka not only criticized Thorndike; his book also was a critique of the major ideas of behaviorism.

Kurt Lewin (1890–1947), also German born, took the spirit of Gestalt theory, added to it some new concepts, and coined a new terminology. He developed a field psychology usually referred to as topological and vector psychology (deriving these terms from the fields of geometry and mechanics). Lewin spent his later years in the United States, where he acquired a considerable following. Because his psychology appears to be the most advanced and systematic field psychology, Chapter 14 is devoted to its expansion especially with reference to learning theory.

As a result of experimentation by the Gestalt-field psychologists, S-R associationists generally are coming to recognize that the earlier atomistic stimulus-response idea, based as it was on the principle of simple reflex arcs, does not explain human behavior adequately. As previously indicated, there is a tendency among contemporary S-R psychologists to speak of "molar behavior," i.e., behavior of the whole organism in contrast to piecemeal, or "molecular," behavior. Such psychologists characteristically refer to "total responses to patterns of stimulation." However, because these psychologists continue to think in terms of a mechanical linking of stimuli and responses, they are still within the basic pattern of S-R associationism. In spite of their adoption of the concept of molar behavior, their point of view tends to be fundamentally different from, and incompatible with, that of Gestalt-field psychologists.

WHAT IS THE PHILOSOPHICAL THINKING BEHIND THE TWO FAMILIES?

It is the purpose of this part of the chapter to explore some of the philosophical implications of the two families of psychology. When a contrast is drawn between their underlying philosophical premises, differences between the two families are made much clearer. Although psychologists have tried during the past century to divorce psychology and philosophy, it is doubtful that this is possible. There is no science so "pure" that it lacks philosophical implications. Even physicists find it helpful to make assumptions about the basic nature of their materials and processes; they too become involved in philosophical formulations.

Since any psychological system rests upon a particular conception of human nature, psychology is deeply involved with philosophy from the very start. Of the various positions a person may take on the question of the basic nature of man, we have seen that two—good-active and bad-active—are prescientific in the sense that they render judgments on man's hereditary moral nature (students may want to review Chapter 2). The issue among contemporary psychologists is whether man is an active creature of instincts (as exemplified in Freudian or neo-Freudian psychology), an essentially passive creature in a determining environment (as implied in S-R associationism), or a purposive person interacting with a psychological environment (as implied in Gestalt-field psychology). Each of the two latter positions harmonizes with a broad philosophical outlook: S-R associationism with philosophic *positivism* or realism,[9] and Gestalt-field theory with a systematic relativism, also called *pragmatism, experimentalism,* or *instrumentalism.*

Realism and S-R Associationism

What is realism? Space permits only the barest treatment. Realists are convinced that the physical world experienced by human beings is real and essentially what it appears to be when observed through the senses. Furthermore, even if there were no human beings around to observe it, it would exist in the same state. Existence is independent of a thing's being

---

[9] Realism as used here connotes the qualities of naturalistic, monistic realism. Although its description also fits some facets of contemporary classical realism, it does not represent adequately that point of view.

known. Realists assume that the physical world is governed by natural laws which operate inexorably and without change. They further assume that a basic principle of the universe is cause and effect; every event is determined by events that have gone before. The universe is a vast mechanism governed by laws which are essentially mechanical in nature.

A realist is likely to assume that there is a kind of hierarchy of the sciences, some being much more objective and reliable than others. He places at the top of the hierarchy physics and chemistry, aided by mathematics. These sciences are regarded as models, which other sciences should emulate. To a consistent realist, nothing should be asserted to be real or meaningful unless, through observation, it can be subjected to objective study, using only publicly verifiable data. If anything exists, it supposedly exists in some amount; if it exists in some amount, it can be measured.

Let us next see how this over-all point of view was transplanted to psychology. Early in human history, people commonly believed in animism, i.e., that all objects, including even rocks, have minds or spirits. Since primitive man had no other way of explaining most types of natural events, animism provided at least some basis for understanding. As people learned more about natural causation, animism declined in popularity. In other words, when human beings came to understand something about gravity, a person no longer needed to attribute a mind and will to a rock to know why it fell on his head.

As time went on, mechanical explanations began to be applied to all sorts of physical events involving nonliving objects. Increasingly the nonliving parts of the universe were believed to consist of atoms in motion, each inert by itself, but subject to the push and pull of lawful forces external to itself.

Living matter, particularly human beings, did not appear to conform to the mechanical concepts applied in the world of nature. Human beings seemed, on the surface at least, to be willful and unpredictable. Thus some kind of mind force was attributed to them. Some persons assumed that all living things have such a nonmaterial life force—a belief referred to as vitalism (described in Chapter 2). Belief in a nonmaterial mind force as applied to human beings (body-mind dualism) led, as we saw in Chapter 10, to a distinctive conception of learning. The idea that learning is a process of disciplining or training minds gave us the classical tradition in education. Although actual teaching under the mind-training approach may appear highly mechanical, the conception of human nature underlying it definitely is nonmechanistic. It assumes a mind substance capable of free will and other spontaneous and "uncaused" behavior.

All associationist psychologies tend to be mechanistic, in the sense that they describe man and thought in the same physicalistic terms as are used by natural scientists. All four psychologies—apperception, connectionism, behaviorism, and reinforcement began as mechanistic theories of learning. Thus, with their coming there was an accompanying move toward rejection of vitalism or any other conception of life inconsistent with realists' interpretation of the universe. Consequently, with the advent of associationistic psychology, psychologists found themselves in increasing sympathy with the tenets of realistic philosophy.

Mechanistic-realistic psychology was an outgrowth of the attempt by S-R theorists to make psychology as "scientific" as physics. The issue between mechanistic and nonmechanistic psychology is nowhere stated more clearly than by the contemporary neobehaviorist D. O. Hebb. Hebb says flatly that psychology's only hope of remaining scientific is to assume that man is basically a mechanism. He says that there are only two alternatives so far as the basic outlook of a psychologist is concerned—mechanism and vitalism. *"Psychology,"* he says, "is the study of the more complex forms of organization in behavior, and of the processes such as learning, perception or emotion which are involved in the organization. . . . *Behavior* is the publicly observable activity of muscles or glands of external secretion as manifested in movements of parts of the body or in the appearance of tears, sweat, saliva and so forth. . . . The *organization* of behavior is the pattern, or combination, of separate items in relation to each other and to environmental stimulation."[10]

Furthermore, with respect to the type of study which psychologists can undertake, he says, "All one can know about another's feelings and awareness is an inference from what he *does*—from his muscular contractions and glandular secretions."[11] To a psychologist such as Hebb, Gestalt-field psychology would appear to be nothing more than "confusionism." The philosophical orientation of a mechanistic psychologist is so thoroughly realistic that any other outlook seems untenable.

Among S-R theorists, much use is made of the concepts *reflexes, reactions, objective measurement, quantitative data, sequence of behavior,* and *reinforcement schedules.* They have used these and similar expressions in an attempt to be rigidly scientific. To them, stimulus and response in psychology are equated with cause and effect in physics.

In his approach to education a realist, and likewise an S-R associationist, is very much an environmentalist and determinist in the sense that he assumes that the surrounding environment should, and inescapably will, control closely the behaviors and learnings of students. Thus, teaching practices advocated by S-R psychologists are closely in tune with the realistic outlook. Such psychologists tend to recommend that

[10] D. O. Hebb, *A Textbook of Psychology,* Saunders, 1958, p. 2.
[11] D. O. Hebb, *The Organization of Behavior; a Neuro-Psychological Theory,* Wiley, 1949, p. xiii.

subject matter be selected by qualified adults prior to the teaching act, that it reflect facts and skills which are useful in contemporary society, and that it be inculcated into students. There is an implicit assumption that, if a given item of subject matter impinges upon a student, there will be a definite and predictable effect. Only secondary, if any, mention is made of such concepts as *student goals, motives,* or *problem solving.*

Relativism and Gestalt-Field Psychology

Relativism has emerged during the past 70 or 80 years and is, in a sense, a reaction against the absolutistic ways which have characterized many facets of man's thinking throughout history. Relativism contrasts sharply with realism. The latter is absolutistic in that its exponents assume the existence of an ultimate reality which consists of fixed natural laws and they define truth as that which corresponds to natural law and consequently is unchanging. Relativists do not assert or deny absolute existence. Rather they define *psychological reality* as that which we *make* of what comes to us. They then deal with reality, so defined, in achieving truth and designing behavior.

Probably the central idea of relativism is that *a thing derives its qualities from its relationship to other things.* A person may look at a patch of grass which is in shadow. Compared with grass in the full rays of the sun, the patch appears dark; but compared with grass at night, it appears light. A homely girl, in the company of girls even more homely, appears pretty. The way we perceive any object or event is colored by the total situation. This principle is actually one with which everyone is familiar. Relativistic philosophy does little more than explore and develop the numerous ramifications and implications of this central idea.

It might appear that if relativism were a valid concept a person could never make a definitive statement about anything, except to say that it "is closer than something else," "is to the left of something else," "is redder than something else," "is smaller than something else."

However, this is not an insurmountable problem. In order to view something relativistically, one simply determines a convenient vantage point —a frame of reference. A man can say that his automobile has 200 horsepower and such an assertion can be quite confident. The unit of measure, one horsepower, is an arbitrary measure—contrived by man and susceptible to future change—but it has definite usefulness as a point of reference. Such relatively fixed points of reference are *relatively absolute.* The word absolute, so used, is an adjective; it means no more than that the point of reference is one of relative fixity or stability.[12]

[12] The present discussion of relativism follows closely that in Ernest E. Bayles, *Democratic Educational Theory,* Harper, 1960; see particularly Chaps. 4 and 7.

If one assumes that things have to be dealt with relationally, rather than as things-in-themselves, a distinctive method of defining truth, or knowledge, and an equally distinctive method of arriving at truth are required. A relativist rejects the notion that man is able to find and use final or ultimate truth. Consequently, he has little, if any, interest in "eternal verities." Relativists regard knowledge as insights developed and held by human beings using human methods. As Bayles points out, the development of the notion that knowledge is a matter of human interpretation, and not a literal description of what exists external to man, reflects a shift from a realistic to a relativistic view of science. In physical science, it is no longer commonly said that an atom has certain properties; rather, one says that it *acts as if* it has these properties.

A scientific law (including a principle of psychology) is a statement which seems true to all or most of those who are competent to study the matter. The relativistic test of truth is anticipatory accuracy, not correspondence to ultimate reality. Thus, in a sense, a scientific law is a generalization about which there is considerable agreement among those scientifically competent in its areas; it is a matter of consensus. Its test, however, is not the consensus but its predictive accuracy. Relativists assume that no scientific law is "sacred"; any law may change, and indeed, over the course of time most will. A significant aspect of the thinking of relativists is their expectancy of change. They are much more likely than realists to think of both nature and culture as undergoing continuous modification.

But what grounds does a relativist have for judging anything true? To quote Bayles, an insight is considered true "if, and only if, the deduced behavior pattern, when tested experientially or experimentally, produces the results which were anticipated." Thus, an insight is true if it proves to be reasonably accurate—if what one supposes will follow from its application actually follows. To put it colloquially, a statement is true if it "pans out." Truth, to a relativist, is not based upon "eternal and universal principles." It is man made, and man will change it as need be. This does not mean that truth is unimportant or ephemeral. It does mean that truth tends to evolve as human experience evolves. It also means that truth sometimes is quite personal and individualistic; what is true for me may not be true for you, even in situations which on the surface look quite similar. However, many relativistic truths are widely agreed upon within groups of various sizes; they are social truths.

Both realists and relativists assume that the most valid method of inquiry is scientific in nature; it is based on testable evidence. But they define scientific method in different ways and, as the foregoing discussion has indicated, seek different ends from it. To a relativist, scientific method is not merely a sequence of steps such as a physicist supposedly uses. Scientific thinking is any form of intellectual pursuit which is based on testable evidence and is productive in relation to the goals of the thinker. To be sure, there are some measuring sticks or criteria of scientific truth; these criteria Bayles has encompassed under the headings of adequacy and harmony. A conclusion, to be properly scientific, must *harmonize* all the data, i.e., it must make the data "jibe," or "add up." If a single pertinent fact seems to "point the other way," if it remains unexplained, then the conclusion is not to be trusted. According to the principle of *adequacy,* all known pertinent facts must be taken into consideration. None may be ignored—no matter how unpalatable it might seem.

A relativist construes science much more broadly than does a realist. He assumes that the scientific way can be applied in a wide range of situations. A relativist does not think in terms of a hierarchy of sciences, with physics, chemistry, and mathematics at the top. He is also more flexible with respect to the kinds of data he will consider. A realist in psychology is likely to admit only data of observable physical objects or substances. Conversely, a relativist in psychology will consider all the data of human experience, including that which may seem introspective.

Why is a relativistic outlook in philosophy in harmony with Gestalt-field psychology? This school of psychology contains strong relativistic elements which naturally align it with relativistic philosophy, as will become clear during our examination of certain aspects of Gestalt-field theory.

Gestalt-field psychology is essentially an emergent synthesis which developed from conflict between the tenets of Roussellian "romantic naturalism" and "scientific realism." As we have seen, Roussellians contend that psychological development is primarily a matter of natural unfoldment. To them, learning is largely equated with unfoldment and is a product of inner urges. It is not imposed by a child's environment. Realistic psychologists see all development as a product of learning and assume that learning comes from the environment; it is conditioning induced by stimuli which impinge upon a child from without.

The only way of bridging the two positions appears to be to assume that a child is what he is because of an interaction between him and his culture. With the emphasis upon interaction, the responsibility for development rests neither with the child alone (as Rousseau would have said) nor with the environment alone (as a realist says). It is person and environment coming together—in a psychological field—where Gestalt-field psychologists find the clue to psychological development.

What has this to do with relativism? Since the number of possible culture patterns is infinite, the possibilities for variety in human development become infinite likewise. Within its biological limits, human nature might become anything. Furthermore, if one accepts the premises of Gestalt-field psychology, he must define reality in a manner entirely different from that of a realist. Reality now consists of the *interpretations* a person makes of himself and his surroundings as he interacts. If reality is to be regarded as interpretations or meanings, rather than pre-existent physical objects, as such, it is obvious that reality will be in a constant state of flux. In 1947, Earl C. Kelley published an extraordinarily provocative little book entitled *Education for What Is Real*. By "what is real" Kelley means our *perceptions* of physical and social objects. Kelley's book depicts concisely and sharply many aspects of the issue concerning the definition of reality. Because this issue is of prime importance, the following section explores several of its facets.

HOW DO THE TWO FAMILIES DEFINE REALITY?

S-R associationists tend to treat reality and existence as identical. The term *existence* refers to what exists or "what is there," i.e., physical objects and processes. The chair on which the reader is sitting may be said to exist, and to an associationist the chair is a good example of reality (not one's impression of the chair, but the chair itself). The chair exists in its own right; the way one perceives it is not relevant to its reality.[13]

Gestalt-field theorists make a distinction between reality and existence. Without denying independent existence of objects, or even of other people's ideas, they insist that each person sizes up or interprets his world in such a way that it will form a meaningful pattern for him, and his interpretation is the reality on which he designs his actions. A Gestalt-field psychologist thinks that a person's knowledge of things is always limited by the impossibility of his ever getting completely "outside himself." He assumes that any perception will be colored to some degree by the purposes and experiences of the observer, as well as by the procedures used in observing the perceived object. None of this should be taken to mean that a person literally makes his world; rather, in any field—science, social relations, morality, even religion—each individual makes, not the world, but his own notions of the world.

In order to understand fully the difference in definitions of reality between the S-R association and the Gestalt-field approaches, it is necessary to explore in some detail the differences between their exponents in their definitions of environment, perception, interaction, and experience. We

[13] The way in which we here use the term *existence* bears no relation to the way it is used by existential philosophers. Their "existence" is a psychological and not a physical concept.

already have suggested some of these differences. We propose now to dig more deeply. Some repetition of what has been said before is necessary.

How Is Environment Defined by the Two Groups of Psychologists?

S-R associationists maintain that a person's psychological and physical environments are identical; his environment consists of all his physical and social surroundings. Because environment is defined in objective, physicalistic terms, presumably anyone can see (or hear, smell, feel, or taste) the environment of anyone else.

In contrast, Gestalt-field psychologists think of a person's environment as psychological, and it consists of what he makes of what is around him. It is that portion of a life space or perceptual field which surrounds a *person* or *self*. A psychological environment includes impressions of parts of the physical environment but not necessarily all of it. It also extends beyond its physical environment. Sometimes a person's psychological environment includes largely memories or anticipations; in this case he is scarcely aware of the physical world currently around him. In Lewin's terminology, he is operating on an "irreality level."

Since each person's perceptual environment is unique, obviously two persons may appear to be in the same location in space and time (or as nearly so as possible) and yet have very different psychological environments. Furthermore, the behaviors of two equally intelligent persons who are confronted with the same "objective facts" may differ drastically because each is different in his purposes and experiential background. Whenever a person has a new experience, he changes his environment and will never again be able to recapture the old environment in its identical form. The Gestalt-field conception of environment explains why in a particular family one son may become a minister and another turn to crime; their interpretations of their world differ radically, even though to an outsider their social and physical environments would appear quite similar.

How Do the Two Groups Define Perception?

S-R associationists define perception in such a way as to make it analogous with taking photographs. The sense organs in literal fashion "read" a person's social and physical surroundings and record this "reading" in the nervous system. After sensing something, a person may derive a meaning for it. But note that, according to an associationist, sensation comes prior to meaning and the two acts, sensing and finding meaning, are regarded as separate. An S-R associationist assumes that sensation may be indiscriminate, in that a person tends to "take in" all aspects of the physical world to which his sense organs are sensitive. Such a psychologist defines perception, then, as a two-step process (sensing and deriving meaning) which focuses on particular objects of the environment only insofar as previous conditioning directs.

A Gestalt-field psychologist, on the other hand, does not separate sensation of an object from its meaning. In his view, a person will rarely sense an object unless it has relevance to some purpose of the person. It is this relevance to purpose, this instrumental quality, of an object which constitutes its meaning. Unless a person sees some meaning in an object, he will pay little or no attention to it. Thus, a Gestalt-field psychologist sees perception as a unitary process, in which sensation hinges on meaning and meaning on sensation, and sensing and finding meaning occur simultaneously. Perception, to a field psychologist, is highly selective. It is always related to a person's purposes at the time of perception. In his goal-seeking behavior, a person actively seeks out those aspects of his environment which will help or hinder him, and usually it is to these that he is primarily sensitive.

Furthermore, to a Gestalt-field psychologist the meaning of a sensation or perception is always related to the total situation. Relationships, and not a summation of individual elements, determine the quality of any event (such as perception). Any psychological event is a result of the interaction of many factors; hence, perception always involves a problem of organization. A thing is perceived as a relationship within a field which includes the thing, the viewer, and a complex background incorporating the viewer's purposes and previous experience. Considering the above notions, it is obvious that to a Gestalt-field theorist the senses do not directly mirror physical objects in their geographical environment. The camera analogy which fits the associationist's idea of perception seems to a field psychologist gross oversimplification.

Is Interaction of Person and Environment Alternating or Simultaneous and Mutual?

The term *interaction* is commonly used in describing the person-environment process through which reality is perceived. Both families of psychology use the term but define it in sharply different ways. Whereas S-R association theorists mean alternating interaction or reaction of organism, then of environment, Gestalt-field psychologists always imply that the interaction of a person and his environment are simultaneous and mutual—both mutually participate at the same time.

ALTERNATING INTERACTION. Alternating interaction begins with a reaction of a person to a stimulus. The person is regarded as a passive receiver of stimuli; his habitual pose is one of waiting or repose. When he receives a stimulus he reacts in whatever way he must—in accordance with the conditioned or innate reflexes which are called into play. When he reacts, it is likely that he will change his physical or social environment in some way. (The environment is also passive, in the sense that it "waits" for him to do something to it.) To an associationist, the temporal sequence of the interactive process is stimulus-reaction-stimulus-reaction, and so on. The chain of S-R's may continue indefinitely. Consider an example. A dog bites a man; the man kicks the dog. Let us suppose the kick conditions the dog not to bite. The dog is friendly toward the next man he encounters, and the man reacts by patting him on the head. The dog may then react by licking the man's hand. The man may then buy the dog a steak. And so on, ad infinitum.

S-R associationists may think of interaction as involving only physical processes. That is, material objects react to other material objects. Interaction between human beings is analogous to the interaction of molecules in a chemical compound. One molecule strikes another, which is deflected against another, which hits another, and so on. The interactive process is regarded as a chain of causes and effects; stimuli are causes and responses are effects.

SIMULTANEOUS MUTUAL INTERACTION.   Interaction, when used by Gestalt-field psychologists, refers to a relationship between a person and his environment in which the person in purposeful fashion tries to see meaning in his environment and use objects in his environment in advantageous ways. As he interprets and uses his environment for his own purposes, both are changed. The person's physical environment may be changed in ways which others may observe; or it may not. In any case, its meaning is changed so that it looks different to the person interacting with it. The person changes in the sense that through interaction he achieves new insights which literally transform him, in however minor ways. Gone from this concept of interaction is the idea of the reaction of a passive organism to a stimulus, and an ensuing chain of S-R's running back and forth from organism to environment. Rather, we now have simultaneous mutual change of person and environment, during which we do not make a sharp distinction between the two. In symbolic terms, this concept is simultaneous mutual interaction—the SMI concept.

Parents and siblings usually constitute important aspects of a child's environment. When a second child arrives in a family, the first child sizes up—perceives—the situation. Whether the first child feels rejected depends not upon the physical stimuli he receives from his parents and the sibling but upon what he makes of the relationship of the parents and the second child. The important question is not Do the parents actually favor child number two? but rather Does child number one "see" child number two as favored over child number one—himself? In this situation, the parents and the other child are key aspects of each child's and parent's environment. The way child number one perceives the situation has important bearing upon the environments of child number two and the parents. Each person in a situation interacts with the others.

Gestalt-field theorists, in their espousal of the concept of SMI, make a sharp distinction between interaction of physical objects in a physical environment and (the subject of psychology) interaction of psychological realities in a psychological environment. To a field psychologist, it is only what occurs in a person's life space which, at that moment (or a longer unit of time), is important to that person. A person interacts by relating himself (as he understands himself) to his interpretation of what is around him. Of course, while interacting, he may move his body and manipulate objects in his physical environment in ways conspicuous to observers. But psychological interaction and physical reaction are two different processes. A person can interact within a psychological field while he is seated in an armchair in front of a fireplace. Human experience is synonymous with an interactive event. It does not necessarily require any kind of motion which an observer can detect.

Any idea can be ridden too hard, and the reader has probably already thought of cases in which the concept of SMI does not seem to fit. For example, a man who is not aware of danger may be shot in the back. It seems fairly clear that in such a case the man has been a passive victim of a feature of his environment which was active in relation to him. However, all this example suggests is that there are situations in which a person has no control over what happens to him. Gestalt-field psychology and relativistic philosophy do not deny this; instead, they operate on the not inconsistent assumption that, whenever a person can, he seeks to manipulate purposefully all those aspects of his environment which at the time mean anything to him. He may or may not be successful, but whether or not he is, his life space will be different as a result of the attempt.

What Is Experience?

Up to this point, we have used the term *experience* without really coming to grips with its meaning. Gestalt-field psychologists regard experience as a pivotal concept in any discussion of the interactive process and the meaning of reality. S-R associationists make little use of the term, especially in connection with any investigation or description which is supposed to be scientific. Most charge that Gestalt-field psychologists use the term *experience* in such a way as to imply a process which does not involve the real physical world but only "mentalistic" copies of it. According to associationists, the concept presupposes a special world of consciousness and, if consciousness does exist, it does not lend itself well to scientific study. An associationist may concede that thought appears to exist, but he is likely to insist that, if human beings are to be studied with true scientific objectivity, most kinds of mentalistic concepts must be ruled out of bounds. The well-known neobehaviorist B. F. Skinner expresses this notion clearly: ". . . the private event [i.e., thought or consciousness] is at best no more than a link in a causal chain, and it is usually not even that. We may think before we act in the sense that we may behave covertly before we behave overtly, but our action is not an 'expression' of the covert response [i.e., thought] or the consequence of it. The two are attributable to the same variables."[14]

What Skinner appears to be saying is that, even if a person does think, his thoughts are inconsequential; his actions, whether or not he thinks, will be part of a cause-and-effect (S-R) sequence which originates and ends outside himself. To Skinner, if thought occurs, it is not a cause of action but rather an irrelevant by-product of stimulation which would have caused the action anyway.

If an S-R associationist were to use the term *experience*, he would have to define it mechanistically. To him, experience could mean no more than the conditioning process by which a person acquires a new response. If a child touches a hot stove and if a link is formed between the sight of a stove and a withdrawal response, then an associationist might say the child has had an experience. No thought needs to have occurred and no insights need to have been developed.

Gestalt-field psychologists use the term *experience* extensively but define it in a way consistent with a relativistic outlook. They regard experience as rooted in insightful behavior. From this point of view, experience is a psychological event which involves acting purposefully with anticipation of the probable or possible consequences of such action. Experience is interaction of a person and his perceived environment. This is what Dewey means when he says, "An experience is always what it is because of a transaction taking place between an individual and what, *at the time,* constitutes his environment."[15] He states further, in connection with experience and learning, that "To 'learn from experience' is to make a backward and forward connection between what we do to things and what we enjoy or suffer from things in consequence."[16] Experience includes an active and a passive element, combined in a peculiar fashion: "On the active hand, experience is *trying.* . . . On the passive, it is *under-*

[14] B. F. Skinner, *Science and Human Behavior,* The Macmillan Company, 1953, p. 279.
[15] John Dewey, *Experience and Education,* Macmillan, 1938, p. 41 (our italics).
[16] John Dewey, *Democracy and Education,* Macmillan, 1916, p. 164.

going. When we experience something we act upon it, we do something with it; then we suffer or undergo the consequences. We do something to the thing, then it does something to us in return: such is the peculiar combination. The connection of these two phases of experience measures the fruitfulness or value of the experience. Mere activity does not constitute experience."[17]

The SMI concept implies a continuity of experience. Every experience both extracts something from experiences which have gone before and modifies in some way experiences which follow. Furthermore, to some degree every experience influences the conditions under which future experiences may be had. Thus, in the case of a reasonably normal person, successive perceptual fields or life spaces tend to be similar to, though not identical with, one another.

It is easy to see why the Gestalt-field concept of experience is in tune with a relativistic philosophy. If life consists of a series of experiences through which a person and his environment are continuously changing, then it is obvious that we must regard life as constant change with no fixed limits. Furthermore, since perception is considered a creative act, human experience can never lead to discovery and assertion of a fixed, absolutistic truth.

WHAT DOES MOTIVATION MEAN TO EACH FAMILY?

Motivation refers to the "mainsprings" or instigating forces of behavior; people do what they do because of motivation. As in the case of concepts treated previously in the chapter, S-R associationists and Gestalt-field psychologists hold contrasting and seemingly incompatible ideas about the nature of motivation. These differences go back to the contrasting conceptions of basic human nature held by the two schools of thought. If one views man and the universe mechanistically, he will prefer a theory of motivation compatible with this opinion; if he views man as a purposeful, reflective, and creative individual, he will have a quite different theory of motivation.

What Is Motivation to S-R Associationists?

As we have seen, associationists tend to regard man as an intricate machine. Machines operate with blind regularity, according to a set of fixed principles. Even a machine as complicated as an electronic brain does not operate purposefully as we usually use the term. An electronic brain does not know what to do until it has been set by a human being. Even electronic brains which can correct their own errors and do other

17 *Ibid.,* pp. 163–164.

seemingly fantastic things still behave as they do because some person has designed and regulated them. In a sense, a machine has no more purpose than a falling rock; it acts, but it has no thought-out goal. S-R theorists generally attribute this same quality to human nature.

To an S-R psychologist, all motivation is assumed to rise directly from organic drives or basic emotions or from a tendency to respond established upon prior conditioning of the drives and emotions. Organic drives, such as hunger, thirst, and sexual need, and the emotions, fear, anger, and "love," supposedly produce behaviors which are both predictable and irresistible. The drives and emotions are "built into" the machine and it can do nothing to resist them. Conditioning produces a series of learned reflexes which spring into action whenever relevant stimuli appear. These conditioned responses operate more or less automatically; a person makes them because he must. Through conditioning, the machine, i.e., the body, has been regulated to behave in a predictable manner. To an S-R psychologist, then, all behavior is stimulus directed, whether the stimulus comes from within the organism or without. Motivation is defined as the urge to act which results from a stimulus. Since behavior is stimulus directed, it is not related to purpose of any kind.

There are certain obvious aspects of the behavior of men or lower animals which do not appear to be explained by the mechanical concepts of S-R theory. One of these is attention. At any given time, a person pays attention to one thing rather than another. At this moment, the reader of this book is "attending" to this page rather than to a television program, a poker game, or a pretty girl. So the fact of attention seems to demonstrate that human behavior is governed by purpose. S-R theorists concede that a person may often respond selectively to one or a small group of stimuli at a time. However, they argue that what appears to be selective response can be explained according to S-R principles and that the existence of purpose need not be assumed. A person selects one response rather than another, according to an S-R psychologist, because of the particular combination of prior conditioning and present physiological drives and stimuli which are operating at the moment of perception. To an S-R theorist, to introduce purpose as an explanation of motivation is to risk introducing some kind of supernatural guiding force and to make impossible a truly scientific approach to the study of behavior.

An associationist's theory of motivation has important implications for education. According to his viewpoint, a child does not have to "want" to learn history in order to learn it. He does have to be persuaded to study it, to repeat the verbal responses which we associate with a knowledge of history. Anyone can learn anything of which he is capable if he will only allow himself to be put through the pattern of activity necessary for conditioning to take place. Thus, an associationist does not talk much about such things as "psychological involvement" or "helping students see the point of learning." Instead, he engages students in activity and assumes that activity with reinforcement automatically produces learning. A teacher carefully plans which learnings (responses) he wants students to develop. He then induces these responses and associates them with stimuli.

What Is Motivation to Gestalt-Field Theorists?

Within the Gestalt-field frame of reference, behavior is a function of a total situation, i.e., a person interacting within a field of psychological forces which includes memories, anticipations, purposes, and interpretation of relevant physical objects and events. Motivation cannot be described as merely an impulse to act triggered by a stimulus. Rather, motivation emerges from a dynamic psychological situation, characterized by a person's desire to do something.

A Gestalt-field psychologist regards motivation as a product of disequilibrium within a life space. A life space includes goals and often barriers to the achievement of these goals. A goal may be either positive or negative—something one wants to achieve, or something he wants to avoid. When a barrier, i.e., any obstacle to the direct and immediate achievement of a goal, whether physical or psychological, appears, a person feels tension. He tries to relieve tension by surmounting the barrier. The tendency to release tension by proceeding toward a goal, including the overcoming of whatever barriers are in the way, is motivation.

The particular form which motivation takes and its intensity are functions of a field of psychological forces in which no distinction can be made between "inner" and "outer." That is, one cannot identify a category of forces which stems exclusively from physiological drives and another category which stems from the outside environment. Hence, a Gestalt-field psychologist objects to the manner in which an associationist attributes motivation to independently acting organic drives and stimuli which originate wholly from outside an organism.

S-R theorists in the Thorndikean tradition make much of pleasure and pain, or satisfaction and annoyance, as instigators of behavior. An organism presumably is so put together biologically that it seeks to achieve pleasurable states and to avoid painful ones. Gestalt-field psychologists are more likely to talk about success and failure as motivators, the former being the "reward" for completing an act. Success and failure are not merely achievements as such but represent the relationship between a person's ambitions and his achievements. If he has a certain level of aspiration and is able to achieve this level, he feels good about it. If he attains success at one level of aspiration, he is likely to raise the level, and to continue doing so as long as he is able to perform successfully.

Thus, goals tend to be self-set and to change in dynamic fashion with each new experience.

Another feature of the Gestalt-field theory of motivation which sets it apart from S-R theory is the emphasis placed on the present situation. Motivation, to the Gestalt-field theorist, grows out of one's contemporary life space—the psychological forces which are operating right then. In contrast, an S-R theorist tends to think of motivation as emerging from an accumulation of historical events, i.e., past conditionings, coupled with currently operating organic drives. An S-R theorist looks backward into a person's life to determine why he behaves as he does now. A Gestalt-field psychologist does not ignore the impact of previous experience on a person's contemporary life space, but in explaining the causes of behavior he focuses on the present scene as the person experiences it. For these reasons, it is common to think of S-R psychology as embodying a *historical* approach and Gestalt-field psychology as embodying a *situational* approach.

A teacher who accepts the Gestalt-field concept of motivation and a teacher who operates within an S-R framework are likely to approach teaching in fundamentally different ways. For one thing, a teacher with a Gestalt-field orientation is concerned always with the problem of personal involvement, i.e., helping students see a need to learn. The personal goals of students will always be relevant. This does not mean that he will cater to their every whim. Often he will try to help them rethink their goals and discard those which are trivial and whimsical. Much of the time he will attempt to arrange the teaching-learning situation so that students will adopt goals entirely new to them. He will not forget that, unless a child realizes a need to learn something, the child either will not learn it at all or will earn it only in a transitory and functionally useless way.

BIBLIOGRAPHY

NOTE: References pertaining to Chapters 11 and 12 are at the end of Chapter 12. These two chapters should be studied as a unit.

12

HOW DO THE TWO
FAMILIES OF LEARNING
THEORY DESCRIBE THE
LEARNING PROCESS?

This chapter continues the analysis begun in Chapter 11 but centers on some of the more technical aspects of the learning theories developed by S-R associationists and Gestalt-field theorists. Some repetition of ideas stated in Chapter 11 is inevitable, but the focus is quite different.

Do animals, including man, learn simply by being conditioned step by step under the tutelage of a teacher or experimenter, or do they learn by surveying their situation and grasping relationships? Let us set up a hypothetical experiment and speculate on how animals will behave. Our subjects will be rats in an elevated maze (see Fig. 11). The alleys are formed of strips of wood without sidewalls. They are raised high enough from the floor so that the rats will not jump off. The gate in the maze is made so that the weight of a rat will cause it to lower and permit the rat to run through.

In order to accustom the rats to the maze and to develop in them preferential tendencies with reference to the three possible pathways to food, we give them some preliminary training. We deprive them of food for 24 hours, then place them in the starting box and permit them to find their way to the food box. They are given 10 such trials per day and soon learn (after trying the various paths) to take the shortest, path 1, to the food.

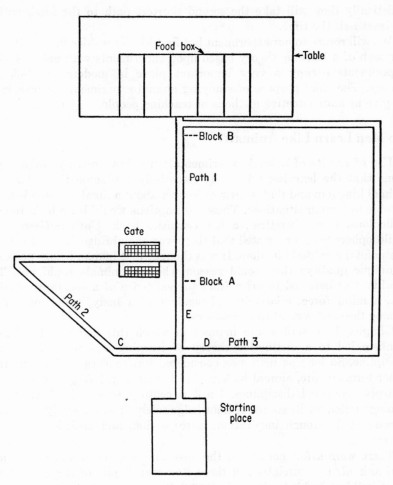

FIG. 11. Ground Plan of Elevated Maze Used by Tolman and Honzik. (From Ernest R. Hilgard, *Theories of Learning*, Appleton-Century-Crofts, 1956, p. 194.)

We then block path 1 at point A. When this is done, the rats will turn back to the choice point (fork in the road) and almost always (about 93 percent of the time) take path 2.

Now, what will the rats do when for the first time the block is placed in the common section of paths 1 and 2 (at point B)? They will return toward the starting place on path 1 and turn at the intersection of the three paths. But will they take path 2 or path 3? Have they sized up the situation and "seen" that the block is on path 2 as well as path 1? If so, they will take path 3. On the other hand, if the rats are operating mechanistically they will take the second shortest path to the food, path 2, at least half the time.

We will return to our experiment but first let us consider the significance for man of a learning theory based upon experiments with animals. Such experiments occupy a very important place in modern psychological theory. The chief purpose of studying animal experiments in learning is to give us more effective methods of teaching people.

Do Men Learn Like Animals?

Use of results of animal experimentation is governed by the assumptions that the learning process is essentially the same throughout the animal kingdom and that what we discover about animal learning is transferable to human situations. These assumptions would have been thought ridiculous, if not heretical, a few centuries back. Until modern times, philosophers took for granted that there was an unbridgeable gulf between man and the animal kingdom. It was thought that human beings possessed a unique quality: they could reason whereas animals could not. This quality was believed to arise from the existence of a substantive mind; i.e., a mind force, relatively independent of a body, which only man, among the earth's creatures, possesses.

Chapter 10 describes the manner in which this belief in body-mind dualism led to a distinctive theory of learning and teaching—mental discipline. So long as man was considered fundamentally different from other forms of life, animal biology and human psychology remained two sharply separated disciplines. Until a century. or so ago, human psychology relied for its source of knowledge solely upon the study of humans —conducted through inspiration, introspection, and intuition, tempered by reason.

There were a few persons of the past who rejected the idea that man and animals are unrelated; of these Rousseau is one of the earliest and most striking. In his book *Émile* (1762) Rousseau strongly implied that a continuity exists between animal and human nature. According to Rousseau's theory of child nature, a human being at birth is a healthy little animal—a creature like other animals of nature.

During the Romantic period (late eighteenth and early nineteenth centuries) many philosophers and literary figures believed that mind permeated the entire universe, including all living things. Furthermore, this universal mind substance was believed to be unitary—everywhere the same. Man possessed more of it than did lower animals, but the difference between human mind and animal mind was one of degree rather than kind. Of course, not all scholars accepted this view. The psychologist Wundt, for example, was convinced that consciousness—a product of mind —was unique to human beings.

It was the work of Darwin and other evolutionists of the nineteenth century that most definitely gave man a place in the animal kingdom. Darwin noticed particularly the close similarity of the bodily structures and functions of man and the lower animals. In his *Descent of Man* he also presented much evidence of the existence of psychological, as well as physical, continuity throughout the animal kingdom. He wrote, "There is no fundamental difference between man and the higher animals in their mental faculties."[1] But in a later section he qualified this opinion by writing, "There can be no doubt that the difference between the mind of the lowest man and that of the highest animal is immense."[2] In spite of the qualification, Darwin appears to have maintained consistently that in their fundamental aspects man and the lower animals exhibit a commonality of both physical and mental characteristics.

Antagonists of the theory of evolution defied Darwin to explain why, if there is a continuity between man and the animal kingdom, man can reason whereas lower animals seem to be governed by instinct rather than reason. Darwin countered with the explanation that much human action, too, is to be interpreted as instinctive in origin and that animals, on their level, exhibit a capacity for reason.

During the latter part of the nineteenth century the idea that there is a continuity among animal species, and that behavioral tendencies, including learning, are broadly similar throughout the animal world, rapidly gained in popularity among biologists and psychologists. Pierre Flourens, we have noted (p. 260), proposed in the nineteenth century that conclusions drawn from animal experimentation should be equally applicable to man. Pavlov made this assumption also, as did his contemporary, Thorndike, in the United States.

In addition to the cheapness and convenience of using lower animals rather than humans in a psychological laboratory, obviously experiments can be performed on animals which our mores would prevent being tried on people. Furthermore, many persons have felt that it was easier to isolate simple units of behavior in lower animals than in human beings; although in humans the units may be substantially the same, they are often combined in a manner too complex for ready study. Thus, it was thought that one might learn more about types of behavior fundamental to the animal kingdom by studying the lower animals than by studying men. For all of these reasons, animal experimentation became extremely popular among psychologists.

In the preceding chapter we describe briefly the general nature of the animal experimentation undertaken by S-R associationists. These psychologists hoped to formulate laws of human learning by observing overt behavior of laboratory animals placed in various kinds of situations such

[1] Charles Darwin, *The Descent of Man,* Appleton, 1920, p. 66.
[2] *Ibid.,* p. 125.

as puzzle boxes and mazes. By the early 1920s, the manner in which behaviorists conducted their experiments came under the fire of Gestaltists.
The nature of the Gestalt criticism is developed in the following section.

Do Animals Learn Like Men?

Whereas the behaviorists assumed that men learn like animals, and
more specifically like their own experimental animals in their own types
of experiment, Gestalt-field psychologists gave the question a reverse
twist: Do animals learn like men? Of course, if there is a continuity between man and the lower animals, both ideas should make equal sense
and both should be answerable in the affirmative. But Gestalt-field psychologists had something else in mind. While not denying the likelihood
of a fundamental similarity in the behavior of man and other animals,
Gestalt-field theorists were interested in raising questions about the whole
approach of the behaviorists.

Gestalt-field psychologists noted that behaviorists usually placed their
animals in situations entirely foreign to them. There was no place for
them to begin a solution and they were permitted a bare minimum of
freedom in which to try. Locks, levers, and mechanical devices used were
above the animals' level of comprehension. In order for them to achieve
the correct procedure it was necessary for them to stumble onto the key
by chance. Because lower animals are less discerning of relationships
which seem important to men than are human beings, they appear, in a
humanly contrived "problem," to make completely random movements.
Thus, the nature of their discovery of the relationship between the release
mechanism and escaping from a puzzle box, on the surface, appeared to
be completely mechanical. Having set the stage against animals display-
ing genuine problem-solving activity, S-R associationists concluded that
learning is a product of a mechanical trial-and-error process.

One of the sharpest criticisms which a Gestalt-field theorist can make
of the behavioristic conception of learning is directed against the tendency
of the latter to deny purpose a central role in learning. To a Gestalt-field
psychologist, learning always involves purpose. The tension which motivates an animal to learn is tension *toward a goal*. Gestalt-field psychologists feel they have abundant experimental evidence to show that learning
is purposive even among animals quite low on the phylogenetic scale.

An animal with purpose does not make random motions—even though
it may appear so on the surface. It tries everything at its command, but
if the problem is too difficult its trial moves will appear to an observer as
random. If one eye of a slug or honeybee is blinded, the animal at first
glance appears to go through meaningless motions. However, more careful
observation reveals that it is demonstrating something other than mere

random response. It assumes a posture which orients its body toward the light source; it flexes its legs on one side and extends them on the other as if it wanted to move in relationship to the light.

Gestalt-field psychologists also criticized experimentation of behaviorists on the ground that it was so arranged that, even if animal learning were insightful, the development of insight would not show. *The real nature of any psychological process can be concealed if the experimenter designs his experiments in line with predetermined conclusions, and this is precisely what the Gestaltists insist S-R associationists are inclined to do.* In an attempt to refute the contention of behaviorists that learning is mechanical—a mere matter of forming the right connections through chance—the Gestaltists designed an entirely different type of animal experiment. Their experiments involved creation of problematic situations which animals might conceivably resolve through development of insight. These situations were geared in difficulty to the presumed potential intelligence of the animals being studied.

Let us now return to the three-path experiment described at the beginning of the chapter. This actually is a classic experiment performed by Tolman and Honzik at the University of California. When the rats backed out of path 1, they did not take path 2 but path 3—the longest path, but the only one now open to the food box. *Of the 15 rats, 14 behaved in this way.* The rats' backing out of path 1 and taking path 3 was an indication of their having "sized up" the situation—of their having developed insight. Using path 3 was a relatively new and creative solution of what, to the rats, was a real problem.[3]

Köhler's famous experiments with chimpanzees further illustrate the Gestalt-field approach to animal experimentation. Köhler spent four years on the island of Tenerife working with chimpanzees. A typical experiment involved suspending food (usually bananas) from the ceiling of a cage and then providing a chimpanzee with a tool or tools with which to knock down or reach for the fruit. The tool might be a pole of adequate length, a pole in sections which had to be joined, or boxes which could be stacked and climbed. Köhler's chimpanzees, rather than gradually acquiring right responses and eliminating wrong ones, seemed at some point in a problem to develop insight into it—to grasp, often rather suddenly, the relationship involved. The chimpanzees seemed to get the idea of "tool use" and to apply it in new situations calling for tool use.[4]

Köhler also experimented with "stupid" chickens and found considerable evidence that even chickens can see relationships and that it is relationships to which they respond rather than specific stimuli. He taught

[3] E. C. Tolman and C. H. Honzik, " 'Insight' in Rats," *University of California Publication in Psychology*, Vol. 4, No. 14, pp. 215–232.
[4] Wolfgang Köhler, *The Mentality of Apes*, Harcourt, Brace, 1925.

chickens to expect food only from the darker of two papers placed side by side. For the lighter paper he then substituted one even darker than the original dark one. In 70 percent of the trials the chickens switched their preference from the originally preferred dark paper to the paper which was still darker, suggesting that they had achieved an insight: "If I go to the darker of two surfaces, I will get food." The chickens had "generalized," i.e., sensed the relationship of darker to lighter *as a general principle* in "food getting."[5]

Two American Gestalt psychologists, Raymond Wheeler and Francis Perkins, performed a great deal of animal experimentation in the 1920s and 1930s. Among their most frequently cited experiments was one with goldfish in which the fish received food after responding properly to a configuration of lighting. The fish learned to pick the light of brightest, medium, or dimmest intensity even though the experimenters kept varying the absolute intensity and the serial arrangement of lights. Wheeler and Perkins report numerous other studies made by themselves and others in which animals ordinarily regarded as not very intelligent learned to respond to relationships in an apparently intelligent way.[6]

The question arises, How far down the phylogenetic scale can an investigator go and still observe animals behaving as if they could generalize, i.e., perceive a relationship? To perceive a relationship one must get the feel of how a thing works. At first thought it would seem that to do this an animal must have a certain minimum of sensory and neural equipment—perhaps at least a brain, even if only rudimentary. However, one well-known American biologist, H. S. Jennings, writing in the early 1920s, concluded differently. Jennings spent much time observing the behavior of protozoa—such as euglenae, paramecia, and amoebae. He found that the actions of protozoa are not only highly variable but also readily modified, and he decided that their behavior could not be explained merely in terms of simple physiochemical reactions. Jennings thought that insofar as their observable behavior was revealing, it was as reasonable to infer the presence of conscious behavior among protozoa as it was among men.[7]

What are we to conclude from all this? One possible conclusion is that an animal experimenter, depending upon his orientation, is likely to arrange his experiment so that animal behavior appears to be either chancelike and mechanical or insightful. A famous philosopher, Bertrand Russell, noted before the end of the 1920s that psychologists could demonstrate two fundamentally different types of response in their animal

---

[5] See Henry E. Garrett, *Great Experiments in Psychology*, Appleton-Century, 1941, pp. 216–219.

[6] Raymond H. Wheeler and Francis T. Perkins, *Principles of Mental Development*, Crowell, 1932.

[7] H. S. Jennings, *Behavior of the Lower Organisms*, Columbia University Press, 1923, p. 335.

experiments, depending entirely on how they arranged the experimental situation. Russell commented humorously: ". . . Animals studied by Americans rush about frantically, with an incredible display of hustle and pep, and at last achieve the desired result by chance. Animals observed by Germans sit still and think, and at last evolve the solution out of their inner consciousness."[8]

The state of affairs with regard to experimentation with lower animals is probably not as indecisive as Russell's comment would lead one to think. Once a student sets his orientation in either an S-R associationistic or a Gestalt-field point of view, he benefits by the broadest possible knowledge of all available experimental, as well as other, evidence. However, a student's psychological orientation will largely determine how results of each experiment contribute to his interpretation of human learning.

Behaviorists have clearly shown that animals can be put in experimental situations where they demonstrate overt behavior which seems trial-and-error, chancelike, blind, and mechanical. There seems to be little question but that human experimental subjects could be put in situations which would cause them to appear to demonstrate the same kind of behavior. The requirement of such experiments seems only to be that the problem presented the learner is one with which his previous experience has in no way equipped him to cope.

On the other hand, the Gestalt-field group of psychologists have demonstrated adequately the one point they wanted to make, namely, that whether one is dealing with the lower animals or man, situations can be arranged in which learning shows an "Aha!" quality. That is, an experimental subject, in learning something, seems to "catch the point" or get the feel of a confronting situation. If man and the lower animals do seem to learn insightfully in situations which permit it, then serious doubt is cast upon the validity of the behaviorist notion that learning is purposeless, mechanical, and chancelike.

Gestalt-field psychologists insist that to describe learning throughout the animal kingdom we do well to begin with human examples. As we examine conscious behavior of ourselves or others, learning often—and perhaps always—appears to be a matter of *seeing through things*, of *gaining understanding*. If we start with the assumption that other animals learn in the same way, we devise experiments which will enable them to reveal such learning.

This does not mean that if we are studying, say, a dog, we dare anthropomorphize him, i.e., attribute to him human characteristics; it does mean that we must guard against mechanizing him, i.e., making a

[8] Quoted in W. D. Commons and Barry Fagin, *Principles of Educational Psychology*, Ronald, 1954, p. 28. Originally in Russell's *Philosophy*, 1927. The Germans referred to are obviously the Gestaltists.

machine of him. The way to study a dog is to "dogize" him, just as in studying a child we should "childize" him. In short, we must consider each animal as well as each human being on its own level. If we always keep this in mind, we can probably make some generalized statements about learning which will hold true with respect to most or even all forms of animal life.

WHAT ARE THE TWO MAJOR CONTEMPORARY VERSIONS OF THE NATURE OF LEARNING?

In Chapter 11, we open discussion of the two major contemporary versions of the nature of learning. We now treat in detail these two currently competing descriptions of learning. As already noted, neobehaviorists conceive of learning as *conditioning* or *reinforcement;* Gestalt-field psychologists think of it as *development of insight.*

Is Learning Conditioning—Reinforcement?

Neobehaviorists use *conditioning* or *reinforcement* to describe the learning process as they understand and interpret it. *Conditioning* is so called because it results in formation of conditioned responses. A conditioned response is a response which is associated with or evoked by a new—conditioned—stimulus. Conditioning implies a principle of adhesion, one stimulus or response is attached to another stimulus or response so that revival of the first evokes the second.

Reinforcement is a special kind or aspect of conditioning within which the tendency for a stimulus to evoke a response on subsequent occasions is increased by reduction of a need or a drive stimulus. A need or drive stimulus, in a sense, occurs between the stimulus and the response with which it is associated. A *need,* as used here, is an objective requirement of an organism. A *drive stimulus* is an aroused state of an organism. It is related to the need which sets the organism into action, and may be defined as a strong, persistent stimulus which demands an adjustive response.

The ultimate goal of neobehaviorists is to reduce learning to physiochemical factors. Learning consists of impressions of new reaction patterns on a pliable, passive organism. Since learning arises in some way from an interplay of organisms and their environment, key concepts of neobehaviorists are *stimulus* (that which is provided by an environment) and *response* (that reaction which is made or given by an organism). Consequently, the problem of the nature of the learning process centers in the relationships of respective stimuli and responses and what occurs between them.

Three representative neobehaviorisms are Edwin Guthrie's *Contiguous*

Conditioning, Clark L. Hull's *Deductive Behaviorism or Reinforcement Theory,* and B. F. Skinner's *Operant Conditioning.* These are alike in their emphasis upon a mechanical treatment of stimuli and responses. They agree that at no time is purposiveness to be assumed. Problems of "purposes" must be explained by natural laws or principles whereby organisms mechanically develop "purposes." However, they differ in their interpretations of stimulus-response relationships in learning procedures. Guthrie is convinced that learning occurs when a stimulus and a response happen simultaneously; Hull centered the essence of learning in what occurs between the stimulus and the response; and Skinner places his emphasis upon the stimulus which follows a response. When we express these relationships symbolically, using S for stimulus, R for response, and O for organism, Guthrie holds to an S-R, Hull to an S-O-R, and Skinner to an R-S learning theory.

Whereas Guthrie's learning theory is conditioning but not reinforcement, Hull's and Skinner's are both conditioning and reinforcement—but of different kinds. Hull called his system deductive because in developing it he, like Newton in physics, deduced or derived a large number of secondary principles of observable phenomena from a small number of primary principles.

Neobehaviorists in education tend not to adhere rigidly to any one of the S-R patterns but to intermix them in applying psychology to teaching procedures. In this way they attempt to achieve an integration of the earlier works of Pavlov, Watson, and Thorndike with that of contemporary S-R associationists. Let us examine very briefly each S-R associationistic theory of learning and see how it would color teaching procedures in a school learning situation.

GUTHRIE'S CONTIGUOUS CONDITIONING.   Guthrie's learning theory is conditioning but not reinforcement. Furthermore, it is a special kind of conditioning which we may identify as *simultaneous contiguous conditioning. Contiguity* means that stimuli acting *at the time* of a response, on their recurrence, tend to evoke that response. Furthermore, if a stimulus occurs contiguously with a response, the response to that stimulus will continue to occur with it until some other response becomes conditioned to that stimulus.

Strengthening of individual connections of stimuli and response—the actual conditioning—supposedly takes place with a single simultaneous occurrence of a stimulus and response. This does not mean that repetition has no place in learning, but that within repetition an increasing number of stimuli are made into conditioners; there is no strengthening of individual connections, but there is enlistment of more.

Guthrie reasons that, since association can occur with one connection and last for life, there is no need for anything like reward, pleasure, or need reduction to explain learning. Thus, there is no place for reinforcement in contiguity theory. To Guthrie, scientific laws deal with observable phenomena only. In psychology these are physical stimuli, and responses in the form of contractions of muscles and secretions of glands, but there is no place for hypothetical intervening variables between stimuli and responses.

A proponent of contiguous conditioning, in teaching people first gets them to perform in a certain way, then while they are doing so gives them the stimuli which he wants associated with that behavior. To teach that man is *Homo sapiens,* a Guthriean would induce his student to say *Homo sapiens* and while he was saying it stimulate him with *man* either spelled out, pictured, or both. The more "man" stimuli he could give the student while he was saying *Homo sapiens* the better it would be. In this teaching-learning process *man* is the conditioned stimulus and *Homo sapiens* is the conditioned response.

HULL'S REINFORCEMENT THEORY.　Hull's learning theory also is stimulus-response conditioning, but of a special kind, called *reinforcement.* In presenting his theory of learning Hull stated, "Whenever a reaction (R) takes place in temporal contiguity with an afferent receptor impulse $(\dot{s})$ resulting from the impact upon a receptor of a stimulus energy $(\dot{S})$, and this conjunction is followed closely by the diminution in a need (and the associated diminution in the drive, D, and in the drive receptor discharge, s_D, there will result an increment $\triangle$ (S→R), in the tendency for that stimulus on subsequent occasions to evoke that reaction."[9]

Within Hullian reinforcement, the stimulus and the response are not simultaneous; the stimulus precedes the response. Furthermore, learning does not take place with a single trial; it is stamped in through a process of repeated need or drive stimulus reductions.

Hull thought that learning occurs through biological adaptation of an organism to its environment in a way to promote survival. A state of need means that survival of the organism is not being adequately served. Drive is a general condition of organic privation arising from lack of food, water, or air, from unhealthful temperatures, from tissue injury, from sex-linked conditions, or from other deficiencies. When needs or drive stimuli develop, the organism acts and the action brings reduction in needs or drive stimuli. Actions—responses—which lead to reduction of needs or drive stimuli are *reinforced;* thus reinforcement is centered in adaptation for survival. However, in life situations there are many reinforcers which do not contribute directly to biological adaptation of an organism. Through *higher-order conditioning* many things and actions come to have

9 Clark L. Hull, *Principles of Behavior,* Appleton-Century-Crofts, 1943, p. 71.

value and can serve as reinforcers. Higher-order conditioning is conditioning based upon previous conditioning.

A child is conditioned to think—say to himself "man" when he sees a man or a picture of a man. This conditioning could have been based upon reduction of drive stimuli. Perhaps he wanted a piece of candy and his parents withheld it from him until he said "man." Now, in ninth grade, "stimulus man" evokes *Homo sapiens,* perhaps through the satisfaction of curiosity, and curiosity is a product of higher-order conditioning; the youth previously had been conditioned to be curious.

SKINNER'S OPERANT CONDITIONING. The unique feature of operant conditioning is that the reinforcing stimulus occurs not simultaneously with or preceding the response but following the response. In operant conditioning, an organism must first make the desired response and then a "reward" is provided. The reward reinforces the response, i.e., makes it more likely to recur. The *response* is *instrumental* in bringing about its reinforcement. The essence of learning is not stimulus substitution but response modification. In learning, there is a *feedback* from the reinforcing stimulus to the previous response. To illustrate, in the training of pets a desired response is reinforced after it occurs—a dog is fed after it "speaks," and this increases the likelihood of its "speaking" in the future.

Note that in operant conditioning the stimulus which produced the response in the first place is not in any way involved in the learning process. The original response is a result of a stimulus, but the nature of this stimulation is irrelevant to operant conditioning. It is only necessary that some—any—stimulus elicit the response for operant conditioning to function. Emphasis is on reinforcing agents, not on original causative factors.

An operant-reinforcement approach to teaching a ninth-grader that man is *Homo sapiens* would be to show the student *man* along with several other more complicated words, one of which is *Homo sapiens.* If the student chooses *non sequitur* or any expression other than *Homo sapiens,* nothing happens. If he chooses *Homo sapiens,* the teacher says "wonderful." This is reinforcement and they proceed to a new "problem."

Within neobehaviorism, learning is nonpurposive habit formation. Habits are formed through conditioning, which attaches desired responses to specific stimuli. A stimulus triggers an action or response, which can take only one form because of the nature of the stimulus, the condition of the organism, and the "laws of learning" involved. Teachers who adopt this mechanistic approach to learning decide specifically what behaviors they want their students, when finished products, to manifest, and they proceed to stimulate them in such a way as to evoke and fix those behaviors.

Is Learning Development of Insight?

The key word of Gestalt-field psychologists in describing learning is *insight*. They regard learning as a process of developing new insights or modifying old ones. Insights occur when an individual, in pursuing his purposes, sees new ways of utilizing elements of his environment, including his own bodily structure. The noun *learning* connotes the new insights— or meanings—which are acquired.

Gestalt-field theorists attack two weaknesses in the theory that learning is conditioning: (1) the attempt of S-R associationists to explain complex interrelated organizations in terms of simpler elements, i.e., to insist that learning consists of an accumulation of individual conditioned responses, each relatively simple in itself, but eventuating in a complicated pattern of habits; and (2) the tendency of S-R associationists to attribute learning to reduction of basic organic drives.

Gestalt-field psychologists view learning as a purposive, explorative, imaginative, and creative enterprise. This conception breaks completely with the idea that learning consists of linking one thing to another according to certain principles of association. Instead, the learning process is linked with thought or conceptualization; it is a nonmechanical development or change of insight.

S-R associationists also sometimes use the term *insight*, but when they do they mean something quite different from what a Gestalt-field theorist means. When used by associationists, the term describes a special and rare kind of learning. To use Woodworth's definition, insight is ". . . some penetration into the [absolutely] true nature of things."[10] But to Woodworth and other associationists, the ordinary form which learning takes is conditioning. The most systematic of the associationists would deny that there can be two entirely different kinds of learning; therefore they prefer to describe *all* learning as conditioning. Since insight obviously implies something very different from conditioning, many associationists do not use the term at all. To them it connotes something intuitive and mystical, something which cannot be described operationally. In contrast, Gestalt-field psychologists do not like to use the term *conditioning;* they regard *development of insight* as the most descriptive phrase available to describe the manner in which learning actually takes place.

The Gestalt-field definition of insight is a sense of, or feeling for, pattern or relationships. To state it differently, insight is the "sensed way through" or "solution" of a problematic situation. Insights often first appear as vague "hunches." We might say that an insight is a kind of "feel" we get about a situation which permits us to continue actively

[10] R. S. Woodworth, *Psychology,* Holt, 1940, pp. 299–300.

serving our purposes, or trying to. When are insights verbalized? Perhaps at once; perhaps never. We probably know many things which we never manage to put into words. This is a problem on which animal experimentation sheds some light. Animals below man cannot talk; they can communicate, but not by putting sounds together in coherent subject-predicate sentences. Yet the evidence indicates beyond much doubt that they learn insightfully when confronted with what to them are problems.

If we define *hypothesis* broadly, we may refer to insights as hypotheses. However, a hypothesis usually is defined as a special kind of verbalized insight. It is a statement which takes the form of a declarative sentence, or in many cases an "if-then" sentence. For example, one might say, "Most redheaded girls have violent tempers" (a declarative statement), or one might say, "If most redheaded girls reach a certain frustration level, they then display a violent temper" (an if-then statement). Hypotheses, defined as verbal statements, are the only kind of insight which we can test in a strictly scientific fashion.

This brings us to a crucial question: Are insights necessarily true? Gestalt-field psychologists do not use the term *insights* in a way to imply that they are necessarily true. Granted, the term sometimes is used this way by others—for example, by Woodworth in the above quotation. But the relativistic orientation of Gestalt-field theorists necessarily leads them to think of insights as trial answers which may or may not help a person toward his goal; they may or may not be true. Truth, relativistically defined, "is that quality of an insight which enables its possessor to design behavior which is successful in that it achieves what it is designed to achieve."[11] Insights derive from a person's best interpretations of what comes to him; they may be deeply discerning or they may not. They may serve as dependable guides for action or they may prove ruinous. Sultan, one of Köhler's chimpanzees, held a box in the air beneath a hanging banana. He then suddenly released his hold on the box and attempted to jump on it to reach the food. Sultan had an insight, but not a true one.

Insights are to be considered, not as literal descriptions of objective physical-social situations, but as interpretations of one's perceived environment on the basis of which subsequent action can be designed. Although insights are not physicalistic descriptions of objects or processes in the environment, they necessarily take account of the physical environment. Their usability depends in part on how well this is done. Insights may misinterpret a physical environment so badly that they are useless as rules of action, in which case they are to be regarded as false.

It is important to understand that insights are always a learner's own.

[11] Ernest E. Bayles, *Democratic Educational Theory,* Harper, 1960, p. 80.

It is true, of course, that they may become his own through adoption. An insight is usable to a learner only if he can "fit it in." He must understand its significance—for him. A teacher cannot give an insight to a student as we serve a person meat on a platter. He may acquaint students with his insights, but they do not become insights for students until students see their meaning for themselves and adopt them as their own.

One objection frequently raised to the Gestalt-field tendency to construe all learning as insightful is that some learning tasks are performed successfully without apparent development of insight—as, for example, when a child memorizes the multiplication tables. A field psychologist concedes that some learning appears highly mechanical, but he goes on to say that it is not necessarily as mechanical as it appears. He argues that even though a child may repeat the multiplication tables until he appears to have memorized them by rote, what the child actually has done is to get the feel of some pattern which is present in the tables. The pattern may lie in the relationship of numbers or perhaps merely in the order in which the student placed the numbers to "memorize" them.

Insight does not imply that for a person to learn something he must understand all aspects of its use. Any degree of "feel for a pattern" is sufficient to constitute insightful learning. For example, in learning to extract the square root of a number, one might develop insight as to *why* the method works. Or the insight gained might be much more superficial; it might be merely a "feel" for the method—the pattern of steps—with no real understanding of the basic algebraic formula $(x + y)^2 = x^2 + 2xy + y^2$.

Some Examples of Insightful Learning

Before he can become a sharpshooter, a rifleman must get a "feel" for his rifle. Often a Tennessee squirrel hunter was slow in learning to be an army rifleman. He had an excellent feel for his squirrel gun, but a squirrel gun was not an army rifle. In his army training he had to change old insights as well as develop new ones. On his squirrel gun his sights were fixed immovably to the barrel. To hit a squirrel he had to take wind and distance into consideration and move the rifle away from a line on the target (windward and upward) to give "Tennessee windage" and "Kentucky elevation." He had developed insights to the point that he could behave intelligently without thinking; he could aim his gun and pull the trigger while giving very little attention to what he was doing.

Since his army rifle had movable sights which, prior to aiming, were to be adjusted to allow for windage and elevation, he was supposed to set his sights and then line them directly on his target. But under pressure of target practice he used his new insights to adjust his sights correctly, then when he began to fire he gave his rifle Tennessee windage and Kentucky elevation. In army terminology he got a "Maggie"—he missed the target completely. He had used two sets of incompatible insights. He could learn to shoot his army rifle accurately only by getting complete feel for his army rifle and leaving most of his squirrel-gun-aiming insights out of the picture.

What is the answer to $\sqrt{(\text{dog})^2} = $? How did you know it was "dog"? Had you ever before worked with square root and dog at the same time? If you knew the answer was "dog," you had an insight into the problem. Perhaps you had never put the insight into words, but you knew that $\sqrt{x^2} = x$ and $\sqrt{4^2} = 4$. Your insight, when verbalized, would run something like, "The square root of anything squared is that thing." Conversely, you may have "learned"—memorized—"The square root of a quantity squared is that quantity" and still not know the answer to $\sqrt{(\text{dog})^2} = $?

How would students study spelling so as to develop insight? Teaching for insight has definite implication for methods in spelling. Groups or families of words might be studied in such a way that students develop feeling for a certain spelling pattern. Once a pattern is discovered other words will be sought which conform to it. *Cat, fat,* and *bat* are "at" words. Now what about *hat, mat, pat, rat,* and *sat?* As students, working cooperatively with their teacher, find other word families, they soon will encounter words which apparently should, but do not, fit a certain family —they find some limitations to an insight. They then seek other words with the same divergence from the "rule" and make a family of them. Or in case there is only one divergent word, they think of it as an exception. As the insights into patterns of spelling are put into words, a class can formulate rules. But now rules will be verbalizations of students' insight as contrasted with meaningless statements memorized at the beginning of study.

Insight and Generalization

Often when an insight is first "caught" it applies to a single case. Even so, a person is likely to assume that the insight may work in similar situations. Suppose, for example, that, after studying a particular situation, we hypothesize, "Mary became a shoplifter because she felt unwanted by her parents." The natural next step is to think, "Boys and girls who feel unwanted at home tend to become thieves." Of course, this generalization is only *suggested.* It is not *warranted* by evidence from a single case. Before generalizations become reliable it is usually necessary that they rest on a number of specific insights, all suggesting the same conclusion. In short, dependable generalizations are usually products of considerable experience. Further, they are prone to change in the course of experience, evolving continuously in the direction of greater usefulness as tools of thought.

A tested generalization is assumed to be valid in any future situation similar to the situations in which it was tested. Tested generalizations have the character of *rules, principles,* or *laws.* Syntactically, generalizations are frequently if-then statements: If we take a given action, then the probability is high that a given consequence will follow. We emphasize that tested generalizations should be regarded as *probabilities.* Although, to behave with foresight, we must assume that our generalizations have predictive value, the predictions are to some degree always based on faith.

As suggested earlier, if-then statements usually also may be expressed in present-tense declarative sentences. For example, when a person says, "An increase in the quantity of money is likely to produce a rise in prices," he may mean exactly the same as if he said, "If the quantity of money in circulation is increased, then prices are likely to rise." In using generalizations as hypotheses in scientific procedure, the if-then form often is preferable. It is more likely than is a simple declarative sentence to suggest operations to be performed, and therefore throw emphasis upon experimental tests.

WHAT IS THE RELATIONSHIP OF BEHAVIOR TO LEARNING?

Behavioristically defined, *"Behavior* is the publicly observable activity of muscles or glands of external secretion as manifested in movements of parts of the body or in the appearance of tears, sweat, saliva and so forth."[12] Gestalt-field psychology gives *behavior* a quite different meaning. It is any change in a person, his perceived environment, or the relation between the two which is subject to *psychological* principles or laws. Psychological behavior involves purpose and intelligence; hence it is not correlated with physical movement. From a Gestalt-field point of view, psychological behavior is not directly observable; it must be inferred.[13]

Learning and change in observable behavior usually occur side by side and obviously are interrelated in some way. Accordingly, S-R associationists contend that any change of behavior is learning and conversely that learning is a change of behavior. Thus, the current practice among many educators of defining learning as "change in behavior" usually reflects an associationist psychology.

Gestalt-field theorists counter that S-R associationists err in making synonymous the observable results of learning and the learning itself.

12 D. O. Hebb, *A Textbook of Psychology,* Saunders, 1958, p. 2.
13 See Morton Deutsch, "Field Theory in Social Psychology," in Gardner Lindzey, ed., *Handbook of Social Psychology,* Addison-Wesley, 1954, p. 191.

They argue that a change in physiological behavior does not necessarily mean that learning has occurred. A person who is struck from behind and knocked down may gain from this experience a healthy respect for dark alleys, but the change in behavior—falling down—is not equivalent to a change in insight. Furthermore, a person may use insights he has had for some time as a basis for change in his present behavior. An author may know that too much coffee is not good for him but persist in drinking coffee until he completes a manuscript and then reduce the amount of coffee he drinks. Probably many changes in the behavior of school children do not reflect change of insight, or at least not the kind of change which the teacher assumes. Johnny may start saying "please" and "thank you" without an insightful grasp of the implications. He may labor hours every night over homework without having his work produce any change of mind about matters embraced in the homework itself. (Of course, the assignments may cause changes in his attitudes toward teachers and school.)

Gestalt-field psychologists maintain that not only may change in behavior occur without learning, but also learning may occur without observable changes in behavior. This is true in any of innumerable situations. There may be no opportunity or occasion for a change in behavior, as when a person decides it would be nice to give more to charity but doesn't have the money to do so. New insights may fail to change a person's behavior if they are competing with old insights which have a stronger hold. Thus one may decide that racial discrimination is bad but continue to practice it. In summary, when a person learns, his behavior usually changes; but it does not follow that for learning to take place a change in observable behavior must take place at the same time, or that from a change in overt behavior we can always accurately infer the full nature of the insight behind it.

Many people with a behavioristic orientation think that doing something a number of times will necessarily affect future behavior. Thus, if one smokes a pack of cigarettes a day for a few weeks he is likely to become a habitual smoker. Gestalt-field theorists deny that this is the case. Doing a thing once or many times will affect subsequent behavior only in the degree to which doing it gives the doer a feeling for the act or insight into the consequences of its performance. It is the thought process, not the action, which is crucial. For this reason, Gestalt-field psychologists emphasize experience rather than behavior, with experience defined as *an interactive event in which a person comes to see and feel the consequences of a given course of action, through acting and seeing what happens.*

The emphasis of S-R associationists upon overt behavior has led to school practices designed to produce a desired kind of behavior and to methods of evaluation which measure overt behavior—and nothing else.

Teachers, or other school authorities, decide which specific behaviors they want students to display. They then stimulate the students in such way as to evoke the desired behaviors. The success of the process is judged by how dependably the behavior can be invoked in the future (usually on tests). Field psychologists protest this approach to education; they argue that a student may learn little more from it than the insights he gains about teachers and schools and about how to play the memory-work game successfully.

WHAT IS THE RELATION BETWEEN LEARNING AND THINKING?

Much is said about the importance of "teaching students to think." This is one objective of education on which people of all shades of opinion *seem* to agree. Agreement ceases when "thinking" must be defined and the methods for promoting thinking specified.

Should students be required to think as part of their activity in school? One group of educators seems to feel that school should prepare students to think, but that during the period of preparation thinking is not necessary. These people usually argue that the purpose of education is to give students background—the factual equipment with which to think at some later time. Proponents of this position often do not make themselves clear as to when thinking should start. Apparently some of them feel that thinking should not begin before the age of 21.

There are others who seem to feel that it is good for students to think part of the time while in school but not all of the time. They often associate thinking with certain courses, like higher mathematics. People of this persuasion may classify courses into two categories: background "fact courses" and courses in which students need to think. The former are usually considered just as important as the latter.

Probably most people who feel that learning may consist of the thoughtless acquisition of facts or skills are oriented in the direction either of mental disciplines or of S-R associationism.

Gestalt-field psychologists feel that learning and thought are closely allied; one does not occur without the other. Change of insight is invariably accompanied by thought of some kind; and thought of any kind invariably produces some change of insight, however small. Since thought occupies a crucial place in the learning theory of Gestalt-field psychologists, we treat this subject in considerable detail.

What Is Thinking?

In its broadest sense, thinking is any conscious behavior which is related in some way to the pursuit of goals. However, there is a level of conscious behavior which can scarcely be called thinking. This is reverie—fanciful musing or daydreaming. It is a more or less undirected association of ideas. Whenever a problem arises, reverie is supplanted by directed or pointed thinking.

Thinking, in its usual sense, is goal-related problem solving. It is an attempt to work through an obstacle in order to find the means to achieve an end. For purposes of analysis, we may distinguish two levels of problem solving. Any line drawn between them is necessarily arbitrary. One level may be termed *simple problem solving*. Simple problem solving does not involve weighty decisions. Examples of problems on this level are expressed in the following questions: Shall I wear a red or green tie today? Shall I have eggs or cereal for breakfast? Shall I drive or walk to work? Shall I spend the evening reading a book or watching a motion picture? We usually solve these problems without lengthy deliberation. Our anxiety level remains low. Once we have made a decision, we are unlikely to worry about it later.

The other level of thinking may be termed *complex problem solving*. It is on this level that we face a problem which is not so easy to settle—that is, unless we decide to ignore it. Complex problem solving usually requires more effort and time and is accompanied by a higher anxiety level. Such problem solving requires us to develop major new insights, or, in layman's language, to undergo a "change of mind." The distinguishing characteristic of this level of problem solving is that each problem presents us with something new. Although many elements of the problem may be familiar, some will be unfamiliar. Each act of complex problem solving requires some degree of originality or creativity. Examples of problems on this level are suggested by questions such as: Shall I encourage my son to go to college? Shall I seek a divorce? Shall I change my registration from Democrat to Republican? Shall I switch my church affiliation? Of course, not all complex problem solving involves questions as weighty as these. Deciding which insecticide to use or which service station to patronize might also require complex problem solving.

What Forms Does Problem Solving Take?

Since simple problem solving pretty well takes care of itself, we shall concern ourselves here with the more complex variety. Problem solving, whether simple or complex, takes various forms. There is more than one route by which we may secure answers to our questions. Not all routes are equally effective, and some which work—in the sense that they lead to answers—are undesirable because their answers are not dependable. Let us consider first some of the roads to truth which often produce unreliable results.

DEDUCTIVE REASON. The terms *reason* and *thinking* often are used interchangeably. Historically, reason has meant something other than reflection, as we now commonly define reflection. Reasoning has been defined as the process of deducing conclusions from given premises. It involves logic alone. In contrast, reflection includes not only logical processes but also the gathering of evidence—empirical or factual data. Reflection combines deduction and induction, whereas deductive reason confines itself to the former.

What is wrong with deductive reason? A conclusion based on reasoning alone can never be any better than the premises from which the reasoning began. If the premises are false, the conclusion will be false—unless through invalid reasoning one reaches a right conclusion from wrong premises. Historically, those who have placed heavy reliance upon reason usually have disdained the careful experimentation and observation which would have been necessary to test the truth of their premises.

The formal use of reason as a road to truth dates back to early Greek civilization. Aristotle originated the classical laws of logic and invented the syllogism as a purported reasoning device. A number of modern writers feel that many of the problems which beset Western civilization are a result of the Aristotelian tradition. Central to this tradition are these propositions:

1. A is A.
2. Everything but A is non-A.
3. Nothing is both A and non-A.

Reasoning which starts from these "laws" has an either-or quality. Either-or reasoning (sometimes called two-valued orientation) occurs when we are able to see only two choices in a complex situation. It causes us to see the world and ourselves only in terms of black and white. One may wonder, for example, if his life has been a success. He can always find some evidence that it has and some evidence that it has not. Either-or reasoning is likely to keep him from seeing that his life has been both a success and a failure. Instead, he is compelled to conclude that it has been *either* a success or a failure.[14]

COMMON SENSE. As we use the term here, *common-sense thinking* is based purely upon sensory data, particularly of a superficial or limited sort. It stops short of seeking deep and complex relationships and confines itself to the way things appear upon cursory examination. It is common sense, for example, to believe that the earth is flat and that the sun revolves around the earth. This is the way it *looks* upon mere inspection.

Common-sense thinking often reflects the fallacy of *post hoc, ergo*

[14] For an excellent treatment of this subject see Wendell Johnson, *People in Quandaries,* Harper, 1946, pp. 6–10.

propter hoc ("after this, therefore on account of it"). Events are given a cause-effect interpretation simply because they are consecutive. For example, a swimming pool is opened to all races. A riot takes place. It would be common sense to conclude that the second event was caused by the first. But this conclusion is not dependable because there may have been present some other causal factor not evident upon casual observation.

It would require many volumes to catalogue all the mistaken beliefs of the past which have seemed a matter of common sense to those who held them. The early common-sense beliefs in alchemy, magic, and witchcraft may seem crude and indefensible today, but many of our present-day common-sense beliefs are probably based on just as little evidence.

INTUITION.   For answers to some problems it has been recommended that we rely upon intuition. Women are supposed to have a well-developed capacity for intuition and men are supposed to be frequent victims of it. What people mean by intuition is not always clear. In this book an intuitive judgment refers to a hypothesis based upon personal convictions; any evidence which supports it is hidden and vague even to the person who states the hypothesis.

What is wrong with intuition? One thing wrong is that no one can describe in objective terms what happens during an act of intuition and there is no way to verify its reliability. Intuitive thought does not make use of publicly verifiable data, runs no tests on its hypotheses, and totally ignores the fact that its assumptions may be false (or debatable). A common feature of intuitive thinking is that the claim that one has been intuitive often occurs *after* the event about which intuitive judgment was rendered. A man who breaks his leg one afternoon may report the next day that on the morning before the accident he had had a premonition of impending disaster. It may be that intuitive judgments which turn out to be true are merely good guesses; the bad guesses are conveniently forgotten.

In spite of the difficulties which intuition presents, we should not rule it out of court summarily. A hunch without any evident basis may be a highly productive starting point. Intuition may be, as Stuart Chase suggests, a "loose term for a half-conscious blend of many minute observations." These "half-conscious observations" may be very good observations, even though not susceptible to verbalization. Intuitive thinking may be a worth-while source of hypotheses. Our only mistake is in taking them authoritatively as if they were established truth.

APPEAL TO AUTHORITY.   We appeal to authority when, rather than thinking a matter through ourselves, we accept without question an answer supplied by someone else. Reliance on authority is legitimate and necessary provided the authorities on whose opinions we rely have themselves used dependable methods in arriving at their opinions. If there is reason to suspect that an authority has used any of the more questionable roads to truth described herein, we should take his word with several grains of salt. In any case, it is always well to be critical of conclusions which we take ready-made from others.

The most common source of authority in public school is, of course, textbooks. Many students regard the utterances of textbook writers as ultimate truth, which is hardly surprising in view of our tendency to elevate textbooks to a central position in our educational system. Second to textbooks, students often consider their teachers authorities and take at face value most of what teachers say.

Often an appeal to authority attempts to uncover the dictates of natural law or some divine or supernatural power which exists above and beyond human experience. An excellent example of how a decision of major importance may stem from this kind of reliance on authority comes from the administration of President William McKinley. Of McKinley's method of solving the problem of whether to seize the Philippines, Charles and Mary Beard say:

> The intellectual and moral methods by which he resolved his perplexity the President later explained. . . . "I walked the floor of the White House night after night," he said, "and I am not ashamed to tell you, gentlemen, that I went down on my knees and prayed Almighty God for light and guidance more than one night. And one night late it came to me in this way—I don't know how it was, but it came—. . . . There was nothing left for us to do but to take them all, and to educate the Filipinos, and uplift and civilize and Christianize them. . . ."[15]

RATIONALIZATION.   Rationalization is the attempt to defend a cherished belief by a largely unrecognized slanting of evidence. Rationalization may make use of well-established facts, but it neglects some of the facts which are both available and pertinent. Rationalization is inventing "good reasons" for what we are already determined to believe. As we shall soon see, scientific reflection differs fundamentally from rationalization. But teachers who say they want their students to think often mean rationalize rather than reflect. Many teachers prize thinking only if there is some advance guarantee that thinkers will not reach unorthodox conclusions about touchy issues.

We find much rationalization in textbooks. Nor is this limited to the United States. Walworth has produced conclusive evidence that history books used in the secondary schools of Mexico, Spain, Germany, Great Britain, Canada, and the United States differ greatly in what the "true facts" are considered to be.

[15] Charles A. Beard and Mary R. Beard, *Rise of American Civilization*, Macmillan, 1930, Vol. II, pp. 375–376.

For example, a book written by Toro for the education of Mexican students treats the annexation of Texas as follows: ". . . The partisans of the South looked toward us to increase their territory, make new slave states out of it, and strengthen their domination; and they resolutely determined to acquire Texas, counting upon the aid of President Jackson, an unscrupulous man who, as a proprietor of slaves, was personally interested in the matter and resorted to every sort of means, even the most immoral, to accomplish his ends. . . ."[16] High school students of the United States may read the more "enlightening" pages of Faulkner and Kepner and learn that "It was hardly to be expected that these aggressive Anglo-Saxon frontiersmen could long dwell in peace under the control of a people representing a very different civilization, and under a weak and inefficient government continually changing as one revolution succeeded another."[17]

No doubt teachers in Mexico, like teachers in the United States, feel that they are teaching the facts and that learning these facts will help students think about their problems. Yet both textbooks cannot be completely right, and both may be largely wrong. The statement that Jackson was *unscrupulous* is as nonfactual as the statement that government in Mexico was *weak and inefficient*.

WHAT IS THE REFLECTIVE METHOD?

There is no essential difference between reflection, as we use it in this book, and scientific process, broadly defined. The term *scientific* does carry a connotation which is less suited to our purposes than does the term *reflective*. In the thinking of many persons *science* implies white-gowned technicians, microscopes and telescopes, chemical tables, and cyclotrons. It suggests precise measurement, use of mathematics, a large amount of rather esoteric wizardry, and neglect of moral values. But *scientific* in its broadest sense covers not only a special kind of gadgetry and techniques but also a unique outlook, attitude, and method of inquiry.

Reflection refers to the essential but non-gadgetlike features of scientific method—to an attitude of mind and a generalized set of operations with which we may approach all problems, whether physical, social, or psychological. John Dewey gave us a classic definition of reflection when he called it the "active, persistent, and careful consideration of any belief or supposed form of knowledge in the light of the grounds that support it and the further conclusions to which it tends. . . ."[18] Dewey conceived of reflection as the kind of thought which embodies the scientific method, defined in its broadest sense. To him, all thinking which is worth while

[16] Arthur Walworth, *School Histories at War,* Harvard University Press, 1938, p. 40.
[17] *Ibid.,* p. 41.
[18] John Dewey, *How We Think,* Heath, 1933, p. 9.

is reflection, as we have defined it. Reflection leads to generalization of a kind which is understood by learners and which has maximum transfer value to new situations.

It is possible to describe reflection as psychological movement through a series of steps. Such movement results in a progressive development of insight about a problem. These steps are as follows:[19]

1. Recognition and definition of a problem. This occurs when we become aware of a goal and an intervening obstacle. Often a problem consists of a newly sensed discrepancy in known data.
2. Formulation of hypotheses. Hypotheses are possible answers. They are invented generalizations which to be used most successfully must be verified by human experience. In a relativistic sense, all scientific generalizations are hypotheses in which greater or lesser degrees of assurance can be placed. They range from hunches based on minimum data to laws which reflect a very high degree of factual verification.
3. Elaboration of logical implications of hypotheses. This includes deducing observations which have already been made—so that hypotheses may be checked against present knowledge; and deducing observations which have not yet been made—so that hypotheses may be tested through experiments yet to be designed.
4. Testing of hypotheses. This involves attempts to verify consequences deduced under step 3 above, in terms of both the data of previous experience and data procured in experimental tests.
5. Drawing conclusions. This consists of acceptance, modification, or rejection of hypotheses, or concluding that as of now the available pertinent evidence does not warrant taking any stand at all.

Although the foregoing steps are present in each completed act of reflection, no one should suppose that a person goes through them in the consecutive, orderly fashion in which they may be listed on paper. Reflection normally is characterized by confusion, hesitation, backtracking, and "going around in circles." In many cases it appears to a thinker that he will never reach a solution at all. And once reached, a conclusion often must be abandoned and the process started all over again. Reflection is seldom easy; at best it is exhilarating and exciting, and at worst it is painfully hard work beset with many frustrating moments.

There is a great deal more to understanding the reflective process than merely listing the steps. Experience of the past few centuries has led to certain conventions concerning how a reflective or scientific process is to be pursued. We use the term *conventions* because there is nothing abso-

---

[19] The formulation presented here is somewhat standard, and its essential form appears in many writings; the specific way in which the steps appear here was suggested to the authors by Ernest E. Bayles.

lutistic about the rules which govern testing of hypotheses. Pragmatically, the rules accepted at present have been shown to lead to more productive results than any alternative rules which have yet been devised. But there is no reason to suppose that the rules of reflection will not continue to evolve as mankind gains more experience. We list some of the more important of these rules together with some needed qualifications.

1. Whenever one insight or conclusion is accepted in preference to another, it is presumed that *reasons exist for its acceptance.* The grounds for acceptance may be scant, but as long as they are better than the grounds any competing insight can offer, they justify its tentative acceptance. What we regard as true does not need to be proved in any final sense; it requires only some supporting evidence.

2. Insights are always *provisional.* That is, all knowledge is assumed to be a product of human experience and hence subject to change. No question is closed to re-examination provided a reason to re-examine it develops. This does not mean that one may not establish principles or laws which are assumed to be valid for a very long period of time. Such principles or laws are not absolutes so long as people remain willing to re-examine them at any time questions arise involving them.

3. Insights are consistent with each other. *We assume that two contradictory insights can never be true at the same time, for the same purpose, and under the same conditions.* This does not mean that one may not switch from one idea to another which is incompatible with it. Changing one's mind is not an example of inconsistency; in fact, a reflective person is known for his flexibility. A person is inconsistent only when he holds two opposites at once and under the same assumed conditions. This rule is apparently the same as what Ernest Bayles calls the "principle of harmony." He states it thus: ". . . The process of testing hypotheses by the use of data is one of asking whether the data agree with the hypothesis. Which hypothesis, if any, causes the data to fall into a thoroughly harmonious pattern? A problem can be considered solved *beyond reasonable doubt* when and only when (1) one proposed solution presents a pattern which harmonizes all the data which have been obtained . . . and (2) there are no data which are incompatible with that proposal."[20]

4. All pertinent, available evidence is examined before conclusions are drawn. An investigator looks at all facts then available, no matter how unpalatable some of them may seem. There is never a slanting, ignoring, or distorting of data to prove a point. Taboos and ungovernable prejudices do not mix with a reflective approach. Dr. Bayles refers to this principle as the principle of "adequacy"—the data must be adequate, i.e., as complete as possible. The crucial datum, of course, is the actual predicated

[20] Ernest E. Bayles, *The Theory and Practice of Teaching,* Harper, 1950, pp. 108–109.

functioning of a hypothesis in new situations. If it "works" in this manner, this is the best thing which can be said for it.

5. The ultimate authority for any scientific conclusion is to be found in perceivable phenomena, as suggested through observation and experiment. This statement can easily be misconstrued and needs considerable qualification. Human beings seem capable of an unlimited range of experience, including what we commonly call mystical. Mystical experiences may be hallucinations (which are common to man) or they may represent some kind of contact or involvement with an "otherworldly" realm accessible at present only to a small proportion of persons. A person who is relativistically oriented does not like arbitrarily to rule out *any* kind of evidence. He prefers, rather, the idea of an "open universe"—in which anything is possible. On the other hand, without better evidence than is now available, those who use a reflective approach remain highly skeptical of evidence which purportedly is derived from a world other than the "here and now."

6. Closely related to the problems stemming from number 5 above is the rule that all operations in a reflective act must be performed openly and in a fashion that will enable other competent persons to repeat them. Each act of reflection must be able to supply its own recipe, so to speak; or, stated in another way, it must be subject to operational description. A mechanic overhauling a carburetor can describe each step along the way, and, if I am bright enough, I can repeat it. So can you, or anyone else. We are saying that scientific reflection is a *public* rather than a private road to truth. This is not the same as saying that there are no private roads: in fact, there may be a great many.

Although the foregoing rules have been described separately, it should be obvious that they are closely interrelated. Each hinges to some degree upon the others. Nor is there any implication that this is a complete "listing" of rules governing the reflective method.

The purpose of rules associated with a reflective approach is to make for "good thinking," which, in the final test, may be judged *only against its results*. The presumed purpose of any act of thought is to provide a person with tested insights which are worth more than the insights formerly held. Prior to the above discussion of reflection, we described several supposedly spurious or incomplete methods of thought; these were judged inadequate solely on the ground that they lead to less reliable or less usable insights than does reflection.

To summarize the chapter, we have suggested that, although animal experimentation has led to conflicting conclusions about learning, apparently it has been demonstrated that all members of the animal kingdom, under the right circumstances, can learn insightfully. Next, we contrasted the two major descriptions of learning: conditioning and development of insight. Finally, we suggested that a Gestalt-field psychologist equates development of insight with thinking, and that there are various kinds of "thinking," the most productive of which is scientific reflection.

BIBLIOGRAPHY

Beach, Frank A., and others, *The Neuropsychology of Lashley*, McGraw-Hill, 1960.
> A selected sample of Lashley's original papers which represents his experimental studies, general theory, and criticism of connectionism. Edwin G. Boring's introduction shows Lashley's contribution to field psychology.

Chaplin, J. P., and T. S. Krawiec, *Systems and Theories of Psychology*, Holt, Rinehart and Winston, 1960.
> A treatment of the evolution of psychological thought, which is traced from classical scholars to the major contemporary theories. Shows the continuity of thought from philosophy and physiology to psychology. Contains a good list of biographical sketches of contributors to psychological thought. Chapters VI and VII are especially pertinent to learning.

Conant, James B., *Modern Science and Modern Man*, Doubleday, 1953.
> An explanation of how every phase of our lives is becoming involved with scientific procedures, and how this revolution in living has carried with it a revolution in scientific outlook. Man, as a scientist, no longer is seeking absolute, but rather, workable, truth; he is becoming relativistic.

Contemporary Approaches to Cognition. A symposium held at the University of Colorado, Harvard University Press, 1957.
> For the advanced student. Includes a range of positions all of which focus on psychological, rather than behavioral, facts.

Frank, Philipp, *Relativity—A Richer Truth*, Beacon, 1950.
> An examination and evaluation of the relativistic outlook, with a foreword by Albert Einstein. A key chapter, Chapter 22, is "How Can an Anti-Metaphysical View of Science Help Democracy?"

Fullagar, William A., and others, *Readings for Educational Psychology*, Crowell, 1956.
> An excellent selection of readings with major emphasis upon learning. Especially recommended are No. 1, "The Nature of Learning Theories," by Hilgard; No. 5, "The Idea of Learning as Development of Insights," by Bayles; and No. 8, "Counseling as a Learning Process," by Combs.

Geiger, George Raymond, *John Dewey in Perspective*, Oxford University Press, 1958.
> By an astute student of Dewey and the "relativistic" position which Dewey helped develop. This book is somewhat easier reading than most of Dewey's works, yet it gives an accurate picture of Dewey's thoughts.

Harris, Theodore L., and Wilson E. Schwahn, *The Learning Process*, Oxford University Press, 1961.
> An exceptionally good book of readings on learning. Emphasizes experi-

mental studies of learning and developmental and evaluational problems related to the learning process.

Hebb, Donald Olding, *A Textbook of Psychology*, Saunders, 1958.

A textbook in general psychology which treats psychology as a biological, not a social, science. Mechanisms of behavior in learning, perception, and emotion are discussed in a thoroughly S-R associationistic manner.

Henry, Nelson B., ed., *The Psychology of Learning*, Forty-first Yearbook of the National Society for the Study of Education, Part II, University of Chicago Press, 1942.

In Section 1: contemporary theories of learning; in Section 2: the implications of learning theories for education. Chapter 7 by T. R. McConnell is an attempt to reconcile conditioning, connectionism, and field theory to form a synthesis of learning theories.

Hilgard, Ernest R., *Theories of Learning*, 2nd ed., Appleton-Century-Crofts, 1956.

A systematic, critical presentation of nine most prominent learning theories current among contemporary psychologists. Four are S-R associationisms and three are of the Gestalt-field family.

Hook, Sidney, ed., *Dimensions of Mind*, New York University Press, 1960.

A symposium of twenty-nine papers on the mind-body, mind-brain problem. Papers are grouped under "The Mind-Body Problem," "The Brain and the Machine," and "Concept Formation." Three major kinds of considerations undergird the papers—nature of experience or "raw feel," traditional dualistic language habits, and results of modern psychology and brain physiology.

Koch, Sigmund, *Psychology: A Study of a Science*, McGraw-Hill, 1959.

A technical but highly informative volume, concerned with the general conceptual formulations of current psychologies. Each approach or theory is represented by a distinguished psychologist.

Kuenzli, Alfred E., ed., *The Phenomenological Problem*, Harper, 1959.

Readings in cognitive-field psychology. Excellent selections for advanced students.

Lindzey, Gardner, ed., *Handbook of Social Psychology*, Vol I, Theory and Method, Addison-Wesley, 1954.

In Part 2, "Contemporary Systematic Positions": excellent presentations of five systematic psychological outlooks which have definite implications for learning as well as for social psychology. Stimulus-Response contiguity, cognitive, psychoanalytic, field, and role theories are presented.

Thorndike, Edward L., *Selected Writings from a Connectionist's Psychology*, Appleton-Century-Crofts, 1949.

A collection of Thorndike's papers to give students a firsthand knowledge of connectionist psychology. His autobiography gives the reader a picture of how educational psychology has developed.

Watson, John B., *Psychology from the Standpoint of a Behaviorist*, 2nd ed., Lippincott, 1924.

An introductory psychology textbook written strictly from a mechanistic, behavioristic point of view.

Watson, John B., *The Ways of Behaviorism*, Harper, 1928.

An explanation of the what and why of behaviorism (which had been growing some fifteen years) and why it opposes mentalistic concepts like instinct and unconscious.

Watson, John B., and William McDougall, *The Battle of Behaviorism*, Norton, 1929.
A debate between McDougall, the eminent psychologist of instinct theory, and Watson, the upsurging behaviorist. The sharp conflict between mentalistic and physicalistic psychology becomes clear.

Wertheimer, Max, *Productive Thinking*, enlarged ed., edited by Michael Wertheimer, Harper, 1959.
An analysis of the thinking process, by one of the three leading Gestalt psychologists. He developed the differences between associationistic and field study of thinking and showed how Gestalt psychology and reflective thinking are closely related.

Wolman, Benjamin B., *Contemporary Theories and Systems in Psychology*, Harper, 1960.
A comprehensive picture of contemporary psychological theory. It emphasizes concept formation, relationship of psychology to other sciences, and methods of research. Chapters 1–4 present S-R associationistic theories and Chapters 10–13 Gestalt-field theories.

13

HOW DOES SKINNER'S OPERANT CONDITIONING WORK?

Let us each picture ourselves as a fourth-grader, Dale Cooper, in a possible classroom of the year 1975. At the first bell students enter the room; at the second bell they become silent. When opening exercises have been completed, the teacher says, "Arithmetic." Dale has been conditioned at this signal to place his arithmetic cylinder on his teaching machine, find where he left off yesterday, and proceed with conditioning himself to solve arithmetic problems. After 20 minutes the teacher says, "Reading," and in another 20 minutes "Spelling." Each word is the appropriate stimulus for Dale to change cylinders on his machine. Then comes recess. At the sound of a bell with a different tone from that of the one which brought students into the room, they go out to the playground. Here, playground equipment has been adequately mechanized and sequenced so that there is little need for a teacher or any other supervisory personnel. The teacher uses the recess period to check, repair, and lubricate the machines.

The psychology which would support the emphasis on teaching machines for Dale's education has been developed by a professor at Harvard, B. F. Skinner (1904—). Skinner has found *operant conditioning* highly effective in training animals and he is confident that it promises equal success when used with children and youth. In operant conditioning, teachers are considered architects and builders of students' behavior.

314

Learning objectives are divided in a large number of very small tasks and reinforced one by one. Operants—sets of acts—are reinforced—strengthened—so as to increase the probability of their recurrence in the future. In this process it is of prime importance that teachers employ properly timed and spaced schedules of reinforcement.

Professor Skinner considers it the purpose of psychology to predict and control *behavior* of individual organisms. He insists upon limiting psychological study to observable behavior of organisms; his only data are those acquired by sensory observation. He opposes the use by psychologists or teachers of such terms as *will power, sensation, image, drive,* or *instinct;* these refer to supposedly nonphysical events. *Behavior* is ". . . the movement of an organism or of its parts in a frame of reference provided by the organism itself or by various external objects or fields of force."[1]

Skinner's psychology is a strictly engineering type of science which supposedly is devoid of theory of any kind. He insists that psychology is a science of overt behavior and only overt behavior. He defines learning as a change in probability of response. In most cases this change is brought about by operant conditioning.

Operant conditioning is the learning process whereby a response is made more probable or more frequent; an *operant* is strengthened—reinforced. Reinforcement is explained in Chapter 12, p. 292. An operant is a set of acts which constitutes an organism's doing something—raising its head, pushing a lever, saying "horse." In the process of operant conditioning operant responses are modified or changed. Reinforcement means that the probability of the repetition of certain responses is increased.

Skinner thinks that nearly all human behavior is a product of operant reinforcement. In everyday life, in various fields including education, people constantly change the probabilities of responses of others by arranging reinforcing consequences. Operant reinforcement improves the efficiency of behavior. Through it we learn to keep our balance, walk, play games, and handle tools and instruments; we perform a set of motions, reinforcement occurs, and the likelihood of our repeating the motions is increased.

Whenever something reinforces a particular form of behavior, the chances are better that that behavior will be repeated. The task of psychologists is to gain more understanding of conditions under which reinforcement works best. To the many "natural" reinforcers of behavior a host of artificial reinforcers may be added. "Any list of values is a list of reinforcers—conditioned or otherwise. We are so constituted that under certain circumstances food, water, sexual contact, and so on, will make any behavior which produces them more likely to occur again. Other

[1] B. F. Skinner, *The Behavior of Organisms,* Appleton-Century-Crofts, 1938, p. 6.

things may acquire this power. . . . An organism can be reinforced by—can be made to 'choose'—almost any given state of affairs."[2]

HOW HAS SKINNER USED ANIMALS TO STUDY OPERANT REINFORCEMENT?

In general, experimental psychologists have not related their laws and theories to instances of learning in real life.[3] However, Professor Skinner and his associates have experienced remarkable success in training animals. It is probable that even professional animal trainers, through study of the procedures used in operant conditioning, could improve their techniques. In one college class period, by presenting food to a hungry pigeon at the right time, Skinner has implanted in the bird three or four well-defined responses such as turning around, pacing the floor in a figure-eight pattern, stretching the neck, and stamping the foot.

Skinner's basic thesis is that, since an organism tends in the future to do what it was doing at the time of reinforcement, one can, by baiting each step of the way, lead it to do very much what the experimenter wishes it to do. Using this thesis as a basis for his procedure, he has taught rats to use a marble to obtain food from a vending machine, pigeons to play a modified game of tennis, and dogs to operate the pedal of a refuse can so as to retrieve a bone.

Skinner has centered his study on lower animals because their behavior is simpler, conditions surrounding them may be controlled better, basic processes are revealed more readily and can be recorded over longer periods of time, and observations are not complicated by social relations between subjects and the psychologist.[4]

The "Skinner box" is a simple box which was made to contain a rat, a lever, and a device for delivering a pellet of food each time the rat pressed the lever. Recording devices are set outside the box so that the experimenter can go home at night and see in the morning what the rat has been doing. There also are Skinner boxes for the study of pigeons and other animals. A rat or pigeon learns rapidly in a Skinner box because in the box there is little else for him to do. Skinner says, "The barest possible statement of the process is this: we make a given consequence contingent [dependent] upon certain physical properties of behavior (the upward movement of the head), and the behavior is then observed to increase in frequency."[5]

[2] B. F. Skinner, *Cumulative Record,* Appleton-Century-Crofts, 1959, p. 33.
[3] See Donald K. Adams *et al., Learning Theory, Personality Theory, and Clinical Research,* Wiley, 1954, p. 2.
[4] B. F. Skinner, *Science and Human Behavior,* The Macmillan Company, 1953, p. 38.
[5] *Ibid.,* p. 64.

A pigeon's behavior can be reinforced in such a way that neck stretching will become habitual. The pigeon is placed in a cage so that the experimenter can sight across its head at a scale pinned on the far wall of the cage. The height at which the head is normally held is established on the scale; then some line, which is reached only infrequently, is selected. The experimenter, keeping his eye on the scale, quickly opens the food tray whenever the bird's head rises above the established line. As a result, learning occurs; . . . "we observe an immediate change in the frequency with which the head crosses the line. We also observe, and this is of some importance theoretically, that higher lines are now being crossed. We may advance almost immediately to a higher line in determining when food is to be presented. In a minute or two, the bird's posture has changed so that the top of the head seldom falls below the line which we first chose."[6]

By training two pigeons separately to do their parts in a total performance, Skinner has constructed a social scene within which competition is exemplified by two pigeons playing a modified game of ping-pong. He accomplished the training through operant reinforcement. First, the pigeons were reinforced when they merely pushed the ball. Then when the ball got by one pigeon the other was reinforced. He also has trained pigeons to coordinate their behavior in dancing in a cooperative manner which rivals the skills of most able human dancers.

Reinforcement procedures may vary according to intervals of time and the number of responses between reinforcements. A schedule of reinforcement is a pattern of "rewarding" behavior based upon a fixed time interval and a fixed number of responses between "rewards." In a laboratory, Skinner and Ferster have obtained performances appropriate to each of nine different ratio-interval schedules. When a stimulus is presented the pigeon executes the performance appropriate to its reinforcement schedule. Then when another stimulus is presented, the pigeon executes the performance appropriate to its specific schedule. Skinner thinks that this achievement makes more plausible the extension of laboratory results to daily life. To him, learning, in the everyday life of people, is more complicated but nevertheless of the same basic nature as an animal's learning through operant conditioning.[7]

In operant conditioning experiments, the species of organism studied has made surprisingly little difference. "Comparable results have been obtained with pigeons, rats, dogs, monkeys, human children, and most recently, . . . human psychotic subjects. In spite of great phylogenetic differences, all these organisms show amazingly similar properties of the learning process."[8]

[6] *Ibid.*, pp. 63–64.
[7] See Skinner, *Cumulative Record*, pp. 147–148.
[8] *Ibid.*, p. 148.

WHAT PSYCHOLOGICAL THEORY UNDERLIES SKINNER'S TEACHING PROCEDURES?

Throughout his study and writings, Professor Skinner has adhered rigorously to a basic conviction that psychologists should restrict their study to the correlations between stimuli and responses and not meddle with any "make-believe" psychology which constructs intervening physiological or mental links between stimuli and responses. Adherents of Skinner's position consider study of these intervening variables ". . . a dummy physiology doing duty for truth when facts are missing."[9]

In a sense Skinner's psychology, operant behaviorism, is a modern extension of the earlier stimulus-response psychologies—connectionism as developed by Thorndike and behaviorism as developed by Watson. Thorndike dealt with both physical and mental elements but was always mechanistic in his study of man. Watson, too, was mechanistic; however, he limited his study to the behavior of biological organisms. Skinner, like both Thorndike and Watson, assumes that man is neutral and passive and that all behavior can be described in mechanistic terms. In his study of man and animals, he constantly is mechanistic, elementistic, and associationistic; to him, psychology is *the science of behavior*.

What Is the Meaning of "the Science of Behavior"?

Skinner sees a great and crucial future for a science of behavior. In his view, since a science of behavior is concerned with demonstrating the consequences of cultural practices, there is reason to believe that presence of such a science will be an essential mark of the culture or cultures which will survive in the future, and that the culture most likely to survive is the one in which the methods of science are most effectively applied to the problems of human behavior.[10] Consequently, throughout his work he has striven constantly to be scientific to the nth degree. He sees *science* as ". . . more than a set of attitudes. It is a search for order, for uniformities, for lawful relations among the events in nature. It begins, as we all begin, by observing single episodes, but it quickly passes on to the general rule, to scientific law."[11] Thus, he places himself in line as a contemporary representative of inductive, atomistic science following the earlier pattern of Francis Bacon and John Stuart Mill. One can get the "flavor" of Skinner's work only through reading his books and papers. His frequent usage of the definite article *the* as contrasted with his infrequent usage of the indefinite articles *a* or *an* is quickly apparent. Like other "realistic" scien-

[9] Edwin G. Boring, *A History of Experimental Psychology*, Appleton-Century-Crofts, 1950, p. 650.
[10] Skinner, *Science and Human Behavior*, p. 446.
[11] *Ibid.*, p. 13.

tists, he assumes that this practice adds to objectivity and makes reports of studies more "scientific."

A "REALISTIC" DEFINITION OF SCIENCE. Skinner works on the basic assumption that there is order in nature, including human behavior, and that it is the function of science to *discover* the order; this is the commitment of a *realistic*, as opposed to a *relativistic*, scientist.[12] Within Skinner's realistic outlook, science is concerned with discovery of pre-existent laws which govern the world about us. Knowledge of these laws enhances predictability, and thereby control, of the variables which cause events to occur. This supposedly is as true in psychology as in physics or chemistry. Thus, man, through discovery of laws and organization of them into systems, enables himself to deal effectively with aspects of the naturalistic world.

Skinner recognizes that ". . . it is time to insist that science does not progress by carefully designed steps called 'experiments' each of which has a well-defined beginning and end. Science is a continuous and often a disorderly and accidental process."[13] Nevertheless he leaves unrecognized the relativistic principle that *reality* consists of that which we make of what comes to us and is ". . . definable as something which might, should, or does make a difference to someone or something."[14]

MAN, A SUBJECT OF SCIENCE. According to Skinner, it is not to be assumed that human behavior has any peculiar properties which require a unique method or special kind of knowledge. The variables of psychology, like the variables of any other science, must be described in physical terms. In Skinner's psychology, the dependent variable in a situation is the behavior of an individual organism. The independent variable consists of external conditions of which the behavior is a function. This means that behavior operates upon the environment to generate consequences; *it* behaves.

The laws of the science of psychology are as definite as those of any other science. Skinner says, "It is decidedly not true that a horse may be led to water but cannot be made to drink."[15] He thinks that, through applying the laws of psychology and arranging a history of severe deprivation, it could be made absolutely sure that drinking would occur; likewise, a desired behavior can be caused in a human being.

Skinner's goal in psychology is to achieve the degree of prediction and control in regard to human behavior that has been achieved by the physical sciences. The scientist of behavior evaluates probability of behavior

[12] Skinner, *Cumulative Record*, pp. 88–89.
[13] *Ibid.*, p. 98.
[14] Ernest E. Bayles, *Democratic Educational Theory*, Harper, 1960, p. 94.
[15] Skinner, *Science and Human Behavior*, p. 32.

and explores conditions that determine it. Through gathering data in regard to the frequencies of responses which have already occurred, he is able to make accurate statements about the likelihood of occurrence of a single future response of the same kind; frequency of response indicates probability of response. "We are concerned, then, with the causes of human behavior. We want to know why men behave as they do. Any condition or event which can be shown to have an effect upon behavior must be taken into account. By discovering and analyzing these causes, we can predict behavior; to the extent that we can manipulate them, we can control behavior."[16]

The problem of predicting whether a man will commit suicide is of the same nature as the problem of predicting the probability of explosion of the first atomic bomb. The basic datum in scientific analysis of behavior is probability. However, the actual observed dependent variable is frequency of response. Since much important human behavior occurs only once, it cannot be studied in terms of frequencies. A man may marry only once, he may engage in a business deal only once—he will commit suicide only once. So, like the probability of the first atomic bomb explosion, some behavior cannot be stated in terms of frequency. Nevertheless, it can be evaluated in terms of probabilities of many of the component events which can be based upon data in the form of frequencies, and any behavior may be studied in terms of its component parts.[17]

How Is the Science of Behavior Related to Determinism?

Skinner's psychology implies a strictly naturalistic determinism. He notes that a scientific conception of human behavior dictates one practice and a philosophy of personal freedom another; and that a scientific conception of human behavior entails the acceptance of an assumption of determinism. Determinism means that behavior is caused, and that the behavior which appears is the only kind which could have appeared. Skinner emphasizes that the same type of determinism which is commonly accepted as applying to machines applies equally to human beings. As machines have become more lifelike, living organisms have been found to be more like machines. Today, many machines are deliberately designed to operate in ways which resemble "human behavior." "Man has, in short, created the machine in his own image."[18] Since mechanical calculators now solve equations too difficult or too time consuming even for human mathematicians, human beings have lost much of their uniqueness.

Determinism carries with it the implication that environment deter-

16 *Ibid.*, p. 23.
17 Skinner, *Cumulative Record*, p. 76.
18 Skinner, *Science and Human Behavior*, p. 46.

mines an individual even when he alters his own environment. "It does not matter that the individual may take it upon himself to control the variables of which his own behavior is a function or, in a broad sense, to engage in the design of his own culture. He does this only because he is the product of a culture which generates self-control or cultural design as a mode of behavior."[19]

Skinner says, "The scientist, like any organism, is the product of a unique history."[20] He considers science of major importance in human affairs but recognizes that even scientists and science are not free. Science, too, is a part of the course of events and it cannot interfere with that course. Thus, science and scientists must be explained in any adequate account which science gives of human behavior in general. Science supplies an account of processes of which it itself is an example.[21]

HOW IS OPERANT CONDITIONING NONPHYSIOLOGICAL AND NONPHENOMENOLOGICAL?

A system of operant conditioning has no place for study of either physiological or phenomenological psychology. *Physiological psychology* is devoted to study of physiological, neurological, and biological functions within an organism. *Phenomenological psychology* centers upon what events mean to the persons involved. In a sense it is similar to physiological psychology in that it, too, is centered upon what takes place within a person. However, it differs sharply from physiological psychology in that major emphasis is placed upon the process of experiencing. Because Skinner rejects both physiological and phenomenological psychology, his friends sometimes speak of his dealing with the "empty organism."

NONPHYSIOLOGICAL PSYCHOLOGY. Skinner is convinced that the practice of looking inside an organism for an explanation of behavior has tended to obscure the variables which lie outside the organism and are immediately available for scientific analysis. These variables outside the organism are in its environmental history and its immediate environment. Their study permits behavior to be explained scientifically just as behavior of nonliving objects is explained scientifically by physicists. These independent variables are of many sorts and their relation to behavior is often subtle and complex; nevertheless, according to Skinner, it is only through analyzing them that we may hope to reach an adequate account of behavior.

Since all statements about the nervous system are not expressed in the

---

[19] *Ibid.,* p. 448.
[20] Skinner, *Cumulative Record,* p. 99.
[21] Skinner, *Science and Human Behavior,* p. 446.

same terms and cannot be confirmed by the same method of observation as the facts for which they are supposed to account, they are theories. Thus, Skinner feels that they can make little contribution to a scientific psychology. In the present stage of science a neurological explanation of behavior is impossible. However, this fact in no way implies that a scientific psychology of learning cannot be established separate from any neurological theory.

NONPHENOMENOLOGICAL PSYCHOLOGY. Statements about mental events, like neurological statements, also are theoretical. Thus, Skinner belittles attempts of psychologists to infer what a physical situation *means* to an organism or to distinguish between the physical world and the psychological world of experience. He constantly emphasizes that events affecting an organism must be capable of being described in the language of physical science.[22] To him, the "free inner man" who is held responsible for the behavior of the external biological organism is only a prescientific substitute for the kinds of external causes of behavior which are susceptible to scientific analysis. Hence there is no place in scientific psychology for study of the personal experience of a man.

Skinner sees the practice of some scientists, who indicate that they are describing only half the universe and that there is another half—a world of self, mind, or consciousness—as a part of the cultural heritage from which science has emerged but which now stands in the way of a unified scientific account of nature. Even in discussing the higher human function, thinking, Skinner sees little need for the concept *self*. He recognizes that behavior is a function of the environment, that environment, then, presumably means any event in the universe capable of affecting the organism, and that a very small part of this universe is private, i.e., it is enclosed within the organism's own skin. Thus, some independent variables, for example, an aching tooth, may be related to behavior in a unique way. However, he sees no reason to suppose that the stimulating effect of an inflamed tooth is essentially different from that of a hot stove.[23]

Since the self is not identical with the physical organism, such a concept is not essential in any analysis of behavior. The concept may have had an early advantage in representing a relatively coherent response system, but it is hazardous in that it may lead us to expect consistencies and functional integrities which do not exist. "The alternative to the use of the concept [self] is simply to deal with demonstrated covariations in the strength of responses."[24]

In opposing the "inner man" concept of human behavior Skinner notes the similarity of the inner man concept to a "God within" which does not

22 *Ibid.*, p. 36.
23 *Ibid.*, p. 258.
24 *Ibid.*, p. 286.

occupy space and thus may be multiplied at will, as is done in the Freudian pattern. He points out that as more and more of the behavior of organisms has come to be explained in terms of stimuli, at each stage of scientific development of psychology, some part of the control of the organism has passed from a hypothetical inner entity to the external environment. "The 'will' has retreated up the spinal cord, through the lower and then the higher parts of the brain, and finally, with the conditioned reflex, has escaped through the front of the head."[25]

In Skinner's system there is no place for the statement that behavior is under the control of an incentive or goal. A scientific psychology, as Skinner defines it, replaces statements which might use such words as *incentive, goal,* or *purpose* with statements about conditioning. Instead of saying that a man behaves because of the consequences which are to follow his behavior, we simply state that he behaves thus and so because of the consequences which have followed similar behavior in the past. When one is "looking for something" he is emitting responses which in the past produced something as a consequence. When one says, "I am looking for my glasses," what he really means is ". . . 'I have lost my glasses,' 'I shall stop what I am doing when I find my glasses,' or 'When I have done this in the past, I have found my glasses.' "[26]

Since the terms *pleasant* and *satisfying* do not refer to any physical property of reinforcing events, and physical sciences use neither of these terms nor their equivalents, they, too, should be deleted from the language of a science of psychology. Furthermore, since behavior is always the behavior of an individual, a science of behavior which concerns only the behavior of groups is not likely to be of help in understanding particular cases. Thus, "A 'social force' is no more useful in manipulating behavior than an inner state of hunger, anxiety, or skepticism."[27]

WHAT IS THE NATURE OF OPERANT CONDITIONING OR REINFORCEMENT?

In the pigeon experiment, the process of *operant conditioning* is the change in frequency with which the head is lifted to a given height, the *reinforcer* is food, and the *reinforcement* is food presentation when the response is emitted. The *operant* is the behavior upon which the reinforcement is contingent—the height to which the head must be raised.

In operant conditioning, the important stimulus is the one immediately following the response, not the one preceding it. Any emitted response which leads to reinforcement is thereby strengthened. It is not the specific S-R tendency that is strengthened, but rather the *general tendency* to

[25] *Ibid.,* pp. 48–49.
[26] *Ibid.,* p. 90.
[27] *Ibid.,* p. 36.

make the response. A rat presses a lever and gets food. Because of this, the rat will be more likely to press the lever again. "What is changed is the future probability of response in the same *class*."[28] The operant as a class of behavior, rather than the response as a particular instance, is reinforced. Since each reinforcement builds up a reserve of responses, a pigeon may continue to raise its head or a rat to press the lever several, or even many, times after food has ceased to appear.

The law of operant conditioning is that, if the occurrence of an operant is followed by presentation of a reinforcing stimulus, the strength—probability—is increased. What is strengthened is not a stimulus-response connection; the operant requires no specific eliciting stimulus. Insofar as the organism is concerned, the only important property of the operant contingency is time; the reinforcer follows the reponse. How this is brought about does not matter. The process of operant conditioning may be described adequately without any mention of a stimulus which acts before the response is made. In reinforcing a pigeon's neck stretching it is necessary only for one to wait for neck stretching to occur. It is not necessary for the experimenter to elicit it.

In operant conditioning, the subject's seeing a connection is in no way essential. Skinner considers Thorndike's expression "trial and error learning" to be superfluous and out of place. As he has observed the behavior of pigeons and other animals, he has seen no reason to call the movements being taught "trials" and any movements which did not achieve a specified consequence "errors." "The statement that the bird 'learns that it will get food by stretching its neck' is an inaccurate report of what has happened."[29] A Gestalt-field explanation of how the bird learns, of course, would be just this.

Skinner observes that the behavior which is more likely to be reinforced is the more likely to occur. Presence of a cat is the occasion upon which the response "cat" is likely to be reinforced. However, a stimulus eliciting "cat" is in no way an essential part of the operant conditioning process. Operant reinforcement of a behavior is contingent—dependent—upon a response, not the stimulus which gave rise to that response. The response *c-a-t* is reinforced after it is uttered. The stimulus involved here is a discriminative, not an eliciting, one. "The discriminative stimulus does not elicit a response, it simply alters a probability of occurrence."[30] It is not correct to say that an operant reinforcement strengthened the response which preceded it; the response has already occurred and cannot be changed. What has been changed is that the probability that that class of responses will occur in the future has been increased.

[28] *Ibid.*, p. 87.
[29] *Ibid.*, p. 64.
[30] *Ibid.*, p. 110.

Skinner revised Thorndike's law of effect. "Instead of saying that a man behaves because of the consequences which *are* to follow his behavior, we simply say that he behaves because of the consequences which *have* followed similar behavior in the past. This is, of course, the Law of Effect or operant conditioning."[31] The law of effect exemplified in operant conditioning simply specifies a procedure for altering the probability of a chosen response. By progressively changing the *contingencies of reinforcement* in the direction of the desired behavior, one can see learning occur.

What Are Contingencies of Reinforcement?

A contingency of reinforcement is a sequence in which a response is followed by a reinforcing stimulus. The basic three-term contingency of operant conditioning is response, stimulus, and reinforcement in that order. In a contingency the occurrence of an operant—response—is *followed by* presentation of a reinforcing stimulus, and the strength—probability—of recurrence of the operant is increased. The three-term contingency of operant reinforcement occurs when a child is taught to read; a given response is reinforced with "Right" or "Wrong" according to how the student responds to the appropriate visual stimulus—word or sentence.

The key to successful teaching or training is to analyze the effect of reinforcement and design techniques which manipulate the process with considerable precision—to set up specific reinforcing contingencies. In this way the behavior of an individual organism may be brought under precise control. Implicit in operant behaviorism is the conviction that "When all relevant variables have been arranged, an organism will or will not respond. If it does not, it cannot. If it can, it will."[32]

How Does Operant Differ from Respondent or Reflexive Conditioning?

Reflexive learning involves such situations as are described in the Pavlovian dog studies. Essentially it is a process of stimulus substitution. An organism supposedly responds reflexively to a natural or unconditioned stimulus. A new stimulus is presented along with the original stimulus and the organism comes to respond to the new stimulus in the same way it formerly did to the original one. The new stimulus becomes a conditioned stimulus; the organism has learned. In reflexive or respondent conditioning the key stimulus is the one which precedes the response. Whereas reflexive learning is an S-R process, operant learning is an R-S process.

In operant learning, the significant stimulus is that which immediately

---

[31] *Ibid.*, p. 87.
[32] *Ibid.*, p. 112.

follows the response. Any modification of the environment is a stimulus. Operant behavior is that behavior which operates upon the environment to generate consequences. Notice that in this process not the person or the environment but it—behavior—behaves; behavior is a phenomenon of nature. Just as wind blows, behavior behaves.

Although Skinner acknowledges two kinds of learning—operant and reflexive—he places far greater emphasis upon operant learning, which is under the control of its consequences. He sees most human behavior and consequently nearly all human conditioning or learning as operant. He feels that, if all the behavior which falls into the pattern of simple reflexes were assembled, it would represent only a very small fraction of the total behavior of an organism. He is convinced that early investigators overworked the principle of reflexive conditioning and made exaggerated claims for it. However, he warns that the area of reflex behavior should not be overlooked. To ignore completely the principle of the conditioned reflex would be unwarranted. But "It is neither plausible nor expedient to conceive of the organism as a complicated jack-in-the-box with a long list of tricks, each of which may be evoked by pressing the proper button. The greater part of the behavior of the intact organism is not under this primitive sort of stimulus control. The environment affects the organism in many ways which are not conveniently classed as 'stimuli,' and even in the field of stimulation only a small part of the forces acting upon the organism elicit responses in the invariable manner of reflex action."[33] The environment is so constructed that certain things tend to happen together. Respondent conditioning is the effect of this phenomenon upon behavior. When certain events like the color and taste of ripe fruit occur together, an organism responds in the same manner to either stimulus, color or taste. It has learned this through respondent conditioning. However, the importance of this kind of learning has been emphasized far too much. Behavior such as eating a meal or driving a car shows but little respondent character; most of it is operant in nature.

WHAT ARE THE PROCESSES OF OPERANT REINFORCEMENT AND EXTINCTION?

In operant conditioning, an operant is strengthened through its *reinforcement* or weakened through its *extinction*. The psychologist's task is simply to account for probability of responses in terms of a history of reinforcement and extinction. The effect of *reinforcement* always is to increase the probability of response. Extinction is the reverse of reinforcement. When a reinforcing stimulus no longer occurs following a response, the response becomes less and less frequent; this is operant *extinction*.

[33] *Ibid.*, pp. 49–50.

"Conditioning builds up a predisposition to respond—a 'reserve'—which extinction exhausts."[34]

What Are the Two Kinds of Reinforcers?

Any stimulus whose presentation or removal increases the probability of a response is a reinforcer. Consequently, there are two kinds of reinforcers or reinforcing events—positive and negative. A positive reinforcer is any stimulus the *presentation* of which strengthens the behavior upon which it is made contingent; a negative reinforcer is any stimulus the *withdrawal* of which strengthens that behavior. Since in both cases responses are strengthened, reinforcement is taking place. A positive reinforcement consists of presenting a stimulus, of adding something—food, water or a teacher's smile—to an organism's environment. A negative reinforcement consists of removing something—a loud noise, an electric shock, or a teacher's frown—from the situation. In both of these cases the probability that the response will recur is increased.

Although in lay usage both positive and negative reinforcers are "rewards," Skinner warns against defining a positive reinforcer as pleasant or satisfying and a negative reinforcer as annoying. "It would be as difficult to show that the reinforcing power of an aversion stimulus is due to its unpleasantness as to show that the reinforcing power of a positive reinforcer is due to its pleasantness."[35] When a person reports that an event is pleasant, this simply means that the event is of such kind that it reinforces him. Physical science uses no such terms as *pleasant* and *unpleasant* or their equivalents. The terms in no way refer to physical properties of reinforcing agents.

Is Punishment Reinforcement?

Punishment is a basically different process from reinforcement. Whereas reinforcement involves presentation of a positive reinforcer or removal of a negative one, punishment consists of presentation of a negative stimulus or removal of a positive one. Again, whereas reinforcement is defined in terms of strengthening of response, punishment supposedly is a process which weakens a response. Putting it succinctly, when a stimulus is involved in strengthening a response there is reinforcement; when a stimulus is presented or withdrawn in an attempt to weaken a response, there is punishment.

Results of experiments indicate that punishment does not permanently reduce a tendency to respond. Thorndike's experiments with human subjects indicated that a reward strengthened the behavior which preceded it

---

[34] Skinner, *Cumulative Record*, p. 53.
[35] Skinner, *Science and Human Behavior*, p. 173.

but that punishment did not weaken it. Through reward, behavior may be stamped in; but the converse, that through punishment it can be stamped out, does not hold. Whereas reinforcement can be controlled to good advantage, in the long run punishment works to the disadvantage of both the punished organism and the punishing agency. Its results are neither predictable nor dependable. Extinction—permitting a behavior to die out by not reinforcing it—and not punishment is the appropriate process for breaking habits.

What Are the Types of Operant Reinforcement?

There are two rather distinct types of operant reinforcement—stimulus discrimination and response differentiation. Nearly all human learning can be classified under these two. However, the process of respondent (reflexive) conditioning must not be completely ignored.

Through operant reinforcement a relatively complete new unit of behavior may be learned or an existing unit of behavior may be refined. In general, reinforcement which leads to behavior acquirement is a process of discrimination of stimuli, whereas behavior refinement or skill development is a process of differentiation of response.

DISCRIMINATION OF STIMULI.   Operant discrimination is a change in behavior as the result of changes in the environment—stimuli—of the organism. A pigeon can be made to be more likely to respond by stretching its neck at times when a light is on. This probability is increased by discrimination. Imitative behavior is an example of the result of discriminative operant reinforcement. Such behavior does not arise because of any inherent reflex mechanism but develops in the history of the individual as a result of discriminative reinforcements. The visual stimulation of someone waving a hand is the occasion upon which waving a hand probably received reinforcement. The reinforcement, not the stimulation from the other person's waving his hand, is the cause of future hand waving in similar situations. Because objects in shop windows into which other people are looking are likely to reinforce looking into such windows, when a person sees other people looking into a shop window he too is likely to look. Taking an interest or attending are only some other expressions that are commonly used to describe the consequence of discriminative operant reinforcement. "Attention is a controlling *relation*—the relation between a response and a discriminative stimulus. When someone is paying attention he is under special control of a stimulus."[36]

DIFFERENTIATION OF RESPONSE.   Skills are improved through differences in reinforcements of varying responses. Many differentiation reinforce-

[36] *Ibid.*, p. 123.

ments may be supplied automatically by mechanical exigencies of the environment of an organism. To throw a ball skillfully, a person must release it at the proper moment; instances in which release comes before or after the proper moment are not reinforced. However, in more complex skill learning, reinforcement must be supplied by a teacher. In this process, reinforcement which develops skill must be immediate. "By reinforcing a series of successive approximations, we bring a rare response to a very high probability in a short time."[37]

Through the procedure of operant conditioning, within which differentiation of response is reinforced, a hungry pigeon well adapted to the experimental situation and the food tray usually can be brought to respond by pecking a specific spot in two or three minutes. To get the pigeon to peck a specific spot as quickly as possible, the bird is given food when it turns slightly in the direction of the spot. This increases the frequency of turning toward the spot. Reinforcement is then withheld until the bird makes a slight movement toward the spot. Then positions which are successively closer to the spot are reinforced. Then reinforcement is given only when the head is moved slightly forward, and finally only when the beak actually makes contact with the spot.

In target practice a rifleman needs a report of the accuracy of the shot from time to time to maintain the reinforcing power of feedback. However, after some practice he eventually knows before the target is hit whether the shot was good or bad. His own behavior generates a stimulating feedback. Hits and misses generate different forms of this feedback. Likewise, good form in bowling is reinforced by feedback from the bowler's body.

What Is Extinction?

We know that, in general, when we engage in behavior which no longer "pays off," we find ourselves less inclined to behave in that way again. If we get no answers to telephone calls, we eventually stop telephoning. In operant behaviorism this phenomenon would be described by saying that when reinforcement is no longer forthcoming, a response becomes less and less frequent. This is the process of operant extinction.

Operant extinction takes place much more slowly than does operant reinforcement. However, as an organism responds less and less, a uniform process of extinction may be detected. Since behavior during extinction is a result of the conditioning which had preceded it, extinction occurs quickly when only a few of a given response have been reinforced and is greatly protracted when there has been a long history of reinforcement.

The extinction process includes the interesting phenomenon of spontaneous recovery. Even after prolonged extinction, an organism, at the be-

[37] *Ibid.*, p. 92.

ginning of another session of an activity in which it had been trained but now is no longer being reinforced, often will respond at a higher rate for at least a few moments.

Sometimes an extinction curve is disturbed by an emotional effect. Failure of a response to be reinforced not only leads to operant extinction but also may be accompanied by a reaction commonly called frustration or rage. A pigeon that has failed to receive reinforcement flaps its wings and engages in other emotional behavior. A mechanic, who is in the habit of having bolts unscrew when he turns his wrench, vents his spleen when one breaks off instead. However, after exercising his vocabulary he turns back to the next bolt. Likewise a pigeon or rat will turn again to the operating key of the box when the emotional response has subsided. Extinction curves often show cyclic oscillation as the emotional response builds up, disappears, and builds up again.

Whereas the mere passage of time after reinforcement has surprisingly little effect upon loss of the act or habit, extinction is an effective way of removing an operant from the repertoire of an organism. When unaccompanied by extinction, forgetting takes place very slowly if at all. Note the key difference here: Whereas mere forgetting is the losing of a habit through the passage of time, extinction requires that the response be emitted without reinforcement. "In human behavior skilled responses generated by relatively precise contingencies frequently survive unused for as much as half a lifetime."[38] The commonly heard assertion that early experiences of a child determine the personality of the mature person implies that the effect of operant reinforcement is very durable and that in human beings operant extinction is unlikely to occur on a large scale.

The resistance to extinction generated by intermittent reinforcement of a response is much greater than that achieved by the same number of reinforcements given for consecutive responses. If we only occasionally reinforce a child's good behavior the behavior survives after reinforcement is discontinued much longer than if we had reinforced every instance up to the same total number of reinforcements. Since intermittent reinforcement generates longer extinction curves than does continuous reinforcement, there is no simple relation between the number of reinforcements and the number of unreinforced responses necessary for extinction.

HOW MAY OPERANT CONDITIONING BE APPLIED TO SCHOOLROOM PRACTICES?

Skinner is convinced that operant conditioning, so fruitful when applied to animal training, promises equal success when used in schools. He feels that the most efficient control of human learning requires instrumental aid.

[38] *Ibid.*, p. 71.

He is appalled at the present inefficient practices in schools and recommends a procedure whereby they can be corrected. He recognizes the *first* task of teachers to be to shape proper responses, to get children to pronounce and write responses properly. But he sees their *principal* task as bringing proper behavior under many sorts of stimulus control. "Teaching spelling is mainly a process of shaping complex forms of behavior. In other subjects—for example, arithmetic—responses must be brought under the control of appropriate stimuli."[39]

What Are the Shortcomings of Current Educational Practice?

Skinner believes that it is in bringing correct responses under stimulus control that the greatest inefficiency of current teaching procedures occurs. "In education we design and re-design our curricula in a deperate attempt to provide a liberal education while steadfastly refusing to employ available engineering techniques which would efficiently build the interests and instill the knowledge which are the goals of education."[40]

Skinner notes some current weaknesses in educational practices: (1) Behavior is dominated by aversion (escape) stimulation; (2) too great a lapse of time exists between behavior and its reinforcement; (3) a skillful program of reinforcement which moves forward through a series of progressive approximations to the final complex behavior desired is lacking; and (4) reinforcement of desired behavior occurs much too infrequently.

BEHAVIOR DOMINATED BY AVERSION STIMULATION. Although the type of threatened displeasure or pain has been changed in the past fifty years, behavior in the lower grades is still dominated by aversive stimulation—a child is trying to escape or keep away from something. Fifty years ago a child read numbers, copied numbers, and memorized tables to escape the birch rod or cane, i.e., as far as the child was concerned, he did these things to avoid or escape punishment. Today a school child behaves the way he does primarily to escape the threat of a series of minor distasteful events—the teacher's displeasure, criticism or ridicule by his classmates, a poor showing in competition, low marks, or a trip to the principal's office. When children are dominated by this atmosphere, getting the right answer is in itself a rather insignificant event. Thus, the emphasis in teaching and learning is not centered where it should be—in operant conditioning.

EXCESSIVE TIME LAPSE BETWEEN BEHAVIOR AND REINFORCEMENT. Unless explicit mediating behavior has been set up, the lapse of only a few seconds between a response and its reinforcement destroys most of the effect. A grade on a test taken near the end of the week is too far away

---

[39] *Cumulative Record*, p. 165.
[40] *Ibid.*, p. 228

from the behaviors the students emitted—sent out—in studying the subject matter earlier in the week. Reinforcing stimuli should follow the response immediately.

Through use of the generalized reinforcer—approval—schools and society reinforce acquisition of the type of behavior learned in school. This is done by awarding grades, promotions, keys, diplomas, degrees, and medals. Skinner notes that these reinforcers do reinforce going to school and gaining a diploma or degree; their shortcoming is that they seldom if ever reinforce the subject matter elements themselves.

ABSENCE OF A PROGRAM OF SERIAL REINFORCEMENT.   A carefully planned program of teaching supposedly should move forward step by step by reinforcing a series of progressive approximations to the final behavior which is desired. To bring a human organism into possession of mathematical behavior most efficiently, a long series of reinforcement contingencies is necessary. Since a teacher has only so much time, he cannot deal with a pupil's responses one at a time and it is usually necessary for him to reinforce the desired behavior only in blocks of responses.

INFREQUENCY OF REINFORCEMENT.   Perhaps the most serious criticism of current classroom procedures is the relative infrequency of reinforcement of the desired acts of students. It is just not humanly possible for one teacher to provide an adequate number of reinforcement *contingencies* for a class of 30 or 40 children. Skinner estimates that, although adequate efficient mathematical behavior at the level of the first four grades requires requires somewhere between 25,000 and 50,000 reinforcement contingencies, a teacher at best could provide only a few thousand. Thus, even our best schools may be criticized for their inefficiency in teaching drill subjects such as arithmetic. Advances recently made in the control of the learning process, Skinner believes, suggest that classroom practices should be thoroughly revised.

What Are the Relevant Considerations in Conditioning— Teaching—a Child?

In order to plan a procedure for inculcating certain desired behavior in a child, certain specific questions need to be answered: (1) What behavior is to be established? (2) What reinforcers are available? (3) What responses are available? (4) How can reinforcements be most efficiently scheduled?[41]

BEHAVIOR TO BE ESTABLISHED.   To teach efficiently the first job of a teacher is to determine carefully just what it is he plans to teach at a specific

[41] *Ibid.*, pp. 152–153.

time. A teacher is the architect and builder of behaviors. He must decide what he wants to teach, then teach it. His objectives are specific, and they are defined in terms of desired behaviors. Thus, in determining achievement of objectives of a school, operant behaviorism requires a teacher-centered classroom.

REINFORCERS AVAILABLE. What does a school have in its possession which will reinforce a child? Since the sheer control of nature in itself is reinforcing, the material to be learned may provide considerable automatic reinforcement. Children play for hours with mechanical toys, paints, and puzzles. These feed back significant changes in the environment and are reasonably free of aversive properties. Automatic reinforcement from manipulation of the environment is probably rather mild. However, in teaching, the net amount of reinforcement in each contingency is of little significance. When properly and carefully used, a series of very slight reinforcements may be tremendously effective in controlling behavior.

In addition to automatic reinforcement arising from manipulation of the environment, some other reinforcers are available and often used. A child behaves in a certain way and the behavior is reinforced by its immediate consequences. Reinforcement may follow from a child's excelling others. However, when he is competitively "rewarded," the reinforcement of this child is, of necessity, aversive—"punishing"—to others. The good will and affection of the teacher also may be reinforcing. A positive "reward" or "consequence" (stimulus) strengthens the behavior that is part of the contingency including that stimulus; it supposedly has nothing to do with organismic purpose.

RESPONSES AVAILABLE. In planning a program of progressive approximations that will lead to the desired final form of behavior a teacher must have an inventory of responses which are available throughout the conditioning process.

MOST EFFICIENT SCHEDULING OF REINFORCEMENTS. To schedule reinforcements efficiently means to make them contingent upon the desired behavior. Here two considerations are involved: gradual elaboration of extremely complex patterns of behavior and maintenance of the behavior in strength at each stage. "The whole process of becoming competent in any field must be divided into a very large number of very small steps, and reinforcement must be contingent upon the accomplishment of each step. . . . By making each successive step as small as possible, the frequency of reinforcement can be raised to a maximum, while the possibly aversive consequences of being wrong are reduced to a minimum."[42]

42 *Ibid.*, p. 153.

Skinner contends that the necessary requirements for adequate reinforcement are not excessive but they probably are incompatible with current realities of present-day classrooms. Experimental studies of learning have indicated that, in order to arrange the contingencies of reinforcement which are most efficient in controlling learning in an organism, mechanical and electrical devices must be used. As a mere reinforcing mechanism, a teacher is out of date—and would be even if he devoted all his time to a single child. Only through mechanical devices can the necessarily large number of contingencies be provided. "We have every reason to expect, therefore, that the most effective control of human learning will require instrumental aid."[43]

How Do Teaching Machines Work?

In Skinner's view, education must become more efficient to a degree that cannot be accomplished merely by our building more schools and preparing more teachers; adequate systems of labor-saving capital equipment, i.e., teaching machines, must be developed. He is critical, too, of traditional education which makes students more and more the passive receivers of instruction. Teaching machines, he feels, encourage students to take an "active" role in the instructional process—they must press buttons and turn knobs.

REQUIREMENTS OF AN APPROPRIATE TEACHING MACHINE. Skinner thinks that, in light of modern psychological knowledge, an appropriate teaching machine has two basic requirements: First, a student must compose his response rather than select it from a set of alternatives.[44] Second, in acquiring complex behavior, a student must pass through a carefully designed sequence of steps; each step must be so small that it always can be taken, yet in taking it the student must move somewhat closer to fully competent behavior, and the machine must operate so as to make sure that steps are taken in a carefully prescribed order.[45]

OPERATION OF A TEACHING MACHINE. Skinner anticipates no particular difficulty in producing workable teaching machines. The necessary contingencies may be arranged either mechanically or electrically. Let's see how he describes a teaching device:

The device consists of a box about the size of a small record player. On the top surface is a glazed window through which a question or problem printed on

[43] *Ibid.,* p. 154.

[44] In the 1920s Sidney L. Pressey developed a teaching machine which students used in taking and scoring multiple-choice tests; they selected, but did not formulate, the answers.

[45] Skinner, *Cumulative Record,* p. 161.

a paper tape may be seen. The child answers the question by moving one or more sliders upon which the digits 0 through 9 are printed. The answer appears in square holes punched in the paper upon which the question is printed. When the answer has been set, the child turns a knob. The operation is as simple as adjusting a television set. If the answer is right, the knob turns freely and can be made to ring a bell or provide some other conditioned reinforcement. If the answer is wrong, the knob will not turn. A counter may be added to tally wrong answers. The knob must then be reversed slightly and a second attempt at a right answer made. (Unlike the flash card, the device reports a wrong answer without giving the right answer.) When the answer is right, a further turn of the knob engages a clutch which moves the next problem into place in the window. This movement cannot be completed, however, until the sliders have been returned to zero.[46]

What Are the Advantages of the Use of Mechanical Teaching Devices?

Skinner claims a long list of advantages available through use of mechanical teaching devices in present-day classrooms. (1) Reinforcement for the right answer is immediate. (2) Provided traces of earlier aversive control can be erased, mere manipulation of the device probably will be reinforcing enough to keep an average pupil at work for a suitable period each day. (3) All at one time, a teacher may supervise an entire class at work on such devices; yet each child may complete as many problems as possible in the class period and progress at his own rate. (4) Any child who is forced to leave school for a period may return at any time and continue from where he left off. (5) Each child may advance at his own rate and when he gets too far ahead of the class may be assigned to other tasks. (6) Through carefully designing materials, teachers may arrange problems in a serial order in the direction of an immensely complex repertoire. (7) Since the machines record the number of mistakes, tapes can be modified to enhance their effectiveness. (8) Knowing just what each student has done, a teacher can apply necessary supplementary reinforcement at the greatest vantage point.

Can Machines Teach a Child to Think?

Skinner emphasizes that thinking or originality is not absence of lawfulness and it should never be considered a spontaneous process. He points out that as long as thinking is identified with spontaneity or lawlessness it is a hopeless task to attempt systematically to influence a child's thinking in any way. Thinking, like the rest of the behavior of an organism, is a lawful process. Thus, verbal behavior, in terms of which human thinking eventually must be defined, should be treated in its own right as a substantial goal of education. In inculcating this behavior, learning devices

[46] *Ibid.*, p. 154.

can teach verbal thinking, i.e., establish the large and important repertoire of verbal relationships encountered in science and logic.

Skinner thinks it is of critical importance for us to realize that, in operant behaviorism, thought is not some mysterious process which is the cause of behavior, but the behavior itself. Man thinking is man behaving, and human thought is operant, not reflexive, behavior. "Shakespeare's thought was his behavior *with respect to his extremely complex environment.*"[47] "In the broadest possible sense, the thought of Julius Caesar was simply the sum total of his responses to the complex world in which he lived."[48]

Skinner observes that study of what traditionally has been called the human mind is more appropriately a study of concepts and methods which have emerged from an analysis of behavior. Thinking behavior is verbal or nonverbal, overt or covert. It is primarily the verbal behavior of men which has survived in recorded form, but from this and other records we can know something about their nonverbal behavior. When we say that Caesar thought Brutus could be trusted we do not necessarily mean that he ever said as much. Rather he behaved verbally and otherwise as if Brutus could be trusted. The rest of his behavior, his nonverbal plans and achievements, were also part of his thoughts.

Although in earlier behavioristic analyses thinking was identified with subaudible talking, Skinner feels that nothing is gained by so doing. There are difficulties in assuming that covert behavior is always executed by the muscular apparatus responsible for the overt form. Furthermore, the data which give rise to the notion of covert speech can be treated, as such, with a high degree of rigor. Rather than identifying thinking with *talking,* a better case can be made for identifying it with a special kind of *behaving,* that which automatically affects behavior and is reinforcing because it does.

Thinking is more productive when verbal responses lead to specific consequences and are reinforced because they do so. Just as a musician plays or composes what reinforces him audibly or an artist paints what reinforces him visually, a speaker or writer, engaged in verbal fantasy, says that which is reinforced by hearing it, or writes that which is reinforced by reading it. However, it must be recognized that in any case the solution to a problem is simply a response which alters the situation so that another strong response can be emitted. "Reinforcing contingencies shape the behavior of the individual, and novel contingencies generate novel forms of behavior."[49] Thus, man's present better control of the world

---

[47] B. F. Skinner, *Verbal Behavior,* Appleton-Century-Crofts, 1957, p. 450.
[48] *Ibid.,* pp. 451–452.
[49] *Ibid.,* p. 255.

could be described and expressed just as well by saying that the environment now is in better control of man.

The key to effective teaching of thinking, as well as any other behavior, is immediate feedback. To teach thinking, we should ". . . analyze the behavior called 'thinking' and produce it according to specifications. A program specifically concerned with such behavior could be composed of material already available in logic, mathematics, scientific method, and psychology."[50]

BIBLIOGRAPHY

Galanter, Eugene, *Automatic Teaching: The State of the Art,* Wiley, 1959.
 A collection of papers, one by B. F. Skinner, which treat the experimentation, analysis, and programing related to machine teaching.
Hilgard, E. R., *Theories of Learning,* 2nd ed., Appleton-Century-Crofts, 1956.
 In Chapter 4, "Skinner's Operant Conditioning": a descriptive interpretation of Skinner's operant conditioning theory of learning.
Holland, James G., and B. F. Skinner, *The Analysis of Behavior,* McGraw-Hill, 1961.
 A programed textbook for an introductory course in psychology to be used as a substitute for a teaching machine. A student supposedly is to learn the basic terms and principles of behavioristic conditioning; he writes the correct answer to a question, then is reinforced by finding it on the next page.
Skinner, B. F., *The Behavior of Organisms,* Appleton-Century-Crofts, 1938.
 Skinner's early systematic statement of operant behavior and conditioning.
Skinner, B. F., *Walden Two,* Macmillan, 1948.
 A novel proposing and describing a community within which maximum use is made of conditioning to control human welfare. It deals with the educational and social implications of behaviorism.
Skinner, B. F., *Science and Human Behavior,* Macmillan, 1953.
 An application of "realistic" scientific method to a study of human behavior centered around operant conditioning. "Scientific Analysis" is extended to the behavior of people in groups and the operation of controlling agencies such as government and religion. Its final section analyzes education as a process of control of human behavior.
Skinner, B. F., *Verbal Behavior,* Appleton-Century-Crofts, 1957.
 An explanation of how verbal behavior, including thinking, takes its place in the larger field of human behavior; it too is learned through operant conditioning. Ways of manipulating verbal behavior of individuals are treated.

[50] Skinner, *Cumulative Record,* p. 173.

Skinner, B. F., *Cumulative Record*, Appleton-Century-Crofts, 1959.
  A series of Skinner's papers which reflects the implications of his position. Part III, "The Science of Learning and the Art of Teaching" and "Teaching Machines," is particularly pertinent to this chapter.
Skinner, B. F., "A Case History in Scientific Method," in Sigmund Koch, *Psychology: A Study of Science*, McGraw-Hill, 1959.
  Skinner's own personal history illustrating his philosophy of science and psychology of behavior. He relates how he was operant-conditioned to perform in certain ways as he studied the conditioning of animals. The chapter is interesting reading. See pp. 359–379.

14
WHAT IS THE COGNITIVE-FIELD THEORY OF LEARNING?

Chapters 10, 11, and 12 are devoted to discussion of some possible descriptions of how man learns. In Chapter 10 some reasons are presented for studying the various learning theories; readers then are introduced to *mental discipline, natural unfoldment,* and *apperception.* These three outlooks toward learning, although now seldom promoted in teacher education institutions, continue to be reflected in many present-day school practices. In Chapters 11 and 12, the two major contemporary families of learning theory, S-R association and Gestalt-field theory, are described in a general way. Chapter 13 describes a systematic example of the S-R associationist family, Skinner's operant conditioning. This chapter takes up a representative of the Gestalt-field family, the cognitive-field theory of learning, exemplified in the thinking of the late Kurt Lewin.

The cognitive-field theory represents a relativistic, as opposed to an absolutistic (mechanistic), way of viewing man and the learning process. Readers are warned that should they attempt to understand its concepts mechanistically, they will not grasp this theory. A mechanist attempts to explain all the fullness and variety of a universe in terms of machine-like objects and movements. Thus, a mechanist in psychology reduces all human activities to movements, usually in terms of stimuli and responses. He considers a person an organism which is a product of its unique history of stimulus-response patterns. Just as an automobile is built by workmen who assemble its respective parts, a person is educated by teachers who feed into his physiological make-up the various aspects of environment which supposedly make him what mechanistic teachers want him to be.

The basic principle of *relativism* is that nothing is perceivable or conceivable as a thing-in-itself. Rather, everything is perceived or conceived in relation to other things. That is, a thing is perceived as a figure against a background, experienced from a given angle or direction of envisionment. Consequently, relativism means that psychological reality is defined, not in "objective," physical terms, but in psychological, perceptual terms. So defined, reality consists of what one makes of that which comes to him through his senses or otherwise.

See if you can get the point of this story. What is the significance of the third umpire's statement? What makes a ball a ball and a strike a strike? "The story concerns three baseball umpires who were discussing the problems of their profession. The first umpire said, 'Some's balls and some's strikes and I calls 'em as they is.' The second umpire said, 'Some's balls and some's strikes and I calls 'em as I sees 'em.' While the third umpire said, [I sees 'em comin' across and] 'some's balls and some's strikes but they ain't nothin' till I calls 'em.' "[1]

The cognitive-field theory of learning is closely related to, and derived from, *cognitive* and *field* psychological theories.[2] *Cognitive* is derived from the Latin verb *cognoscere*, which means "to know." Cognitive theory deals with the problem of how people gain an understanding of themselves and their environments and how, using their cognitions, they act in relation to their environments. Field theory centers on the idea that all psychological activity of a person occurs in a field; it is a part of a totality of coexisting factors which are mutually interdependent.

A field consists of the concurrent interrelationships in any one situation. A field situation is perceived in such a way that any change in the field depends upon the field at that time. An astronomer uses "field" to describe the universe and predict the orbit of stars. A biologist relates the function of cells to their location in a growth "field." A physicist uses "field" in his study of the structure of an atom. To a psychologist "field" means the total psychological world in which a person lives *at a certain time.* It includes matters past, present and future, concrete and abstract, actual and imaginary—all interpreted as simultaneous aspects of a situation.

A cognitive-field theory of learning often is called merely *field theory.* However, since it describes how a person gains understanding of himself

---

[1] Hadley Cantril, "Perception and Interpersonal Relations," *American Journal of Psychiatry*, August, 1957, p. 126.

[2] See Gardner Lindzey, *Handbook of Social Psychology*, Addison-Wesley, 1954, Vol. 1, Chaps. 3 and 5.

and his world in a situation where his self and his environment compose a totality of mutually interdependent, coexisting facts, *cognitive-field* is more truly descriptive of the learning process. Within cognitive-field theory, learning, briefly defined, is a relativistic process by which a learner develops new insights or changes old ones. In no sense is learning a mechanistic, atomistic process of connecting stimuli and responses within a biological organism.

Insight, concisely defined, is a basic sense of, or feeling for, relationships. Although there is nothing about the term *insight* which requires it to be *right* in any absolutistic sense, it is a grasp of a thing which often does go deeper than words. Thus, it is a realizing sense of a matter. Insight into a matter is its meaning. Meaning, so used, denotes that to which a matter or idea points or what it signifies. The insights of a person are not equated with his consciousness or awareness or his ability to describe them verbally; their essence is a sense of, or feeling for, pattern in a life situation.

Development of insight means getting the feel of a matter, grasping the idea, catching on to or seeing through a situation. An insight is acquired through doing something and seeing what happens. The focus of the learning is on the seeing, not, as has been assumed by S-R associationists, on the doing. Seeing, here, is broadly defined to mean catching the point or getting the idea. Any or all of the senses may be involved. The sensory action may be so rudimentary that the person involved may not realize it is going on at all; he may think he is learning through the "mind's eye."

During World War II, one of the authors watched a group of "noncoms" teaching recruits in basic training to fire Army rifles (the author was one of these "rookies"). Army rifles have a powerful recoil or kick. A soldier is supposed to "squeeze" the trigger gradually and smoothly until the rifle fires. Recruits usually anticipate the recoil and jump before the shell explodes; thus, their aim is completely spoiled. The problem for a noncom was to teach his "pupil" not to make the anticipatory jump. Recruits were convinced that they really did not jump until after the explosion and thus hours of blankety-blankety-blanks had little, if any, effect. Corporal Jones helped his "pupil" gain an insight. He "scolded" him several times for jumping, with no avail. Then while his pupil's attention was diverted to a fellow sufferer, the corporal slipped a fired cartridge into the firing chamber. The recruit aimed, started to squeeze, and again jumped out of his skin. He had gained an insight. He was jumping before his rifle fired and thus ruining his aim. His jumping before the rifle had fired then ceased.

Cognitive-field psychology explains development of insight as change in cognitive structure of a life space. To think of learning as development of insight and apply the thinking to school situations most advantageously, we need a psychological structure upon which to build our thinking. This is provided by cognitive-field psychology. A person's *insights* collectively constitute the *cognitive structure* of his life space. *Cognitive structure* means the way a person perceives the psychological aspects of the personal, physical, and social world. Such a world includes a person and all of his facts, concepts, beliefs, and expectations. Consequently, the cognitive structure of life spaces figures in development of language, emotions, actions, and social interrelations.

WHAT IS COGNITIVE-FIELD PSYCHOLOGY?

The development of cognitive-field psychology is attributed largely to Kurt Lewin and his associates and students. Lewin (1890–1947), a native of Germany, received his doctorate at the University of Berlin, where he was later professor of psychology and philosophy. In 1932 he came to the United States. He taught at Stanford, Cornell, and Iowa, and in 1944 became director of the Research Center for Group Dynamics at the Massachusetts Institute of Technology. His students now are working at the Research Center for Group Dynamics, University of Michigan, Duke, Kansas Universities, and other institutions.

Lewin considered psychology a science closely related to everyday life. He wanted most of all to study the various problems of the social sciences involving minority groups, political organizations, and international and intercultural relations. In the course of applying his psychological theory to problems in these areas he became interested in "teaching" and "learning." In keeping with his interests, he developed some new problems for psychology and was highly creative in his methods for solving them. As a leader in development of methods of group dynamics and action research, he thought that actual experiments with groups could be performed under precisely controlled conditions. His study of the effects of various social climates on youth is an example of an experiment in group dynamics. This study was conducted with groups of boys in a boys' club. By means of the relationship of a leader to his respective group, anarchic, autocratic, and democratic social climates were experimentally developed. Careful note was made of the behaviors of the boys in each social climate (see Chapter 1, p. 13). The process required to change the social climate of a group from one form to another also was studied.[3] In many circles, action research has become an accepted method of scientific procedure; group studies are so performed that key individuals in the social situation being investigated, through serving as recorders, observers, and analyzers, actively participate in conducting the study. Through this

---

[3] See Kurt Lewin, *Resolving Social Conflicts,* Harper, 1948, pp. 71–83.

method teachers may systematically study the student-teacher relationships which exist in their own school.

The center of Lewin's psychological interest was in the motivating conditions of person-environment situations. Furthermore, he was extremely interested in democratic principles and practices. It is no accident that his psychological system provides a foundation for a psychology of learning germane to American democratic society. Although field theory is applicable to all fields of psychology, it is particularly useful in social, personality, and educational psychology.

Lewin thought that during its development psychology somehow had missed much of what was at the heart of scientific modes of thought. He was convinced that the various S-R associationisms represented an inadequate approach to the study of psychology. Thus, he developed his "field psychology" in such way as to make it fundamentally different from the various S-R associationisms. Whereas S-R associationisms study psychology as a series of events, the very term *field* of field psychology implies that, psychologically interpreted, everything happens at once. Within field psychology, behavior has a unique meaning; it is described, not in physical terms, but in terms of what exists for the person being studied.[4]

Lewin's goal was to make the concepts of field psychology of sufficient scope to be applicable to all kinds of behavior and yet specific enough to permit representation of a definite person in a concrete situation. He observed that conventional laws of S-R associationistic psychology are based on statistical predictions, and that statistical predictions may apply to the average of children or to the typical behavior of an age group, but they do not anticipate what a given person will do in a specific situation. He thought that objectivity in psychology demanded representing the field adequately and accurately as it exists for an individual at a particular time. Consequently, to be objective in psychology one must be subjective; one must observe situations as the person being studied views them.

What Is the Method of Cognitive-Field Psychology?

Lewin's *field* psychology more precisely is called *topological and vector* psychology. In developing his psychology he borrowed ideas and concepts from other disciplines, namely, geometry and physics. Key concepts which he borrowed were "topology" from geometry and "vector" from physics. In using these and related concepts, he did not adhere rigidly to the definitions of their mother sciences but construed them in a manner most useful to his system of psychology.

Some scientists have criticized Lewin for giving these terms a somewhat

[4] See pp. 349–350 of this chapter.

different meaning from what they have in other areas of knowledge. Lewin has answered their criticism by stating that scientists in any area should use any concept in the ways that lend themselves most effectually to pursuit of their problems. Relativists encourage cooperation among all scientific endeavors, but they do not insist that any area of science be restricted by the specific laws, principles, concepts, and definitions of a sister science.

Through use of topological and vector concepts, Lewin pictured psychological reality in terms of field relationships of a person and his environment. In so doing he applied the method of field theory as it had been developed in the physical sciences. However, since concepts of the physical sciences did not lend themselves to a science of psychology, he did not use the same concepts and facts as did field theorists in sister sciences.

What Is the Role of Theories and Laws in Cognitive-Field Psychology?

In contrast to the professed practice of most S-R associationists, including Skinner, Lewin made much use of hypotheses and theories. To him, scientific method included not only the processes of observation and classification of data, but also formulating and testing hypotheses. Letting the facts speak for themselves was not enough. He wanted to develop considered hunches and see whether they would check out. Consequently, collection and classification of behavioral facts was deemed an inadequate process for answering questions involving conditions and causes of events. Lewin agreed with S-R associationists that research should begin with careful observation. However, since he emphasized the importance of inferring the motives of people being studied, his observation was done in a different way and for a different purpose.

> Only with the help of theories can one determine causal interrelationships. A science without theory is blind because it lacks that element which alone is able to organize facts and to give direction to research. Even from a practical point of view the mere gathering of facts has limited value. It cannot give an answer to the question that is most important for practical purposes—namely, what must one do to obtain a desired effect in given concrete cases? To answer this question it is necessary to have a theory, but a theory which is empirical and not speculative. This means that theory and fact must be closely related to each other.[5]

Lewin's purpose was to formulate laws—relationships—predictive of behavior of individual persons in their specific life spaces. He was convinced that in order to understand and predict behavior, one must consider

[5] Kurt Lewin, *Principles of Topological Psychology*, McGraw-Hill, 1936, p. 4.

a person and his environment a pattern of interdependent facts or functions. Furthermore, he regarded as lawful all events which occur in a person's life space, even those occurring only once. Thus, instead of placing emphasis on a mathematical average of as many different cases as possible, he centered attention on careful, full descriptions of particular person-environmental situations. "The general laws of psychology are statements of the empirical relations between these constructive elements or certain properties of them. It is possible to construct an infinite number of constellations [life spaces] in line with these laws; each of these constellations corresponds to an individual case at a given time."[6]

What Are Some Essential Features of Cognitive-Field Psychology?

There are some features of field psychology which make it distinctly different from any of the mechanistic psychologies. The foremost of these features is its unique approach to the study of perception and reality. Other important characteristics are interpretation of intelligent behavior as purposive, emphasis upon psychological functions rather than objects, a situational as opposed to a historical point of view, and stress upon the principle of contemporaneity. We expand each of these points in the following sections.

1. PERCEPTION AND REALITY DEFINED RELATIVISTICALLY. The field, i.e., life space, which influences an individual is described, not in "objective," physical terms, but in the way it exists for that person at that time. Thus, there is no attempt to relate behavior to a biological organism and its physical or geographical environment as such. In field psychology, the psychological concept *person* is much broader than is the biological concept *organism*. A life space or field consists of the content of an individual's perception. Neither the organism nor the environment alone is the one main factor. Rather, a person and his environment are simultaneously interacting and participating in perception; they constitute an SMI (simultaneous mutual interaction).

Perception, here, is interpreted in its broadest possible sense. It does not mean mere consciousness. There is evidence from observation of human and animal behavior that one cannot use consciousness as the sole criterion of what is a part of a life space. A child playing in his yard behaves differently when his mother is home and when she is out, yet he probably at no time verbalizes—is specifically conscious—of her being home or away. Children in a schoolroom with teacher A conduct themselves quite differently from when they are with teacher B. Yet they may at no time

[6] Kurt Lewin, *Field Theory in Social Science,* Harper, 1951, p. 61.

consciously formulate the two patterns of behavior. Likewise dogs and other animals size up situations and do the best they can for themselves; however, there is little if any evidence that in so doing they carry on a conscious process. Perception, then, must be construed to cover all the different ways one has of getting to know his environment.

In *apparently* the same situation, a person at different times may perceive quite different aspects of a situation and behave accordingly. Furthermore, provision of opportunity for one to perceive certain aspects of a physical or social environment in a certain way by no means guarantees that that particular perception will occur or that the perception which does occur will have anything like a one-to-one relationship to the objective environment as it appears to someone else. Drs. Adelbert Ames, E. Engel, and Hadley Cantril have performed experiments at the Institute for Associated Research, Hanover, New Hampshire, which show that in perception nothing is absolutely fixed. Rather, one interprets everything in terms of the situation as a whole. What one perceives—his reality— consists of what he makes of what seems to be himself and his environment. Depending on the habits—insights or understandings—he brings to a particular occasion, he seems to give meaning and order to things in terms of his own needs, abilities, and purposes.[7]

A description of two experiments performed at the Hanover Institute will give some idea of the nature and significance of these studies. Dr. Engel was curious to see what would happen when a person viewed two different pictures through a stereoscope. One set of his "stereograms" consisted of pairs of small photographs of football players, one to be viewed by the right eye, the other by the left. There was enough similarity in the pairs of pictures for a subject to get binocular fusion. However, when a person looked into the stereoscope and described the face he saw, it was neither of the faces represented by the photographs. Instead, he described a new and different face, usually made up of the dominant features of both faces he was viewing with separate eyes.

Dr. Cantril reports experiments with a pair of stereograms. Each stereogram was a photograph of a statue in the Louvre; one the Madonna with Child, the other a lovely young female nude. A typical viewing of the pair of stereograms proceeded as follows: The subject first saw only a Madonna with Child, then a few seconds later exclaimed, "but my —— she is undressing." She had somehow lost the baby she was holding and her robe had slipped from her shoulders. "Then in a few more seconds she lost her robe completely and became a young nude." Sometimes the process is reversed. Other people never see the nude and others never see the Madonna. Apparently, what a person "sees" in a situation depends

[7] These experiments are summarized in Alfred Kuenzli, *The Phenomenological Problem*, Harper, 1959, Chap. 8.

upon his needs, abilities, purposes, and insights as well as upon what is "out there."

Since reality, relativistically defined, consists of what one makes of what comes to him through his senses or otherwise, one's person is what he makes of himself, and his environment consists of what he makes of that which surrounds him. In keeping with his relativistic outlook, a field psychologist shuns the use of concepts implying fixed traits or rigid habits of personalities. He recognizes the difficulty of man's ever getting outside himself sufficiently to make final statements about what is absolutely real or true. Since he regards truth as tentative and instrumental (not final), he shies away from making dogmatic statements about the nature of man and the universe. Rather, a statement is considered true because of its accuracy in prediction and the consensus of people competent in its area in regard to the possible consequences of acting on it—its usefulness. It should be emphasized here that a relativistic definition of truth in no way discounts the value of truths. Rather, it supposedly defines truth in a more discerning manner.

2. PURPOSIVENESS OF BEHAVIOR. Within cognitive-field psychology *purposive* is nearly a synonym for *intelligent*. A unique characteristic of human beings is their capacity to pursue long-sighted, as well as short-sighted, self-interests. Field psychologists recognize the significance of this fact. When a child is behaving purposively, he is pursuing his goals in light of the insights he has available; he is behaving intelligently. The goal or goals toward which a child strives psychologically exist in his present life space. The phenomenon of goal is such that expectation—not actual realization—is its essence. Although the content of a goal may be in the future or may not occur at all, this goal as a psychological fact necessarily lies in the present life space. A student's goal to become a teacher is a goal toward teaching as he now sees it. This goal may be a far cry from teaching as it eventually is experienced.

The *purposiveness* of cognitive-field psychology is *immanent*, not *transcendental*, to the world of experience; it prevails in workaday life situations. That is, careful study of children, as well as of other animate beings, in life situations indicates that if they are active at all they are trying to do something, and that, through our anticipating what they are trying to do, we can predict most accurately what they are going to do. Whether there is transcendental—supernatural—purpose in the universe is another problem which is related only indirectly to the concept *purposive* as developed in field psychology. Relativistic purposiveness is immanent.

3. EMPHASIS UPON PSYCHOLOGICAL FUNCTION. A third important feature of cognitive-field psychology is its emphasis upon psychological functions or events as contrasted with objects or movements. A fallacy of S-R asso-

ciationists, noted by relativistic field theorists, has been their tendency to describe the character of an activity by its physical aspects only and to neglect the great effect of the psychological setting. For example, experiments on satiation clearly indicate that fatigue often is largely a matter of psychological boredom, not physical tiredness. Moving one's arm in an identical way while making certain lines may have different psychological and physiological effects, according to the meaning of this activity to him. The act of repeatedly making a pattern of four lines may have become disintegrated and the arm fatigued as a result of oversatiation. Then a change of the same movements to making a different pattern of lines or a picture from these lines suffices to bring a reorganization of the activity and erase the bodily symptoms of fatigue. If the meaning of an activity is changed by imbedding it in a different context, bodily symptoms of fatigue tend to disappear.

Psychological is understood to mean in accordance with the logic of a growing mind or intelligence. To be psychological in his pursuits, a field psychologist must look at the world through the eyes of a learner. To describe a situation psychologically, one must describe the situation which confronts an individual. Such a situation is viewed as a pattern of person-environmental relationships which provide and limit opportunity. Once the person-environmental structure is established, the problem is to use constructs and methods adequate to deal with the underlying dynamics of behavior and to do this in a scientifically sound manner.

A construct is an invented idea. It is a generalized concept not directly observed but formed from data that are observed. Its purpose is to correlate a broad range of data which have some basic functional similarity, despite marked superficial differences. Need, psychologically defined, is an example of a construct. It has no length, breadth, thickness, or mass, yet it is a crucial, functional concept in studying human activity. Lewinians speak of observable data as *phenotypes* and unobservable, constructual representations as *genotypes*.

A functional definition of psychological behavior opens the way for extensive use of systematic constructs. Whereas an S-R associationist supposedly restricts his generalizations to those based on the use of "objective" data, a relativistic field psychologist knowingly uses constructs which go beyond the observable data. Constructs provide a means of bridging the gap between general laws which cannot be observed and the functions of individual persons which can be gathered as data. Thus, through the use of a few constructs the essence of an individual case can be adequately represented.

4. SITUATIONAL EMPHASIS.   A fourth definitive characteristic of cognitive-field psychology is that a study always begins with a description of a

situation as a whole—the field—and proceeds to specific and detailed analysis of various aspects of the situation. At no time are aspects of a field viewed as isolated elements. In the study of a life space with its various constructs, the idea constantly is kept to the forefront that no two constructs or concepts are mutually exclusive, but that everything to some degree and in some sense is dependent upon everything else. Readers again are cautioned that, should they slip into giving the constructs independent physical or biological existence, they will be attempting to understand a relativistic psychology in mechanistic fashion.

5. PRINCIPLE OF CONTEMPORANEITY. The fifth essential feature of cognitive-field psychology is the one most often misunderstood. Contemporaneity literally means all at one time. A psychological field or life space is a construct of such nature that it contains everything psychological which is taking place in relation to a specific person at a given time. The unit of time, microscopically viewed, is a moment; however, macroscopically considered, it may cover hours or even weeks. Whatever the length of time, everything is going on at once—that is the meaning of *field*. Readers are urged neither to reject the concept of contemporaneity summarily nor to give it an oversimplified interpretation.

Use of the concept *psychological field* implies that everything which affects behavior at a given time should be represented in the field existing at that time, and that only those facts can affect behavior which are part of a present field. A person's psychological field which exists at a given time contains, as well as the environment of the present, the views of that individual about his future and his past. It should be emphasized that any psychological past or psychological future is a simultaneous part of a psychological field existing at a given time. Psychologically, there is no past or future except as it enters into the present. "Since neither the [physical] past nor the [physical] future exists at the present moment it cannot have effect at the present."[8]

An individual's views about the past, as about the rest of the physical and social world, are often incorrect; nevertheless they constitute a significant psychological past in his own life space. Furthermore, the goals of an individual as a psychological fact lie in the present and they too constitute an essential part of his life space. The content of the goals may lie in the future and they may never occur. The nature of an expectation is not dependent upon the event's coming to pass. If an Indian warrior were brave so that in the future he would go to the happy hunting ground, whether or not there actually existed a future happy hunting ground would have no bearing on his being brave. His happy hunting ground is a part— a goal region—of his contemporaneous life space.

[8] Kurt Lewin, *Principles of Topological Psychology*, McGraw-Hill, 1936, p. 35.

The principle of contemporaneity means that psychological events are determined by conditions at the time behavior occurs. One cannot derive behavior from either the future or the past as such. Both S-R association-ists and field psychologists see little basis for future cause of events. However, field psychologists differ sharply from S-R associationists in their insistence that derivation of behavior from the past is equally metaphysical—beyond the realm of science. Since past events do not now exist, they, as such, can have no effect on the present. Thus, influence of a future can be only anticipatory, and effects of a past can be only in-direct. However, through continuity of life spaces, past psychological fields do have their "trace"—residue—in a present field which influences a per-son's behavior. *Trace* is a region or condition of a present life space which has *similarity* to a characteristic of earlier life spaces. In other words, *trace* means that there is some similarity of regions of succeeding life spaces. When a person uses an earlier acquired insight in solving a current problem, the insight is an example of trace.

The principle of contemporaneity has definite implications for educa-tion. When through continuity the past enters into the present, knowledge of the past and its heritage is of great value and significance. However, the mistake of making records and remains of the past *in themselves* the central materials of education is that it cuts the vital connection of present and past. Thus, it tends to make the past a rival of the present and the present a more or less futile imitation of a past which can never be known in its absolutely exact form. Lewin's principal construct to represent a contemporaneous situation is *life space*.[9]

WHAT IS A LIFE SPACE?

Life space is a scientific formulation developed for the purpose of expressing what is possible and impossible in the life of a person and an-ticipating what is likely to occur. It represents the total pattern of fac-tors or influences which affect behavior at a certain moment. Behavior means any change in a life space which is psychological—in accordance with a growing intelligence. A person's life space represents the total world in which the person lives. This may include his precepts, knowledge, and beliefs; his forward and backward time perspective; and abstract ideas as well as concrete objects. Man's universe has become largely symbolic in nature. Thus, a life space includes not only physical reality but also language, myth, art, and religion.

Lewin's basic formula is $B = f(P, E)$. Behavior, B, is the f, function; P, psychological person; and E, psychological environment. A psychologi-cal person and his psychological environment, so formulated, constitute a life space. A life space or psychological field is not defined in terms of

[9] See pp. 364–369 for definitions of Lewin's constructs.

mere consciousness or awareness; neither is it an organism in an environment. Rather, it is a dynamic whole of such nature that a change in any part affects other parts, and every change depends upon the whole; it is a totality of coexisting facts. Psychological person and psychological environment are not mutually exclusive; however, they may be considered to function as subwholes of a psychological field or life space. A life space is surrounded by a foreign hull—the aspects of the physical and social environment which to that person at that moment are not psychological. The foreign hull of a life space consists of all the potential perceptions as contrasted with the functional perceptions of a person's unique field.

In a life space, a person and his environment are in simultaneous mutual interaction (SMI) and are mutually interdependent. Each depends upon the other for its nature and functions; it is impossible to treat one adequately without also treating the other. One's

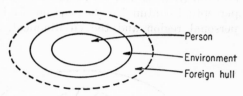

Fig. 12.   A Life Space.

person is definitive of one's environment and likewise one's environment is definitive of oneself. A person, his environment, and the foreign hull of his life space may be represented by concentric figures. A person is within his environment and both are within the foreign hull as shown in Fig. 12.

What Is a Person?

A psychological self or person is a crucial aspect of a life space. Under no circumstances is a person considered identical with an organism. Thus, a person is not limited to a mind or body; neither is it a mind and body. Rather, a person is *a consciously behaving self*. It is the center of abilities and needs; it is what a child means when he says "I" or "me." The concepts *self* and *person* are used interchangeably and may be considered synonyms. Teachers more often think of Billy Smith and Sally Anderson as persons. However, Billy and Sally, when thinking of themselves, are more likely to use the term *self*. A person is in no sense an abstract ego or self which can be experienced apart from any social context. It is within the social living of an individual that a self emerges and continues to change throughout life. It may be said that the basic human need is for preservation and enhancement of this emergent self or person. One even owns a "loyal" dog in order to enhance and give constancy to his psychological self or person.[10]

[10] See Chapter 7, pp. 173–175, for further expansion of the concepts *self* and *ego involvement*.

A person may be represented as a differentiated region of a life space. The field of a newborn baby is something like "one big blooming buzzing confusion." Then as one lives his life, although he may not think of it in these specific terms, his total situation is structured as his *self*—person— and his *environment*. Some aspects of experience involve the central core of a person; they are very near and dear to him. Others are of a less vital, peripheral sort. We may think of a person as structured in outer and inner layers. Some experiences involve only the more peripheral areas, whereas others embrace the most central regions of a psychological person.

Psychologically, a person is composed of (1) a motor-perceptual stratum (region) and (2) an inner-personal stratum (region). The motor-perceptual stratum has the position of a boundary zone between the inner-personal region and the environment. It represents the knowing and

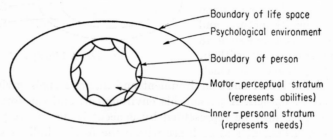

FIG. 13. A Structured Person in a Life Space.

manipulative abilities of a person. *Motor-perceptual system* denotes the phenomenon which a mechanist would see simply as body or organism. A mechanist, that is, would set his pattern of thinking in a physiological rather than a psychological frame of reference. In a sense, the motor-perceptual system is the tool of the inner-personal system. Like regions of the environment, it provides opportunity and limits opportunity. However, it is more closely identified with the self than is the environment. Whereas abilities are centered in the motor-perceptual system, needs are centered in the inner-personal system. Since the motor-perceptual region is between the inner-personal region and the environment, it performs functions of both person and environment. This means that a person acts in relation to his environment and simultaneously realizes the consequences of so doing.

The form which the development of selfhood takes depends upon the interaction of a person and his environment. An organism, in a sense, is an aspect of each—person and environment. Furthermore, whether something belongs to the self or to the environment depends, among other things, upon present needs and other factors of the inner-personal region. "Needs or other states of the inner-personal regions can influence the environment only by way of a bodily expression or a bodily action, that is, by way of a region which one can call the motor region."[11]

What Is a Psychological Environment?

The psychological environment of a life space consists of everything psychologically outside an individual person which means anything to him. It is made up of everything in which, toward which, or away from which a person can change his psychological position. "Environment is understood psychologically sometimes to mean the *momentary situation* of the child, at other times to mean the *milieu,* in the sense of the chief characteristics of the permanent situation."[12]

What Is a Foreign Hull?

A foreign hull is composed of those aspects of an organism's environment which are observable by the one studying the particular person but which at that moment have no significance for the person being studied. Thus, it is the complex of all nonpsychological factors surrounding a life space. It is made up of physical and social factors which, at the time being considered, are not subject to a person's psychological conceptualization, but which may at any time become parts of his psychological field. Thus, it is that part of his physical and social environment which, at the moment under consideration, is not included in his psychological environment. The physical and social conditions of the foreign hull limit the variety of possible life spaces. Anything which appears to be in a child's physical environment, but of which he is completely oblivious, is in the foreign hull of his life space. However, if he reacts to that thing in any way, either positively or negatively, it is no longer in his foreign hull but in his life space proper. Should Billy have only contempt for Miss Smith, she is in his life space just as much as if he loves and respects her.

Nonpsychological factors observed only by an outsider can at the next moment become psychological for the person being studied. A characteristic of the parts of a life space and their regions is permeability. There can be movement both ways through the boundary of a person or a life space or through any of their regions. For an aspect of the physical world to influence the intelligent behavior of a person, it must be moved from a foreign hull into his life space through his interaction with it.

Continuity of Life Spaces

A life space is of a moment's duration. One moves through a series of life spaces. In dynamic human beings, we would not expect consecutive

[11] Lewin, *Principles of Topological Psychology,* p. 177.
[12] Kurt Lewin, "Environmental Forces," in Carl Murchison, ed., *Handbook of Child Psychology,* Clark University Press, 1933, p. 592.

life spaces to be identical. However, we can anticipate some degree of similarity and continuity of life spaces as the experiences of one moment shade into those of the next. For practical schoolroom procedures, depending upon the purposes being pursued, we assume a fixity of life spaces for longer periods than a moment—perhaps a class period, a week, or a month.

Within a series of overlapping life spaces, a person's life is a continuity of psychological tensions, locomotions, and new equilibriums. When there is an increase of tension in one part of a life space relative to the rest of the system, disequilibrium occurs. When a person finds himself in a state of disequilibrium and attempts to return to equilibrium, psychic energy is expended; he engages in psychological locomotion. Should tension throughout the system become completely equalized, output of energy would cease; the total system would come to rest.

Of course, throughout a life span this absolute balance is never achieved. Since a person is intelligent and purposive, he expands and restructures his life space and consequently new disequilibriums emerge. This process gives a dynamic nature to human living which makes it immensely interesting and challenging (see Chapter 7, page 175).

HOW IS LEARNING DEFINED IN COGNITIVE-FIELD THEORY?

Kurt Lewin was interested primarily in a study of human motivation. Thus, his field theory was not developed as a theory of learning, but more as a theory of motivation and perception.[13] However, he was concerned with the application of his theory to learning situations and he did some writing in this vein. To develop a cognitive-field theory of learning, one must, while borrowing heavily from the ideas and constructs of Lewin, to some degree deviate from his usages in order to center thinking upon a psychology of learning.

Whereas S-R associationists tend to consider learning a separate psychological process, field theorists see it as one of the several interdependent functions within the framework of life spaces. Since, in field psychology, learning and development are nearly synonymous concepts, there is much in common between this section on cognitive-field theory of learning and the section of Chapter 7 which treats development within a relativistic frame of reference.

Field psychology is a purposive psychology; it assumes that intellectual processes are deeply affected by an individual's goals and that learning activity, including habit formation, is goal directed. Goal or purpose, therefore, is central to cognitive-field learning theory. This contrasts

[13] The more technical terminology and aspects of Lewin's field theoretical approach to psychology are presented in the later sections of the chapter, pp. 364–370.

sharply with S-R associationisms, which either ignore goal or purpose completely or make it only peripheral and incidental. Associationists have tended to consider any concept of goal direction or purposiveness *teleological*. To them, *teleological* means deriving present behavior from the future and consequently sounds mystical and superstitious. Thus, associationists have placed emphasis upon past events as the cause of present behavior. Since field psychology is goal centered, cognitive-field theorists inveigh against use of such mechanistic terms as *reflex arc, connectionism, conditioning, associationism,* and *reinforcement*.

Cognitive-field theory involves the kind of generalizations about learning which may be applied to actual persons in school situations. It is associated with the knowing and understanding functions which give meaning to a situation. It is built around the purposes underlying behavior, the goals involved in behavior, and persons' means and processes of understanding themselves as they function in relation to their goals. Factors of a life space acquire meaning as a person formulates his goals and develops insights into ways of achieving them. Thus, this is a "goal-insight"[14] theory of learning.

Why Is Cognitive-Field Theory Contrasted with S-R Associationisms?

Cognitive-field theory is so developed as to contrast rather sharply with the various associationistic or stimulus-response theories. Advocates of this theory do not deny existence of neural couplings but they do challenge the importance of the concept; they assert that it is inadequate to explain the learning process. Their position continues to be supported by research. In 1958 K. S. Lashley (1890–1958), who had devoted a lifetime to study of nervous function, stated: "I cannot pretend to have formulated a complete and satisfactory account of how the brain thinks. I recognize gaps and inconsistencies in my formulation of the problems, and the hypotheses that I have suggested will probably collapse under the weight of additional evidence."[15]

Lewin performed his early research with associative learning. He discovered that for terms or ideas to be associated—to have a connection formed between them—they had to belong to the same tension system. He found no force within mere association of items which leads to their reproduction; reproduction of acts or thoughts must be motivated. Thus, he contended that items are linked together in "memory" not through con-

---

[14] See Ernest E. Bayles, *Democratic Educational Theory,* Harper, 1960, Chap. 3.
[15] Karl Spencer Lashley, Selected Papers of, *The Neuropsychology of Lashley,* edited by Frank A. Beach, Donald O. Hebb, Clifford T. Morgan, Henry W. Nissen, McGraw-Hill, 1960, pp. 541–542.

nections or associations but by the way they fit into the field organization or the task as a whole—by their configuration.

Since cognitive-field theorists are convinced that psychological activity depends upon energy related to psychological tension systems, to them no mere coupling principle can adequately explain psychic activity. They challenge forcefully the principle of adhesion, the attachment of one thing to another so that revival of the first brings forth the second. Consequently, they think that "reward" and "punishment" do not stamp in and stamp out associations. Rather, they bring changes in the valences— values—of parts of the psychological environment and in the tension systems of the person in relation to his environment.

Perception of situations, not physical events as such, is the immediate cause of behavior. A psychological tension system exists whenever a psychological need or intention appears. As a need or intention is fulfilled, tension is released. The strength of a need correlates with a psychological force, which force has two basic results. It leads either to psychological movement of the person in the direction of the force or to a change of his cognitive structure corresponding to such a locomotion. This means that release of tension may be achieved either through reaching a goal or through restructuring one's life space, i.e., through learning to "see things differently."

A high school girl has a driving ambition to become a movie star; thus in her life space there is a pressing tension between herself and stardom. Assuming that, like most girls, she does not have "the stuff" to become a movie star, tension must be relieved through some other course. She might reconstruct her life space so as to substitute a reachable goal for her earlier unattainable one. Or she might achieve a more drastic reconstruction and change her goals so that there is nothing left of stardom or any substitute.[16] Such reconstruction of a life space is the essence of the learning process. Learning, so construed, is a change in the cognitive structure of, or insights in regard to, one's life space, which consists of a person and his environment.

How Is Learning a Change in Insight or in Cognitive Structure?

Insights may be verbal, preverbal, or nonverbal. One may gain an insight before he has words to express it, one may have a complete and exact verbalization involving no or little insight, or the insight and the verbalization may be achieved simultaneously. There is evidence that even nonverbal animals solve mazes by formulating a series of cognitive structures and testing them, and that they solve their problems through gain-

[16] Psychological conflicts from a field point of view are discussed in more detail in Chapter 18, pp. 463–464.

ing insight into their situations. By being given food, a dog is taught to "sit." Later he wants a toy which he sees on a table. He goes to the table, assumes his "sitting" position, and barks.[17]

It is an insightful process when a ball player gets a feel for the correct swing of his bat, when a little child discovers how to dress himself, when a boy or girl learns to drive an automobile, when a child gets the idea of multiplication, perhaps through addition, or when a college student learns how to "read" Shakespeare.

It is in connection with goal-directed behavior that insightful learning occurs. One's direction or purposeful activity in his life space is dependent upon its cognitive structure. Remember that a life space contains a person (self) as well as his environment, and that through gaining and changing insights he cognitively structures both. A completely new situation would be cognitively unstructured; a person would have no knowledge of what would lead or point to what. Thus, at that moment his behavior would be completely random. (This is the position of an animal when it is first placed in a "problem box.") However, rarely, if ever, does a person function in a completely unstructured situation. More often we find students in situations which are inadequately or inharmoniously structured. This means that they have problems and need to extend their learning—change cognitive structures.

A person's behavior in a relatively unstructured situation would appear exploratory, vacillating, and contradictory. An adolescent, for example, vacillates between a child's and an adult's world, neither of which to him is well structured. Newly acquired adult regions of his life space will not fit into a child's world, and some of the child's regions to which he clings will not fit in the adult world he is, at times, attempting to enter.

A child's behavior, to a very large degree, depends upon the cognitive structure of his life space. Learning results in building psychological traces which contribute to the structure and dynamics of future life spaces and thus affect future performance. Memory processes refer to cognitively structured similarities between an individual's life spaces which exist at different times. It is because of the continuity of life spaces and their cognitive structures that learning is of value to a person. Good insight into a present life space or situation tends to provide excellent foresight into the cognitive structure of future life spaces. Suppose a college student wishes to understand and appreciate principles of human development and learning and to prepare himself to apply them in future teaching situations. An excellent procedure would be for him to acquire a deep understanding of himself, his environment, and their relationships in his current series of life spaces.

Learning is a process whereby, through active experience, insights are

17 Insight is defined on pp. 296–300.

changed so as to become more serviceable for future guidance. Human beings, when behaving intelligently, are assumed to be purposive and their learning is related to their purposiveness. According to cognitive-field psychology, a child in a learning situation is not unfolding according to nature; neither is he being passively conditioned always to respond in a desired manner. Rather, at his level of maturity and comprehension, he is differentiating and restructuring himself and his environment; he is gaining or changing insights.

Learning is a dynamic process; a constantly expanding world of understanding is reaching out to encompass a constantly expanding psychological world. At birth, a child's world is very small. But on his level he is trying to understand that small world. He is trying to understand how to get food. Soon he will be seeking warmth. Later he will seek means of getting attention. When he is an adult, in order more adequately to influence his own adult destiny, he will seek insights into his world as it affects him. Hence, to one with a cognitive-field approach, learning means development of a sense of direction or bearing which can be used, when occasion offers and if found desirable, as a guide for conduct. This all means that learning is enhancement of intelligence.

Lewin considered learning to consist of four types of change, namely, change in cognitive structure, change in motivation, change in group belongingness or ideology, and gain in voluntary control of musculature or learning skills. He distinguished between the first two rather sharply. Thus, he tended to separate cognitive and motivational problems. To him, change in cognitive structure meant development of perceptual knowledge. It was centered in the topological—structural—aspects of a situation. Change in motivation, in contrast, meant learning to like or dislike certain areas—aspects of a life space. However, he recognized that even changes in motivation arise from changes in cognitive structure; to change the valence of an activity for a child, one must change the cognitive structure of that child's life space in regard to it.

Growing into a culture through one's change in group belongingness and ideology and his development of skills also involves primarily perceptions of oneself and the people and objects around him. Thus, these two types of change, too, are principally a process of change in the cognitive structure. Consequently, in treating learning, Lewin's pivotal concept was change in cognitive structure. In 1945 he wrote, "A change in action ideology, a real acceptance of a changed set of facts and values, a change in the perceived social world—all three are but different expressions of the same process."[18]

The cognitive structure of a life space corresponds to the meaningful

18 Lewin, *Resolving Social Conflicts, op. cit.,* p. 64.

knowledge of a person, knowledge being defined in the broadest sense possible. A change of cognitive structure may occur in any part of a person's life space, including the psychological past, present, or future. By defining all learning as essentially a process of developing cognitive structure or insights, we escape the dangers of forming a dichotomy—split—of knowledge and motivation. The formation of this dichotomy has led in the past to a rather sharp distinction between learning of facts and development of personality, character, and attitudes. Ideas involving emotional, motivational, and imaginative functions ultimately are as necessary in "factual" mathematical, scientific, and historical pursuits as they are in literature and the fine arts.

DIFFERENTIATION AND GENERALIZATION. Changes in cognitive structure are of three types: differentiation and its complement—generalization—and restructurization. Differentiation is the process in which regions are subdivided into smaller regions. An example of differentiation in early life is a child's distinguishing parts of his body—arms, legs, head, and trunk. In differentiation of unstructured areas, previously vague and unstructured areas of a life space become cognitively structured and thus more specific. A person makes more sense of what, to him, was previously a "blooming, buzzing confusion." As a child grows he differentiates himself—his person—from his environment, different aspects of his person and environment from each other, and an irreality level from the reality level of his life space. When he realizes that there is no Santa Claus but continues to talk about him, he is differentiating irreality from reality. In contrast, a very young child does not make this distinction; everything is "real."[19] In this way a child distinguishes and identifies significant features of himself and his environment. Also, during a person's psychological development, through differentiation his time perspective enlarges. He differentiates past and future time regions of a present life space and thereby brings a more and more distant past and future to affect present behavior.

One generalizes when he forms a concept which includes previously differentiated aspects of himself or his environment. Generalization arises through categorization of subregions into a unified region of one's life space. When a child learns that cats, dogs, horses, and birds are animals or a student learns that his hopes, dreams, beliefs, and anticipations are all subregions of a "future" region in his contemporaneous life space, he is generalizing.

[19] See Kurt Lewin, *Field Theory in Social Science*, Harper, 1951, pp. 245–246. Reality-irreality refers to strata of a life space. Different degrees of irreality correspond to different degrees of fantasy; they include wishes and fears. Reality levels are characterized by relative rigidity, irreality levels by greater fluidity.

RESTRUCTURIZATION.   A person not only differentiates and generalizes his life space into new regions but simultaneously changes the meanings of respective regions in relationship to himself and to one another. Restructurization means that one defines or redefines directions in his life space; he learns what actions will lead to what results. He does this through perception of significant relationships of different functional regions of his life space. Consequently, restructurization consists of separating certain regions which have been connected and connecting certain regions which have been separated. (Remember that regions are defined as functionally distinguishable parts of a life space.)

When we were quite young, most of us differentiated people from their environments. Later we differentiated people into various races, classes, and groups. Perhaps about the same time we generalized them into Republicans and Democrats or Christians and non-Christians. As a person learns, he continues to differentiate and generalize himself and his environment, but he also restructures the differentiated and generalized regions of his life space so as to give them new meanings.

What Is Habit?

Habit is assumed to be goal directed. It is fluid, effective, efficient action arising through a person's operating on the basis of the insights he possesses. Habit is not a fixed sequence of acts which can be explained adequately as a system of preformed pathways in the nervous system. (Of course, some sort of concomitant neural action is not denied.) When one operates in terms of the insights or cognitive structure he has, habit is manifested. Change in cognitive structure through differentiation, generalization, and restructurization means a change in meaning. When an event has meaning its psychological position and direction are determined; one knows what actions will lead to what results. This is the basis of habit. The habits of a person at a given time constitute a significant function of his life space. Habit enables one to behave intelligently without thinking. Often there is not time to think; indeed, thinking then might be disastrous. What happens when your car is closely following a large truck going 70 miles per hour and the truck stops abruptly?

What Is Intelligence?

Cognitive-field psychologists define intelligence as ability to respond in present situations on the basis of anticipation of future possible consequences and with a view to controlling the consequences which ensue. One's intelligence so defined consists of the number and quality of his insights. Within this frame of reference, successful behavior rightfully may be called intelligent only when a person might have done otherwise and his actions were premised upon his envisioning what he was doing and why. Learning is enhancement of one's intelligence. This means that all of its forms—development of logical organization, social insight, appreciation, information, and skills—have a common element. They all involve a change in the experiential situation of a person which gives him a basis for a greater predictability and control in relation to his behavior; they enhance his intelligence.

Whereas S-R associationists are prone to think of intelligence as something substantive—nounlike—with which a child is born and which can be changed little if at all, cognitive-field psychologists place greater emphasis upon the adjective *intelligent* or the adverb *intelligently*. Behaviorists and connectionists consider children, in their essential nature, passive pieces of protoplasm, more or less sensitive to external and internal stimulation. The ones with the highest number of receptors and the most sensitive receptors are deemed most intelligent; they react the quickest and most accurately when their "triggers" are pulled.

As an adjective *intelligent* is descriptive of effectual behavior. An innate specific intelligence is not necessarily postulated at all. The intelligence that any intelligence test measures consists of a person's insights and his ability to use them in situations. These insights are in no way innate but are acquired as a dynamic person interacts with his psychological environment. There is little psychological basis for the assertion that IQ is innately constant. The organism which plays its part as a person develops insights has genetic qualities, but these are biological, not psychological, traits.

How Does Intelligent Behavior Differ from Nonintelligent Behavior?

Cognitive-field psychologists view an intelligently behaving person as one who acts as if he is pursuing a purpose and has some foresight as to how it is to be achieved. Nonintelligent behavior arises when a person is pushed or pulled about as an inert, nonliving object, just as a stone dislodged from a place of support falls to a lower lodgement. Let us picture a man straddling a pole and attempting to raise it from among a pile of similar poles. He is behaving intelligently. As the poles are moved, their position changes and suddenly a group of poles falls on the far end of the pole he is lifting; another group in the center serves as a fulcrum and the poles raise him into the air. When he is raised into the air, he displays nonintelligent behavior. He is behaving—moving—but there is no connection between this specific movement and his foresight of consequences. In intelligent behavior, an activity is carried forward to a goal through a process by which one constantly searches out the conditions for the next step all along the way. Intelligence, then, is largely a matter of foresight.

What Is Thinking?

Thinking involves time and a series of life spaces. It is a process whereby an individual remakes old habits and forms new ones. It includes finding, elaborating, and testing hypotheses. Whereas in S-R association-isms creative thinking and imagination really are not "creative" (they represent formulation of new relationships of old materials), in cognitive-field psychology progress in thinking is considered a truly creative event. In this event there is psychological locomotion. A person is oriented to-ward a goal and there is structuring or restructuring of the field. Thus, thinking arises in a situation where a person feels a need—has a goal. In place of a clear path to that goal he encounters a forked road or no road; the problem presents itself as an unclear, unstructured region. In thinking, then, there is a transformation or restructurization of the total field aris-ing through perception of the total situation. We think our way into a system of living. Progress in thinking means that one is fortunate enough to approach a solution by a new, more productive path. Through thinking one achieves fruitful changes in the cognitive structure of his life space—he gains new insights and he changes old ones.

WHAT IS THE MEANING OF COGNITIVE-FIELD PSYCHOLOGY FOR A SCHOOL SITUATION?

Advocates of cognitive-field psychology think that a teacher should teach, not baby-sit or dictate. A baby-sitter usually performs a custodial function but teaches children little, if anything. A dictator imposes the "right" answers. A teacher, in contrast with both, should perform his special teaching role in a process of student-teacher mutual inquiry.

The role of a teacher should be similar to that of a head scientist in a scientific laboratory; he should lead children in such manner that he helps them formulate and solve problems. To accomplish this, he should have a rich, extensive background of varied knowledge; he should be alert to the habitual attitudes and outlooks students are developing; and his ideal should be to promote an atmosphere which fosters maximum insightful growth. This means that he should be able to judge which attitudes or insights are conducive to continued growth and which are detrimental. He also should have sympathetic understanding of students as persons and should develop an accurate idea of what actually is going on in the minds—life spaces—of those whom he is teaching.

Topology of a life space shows the various possibilities for psychological movement or action; *vectors* show the moving forces within the topologi-

cal structure. To understand the behavior of a child, one must determine
the psychological position of the child's person in reference to the goal
regions of his life space. This entails knowing the child's social position
within and outside various groups, his position in relation to various ideas
and activities, and the role of physical objects in his life space. The
relative region of a life space in which a child is located determines the
qualities of his immediate surroundings. It sets the possibilities for the
child's next step in his psychological life—his topology. It also determines
his *vectors*—what step or event means action toward and what step means
action away from his goals.

A student's life space on a given evening, topologically, may contain a
TV set, a book, and a movie. Vectorially, each object and activity has
some degree of valence—alluring or repelling power. Should he go to the
movie, this means that movie valence is greatest of all. When one behaves intelligently, he does what he wants most to do; if he does not want
to do it more than he wants *not to do* it, he does not do it.

In a cognitive-field approach to the study of a school situation, a
teacher and his students each is considered as a person *and* his life space.
The goal of a teacher should be to have a common intersection of these
life spaces. The way to peripheral regions of a person is quite accessible in
ordinary conversation. However, it is more difficult to reach more central
regions, i.e., those needs near and dear to him. To gain an understanding of
each child and his cognitive world, a teacher has to develop a sort of
disciplined naïveté. In order adequately to see Tom through he must see
through Tom. He must see Tom's person and environment as Tom sees it.
When a teacher gains rapport with a child—when he gains his confidence—his influence can extend to the child's central regions and he is in
a position to speak of the child's needs. What a child needs depends
primarily upon how he sizes up himself and his material and social
environment.

For a teacher to analyze a psychological situation, he should describe
the structure of a person and his environment and ascertain their dynamic
properties—what they have to do with the child's behavior. A teacher
must see the relationships between the various regions or parts of the
child's life space. He must establish the nature of the respective factors
residing within, at, and outside the boundary. Factors outside the boundary of a life space, the foreign hull, are those which may be perceived by
others but at the moment have no place in the perceptual world of the
person being studied. Knowing these facts helps a teacher determine what
is possible and what is not, and what might happen and what might not.
Then, to understand and accurately predict behavior, a teacher, in addition to understanding the structure of the child's field, i.e., the interposi-
tional relationships between the parts in his life space, must also ascertain

the dynamic properties of the child's life space—the valences of his goals and the barriers to his goals.

Now what does all this mean in a school situation? Let us return to the schoolroom described in Chapter 7. "Alice is so absorbed with her teacher and school work that she is oblivious to everything else about her including the other children." The teacher is central in Alice's life space. Alice's school work also is far within the border of her life space. The other children and everything else in the room that is not part of Alice's school work are in the foreign hull of her life space. "Helen is a social butterfly; she wants the attention of most of the children in the classroom. She does give attention to the teacher from time to time, but right now she is concerned with other things." The other children are in Helen's life space; the teacher is at the margin, sometimes in and sometimes out. "John's body is in the classroom but 'psychologically' John is riding a shiny new tractor which is being operated in the field adjoining the school." John's school environment and his psychological environment have little in common. Whereas nothing within the room is in his life space, the tractor is as central as it can be and its valence is very high.

WHAT ARE THE KEY CONCEPTS OF FIELD OR TOPOLOGICAL AND VECTOR PSYCHOLOGY?

Readers will find this section, which explains why field psychology is more specifically named "topological and vector psychology," somewhat technical and perhaps difficult. However, should they seek sharper insights into the deeper implications of field theory, this section will greatly enhance their understanding.

Lewin said, "Topological and vectorial concepts combine power of analysis, conceptual precision, usefulness for derivation and fitness for the total range of psychological problems in a way which, in my opinion, make them superior to any other known conceptual tool in psychology."[20] He felt that topological and vector, or field, psychology was characterized by a set of concepts or constructs which permitted representation of psychological reality in a highly adequate fashion. He wanted concepts broad enough to be applicable to all kinds of behavior and at the same time specific enough to represent a definite person in a concrete situation. This system implements a person's being represented as separated from and yet enclosed within a larger totality—his life space. Thus, it enables one to represent adequately a psychological situation which includes a person, his environment, his needs, his goals and their dynamic interrelations.

[20] Kurt Lewin, "Field Theory and Learning," in Nelson B. Henry, ed., *The Psychology of Learning,* Forty-first Yearbook of the National Society for the Study of Education, Part II, Public School Publishing Co., 1942, Chap. 6, p. 219.

For one to grasp fully the ideas of a relativistic, field psychology, it is essential that its key concepts be defined precisely as they are used in this frame of reference. In studying these concepts, readers should keep in mind the essential idea of field psychology: the meanings of all its constructs are mutually interdependent. Each depends for its meaning upon the meanings of all the others.

Furthermore, it should be remembered that a diagram of a life space is figurative. It is difficult, perhaps impossible, to show everything at once. A complete and accurate image of a life space would show all of the psychological facts and constructs in a momentary situation represented by a differentiated person and a differentiated environment. A differentiated person or environment is one structured or functionally divided into various aspects as perceived by the one being studied. Some differentiated aspects of a person are friends, ambitions, self-aggrandizement, and needs and abilities to know about various matters and to carry out activities of different kinds. A differentiated environment contains everything perceived by the person at the time under study.

Lastly we should guard against reifying or making physical things of the psychological constructs whose purpose is to symbolize relationships primarily functional in nature. For example, we should at no time think of a psychological person as synonymous with a biological organism or of a psychological and a physical environment as the same concept.

What Are the Three Pivotal Concepts of Field Psychology?

The three pivotal concepts of cognitive-field psychology are life space, topology, and vector. Whereas *life space* is treated in some detail on pages 350–351 of this chapter the concepts *topology* and *vector* have heretofore been only briefly defined. In this section *life space* is summarized, then *topology* and *vector* are explained in greater detail.

LIFE SPACE. Life space contains the whole of one's psychological reality—what one makes of what comes to him. It includes everything that one needs to know about a person in order to understand his concrete behavior in a specific psychological environment at a certain time. The psychological environment and the person constitute the situation as perceived by that person. Emergence of the properties of a life space depends partly upon the state of the individual as a product of a continuity of life spaces and partly upon his interaction with his physical and social surroundings.

TOPOLOGY. Topology is a nonmetrical geometry which encompasses concepts such as inside, outside, and boundary but has no dealings with length, breadth, or thickness. No distances are defined. Rather topology is concerned with the relative position of the geometric figures being considered. "Topologically there is no difference between a circle, an ellipse, a regular or irregular polygon with any number of sides. . . . A drop of water and the earth are, from a topological point of view, fully equivalent."[21]

Two basic concepts which topological space denotes are connectedness and part-whole relationships. Topologically, things may be next to, inside, or outside one another. Size or shape has no significance in a topological figure. The life spaces in Fig. 14 are topologically equal. Each is a completely bounded area within a larger bounded area.

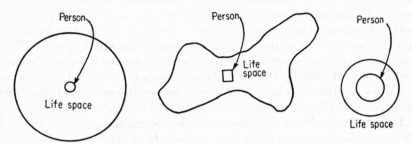

Fig. 14.　Topology of Life Space—Three Equal Figures.

Topological concepts are used to represent the structure of a life space, to define the range of possible perceptions and actions. This is accomplished by showing the arrangement of the functional parts of a life space. The parts are shown as various regions and their boundaries.

In addition to the person whose life space is being studied, regions represent activities like eating, going to the movies, and making decisions; more passive incidents like being fired or being rewarded; and social entities such as family, church, school, and gang. If the region "going to the movies" is located in a person's life space, the person is either engaging in or thinking about engaging in that activity. If "being fired" is in his life space, he is perceiving that incident and its consequences. "Church" in a life space involves what one makes out of what "church" means to him.[22]

VECTOR.　The concept *vector* is borrowed from a system used in mechanics to represent direction and strength as two of the three properties of a force. The third property is its point of application. In psychology a vector represents a force which is influencing movement toward or away from a goal. A force is a tendency to act in a certain way or direction. A vector is a concept equivalent to, and descriptive of, a psychological force. If there

[21] Lewin, *Principles of Topological Psychology, op. cit.*, p. 88.

[22] See Dorwin Cartwright, "Lewinian Theory as a Contemporary Systematic Framework," in Sigmund Koch, ed., *Psychology: A Study of a Science*, McGraw-Hill, 1959, p. 25.

is only one vector—force—there is locomotion in the direction toward which the vector points. However, if two or more vectors are pointing in several different ways, movement is in the direction of the resultant force.

Whereas topological concepts are used to illustrate structurally what is possible, vectorial concepts describe the dynamics of a situation —what is happening or is likely to happen. Thus, vectors deal with the tendencies of a life space to change or resist change. In an illustration of what is happening or likely to happen, a vector may represent either a driv-

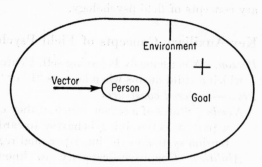

Fig. 15.   A Vector.

ing or a restraining force. A driving force is a tendency to change or move. A restraining force is a barrier or obstacle to psychological locomotion, which opposes some driving force. Both driving and restraining forces may arise from the needs and abilities of the person being studied, from actions of another person, or from the impersonal aspects of a situation.

What Are Some Auxiliary Concepts of Field Psychology?

The pivotal concepts—life space, topology, and vector—and ideas auxiliary to the basic formula—$B = f(P, E)$—are illustrated in Fig. 16. The latter are described in the following glossary of key auxiliary concepts of field psychology. These elements of construction represent ideas, not "objective" self-evident phenomena.

An analysis of the structure and dynamics of the life space of a child in school will reveal numerous interdependent aspects of the situation such as the child's relationships with his teacher and other students, the

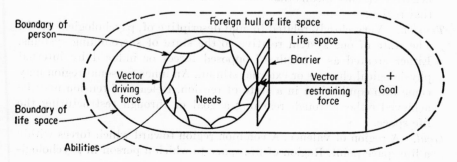

Fig. 16.   Life Space of an Individual.

social pressures arising from his family, and even the consequences of his family's relations with other families. All of these various factors of a situation may be expressed through the use of the key pivotal and auxiliary concepts of field psychology.

Key Auxiliary Concepts of Field Psychology

Person.   A consciously behaving self. Center of abilities and needs. That which a child means when he says "I" or "me."

Person-centered constructs

Needs.   States of a person which, if they exist in relation to a goal, have a part in determining behavior toward that goal. Correspond to a tension system of the inner-personal region of a person.

Abilities.   Cognitive—capacity to know environment. Executive—capacity to manipulate environment.

Environment.   Everything in which, toward which, or away from which a person can make psychological movement—do anything about. Person and environment are mutually dependent upon one another.

Foreign hull of life space.   Complex of all nonpsychological facts which surround a life space. That part of a person's physical environment which, at a particular moment, is not included in his psychological environment. Physical and social raw materials. Foreign hull limits behavioral possibilities.

Cognitive structure.   An environment, including a person, as known by the person. Synonyms are *insight* or *understanding.* Has one dimension—clarity.

Valences.   Positive or negative imperative environmental facts. Properties which regions of a life space have if an individual is drawn toward them or away from them. A region which possesses a positive valence is one of such nature that forces correlated with the valence of that region tend to move the person in the direction of that region. A negative valence means that forces tend to move the person away from that region.

Tension.   Very closely related to, and descriptive of, psychological needs. The state of one system relative to the state of surrounding systems. Either created as a result of opposed forces or induced by internal physiological changes or external stimuli. An inner-personal region may come into equilibrium in a state of tension. Release of tension may be achieved either through reaching a goal or through restructuring the life space.

Goal.   A region of valence. A common region toward which forces within a life space point. Region of life space to which a person in psychologically attracted.

Barrier. Dynamic part of an environment which resists motion through it. That which stands in the way of a person's reaching his goal.

Force. Immediate determinant of the locomotions of a person. The tendency to act in a certain direction. Its properties are strength, direction, and point of application. It is represented by a vector. The strength of a force is related to, but not identical with, the strength of a valence. The combination of forces acting at the same point at a given time is a resultant force. Force is analogous, but not identical with, *drive* or *excitatory tendency* as used in S-R associationisms. (*Drive,* behavioristically defined, is a strong, persistent stimulus which demands an adjustive response.)

What Is Behavior?

In cognitive-field psychology *behavior,* when used, is defined quite differently from the way S-R associationists define it. The latter, in harmony with their interpretation of psychology as a study of the relationships of biological organisms and their physical and social environments, think of behavior as some kind and degree of observable muscular or glandular movement. The movement may be only incipient or covert or it may be overt; nevertheless, its being behavior means that it is physical movement. Were adequate devices available, it supposedly could be observed and measured. Cognitive-field psychologists do not accept this definition of behavior.

In speaking of behavior, cognitive-field psychologists imply psychological locomotion but not necessarily any sort of physiological movement. One may "come closer" to another person, yet exhibit no physical evidence of locomotion. Behavior takes place in a life space, rather than in observable space. Psychological behavior is more or less conscious—verbal or symbolic—and may be equated with experience. Every specific instance of behavior must be viewed as the result of interaction of several pertinent features of a concrete situation. Broadly defined, then, behavior means any change in a life space which is subject to psychological laws. Thus behavior may be a change of the relative location of a person and his environment, a cognitive reorganization of his environment, or a restructuring of his person; it includes any change in valence of any part of his life space.

Psychological behavior and *locomotion* are analogous concepts. *Behavior* describes the simultaneous functions within a life space of an individual. *Locomotion* refers to the relative positions of respective regions of a person's *temporally continuous* life spaces. When we concentrate study upon a person and his current environmental situation, *behavior* adequately denotes changes which occur in a life space. However, when we consider a time element, a person appears to occupy a series of overlapping life spaces. The life spaces usually manifest a continuity; they are similar but not identical. Change in subsequent life spaces is locomotion. Consequently, depending upon whether we are centering our study upon the person-environment interactivity or the psychological continuity of a person's life spaces, we may represent any psychological phenomenon in terms of either behavior or locomotion; behavior centers upon how one sizes things up, locomotion on what one does about it as he moves into new life spaces.

BIBLIOGRAPHY

Bigge, Morris L., "The Harmonies and Conflicts of Principles of Topological and Vector Psychology with the Tenets of Three Educational Philosophies," unpublished doctoral dissertation, University of Kansas, 1951.
    Comparison of Lewin's principles of topological and vector—field—psychology with the tenets of idealism, realism, and pragmatism. They harmonize most closely with pragmatism; however, there are realistic overtones.
Bigge, Morris L., "A Relativistic Approach to the Learning Aspect of Educational Psychology," *Educational Theory*, July, 1954, pp. 213–220.
    A proposed harmonization of the topological and vector psychology of Lewin with the pragmatic educational philosophy of John Dewey and Boyd H. Bode. It suggests that a relativistic approach to learning theory is highly predictive of individual behavior.
Bigge, Morris L., "A Relativistic Definition of Stimulus-Response," *Journal of Educational Psychology*, December, 1955, pp. 457–464.
    Implications of situational psychology for relativism. *Stimulus* and *response* gained their currency within mechanistic approaches to learning. If they are to be retained within relativism, they should be redefined. Stimulus does not occur first, followed by response; nor vice versa. Rather, the two operate simultaneously. Stimulus is environment centered and response is person centered.
Combs, Arthur W., and Donald Snygg, *Individual Behavior: A Perceptual Approach to Behavior*, rev. ed., Harper, 1959.
    Descriptive paragraph in bibliography for Chapter 7.
Hilgard, E. R., *Theories of Learning*, 2nd ed., Appleton-Century-Crofts, 1956.
    In Chapter 8: an interpretation of learning within field psychology.
Kuenzli, Alfred E., *The Phenomenological Problem*, Harper, 1959.
    Descriptive paragraph in bibliography for Chapter 7.
Leeper, Robert W., *Lewin's Topological and Vector Psychology, a Digest and Critique*, University of Oregon, 1943.
    Presentation and criticism of Lewin's topological and vector psychology. Also an attempt at revision of Lewin's statements on some points. Leeper recognizes Lewin as a trailblazer but thinks some re-examination is in order.

Lewin, Kurt, *Principles of Topological Psychology*, translated by Fritz and Grace M. Heider, McGraw-Hill, 1936.

One of the two basic books written by Lewin in German and translated into English. It contains practically all of the structure of his field psychology but is more difficult to read than are his later works. The latter pages contain a valuable glossary of field concepts.

Lewin, Kurt, *Field Theory in Social Science*, Harper, 1951.

Descriptive paragraph in bibliography for Chapter 7.

Lindzey, Gardner, ed., *Handbook of Social Psychology, Vol. I, Theory and Method*, Addison-Wesley, 1954.

In Chapter 5: an excellent description by Morton Deutsch of field theory as it has been developed by Lewin and his students. Chapter 3 on cognitive theory and Chapter 6 on role theory contribute to understanding of the field position.

Sherif, Muzafer, and Carolyn W. Sherif, *An Outline of Social Psychology*, Harper, 1956.

Descriptive paragraph in bibliography for Chapter 7.

Tolman, Edward Chase, *Collected Papers in Psychology*, University of California Press, 1951. Also published in 1958 under the title *Behavior and Psychological Man*.

Papers reflecting Tolman's unit of psychological study as molar behavior purposively organized. Tolman's ideas bridged S-R associationism and cognitive-field theory. He accepted many field concepts such as purpose and insight but remained a behaviorist. He was critical of S-R connectionistic theories.

15

HOW IS LEARNING
RELATED TO TEACHING?

In previous chapters we have described several more or less systematic outlooks in psychology, each of which includes a theory of learning. We have seen how much in contrast are the chief tenets of the two major families of learning theory—the one leading to teaching which is highly mechanistic and the other leading to teaching with emphasis upon reflection and creativity.

This chapter focuses upon principles of learning which are not usually clearly attached to either S-R associationism or the Gestalt-field outlook. They are widely stated in textbooks of educational psychology, irrespective of the over-all orientation of psychologists. Although we shall see that the manner in which these principles are interpreted and used is influenced by whether one is an exponent of associationism or of field psychology, in the main they lead to somewhat similar classroom results.

The principles to be presented in this chapter are close to classroom practice in the sense that they provide rather specific directives to teachers. In this respect, the present chapter is a bridge between the relatively abstract theory of preceding chapters on learning and the largely "how-to-do-it" emphasis of Part IV, which follows.

Before moving into an elaboration of these widely accepted principles of learning, we should make it clear that most psychologists, and particularly those with the widest reputation, are interested as much as ever in "system building," i.e., constructing a body of theory which is cohesive and internally consistent and within which all elements, even minor ones, harmonize with the central premises. Examples of such persons on the side

372

of field psychology are John Dewey, Boyd H. Bode, E. C. Tolman, Ernest E. Bayles, H. F. Wright, Arthur Combs, Donald Snygg, Carl Rogers, Nathaniel Cantor, Gardner Murphy, Kurt Lewin, R. G. Barker, and R. Lippitt. On the side of associationism are Edward L. Thorndike, John B. Watson, E. R. Guthrie, P. Sandiford, A. I. Gates, C. L. Hull, K. W. Spence, B. F. Skinner, and D. O. Hebb.

These persons, like prominent figures in all the other social and natural sciences, recognize that scientific progress has thrived on systematization, such as the theory of relativity in physics. Nevertheless, most scientists recognize a different level of principle—what we might call "working principle" because of its immediate applicability in practice. The chief condition which a working principle must meet is that it not be inconsistent with the major system to which its practitioners are committed. However, it may be equally consistent with more than one competing system.

The principles to be described have been selected from a wide range of literature. They are not presented as an inclusive listing of "working principles" of learning; they represent but a sampling of some of the useful statements which can be made.

HOW MAY WE IMPROVE MOTIVATION?

When a person develops a state of tension resulting from unsatisfied need, we say that he is motivated. Motivation may spring from a variety of needs, ranging from those which are largely physiological in origin to those which are primarily psychological, such as a conflict in religious belief. The person's aim becomes the reduction of tension, which can occur only as the need is satisfied or partially satisfied.

Obviously, motivation plays a central role in learning. Students who are motivated work purposefully and energetically. They display few if any "discipline" problems. A teacher who can keep his students well motivated has won more than half the battle.

The Role of Personal Involvement

Where possible, through the medium of a democratic classroom climate, a teacher's task is to help induce personal involvement. Because of the interactive character of the most productive classroom situations, both students and teacher eventually test their attitudes, values, beliefs, skills, or knowledge. Specific techniques for doing this are described in Chapter 19.

After saying this, we would be unrealistic if we failed to concede that such a step is easier to describe than to achieve in practice. In virtually every school subject, a few students will appear well motivated; likewise, a few will appear to have no motivation toward learning and in spite of a teacher's best efforts will remain that way. Another group will respond more or less well to the teacher's efforts to produce motivation. It is among this middle group that teachers feel their greatest sense of accomplishment or frustration.

Extrinsic vs. Intrinsic Motivation

We have dealt with this subject elsewhere and present here only a brief review. Intrinsic motivation is that which arises when the resolution of tension is to be found in mastering the learning task itself; the material learned provides its own reward. A boy who studies the construction of model airplanes diligently so he can make a model is experiencing intrinsic motivation. Extrinsic motivation occurs when a person pursues a learning task, but for reasons which lie outside of it. If a boy studies model airplanes because he thinks it will please his father, an ex-pilot, rather than because of a personal interest in model planes, he is moved by extrinsic motivation. After making the distinction, it is necessary to point out that in most learning situations motivation cannot be dichotomized so neatly. It is a function of the total situation and hinges on some blend of personal concern for the work itself and concern for extrinsic factors. As a practicable working principle, motivation is probably always a function of an interactive situation.

Obviously, both emphases on motivation *work* in the sense that they both lead to learning. However, educational psychologists condemn extrinsic motivation as undesirable because, since the material learned does not in itself serve any purpose of the learner, he tends to forget it as soon as his extrinsic purpose is met. In addition to poor retention of material learned, extrinsic motivation usually leads to careless, inaccurate learning. The learning task is hurried through as quickly as possible so that the reward may be obtained. If Johnny tries for a B in arithmetic because his father promises him a one-dollar reward, Johnny is not likely to care how he gets the B—copying someone else's answers is as good a way as any. This appears to be the working out of Thorndike's law of effect and is incompatible not only with the tenets of field psychology but with what is usually recognized in the literature as the best of modern school practice.

In spite of the undesirability, on psychological grounds, of an emphasis on extrinsic motivation, in some situations many teachers feel they have no choice but to employ it. When this is the situation, teachers may be undecided as to whether to use rewards or punishments. A number of studies—in the Thorndike tradition—have been conducted in an attempt to determine whether it is more effective to praise students for what they learn or blame them for what they do not learn. After reviewing these studies, Stephens decides that the evidence is so conflicting that no definite conclusion can be drawn. The only conclusion which seems warranted is that either praise or blame is usually more effective in promoting learning than a policy of ignoring the achievement or lack of achievement of students.[1]

The Role of Success

Although occasional failure, including in some cases even punished failure, is not inimical to the progress of learning, fairly regular success is a *must*. As Pressey and his associates put it, "Learning feeds on success."[2] Unless motivation is extraordinarily high, a continuous succession of failures discourages students to the point where frustration blocks further effort.

However, too much can be made of the role of success. An uninterrupted series of successes may be as bad for the cause of learning as an uninterrupted series of failures. In Chapter 18 we suggest that it is healthful to let students make a certain number of mistakes—provided they are the kinds of mistakes one can learn by.

Related to the question of success vs. failure as a contributor to motivation is the question of whether students should be kept informed at all times of progress. The answer seems to be that a knowledge of progress spurs them on to additional effort, although this would not be the case if the goal were easy and a student found he was on the verge of success with extra time left.

Demotivation Caused by "Pat" Answers

We experience our strongest motivation in situations which are puzzling. If we completely solve the problem facing us, all sense of tension disappears; we cease to be interested because there is nothing to be interested in. Some misled teachers feel that each unit of work, or each class period, should end with a full resolution of whatever issue was under study. They sometimes feel that it is better for a teacher to tell students the "right answers" than to let them leave the class "unsatisfied." No policy could be more effectively calculated to destroy sustained motivation. A truly skilled teacher will see to it that each day students leave class with unanswered questions. Even an entire semester's work should not "wrap up" a subject "for keeps."

[1] J. M. Stephens, *Educational Psychology*, Holt, 1956, p. 303.
[2] Sidney L. Pressey, Francis P. Robinson, and John E. Horrocks, *Psychology in Education*, 3rd ed., Harper, 1959, pp. 355 ff.

Tests as Sources of Motivation

Some teachers feel that in order to keep students working it is necessary to give them frequent tests, both announced and unannounced. We are talking here of tests used for purposes of motivation, not for remedial purposes. Stephens surveys a number of relevant studies and draws a different conclusion.[3] At the college level, the research evidence suggests that tests given once or twice a term produce just as much motivation as frequent tests. In high school the results differ, in that tests spaced about two weeks apart seem efficacious. *Daily tests produce less motivation than no tests at all.* Further, the studies indicate that students learn less in courses in which they are given surprise tests than in courses where test dates and coverage are announced ahead of time.

Of course, tests employed as motivating devices function primarily as extrinsic motivation. A student's primary goal in such a situation is not to learn the subject content for its own sake but to pass the test. Generally speaking, frequent and widespread use of tests for other than remedial reasons indicates commitment to a mechanistic psychology.

Self-Imposed Goals vs. Teacher-Imposed Goals

It is a well-known fact among psychologists that when a person develops goals which he sees as personal to himself, although perhaps involving others whom he cares about, he tends to set ambitious goals. The tendency actually is for most students to set goals that are difficult to the point of being unrealistic—students who have great difficulty with mathematics sometimes choose engineering as their career.

In most school subjects it is not feasible for students to operate as free agents in setting their goals in the course. However, an experienced teacher has a pretty good idea of what an average student can achieve and it makes for better motivation to discuss the objectives of the course with students. Through such discussion, students and teacher both may come to feel more personal involvement in the course objectives.

HOW MAY WE MAKE LEARNING MORE EFFICIENT?

In this book, improving the efficiency of learning means establishing situations in which maximum change of insight may occur in a given time. Although insightful learning may proceed very rapidly, it seldom can be hurried. Some of the most efficient possible learning situations appear on the surface as unnecessarily—even hopelessly—time consuming.

[3] Stephens, *op. cit.*, pp. 300–301.

Readiness and Learning

A young person is ready to learn something when he has achieved sufficient physiological maturation and experiential background so that he not only can learn but wants to. For example, it is physiologically impossible for a child of 3 months to learn to walk. For all except an occasional prodigy, it appears impossible for a child of 2 to learn to read; not only is his neuromuscular system insufficiently developed, but he doesn't want to read. A youth of 12 is not normally ready to study subjects such as calculus, advanced economic theory, or Shakespeare. His lack of readiness is probably more attributable to absence of suitable experiential background than to inadequate development of physiological structures, although until a person is fully matured physically it is usually difficult to say to what extent incomplete development of physical structure is a hampering agent, particularly in the case of primarily "intellectual" learning tasks. There is evidence to suggest that certain school subjects can be taught successfully much earlier than was once supposed—algebra is a case in point.

Much of the research on readiness has pertained to the teaching of reading and arithmetic. When is a youngster old enough to learn to read or to do long division? Although specific figures are frequently given, e.g., a child is often said to be ready to read at the age of 6.5 years, they can be highly misleading. There is great individual variation among children. Some are ready to read at the age of 3; others might as well wait until they are 8.

Serious problems may result from taking data on readiness literally, particularly when virtually all formal education is *mass* education in most countries. It is a matter of administrative convenience to require all children to begin school at about the same age. If Mary, who is ready to read at 3, has been taught by her parents to read, and is reading at, say, a fourth-grade level when she enters the first grade, she is bound to find the school's reading program insufferably dull. She may become a highly bored and frustrated child and so will frustrate teachers and parents. If Johnny is incapable of learning to read at 6½, when we normally begin reading in this country, he may face a year or two of failure and eventually develop a mind-set against reading which will make it difficult for him to learn to read at any age.

Similar problems occur at all age levels. Some persons are never ready for certain learning tasks which are assigned regularly in school. For example, one of the authors was required to take a succession of physical education activity courses while a freshman and sophomore in college. He was *never* ready, in the sense that a combination of poor coordination, poor vision, lack of previous experience, and negative mind-set made it impossible for him to achieve, even at the minimum standards set by the instructors. Fortunately, in physical education classes, a C is usually conferred for regular attendance and harmless conduct.

Our definition of readiness presents the same problem as our definition of intelligence: it is impossible to isolate those factors which are innate and those which are a product of learning. We can only assume that when a person is ready for a new learning, it is because he has developed his ability and interest to the point that he sees the new learning as the next step for him to make.

We do not even have conclusive data on the possible degree to which strong motivation may speed physiological maturing. An average youngster may achieve the necessary coordination to perform a particular physical task at the age, say, of 12; but those who are especially interested in learning the task, and who begin trying it at an earlier age, may significantly accelerate the development of coordination.

Studies indicate that there is nothing to be gained by starting youngsters on a particular learning task earlier than readiness normally permits. Whether readiness for a particular task hinges primarily on genetically controlled maturation or primarily on experience and desire, most children, if started at a task much earlier than it is normally learned in our culture, do not learn it well, if at all. They tend to flounder, making gains which are offset by retrogressions. The one who is started later on the same task may learn so much more rapidly that he quickly catches up with the child started earlier.[4] This apparent fact should not be taken as a denial of the point made earlier: a number of subjects now normally reserved to high school or college could be taught effectively in elementary school if there were good social reasons for doing so. We have mentioned certain aspects of higher mathematics in this connection; foreign language is another example. There are social reasons, however, for keeping the elementary curriculum sufficiently uncluttered to be able to focus on fundamental language and arithmetic skills.

The Role of Practice

Although some learning is of an "Aha!" character, i.e., the learner gets the point in a flash and does not forget it, other learning requires lengthy practice. If a teacher is to help students make the most efficient use of practice he must remember several important principles concerning its use.

First, repetition per se does not teach. Thorndike's original "law of exercise" suggested that animals—and humans—learn an act merely by

[4] A number of such studies are summarized in Glenn M. Blair, R. Stewart Jones, and Ray H. Simpson, *Educational Psychology*, Macmillan, 1954, pp. 114–122.

repeating it enough times. In the 1930s Thorndike himself decided that such a notion had no experimental support and retracted his earlier statement. When we use the term *practice* we refer to trials which have an experimental character, trials in which the action is varied, even though slightly, each time the learner asks himself, "What did I do wrong?" or "How can I do it better?" Pressey, Robinson, and Horrocks cite a study in which the conclusion was drawn that ". . . repetition that occurs in acquiring skill is not repetition of one set of identical elements, but the gradual development of structural features. Instead of doing the same thing over and over, the learner progresses to more advanced stages of performance."[5]

Old-fashioned teachers who kept Johnny after school until he could write 100 times on the blackboard, "It is wrong for boys to spill ink on little girls' hair" undoubtedly taught Johnny something but assuredly not that it is wrong to spill ink on little girls' hair.

Practice may be *massed* or *distributed*. Massed practice means long practice periods. Distributed practice means a succession of shorter practice periods with rest or other forms of activity spaced between.[6] Virtually all of the research evidence seems to show spaced practice to be more efficacious than massed practice. With massed practice both fatigue and boredom reduce attention and cause practice to turn into mere repetition.

In many instances, spacing actually speeds up the learning process. It is fairly common for persons to reach a plateau—a dead end—in learning, and to re-establish progress after a waiting period. One of the authors knows a person who learned to swim "wrong." He never mastered the popular crawl stroke. He began learning this stroke in his 40s but was handicapped by poor coordination—he inhaled when his face was under water and exhaled when it was out. After a summer of near drowning, he again attempted, the following June, the crawl stroke. Surprisingly, in the first trial he did much better. Although gains were slow that summer, the following year, after a winter's rest, he did better still.

Although not usually so interpreted, the experimentation on practice lends more support to the insight theory of learning than to any of the S-R associationistic interpretations of the learning process. The fact that practice, to be effective, must be experimental, that is, accompanied by a questioning attitude, supports the notion that the role of practice is not to strengthen neural connections but to contribute to the development of

[5] Pressey, Robinson, and Horrocks, *op. cit.*, p. 349.
[6] Cronbach's chapter on practice does a good job of summarizing and restating some of the more significant research concerning practice. See Lee J. Cronbach, *Educational Psychology*, Harcourt, Brace, 1954, Chap. 12. Spacing is treated on pp. 367–370.

an insight. We perfect our thought patterns by trying them out experimentally.

One qualification needs to be made in connection with distributed practice as well as distributed study of any sort. Too much has been written about attention span. Some writers state with great specificity, in terms of number of minutes, what the attention span of a person of a given age is. Attention span refers to the length of time which a person can pursue a learning task without having his attention falter seriously. Attention span is obviously a function of the level of motivation, and it is misleading to say, as some psychologists have said, that the attention span of children increases with age. *It increases with motivation.*

We have seen small children work as persistently and diligently at a task as any adult would be likely to do. The difference between childhood and adulthood appears to be that adults are better able to subordinate short-run pleasures in the interest of longer-range pleasures; adults find it easier to "live for the future." Hence, they can more easily develop long-range motivation for a short-range learning task which requires massed practice—like learning a foreign language quickly.

Fatigue does not interfere seriously with learning provided sufficient motivation is present. This statement is true only within limits, for exhaustion can become so intense that even the highest level of motivation flags. Conversely, in the absence of motivation, a rather simple learning task can produce marked feelings of ennui.

Part vs. Whole Learning

This issue dates back to the 1920s, when connectionism was first being challenged by the Gestalt outlook. The standard connectionist approach had been "piecemeal" learning: one begins with individual elements and learns them one by one, eventually assembling them into a whole. It would be wrong to imply that the connectionists originated an atomistic approach to teaching; such an approach dates back much farther than Thorndike. However, associationist thinking in psychology did provide a rationale for the atomistic approach by giving it theoretical support.

The Gestaltists insisted that we learn best when we begin with the largest unit we can comprehend. In studying a poem, for example, instead of beginning with a word-by-word or line-by-line analysis, students should read the entire poem through rather quickly and try to size up its over-all meaning. Once this is done, a Gestaltist would have no objection to an analytical approach; when a person has gained some "feel" for the entire poem, analysis plays a different role: each part is studied with respect to how it fits into the total picture.

The part vs. whole issue has plagued teachers of reading for almost half a century. Should a child learn to read by learning first the alphabet, then how to pronounce syllables, then words, then finally sentences, paragraphs, and themes? Or should he begin with simple themes and strive as rapidly as possible to envision word groups and later entire sentences or paragraphs as units? Under the latter approach (sight reading) students get a feel for pattern and, so the argument runs, learn to read more rapidly and fluently.

As Pressey points out, the experimental evidence to date favors conclusively neither one view nor the other.[7] Most educational psychologists today, even those with an associationist orientation, argue in favor of the "whole" method for all types of material susceptible to such an approach. Yet, as Pressey points out, the relative superiority of one method or the other may hinge largely on the learner's "motivation, . . . patience, and the extent to which he perceives the learning situation as being important and fulfilling a need." Pressey also suggests that intellectual capacity is a significant factor, in that persons with higher than average IQ tend to learn better by wholes. The amount and quality of prior practice also enters the picture: practice in either approach seems to increase one's efficiency in utilizing that approach. Finally, some learning materials lend themselves better to part learning, some to whole learning.[8]

It is the observation of the authors that people who begin a learning task by the "part method" tend at some point in its achievement to move to the "whole method." When this transition is made, progress is likely to accelerate rapidly. A good example of what happens may be found in the learning of typing. The old-fashioned way of teaching typing was first to teach students the location of the letters on the keyboard and how to stroke each letter at will. The next step was to teach them to type syllables. Next came words, then phrases, then sentences. This was the "part method" with a vengeance. Students can learn to type this way. However, they usually hit a plateau, a period of no progress in spite of diligent practice. Rather suddenly—often it comes with a rush in a matter of a few days—a student finds that he is no longer "spelling out" words on the typewriter. In fact, he is typing entire phrases or sentences without attention to individual letters or words. He has moved to "pattern typing." He has suddenly gained a feel for a stroking pattern appropriate to phrases, sentences, or groups of sentences. Now typing speed and accuracy tend to soar.

When a typist can no longer recall where individual letters are on the keyboard he has moved to a fundamentally different approach and apparently the only one whereby a high level of skill can be achieved. One of the authors does all of his writing (except signing checks) on a type-

[7] Pressey, Robinson, and Horrocks, *op. cit.*, pp. 353–355.
[8] *Ibid.*, pp. 354–355.

writer. The only way he can visualize where a particular letter is on the keyboard is to arrange his hands in typing position and stroke a word containing the letter, meanwhile *watching to see where his finger lands* when the letter in question is struck. Sometimes stroking a single word is difficult without stroking a phrase or sentence which contains it.

HOW MAY WE IMPROVE RETENTION?

Most of the studies of retention have been made by connectionists and have been based on a learner's ability to reproduce at some later date a response which he could once make. Studies of recall have included both sensorimotor and verbal responses. In Chapter 1 we suggested that much of what is learned in school is quickly forgotten. Pressey has summed up a number of studies of the recall of verbal responses—the so-called "fact learning" which is so commonly emphasized in schools. He concludes that "At the end of a course, students remember about three-fourths of the facts covered. One year following the conclusion of a course, students remember about one-half the facts covered. Two years following the conclusion of a course, students remember about one-fourth the facts covered."[9] These studies do not take us beyond two years after the learning occurred. There is every reason to suppose that the process of forgetting continues until, for most types of "fact courses," virtually all is lost. There is no research as yet which furnishes a basis for contradicting the opinion of Wrightstone, paraphrased in Chapter 1, to the effect that many school courses might as well not be taken at all if their value is to be judged from any long-range results which we can measure. On the hopeful side, we know with little question that learning can be quite permanent; formal education is not necessarily doomed forever to be largely wasted.

Meaning and Retention

Material which is meaningful to students is remembered much better than material which is not. Defining meaning is not easy, and since this problem is dwelt on at length in Chapter 17, we will say here only that meaningful material is confined to *relations* between facts (generalizations, rules, principles) for which students see some use. Solitary facts are on essentially the same level of meaninglessness as nonsense syllables, and approximately the same forgetting curves apply to both.

Making learning meaningful is a matter of selecting the right content —it must be reducible to principles—and helping students see its applicability in situations which they are concerned about. However, as McDon-

[9] *Ibid.*, pp. 262–263.

ald points out, the learning of *any* kind of organizing principle contributes to retention.[10]

Results of learning meaningful material are apparent enough. Cronbach cites a study in which tests requiring the application of major generalizations to new problems were administered at the beginning of a course in zoology, at the end, and a year later. The respective scores were 35, 65, and 65. There was *no loss* of material learned. In another study, where zoology students were asked to draw conclusions, i.e., infer principles, from experiments not previously studied, the respective scores were 30, 57, and 64. Students did even better after an interval of a year![11]

Stephens sums up the situation very nicely when he says, "If the material is sufficiently meaningful, there may be no forgetting whatever. An important governing principle, like the idea of the conservation of energy, may so help us organize the rest of our ideas that it stays with us for life. Content that is not so brilliantly structured but which still has much meaning will be remembered in proportion to its meaning. Nonsense material is headed for extinction before the last syllable is uttered."[12]

Possibly the whole point is that material which can be learned insightfully, particularly on the level of *generalized insight*, becomes a permanent part of one's personality structure. All school learning *could* be of this nature if teachers understood well enough the basic psychological principles involved.

The Role of Purpose in Forgetting

It is pleasant to be able to forget some things. Any rounded study of retention would have to include study of the extent to which our wishes govern memory. We do not automatically remember new events of experience according to the length or spacing of practice sessions or any other mechanical formula. We do a reasonably good job of remembering what we really want to remember and forgetting what we prefer to forget.

One professor we know makes no attempt to remember his automobile license number. "I have no reason to," he says, "because I have the number on a tag attached to my key chain. It is easier to refer to the tag than to try to keep the number in mind."

Some experiences are so painful that our mental health benefits by either forgetting them or restructuring them in memory so that what we recall does not resemble closely what actually happened. On the other hand, some experiences are so pleasurable that we not only remember them in detail but in memory embellish them. The fish we caught on our

[10] Frederick J. McDonald, *Educational Psychology*, Wadsworth, 1959, p. 192.
[11] Cronbach, *op. cit.*, p. 392.
[12] Stephens, *op. cit.*, pp. 427–428.

Canadian trip of 1951 become larger and more plentiful every year.

With respect to learning in school, where controversial content is concerned, we tend to forget that with which we do not agree and to remember that with which we do. A frequently cited study was conducted by J. M. Levine and Gardner Murphy, in the early 1940s. Students were grouped according to whether they were procommunist or anticommunist in attitude (at that time a student could be safely procommunist). Both groups of students were given both pro- and anticommunist reading references. In a later memory check, the anticommunist students remembered the anticommunist arguments much better than they did the procommunist arguments, and vice versa.[13]

Purposive forgetting and remembering are examples of psychological homeostasis. Through them we preserve our self-organization in a reasonably adequate state. We employ forgetting and remembering to heal psychological wounds, to shore up self-respect, and to make better sense generally out of our psychological world.

The final point of the foregoing sentence perhaps deserves a little elaboration. In Chapter 11 we discussed the Gestalt "law of Prägnanz" and related laws—all having to do with perception. It will be recalled that, according to these principles, when a person perceives fragmentary, incomplete, or unsymmetrical objects he tends to see them as more complete, perfect, and balanced than they actually are. Probably every time we recall an experience we have a repetition of perception, in the sense that we reinterpret what we recall in the interest of making a more pleasing pattern out of it. Virtually all texts in educational psychology cite experimental evidence to support this view. One of the better treatments is on pp. 188–191 in the text by Frederick J. McDonald, cited earlier. Perhaps the main lesson to be had from this research is that forgetting is an active and not a passive process, just as is any learning which has promise of retention.

The Role of Overlearning

A person can learn something well enough to make a perfect score on a test given immediately after the learning; he can then continue practice on the same material for an indefinite time, or at least until boredom poses an insurmountable barrier. It has been found that such overlearning does contribute to retention. Hence, most books in educational psychology list overlearning as a means of improving retention.

It should be noted, however, that, when the material to be learned is sufficiently meaningful, overlearning is never necessary. Overlearning is an antidote for attempts to teach relatively meaningless content.

[13] See McDonald, *op. cit.*, pp. 201–202.

Nevertheless, when a person is faced with a learning task such as acquiring the vocabulary of a foreign language, overlearning may be the sensible course to pursue. Overlearning is measured in terms of the percentage of additional practice spent after initial mastery. According to one study, reported by Stephens,[14] 50 percent of overlearning produced a gain in retention after an elapsed time of 28 days of approximately 25 percent; 100 percent of overlearning contributed only slightly more gain than this, possibly because boredom interfered with its effectiveness. Other studies do not produce the same percentages, but all seem to agree that overlearning contributes to retention.

Spaced Review vs. Cramming

Apparently retention is higher if study periods are spaced methodically over the course of an entire semester than if a student waits until a day or two before the final examination and "burns the midnight oil." Results on the final may be equally good; some students learn to cram quite effectively. But long-range results from cramming are likely to be meager—although tempered, of course, by the interplay of the other factors we mention.

The issue of spaced review vs. cramming is not the same as the issue of distributed vs. massed practice. Studies on the relative effect on retention of distributed and massed practice are inconclusive. The issue is in what temporal relationship to the initial learning should review occur—whether it be distributed or massed. The answer seems to be suggested by the nature of a typical forgetting curve, as shown in Fig. 17. Since the rate of forgetting is much more rapid relatively soon after the initial learning, we may hypothesize that review periods should follow immediately after the initial learning and not be delayed. McDonald cites experimental

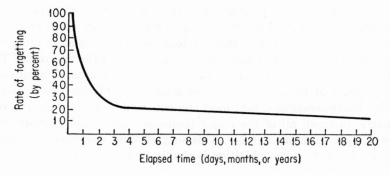

Fig. 17.   A Typical Forgetting Curve.

14 *Ibid.*, p. 429.

evidence to suggest that spaced but frequent reviews immediately following initial learning, followed by widely spaced "brush-ups" during the
period of desired retention, represent the most effective approach.[15]

Readers should remember that when we say "review" we are not referring to repetition; rather, we mean practice with an experimental cast, as
described earlier. Review is even more effective if it seeks to go beyond
the initial learning by tying it in with new learning or interpreting it on a
more sophisticated level. Readers should also remember that the forgetting curve reproduced in Fig. 17 and the present discussion of the role of
practice in improving attention apply primarily to either complicated
sensorimotor learning or verbal learning which is relatively low in meaningfulness and intrinsic motivation. Learning of the most desirable kind
produces a rather flat forgetting curve and does not have to be practiced
to be remembered.

Effects of Intervening Events

A great deal of writing is available on the general subject of the effect
on recall of previously assimilated new items of learning, and conversely,
the effect on recall of new learnings of what was learned previously. When
a second set of learnings intrude upon a first set, and prevent or distort the
recall of the first set, we say that *retroactive inhibition* has occurred.
When a first set of learnings intrude upon a second set, and prevent or
distort the recall of the second set, we say that *proactive inhibition* has
occurred. Since there is a strong tendency for any two sets of related
learnings to mingle with and to influence each other in reciprocal fashion,
some writers prefer not to make the above distinction but rather to use
the term *interactive inhibition*.[16]

Students who read the present book frequently report that, by the time
they have completed the first three chapters, so many different points of
view about key issues in psychology have been presented that they "can't
remember any of it." They then go on to say that they could remember
well enough through the first three or four positions, but after that, with
the addition of still others, they "can't even remember the first ones." This
would seem to be a clear example of interactive inhibition. (Fortunately,
several years of experience using the manuscript of this book prior to
publication demonstrated that most students could learn, by the end of a
semester, to recall all of the major positions treated and to distinguish
them sharply from one another. This suggests that sometimes a suitable
antidote for interactive inhibition is simply more study.)

[15] McDonald, *op. cit.*, p. 197.
[16] See, for example, Arden M. Frandsen, *Educational Psychology*, McGraw-Hill,
1961, pp. 372 ff.

HOW IS LEARNING TRANSFERRED FROM SITUATION TO SITUATION?

Transfer of learning involves the ability to utilize in new situations that which one has previously learned. The assumption underlying our entire public education system is that the knowledge gained when certain learnings are required in schools not only will be available in the future but also will be applied to some degree in the solution of new problems as they arise in further school and life situations. Society supports education only because it assumes that learning in school facilitates learning and thinking in situations outside school.

The basic problem of transfer is: How can we teach for maximum effective transfer of learning? Problems subordinate to the principal one are: (1) How does a person's current learning assist in meeting future learning situations? (2) How does what youngsters learn in school affect what they learn and what they do outside school? (3) Does it have as much effect as it should, and how can it be made more effectual?

More specifically, will an individual carry over the arithmetical abilities he learned in a classroom to the problems he actually meets in business or in tasks about the house? Will a student of algebra automatically apply his algebraic knowledge to the solution of problems in physics? Will a knowledge of health practices insure that a boy will acquire good health habits? Does practice in memorizing, reasoning, persevering, and willing improve the mental process in general? Can one improve his perception, retention, and imagination in all fields by practice in one? If so, what kind of task should he practice?

Since many problems of life cannot be specifically foreseen, schools must give students general preparation to cope with them. Consequently, the critical question of teachers in regard to transfer is not whether it takes place but what conditions enhance the greatest amount of transfer.

The Theory of General Transfer

Prior to the sixteenth century, general transfer of training through mental discipline was widely accepted in educational circles. Transfer supposedly was automatic; when a child's mind had been adequately disciplined, it would function more effectively in any learning, willing, or thinking situation. The idea was that faculties of the mind lie dormant until they are exercised. Such faculties as memory, will, reason, and perseverance are the "muscles of the mind"; like physiological muscles they are strengthened through exercise. Not long ago a colleague of one of the authors, a professor of history, said, "I know that students forget in a few years most of what they learn in their history courses. But this doesn't really concern me much. The main value of history is in the disciplining effect it has on students. That effect will remain with them as long as they live."

The doctrine of mental discipline gave transfer its first highly systematic development. Certain subjects such as Latin and geometry supposedly were endowed with unusual transfer qualities. Since, in mental discipline theory, transfer is assumed to be automatic, once a faculty has been developed it goes into operation whenever its use is appropriate.

The theory of mental discipline has been discredited to the point that school subjects no longer can be justified in terms of improving students' minds through exercise. Evidently there is transfer of *learning* but not the general transfer implied in mental discipline. Methods of solving arithmetic problems can be transferred to solution of problems in algebra. The learning of Latin may, and often does, facilitate the learning of English grammar. However, if experimental research is to be trusted, transfer is not automatic and it is not a matter of disciplining minds.

Herbartian apperception, S-R associationisms, and Gestalt-field theories of learning, while disagreeing on many things, all harmonize in their opposition to mental discipline. Their strongest weapon has been systematic research which tests the results of mental discipline through measurement of just how much memorization strengthens a "memory faculty." Studies developed at the turn of the twentieth century by James, Thorndike, and Woodworth experimentally refuted validity of a mental discipline theory of transfer. Of course, even today mental discipline may be, and often is, defended through philosophic reasoning divorced from research.

Transfer by Identical Elements

S-R associationists attempted to replace the mental discipline theory of transfer with the theory of transfer by *identical elements*. The identical elements theory was developed by Thorndike, who contended that what is learned in one situation is usable in another only to the degree that there are identical elements in the two situations. Identity may be in content, method, procedures, or aims.

Thorndike assumed that, if an S is connected with an R and that same S-R connection is applicable in another situation, it will operate, automatically and mechanistically. An S may be a single stimulus or a group of stimuli, and similarly an R may be a response or a group of responses. Although study of Latin did not discipline faculties of a generalized mind, it supposedly did contribute to transfer to the degree that there are identical elements in Latin and English vocabularies; the "port" of Latin *porto* transfers to the "port" of English *transport*. Consequently, in accordance with identical elements, if Latin is taught at all, emphasis should be upon roots or segments which are identical with those in English.

If one tries to base a school program on this conception of transfer his only choice is to incorporate in the curriculum as many learning tasks as possible which, when reproduced outside of school, will contribute to the effectiveness of living. An entire generation of curriculum makers did, in fact, adopt this approach. They studied American community life much as an efficiency expert would conduct time-and-motion studies in a factory. They then tried to list specific verbal and motor responses which are needed in daily life and to teach these without more than minor modification in school.

This approach to education poses many difficulties, not the least of which is that there are so many kinds of situations in life to be coped with that a school could not possibly teach them all, even in the 12 or 13 years of required attendance. Curriculums became hopelessly cluttered, and in most schools the results of this cluttering remain today. If only identical elements transfer, the work of the school becomes virtually hopeless.

Under such a situation, someone must decide for each school *which* among the hundreds of thousands of possible learnings that might be justified are important enough to be taught. Who is to make this decision? Almost everyone will claim the right—legislators, businessmen, labor leaders, patriotic organizations, unpatriotic organizations, parents, school boards, school administrators, and occasionally even a teacher who has the courage to express an opinion.

Pedro T. Orata has concentrated his professional study upon transfer of learning. In 1941 he said, "The evidence which tends to disprove Thorndike's theory of identical elements continues to cumulate. . . ."[17] He continued, "Not a simple succession of elements is transferred, but rather an attitude of response or a way of seeing the same kind of solution for different problems. Whereas senseless learning does not transfer, meaningful learning does. The process of learning for transfer becomes one of organization and reorganization of experience."

Orata also lists some conclusions that have developed from his studies. He notes that transfer is found in approximately 80 percent of studies, it is not an automatic process which may be taken for granted, and the amount of transfer is influenced by many factors. Factors centered in the learner are age, mental ability, personality, stability attained by a learned pattern, knowledge of direction, attitude toward the learning situation, efficient use of past experience, accuracy of learning, and acceptance of methods, procedures, principles, sentiments, and ideals. Factors centered

---

[17] Pedro T. Orata, "Recent Research Studies of Transfer of Training with Implications for the Curriculum, Guidance, and Personal Work," *Journal of Educational Research,* October, 1941, p. 83.

in the learning situation are meaningfulness of the learning situation, suitable organization of subject matter presentation, and provision for continuous reconstruction of experience.

Identical elements theory affirms that transfer occurs, but apparently does not explain how. Psychic atomism and mechanism are inadequate to explain transfer of learning. Some critics of identical elements theory interpret it as really a fragmented faculty psychology—elements in learning may be construed as small faculties.

Transfer of Generalizations

Almost all of the studies of transfer have shown that at least some transfer does occur, although not of a kind so general as to support the notions of the mental disciplinarians. The question which we now debate is, What is the mechanism of transfer? There is no longer any doubt that transfer is possible, but to take fullest advantage of it we must know just how it operates.

As early as 1905, Charles H. Judd, an American educator, asserted that not only does transfer occur if you let it, but the medium of transfer is the *sensed relationships between the elements of a situation*. A statement of relationships is a *generalization*. It may also be called a *principle, rule,* or *law*. Judd's experiment has become something of a classic; it is described in most textbooks which treat the problem of transfer. He selected two groups of boys comparable in those variables which seemed relevant. One (the experimental) group was instructed in the principle of the refraction of light. The other (control) group was not. Both groups of boys were then asked to hit underwater objects with darts. (At the beginning of the experiment, none of the boys had any skill in throwing darts.)

Both groups of boys were instructed to hit targets placed 12 inches under water. The boys who had had theoretical training in the principles of refraction did as poorly at this task as the control group: they had to learn to throw darts before their theoretical training could help. Once this was accomplished, the target was moved to a position four inches under water. Immediately, the experimental group showed a conspicuous superiority over the control group. Their understanding of the nature of refraction had given them cues as to where to aim the darts in order to hit underwater objects which are not where they appear to be. Judd's experiment and his interpretation of it is related in detail in his various books.[18]

Judd's findings antedated similar findings by the Gestalt psychologists. Köhler, Koffka, Wheeler, Perkins, and other Gestaltists (see Chapter 11

[18] See especially Charles H. Judd, *Educational Psychology*, Houghton Mifflin, 1939, pp. 507 ff.

for an account of the work of these men) all insisted that what animals and human beings tend to learn in any meaningful learning situation is *relationships*. Statements of such relationship are *theories* (or as previously stated, generalizations, principles, rules, or laws), which, as Judd said, are ". . . a kind of summary of many experiences. It [theory] makes possible the proper interrelating and interpreting of a whole body of varied experience."

Since accumulated experimentation has shown that attempts to base transfer on identical elements leads to more problems that it solves, and since the generalization theory of Judd and the Gestaltists seems highly productive as a basis for transfer, virtually all educational psychologists today seem to prefer the generalization theory.

More recent research supports Judd's position. In 1957 Kittell measured the relative effects of three amounts of direction to sixth-grade learners in their discovery of established principles on transfer to differing situations and on retention of learned principles.[19] He concluded that "Evidence from this experiment in conjunction with that of similar experiments indicates that furnishing learners with information in the form of underlying principles promotes transfer and retention of learned principles and may provide the background enabling future discovery of new principles."[20]

However, Judd and most other investigators of the generalization hypothesis stop short of a fully adequate statement of the conditions of transfer. It is increasingly apparent that the achievement of a generalization by a student does not in itself guarantee transfer. Even Cronbach's recent statement stops just short of mentioning that for transfer to occur students must be motivated toward that end. He points out that to facilitate transfer students need to learn general principles, that these principles must be clearly understood, that students must be shown places in which the principles can apply, and that they must be given opportunity to recognize the applicability of the principles in increasingly varied and complex situations.[21] This is excellent as far as it goes, but it still leaves out one ingredient which seems indispensable—the motivation of students. A more refined and practicable statement of the conditions of transfer, and one which divorces transfer fully from a mechanistic orientation, is to be found in the recent writings of Ernest E. Bayles. Bayles tells us that *"Any given item of training will transfer if and when—and only if and when—(1) opportunity offers, (2) a trained individual sees or senses it as an opportunity, and (3) he is disposed to take advantage of the op-*

[19] Jack E. Kittell, "An Experimental Study of the Effect of External Direction During Learning on Transfer of Retention of Principles," *Journal of Educational Psychology*, November, 1957, pp. 391–405.

[20] *Ibid.*, p. 404.

[21] Cronbach, *op. cit.*, p. 272.

portunity."[22] In this statement, we take it that "item of training" may be defined as "an insight susceptible to generalized application."

One may operate on habit, and transfer may occur with little or no reflection. Or transfer may occur in a highly reflective situation. In either case transfer is not automatic. A habit is a skillfully executed application of a principle in a situation wherein application of that principle apparently will help a person achieve a goal. Even habits are not blind, automatic behaviors. Rather, they are precise adjustments to situations which call for them. They are products of tested insights which are used in new situations.

Transfer of learning occurs because of perceptual similarities between two situations. When it occurs it is in the form of generalizations, concepts, or insights which are developed in one learning situation and are usable in others. For learning to be most useful in future situations it is essential that insights that are gained be generalized. But even then we cannot safely assert that transfer of generalizations takes place automatically. For transfer to occur, a learner should not only generalize but understand how the generalization can be used, and he should have a desire to use it.

McConnell says, "The consciousness that one is acquiring meanings and abilities which are widely applicable in learning and living is what creates a frame of mind favorable to transfer. . . . Important as it is, however, this attitude is not enough. One must make an aggressive attempt to interpret new problems in the light of previous experience, and to bring to bear upon the novel situation those understandings and abilities which are relevant and serviceable."[23]

Gertrude Hendrix' new clue to transfer of training is that ". . . it is the intermediate flash of unverbalized awareness that actually counts for the transfer power. . . ."[24] She found that the way a person learns a generalization affects the probability of his recognition of an opportunity to use it. In method I (a conventional method) a generalization was first stated, then illustrated, then applied to new problems. In method II, the generalization was not stated but "drawn out of" the learners by asking questions; teaching was for unverbalized awareness.

In teaching for unverbalized awareness the stage was set in such a way that as soon as the generalization dawned the learner would begin to apply it. Students were asked to find the sum of the first two odd numbers, the sum of the first three odd numbers, the sum of the first four odd num-

22 Ernest E. Bayles, *Democratic Educational Theory,* Harper, 1960, p. 58.

23 Arthur I. Gates, Arthur T. Jersild, T. R. McConnell, and Robert C. Challman, *Educational Psychology,* Macmillan, 1948, pp. 509–510.

24 Gertrude Hendrix, "A New Clue to Transfer of Training," *Elementary School Journal,* December, 1947, p. 200.

bers, etc. As soon as the subject knew the relationship between these sums and the number of odd numbers to be added, he started to gasp a little, or smile, or grew tense. That is, he showed in some way that something had happened to him. (The answer: the sum of the first n odd numbers is n^2.) Furthermore, he began to give succeeding answers rapidly, getting them by the short cut rather than by the laborious process of adding; he revealed possession of the generalization by transfer behavior based on that generalization.

In method III, students were taught as in method II except that subjects were asked to state the rule they had discovered. Arrival at a correct verbalization (method III) took about twice as long as discovery of a generalization on an unverbalized level (method II). In every case included in two experiments, the highest transfer effects were achieved in the group taught by the unverbalized awareness procedure. The lowest transfer effects came from the group taught by the method in which the generalization was stated first, then illustrated, then applied to new problems. Groups who learned by conscious generalization showed up somewhere between the other two groups. Hypotheses emerging from the data are as follows:

1. For generation of transfer power, the unverbalized awareness method of learning a generalization is better than a method in which an authoritative statement of the generalization comes first.

2. Verbalizing a generalization immediately after discovery does not increase transfer power.

3. Verbalizing a generalization immediately after discovery may actually decrease transfer power.[25]

Crucial Points in Regard to Transfer

Transfer of learning may be summarized in six crucial points:

1. Opportunity for transfer may occur in many situations. It is not inherent in any subject but is possible from any field of knowledge.
2. Transfer is not dependent upon exercise with disciplinary subjects.
3. Transfer is dependent upon methods of teaching and learning which use lifelike situations. It is facilitated by teaching for large generalizations which have transfer value.
4. Transfer is not automatic; opportunities for transfer must be recognized, and the person concerned must want to use them.
5. Transfer varies according to difficulty of generalization of subject matter and intellectual ability of individuals.
6. Insights need not be put into words for their transfer to occur.

[25] *Ibid.,* p. 198.

HOW MAY PRINCIPLES OF LEARNING BE APPLIED IN THE TEACHING OF A SCHOOL SUBJECT?

In this section there is an example of teaching which illustrates a good many of the principles stated earlier in the chapter. It makes no attempt to incorporate all of them.

Further explanation of the rationale of this section is needed. In our opinion, most of the empirically based principles of learning now included in textbooks of educational psychology harmonize with the Gestalt-field family of learning theories. Although most writers of books in this field try to steer an eclectic course, choosing equally from the experiments of connectionists and field psychologists and refraining from expressing any preference, the research itself, if viewed objectively, appears to reflect, in the main, Gestalt-field assumptions. This is the case, in many instances, whether or not the researchers concede these assumptions. For example, the whole point of most discussions on motivation is that purpose be brought into the picture; yet purpose has been the forte of Gestalt-field psychology and has been played down by all varieties of associationism. As time goes on, we realize more and more that most examples of readiness are just as much a function of experience and purpose as of maturation. The new conceptions of practice seem to imply field theory rather than associationism. Present tendencies with respect to the part vs. whole issue likewise seem to favor the Gestaltists. The studies of retention, which emphasize *meaning* and *motivation* as the primary bases for retention, are wholly on the side of the Gestalt-field position. The "generalization" position with respect to transfer likewise is most consistent with the Gestalt-field point of view.

One difficulty with studies of learning in the past is that the results obtained depended largely on how closely learning was supervised. If learners (whether pigeons or human beings) are highly restricted, one gets the results which Skinner gets. If learners are allowed a considerable amount of freedom they appear to learn insightfully. The results of learning experiments depend more than most experimenters realize on the design of the experiment, rather than on the actual morphology of the learning process. (This was pointed out in Chapter 12.)

Another relevant comment is that almost all associationists have moved steadily over the years in the direction of a Gestalt-field position. Such movement has often taken the form of adoption of an eclectic position following the original espousal of a connectionist or behavioristic point of view. The evolution in Thorndike's own thought is a striking example of this kind of development. In the 1930s, toward the end of his influential career, Thorndike began expounding the concept of *belongingness.* Although he stated this concept ambiguously, and the word itself was poorly chosen, it appears that he meant something like the Gestalt "law of Prägnanz." His suggestion was that we perceive, and learn, something with more ease if it forms a sensible pattern. Sandiford illustrates this by suggesting that a number sequence of 2, 4, 8, 16, etc., has more "belonging-ness" than 1, 3, 4, 2, 5, 11, 13, 15.[26]

But let us get on with the main task of the section. Our illustration of the teaching of a subject insightfully is taken from the subject of arithmetic, specifically the teaching of the multiplication combinations involving the 9's. We use the 9's because these combinations are generally considered the most difficult. Furthermore, we use arithmetic because most teachers feel that, however one might teach other subjects, arithmetic must be taught by rote.

Let us assume that we are in a fourth-grade class and are ready to attack the 9's. We already have learned the 2's, 3's, 5's, 10's, and 11's, and we have learned them in such way as to have developed insight into the relationships involved in these tables. We can anticipate a kind of dialogue between students and teacher, which might go somewhat as follows:

The teacher reminds students of the tables they know already and has them review these tables until it is clear that they know them well. The review process might appear on the surface as drill in the old-fashioned sense, but there is a fundamental difference. The teacher makes certain that students understand the relationships involved, i.e., relationships of the same general type as those they are about to learn in connection with the 9's. After the review, the teacher suggests that the class advance to the 9's. (Some students are likely to protest that the 9's are more difficult than any of the others.)

The teacher begins writing the tables on the blackboard, at the same time asking members of the class to supply answers which they already will have learned from their study of the other tables. A "side trip" may be necessary to help students grasp the insight that the product of 9×2 is the same as that of 2×9. What appears on the blackboard is something like this:

$$9 \times 1 = 09 \qquad 9 \times 7 =$$
$$9 \times 2 = 18 \qquad 9 \times 8 =$$
$$9 \times 3 = 27 \qquad 9 \times 9 =$$
$$9 \times 4 = \qquad 9 \times 10 = 90$$
$$9 \times 5 = 45 \qquad 9 \times 11 = 99$$
$$9 \times 6 = \qquad 9 \times 12 =$$

[26] Peter Sandiford, "Connectionism: Its Origin and Major Features," in Nelson B. Henry, ed., *The Psychology of Learning*, Forty-first Yearbook of the National Society for the Study of Education, Public School Publishing Co., 1942, pp. 126 ff. See also J. F. Brown and D. D. Feder, "Thorndike's Theory of Learning as Gestalt Psychology," *Psychological Bulletin*, June, 1934.

To this point, the answers supplied are based on students' prior learning of the 2's, 3's, 5's, 10's, and 11's. Let us now envisage the following dialogue:

TEACHER: How do we know the answers to $9 \times 1, 9 \times 2$, and 9×3?
CLASS: Because we know the 1's, 2's, and 3's.
TEACHER: And what about $9 \times 5, 9 \times 10$, and 9×11?
CLASS: We know these because we know the 5's, 10's, and 11's.
TEACHER: The ones that are left are the hard ones, aren't they? What is the answer to 9×7, Jimmie? Tell me without looking at the tables in your book. (Within instruction procedure, when the teacher addresses Jimmie or any other pupil, he anticipates that at least most members of the class are thinking along with the student spokesman.)

Jimmie probably will say nothing but will stare at the teacher, baffled. The teacher may then ask various other members of the class the answer to $9 \times 6, 9 \times 8$, and 9×4. After the class begins to demonstrate a certain amount of bafflement (perhaps approaching the point of mild frustration), the teacher may entice them in this manner: "Would you like to gain enough understanding of the rest of the 9's so that after today you will know the answers to all of them?" The class is likely to respond in the affirmative with considerable enthusiasm.

TEACHER: All right, let's work at this thing together. June, go to the board and write the 10's up to 10×5 right beside the 9's. (The class now will have before it the following combinations.)

$$10 \times 1 = 10 \qquad 9 \times 1 = 09$$
$$10 \times 2 = 20 \qquad 9 \times 2 = 18$$
$$10 \times 3 = 30 \qquad 9 \times 3 = 27$$
$$10 \times 4 = 40 \qquad 9 \times 4 =$$
$$10 \times 5 = 50 \qquad 9 \times 5 = 45$$

TEACHER: When we compare the 9's which we have answered to the 10's, what difference do we see in the answers? What happens in the case of the 9's which did not happen in the 10's?
CLASS: Each step we move up in the 9's, one is lost.
TEACHER: How do you mean?
CLASS: 9×1 is one fewer than 10×1, 9×2, is two fewer than 10×2, and 9×3 is three fewer than 10×3. That is why we get the answers 09, 18, and 27.

Of course, finding this principle may not come as easily as the foregoing dialogue might suggest. The teacher might need to do quite a lot more "fishing," by rephrasing the question and perhaps even offering some hints. The speed with which a class comes to see for itself principles which are new to it depends much upon what atmosphere has been established, and, of course, on the brightness of the students.

The teacher next helps students see that as in the 10's, the first digit goes up one each time, 09, 18, 27. By this time, the stage should be set for supplying the missing answers.

TEACHER: Now think carefully about what we have learned. Since $9 \times 2 = 18$ and $9 \times 3 = 27$, Gary, what is the answer to 9×4?
GARY: 36.
TEACHER: Why?
GARY: Well, if the first number increases by one for each larger table, and if we lose one in the last number of each table upward, it would have to be 36.
TEACHER: You already know the answer to 9×5. Judy, does it check with the idea which we have learned?
JUDY: Sure, the first number will be one larger, and we will have lost five numbers from the second number. That makes 45.

The reader should not be misled by the foregoing hypothetical dialogue. In order to economize on space, students have been pictured as saying the right thing the first time. In an actual classroom situation there would be more hesitancy, more fumbling, more tries on the part of students and teacher. But the process would remain essentially the same.

The class now is ready to deepen its insights in relation to the multiplication process.

TEACHER: Look again at the first digit of each answer. (Teacher points to the 9's through 9×5.) Look at each of these digits in relation to the multipliers, 1, 2, 3, 4, and 5. Do you see anything interesting?
GARY: Why, the first digit of the answer is always just one number smaller than the multiplier.
TEACHER: Why do you think this is so?
GARY: Would this be caused by losing a number each time—I mean, losing a number as compared with the 10's?

The teacher has succeeded in evoking the insight (at least in Gary) that when one multiplies by 9 rather than 10, there is a loss of one at each step, including the first. The answers "never catch up," so to speak. They keep falling behind, but according to a definite and predictable pattern.

Still another relationship may be taught the class:

TEACHER: Look carefully at the answers which we have so far. (The teacher points to 09, 18, 27, 36, and 45.) Add the two digits of each answer and see what happens.
CLASS: The sum of the digits is the same in each answer. The sum is always 9.
TEACHER: Yes. $0 + 9 = 9$; $1 + 8 = 9$; $2 + 7 = 9$. Why is this so?
CLASS: $9 \times 1 = 9$, then the first digit always increases by one, and the second digit decreases by one. They kind of balance each other, so the sum remains the same.

By this time the stage has been set for teaching the remaining combinations involving the 9's. When asked the answer to 9×7, students should reason that the first digit of the answer will be 6 $(7 - 1)$ and that the second digit should be 3 $(9 - 6)$. The class now should be able to complete the table through 9×10 easily. At 9×11, the first digit of the answer becomes two less than the multiplier. (Why?) Furthermore, the sum of the two digits of the answer does not equal 9, as it did in each preceding step. (Again, why?) Students will know the answer is 99. The problem is, why? Answer: $9 \times 10 = 90$; at 9×11 "we start around again"— $90 + 9 = 99$. At 9×11 the first digit of the answer has lost two from the multiplier: $11 - 2 = 9$, so in 9×12 the first part of the answer is $12 - 2$ or 10. For the sum of the digits to add to 9, the last digit is 8. Thus, $12 \times 9 = 108$. This can be extended into a game.

$$13 \times 9 = 117$$
$$14 \times 9 = 126$$
$$15 \times 9 = 135$$

The class members now are ready to test their new insights to see whether they will work. The teacher may suggest to his better students that they put into words the insights they have learned. However, it should be borne in mind that it is not always necessary for one to put an insight into words in order to use it.

In what specific ways does this lesson in arithmetic differ from traditional procedures used in teaching the multiplication tables? The answer to this question will express the significance of field psychology for learning and teaching. This lesson reflects the teacher's assumption that learning is an insightful process. The teacher is attempting to aid students in improving their understandings or insights in regard to multiplying by 9 and doing it in such a way as to heighten their abilities to achieve new insights independently; he is not merely giving students a gimmick.

BIBLIOGRAPHY

Coladarci, Arthur P., *Educational Psychology: A Book of Readings*, Dryden, 1955.
  Carefully selected readings, many of them pertinent to the subject of learning. Reading 1 may help students tie together much of the present book. Also recommended are 2–4 and 23–33.
Cronbach, Lee J., *Educational Psychology*, Harcourt, Brace, 1954.
  A popular general text in educational psychology. Eclectic in orientation. Treats most of the topics covered in the foregoing chapter.
Fullagar, William A., and others, *Readings for Educational Psychology*, Crowell, 1956.
  One of the best compilations of readings. Part I is "must" reading for all students of the present text. See annotation at the end of Chapter 12.
Henry, Nelson B., *The Psychology of Learning*, Forty-first Yearbook of the National Society for the Study of Education, Part II, Public School Publishing Co., 1942.
  Explanations of the major schools of thought, by their respective exponents. In Chapter VII, T. R. McConnell attempts a reconciliation of competing theories. Section II (pp. 289 ff.) is steadily relevant to the foregoing chapter.

Krech, David, and Richard S. Crutchfield, *Elements of Psychology*, Knopf, 1958.
A massive volume with several sections bearing on the previous chapter and Part IV to follow. See especially Part III, "Adaptive Behavior."

Lee, J. Murray, and Doris May Lee, *The Child and His Development*, Appleton-Century-Crofts, 1958.
Cited previously, but steadily relevant to this book. Part III pertains to the foregoing chapter. See annotation at end of Chapter 6.

McDonald, Frederick J., *Educational Psychology*, Wadsworth, 1959.
A first-rate general text in psychological foundations. To supplement the foregoing chapter, concentrate on Part II.

Morse, William C., and G. Max Wingo, *Studying Psychology and Teaching*, Scott, Foresman, 1957.
A workbook with readings. One of the better selections pertinent to much of the present volume. Don't skip the selections on pp. 274 ff.

Pressey, Sidney L., and others, *Psychology in Education*, 3rd ed., Harper, 1959.
A general text in educational psychology which has become something of a classic. Eclectic in view, but highly readable and useful at the classroom level. Rather steadily relevant to material in the foregoing chapter. See especially Part II.

Remmers, H. H., and others, *Growth, Teaching and Learning, a Book of Readings*, Harper, 1957.
In Part I: several readings which are relevant to the foregoing chapter. See especially those by Kramer, Trow, Tiedeman, Ryans, Woodruff, Tuttle, and Blair.

Stephens, John Mortimer, *Educational Psychology*, Holt, 1956.
A first-rate text written within a connectionist framework. See Part III. Chapters 8 and 9 may help students understand better the various positions treated in Part III of the present text.

Tilton, J. W., *An Educational Psychology of Learning*, Macmillan, 1951.
One of the most sophisticated books yet written in the area. Tilton leans toward field theory but makes a serious attempt to integrate opposing positions with it. An original book, worth anyone's study. Entire book is relevant to the preceding chapters of Part III.

Wheeler, Raymond, and Francis T. Perkins, *Principles of Mental Development; A Textbook in Educational Psychology*, Crowell, 1934.
A book intended to refute atomism and mechanistic preconceptions based upon absolutistic methods of thinking. It derives from Gestalt in psychology and organismic thinking in biology. If nothing else, students should read the preface.

Wolman, Benjamin B., *Contemporary Theories and Systems in Psychology*, Harper, 1960.
An exceptionally good comparative psychology which treats all the major scientific systems. The author makes a case for eclecticism. This type of book may be used as a capstone for all the preceding chapters of the present volume, although in rejecting systematization Wolman departs from our own viewpoint. Not for beginning students.

PART
IV

HOW IS PSYCHOLOGY
USED IN THE
CLASSROOM?

A textbook on the psychological foundations of education would be incomplete without a section on classroom application of psychological principles. In Part IV we try to avoid merely providing students with a "bag of tricks." In each chapter we present statements of theory—in some cases summary restatements of theory presented earlier in the book—and move on to discussion of the implications of theory for classroom action. In no instance are theory and practice divorced. At the same time, practice is given serious attention; Chapters 17, 18, and 19 essentially are "how-to-do-it" chapters.

Chapter 16 raises questions about present points of confusion in American education and poses a single overarching goal—promotion of intelligent behavior—which could help to restore a sense of direction. Thus, it provides background material essential to later chapters.

Although most of the chapters in Part IV harmonize best with a cognitive-field point of view, readers should note that Chapter 17 is built largely around the thinking of the late Henry C. Morrison, who may be identified as an "idea associationist" in the Herbartian tradition.

PART IV

HOW IS PSYCHOLOGY USED IN THE CLASSROOM?

16

HOW IS TEACHING
RELATED TO INTELLIGENT
BEHAVIOR?

Owing to the historical sequence of emerging psychologies of learning, the psychological underpinnings of modern education are extremely diverse and inconsistent. Once a point of view is developed and popularized, centuries are required for its influence to cease to be felt. As new positions are developed, they do not displace the old; they are grafted on to it. The eventual result is a hodgepodge of bewildering complexity. In the resulting educational atmosphere, one of the most perplexing problems involves the relationship of teaching to intelligence. Consequently, a key to significant differences in outlooks of teachers is the way they define, treat, and foster *intelligence*.

Representatives of all schools of thought take at least some interest in intellectual development of individuals. However, they do not all define intelligence in the same way, and they differ sharply in regard to whether intelligence should be the immediate end of education or merely a subsidiary goal or by-product. Each psychological position has its own characteristic way of defining intelligence and evaluating a proposal that promotion of intelligence be the central goal of education.

We take the position that the most useful way for teachers to define intelligence is as capacity to act with dependable foresight and that it is a product of the interaction of a person and his psychological environment. Hence, a person's intelligence is capable of improvement with education.

WHAT ATTITUDES HAVE BEEN TAKEN HISTORICALLY TOWARD THE NATURE AND PROMOTION OF INTELLIGENCE?

Prior to the 1700s it was thought that little, if anything, could be done to improve the intelligence of an average man. Until the coming of the "Age of Enlightenment" of the seventeenth and eighteenth centuries, it was generally assumed that attempts to improve the quality of the intellect of an ordinary person were doomed to defeat. This pessimistic and fatalistic view of the human race dated from ancient times. However, a much more optimistic view developed in the eighteenth century. Liberal thinkers of France, England, the American colonies, and elsewhere, influenced by Locke's *tabula rasa* theory of sense empiricism, concluded that the intelligence of any normal person could be improved indefinitely through education. Faculty psychology, too, contributed to this line of thinking; intelligent behavior was assumed to be a product of the use of certain faculties (such as reason, memory, and imagination), which were strengthened by exercise.

Those who were optimistic about improvement of intelligence tended to favor extension of education to the lower classes and improvement of education for everybody. However, the mental discipline approach to learning was at that time the only one known; hence, those who felt that education could improve the intelligence of students assumed that benefit could come only from disciplinary drill or reading of the classics.

So far as eighteenth-century school people were concerned, improvement of intelligence could hardly have been much of an issue. For one thing, the concept of intelligence was not well developed. Nothing like a modern definition, in operational terms, of what it means to be intelligent was available. For another thing, the aims of education were many, and production of "thought power" was by no means given central place. Moral training probably was regarded as more central to the educational enterprise. Today, however, in much of the literature of education, development of the capacity to think, i.e., to make intelligent decisions, is a paramount goal. This is not to say that moral education is disregarded but rather that the method of intelligence is recommended in this area as well as in others.

Why do so many educators of today stress development of intelligence as a primary goal of education? One reason is the relation between the level of general intelligence and successful functioning of democracy. This relationship has been noted for many centuries, often for the purpose of proving that, since the masses were so lacking in intelligence, democracy was an impractical ideal. However, by the late eighteenth or early nineteenth century, democracy had come to be widely accepted in a few countries not only as an ideal social arrangement but also as a practical system of human relations. Those who thought democracy practicable, like Thomas Jefferson, felt that its potential for good could be realized only as the masses were educated. Jefferson recommended free public education—not much, but a little—for everyone. His assumption was that a system of free, compulsory public education would raise the general level of intelligence.

Possibly most people today would say that intelligent behavior among the masses is prerequisite to successful functioning of democracy and that education is essential to mass intelligence. It is likely that the average person does not have a very clear conception of what it means to be intelligent. He is for intelligence up to a point; but when its application has reached a certain intensity and comprehensiveness, he becomes frightened of it. He regards a limited amount of intelligence as a necessity and any amount in excess as subversive.

Many social scientists and other students of society, while committed personally to democratic values, are not now so much concerned with the use of intelligence to bolster democracy as with its use to insure human survival. Perhaps there are few who fear that *Homo sapiens* will disappear from earth; but a great many highly educated people genuinely fear that human existence may degenerate to a kind of brute level. They are alarmed because of the failure of man, up to the present, to eliminate certain threats to his continued civilized existence. The greatest such threats probably are uncontrolled population growth and atomic war.

Although there might be disagreement as to the seriousness of problems now confronting mankind, there probably would be little objection to the statement that numerous social difficulties exist which people have so far failed to alleviate to any significant degree. In addition to population growth and war, we should include in our list extreme poverty and outright hunger in large parts of the world, political and economic centralization, growing mechanization of life in industrial countries, and increasing pressures toward conformity.

To what extent can gains in the general level of intelligence help us achieve solutions or partial solutions to problems like these? No one can answer with certainty. In some areas of life we allow intelligence to operate in comparative freedom. In science and technology the method of intelligence seems firmly established. A scientist or technician is rewarded for discovering flaws in old scientific or technical ideas, particularly ideas relating to design and manufacture of material goods. An inventor who devises a new military weapon or a new design for an automobile motor may become a national hero. It does not matter seriously that his invention makes obsolete all that has come before it. Here, at least, intelligence is highly rewarded.

But as James Harvey Robinson pointed out, ". . . Our most important opinions—those, for example, having to do with traditional religious and moral conviction, property rights, patriotism, national honor, the state, and indeed all the assumed foundations of society—are, as I have already suggested, rarely the result of reasoned consideration, but of unthinking absorption from the social environment in which we live. Consequently, they have about them a quality of 'elemental certitude,' and we especially resent doubt or criticism cast upon them."[1] Thus, we live in a paradoxical world. We use the method of intelligence with boldness and zest in certain areas of living and we reject it with great determination in others.

Each basic psychology of learning—mental discipline, natural unfoldment, apperception, S-R associationism, and cognitive-field psychology—has its unique meaning for the concepts *intelligence* and *intelligent*. During the development of modern education, each psychology has had its turn at the center of the stage. With every change in dominant psychology, schools have shown the consequences of the meaning of intelligence then in vogue. Consequently, confusion in regard to the nature of learning has carried with it a parallel confusion concerning the nature and meaning of intelligence.

Mental Discipline and Intelligence

According to the doctrine of mental discipline, the chief purpose of education is to strengthen the mental faculties, especially will and reason, through appropriate kinds of drill. Although mental disciplinarians often fail to define their terms carefully, it is evident that their view of the meaning of intelligence is different from that of persons who reject this approach to education. To mental disciplinarians, intelligence is a condition characterized by relatively high development of the faculty of reason. An intelligent man is a highly rational man. The faculty of reason, when well exercised and developed, supposedly qualifies its owner to reason intelligently—accurately and logically—in regard to any matter.

Until the end of the nineteenth century, American formal education was dominated by the doctrine of mental discipline. During this period, education was regarded as necessarily unpleasant. The schoolroom atmosphere was at least austere and sometimes harsh. Teachers usually were dictators, sometimes benevolent, sometimes even spiteful. Children were expected to be respectful and obedient and to accept at face value whatever a teacher told them. Curriculums were relatively fixed, with an almost exclusive emphasis in elementary schools on the fundamental skill subjects and in secondary schools on such "disciplinary" subjects as Latin, history, and mathematics.

[1] James Harvey Robinson, *The Mind in the Making,* Harper, 1921, p. 61.

There always have been persons who opposed austere, disciplinary education. Undoubtedly some of these dissenters rejected mental discipline because they felt sorry for children. They deplored extremely difficult assignments, stern rules governing conduct, and severe punishments. However, kindness toward children was not likely to be carried very far in a culture based upon the psychological and philosophical premises of Puritanism and kindred outlooks. One who accepts the "bad-active" principle of human nature logically regards it as a favor to a child to "break his spirit." If a child's natural impulses are evil, crushing these impulses should help the child—not only to acquire immortality, but also to prosper here on earth.

The two most influential groups in the United States who continue to favor a disciplinary approach to education are some church officials, particularly those dedicated to parochial education, and those liberal arts professors who are under the influence of faculty psychology and the classical tradition in education. In addition to these there are many thousands of persons, including some public school teachers, who gravitate toward a theory of mental discipline. All of them to some degree assume the validity of faculty psychology. They think that learning is a matter of strengthening, or disciplining, the faculties and that certain faculties combine to produce intelligent behavior.

Persons whose theory of mental discipline is tied to a theology are likely to stress strengthening of faculties such as will, moral discernment, and religiosity. Those whose theory of mental discipline is related to a nonreligious humanism, e.g., "pure" classicists, are likely to stress such faculties as reason, memory, and imagination, all of which might work together to produce "intellectual capacity."

Professor Arthur Bestor, who may be called a modern classicist, writes as follows: ". . . The school exists to provide intellectual training in every field of activity where systematic thinking is an important component of success. It exists to provide it for every citizen who has the capacity and the will to apply intellectual means to the solution of the problems that confront him."[2] Repeatedly in his writings Professor Bestor reiterates his contention that the foremost role of schools is "intellectual training." Other modern classicists who argue in the same manner are Robert Hutchins, Mortimer Smith, and Bernard Iddings Bell.

Roussellian Natural Unfoldment and Intelligence

Any drastic departure from a disciplinary approach to education is possible only with adoption of fundamentally different assumptions about

[2] Arthur E. Bestor, Jr., "Anti-intellectualism in the Schools," *New Republic*, January 19, 1953, pp. 11–13.

the nature of man and the universe. As we have seen, Rousseau supplied these assumptions. Let us follow the train of thought which emerged as a result of Roussellian influences.

If man is a part of nature, and if all of nature is intrinsically good, then man is naturally good. (This line of reasoning is developed in considerable detail in Chapter 2.) If a child is born good, and his natural tendencies lead him to remain so, then it follows logically that children should be reared *permissively;* there is no need for their being disciplined at any time. A permissive classroom is one in which there is *unlimited freedom.* A permissive situation is laissez faire—meaning literally "let people do what they choose." *Permissive* may be considered the opposite of such terms as *teacher-centered, centralized, directed,* and *autocratic.*

Permissiveness should not be confused with democracy. A democratic group is led; it may be subject to a variety of restraints. In a democratic classroom there is not unlimited freedom but, rather, equally limited freedom. We may think of democracy as an emergent synthesis arising from the inadequacies of both anarchic—laissez-faire—and autocratic forms of organization.

How exponents of natural unfoldment define intelligence is not entirely clear. Conceivably, they might employ any of the extant definitions. What is clear is that they regard the development of intelligence as something which "just naturally happens." To be consistent with their over-all outlook, they would reject any kind of formal teaching for the purpose of stimulating intelligence. They would stress student-planned activities, including highly permissive types of projects, as the means for releasing or developing intellectual performance.

Eighteenth-century Roussellian "romantic naturalism" greatly influenced nineteenth-century thinking of leaders such as Pestalozzi and Froebel and reasserted itself in twentieth-century "Progressivism." Not only did Heinrich Pestalozzi (1746–1827) favor broadening the elementary curriculum by adding subjects with a natural appeal to children; he also believed that children should learn actively through inquiry and investigation. Compared with practices which were to develop in the twentieth century, Pestalozzi's approach to teaching does not appear highly permissive. However, it was much more "child centered" than most elementary education of that century.

Friedrich Froebel (1782–1852), a German educator and founder of the kindergarten, appears to have favored permissivism more than did Pestalozzi. Froebel said, "What one tries to represent or do he begins to understand." This seems to mean that "we understand what we do for ourselves." There surely is merit in such an idea; however, Froebel developed the idea to mean that children can set their own standards and should be allowed to do so. All self-initiated activity is creative, he argued, and can be justified on educational grounds. The curriculum he advocated consisted almost entirely of relatively spontaneous, free activity.

Without some qualifications, the foregoing statement would be an exaggeration; Froebel apparently did feel that certain activities were more valuable than others. He listed a large number of such activities, including games, plays, handwork, collecting, music, gardening, storytelling, construction projects, and democratic self-government. However, in a Froebelian kindergarten children were more free than in any previously known school. Here teaching practices *looked* different, dramatically different. Anyone could sense the difference in atmosphere between a school where children were encouraged to do what they liked and happiness and gaiety were promoted and a school where the teacher was a dictator deliberately trying to make life unpleasant for children.

Herbartian Apperception and Intelligence

There are two broad types of associationisms: (1) early mentalistic associationisms which had association of ideas in a mind as their focal point, and (2) more modern physicalistic associationisms which concern themselves with formation of connections in a brain and peripheral nervous system or between organic responses and environmental stimuli.

Herbartian apperception has been the leading example of the first type of associationism. Although Herbart's associationist psychology was built on fundamentally different premises from the natural unfoldment theory of followers of Rousseau, it was equally incompatible with mental discipline. Hence, Herbartian teaching, like Roussellian permissiveness, can be considered a counterinfluence to mental discipline. The formal, rigid approach of Herbartians, however, coupled with what appeared to be emphasis upon rote memorization, made their teaching appear on the surface much like the kind of education practiced by the mental disciplinarians. Herbart's prescription for good teaching, as implemented by his followers, became highly mechanical. Both apperception and mental discipline made a teacher equally central and dominant in the educational process. The Herbartian five steps seemed to put teaching on a different plane from that of mere drill and rote memorization. However, the Herbartian teachers were like all other associationists in one respect: the teacher was the dominant figure and students were permitted little opportunity for creative reflection.

Psychologists in the tradition of early associationism had a characteristic manner of defining intelligence. Remember that they regarded learning as a process of storing away ideas. Hence, they equated intelligence with capacity to associate and retain ideas and call them forth when needed in proper association with one another. To them a mind acts somewhat the way a boy managing his marbles does: except for those in use, he keeps them put away, but they are stored in a sufficiently organized manner so that the boy can easily get his hands on his favorite "shooters" as well as his cheap, expendable glass marbles when he needs them. *Intelligence* refers to a person's general effectiveness at storing "mental marbles" in organized fashion and selecting efficiently those which he wants to use as the need arises. The active nature of intelligence, however, resides in the "marbles," not in the container.

S-R Associationism and Intelligence

In the first quarter of the twentieth century the two dominant S-R associationistic psychologies were Watsonian behaviorism and Thorndikean connectionism. Today's S-R associationisms are modifications and refinements of these two earlier psychologies.

If we permitted them to substitute "physical bonds" for "ideas in association," the later associationists would accept about the same definition as apperceptionists. To them, a person's capacity to form links in the nervous system between stimuli and motor responses, to retain these links, and to repeat the proper sequence of motion when confronted with a stimulus at any time in the future constitutes intelligence. Since, to them, intelligence has a physiological basis and a given person's neural structure is not likely to change, it is only logical to suppose that the potential of an organism for intelligent behavior will not change. And indeed this is what the generation of associationists who were in the forefront during the 1920s and 1930s did believe.

S-R associationists regard intelligence as an innate, relatively fixed neural structure; once physiological maturity is reached it does not change. It is measured by tests which attempt to sample what a person has learned as well as how effectively he can solve problems (most of which involve one's ability to see relationships). Once a person's "mental age" is derived by means of such a test, an IQ score is obtained by dividing mental age by chronological age and multiplying by one hundred. Intelligence, so measured, supposedly is innate, and IQ supposedly is constant throughout life.

John B. Watson was convinced that in any normal person the capacity for forming neural bonds was so great that he would never make full use of it. He therefore assumed that an average person does not learn up to capacity, and the amount he does learn is purely a function of the environment. Watson believed, then, that almost any normal person could acquire the same complicated conditioning that, say, a skilled surgeon (or even a philosopher) could achieve. Thus, on the matter of intelligence, Watson was an environmentalist.

Watson's followers were less optimistic. Generally speaking, American behaviorists have assumed not only that intelligence is a fixed capacity but that the limitations of neural structure do prevent most persons from performing above a given (and definable) level. These psychologists place great faith in the ability of intelligence tests to reveal the level for any particular person.

Implications for education of this mechanistic concept of intelligence are clear. First, education can do only so much; each person is limited by his inborn neural structure. Second, all education can do is take advantage of what capacity a child has for forming dependable S-R linkages. His capacity for intelligent behavior depends upon how many good links can be formed and retained. Hence, the best—in fact, the only—way education can serve the cause of intelligence is to condition children effectively.

In a classroom situation where the guiding educational psychology is based upon S-R associationism, conditioning takes the form, for the most part, of committing facts to memory and selecting the proper one of several suggested answers. Students learn to repeat verbal statements when given the appropriate stimulus. Obviously, there is little which is reflective or creative about this, but persons who operate in terms of an associationist psychology have never regarded learning as basically reflective or creative. Associationists, however, do assume that conditioning may be the basis for future intelligent behavior.

Any psychology which explains mental functioning as either an association of ideas or an association of stimuli and responses is likely to lead to a characteristic manner of classroom instruction. Such psychologies (all the associationisms) usually assume that learning is a mechanical process which can operate only in the presence of an environment directing it. Hence, a teacher who accepts an associationist psychology selects ahead of time the precise ideas or responses to inculcate in his students. Through drill or exercises students reproduced the desired ideas or responses until they are fixed. Then, as a final step, the teacher tests the students to see whether they can accurately reproduce the learned material.

Appropriate responses become the associationistic basis of courses of study, textbooks, and unit plans. A teacher's role is to get the responses fixed in students. If, like Thorndike, one defines a habit as a fixed way of responding to a given stimulus situation, then the object of education under S-R associationistic psychology becomes the fixation of as many habits as possible as permanently as possible. Successful teaching of a maximum number of habitual responses seems to require somewhat rigid time scheduling and minimum indulgence of students' natural interests.

Classrooms of teachers educated in associationistic psychology often have the appearance of classrooms of mental disciplinarians. The chief difference, perhaps, is that an associationist includes "practical" subjects, like shop and home economics, whereas a mental disciplinarian, influenced by the classical tradition, stresses subjects like philosophy and classical literature to discipline immature minds.

Cognitive-Field Theory and Intelligence

As stated earlier on pp. 127–128 of Chapter 5, the cognitive-field definition of intelligence is one's capacity for accurate foresight as it is revealed in one's ability to solve problems in areas of concern. This conception of intelligence assumes that problem-solving ability, although influenced by hereditary factors, is susceptible to change in a normal person and can improve through education. If one's education includes not only opportunity for problem solving but also opportunity to study the problem-solving process as a process and to achieve generalized insights about it, most new problems, it is assumed, will be approached more intelligently than they would have been before. As a person acquires more, and more adequate, generalized insights he becomes more intelligent.

Capacity for accurate foresight is closely related to the quality of one's perceptions. We cited in Chapter 5 a highly provocative article on this subject published by Arthur Combs in 1952.[3] Combs begins by stating that there is a growing tendency in psychology to view behavior as a function of perception. Anything which limits the scope and clarity of a person's life space—perceptual field—detracts from his capacity for intelligent action.

At any given time the nature of our perceptions is influenced by certain factors. First, our perceptions are affected by our purposes at the time; what seems relevant one time will be quite irrelevant another. Often we unknowingly distort "what is there" in an attempt to serve our purposes better. Second, there are physiologic limitations to perception. Some of these are not obvious and are difficult to demonstrate—such as differences in the functioning of neural structures in persons who appear physiologically normal. Other physiological differences are obvious: e.g., the near-sightedness of one of the authors often leads to behavior which to an observer appears "stupid." Exhaustion or illness, too, can significantly limit the quality of perception. Third, the range of experience which is represented in a person's life space makes a profound difference in what is perceived. One who lives in a stimulating environment has a great advantage over one who does not.

If Combs' thesis is valid, learning necessarily plays a major role in determining a person's habitual level of intelligence. In fact, the range of intelligence among persons who are not physiologically defective may be

[3] Arthur W. Combs, "Intelligence from a Perceptual Point of View," *Journal of Abnormal and Social Psychology,* July, 1952, pp. 662–673.

explainable largely by differences in learning. At least, we have no conclusive evidence to the contrary. In any case, we now have good reason to believe that virtually everyone can make significant gains in intelligence under the right environmental circumstances. Combs emphasizes the role which our perceptions of self play in intelligent behavior; a person who becomes convinced that he has certain limitations tends to have these limitations, and a self-confident person, in contrast, is likely to perform at an increasingly high level.

Exponents of cognitive-field theory, more than representatives of any other system of modern psychology, have emphasized that capacity for intelligent behavior is modified by learning. Advocates of the cognitive-field position do not like to talk in terms of any limitations of intelligence. For example, Combs and Snygg tell us, ". . . the possibilities for human perception seem almost infinite. Given a healthy physical organism to provide the vehicle for perception, enough time, a stimulating environment, challenging and fruitful problems, and a non-restrictive self concept, there seems no end to the perceptions possible to the individual."[4] Given the proper conditions there is no reason why the intelligence of a person should not increase during his entire lifetime. Of course, old age may produce physiological deterioration which reduces the capacity for differentiating new perceptions. On the other hand, it is possible to cite numerous cases of persons who have retained a remarkable capacity for intellectual growth and creativity until the age of 90 or beyond.

In consideration of the foregoing point of view concerning flexibility of intelligence, a word of caution is necessary. It is by no means easy for a person continuously to improve the number and quality of his perceptions. Although one's perceptual field, or life space, undergoes continuous modification, these changes tend to apply to minor attitudes, values, and beliefs —to items which are not central to one's personality structure. Religious convictions, for example, are not likely to change readily—not, for example, like one's taste in clothing or automobiles. The essential ingredients for continued growth in intelligence are *open-mindedness to new ideas and willingness to criticize one's most cherished convictions.* Since for most persons attainment of these ingredients is very difficult, their intelligence quotients, as revealed by any known measuring device, do not change markedly over the course of time; and in the case of some persons the IQ remains stable, or may even regress. There is reason to suppose, however, that one's degree of open-mindedness and one's ability for self-criticism *are largely a function of his education.*

In discussing intelligence we have said nothing about another dimension of experience—emotion. Faculty psychologists have treated emotional capacities as separate faculties, able to operate quite independently of

[4] Arthur W. Combs and Donald Snygg, *Individual Behavior,* Harper, 1959, p. 216.

other faculties. The faculty of reason, too, was susceptible to independent development; and for reason to function efficiently it must be freed from entanglements with emotion.

Likewise, associationists have tended to separate emotion and thought. They think of all behavior as a product of conditioning. A person could be conditioned, they thought, to be coldly objective when decisions had to be made; or he could be conditioned to make decisions "emotionally." Both of these outlooks can be criticized because of their separation of thinking and feeling (emotion).

To cognitive-field psychologists, thinking never occurs apart from feeling. A person who habitually displays a high level of intelligence experiences emotion as he thinks. Emotion is one aspect of the process we call thinking. Of course, some types of feeling, if experienced with intensity, may hinder rational decision. One of the most common is the fear a person feels when he thinks some aspect of his self is under threat. However, the most careful thought may be accompanied by considerable amounts of fear, discouragement, elation, or other feeling states.

How a teacher conceives the nature of intelligence has great bearing upon how he teaches. Furthermore, whether a teacher is an exponent of mental discipline, natural unfoldment, apperception, S-R associationism, cognitive-field theory, or some combination of these greatly affects how he defines the aims of education, organizes a curriculum, and conducts classes. Most teaching procedures reflect influences of a combination of learning theories. But quite often teachers do not recognize the inconsistencies which their teaching represents. Consequently, there tends to be considerable confusion over the proper relationship of teaching and intelligence.

WHY THE CONFUSION CONCERNING TEACHING AND INTELLIGENCE?

Obviously, there are many contradictions in policies and operations of American education. However, so far as the psychology of teaching and learning is concerned, the one central contradiction is an *incompatible marriage of society-centered, authoritarian traditionalism and child-centered permissiveness.* Traditionalism is an approach to teaching based upon either mind training or the passive assimilation of factual content through drill. Child-centered permissiveness is the approach to teaching based upon giving children free reign to design their own learning activities, with steady emphasis upon self-expression and reliance upon self-control. Child-centered permissiveness considers intelligence innate ability which naturally unfolds as a person develops through successive saltatory stages. Traditional teaching, in contrast, proceeds on the assumption that societal imposition is essential to intellectual growth; minds must be trained, apperceptive masses must be built, or organisms must be conditioned.

In the conflict between *traditionalism and child-centered permissiveness, neither has been able conclusively to win the field. Consequently, as a convenient* modus vivendi *both outlooks have come to be practiced side by side.* A teacher may rely for a while on highly traditional instruction—as if a psychology of learning on which traditionalism is based were valid. After a time he may begin to feel guilty. After all, one's teaching should be up to date! This rationalization is likely to be assisted by the fact that students are becoming restless. So the teacher shifts gears. He assigns handicraft projects and for a few days allows students relatively free expression—as if a psychology of learning upon which free expression is based were also valid. The rub lies in the disharmony of the two psychologies; since they rest on incompatible assumptions about the nature of human beings, they cannot both be valid.

This is not to suggest that students will not learn something under either approach. They possibly may learn equal amounts under both, whether much or little. The point is that the learning process which actually is operating may be quite different from what a teacher assumes it to be; students may be learning things in ways the teacher does not suspect and does not want. The teacher is caught, usually unknowingly, in a situation which he does not understand. What may happen can be illustrated with a concrete example.

How Is Confusion Apparent in Today's Schools?

Mrs. R had taught for 25 years in the same city school system. She was regarded favorably by her administrator and by most of her students. Her areas of specialization were social studies and English.

Mrs. R began a unit pertaining to the geography and the culture of France by assigning the textbook chapter on France. She stressed the importance of memorizing factual details, such as the leading rivers, towns, industries, and seaports. She also told her students that they must learn some of the facts of French history, such as the dates when various heads of government were in office. All of these facts were given in the textbook and in reference books available in the room. At the conclusion of the unit, Mrs. R gave a test consisting of true-false items on the facts.

Daily recitation involved question-and-answer sessions in which Mrs. R asked students to recall facts given in the textbook. On one occasion the class was permitted to play a game. The class was split in half, and the halves took positions on opposite sides of the room. From each group a "questioner" was chosen. His job was to ask questions about France of students in the other group. When a student missed a question, he had to take his seat, as in a spelldown. The questions asked involved highly specific facts of the kind which Mrs. R had stressed as being important.

On two different days students worked at their desks with dittoed sheets supplied by Mrs. R. These were verbatim copies of textbook material, except that two or three words were omitted from each sentence. Blanks were substituted for the words, and students were required to refer to the text and fill in the blanks with the rights words.

In addition to the work in class, Mrs. R assigned each student a project. Projects were to be originated by the students and completed outside of class, with no help from Mrs. R. Mrs. R gave no specifications, except to say that projects must involve some kind of handwork and must bear some relationship to France or French history.

After several rather turbulent days spent in trying to find a project, one of the students, Sally, hit upon the idea of etching a map of France on a piece of plywood with a woodburning set. After etching the map, her plan was to paste pictures on the wood indicating industries or products of particular provinces. Since Sally did not draw well, she persuaded her father to sketch in pencil on the plywood the outline of France, with its rivers, provinces, and major towns. She then selected one of the woodburning styli and began tracing in the sketched map. In the process, she burned a severe blister on one finger. After a number of tearful requests, her father finished tracing the lines on the map with the stylus.

After searching through a good many magazines, Sally discovered that she could not find pictures representing a range of French industries and products. The products portrayed most often were alcoholic beverages— wine, champagne, and brandy. Her father suggested that she confine the pictures to one industry and make use of the pictures of alcoholic beverages.

The teacher accepted the map and gave Sally a mark of B for it. However, when it came time to display the various projects on classroom walls and tables, Mrs. R put Sally's map away in a cupboard. Mrs. R is a teetotaler.

A few months later Sally's father asked Sally what she remembered from her study of France. Her reply was, "I learned that you have to be awfully careful with a woodburning set or you will burn yourself."

The foregoing illustration is reasonably typical of all the units studied in this class during the course of the year. Note that it combined more or less rote fact learning with supposedly free activity. Most of the time the class was fact centered and teacher dominated, but where the projects were involved the teacher veered to a highly permissive approach. Such vacillation between teacher-dominated drill on facts and relatively undirected project work characterizes much of today's teaching.

To summarize, we may say that today's teaching often reflects an incompatible marriage: *the wedding of teacher-dominated drill over highly specific factual material and relatively undirected project work.* It is based on different, and incompatible, psychological assumptions. Now, how has the rise of such self-contradictory teaching occurred and what is to be done about it?

How Has John Dewey Influenced Teaching Practices?

John Dewey generally is considered America's foremost twentieth-century philosopher. His approach to philosophy was unique in that he was convinced that we should be able to validate any tenable philosophical position by placing it in operation in our public schools and reaping beneficial consequences. Dewey's thinking developed at the same time that S-R associationism and Gestalt-field theories were being advanced. Exponents of both schools of psychology have attempted to harmonize their respective theories with Dewey's relativistic philosophy. This practice has given rise to much conflict and confusion and many contradictions in the thinking of modern educators.

Dewey thought that the primary goal of teaching should be improvement of intelligence. Consequently, his psychology placed central emphasis upon teaching students an inclination toward, and the skills necessary for, reflective thinking. Dewey's book *How We Think* reflects his central pedagogical interest. He argued that teachers should stimulate students to think by maneuvering them into problematic, or "forked path" situations. Such situations have the qualities of raising doubts about existing convictions and requiring students to seek alternative solutions, each to be studied on its own merits.

In addition to his positive emphasis on development of capacity for accurate foresight—intelligence—Dewey attacked much of the formalism inherent in both mental discipline and the mental and physical associationisms. He insisted upon treating children kindly, recognizing their interests, and encouraging them to participate actively in the educative process. Because this personal emphasis is stated so strongly in some of Dewey's works, such as *Democracy and Education*, many of his "followers" associate Dewey with those who argue for highly permissive treatment of children. However, careful reading of Dewey, especially of books written during his middle and later years, leads one to conclude that it is a grave mistake to place Dewey among the Roussellians. Dewey's concept of a democratic classroom was not one of laissez faire any more than it was one of cloaked autocracy.

However much quarreling there might be about Dewey's exact position on teacher-student relationships, there is general agreement that his impact served to weaken the arguments of mental disciplinarians and all other formalists. Dewey's philosophy and psychology seemed to demand introduction of much greater flexibility and freedom in classrooms.

It is probably easy to overestimate the immediate influence of Dewey on American education; many classrooms show very little, if any, Dewey influence. Probably one reason is the fact that Dewey's thinking was complex and his writing extraordinarily hard to read. Many "followers" undoubtedly never understood what Dewey meant about some matters. They tended to overemphasize out of all proportion the small streak of Roussellianism which appeared in Dewey's early writing and to ignore Dewey's constant, tough-minded insistence on placing reflective thought at the heart of the educative process. Often they introduced innovations into education which they attributed to Dewey's inspiration but which actually were inspired by educational reformers who preceded Dewey by a long time.

The Progressive Education Association was the chief organization within which contradictions in educational thinking, particularly in regard to the role of schools in relation to intelligence, became apparent.

WHAT WAS THE PROGRESSIVE EDUCATION MOVEMENT?

Progressive Education has deep historical roots in both the United States and Europe. The revolt against what seemed to be mechanical, rote teaching and learning reached such proportions by the time of World War I that the situation was ripe for launching an organized movement for a new kind of education. Hence, the Progressive Education Association was founded in 1919, had its first national conference in 1920, and established its journal, *Progressive Education*, in 1923.

Francis W. Parker often is considered the pioneer of Progressive Education in this country. Parker was director of the Cook County Normal School of Chicago. He urged that his students, as teachers, develop and employ a theory of education along the lines developed by Pestalozzi and Froebel. Parker wanted the native endowments of a child, rather than formal school subjects, made the center of attention in a school. He displayed a reverence for childhood of such magnitude that he could not think in any terms other than those of a child-centered school.

In 1901, a well-to-do admirer of Parker financed a private school in Chicago for implementing Parker's ideas. Over the years, the Francis W. Parker School graduated hundreds of boys and girls. Many of them became distinguished citizens. The school also attracted numerous visitors from this country and abroad. Parker died in 1902.

In 1894 Dewey became head of the Department of Psychology,

Philosophy, and Education at the University of Chicago. In 1896 he established his experimental school, the University Elementary School, at the University. From this time on, he was claimed as the guiding light of the Progressive Education movement. In his book *School and Society* (1899) he advocated introduction of activity programs into schools through which students might learn, through experience, greater freedom of creative expression and attention to social as well as academic aims. However, Dewey did not in this book advocate Roussellian permissivism.

What Were the Key Tenets of Progressive Education?

What did the early Progressives believe? Mr. Cobb has summarized the Progressive creed under 10 major points. He maintains that these 10 points represent principles upon which virtually all Progressives agree; extreme views which reflect personal idiosyncracies are omitted.

1. Health must come first. This principle means much more than the mere promotion of bodily fitness through calisthenics and proper medical care. It means that ". . . the school life from beginning to end should be adapted to the developing nervous system of the child. It means movable seats; more freedom of movement in the classroom; elimination of strain from academic work; abundant handwork and motor-activity of different kinds to balance the head work; avoidance of large classes with their overstimulation for small children; longer recesses and more use of the out-of-doors; and close cooperation between school and home for detection and cure of pathological conditions, whether of body or of mind."[5]

2. Learning comes from doing: let the hands aid the brain. According to this principle, activities should be introduced into all subjects insofar as possible. This means physical activities—work with the hands. Cobb says that this principle is justified because a majority of children in today's world are "motor-active and love doing rather than reading."

3. Classrooms should be freed from unnatural restraints, and "exterior compulsions" should be transformed into "interior compulsions." A great amount of freedom with respect to both the work and general discipline characterizes a Progressive school. Specifically, Cobb says, ". . . The children feel the school to be theirs. They help make the rules which govern their own academic and social conduct. . . . Progressive education introduces into the school life the freedom and democracy which have long since been expressed in political life and which are now manifesting themselves in the home. . . . Children are best behaved when they learn to control themselves. . . ."[6]

4. Education should be adapted to the differences of individual children.

[5] Stanwood Cobb, *The New Leaven,* John Day, 1938, pp. 17–18.
[6] *Ibid.,* p. 19.

Progressive schools, according to Cobb, do not merely allow for differences in personality; they encourage such differences. Such schools continually fight against standardization and conformity. Each child is assumed to be unique and to require unique treatment.

5. Group-consciousness and social-mindedness should be developed in children: social adjustment and character training are as important as academic progress. Progressive schools, as Cobb sees it, de-emphasize competition. Progressive teachers abhor the use of competitive marks and rewards. They seek to develop in children social and cooperative, rather than competitive, aggressive, and exploiting, qualities. To achieve this end, much use is made of group projects.

6. A child should have abundant opportunity for creative expression. "Education should be a process of expression rather than of impression—a natural unfolding of the powers and potentialities of the child." Self-expression calls for much use of the arts, although not in any formalized way: "Expression first, with form subservient to it."

7. A child should be enabled to acquire thorough control of the tools of learning rather than merely to acquire facts. In Progressive schools the emphasis is not on fact learning but rather on the learning of research methods. Children are taught to know how and where to gather required information, and how to use it.

8. The method of creative expression should be introduced into academic work, so that education shall be joyous. Mr. Cobb is not as definite as he might be about what he means here. He suggests that the same principles employed in the teaching of art should be applied to academic subjects "so as to introduce inspiration and creativeness as preliminary to the acquirement of technique by drill." If this is done successfully, children will "work hard" and "accomplish marvels."

9. The tyranny of marks and examinations should be abolished. We shall let Mr. Cobb speak for himself on this point: "Progressive schools do not entirely abolish marks and tests, but use them in such a way as to eliminate strains and anxieties. Progressive educators as a rule use no marks in the classrooms. . . . Children are encouraged to express themselves and to compete, not with other children, but with themselves to surpass their previous records and achievements."[7]

10. The teacher should be a leader and a guide, not a taskmaster. A teacher should be of the "artistic rather than of the bureaucratic temperament." He should have a personality which will permit awakening the creative gifts in children. This means he will be a friendly helpmate who tries to encourage and stimulate. He tries to erase the old-fashioned barriers between teacher and students.

An analytical reader can see a strong element of Roussellian "natural

[7] *Ibid.,* pp. 23–24.

unfoldment" along with a lesser element of authoritarian imposition in these 10 principles. Although Cobb and virtually all other Progressive educators do not advocate turning children loose to do entirely as they please, they reiterate time and again the need to encourage self-expression. Under item 6, Cobb makes the point in typical Roussellian language: "Education should be a process of expression rather than impression—a natural unfolding of the powers and potentialities of the child."

Confusion Within the Progressive Education Movement

One of the few defensible statements which can be made about the Progressive Education movement is that it embraced a diversity of views, united only in that they were all opposed to a mental discipline approach to teaching. The movement represented a revolt against the notions that children are innately bad, that child nature must be remolded, that this can be done only through the stern discipline of rod and unpleasant subject matter. The movement likewise represented a revolt against learning characterized exclusively by drill and rote memorization, or mechanical procedures.

During the early years of the movement, the urge to rebel was so strong in the minds of members of the Association that they failed to see clearly the differences among themselves. The Roussellians, whom some persons have labeled the "super-Progressives," were at the beginning, and remained, perhaps the dominant element in the movement. However, during the 1930s and 1940s an important non-Roussellian segment within the Association began to see clearly the implications of the Roussellian overtones of the movement. This group began to protest and to withdraw support. One of the more important of these critics was Boyd H. Bode, who spent the latter part of his professional life at Ohio State University. In his book *Progressive Education at the Crossroads* Bode attempted to state the crucial issue as he saw it.

Progressives, Bode said, talked and acted as if educators could determine the aims of education merely by studying children. Such study, the Progressives felt, would reveal the needs of children. Reference, of course, is to so-called "child-centered needs"—needs based upon instinctive urges. Once the needs of children were known, a curriculum could be devised to cater to them. Bode countered this view by arguing that needs arise out of interactive situations, and hence neither the social nor the physical environment can be disregarded. No formulation of children's needs is possible apart from a study of the culture in which a child lives.

For example, according to Bode, we live in a culture which is straining to become more democratic and so requires from its members certain kinds of attitudes, values, beliefs, and knowledge. The schools in the United States have an obligation to teach thought patterns compatible with democracy. However, since each person's needs arise from interactive situations, a teacher cannot be guided only by the demands of the culture. Rather, he must study each child in an attempt to see what "needs" arise from the mutual impact of perceptual selves and cultural forces. (The situational concept of needs is described in the last part of Chapter 9.)

Bode did not stop with Dewey's psychological formulations; he developed psychological concepts in his own way, introducing a terminology similar to that used by some of the field psychologists. His over-all point of view, however, is clearly derived from Dewey.

The followers of Dewey, or at least one group of them, irritated by the persistently Roussellian tendencies of other members of the Progressive Education Association, became increasingly intransigent. Ultimately, many of them dissociated themselves entirely from the Progressive Education movement or, if not that, remained as rebels within the ranks. The disharmony within the movement tended to confuse not only the general public but school teachers and administrators as well.

A point of view other than Roussellian unfoldment or that of Dewey could also be detected within the Progressive Education movement, based upon a quite different school of thought in psychology—Thorndikean connectionism. We note in Chapter 2 that Thorndike was extremely influential in teachers' colleges during the 1920s and 1930s. His textbook in educational psychology was the first in its subject to be published in this country and enjoyed nation-wide usage. Although Thorndike's connectionism seems to represent an entirely different theoretical viewpoint from that of either Roussellian or Deweyan psychology, nevertheless it was adopted, at least in part, by numerous persons who identified themselves with Progressive Education. Most of the persons who did this were teachers and administrators without a sophisticated grasp of the ramifications of different psychological viewpoints. Hence, they were unaware that Thorndike's psychology logically calls for an approach to teaching quite incompatible with either the Roussellian or the Deweyan approach. However, a great many professors of education also were not immune to this kind of eclecticism.

For example, William H. Kilpatrick, a well-known figure in the Progressive Education movement, went through stages of promoting a connectionist psychology. Kilpatrick's influential *Foundations of Method* (1926) unequivocably states a Thorndikean connectionist psychology, rooted in the reflex-arc concept. Although Kilpatrick later veered to a configurational psychology of the Gestalt-field pattern, his *Philosophy of Education* (1951) contains a reaffirmation of his debt to Thorndike's laws of learning.[8] Kilpatrick's basic premises appear to be inconsistent. An associationist psychology, such as Thorndike's connectionism, harmonizes

[8] William H. Kilpatrick, *Philosophy of Education*, Macmillan, 1951, pp. 256–257.

with a neutral-passive conception of human nature as developed by John Locke. But when Kilpatrick discusses what part a child is to play in the educative process he usually advocates permissivism. Time after time in his writings he has urged that children be allowed free choice in determining what to do and how to do it. Thus, he seems to assume validity of the Roussellian good-active concept of human nature, which is incompatible with the Lockian view. It should be noted, though, that Kilpatrick is not consistently an advocate of permissivism; at times he says dictation by a teacher is necessary.[9]

One of the slogans popularized by Progressives in education is "Children learn by doing." The implication of this statement seems to be that learning accompanies action—any action. This is the kind of statement which a connectionist or behaviorist, but not a Gestalt-field theorist, would make. To the latter, overt action is not necessary to get change in insight and, in fact, often is not accompanied by learning at all. The "activity programs" which so often characterized curriculums of Progressive schools, as well as the concept of project teaching (as popularized by Kilpatrick), seem much more in the tradition of an associationist psychology than in the Gestalt-field tradition.

What Are the Psychological Implications of Contemporary Educational Procedures?

Although Progressive Education is now virtually defunct as an organized movement (it ceased publication of its journal in the summer of 1958), it has unquestionably been highly influential in American education. Its impact may be observed almost everywhere. However, the movement has not been fully victorious. Almost any school still retains practices that are in keeping with the tenets of mental discipline and apperception. During the 15 years prior to this writing, traditionalism—as exemplified in mental discipline and apperception—even enjoyed a marked upsurge. All the reasons for this are not entirely clear, but one reason would seem to be the generally conservative temper of the country during the period. Another reason was the inadequacy, in the minds of the public, of some of the practices of Progressivism.

Since Progressivism itself is eclectic in its psychological background (a combination of natural unfoldment, Dewey's personal-social psychology, and Thorndike's connectionism) and since traditionalism is also a combination of divergent positions (mental discipline, with both its classical and faculty psychology emphases, and the associationist psychologies)

---

[9] This analysis is supported in Josefa P. Estrada, "A Critical Comparison of the Educational Philosophies of John Dewey and William Heard Kilpatrick," unpublished doctoral dissertation in the School of Education at the University of Kansas, 1958. For a one-chapter analysis of Kilpatrick, see Ernest E. Bayles, *Democratic Educational Theory*, Harper, 1960, Chap. 15.

it is evident that the psychological underpinnings of contemporary educational procedures have been inherently self-contradictory.

Even though the inharmonious elements in present-day educational psychology are not recognized by many persons who are in charge of our schools, steps in the direction of development of an adequate and harmonious psychological basis for education would definitely contribute to the quality of education and a greater enhancement of human intelligence. Perhaps a more adequate psychological basis for teaching is to be achieved through emphasis upon *the method of intelligence.*

WHAT IS THE METHOD OF INTELLIGENCE?

In harmony with cognitive-field psychology, the primary aim of education is *to foster intelligent solution of all manner of problems which confront people.* Schools should give major attention to communicating to students the *method of intelligence* so that they may use it where they will.

It may seem at first glance that this objective of education is just as sweeping, overly general, platitudinous, and meaningless as the high-sounding objectives in the lists which one encounters so often. However, we have already gone a long way in the present book to state in operational terms what it means to behave intelligently. Chapter 12 concludes with a section in which we describe an act of reflection in step-by-step terms and state some of the assumptions governing the reflective process. Later chapters in the present section of the book carry this discussion farther by showing the operations a teacher performs when he promotes reflection. A person who acts reflectively acts intelligently—in fact, for our purposes here we may consider the two terms virtually interchangeable.

To many persons, a single statement of the primary objective of education will seem to by-pass a large number of specific and valid objectives with which schools must be concerned. Surely, it will be argued, a class in say, woodworking must have its own specific objectives and these will differ drastically from the specific objectives of a class in English literature. We grant that this argument can hardly be denied; but our intent here is to focus on an aim of democratic education which applies to any subject field and the achievement of which hinges on a grasp of fundamental psychological principles.

Is Education for Intelligence Too Risky?

This question is likely to inspire the quick retort, "How can a gain in intelligence be risky? Does not the risk lie in a failure to improve intelligence?" The retort usually ignores the full implications of educating for intelligence. In order to make these implications clear, it will be necessary to clarify further and to amplify our definition of intelligence.

Among other things, but perhaps most centrally, intelligent behavior is acting with foresight—that is, with regard to consequences. This implies ability to foresee, to forecast, to see ahead, which is possible only with the aid of experience. Experience gives us generalized insights—general ideas, rules, principles. For example, experience with thunderstorms leads to the generalization that lightning tends to strike high, exposed places. This generalization can be used during future storms to forecast where lightning is most likely to strike. We may then behave intelligently—stay away from high, exposed places if we want to live, or seek such places if we prefer suicide.

So much for how the general principle of foresight works. But there is more to intelligence than this. Certain rules govern the formation of experientially derived generalizations and their application in new situations. They are the rules of the scientific process itself. One rule is that there can be no limitations on the possibilities of a situation: an experience may seem to suggest a rather obvious insight; nevertheless, the insight may be wrong. Of the possible insights suggested during an experience, which is the best? Obviously, it may be a highly unorthodox or socially unpopular one, as is evidenced by the frequency with which, historically, shocking ideas have proved eventually to be the most accurate —or wise (for example, Galileo's hypothesis about the solar system).

If experience is to enhance intelligence, it should be clear that one must approach life situations with an open mind and that the prevailing intellectual climate must permit completely free exploration. There can be no censorship, no tabooed lines of thought. All available pertinent evidence must be regarded as worthy of scrutiny.

Furthermore, there appears to be a correlation between capacity for intelligent behavior and capacity for critical thought. An intelligent person is always something of an iconoclast—he is suspicious of all that is settled and taken for granted. He enjoys examining ideas which frighten persons of lesser intelligence.

Still further, he likes to turn the light of intelligence on any and all areas of life, particularly the "closed areas" (see Chapter 4, pp. 107–108). Also, a positive correlation seems to exist between intelligence and creativeness. An intelligent person tends to get fresh ideas, to think in novel terms. His solutions to problems frequently have an original flavor. The method of intelligence has been designated aptly as "that peculiar species of thought which leads us to *change* our mind."[10]

10 Robinson, *op. cit.*, p. 49. Robinson was one of a group of late nineteenth- and early twentieth-century intellectuals in the United States who were influenced by John Dewey and his psychological conceptions.

To drive our point home, we might illustrate the difference between an intelligent and an unintelligent approach to a specific problem. A few years ago a major controversy raged in the Pacific Northwest over whether the Snake River should be dammed and power installations built by the federal government or by a private power company (the notorious "Hell's Canyon controversy"). The arguments offered in connection with this issue provided excellent examples of intelligent and unintelligent approaches to problem solving. On both sides of the dispute there was name calling and a tendency to impugn the motives of the opposition. This activity was not intelligent because it contributed nothing to a sensible solution of the issue.

The proponents of private development labeled the plan for government development "socialistic." This behavior was unintelligent because it substituted a poorly defined, extraneous issue for the real one, namely, how could people of the Northwest get maximum electric power, flood control, and irrigation at minimum cost. Some of the proponents of government development claimed that those who wanted private development were agents of a private power lobby which was trying to extend its grip over the economy for selfish purposes. This was equally unintelligent behavior, for the same reasons.

Those who approached the problem intelligently kept their sights at all times on the objectives of the project: a combination of cheap power, water for irrigation, and flood control. They then tried to work their way to a conclusion which would be in accord with all the pertinent facts. Necessarily, they drew heavily upon previous experience by studying examples of both public and private river development, comparing the effectiveness of each, and then trying to determine whether factors unique to the northwestern situation would invalidate conclusions drawn from the results of experiments elsewhere. They refused to be sidetracked by ideological issues irrelevant to the main problem. Their approach was flexible and pragmatic. Needless to say, different persons might approach a given problem intelligently and yet come up with different conclusions, as was the case in the Hell's Canyon controversy.

In a school situation, it should not be too difficult for an impartial observer to determine whether a teacher is trying to promote habits of itelligence. Obviously, a teacher who gives his students pat answers which are not to be questioned is not serving the cause of intelligence. Nor is a teacher who refuses students access to relevant categories of facts for fear study of all the facts might lead students to adopt conclusions unsanctioned by the teacher or community. Apparently, in a number of communities, school boards or community pressure groups want students to behave intelligently only in certain "safe" areas and fear the general extension of the method of intelligence.

What Are Some Requirements for Educating for Intelligence?

If he accepts the analysis of cognitive-field psychology on the matter of intelligence, what can a teacher or counselor do to promote intelligence among students? The main avenue for achieving this aim is, of course, reflective teaching and counseling. Specific techniques of reflective teaching are treated in Chapter 18. But reflective teaching by itself may be insufficient. In the case of youngsters with certain types of handicaps, reflective teaching alone may have little effect in enhancing intelligence. Combs and Snygg list several concerns which should be taken into consideration; the following points are suggested by them. (We have added and deleted and take full responsibility for departure from Combs and Snygg's treatment.)

1. Do everything possible to improve students' physical condition. Various studies have shown that improvements in health may lead to marked gains in IQ scores as well as in capacity for steady intellectual growth. Of especial importance is the problem of faulty sensory equipment. The quality of perception is closely related to how well one's senses are functioning. A child with impaired vision or hearing may appear stupid; with the necessary correction, he may make startling gains.

2. Make certain that students have maximum opportunity for achieving new and higher-quality perceptions. Perception occurs only when a meaning is grasped. If a learning situation is meaningless because of its nature, it can hardly be expected to lead to gains in intelligence. We treat the problem of meaning in connection with "understanding level" teaching in Chapter 17. Readers should not underestimate the importance of meaningfulness of experience.

The meaning of course materials may escape some students, not because it would be impossible for them to make sense of the materials, but because anxiety about other matters or distractions of some sort may prevent their giving the necessary attention. Classroom atmosphere itself may interfere with perception. In the now famous experiments of Lewin, Lippitt, and White, it was demonstrated that in the United States either an authoritarian or a laissez-faire classroom is less favorable for effective perception than is a democratic one.

3. The capacity of a person to improve his perceptions may be increased if some of his most pressing goals are met. If a child desires something strongly, he may be able to think only about his want. A child or youth's most urgent wants may involve out-of-school matters over which a school has little control; however, a school may aid a great deal in the satisfaction of certain kinds of wants. For example, a child who is starved for love, prestige, or friendship may find gratification through steps which teachers

or counselors can take; as a result, his ability to perceive in, say, the area of geography may increase.

An excellent example of how satisfaction of a pressing want may improve over-all performance is found in the experience of unmarried and married college students. In study after study it has been demonstrated that typically the work of a college student improves as a result of marriage. Of course, some of the gain is attributable to the increase in his responsibility—his greater need to do well. However, college counselors, on the basis of interviews with students, seem inclined to attribute part of the gain to the simple fact that with marriage satisfaction of a student's heterosexual desires ceases to be a time-consuming distraction.

4. We can help a student achieve more useful perceptions if we stop trying to hand perceptions to him on a platter. Most of the time, as Combs and Snygg put it, "He [the student] is lectured, required, shown, exhorted, and coerced to perceive what someone thinks he should." It would seem that, if a student can be made to feel a problem and if he is then given considerable leeway in exploring solutions, his capacity for achieving new perceptions is greater than if less freedom prevails. The foregoing statement is in no sense advocacy of the ultrapermissive, child-centered approach to education advanced by Roussellians. It means that the more opportunity we can give students for relatively *independent* perceptual situations, the more likely we are to foster intelligence.

5. Schools should do what they can to help children achieve adequate concepts of self. This may well be the most important of the recommendations we can make. To a large degree a person's achievement is limited to what he thinks he can achieve. Virtually everyone eventually develops definite ideas about his limitations. It seems likely that, more often than not, people "sell themselves short." Parents or teachers often act as if they think children are lazy and dull. If this happens frequently enough, children come to accept this evaluation of their abilities. As Combs and Snygg ask, "What differences in the richness and variety of perception might result from a generation of people with 'I can' rather than 'I can't' conceptions of themselves?"

6. Teachers and counselors should make every possible attempt to relieve threat whenever it is suspected that a child is handicapped in his perceptions by it. By "threat" we are not referring necessarily to the threats a teacher might hold over students: "If you don't learn your 6's by Monday, I will keep you after school." Rather, we mean anything in a child's life space which he sees as endangering his self-respect, or the integrity (inner harmony) of the inner-personal area of his life space. The most pressing threats, in this sense, are ideas which appear to jeopardize present self-structure. Awareness of an inconsistency in one's beliefs is

often threatening; in this case, feeling of threat can be relieved only by achieving some reconciliation of the incompatible beliefs.

Obviously, any situation calculated to produce serious reflection contains some degree of threat to established convictions. Otherwise, why bother to reflect? What we are referring to in this section, however, is threat of such magnitude that all a child's efforts must be devoted to combating it. Threat of this kind is often quite irrelevant to the learning task before a child. It may reflect a family situation or inadequate relations with peers. A child who carries too heavy a burden of threat usually displays a rigid, defensive mind-set. He finds it virtually impossible to be open-minded about anything. Chapter 19, on schoolroom "climate making," deals extensively with steps teachers and counselors may take to reduce threat.

HOW CAN SCHOOLS MORE EFFECTIVELY PROMOTE INTELLIGENCE?

Learning situations may be classified according to where they are placed on a continuum which ranges from "thoughtless" to "thoughtful." It is convenient to divide the total range of learning situations, however, into three broad classifications—memory-level, understanding-level, and reflection-level learning.

1. *Memory-level learning.* Memory-level learning is the kind of learning that supposedly leads to committing factual materials to memory and nothing else. We all know how this can be done; it is possible for a person to memorize virtually any type of material, including that which seems quite nonsensical. The more meaningful the material to be learned, the easier it is to memorize. Furthermore, the more meaningful the material learned, the longer it tends to be retained. However, a collection of nonsense syllables might conceivably be remembered for a lifetime if a person had sufficient reason for retaining it.

At first glance, rote-memory learning seems to exemplify the S-R theory of learning; simple linkages are formed between stimuli and responses with no particular thought or purpose involved. A cognitive-field psychologist denies that this is the case. He insists instead that insight of a sort is always present, if anything is learned at all. What characterizes rote learning, to a cognitive-field theorist, is that the insights acquired usually have no significant relationship to the material being studied. However, the learned material is patterned by the learner during the process of his learning it. Even "nonsense syllables," when learned, are not completely nonpatterned.

The capacity to memorize and retain material probably bears no relationship to the capacity for intelligent behavior. Geniuses are notoriously forgetful, although not usually in their areas of major interest. Conversely, a mentally defective person may be highly proficient in memorization. One of the authors once had an opportunity to study a 13-year-old girl with the mental capacity of an imbecile. Polly had a quite brilliant memory of the "shotgun" variety. That is, she memorized indiscriminately anything she heard, and could often repeat verbatim an overheard conversation or a radio newscast after hearing it once. She could recite faultlessly the words of every popular song being broadcast at the time. Nevertheless, Polly's "thought power" was so impaired that if asked to close an outside door of the house she could not tell on which side of the door to stand to avoid shutting herself outdoors.

Every experienced teacher can recall numerous students who developed a considerable capacity to memorize standard curricular materials in most or all school subjects. Such students usually make high marks. However, when put in situations requiring reflection, they may be at a loss. If, occasionally, they take a course from a teacher who employs problem-centered teaching, they may become extremely frustated and do poorly. Conversely, an experienced teacher can recall students whose marks were spotty but who achieved magnificently once they got out of school. There is a fairly good chance that in such cases poor achievement in school is a result of rebellion against required rote memorization.

Memory-level teaching may, of course, contribute indirectly to intelligent behavior. If memorized facts become pertinent on an occasion when a problem requires solving, they contribute to usable background and hence to the effectiveness of the problem solving. However, memorized facts usually contribute little. One reason is that, as already suggested, they tend to be forgotten quickly. Another reason is that a large proportion of the facts memorized in school are irrelevant to future thought needs.

It is no longer a matter for speculation that not much in the way of durable or useful results can be expected from memory-level instruction. Its contribution to intelligent behavior is too unpredictable and undependable for us to set much store by it as a favored instructional procedure. Yet there is no reason to suppose that most teachers are dedicated to any other approach. No matter how much talk is raised against straight memory-level instruction, there are numerous pressures placed on teachers to confine teaching to this level. Furthermore, they may have no vision of anything different. The chance of a prospective teacher's experiencing much instruction in college on a level above sheer memorization is not very great; it would be possible for a person to complete a college education and never once experience a class taught on any other level.

In spite of all the legitimate criticisms we may make of rote memorization, it would be unrealistic to suppose that a teacher can always avoid it. In any ordinary school situation, on occasion even the most imaginative teacher will have no better approach than memory-level teaching. This may occur on days when lack of time has prevented planning anything else. Or it may occur when the teacher does not know how else to handle the material to be covered.

It is perhaps defensible to argue that material which can be treated only on a memory level should not be included in the school curriculum, but for as long as one can see ahead, teachers will be asked to teach subject matter which is difficult to make problem centered or even meaningful. One also can ask, Can the fundamental skills, such as spelling, be taught otherwise than through a process of straight memorization, using drill procedures? Generally speaking, they *can* be taught more efficiently through other procedures. However, much more study will be required to develop procedures for all the fundamental skill subjects which will get us entirely away from memorization by rote.

2. *Understanding-level learning.* The term *understanding* has been used so ambiguously by psychologists and educators that teachers are likely to use it rather glibly, without being able to define it clearly. A teacher may ask his students, "Are you sure you understand this?" and not himself know the meaning of his question. One may be fairly sure his students do not know either.

Although a careful analysis of the nature of understanding must wait until Chapter 17, which is devoted to understanding-level learning, our purposes require a short definition here. A common definition of understanding is "seeing the use to which something may be put." For example, if Johnny knows a use to which he can put his knowledge that Columbus sailed to the West Indies in 1492, we may say that he "understands" the date.

A more sophisticated definition retains the idea of purposeful use but includes another element: the relationship between the general and the particular. A fact or group of facts is said to be understood if their evidential relationship to a principle is seen. That is, if a student sees that a particular fact either supports or casts doubt on some principle, he understands the fact. Likewise, the ability to hypothesize further facts from a principle is evidence of understanding.

Now what is understanding-level teaching? It is teaching that seeks to acquaint students with the relationships between the general and the particular, between principles and solitary facts, and which also shows the uses to which principles may be put. When a teacher tries to teach students *rules* governing the use of, say, subjunctives, he is trying to keep his instruction on an understanding level. If he succeeds, his students will be able to identify cases in which a particular rule applies and use the rule as a guide. We are seeking the same thing when we try to teach rules of spelling, rules for dividing fractions, or rules for repairing a motor. We are likewise operating on the same level when we teach theories in physics, chemistry, or football. (A rule or principle is at the same time a theoretical statement—by definition.)

A contrast may be drawn between understanding-level and memory-level teaching as follows: if understanding-level teaching is successful, students will know, in addition to facts, the principles by which the facts are related; memory-level teaching tends to ignore principles, or at best handles them on such a superficial level that they have no meaning.

From the standpoint of an educational psychologist, understanding-level teaching is much to be preferred over memory-level teaching. In fact, few educational psychologists would settle for anything less. They would argue that much of the inefficiency in education which research has exposed stems from the way most school subjects are organized and presented. Subjects often remain meaningless to students, not because of the intellectual deficiencies of students, but because a human mentality works in such a way that the subjects, *as organized and taught, have little meaning for them.*

Understanding-level teaching gives students a tool for more intelligent behavior. It equips them with generalized insights which can be applied in problematic situations inside and outside of school. It provides them with a mental kit of rules. If the rules learned are the best which are known at the time—by people in a position to have expert knowledge—then students have at least gained something from their education.

By this time readers may have sensed that there is still something lacking. Understanding-level teaching, if it remains merely that, depicts the student as a passive and the teacher as an active agent. A teacher tells, a student listens. Understanding-level teaching may be highly uncritical and authoritarian. The principles taught by the teacher may be wrong— and sometimes are. Understanding-level teaching may lead to more intelligent behavior on the part of a student but it does not carry with it the quality of experience needed to enhance intelligence to the fullest.

3. *Reflection-level learning.* Reflection-level learning leads to understanding, but with reflection the search for understanding is pursued in different fashion from that described in the preceding section. Instead of being given a collection of facts and generalizations by a teacher, students are confronted with something which is unclear or puzzling. Reflective learning may begin with what a student brings with him to school—his own attitudes, beliefs, values, and knowledge. If he can be convinced that there is something seriously inadequate about his present mental furniture, he may be led to reflect. Or reflective learning may begin with some

observed inadequacy in the subject matter: inconsistency, incompleteness, irrelevance, etc. In any case, a problematic situation appears about which a student centers his thinking and research. In the process, he examines facts and generalizations, and, we hope, he tries to seek out new ones.

There are these crucial differences between understanding- and reflection-level teaching: the latter requires more active participation of students, more criticism by them of conventional thinking, and more imagination and creativeness. The classroom atmospheres associated with the two approaches differ markedly. Reflective teaching and learning lead to the development of a classroom atmosphere which is more alive and exciting, more critical and penetrating, more open to fresh and original thinking. However, the type of inquiry pursued in a reflective classroom may be even more rigorous—and more "work producing"—than that pursued in an understanding-level classroom. In contrast a memory-level classroom is easy on everyone, teachers and students alike, unless they are overcome with boredom.

One reason why reflective learning is more consistent with the requirements of intelligent behavior is that intelligence usually implies behavior which is active, exploratory, and original. This is not to suggest that intelligent behavior ignores established facts and ideas. It never cuts completely loose from the past. But it does have a tendency to seek something better than what is commonly accepted.

Many will argue that this chapter states a hopeless ideal. They will insist that an average man is incapable of showing any more intelligence than he now does. This argument can command impressive supporting evidence; after all, what indications are there today that an average adult approaches critical issues intelligently? To all indications, he does not. But at this point we feel impelled to adopt the essential optimism of James Harvey Robinson when he says that the only hope of civilization is the application of human intelligence to the solution of human problems. What other choice do we have except to try this remedy?

BIBLIOGRAPHY

Bayles, Ernest E., *Democratic Educational Theory*, Harper, 1960.
Exploration (in Chap. 15) of the vacillation of some educational progressives between outlooks essentially Roussellian and Thorndikean.

Bode, Boyd H., *Progressive Education at the Crossroads*, Newson, 1938.
An exposition of the inner contradiction within the Progressive Education movement. The harmony of Dewey's and Kilpatrick's views is questioned.

Bronowski, J., *Science and Human Values*, Messner, 1956.
A splendid little book on the philosophy of creativity, democracy, and science. The orientation is relativistic. Relevant here because it defines "scientific" in such broadly humanistic terms that few would object to holding the teaching of a scientific outlook as a central goal of education.

Combs, Arthur W., and Donald Snygg, *Individual Behavior*, Harper, 1959.
Presentation of a comprehensive field psychology in which intelligence is seen as a function of interaction. This popular book has become a standard reference.

Dewey, John, *The Quest for Certainty*, Minton, Balch, 1929.
Dewey's assertion (as elsewhere) that intelligent action is the sole ultimate resource of mankind in every field whatsoever.

Dewey, John, *Experience and Education*, Macmillan, 1956.
A short, lucid book which is steadily relevant to this volume. Dewey explicitly rejects both traditionalism and progressivism in education and urges a third, and distinctively different, course.

Hartmann, George W., *Educational Psychology*, American Book, 1941.
In Chapter 6, "Increasing the Effective Intelligence Level of Individuals and Groups": discussion bearing directly on the thesis of the foregoing chapter, namely, that education designed to raise the level of intelligence is a practicable goal.

Kelley, Earl C., *Education for What Is Real*, Harper, 1947.
A report on experimental work done by Dr. Adelbert Ames of the Hanover Institute on the nature of perception. The findings demonstrate the psychological invalidity of "standard" approaches to education.

Robinson, James Harvey, *The Mind in the Making*, Harper, 1921.
A classic fully as relevant today as when it was published. Perhaps the most forceful plea ever made for educating for intelligence. All prospective teachers should be familiar with this little volume.

Rugg, Harold O., and Ann Shumaker, *The Child-Centered School*, World Book, 1928.
A presentation of the issue of authoritarian vs. laissez-faire vs. democratic learning situations. The authors speak for the latter, but define it to involve less restraint and direction than most present-day democratic teachers would accept.

Washburne, Carleton W., *What Is Progressive Education?* John Day, 1952.
A brief readable statement in defense of Progressive Education. Washburne associates Progressivisim with Dewey and states that Dewey's and Kilpatrick's ideas are in harmony. Today many would dispute these contentions.

Woodring, Paul, *A Fourth of a Nation*, McGraw-Hill, 1957. (See also Woodrings's *New Directions in Teacher Education*, Fund for the Advancement of Education, 1957.)
An effective appraisal of certain contradictions in American education, although Woodring's solutions may be somewhat less than desired.

17

HOW MAY TEACHERS TEACH FOR UNDERSTANDING?

Of the three levels of learning described in the previous chapter, we devote individual chapters to only two: understanding-level and reflection-level learning. Since many teachers have not had a great deal of classroom experience with either understanding- or reflection-level teaching, the procedures involved in each require thorough treatment. To the extent that memory-level learning can ever be justified, the problem of teaching on this level pretty well takes care of itself; a teacher need only teach as he himself usually has been taught.

One reason why teachers have difficulty achieving understanding-level teaching is that even though *understanding* is one of the more common words, it is rarely defined adequately in texts in educational psychology. Also, its everyday meaning, such as is intended when one says, "Yes, I understand you" (that is to say, "I know what you are talking about"), is inadequate for our purposes. Understanding, as a product of the learning process, involves much more.

WHAT IS UNDERSTANDING?

The *American College Dictionary* includes the following definitions of the verb *to understand:* "1. to perceive the meaning of; grasp the idea of; comprehend. 2. to be thoroughly familiar with; apprehend clearly the character or nature of. 3. to comprehend by knowing the meaning of the words employed, as a language. 4. to grasp clearly as a fact, or realize."

A serious student of psychology will be dissatisfied with definitions of this kind. Although helpful to a degree, they are not sufficiently operational. That is, they do not show what a person does, what psychological steps he takes, when he comes to understand something. In the sections to follow, we present two key definitions and then show how they may be combined into one.

Understanding as Seeing Relationships

This definition of understanding is implied in the first category of dictionary definitions. One meaning given in the dictionary for *comprehend* is "to take in or embrace"; the Latin root is *comprehendere*, meaning "to seize." In other words, we have here the idea of reaching out and gathering in individual items. As they are pulled together, they are understood. The definition implies still more, however; it implies inclusion or embracement of a group of particulars under a single overarching idea. If this definition seems too abstruse, perhaps the following illustration will help.

John M. is a beginning teacher. He has had little experience working with children and none with a group as diverse as his sixth-grade class. He notices that some of his students steal and others seem scrupulously honest. Some come to school dirty and unkempt, others are always well washed and well groomed. Some speak ungrammatically, others consistently use "school teachers' English." Some use "dirty language," while others seem to use only language which would be approved in a Sunday school class.

For a long time, these differences in students puzzle John. But as a result of back-to-school nights, occasional contacts in the community with parents, and information received from other teachers, he finds that the habits of his students are very much like those of their parents, or, if not that, like the prevailing pattern of behavior within the socioeconomic group to which the parents belong. John gradually begins to form some generalizations—general ideas—to explain the individual Marys and Jimmys in the class; he restructures his life space.

One of these generalizations is that "Much in the behavior of children can be explained by the nature of the social class into which they are born." Certain corollary generalizations are also helpful: "Almost without exception, 'lower-class' children use 'rough' language." " 'Middle-class' children do not reveal as great an overt interest in sex as do 'lower-class' children." "On the average, 'middle-class' children get better marks than 'lower-class' children."

Note how John M. has changed the way in which he perceives his students. He has come to group or classify students in a more meaningful manner. He understands little Mary better because she is a member of a general classification: lower-middle class, Suburbia, U.S.A. There are other little Marys who exhibit the same habits and who can be placed in the same classification. Because of certain things they have in common, John M. has grouped these students into a "class"; he has "pulled them together." As is illustrated in the foregoing paragraph, he sees each individual child in relation to appropriate generalizations.

Seeing solitary facts in relation to a general principle is the essence of understanding implied by our first definition of the term. Although we are about to suggest that there is significantly more to understanding, teaching probably would be much more effective than it is now if all teachers grasped even this limited definition. Too few teachers realize that any item of factual knowledge is quite meaningless unless students see how it is embraced by a general principle. Every fact must be seen as either supporting or casting doubt upon a principle or it means nothing. Yet entire textbooks have been written which contain little more than "descriptive facts." Teachers often labor away a professional lifetime without trying to teach students the generalizations which would be necessary for them to "pull together" the facts they are required to memorize. One reason why Herbart, in retrospect, appears such a significant figure for his times is that his instructional steps were designed to teach students how to move from individual facts to generalizations (principles) and to use these generalizations to interpret new facts. Herbart's insight concerning the crucial role of generalizations places him far ahead of even many contemporary educators.

Understanding as Seeing the Tool-Use of a Fact

Let us now look at a second definition of understanding. We may say that a person understands something if he sees how that thing can be used to fulfill some goal. (*Thing* is used here in its broadest sense of "any existent"—any object, process, idea, fact, etc.) As soon as a person sees what something is for, he understands it. Of course, the degree of one's understanding is always relative. If I know that a camera takes pictures, I have begun to understand a camera, but, if I am going to use a camera successfully, I need to know the details of its operation. I shall need to know the consequences of using different types of lenses, film emulsions, lighting, and picture compositions.

Note that according to this second definition, *purpose* is always involved in understanding. One has to have a goal, and he must see that which he seeks to understand in relation to that goal. He must see how what he is trying to understand can be made to help in achieving the goal, or how it can be kept from hindering such achievement. It is as important to understand things which get in our way as it is to understand things which help us along. A rattlesnake may be understood as something to be avoided just as a good steak dinner may be understood as something to add savor to life.

This second definition of understanding harmonizes well with the cognitive-field outlook. According to this outlook, each individual, when behaving intelligently, is trying to "size up" his life space in terms of how its various functional regions—parts—can be made better to serve his purposes. The chief of these purposes we labeled in an earlier chapter "maintenance and enhancement of a self," i.e., progressive improvement of a person's ability to structure and use his psychological environment for his own purposes. One continuously experiments in the sense that one tries first one course of action and then another, preserving only those which work. It is from this experimentation that understanding grows. Through experience, the features of each person's environment progressively develop a "pointing quality"—dark clouds "point" to rain, Johnny's outthrust jaw and angry squint "point" to a poke in the jaw for Freddy. This pointing quality which we give to elements of our environment permits us to behave intelligently—we can act with foresight because there are all kinds of signposts along the way. The pointing quality of things tells us the consequences of using them, which is to say, how to use them with maximum effectiveness.

Understanding as Seeing Both Relationships and Tool-Use

It is important to realize that understanding as seeing the relationship between the particular and the general and understanding as seeing the tool-use of things are not incompatible. Not only are they not incompatible; it would appear that, in order to have a fully adequate definition of understanding, we need to incorporate the latter into the former.

Because it ignores the role of purpose, understanding as seeing relationships is not an adequate concept. Suppose one sees the relationship of certain specific facts to the principle of flotation, as we portrayed in the example of a Herbartian lesson plan in Chapter 10 (pp. 250–251). A student reaction to a forced acquaintance with such relationships might simply be, "So what?" and no attempt would be made to delve deeply into the implications of the principle, to remember it for future use, or to transfer it to new situations. In other words, understanding which confines itself to seeing relationships between particulars and a general is a fragile and superficial achievement. But suppose a student is a boat hobbyist. He builds boat models and operates them upon a local lake. He is involved in developing a design and needs to know how much of the boat will be submerged when it is carrying four persons whose average weight is 130 pounds. To this student the principle of flotation, and the concrete facts subsumed under it, will seem of vital importance.

Thus, what we may label "full understanding," "true understanding," or better, perhaps, "functional understanding" is much more likely to occur if a learner, in learning generalizations and the specific facts pertinent to them, sees how some purpose is served thereby. In effect, we cannot divorce the problem of teaching understanding from that of developing motivation.

If understanding is best achieved when we want to use that which is to be understood, it is equally true that when motivation toward understanding is present, what is understood will inevitably consist primarily of principles derived from a pattern of specific facts. We must restate at this point an assertion made in Chapter 12 about the nature of insights. Among other things, it will be recalled, specific insights tend to be generalized. As soon as one achieves an insight the thought comes to mind, "Possibly this idea will work in other—or all—similar situations." The insight's general value is tested through repeated use in similar situations. If it fails to work, it will be discarded as having extremely limited worth. If it seems always to work, it will become a valued possession. Of course, most insights "pan out" in the form of degrees of predictability; they fall somewhere between the two extremes just suggested.

We now have pushed our analysis to the point where we can offer a third definition of understanding. *Understanding occurs when we come to see how to use productively, in ways which we care about, a pattern of general ideas and supporting facts.* This is the definition used throughout the rest of the chapter. Furthermore, when we use the verb *to mean* and the noun *meaning,* we intend them as equivalent to "to understand" and "understanding."

Understanding as a Noun

So far we have been discussing what the verb *to understand* means. In the literature of education, we also regularly encounter the noun *understanding* or *understandings*. The noun form refers to the *product* of acts of understanding. We go through an experimental process of trying to see how certain relationships may be put to use. We find a relationship between something done and the consequences of doing it. This is our understanding.

An understanding is a generalized insight. Often it may be put into words but not always. The understandings a person achieves about a golf swing, jumping the high hurdles, or casting a fly may lie, in part, in a "feel for the act" which would be difficult to verbalize. On the other hand, most persons who have thought about such achievements are able to make statements about the probable consequences of approaching them in alternative ways. Other names for generalized insights are *general ideas, concepts, principles, rules, laws, generalizations, and theories.*

A word of warning about the use of the word *generalization* is in order. Whenever we use the word in this book it is used synonymously with generalized insight. However, generalization often refers to a "sloppy" statement—a statement based on inadequate evidence. For example, "You are only generalizing" sometimes means that we should not take the statements seriously. This is a very imprecise use of language which students should guard against. What people really mean by such statements is not that a person has "generalized" but rather that he has been merely vague or unclear. Since generalization is the only possible basis for intelligent behavior, the highest possible quality of generalization should be demanded in all situations.

Much has been written about teaching for understanding, but unfortunately many teachers and administrators do not seem to understand the basic psychological problems involved. "Understandings" have all too often been regarded as prefabricated concepts to be poured into students by teachers and textbook writers. Of the various educators whose primary interest has been teaching for understanding, Henry C. Morrison (1871–1945), a professor of education at the University of Chicago from 1919 to 1937, probably has made the greatest contribution. Much of the following section is devoted to Morrison's ideas and to an analysis of how they compare or contrast with others appearing in this book.

WHAT ARE MORRISON'S IDEAS CONCERNING TEACHING FOR UNDERSTANDING?

Morrison appears to have been a latter-day Herbartian. However, his ideas represent considerable refinement over those of Herbart. His psychology basically is an *idea-centered associationism* with considerable sophistication. He retained the Herbartian terms *apperception* and *apperceptive mass,* but the steps of the teaching-learning process which he envisioned are not precisely the same as Herbart's, and his conception of the learning process, as such, is much more advanced.

The Nature of Learning According to Morrison

Within an idea-centered frame of reference Morrison describes various types of learning, including conditioning, "bonding," and trial and error.[1] However, the kind of learning he felt schools should promote is not any form of conditioning but a special form of what he referred to as

[1] Henry C. Morrison, *Basic Principles in Education,* Houghton Mifflin, 1934, Chap. 4.

personality adaptation. This seems to place him in the camp of the eclectics. He borrowed freely from various schools of thought, yet to call him an eclectic would be an oversimplification. Through emphasis upon *personality adaptation,* to some degree he developed a synthesis of prevailing outlooks on learning.

Biological adaptation in its most general sense means both a process and a product. The process occurs whenever an organism achieves a better adjustment to the conditions of life. The adjustment itself may be called an adaptation—a change in an organism which throughout the future will enable it to cope with its environment more effectively. Adaptations may be in both structure and function. An animal's eye is a marvelous example of a structural adaptation. Structural adaptations tend to make functional adaptations easier. The latter are changes in behavior, either instinctive or learned, which help an organism cope better with its environment.

According to Morrison, each of the various types of learning is an adaptive mechanism. But remember that Morrison was interested primarily in human beings and their formal education. He felt that it is the business of teachers to produce in students a special kind of adaptation. Here we must distinguish between what he called an adaptive response and true adaptation. An adaptive response is a habit learned more or less by rote which its bearer does not understand and therefore uses blindly. Morrison thought that much human behavior is on this level. But he deplored any kind of teaching which leaves students only with adaptive responses instead of personality adaptations.

The proper task for education, said Morrison, is the creation of true adaptation, which is a *permanent change in outlook.* Or, put in language which Morrison frequently used, it is *personality change.* He was using the term *personality* to mean a total person in its psychological and sociological sense, not to indicate those superficial aspects of a person's make-up which we sometimes signify when we say, "John has a nice personality." Specifically, Morrison said personality is the "sum total of what an individual has come to be by learning the cultural products of social evolution."[2]

Adaptive responses, as just defined, do not involve true learning but rather only pseudo learning. In Morrison's words,

All down through the ages, from Greek times at least and probably earlier, the one consistent meaning found in the writings of those who have been and are trying to think straight about the matter [i.e., what learning is] is the notion that *learning is becoming* and that the product is a new birth in the individual, a changed point of view, a new taste or set of values, a new inward ability. . . .

[2] *Ibid.,* p. 39.

Thus, *every step in the development process for which we use the term education is a piece of learning, or a learning product, and the learning process is the change in personality which constitutes a new insight, or sense of value, or ability.*[3]

Evidently the kind of learning Morrison envisioned is quite similar to the gaining of generalized insight, as it is described in Chapter 12. Although Morrison's theory of learning is not the same as that implied by cognitive-field theory, it is clear that he did regard learning as insightful. In fact, he uses the term *insight* with some frequency (as, for example, in the second paragraph quoted above).

We offer one more relevant quotation:

. . . learnings are always in the nature of new points of view or else acquired capacities for getting experience and reacting adaptively to external circumstances. They may involve knowledge and sundry arts, but it is what comes out of knowledge and the arts that counts.

They are not primarily content in memory, albeit the circumstances under which they are acquired are as truly a part of the memory system as are any other experiences. They are in memory because they have figured in experience; they are not learnings merely because they are a part of memory. Hence, learnings are not information, but rather in part what may have arisen out of information.

They are not acquired adaptive responses, but every true learning makes possible innumerable adaptive responses, as experience of life varies. . . .

They are not habits, although habits may arise out of personal learnings and be controlled by the latter. Nor are they conditioned responses, which are organic and the very opposite of personal learnings.[4]

One of Morrison's key contentions has met with considerable objection. It is that true learning results in permanent learning products—that is, when true learning has occurred the consequences are never lost. "The ultimate test of a product of learning which has involved a genuine adaptation is that it is not lost, otherwise than through its transformation into new adaptations or through the rise of pathological inhibitions. It is never lost by simply fading out."[5] This view of the permanence of learning harmonizes with the thinking of most contemporary Gestalt-field psychologists. Furthermore, it contrasts with the view of most S-R associationists, who hold that the product of learning is conditioned actions which tend to disappear when they are practiced and not reinforced (the process of "extinction"). Morrison would say that a learning which has to be reinforced to prevent its extinction was not a real learning in the first place.

[3] *Ibid.*, p. 38.
[4] *Ibid.*, pp. 239–240.
[5] Henry C. Morrison, *The Practice of Teaching in the Secondary School*, University of Chicago Press, 1931, pp. 21–22.

Let us see how these ideas might apply to some common school practices. If a student is able to pass an examination at the end of a course, most teachers would say he has learned something. If he makes a perfect score on the examination, they would say he has learned a great deal and they would be delighted at their own effectiveness and at the student's capacity and diligence. However, it is almost always the case that if a student takes the same examination a year later he will do poorly on it; 10 years later he probably will fail it miserably. What is the usual interpretation? Most teachers and administrators take this outcome for granted. They say it is to be expected that much learning will be forgotten.

In contrast, Morrison and many contemporary psychologists would say that a student actually learned little, if anything, in such a process. Morrison stated repeatedly that it is possible for students, in spite of high grades and "graduation with honors," to go all the way through school without really learning anything which was intended. He personally felt that no more than about 10 percent of students achieve much true learning from their school courses; and those who do, achieve it in spite of their teachers and textbooks rather than because of them.

According to Morrison, ability to transfer learning is as important a test of its presence as is permanence. Unless what one has gained in school is used habitually in the ordinary activities of life, nothing was gained in the first place. We can evaluate the amount of transfer which has occurred by asking questions such as these:

Does he [i.e., the typical "educated" person] accept the ordinary cant of the day as his opinion? Most people do. Or does he critically examine the facts, apply the principles which he is supposed to have learned in school, and render an opinion in which all reasonable educated persons must concur? Does he hold opinions on all subjects under the sun, as the illiterate is prone to do, or does he distinguish between those fields in which he is entitled to hold opinions and those in which he can have no possible basis for opinion? If he has been credited with certain courses in economics, does he apply economic thinking to the interpretation of commercial situations in which he finds himself, and to the decision which he makes when he votes for a new tax, or does he live the life of the economic opportunist? If he has been credited with certain courses in English literature, are his attainments reflected in his choice of cultural reading or does he solace his leisure exclusively with the Sunday newspaper and the ephemeral story of the day? . . .[6]

If we grant Morrison's conception of the process of learning, we must also concede that once true learning has occurred it will be retained and it will transfer. This is the case because Morrison sees true learning as a remaking of a personality, as a change of insight which leaves a person forever changed. Let us next explore in more detail what a person achieves when he gains true learning.

[6] *Ibid.*, p. 31.

Morrison's Concept of Understanding

To be able to recall something does not mean to understand it. Often just the contrary is the case. A person might be a "walking encyclopedia" and not understand any of the vast content of his memory. Morrison distinguished sharply between education and erudition. People, he observed, typically have held that "knowledge and information are synonymous with education, that the more an individual knows in the sense of erudition the better educated he is."[7] He then took several pages to scoff at this point of view, ending his criticism with the observation that the confusion between education and information-collecting leads schools to try merely to inform students instead of giving them the "insights upon which intelligence is founded."[8]

What are these insights, or understandings, with which Morrison was concerned? To him, understandings were generalizations, rules, principles, concepts—whatever we choose to call them. They suggested an "if-then" relationship—if I perform action A, then action B is likely to follow. Morrison clarified his position with an illustration of how a person might come to understand the function of valves in a pump. In ordinary instructional practice, a student might be asked to memorize the location of valves in a particular pump. But this is not understanding; "all pumps are not alike." To achieve understanding, a student must learn the principles governing operation of valves. If he knows what valves do— not in one pump but in all pumps—he will understand the valves, no matter what kind of pump is involved. When he is confronted with a pump situation and asked to describe action of valves, what he then does is not a matter of recall but one of prediction.

In this pump-valve situation we have almost all the elements of understanding, as set forth earlier in the chapter. We have particulars—facts— in the form of specific pumps with specific valve arrangements. But the specifics are made meaningful by generalizations or principles. Furthermore, the principles sought are cause-effect relationships. They describe the habitual consequences of a given action. Thus, an understanding is not only a generalization adduced from specific facts, but insight into how it may be used in future situations.

Morrison interpreted the role of motivation in a fashion different from that of contemporary field psychologists. He appears to have assumed that students will understand the operation of valves just as well whether or not they lack a feeling of personal involvement with valves. However, it seems reasonable to suppose that a generalization is always more meaningful, and hence more useful, if a learner feels a personal urge to master

[7] Morrison, *Basic Principles*, p. 338.
[8] *Ibid.*, p. 340.

it. It is difficult—perhaps often impossible—to teach children to understand something about which they do not care. Morrison took care of the problem of motivation—to his own satisfaction—by suggesting that learning on an understanding level, as contrasted to memory-level learning, tends to generate its own appeal. No doubt there is an element of truth in this, but motivation is not something which can be taken for granted.

Nonteachable Subject Matter

Since it is impossible to deduce principles or rules from some kinds of subject matter, such as most collections of "descriptive facts," evidently some kinds of subject matter never can be understood. Such subject matter is intrinsically lacking in any basis for understanding—in other words, it is inherently meaningless. Morrison refers to such subject matter as "non-teachable material" and cites examples in textbooks. He has this to say, for example, about some history textbooks:

> Perhaps the most striking example of non-teachable material is to be found in the older texts in history. Nearly all of them were made up of this sort of content from beginning to end. They were chronicles of a meager sort but not histories. They recorded events in chronological order of occurrence, but they failed utterly as a class to interpret the past as an intelligible evolutionary process. *There was nothing to be learned because there was nothing to be understood.*[9]

Perhaps Morrison is unnecessarily kind when he says "older texts." Within a frame of reference of teaching for understanding many of the newer texts in history are also largely unteachable, as are many newer texts in other fields. Furthermore, the psychology of meaning has been so poorly understood by teachers and administrators that they find it difficult to judge whether text or other material is teachable. Consequently, our schools have spent a substantial amount of time, and continue doing so, trying to teach children that which cannot be taught.

Morrison's Recommended Teaching Procedure

Fundamental to comprehension of Morrison's teaching procedure is an understanding of his concept *mastery*. The outcome of all teaching is mastery—not mere memorization of facts, but mastery. Mastery is reached only when planned understandings have been grasped thoroughly. An understanding, as we have seen, is a generalization seen in relation to the pertinent facts and to the uses to which it might be put.

Each subject field, according to Morrison, is to be divided into units. Each unit should present a specific understanding with such thoroughness that mastery is achieved by most students. Note that Morrison did not

[9] *The Practice of Teaching in the Secondary School*, p. 101. (Italics ours.)

mean by a "unit" what is commonly meant today. In contemporary parlance, a unit usually is a block of work which, to a teacher or textbook writer, comprises a logical work task. A unit, therefore, is typically conceived as simply a piece of work, based upon a certain quantity of related facts in a textbook or other source. Morrison's conception of a unit of work was *psychological*. To him, a unit was a generalization and its related facts, *as a student should come to see them*. A unit was never "covered" until all or almost all students thoroughly understood the generalization—its origins in fact, its probable reliability, and the kinds of situations in which it could be used in the future.

Some subjects contain many units, each of which may be grasped by most students in a fairly short time (as algebra). Others contain only one unit, i.e., the whole subject must be mastered before a student has anything worth while (as a foreign language). The point is, a unit represents an insight which is relatively complete in itself. This insight may be relatively simple and readily grasped, or it may require years of study. Hence, a unit, as Morrison conceives it, may require anywhere from a class period to many years to be mastered.

Each unit is developed according to a sequence of steps, which, although Morrison disclaimed their relationship to the famous five steps of the Herbartian method, are nevertheless reminiscent of the Herbartian steps. The steps, as Morrison described them for a "science type" unit, are *exploration, presentation, assimilation, organization,* and *recitation*.

1. *Exploration.* This is the process of determining what students already know about the understanding which the unit is intended to convey. It involves testing, questioning, or discussion. Its purpose is to promote economy; it helps a teacher know when not to reteach a subject because it is already understood, and when not to waste the time of students by launching into a subject for which they do not have necessary background. Exploration also develops what Morrison called "apperceptive sequence." Students review what they know, discover how it is inadequate, and contemplate the kinds of knowledge which would fill in the gaps. Exploration is intended to help students arrange subject matter, not in a "logical" sequence as viewed by a teacher or textbook writer, but rather in a "psychological" sequence, one which makes sense to students. A third role of exploration is orientation of the teacher. Exploration should give a teacher a sense of direction in determining how a new unit is to be approached.

2. *Presentation.* In this step the teacher presents the new material in a brief form, i.e., he hits the high spots, through informal explanation during which he attempts to maintain continuous rapport with the class. Detailed content, for the time being, is ignored. Following the presentation, the teacher tests students to see how many failed to grasp the

material presented. If necessary, the presentation is repeated. *The point is, at no place along the way does the teacher go on to a new step until all or most students fully understand what they have covered up to then.* Sometimes it may be beneficial to re-present material as many as three times.

3. *Assimilation.* After a student has successfully passed the presentation test, he moves to assimilation. In this step he incorporates the new unit into "that complex of attitudes toward the world which constitutes his intellectual self. In brief, he makes the new understanding his own by prolonged contact with the assimilative material."[10] Morrison implied that the key here is thoroughness of study. Study materials are comprehensive; in fact, everything pertinent and available is brought into the picture. A textbook alone rarely is enough.

During the assimilation period, students do much work at their desks (or, preferably, study tables); however, trips to the library or elsewhere for source materials are not precluded. A classroom is equipped as a laboratory with necessary study materials close at hand. Field trips or resource persons from outside may be used to supplement the assimilative material of the classroom.

The work of students is highly individualized. Each works at his own rate. Those who achieve mastery of a unit early may be permitted to do voluntary projects, to work on other courses, or to do free reading. The teacher circulates around the room giving help as needed. As Morrison described it, the atmosphere seems very much like that of a scientific laboratory whose head scientist is the teacher. The teacher asks many questions of individual students in an effort to clarify their thinking and as a check on their progress. Occasionally, so many students will appear troubled by a single point that the teacher stops his individualized tutoring and makes an explanation before the entire group.

The assimilation period basically is a time of supervised study; however, it is a special kind of such study. Both teacher and students are more active than is the case in a traditionally supervised study period during which the teacher sits at his desk grading papers and students work on anything they wish—or nothing. According to Morrison's conception of supervised study, the level of interaction between teacher and pupils is high. Such a period is very much *alive.*

The fundamental object of the assimilation period is for students to see numerous particulars in relation to the generalization on which the unit is based. The teacher continually pushes students in this direction. One test of whether facts have been generalized is to determine whether students are applying the generalizations in other situations—in other classes and outside school. If teachers are to know how much transfer is oc-

[10] *Ibid.,* p. 282.

curring, they need to be in close consultation with one another and in close contact with the community.

Each unit of work—Morrison's mastery unit—must have a teaching structure, that is, an organization to provide apperceptive sequence. Morrison recommended use of guide sheets. Some textbooks are themselves so constructed that they can serve as guide sheets. But most are not, and in these cases teachers must make their own. Guide sheets usually will refer students to a variety of books in addition to the text. What, basically, is a guide sheet? In Morrison's words, ". . . the guide sheet is a series of problems focused upon the several elements in succession and upon the unit as a whole, that is to say, so chosen that the solution of each is a bit of practice in thinking out the unit [of] learning. Necessarily, each problem is an application of the principle or principles being learned."[11]

In examples given by Morrison, each guide sheet begins with a reference to the understanding (generalization or principle) upon which the unit is centered, then poses a series of situations in which students are to apply the understanding. These situations are all practical in the sense that they could actually arise in connection with either other school classes or out-of-school events. Morrison referred to his guide sheets as "problem-centered" and as calling for "reflective thinking." However, we shall see later that problem-centeredness and reflection, in their truest sense, involve more than Morrison envisioned.

The culmination of each unit for a student consists of his taking, and successfully passing, a "mastery test." A mastery test focuses directly on the understandings sought. It is not a test of factual recall. Rather, it measures how well students have grasped the understandings, usually by requiring some kind of application of principles to new situations. Any student who is unable to achieve a near perfect score on the test simply has not mastered the unit. Those who do perform capably are assumed to have mastered the unit and are ready to move on to the next. Those who do not must continue the unit until they can score sufficiently high on the mastery test. If some students never manage to score appropriately on the mastery test, it must be assumed that they do not have the background for the unit. These cases must be studied individually to determine where each student needs to be "restarted." They will be given remedial work until they are ready to retry the unit with a fair chance of success.

4. *Organization.* When a student passes a mastery test and thus terminates a period of assimilation, the next step is to determine whether he can reproduce the essentials of the unit in writing without any help whatsoever from books, notes, charts, or teacher. Morrison referred to

[11] *Ibid.*, p. 305.

this written reproduction of the unit as the *period of organization*. He commented that "The final step in the mastery of any understanding is taken when we 'write ourselves clear-headed' about it." He suggested that the written reproduction of a unit be in outline form and focus on the logical argumentation supporting the understanding sought in the unit. Uniformity of outlines among students is not to be anticipated, but it is expected that the outlines will demonstrate a sound grasp of the understanding. Some students will find it necessary to rework their outlines several times.

To put a line of argumentation supporting a principle into outline form is not easy for most students. Morrison felt that students are not ready to begin such a process until the fourth grade, and that not until they reach junior high school are they able to do a passable job on the first attempt without help.

The step of organization is especially essential in subjects of extensive content, i.e., subjects which embrace a large number of elements in one learning unit. In certain other subjects, such as arithmetic, mathematics, and grammar, written reproduction of a unit tends to be pointless. Hence students can move directly from assimilation to the last step, *recitation*.

5. *Recitation*. Recitation is pretty much the reverse of the first step, presentation: now each student presents orally to the teacher and his classmates a condensed version of the understanding taught in the unit. Note that the step of recitation, in Morrison's plan, is mastery recitation; it bears little resemblance to routine daily recitations which one encounters so often in classrooms. In a traditional daily recitation, students reproduce some fragment of a meager textbook account which was assigned them the day before. They cannot possibly have much understanding of the material. Largely memory-level learning is involved. In contrast, recitation in a mastery unit is the culmination of thorough study which has led to permanent insights; students who have covered the unit successfully can therefore rise to their feet and "know whereof they speak." When students recite they may use the blackboard or demonstration apparatus. They also may use notes if they wish—their own, of course.

Morrison pointed out that neither organization nor recitation should be regarded as a "test." The crucial test is the written mastery test at the end of the assimilation period. It is hard for us to believe, however, that the steps of organization and recitation would never provide worth-while additional evidence of whether mastery had actually been achieved. Morrison did say that these two final steps should be kept short; they represent summarization, not full reproduction of the assimilation process.

Recitation may take the form of a written paper. In this case, what is written is distinctively different from what was written during the step of organization. Organization requires outline form; its purpose is to help students, on their own, to see the unit "whole" or arrange its elements sensibly. Written recitation may resemble a short book chapter or journal article. Or, to keep it informal, it might be in the form of a letter to a friend. To economize on class time and prevent boredom, often it is well to require only a few students to make oral presentations and the remainder of the class to submit papers.

Some General Considerations

One of Morrison's major emphases was on unrestricted thoroughness. A teacher obviously cannot say in advance how much time a mastery unit will take; it will take whatever time is required to get the class through the mastery test with scores approaching perfect, plus a few days more for organization and recitation. True learning which results in personality adaptations simply cannot be fitted to a time schedule. After deploring attempts by administrators to attach a time allocation to every item in the curriculum, Morrison says,

> . . . the learning process refuses to be constrained in any such artificial fashion. Water will not run up hill merely because we wish it would do so. A given series of essential learnings is not necessarily acquired in a given restricted time merely because such would be administratively convenient. The constant is the learning; the variable is the time required. The emergence of the adaptations in personality which constitute education, and which severally are the objectives of teaching, is a lengthy growth process. . . .[12]

Most teachers feel constant pressure to "move along" in order to have the textbook or course of study "covered" by the end of a semester. One of the authors recalls visiting a student teacher a few years ago. The class was American history. In a single 50-minute class period the student teacher made mention of more than 30 separate facts, any one of which, to have been given real meaning (if indeed such were possible at all) would have required one or more class periods. When the author criticized the student teacher he was told, "I had to do it. My supervising teacher insists that we treat everything in the book, it is May already, and we have five more chapters to cover." It was improper to be harsh with the supervising teacher because he in turn was under pressure by his department head to "finish" the book, and the department head was under instructions from the principal to see to it that all his teachers "finished the course."

A teacher's trying to operate on a predetermined time schedule almost inevitably leads to what Morrison called "lesson learning," "lesson reciting," and "lesson testing." Lesson learning is reading an assignment and

[12] *Ibid.*, p. 69.

memorizing as much of it as possible in the available time. Lesson reciting is saying it back to the teacher. Lesson testing is testing to determine how much of the lesson remains in memory after a certain length of time. This is what some persons have called "learning by rote," but if we accept Morrison's definition, it should not be dignified by the name *learning* at all.

Morrison stressed the notion that one may demonstrate observable progress toward what appears to be a learning goal without achieving true learning. Students can go through the motions but remain quite unchanged inwardly. When rigid time scheduling becomes a part of curricular planning, performance may seem rather impressive because students appear to get "a lot done"—make many moves. But this is performance—overt behavior—and not learning. Changes in observable behavior and changes in insight are not synonymous.

The answer to the dilemma posed by time scheduling would seem to lie in trimming curriculums drastically. In a typical public school, at any grade level, we often try to cover entirely too many topics. We bombard students with content, making little distinction between essential and superficial matters. Morrison suggested, "It is no doubt true that the full period of schooling must be carried out within the years during which young people are growing to physical maturity, and there is much to be learned, but that properly implies the reduction of the program of studies to the learnings which are essential in the fundamental structure of the civilized personality and which govern the great mass of learnings which every individual acquires independently of schooling."[13] He then went on to say that, in building a curriculum, the first thing to do is determine which learnings are absolutely essential and then assign to each however much time is necessary to teach it on a mastery level. If there is time left, other less essential learnings may be added.

It would be unrealistic indeed to suppose that curriculums will be easily reduced to a level where much true learning will occur. Too many vested interests are involved, and, unfortunately, many people with vested interests know so little about the learning process that they do not realize how today's crowded curriculums obstruct occurrence of much genuine learning. For example, in most states it is written into state law that students be instructed in the effects of alcohol and narcotics. Typically, units designed to meet this requirement extend from one to five days. How would it ever be possible to produce fundamental changes in students' attitudes in one, or even five, 50-minute periods? Nevertheless, with no consideration of the implications of an adequate psychology of learning, numerous topics have been placed in curriculums by various legislative bodies.

[13] *Ibid.,* p. 70.

Not only state legislatures but also state departments or boards of education, or state superintendents, usually have authority to spell out topics to be included in a public school curriculum. Typically, they use this authority quite freely even to the point of listing topics which must be included in a given course. Add to this the fact that local interests always can suggest new courses to offer and additional topics for present courses, and it is understandable why principals and teachers feel constant pressure to add to schools' offerings without corresponding freedom to delete. *Only when teachers, administrators, and the public generally come to understand that you can't really teach anything if you try to teach everything will the situation be remedied.*

HOW ARE WE TO EVALUATE MORRISON?

The Morrison approach has certain weaknesses as well as certain strengths. Morrison's leading weakness was his apparent failure to pay due attention to purpose in human behavior. He largely disregarded the fact that man is, first and foremost, a goal-seeking individual. This attitude probably was a consequence of his attachment to an associationist psychology. The idea that teachers should motivate students through promoting their personal involvement with the subject matter, and the desirability of doing this, seems not to have occurred to Morrison. In spite of the strong merits of his whole approach, it would be even more effective if it provided a greater place for the psychology of motivation.

Even though Morrison talked of reflection by students, his recommended procedure does not appear designed to lead to genuine reflection. The Morrison system does not offer or permit student choices. Students are given learning materials with which they wrestle until they understand the key principles. This is not the same as helping students weigh contradictory or contrasting ideas and gradually evolve answers to questions which, so far as the students are concerned, had no answers at the beginning of study. *Whereas reflective teaching focuses on issues, Morrison's units centered on answers.* Thus, Morrison seems to have had nothing to say about the role of issues in the teaching-learning process.

Although, in the modern sense of the term, Morrison's mastery approach is not reflective, it has much to commend it. In many situations teachers find it impossible to use a reflective approach—either they don't see how it can be done, or they do not have the background, time, or skill in discussion leadership to make it work. In all these situations, Morrison's ideas can serve as a source of direction.

The idea of *mastery teaching*, with its emphasis on students' relating individual facts to principles and its attention to thoroughness, represents a vast improvement over much of the instruction now given in our public schools. Instruction often tends to be extremely superficial—to hop, skip, and jump over subjects of vital importance. To achieve any significant improvement, teachers must be convinced of the validity of the mastery idea and administrators must be convinced that rigid time scheduling of a curriculum may gravely interfere with learning. Some time scheduling there must be, but administrators could grant teachers far more autonomy than they now have concerning what should be included in a given course and the time which should be spent on each item.

The next chapter, on reflective teaching and learning, assumes as largely valid many of Morrison's ideas: the nature of understanding (with some qualification, as stated on p. 444), the insightful character of learning, and the need for thoroughness if anything is to be learned at all. But it adds two more ingredients to the teaching-learning process: reflection, as it is defined in Chapter 12, and a possible solution to the problem of motivation.

BIBLIOGRAPHY

Bruner, Jerome S., *The Process of Education*, Harvard University Press, 1960.
    The chairman's report of the major themes, principal conjectures, and most striking tentative conclusions of a 1959 conference of 35 natural scientists, psychologists, and educators on teaching science and mathematics in elementary and secondary schools. The report emphasizes teaching for understanding the *structure*—pertinent relationships—of a subject matter rather than for mastery of facts and techniques.

Bruner, Jerome S., and others, *A Study of Thinking*, Wiley, 1956.
    A study based on research carried on at the Institute for Advanced Study (Princeton) and at Harvard. Focuses on the formation and use of concepts. Technical, but an average student can read the introduction with profit. "Anticipatory categorizing" is "understanding" as we define it in the foregoing chapter.

Kecskemeti, Paul, *Meaning, Communication, and Value*, University of Chicago Press, 1952.
    A highly sophisticated and difficult book from which advanced students may get some value. The author is familiar with a field approach, but his treatment appears eclectic.

Morris, Charles, *Signs, Language, and Behavior*, Prentice-Hall, 1946.
    On p. 19: a statement on meaning worth pondering.

Morrison, Henry C., *The Practice of Teaching in the Secondary School*, University of Chicago Press, 1932.
    Morrison's theory of education, with a detailed statement of his idea of the "mastery unit."

Morrison, Henry C., *Basic Principles in Education*, Houghton Mifflin, 1934.
    The bases of Morrison's theory of teaching and learning. See Chapter 4 for his concept of adaptation—learning with understanding but not reflection.
Ogden, C. K., and I. A. Richards, *The Meaning of Meaning* (London), Routledge & K. Paul, 1949.
    A classic but somewhat obsolete because of advances in the psychology of perception.
Osgood, Charles E., and others, *The Measurement of Meaning*, University of Illinois Press, 1957.
    Technical, but provocative. Chapter 1 contains a section entitled "Meanings of 'Meaning.'"
Reichenbach, Hans, *The Rise of Scientific Philosophy*, University of California Press, 1951.
    In Chapter 2: a stimulating and readable discussion on the role in thought of generalization.
Ushenko, Andrew, *The Field Theory of Meaning*, University of Michigan Press, 1958.
    A highly technical discussion which attempts to harmonize the theory of meaning with field psychology. For advanced students.

18

HOW MAY TEACHERS TEACH REFLECTIVELY?

What distinguishes reflective from nonreflective teaching and learning is the presence of a problem which students feel a need to solve. At the outset of a study, a real question develops for which they have no answer, or at least no adequate one. Because problems play a central role, this approach often has been called problem-centered teaching. The accompanying learning process is problem-centered learning.

When reflective teaching is successful, students emerge with an enlarged store of tested insights of a generalized character and an enhanced ability to develop and solve problems on their own. The latter product is even more important than the former. If only the first were accomplished, no claims could be made for reflection-level teaching which cannot also be made for understanding-level teaching as described in Chapter 17. However, within genuine problem-centered teaching, students learn the nature and techniques of the process of problem solving itself. If well taught, problem solving approaches and procedures carry over to a wide range of problems other than those studied in school.

An understanding of how to solve problems according to principles of scientific reflection is perhaps the most useful intellectual tool a person can possess. If the central goal of education is to foster intelligence, reflective teaching should be the core approach used by teachers everywhere. Let us visit a college class in introductory psychology being taught *reflectively* and see whether we can discern what is unique to reflection-teaching procedures.

The problem of immediate concern to the class is, What is the nature of *mind?* Most of the students previously have adhered to a dualistic view of mind and body; they have held the idea that man is composed of two distinctly different kinds of substances—mental and physical. As mutual inquiry proceeds, the following discussion between the teacher and various class members ensues. When a student speaks, he probably is verbalizing the thoughts of most of his classmates. The teacher's goal is to help the students sharpen their insights in regard to the meaning of *mind*. The teacher speaks first.

"Mr. J., do you have a mind?"

"Why yes, I think so."

"Then, possibly, you can tell us what is mind?"

"It is the thing with which we think."

"You have said that mind is a thing. But a chair and a table are things. You were not referring to this type of thing?"

"No! I really meant that we think with the mind."

"What about the use of gray matter? Don't we think with our brains?"

"Well, yes."

"Then, if we think with our minds and we also think with our brains, they must be the same thing."

"No, they are not the same."

"In that case we must arrive at the conclusion that the mind is not a thing and we do not think with the mind?"

The teacher continues. "Are we able to store ideas and knowledge in the mind or are they stored in the brain? We are able to use our memory and imagination. Aren't these two different phases of thinking?"

"Yes."

"We have just said that we think with our brain. Thus, our ideas seem to be stored in the brain and not in the mind. Besides, there are ideas and knowledge in your textbook. But certainly your textbook does not function in any way like a mind. Is the mind separate from the body?"

"Yes, it seems to be."

"What makes you think so?"

"Well, we always think of mind as one thing and body as another."

"But we agreed that mind is not a thing."

"It just makes common sense."

"Is common sense a valid method by which to judge truth?"

"No!"

"You know that it was once common sense to believe that the earth is flat and that it is the center of the universe. You said that the mind is separate from the body or that it seems that way. Have you ever said to yourself that you are going to raise your arm and your arm rises?"

"Yes."

"And you have seen the effect of physical illness upon mental processes. Then, how can the mind and body be considered as separate? Obviously, there must be some connection if we continue to hold this theory.

"Has anyone ever seen electricity?"

"No."

"Will electricity flow through a copper wire?"

"Yes."

"And you know other facts about electricity and what it will do. This description of what electricity can accomplish makes it possible to describe electricity. Let us see if we can apply this same technique to our problem of mind.

"You have said that you have a mind. What did you mean when you said that you have a mind? Did you mean that you act as if you have a mind?"

"Why, yes."

"How would you describe that action?"

"I act normally."

"In other words, the difference between the way you behave and the way someone behaves who we say has lost his mind is that you act in a sensible way. And how do you act if you are sensible?"

"I am reasonable."

"You say act reasonably. But this does not completely describe your action. Therefore, let us look at your behavior from another angle. Imagine that you are looking at a tree. How do you know that the tree is a tree?"

"It looks like a tree and everyone agrees that it is a tree."

"Are you suggesting that such a simple object as the tree has a number of specific meanings?"

"Yes."

"For instance, you will know that a tree isn't metal, that it grows, that it has leaves in summer, and much other material of factual nature. In addition, you won't mistake a tree for anything else. Now, what does this tell you about the way you should behave with reference to a tree? What would you do with a tree?"

"I might cut it down for lumber."

"And you might use it for shade. But in any case, you will not try to eat a tree and you will avoid it if it stands in your path? If you understand the meanings which ordinarily are attached to the word tree and you act accordingly, it might be said that you are behaving intelligently. Couldn't this understanding of meaning be the function which we think of as mind?

"Thus, we have arrived at our definition that mind is a function. We take it to be the function which makes it possible for us to anticipate future consequences of present or proposed lines of action. What is meant by predicting future consequences? Don't we mean that we try to comprehend meaning and use foresight? Then, if we act on the basis of our predictions can we be said to act intelligently?"[1]

Because of space limitation the discussion between students and teacher is to some degree in outline form. In actual practice there would be more "side trips," and many statements would be made which were not pertinent to the problem at hand. The latter part of the discussion particularly would be more involved and much longer than is reported.

Now, just what is there about this teacher-student reflective classroom procedure which makes it different from either memory- or understanding-level teaching? *Perhaps it could be summarized by describing the classroom atmosphere as one of teacher-student mutual inquiry within which genuine problems are developed and solved.*

Problem-centered teaching, then, involves problem raising and problem solving. In problem-centered or reflective classes, instruction begins with

[1] Unit originally written by Leslie A. McKinnis quoted from Ernest E. Bayles, *The Theory and Practice of Teaching*, Harper, 1950, pp. 272–274.

introduction of an "I don't know," or problematic situation—one in which students are faced with a question they cannot answer. The problem should be so compelling that students really will want to study it, but not so overwhelming that they want to give up; it should generate an urge to analyze the possible obstacles and dilemmas in the situation, to understand them, and to devise means for resolving the difficulties. After aiding students in raising a problem, the teacher then helps them investigate it until an answer is found. Problem solving consists of the steps of formulating hypotheses and testing them with all available pertinent evidence. Facts are gathered in profusion, but teachers make no attempt to encourage fact learning or fact recall *as such*. Problems which make for ideal classroom study involve situations which are difficult enough to be challenging, yet simple enough so that most students in a class will be able to cast and test hypotheses leading to a solution.

WHEN IS A PROBLEM A PROBLEM?

Too many teachers who have attempted a problems approach have not adequately understood the psychology of learning as it relates to problem-centered study. Older psychologies—mental discipline, idea association-ism, and S-R associationism—had little to say about problem-centered study. Nor have neobehaviorists, with their more sophisticated S-R associationisms, contributed much understanding of reflective teaching. Prior to the twentieth century, Herbart probably came closer than any other psychologist or educator to formulating a problem-centered approach to teaching, but Herbartian teaching was still not problem centered or reflective in any true sense.

Often "problem-centered teaching" has failed because what teachers have chosen as "problems" have not actually been problems in a psychological sense. Contributions of Gestalt and field psychologists enable us to understand better what happens to a person psychologically when he has a problem. A learning problem is not just an objective issue to be resolved; it must involve *psychological tension in a learner*.

If a learning problem can be defined successfully in psychological terms, this should help to resolve a common dilemma which arises in connection with a problem approach in teaching. The dilemma is this: students have a great variety of real problems, but often the "problems" which teachers think students should study arouse no tension in students; and if students do feel personally some of the problems posed by a teacher, they feel some much less intensely than others. Consequently, the motivation which should accompany problem study often does not develop; students remain cold and uninterested and their work proves to be lackadaisical. An analysis of pertinent psychological factors should help readers understand what lies behind this dilemma.

Some problems may be designated as *personal* in that students are personally involved and so experience tension, which is the essence of a true learning problem. While they are experienced, these problems hold a dominant place in the life spaces of students. Another category of problems may be identified as *social* or *societal;* they represent social needs which some adults believe exist in a community, region, or nation. They constitute part of the social matrix and, as such, are at least in the foreign hulls of the life spaces of students. But often they constitute no part of their actual life spaces.

These problems are felt personally by someone or they never would have been identified as problems in the first place; but commonly they are perceived only by some adults, and sometimes only by experts in fields of knowledge relevant to specific questions. To students, societal problems often seem quite remote; the students' function of living does not bring them into play. Posed by a teacher, such problems, unless students feel themselves personally involved, are not real problems at all.

Students Not Motivated by "Other Persons'" Problems

Reactions of students to the two types of problems—personal and societal—are likely to be quite different. A student can see the point of studying problems in which he is personally involved. The necessary emotional steam already exists; often all a teacher needs to do is direct study so that it will be as mature as possible. But when students are asked to study problems which they do not accept as their own, they are likely to remain unresponsive; furthermore, since no personally felt goals are involved, an inwardly motivated search for solutions is unlikely. Because of this detachment, relevant facts are seen not as data contributing toward a solution but only as lessons to be learned. Consequently, the quality of learning which results when students study someone else's problems is likely to be little different from that produced by conventional textbook-recitation teaching.

Textbook writers often include "problems" at the ends of chapters. Several years ago one of the authors paraphrased the following list of such "problems" from a social studies textbook.

To learn about the public utility companies of your community.
To see how many articles devoted to farming and rural life appear in the local newspaper.
To find out how many ways there are to send money from one city to another.
To find out what instructions are given to Boy Scouts for the protection of forests.

To learn more facts about life insurance.
To determine the advantages and disadvantages of good roads.[2]

There is little reason to suppose that, without skillful preliminary discussion led by a teacher, any of these "problems" as stated will induce any significant kind of psychological tensions in students. All too often textbook writers, preparers of syllabi and courses of study, and classroom teachers themselves label as problems exercises which, no matter what their potential in the teaching-learning process, cannot function per se as true psychological problems for students.

Since study of other people's problems results in learning which qualitatively is little different from traditional fact-memorization, some writers have suggested that teachers exclude from study any problem in which students do not already feel involved, confining instruction to problems which students, because of their life situations, spontaneously feel. Thus, they argue that the role of a teacher is to help students define carefully problems which, for them, already exist, and then to help them conduct whatever research and discussion seem to be appropriate in solving these problems. Although it should not be denied that in any school there is an important place for this kind of problem study, exclusive emphasis on it is highly reminiscent of the Roussellian natural unfoldment outlook. There is a strong flavor of "letting students do as they please." Of course, in the hands of a capable teacher, considerable freedom may be permitted students in *selection* of their problems and at the same time considerable rigor demanded in their study.

Certain persons prominent in the Progressive Education movement of the 1920s and 1930s endorsed a highly permissive approach to teaching. It was at this time that the concept of the "child-centered school" developed. One of the authors once visited a class in a Progressive school in which the teacher asked the class, quite literally, "Well, boys and girls, what do you want to study next?" After a period marked by considerable confusion, the students agreed that they wanted to study American Indians—a subject to which they had devoted units on numerous past occasions.

Need for Classroom Study of Serious Societal Problems

Exclusion of the whole range of adult-felt concerns from classroom study, when it occurs, troubles most persons. One might defend confinement of problem-centered study to problems which students already feel on the ground that it teaches them a method of problem solving which will be useful all through life. However, there are a number of persistent

[2] Maurice P. Hunt and Lawrence E. Metcalf, *Teaching High School Social Studies,* Harper, 1955, p. 44.

societal problems which, for the good of the community, state, and nation, students should come to understand and appreciate. Study of those problems which normally only specialists or other adults are concerned about may be of great importance in preparing students for intelligent citizenship. But how can we motivate students to study, in a serious and sustained way, problems which do not seem real to them? *In this question is the crux of problem-centered teaching.* Failure to give serious consideration to it is the reason why a problems approach so often bogs down, why students "goof off," and why, after having tried "problem-centered teaching" teachers frequently return to "teaching the facts straight."

In recent years, teachers have tried to devise ways of interesting students in problems which intrinsically are not interesting to them. "Solutions" to the enigma in which teachers find themselves have included suggestions that they explain to students just how the problems are bound to affect them eventually, that students be confronted face to face with the problems (as when we take a class to visit a slum), and that teachers use more eyecatching teaching materials (such as pictures).

But as every practicing teacher knows, these "solutions" often fail to produce real intellectual involvement. Students still do not feel the problems as their own. Of course, some students always will do whatever work a teacher assigns, and seemingly do it with enthusiasm. But what seems to be intellectual involvement and a desire to study a genuine problem often is a desire to achieve other goals such as high marks, praise, and social status.

At this point, we should distinguish between what psychologists often call *extrinsic motivation* and *intrinsic motivation*. When a job is done for outside reasons, for reasons not inherent in the job itself, motivation is said to be extrinsic. If Johnny washes his neck not because he wants to feel clean but because he is threatened with a spanking, we have extrinsic motivation. But if a job is done because doing it is somehow satisfying, if the job carries its own reward, if it is done for its own sake, then we say that motivation is intrinsic. If Johnny washes his neck not because of outside pressures but because he likes the feel of a clean neck, or enjoys the act of washing, we have intrinsic motivation.

When a learning goal is extrinsic, it is obvious that once the goal is met there ceases to be any point in remembering the learned material. If certain facts about a gasoline motor are learned only for the purpose of passing a test, as soon as the test is passed the reason for knowing the facts no longer exists. When motivation is wholly extrinsic, no matter how hard the study, we may expect that retention, understanding, and transfer will be much less than when material is learned for the sake of the learner.

Instead of striking out blindly and trying everything he can think of, willy-nilly, to motivate students to study seriously what does not seem to them any of their own concern, a teacher could try a drastically different approach; he could view his teaching problems in the light of a clear and adequate understanding of the learning process. Basic to such understanding would be knowledge of what it means for a person to experience a problem as a felt tension or anxiety, and formulation, based on this knowledge, of an approach to teaching which holds promise in many cases of effectively translating the "problems of others" into the problems of students.

How Is a Problem a Felt Tension or Anxiety?

To have a problem, a person must first have a goal or goals which he accepts as his own. A problem arises when he finds it impossible to proceed quickly and directly to the goal. When he cannot achieve his goal readily, it is either because he sees no open path to it or because he sees two or more competing paths, or two or more competing goals, and cannot decide which to pursue. These are the familiar "no-path" or "forked-path" situations described by John Dewey, and diagramed here.

No–Path Situation
(obstacle appears insurmountable)

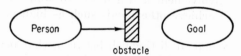

Forked–Path Situation A
(alternate, but equally attractive, goals)

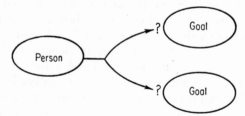

Forked–Path Situation B
(single goal; alternate, but equally attractive, paths)

Dewey's Problematic Situations.

Problematic Situations Defined in Lewinian Terms

Lewinian concepts and terminology also may be used to express the basic elements of a problematic situation. Either there is a goal region in a person's life space which has a positive valence and a barrier between his person and the region of positive valence, or there are several conflicting goal regions toward which or away from which a person might want to make psychological movement. These two types of situations are barrier or no-path situations and conflicting path situations and are also shown in diagram.

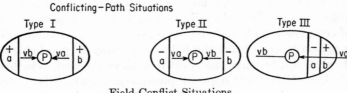

Barrier or No-Path Situation

1. Person
2. Psychological environment
3. Goal, region of positive valence
4. Barrier
5. Vector of driving force toward goal
6. Vector of restraining force of barrier

Conflicting—Path Situations

Field-Conflict Situations.

Conflicting-path situations lend themselves best to reflective or problem-centered teaching. In a Type I situation a person has two conflicting goals or two opposite regions of his life space both with positive valences. Vector vb represents a psychological force equal to the valence of region b; vector va represents a force equal to the valence of region a. In Type II situations the person is faced with two opposite significant regions of his life space each having a negative valence; he wants to escape both. In Type III situations a region of positive valence and a region of negative valence are in the same psychological direction from the person; they are functionally similar. Movement toward or away from those regions will be determined by the relative strength of the two forces at the time of movement.

Superficially, Type I and Type II situations appear much alike; however, they are crucially different. A person in a Type II situation is like a ball being pushed from opposite directions by two sticks; once it gives a little, it flies off to the side out of the picture. A person in such a situation is trying to escape two opposite negative driving forces and so is "between the Devil and the deep blue sea." He is likely to become completely frustrated and, like the ball, leave the field. In contrast, a person in a

Type I situation, like a ball being pulled in opposite directions, usually will stay in the field, i.e., remain engaged with the problem and try to resolve his conflict. He is influenced by two goals, both with positive valences. The goal toward which he moves is the one with higher values (Should his two opposing goals be exactly equal, would he be like the donkey who starved to death while standing exactly halfway between two stacks of hay?)

What Level of Tension Is Best?

A characteristic of the kind of goal-centered situation which we have described above is the presence of a certain amount of felt tension or discomfort. A person confronted with a no-path or forked-path situation feels to some degree doubtful, puzzled, bewildered, uncertain. How strongly he feels this way depends upon at least three factors: (1) desirability of the goal or goals; (2) apparent difficulty of the obstacle; and (3) his own personality make-up. Depending upon circumstances, desire to move toward the goal in a problematic situation (such as is diagramed) may range from a mild and easily cast off tickle to a powerful urge capable of commanding all one's resources. Or a problematic situation may cause a person to flee—leave the field—physically or psychologically, or both. He gives up; he makes no effort to achieve the goal. Whether a person finds himself between opposite positive goals which he is trying to achieve or opposite negative aversions which he is trying to escape depends largely upon how he construes himself and his environment.

In a sense a teacher must be a tightrope walker. He will get best results if he keeps his students under a "full head of steam." When he has involved them to the point that, during discussions, they sit on the edges of their seats, arms waving and eyes glistening, all wanting to talk at once, he has a potentially fine teaching situation. When he achieves this kind of situation, he may be sure that intrinsic motivation, at its best, is operating. However, there is a rather fine line between this type of situation and situations in which students either become so excited that their emotions are chaotic, feel despair because the problem posed is too difficult, or are bored because it is too easy. In any of these instances, a worth-while teaching-learning situation can evaporate suddenly. The situation either gets out of hand or students become apathetic.

Necessity for maintaining control of students cannot be overemphasized. One of the difficulties which commonly arises when a teacher attempts reflective teaching is loss of control. Any class engaged in problem-centered study will seem rather disorderly, but teachers often mistake unproductive chaos for healthy, work-related disorder. When youngsters are either bored or highly excited, they are difficult to manage. A teacher following the reflective approach usually learns from experience when it is time to sidetrack a discussion that is producing too much heat.

What Problems Pose Issues?

Whenever two or more competing alternatives are at stake, there is an *issue*. And since, by definition, all issues are "controversial," *controversy is a fundamental aspect of any truly problem-centered teaching.* Controversy invariably leads to conflict, of which we may distinguish two levels. *Interpersonal* conflict arises when individuals or groups hold beliefs sharply opposed to those of other individuals or groups. We often refer to conflicts on this level as "controversial issues." Persons on each side of an interpersonal conflict, or dispute, may be quite consistent in their own outlooks, even though in sharp disagreement with the opposing position. In our culture such conflict arises between capital and labor, among social classes, among racial, religious, and ethnic groups, among age groups, and sometimes between the sexes.

Interpersonal conflict tends to become internalized within the personalities of individuals so that they are at war with themselves. Caught in a culture in which interpersonal conflict is always present, they often accept as true and good *both* sides of many issues, thus incorporating cultural conflicts into their own personalities. When they become aware of their incompatibilities of outlook, the resulting internal struggle may be referred to as *intrapersonal* conflict. Although the content of an intrapersonal conflict may be no different from that of an interpersonal conflict, it may exact a greater toll because it can lead to disintegration of personality.

Naturally, we do not expect conflict, on the extreme levels just mentioned, to exist in learning situations which are wholesome. But for a reflective learning situation to exist at all, issues must come to be felt by students so that they find themselves to some degree in *controversy with themselves*. Each individual must be attracted to some extent by two or more competing hypotheses and feel temporarily unable to make a choice between them; otherwise, no problem exists for him. This seems so elemental as to be obvious. However, numerous teachers have encouraged students to work on "problems" but at the same time have refused to let them discuss controversial matters or read controversial material—insofar as these actions could be prevented. Teachers—and administrators too—simply do not always see the connection between reflection and controversy.

It is easy to apply an issue- or controversy-centered concept of a problematic situation to events in lives of students. If a boy wants to date a girl and she has persistently remained aloof, he is likely to entertain a variety of plans (hypotheses) for handling the situation. He may consider having a friend intercede for him, developing a new conversational "line," learning to dance better, or, if all else fails, joining the French Foreign Legion. The conflict in his own thinking which results from indecision over which course to pursue may become quite intense. Where strongly felt ends are at stake, then, it is easily seen how learning problems, which involve indecision over how to reach a goal, may arise.

We have been considering when a problem is a problem and how it is a felt tension or anxiety. We now turn to description of the basic procedure for reflective teaching, which includes both problem-raising and problem-solving aspects. Such matters as creating proper emotional climate for reflective teaching and maintaining control of the situation are better treated as part of *group dynamics;* this is the subject of Chapter 18.

HOW DOES PROBLEM RAISING PROCEED?

For a student, a problem arises whenever he can be induced to feel dissatisfied (that is, in doubt) with some one or more of his present attitudes, values, beliefs, or items of knowledge. Introduction of dissatisfaction produces a forked-path or a no-path situation. Is the questioned attitude, value, belief, or knowledge valid, or is it not? Is some alternative more promising than others? In adherence to a certain pattern of thought, is there a basic contradiction which stands in the way? In this sort of situation it is the element of uncertainty that provides the problematic aspect. The goal of learning now becomes the desire to remove doubt, to restore a degree of certitude.

Very often, doubt can be induced by leading a student to see that he simultaneously holds contradictory attitudes, beliefs, or items of knowledge, or that his behavior does not square with what he says are his convictions; by being made aware of his inconsistency, he is made doubtful. There appears to be something in the make-up of most persons in our culture—not yet well understood—which, once inconsistency is clearly recognized, produces a desire for consistency, a desire for a sense of personal harmony, for integration of self. When, over long periods of time, people display gross inconsistencies without appearing to feel unhappy, it is usually because they simply do not see themselves as being inconsistent.

The foregoing paragraph requires qualification. If we are to judge from experience common to us all, a frequent—in fact, the usual—response to awareness of inconsistency is irritation or anger. This is particularly likely if an emotionally charged issue is involved. However, a person's reaction when he is confronted with his own inconsistencies depends largely on how the confrontation occurs. There are appropriate techniques for helping people see their inconsistencies; an elaboration of them is a major theme of the next chapter.

A person may not entertain any mutually incompatible ideas about a particular subject and yet be wrong about it. His thoughts may be inadequate because they ignore more or less conclusive facts. For example, a person who thinks that Ulysses S. Grant was a teetotaler and Calvin Coolidge a drunkard either is ignorant of established historical facts or chooses to ignore them. A teacher who has the necessary skill often can make students dissatisfied with some of their present beliefs by showing how they are contradicted by factual evidence. This induces the same psychological situation, basically, as confrontation of students with self-inconsistencies.

How May Contradictions and Loopholes in Thinking of Students Be Exposed?

Before a teacher can do much about helping students see their inconsistencies, he needs a pretty good idea of what to expect, what kinds of contradictions his students are likely to hold. This knowledge will enable a reasonably skillful teacher to pursue a line of questioning which exposes a student's inconsistencies to himself and at the same time enables the student to save face. One such line of questioning has been labeled the *subject matter switch*.

A subject matter switch is performed when we generalize, or reduce to principle, a particular idea, then demonstrate how a further thought is incompatible with the principle and, consequently, with the first idea. For example, a student expresses the opinion that "Government price supports for cotton are ridiculous." The teacher then seeks agreement with the principle that "The federal government should not interfere with the economy." If the student agrees, the teacher then places the principle in a different context, i.e., gives it different subject matter, with a question like, "Do you favor a protective tariff on cotton?" The student, who also adheres firmly to the principle "A high protective tariff brings prosperity to a nation," is thus placed in a position which forces some kind of revision (if he attempts to extricate himself) of one or both of the contradictory opinions.

The foregoing example is hypothetical and, of course, very much simplified. To make the contradiction explicit to most students in a class, much more discussion would be necessary. Furthermore, this example, and any other which we might substitute, can be misleading. A teacher may ask questions which appear to reveal a contradiction that actually does not exist. If a student is permitted to qualify his opinions by introducing exceptions, he may extricate himself readily without having to do any serious thinking. On the other hand, the general technique of the subject matter switch is useful, and every teacher should experiment with it. Often, when it does not provoke the particular student who is trapped by it to constructive thought, it will motivate other students in the class.

In the preceding sentence we use the word *trapped* advisedly. Yet some explanation is needed. A teacher who wishes to teach reflectively is probably justified in using any device which works to get reflection going. Some devices may seem so teacher centered—i.e., the teacher is so fully in charge—that the whole procedure appears to be rigged in favor of the teacher's biases. But remember that this is only the beginning. When it comes time to cast and scrutinize hypotheses and draw conclusions there can be no rigging. Although the teacher performs key functions throughout the process, the relationship between students and teacher is interactive. Students remain free to reach whatever conclusions they choose, when the teacher has seen to it that they have given reasoned consideration to alternatives and the data which support them.

Another means of inducing students to feel problems is to introduce them to data from outside their life spaces which have the effect of making them doubt some attitude, value, belief, or supposed item of knowledge. In other words, the teacher asks students to read a book, to watch a television program or motion picture, to go on a field trip, or to engage in some other activity which confronts them with facts contrary to what they have taken for granted. Of course, this approach, like any other, may not work; students may refuse to admit the new facts into their life spaces. Unless they recognize the significance of the facts and truly come to doubt, no problem is created. Use of negative evidence to shake the confidence of students in their own knowledge and beliefs is often more effective if evidence comes from some source other than the teacher, for example, other students or reading references.

We wish to emphasize the role of question asking in any problem-centered teaching. Students (and often the teacher) ask questions persistently but the teacher usually refuses to offer fixed answers. The essence of a problematic situation is that there is something in it which is unknown. The unknown can be uncovered only after right questions are asked. One of the best questions is also the simplest: "Why?" "*Why* did you say that?" "*Why* do you have the opinion you have stated?"

How Are Societal Problems Converted into Personal Problems?

In the earlier sections of this chapter we discuss two types of problems, personal and societal, we point out that students are not motivated by other persons' problems, and we note that tension always is involved in a genuinely problematic situation. Our question now is, How may a reflective approach to learning serve to build a psychological bridge between adult-societal and student-personal concerns?

There are numerous areas of adult and societal concern, probably almost the whole gamut of adult interests, about which students normally have attitudes, beliefs, and some knowledge: politics and government, international affairs, economics, business, labor and employment, pure and applied science, religion and morality, various arts, and personal relations. Ideas which students have acquired often are sketchy, disorganized, and poorly understood; nevertheless they do have attitudes, beliefs, and a little knowledge about most things with which adults are concerned. This can be demonstrated by a reasonably free classroom discussion of any one of these subjects.

When students appear in public school classrooms, the *total* knowledge they have, or think they have, is usually more than teachers realize. With modern media of communication, frequent opportunities for travel, and continuously rising educational levels of parents, it seems likely that a great many—perhaps almost all—youngsters have more factual knowledge than they can make sense of. *One of the major jobs of a modern school is to help students make sense of the welter of information which they acquire outside of school.*

Although students willingly make statements about matters in such areas as government, economics, international affairs, and the relationship of science and religion, commitment which they feel toward such statements varies greatly. In some instances, commitment is slight; the student would abandon a pet idea without much hesitation or thought. At the other extreme, statements may represent convictions so highly cherished that students strongly resist bringing them under critical scrutiny.

Beliefs and attitudes that students hold concerning matters also of concern to adults constitute the psychological bridges between youth and adult interests. If a student feels enough personal attachment to a belief to care, the moment the belief becomes a subject of doubt he is likely to want to start thinking about it. At that point, if teaching is skillful, he can be led to want to study a subject about which he previously felt little or no curiosity. For example, if a considerable number of students in a class think that "most businessmen are dishonest," and the teacher can create sufficient doubt of this notion, students may want to make a study of business practices. They may want to know what motivates businessmen, and what the consequences of such motivation are. There is no telling where critical analysis of such a problem might lead—perhaps into inquiries about fundamentally important aspects of our economy.

The point is that by using students' present attitudes, beliefs, and knowledge as the "foils" of our teaching efforts, we often can arouse genuine interest in situations which otherwise would never be felt by students in any way to be problematical. Thus, where students at first feel no personal goal or involvement, a learning problem can be created. There is a way in which genuine student involvement often can be achieved. Students can be led to see their problems involving the subject matter of the social sciences, natural sciences, and humanities. "Other people's problems" can be brought to be "my problems."

HOW DOES PROBLEM SOLVING PROCEED?

Problem-centered teaching does not end with induction of psychological tensions. Helping students feel problems is only a beginning; this first step provides motivation and direction for the inquiry which is to follow. Once doubt has been induced, students are encouraged to formulate as many hypotheses as possible which might resolve discrepancies in thought that have been exposed. Or, in many instances, students will formulate questions, i.e., "negative" hypotheses, the answering of which will solve the problem. Next, students are encouraged to examine the hypotheses (or answer questions) in the light of all obtainable pertinent evidence. Formulation and testing of hypotheses should be conducted in an atmosphere which, insofar as possible, resembles that of a scientific laboratory. That is, the same open-minded and objective attitudes which characterize any scientific investigation should prevail. (It may be useful at this point to review material in Chapter 12 on the nature of thinking, pp. 307–310.

In the process of testing hypotheses, we should note carefully, a teacher does not play the role of a softhearted baby-sitter. At times he must be quite tough-minded in his insistence that students examine and think about all pertinent available evidence. He also must guard against snap conclusions and any other liberties which students might want to take with the reflective method.

Ideally, problem-centered study should culminate in at least a tentative conclusion about how a problem might be alleviated or solved; however, in many instances a definite conclusion will not be achieved. Certain warnings should be issued at this point. It goes without saying that a teacher will encourage tentativeness of conclusions. An irrevocable conclusion is like a locked door, whose key someone has thrown in the ocean. Students should be taught that the door to knowledge must always be left unlocked or even ajar.

Nevertheless at the termination of an inquiry, a conclusion should be a warranted assertion; it should provide greater predictive accuracy than any alternative hypotheses which has been entertained and examined. A conclusion may involve reacceptance of the idea originally brought under question, its modification, or formulation of a substitute idea. The important thing is that students push their thinking farther than it had gone before. Reaffirmation of an idea which a teacher has induced students to doubt is, of course, acceptable, provided that in the course of their study they come to understand the idea better and to have a better grasp of pertinent evidence.

We should stress two points regarding the over-all process of problem-centered study. One relates to thoroughness and the other to orderliness. When a teacher and a class of ninth-graders purport to "solve" some highly difficult problem during the course of a unit of study which covers a period of, say, three days, we can only feel that the procedure has been a travesty on education. It is conceivable that students might inform themselves a little better, might push their thinking forward a little more, in this length of time. But to talk about their achieving *solutions* so quickly is nonsense. True problem-centered teaching, like any teaching which leads to understanding, is necessarily an unhurried procedure. It is very difficult, and usually impossible, to pursue problem-centered teaching in situations characterized by rigid scheduling of time or of units to be covered. (Henry Morrison's comments are apropos here—see p. 450.)

To make problem-centered teaching click, a teacher may need to make several false starts; when one plan for bringing students to feel a problem fails, he tries another until he hits on one that works. The period during which a given problem is studied is necessarily rather unstructured and it frequently is impossible to predict how soon a class will devise anything resembling an answer. Even though a problem has been under study a week or more and nothing educational seems to have happened, so long as the teacher feels there is still a chance that some insights will emerge, study should be continued.

The length of time students struggle with a problem depends upon their age and maturity. First-graders need to come to a conclusion soon after they develop a problem, perhaps the same day. College seniors may accomplish their best learning when they have struggled with a problem for a semester or longer.

As a practical matter, of course, there must be limits to thoroughness. Something like a "law of diminishing returns" operates in education; in connection with each problem, a time will be reached when further pursuit of the problem will obviously not be worth the time and effort involved. Other equally important problems may be pressing for attention.

Most textbooks and courses of study contain entirely too many topics for each to be treated in problem-centered fashion. Thus teachers who wish to experiment with problem-centered teaching must free themselves somewhat from standard printed guides (textbooks, courses of study, state curriculum frameworks). This does not necessarily mean ignoring such guides, which seldom is possible anyway, but rather using them judiciously with clear recognition that they need not be followed literally.

Let us now turn to the question of orderliness. Problem-centered study is rarely, if ever, as orderly as written descriptions of it imply. To realize this, one needs only to listen carefully to a group discussion of some matter about which most members of the group have considerable personal concern. Hypotheses are advanced, evidence is stated, and conclusions are suggested in what appears on the surface to be random order. Thought, even for the best-organized persons, is seldom completely ordered in a one-two-three fashion. Although we may list a series of steps involved in reflective thinking (corresponding to steps of scientific procedure), they are rarely taken in their "logical" order. A thinker moves continuously back and forth from problem to hypotheses to evidence to conclusions in varying order, and at any given moment an idea may strike him which sets off an entirely different train of thought (sometimes about a quite different problem).

In good group inquiry there are always two types of discussion in progress—one the public discussion which an observer can hear, the other a series of private discussions in which each interested student debates the issue with himself. Most of the questions and assertions which are uttered aloud emerge from, or are influenced by, the private, silent debates. An aim of vocal discussion is to help each individual in the classroom, including the teacher, push forward the thinking he is doing privately. Hence, during the course of a single discussion, Mary may reach a conclusion which seems satisfactory to her, John may have his faith badly shaken in a conclusion he once had, and Fred may merely formulate a hypothesis. In each case, the student may have thought the problem through to a point farther advanced than any previously reached by him. Hence, in a discussion which appears chaotic to an observer, individuals may achieve a considerable amount of pointed thinking.

After stressing the inevitable appearance of disorderliness which characterizes most highly motivated discussions, we must not forget that a teacher is obligated to preside in such way as to see that appropriate questions do get asked, that obvious hypotheses are not ignored, that pertinent evidence is not glossed over, and that conclusions are presented and debated (where conclusions seem warranted). In short, he is obligated to see that all aspects of reflective study are evidenced at some time during the public part of a discussion. Only then will individual students have available for their private reflection all that a group study situation can contribute.

Although in the foregoing paragraphs we have concentrated upon the discussion aspect of problem-centered teaching, we wish to emphasize that problem-centered study in school may encompass a variety of activities. It is likely to include periods set aside for individual or group research, home study, trips, and guest speakers. It may include considerable talking, explaining, and illustrating on the part of a teacher—

provided the teacher promotes an atmosphere of mutual inquiry. An informal lecture can be a useful tool for providing data for consideration and for instigating reflection and keeping it moving among students.

WHAT ARE STUDENTS MOST EAGER TO THINK ABOUT?

Although students may have a number of special interests related to such things as professional preparation, part-time jobs while in school, and school affairs, probably most of them also have strong curiosity regarding areas of culture of concern to everyone, adults and children alike. Certainly areas of greatest common concern for adults and young people alike are the so-called "closed areas" of culture. (You may want to review the discussion of closed areas in Chapter 4.) The term *closed* means, essentially, "closed—or somewhat closed—to reflection." The reason for closure is that these are areas of culture in which people hold values and beliefs which they care very strongly about and do not wish to see jeopardized. Therefore, closed areas are characterized by strong prejudices, emotionalism, and considerable irrationality. Such areas of belief include sex, religion, morality, race, social class, nationalism and patriotism, evolution and scientific causation, and socioeconomic ideologies. There are of course many more.

Students tend to hold definite attitudes, values, and beliefs, and to have more or less knowledge or pseudo knowledge in these areas. Frequently they are strongly committed to the notions which they accept. Most experienced teachers are aware that many issues in these areas seem of vital concern to young people, particularly during adolescence, when development of a coherent set of values seems imperative for most youth. Although adults often act as if young people should not be concerned with areas where taboos operate, many studies indicate that youth are at least as interested as adults in these subjects.

Teaching in the verboten areas requires much intelligence and skill. Effective study may be hampered by such factors as a teacher's own ignorance and prejudice, lack of adequate facts, and pressures from school authorities and community. Unless skillfully handled, study in touchy areas of controversy may elicit from students only highly emotionalized reactions with little or no real reflection. For these reasons, teachers tend to detour closed areas and students have little opportunity in school to study issues which are most vital to them. Consequently, "study" of these issues usually confines itself to student "bull sessions" off or on school premises.

Problem-centered teaching does not depend alone on exploiting verboten areas of culture. It is only necessary that ideas which students care something about be made the subject of critical inquiry. One of the writers recalls a situation in which, because of the demise of several fish in the classroom aquarium, a class of fourth-graders embarked upon an enthusiastic study of the biology and ecology of fish life. The students had been caring for the fish according to what they thought were "right principles" (which included the assumption that fish need to eat as much in proportion to size as do fourth graders). The question posed by the teacher, "Why did the fish die?" launched the study.

An important principle of problem-centered teaching is involved in the foregoing illustration. The teacher, whether or not by design, allowed the children to make a mistake—to overfeed the fish. Making a mistake often encourages us to re-examine something we had regarded as true. Teachers usually do not let students make enough mistakes. They tell them the "right way" and students follow more or less blindly. It is often much more educative to let students do something their own way and experience the consequences. Naturally, some situations preclude this. A shop teacher might achieve maximum motivation for study of safety practices by first allowing a student to cut off a finger with a power saw; but he would not be morally justified to use such means to establish an efficient learning situation.

Determination of which subjects, or which topics within a subject, should be handled as problems cannot be made without reference to a specific classroom situation. In each case, a teacher should reckon with the maturity and experiential background of students, community attitudes, his own preparation and skill, and anticipated consequences of having a class delve deeply into the subject.

IN WHAT SUBJECT FIELDS IS PROBLEM-CENTERED TEACHING APPLICABLE?

Many teachers see problem-centered teaching as a possible approach to instruction in a very limited number of courses, such as social studies, literature, industrial arts, or home economics. These teachers are unable to imagine the use of problem-centered teaching in such subjects as mathematics, physics, music, physical education, and foreign language.

With respect to subject areas, it appears that the essential characteristics of problem-centered teaching have enough flexibility to be employed in all school subjects, including those which seem on the surface to be rather cut and dried. Problem-centered teaching does not require development of elaborate unit plans. It emerges whenever a teacher, through adroit questioning and use of negative evidence, induces students to doubt that which they now accept, and then helps them analyze reflectively the issue which has arisen. In most conventional subjects, opportunities regularly appear where a teacher can operate in this manner. Passages in a textbook, assertions made by students, a news story, a motion picture or TV show—any of these may serve at times as a "springboard" for creation of problems. Problem-centered teaching seems to spring into existence in those situations where minds of teacher and students engage. *It grows more from a unique relationship between teacher and students than from any different nature of formal course materials.*

Of course, some courses and some types of course organization lend themselves more readily to problem-centered teaching than do others. A course which has been construed broadly—that is, whose subject matter is not narrowly prescribed—is probably a better tool than is a more narrow course. Thus, as usually defined, general business is a better course for reflection-level teaching than is shorthand; problems of democracy better than economic geography; history and philosophy of mathematics better than algebra; world literature better than freshman composition. This difference, however, is not inherent in the nature of the subject matter as such but lies in the frame of reference within which it customarily is treated.

A course in which problem-centered teaching is used cannot be bound rigidly to a textbook. Real problems are psychological; data used in solving them are rarely organized in the same pattern as textbooks and courses of study. The "logical" organization of a book simply does not usually coincide with the logic of live thought. Hence, courses are best which may be allowed to cut across subject matter lines whenever the cutting across makes sense in terms of the particular problem being studied. This is perhaps the most definable rationale of a core curriculum, which is not the same as saying that at present reflective teaching is common in core classes. Furthermore, since much of the content of textbooks available at present tends to be irrelevant to critical analysis of ideas, attitudes, and beliefs, certain kinds of problems can best be handled if a teacher is not required to follow a textbook closely.

HOW DO PROJECTS, UNITS, AND PROBLEMS DIFFER?

The "project method" was popularized by William H. Kilpatrick in the 1920s.[3] Some writers loosely—in fact, much too loosely—discuss projects, units, and problems as if they were all the same. We should make a clear distinction between these terms.

A project is an individualized work assignment. Although all members of a class may be given the same general kind of task, each student is free to arrange variations. Furthermore, although there may be a deadline for

[3] Kilpatrick described this method in 1918. See "The Project Method," *Teachers College Record,* September, 1918.

completion of a project, students work on an individualized time schedule. Projects involve physical activity and almost always result in some kind of physical product. Examples of projects are making a table, as in a shop class; raising a calf, as in an agriculture class; making an insect collection, as in a biology class; making a clippings scrapbook, as in a social studies class.

A unit, in its most general sense, is a collection of subject matter which is unified by a single theme. The unit concept has been applied extensively in courses of an academic or semiacademic nature, such as English and social studies. In a given course, units constitute the organizational foci. A succession of units, arranged sequentially in some presumably logical fashion, give a course its form. Obviously, unit organization is designed, among other things, to make a course independent, or relatively independent, of a textbook. Since teachers themselves usually are responsible for developing each unit and collecting teaching materials to go with it, a unit organization offers considerable flexibility. Units may be selected and designed to fit a particular situation. Educators have devised a great variety of unit plans, the nature of which depends largely on how the educator defines the learning process and what he sees as the goals of education.

Morrison's mastery units, as discussed in Chapter 17, are but one conception of what unit teaching means. So far as contemporary practice is concerned, most teachers view a unit as very much like a textbook chapter except that, to a large degree, it is their own creation. They see a unit of work as simply a block of subject matter dealing with a common subject. For example, a geography course may contain a unit on France. This simply includes all the factual data on France which the course provides, pulled together in a bundle so that they can be studied together.

Project and unit teaching *are not necessarily problem centered or reflective*. Both project and unit approaches to teaching may fail to confront students with issues and to challenge independent thought. Furthermore, as popularly conceived, projects and units may not even lead to learning on an understanding level. The outcome of project and unit teaching depends almost entirely on the wisdom of the particular teacher involved.

Popularization of project teaching and unit teaching may have done more harm than good in the sense that, to many teachers, these approaches have been seized upon as the heart of the educational process. A teacher may develop a collection of projects and units which look good to him and consider his major teaching problem solved. Consequently, project and unit teaching may misdirect a teacher's effort. Instead of regarding as all-important the development of the kind of unique interaction among teacher and students which leads to reflection and understanding, he is likely to focus on the more or less mechanical arrangement of pre-determined subject matter so it will look neat on paper. Teachers so occupied lose sight of what is central in all learning: the intelligent interplay of a person's ideas with those of others.

Project and unit teaching makes most sense when each project or unit is conceived as encompassing a general idea or insight plus available relevant data needed to give it meaning. But when viewed in this fashion, projects or units can hardly be designed in advance of the time when a student begins to grapple intellectually with a problem. The project or unit evolves as study proceeds.

HOW EFFECTIVE IS REFLECTIVE TEACHING?

A person who experiences reflective learning should thereby gain an increased store of generalized insights related to the subject studied; and these should be incorporated at the personality level so that a permanent change in him occurs. Furthermore, he should show a greater disposition and ability than before to apply the method of scientific reflection to problems outside the school subject in which reflective learning occurs.

It is difficult to measure insightful changes which occur in people as a result of school experiences. The most significant changes may not be evident in a person's outward behavior while he is still in school. Perhaps our best source of evidence as to the effectiveness of reflective learning is the subjective reactions of students themselves. How does a student feel toward a course taught reflectively compared to one taught on a memory or understanding level? The authors' experience has been that students react to reflective teaching in various ways but usually with intensity. Some of them despise their first experience in a reflectively taught course— but not because of boredom. Students who actively dislike reflective situations usually do so because they are encouraged to think about ideas which they prefer not to expose to rigorous examination. Other students, usually a majority, express gratitude for having been "made to think." Some conclude that they "will never again be quite the same."

In addition to the unique nature of its teaching-learning process, there are other advantages of reflective teaching. If conducted in the right manner, it produces a high level of motivation in most students. This leads them to work with a great deal of perseverance and tends to eliminate discipline problems. The authors have seen students become so "fired up" in problem-centered classes that they did twice as much work as would normally be expected, sometimes to the point of neglecting other classes. Work in a reflectively taught class also is likely to be more self-directed and self-sustained than in nonreflective classes. That is, students voluntarily dig for information in libraries and elsewhere. They hold frequent out-of-class discussions concerning their work in class, with cross-fertilization of ideas contributing to learning.

Of course, not all attempts at reflective teaching may work out as well as foregoing paragraphs suggest. In fact, the "problems approach," as it has been called, is in bad repute among some teachers and administrators. One of the charges leveled against it is that students fail to acquire the basic background—principles and facts—essential to a subject. It might seem logical to assume that, on a test designed to measure recall of facts, students taught on a memory or an understanding level would fare better. However, if we are to take at face value a group of studies extending from 1940 into the 1950s, this apparently is not the case. These studies, all designed to test the results of reflective teaching, have been reported by Bayles.[4]

The studies were conducted by public school teachers in Kansas and Missouri and culminated in the form of master's theses. Four of the six studies reported were conducted in high school social studies and the other two in fifth- and sixth-grade classes.

The general procedure was as follows: Students were given IQ tests to determine the average IQ of a class. Only those classes were used which were approximately "average." Then, insofar as the teachers were able to do so, the classes were taught reflectively. The teachers measured the effects of reflective instruction by giving various standardized achievement tests and by observing such changes of students' overt behavior as made it possible to infer the quality of their learning.

The control group used in evaluation of test results was in each case the group upon which the test had been standardized. All tests used had been standardized on groups of students of average or better IQ. The control against which teachers judged student behavior was much more subjective—the behavior of students of other classes which the teachers had taught in conventional fashion. However, since each of the teachers was experienced and able, subjective impressions reported by them were considered worthy of respect.

The results of each study were very clear cut. Irrespective of whether the achievement tests emphasized fact recall or the application of principles, students who had been taught reflectively scored conspicuously higher in almost all cases than the national or regional norms. Those who did not actually score higher than the norms made exceptionally large gains during the school term. With respect to informally gathered data, teachers reported the following results: (1) apparent heightened interest

[4] "Experiments with Reflective Teaching," *Kansas Studies in Education*, April, 1956. This monograph is reproduced in essentially its original form in Chapter 1 of Bayles' book *Democratic Educational Theory*, Harper, 1960.

among students; (2) more work done; (3) more voluntary reporting of data which had been encountered out of school—data gathered from radio, newspapers, magazines, etc.; (4) increased tendency to be critical—to demand evidence; (5) increased participation in discussions, particularly among students formerly reticent; and (6) much more reading. Some of the teachers obtained librarians' records of magazines and books checked out by students; they found that those in their reflectively taught classes were reading more than any other students in school.

To measure the amount of gain during a term, one of the investigators continued for a period of six years to give achievement tests to respective classes at the beginning and end of each school term. She found that the net gain in learning increased from year to year. This indicated that with continued experience with reflective teaching a teacher becomes more effective. If the six teachers participating in these studies had had several years of reflective teaching experience behind them (most were trying it for the first time), it seems likely that the studies would have revealed even more spectacular results.

Many teachers, when discussing the merits of reflective teaching, argue that it works only with the best students. One of the studies reported by Bayles suggests that this is not true; in the instance reported, reflective teaching was used in a class containing a wide range of ability. *Students of low ability made greater percentage gains than did those of high ability.* However, the investigator concluded that her teaching had not been pitched on a challenging enough level for the high group. Probably a safe conclusion is that reflective teaching, when effective, tends to bring students of all levels of ability up to maximum or near maximum performance.

We shall mention only one more conclusion, but it is a significant one. The teachers who participated in the studies which Bayles reports adapted reflective teaching to school situations which were quite conventional. The fact that they achieved good results suggests that effectiveness of teaching in our public schools could be greatly increased without drastically upsetting the conventional framework of subject matter and school organization. It is reasonable to assume that, in a school administratively committed to reflective teaching, results would be even more impressive.

IS AN EMERGENT TEACHING THEORY AND PRACTICE POSSIBLE?

The primary purpose of a course in psychological foundations of education is to aid students in critically evaluating psychological theories from the point of view of their applicability to classroom practices. Aspects of theories of learning and teaching may supplement one another or they may be in open disagreement. The scholarly and sincere psychologist X may find himself opposed to virtually every idea of the equally scholarly and sincere psychologist Y. Disagreement among psychologists may be frustrating to students. On the other hand, in the fact of disagreement lies one of the challenges of such study. Only to the degree that a student is willing to think for himself can he emerge from his studies with something worth while.

When we study the major outlooks in regard to learning and teaching which have arisen in Western civilization and are still with us, it becomes quite evident that actual educational procedures often reflect inconsistent hodgepodges of bits of several systematic theories developed from time to time. Thus, educators often are not able to provide real educational leadership because they themselves are not certain of where they think they are headed.

An educator has three possible choices of action. He may conform rigidly to one systematic theory of teaching and learning—mental discipline, natural unfoldment, apperception, S-R associationism, or Gestalt-field theory; he may eclectically borrow freely from the various outlooks and integrate his ideas into a mosaic or patch work which is available for him to draw upon as need arises; or he may develop an *emergent synthesis,* a genuinely new outlook which benefits from knowledge of all previously developed psychological theories but is not an eclectic compromise between them. An *emergent* is something novel which appears in the course of evolution of ideas. When an emergent outlook reflects the results of the interplay of conflicting ideas and arrives at something new, it is a synthesis.

A relativistic cognitive-field psychology may come to function as an "emergent synthesis" capable of circumventing the difficulties underlying other positions and at the same time providing a base for a set of school practices which are adequate and internally consistent. This promising possibility should at least be examined carefully by prospective teachers.

How Defensible Are the Premises of Mental Disciplinarians?

People who make moralistic judgments about the nature of human nature ("man is born evil") encounter great difficulty in attempting to prove their thesis scientifically. However, whether a person's study of geometry strengthens his thinking faculty is susceptible of scientific test. But attempts to support mental disciplinary propositions experimentally appear to have been unsuccessful. Within a frame of reference of faculty psychology or classicism, mental discipline seems quite harmonious; however, we may question its adequacy for schools in a modern scientific age. (An outlook or thought pattern which is scientifically most satisfactory is one which is both adequate and harmonious in light of all obtainable pertinent data.)

What Are Strengths and Weaknesses of Apperception?

Apperceptionists, in considering a child a passive mind, probably opened the way for S-R associationists' treating a child as a passive piece of protoplasm. Apperceptionists did recognize the principle of activity, but they attributed the activity to ideas, not persons. Thus apperception implies a policy of student indoctrination; the teacher, a specialist in mental chemistry, fills the apperceptive masses of his students with *proper* ideas. Apperception is indeed internally harmonious, but we can question its adequacy, particularly for schools in a democratic society.

How Adequate is Neobehaviorism?

Thorndike's psychology, and that of later behaviorists and neo-behaviorists, likewise is harmonious but probably not adequate. Connectionistic and behavioristic psychologies are "scientific" in the sense that, in the main, propositions which emerge from them are susceptible of scientific test. Results of an education based upon them likewise can be rather objectively measured. We provide an evaluation of these psychologies, as psychologies of learning, in Chapter 12.

One of the main criticisms of connectionistic and behavioristic psychologies, when they are used as guides in teaching, lies in the poor results which follow. This does not mean that, when teaching takes the form of more or less mechanical drill, students do not learn anything. The amount they learn seems to depend largely on how highly motivated they are.

Traditional education generally represents an amalgamation of mental discipline, apperception, and S-R associationism. Aspects of these three positions that are followed sometimes blend and sometimes clash. However, in that all three imply a teacher-centered, autocratic procedure in teaching, they are alike.

Studies which have been made to date, including the famous Regents' Inquiry of the State of New York of the 1930s, show that traditional approaches to education (whether based on mental discipline, apperception, or behavioristic drill) teach an average student very little which is permanent and meaningful. Thus traditionalism can be depreciated on the ground that it represents great waste of children's time and taxpayers' money.

Is Progressivism the Answer?

Can anything better be said of the ultra permissivism advocated by one group of educational progressives? Are the educational results of this approach demonstrably superior to those of traditionalism? They probably are more difficult to measure because they are more intangible. Traditionalists at least can measure their results in terms of highly specific knowledge and skills. Claimed fruits of permissivism are changes in attitudes and values such as are involved in democratic living, inclination toward self-expression, and creative thought. Results of this kind are not unmeasurable, but they are much more difficult to measure than are memorized facts.

A teacher who favors a large degree of permissivism may do so simply out of a feeling of sentimentality toward children. In this case, being able to watch children enjoy themselves in an uninhibited way may be reward enough in itself to the teacher. However, this does not answer the question of whether children experiencing a permissive type of teaching are actually learning that which will enrich their lives most or make them the best possible citizens or workmen.

How Does Cognitive-Field Psychology Eliminate Weaknesses of Both Traditionalism and Permissivism?

Although perhaps not without some distinctive weaknesses of its own, teaching based on cognitive-field psychology appears to be an emergent position which, if widely adopted in our schools, might eliminate some of the inadequacies of an earlier period. The approach to teaching implied by this psychology, although in many respects distinctively different from other approaches, should at the same time have some appeal for traditionalists and Progressives alike.

In contrast to behaviorists, field psychologists are interested mainly in reflection and the ways in which its quality can be improved. An educational program consistent with a cognitive-field psychology focuses on teaching students to think more effectively in a wide variety of situations; it entails problem-centered teaching.

A large group of liberal arts scholars in the United States, too, want to teach students to think more effectively. Most of these persons, however, are inheritors of the classical tradition in education and to the extent that they think in psychological terms they still cling to a faculty psychology. Basically, they are "mental disciplinarians." But if they were to make a careful study of psychology, in relation to contrasting philosophies of education, it seems likely that the only modern school of thought in psychology which they could accept would be a cognitive-field psychology. It is the contemporary scientific psychology which harmonizes best with their professed aim of giving education an intellectual emphasis. Joseph Wood Krutch, a prominent liberal arts scholar, literary critic, and author, has written a book pleading for rejection of mechanistic psychologies (such as connectionism and behaviorism) and for adoption of a non-mechanistic psychology whose main interest would be study of reflective and creative mental processes.[5] Widespread acceptance of cognitive-field psychology would restore an intellectual emphasis in education and at the same time provide a psychological basis for education free of the criticisms validly made of the old "mind training" approach.

Is there anything about the educational implications of cognitive-field psychology which might please the neobehaviorists? Remember that behaviorism implies an education in which students learn as many useful responses as possible. Education is construed as "building background." The accumulated background functions as a reservoir from which the person fishes out the appropriate response when needed. Cognitive-field psychologists certainly do not object to having students learn facts and remember them for future use. However, their emphasis is upon the students' growing to see the world and themselves differently, and facts are acquired and used in the process. They emphasize that facts are best learned when they are regarded by the learner as instruments for serving purposes which he feels are important—when they are connected with problem solving. True, a background of factual information or skills is regarded as useless unless it has sufficient pertinence to the common problems of life to furnish hypotheses for solving them. But a growing number of teachers, including those educated in the behaviorist tradition, would accept the legitimacy of these claims.

Adoption of cognitive-field psychology as a basis for teaching would lead to greater student participation than is permitted by traditional teachers, but participation of a different kind from that advocated by Roussellians. In contrast with either authoritarian or laissez-faire classrooms, the ideal classroom of cognitive-field psychologists would be democratic. Although field psychology is not a compromise between the psychologies underlying traditionalism and permissivism, it does lead to a kind of middle position: a position which permits students a considerable amount of freedom but only within certain confines. The precise balance between authority and freedom should be even more clear to students after they have read Chapter 19.

It is possible that cognitive-field psychology may come to command the support of both those who feel that teachers should be centers of authority and those who feel that classrooms should be child centered. Both traditionalism and permissivism are extreme positions which have been widely attacked. The former is criticized on the ground that it does not permit children enough freedom for intellectual exploration and the latter on the ground that it assumes that adequately worth-while learning will necessarily result if children are given free rein and allowed to plan

[5] Joseph Wood Krutch, *The Measure of Man,* Bobbs-Merrill, 1954.

their own activities. So far as the relationship between teacher and students is concerned, cognitive-field psychology offers a more moderate course than either traditionalism or permissivism. A common, constant purpose of cognitive-field psychology is enhancement of intelligence as teachers aid students in changing or reconstructing the cognitive structures of their life spaces.

BIBLIOGRAPHY

NOTE: Several of the titles listed at the end of Chapter 1 on the nature of good teaching are equally relevant to Chapter 18. See, for example, Barzun, Cantor, Highet, and Rasey.

Anderson, Harold H., ed., *Creativity and Its Cultivation,* Harper, 1959.
    Addresses presented at the Interdisciplinary Symposia on Creativity, Michigan State University. Addresses by top authorities covering numerous facets of the subject. Excellent.
Bayles, Ernest E., *The Theory and Practice of Teaching,* Harper, 1950.
    In Part III: descriptions of teaching strategy to promote reflective learning. Not to be neglected are Parts I and II on theory, unless one is already familiar with Bayles' more recent book, *Democratic Educational Theory.*
Bruner, Jerome S., "The Act of Discovery," *Harvard Educational Review,* Winter, 1961.
    A consideration of discovery—finding out for oneself—in school, and of the kind of classroom and style of teaching that encourages discovery.
Burton, William H., and others, *Education for Effective Thinking,* Appleton-Century-Crofts, 1960.
    A key reference, not only in connection with the foregoing chapter, but in connection with the entire book. The theoretical basis is laid down in Parts I and II. Part III discusses teaching to think in a number of specific school subjects.
Cantor, Nathaniel F., *The Learning-Teaching Process,* Dryden, 1953.
    A splendid book on what is good teaching. Relatively nontechnical, compared with Cantor's book cited in Chapter 1.
Columbia Associates in Philosophy, *An Introduction to Reflective Thinking,* Houghton Mifflin, 1923.
    Still one of the best books in its field. Chapter 1 defines reflection and the remainder of the book presents "case studies" of reflection in action. Covers a number of different subject areas.
Hildreth, Gertrude H., *Educating Gifted Children,* Harper, 1952.
    An account of practices at Hunter College Elementary School. Chapter IV describes teaching methods. The emphasis is on reflective learning, and the approaches employed are applicable to all normal children and youth.
Hullfish, H. Gordon, and Philip G. Smith, *Reflective Thinking: The Method of Education,* Dodd, Mead, 1961.
    A noneclectic argument to the effect that unless education dedicates itself

to teaching students to think, it dedicates itself to nothing at all. Highly recommended reading.

Hunt, Maurice P., and Lawrence E. Metcalf, *Teaching High School Social Studies*, Harper, 1955.

In Part One: a general treatment of reflective teaching which applies equally to all subjects and grade levels. Chapter 8 is perhaps most directly pertinent to the foregoing chapter.

McBurney, James H., and Kenneth Hance, *The Principles and Methods of Discussion*, Harper, 1939.

One of the best treatments of "reflective discussion." The authors reject any discussion which is a mere pooling of ignorance.

19

WHY IS CLIMATE MAKING A PART OF METHOD?[1]

A teacher's success in inducing reflective learning hinges upon his ability to bring students to be involved in issues and yet be curious and open-minded in regard to their resolution. The aim of this chapter is to consider how to keep learners involved to the point of perplexity and yet not frustrate them, and to explore ways in which they can be made more receptive to points of view based on evidence more scientific than the common run.

For this purpose we shall draw rather heavily from experience in fields outside formal education. Specifically, we shall survey briefly some findings from psychiatry which bear on the problem of reducing emotional blocks to learning. We shall also examine the area of study known as "democratic group leadership" in an attempt to see what an understanding of the dynamics of democratic adult groups may reveal concerning classroom practice. It should be noted at the outset that we make no attempt to apply directly to classroom practice the procedures which have been developed for use in therapeutic groups or normal adult groups. Many of these procedures are inapplicable in school classes. However, experience with them does suggest important clues for making learning more reflective, functional, and permanent.

[1] This chapter, with minor changes, is reproduced from Maurice P. Hunt and Lawrence E. Metcalf, *Teaching High School Social Studies*, Harper, 1955. Although there has been a continuing output of literature pertinent to the subjects treated here, the recent literature does not seem to add substantially to the basic facts and ideas set forth in the 1955 volume.

HOW MAY CONFLICT BE RESOLVED FROM A PSYCHOANALYTIC POINT OF VIEW?

Psychotherapists differ in their interpretation of causes of emotional conflict. Freudians attribute conflict to a combination of instinctive drives and early childhood experiences. Neo-Freudians are more inclined to emphasize a patient's present environment as a source of conflict. Therapists likewise differ in their approach to treatment, one group assuming that therapy should expose and help a patient reinterpret early experiences in life, and another that therapy should focus on changing a patient's contemporary life situation. Another source of disagreement is in the question of how directive a counselor should be during counseling sessions. Still another issue relates to whether, in treating certain forms of mental illness, individual or group therapy is the more valuable. Because they are particularly pertinent to our present problem, we shall explore briefly the last two of the issues mentioned.

Directive vs. Nondirective Therapy

In the language of psychotherapy, the issue posed here is between directive and nondirective (or patient-centered) therapy. What is probably the first attempt at careful description and defense of a nondirective approach to therapy was made by Rogers.[2]

We can best describe nondirective therapy through comparisons and contrasts. Rogers suggests that virtually all historical approaches to psychotherapy place a therapist in an authoritarian position with reference to a patient. These approaches assume that a counselor can and should determine a socially accepted goal for a patient and help him rearrange his personality structure or his life situation so that he can achieve it. A patient may be told what to believe and do by subtle and indirect methods, but told he is nevertheless.

Nondirective therapy avoids substituting a therapist's purposes for a patient's. A warm and permissive atmosphere is created in which a patient feels perfectly free to talk about his problems. The counselor accepts, recognizes, and clarifies feelings expressed by the patient, who talks his way through his problems, moving successively from a phase of "blowing off steam" to a phase of better self-understanding and heightened capacity for reflective handling of his own problems. Although nondirective therapy places more emphasis upon emotional adjustment than do some other approaches, it is assumed that an *outcome of therapy will be reflectively achieved insight*. The responsibility for this outcome is placed squarely on patients; whatever decisions they make are theirs alone.

[2] Carl Rogers, *Counseling and Psychotherapy*, Houghton Mifflin, 1942.

We shall confine ourselves to one further point: in contrast to Freudian approaches to the theory of neurosis, nondirective therapy assumes that, rather than being largely internal and psychic, conflicts have a large cultural component. That is, they are mostly a result of one's present relationship with his environment: they grow from "some new cultural demand which opposes individual need."[3] This appears to be saying much the same as is said elsewhere in the present book: that most emotional conflicts are a result of a person's internalizing, or incorporating within the self, discrepancies of his surrounding culture, i.e., conflicting beliefs and behaviors.

A nondirective approach to psychotherapy has important implications for teaching. Although a teacher probably should not be "nondirective" in the sense described by Rogers, the idea of encouraging individuals (including students) to formulate their own purposes and solve their own problems in the presence of an adult who, rather than dictating, merely gives encouragement has broad significance for group management in a democratic society. Limitations of the Rogerian outlook for school use will be treated later in the chapter.

Individual and Group Counseling and Behavioral Change

Psychological counseling which acquaints a patient with "the facts" concerning his situation may fail to produce logically implied changes in behavior. For example, Rogers says, "It has come to be recognized that we do not change the client's behavior very effectively simply by giving him an intellectual picture of its patterning, no matter how accurate."[4] Change in knowledge leads to the adoption of new values. But if a situation rewards old values, they will continue to dominate the new. When this is the case, behavior reflects the old values and remains unchanged.

One reason a counselor may not succeed in bringing about significant changes in behavior is that the behavior of every individual is firmly rooted in the persons with whom he associates. That is, actions of a patient are largely controlled by groups to which he belongs and can be changed only as behavior of the groups themselves changes.[5]

A deep-seated desire of human beings is for security. A common means of achieving security is through membership in a group. When a person feels that he has a place in a group, that he "fits in," that he is wanted, he feels secure. As Lewin points out, "The social climate in which a child lives is for the child as important as the air it breathes. The group to which a child belongs is the ground on which he stands. His relation to the

---

[3] *Ibid.*, p. 54.

[4] *Ibid.*, p. 27.

[5] As used in this chapter, *group* means two or more persons in *psychological interaction* with each other. Related terms are *in-group*, *primary group*, and *face-to-face group*.

group and his status in it are the most important factors for his feeling of security or insecurity."[6] One achieves membership in a group by conforming, at least to a degree, to the mores of the group. To be accepted in a group of thieves, one must act like a thief; to be accepted in a group of saints, one must act like a saint.

This is not to say that an individual is completely subject to group control. He may develop beliefs and values which are novel to a group and may get them accepted by others in the group. With widening acceptance, the new beliefs and values become effective in controlling group behavior. The extent to which an individual can project his own unique personality into group life, and thereby change a group, depends on the situation, e.g., whether the group is itself democratic and the extent to which the larger culture outside the group is hostile or friendly to the changes, and on his own capacity for persuasion. A modern sociologist is likely to regard the process of interaction itself as the basic social datum; every group is constantly shaping individuals in it and simultaneously is being shaped by them.

Though interaction is always present, we cannot imagine that large changes will occur in individuals outside their relationship to their primary group associations. A psychotherapist is constantly aware of the fact that there is little he can do to help a patient reorganize his personality *as an individual.* Such reorganization as may occur must fit exigencies posed by a patient's associations—the various needs and pressures, often highly subtle and complex, which grow out of the fact of group membership itself. This is particularly the case where values are concerned, and even more particularly, values in "closed areas."

During World War II, experiments in group psychotherapy were undertaken out of necessity. There were not enough therapists or facilities for individual counseling. The results of counseling with groups of patients were often gratifying. Now, in certain situations group therapy is seen as having advantages over individual therapy.[7] The reason appears to lie in the previously mentioned supposition that it is easier for an individual to change his values and behavior if other persons with whom he is in intimate contact are also changing.

There is disagreement as to whether in group therapy the therapeutic effect comes primarily from the relationship of each member to the therapist or from relationships of members to each other, but the latter interpretation seems to be growing in popularity. In some instances a patient can express himself more freely in a small face-to-face group than in individual relationship to a counselor, perhaps because he feels less alone, the group gives him courage, and other members have established prece-

[6] Kurt Lewin, *Resolving Social Conflicts,* Harper, 1948, p. 82.
[7] See Leon Gorlow and others, *The Nature of Nondirective Group Psychotherapy,* Teachers College, Columbia University, 1952, p. 8.

dents for speaking frankly. Through the give-and-take of free discussion some persons may come to see their own problems better than through individual counseling situations. Patients accept censure, suggestions, and guidance from each other more readily and with less disturbance and hostility than from a therapist. "One of the most important constituents of the ground on which the individual stands is the social group to which he 'belongs.' "[8]

A group situation may also stimulate one to deal openly and creatively with his own conflicts. Foulkes summarizes this possible therapeutic effect of a group: ". . . Lectures, exhortations, sympathy, pity, advice, medicaments, explanations, encouragement, all can help a little, but they cannot move the patient out of his fortress of entanglement. In the long run, they can only help him to entrench himself deeper in it. . . . If he is, however, brought into a situation, which he himself is continuously helping to create, to shape, he is forced to come out into the open with his own reactions and their contradictions."[9]

Whether a patient benefits more from group than from individual therapy depends in large part on the nature of his illness. Group therapy is regarded as of limited usefulness for the mentally unbalanced and probably for extreme neurotics. The nearer a patient is to normality, the more effective group therapy is likely to be. Its greatest value may be, as Hobbs points out, "in the neglected field of therapy for the normal person with debilitating situational conflicts. . . ."[10]

What is the significance to classroom teachers of clinical experience in individual and group psychotherapy? The hypothesis is suggested that a wide range of personally felt problems may be handled successfully among normal persons, including adolescent youth, with resultant permanent changes in outlook and behavior, if they are encouraged to air problems freely in the give-and-take atmosphere of a face-to-face group. Although this general idea is not new, modern psychiatric practice offers clues as to the most effectual managerial techniques for such learning situations.

WHAT IS THE DEMOCRATIC GROUP-LEADERSHIP MOVEMENT?

Related to the development of group psychotherapy is the democratic group-leadership movement. This movement embraces a body of experi-

[8] Kurt Lewin, *Resolving Social Conflicts,* Harper, 1948, pp. 145–146.
[9] S. H. Foulkes, *Introduction to Group-Analytic Psychotherapy,* Heinemann Medical Books, 1948, p. 70.
[10] Nicholas Hobbs, "Group-Centered Psychotherapy," Chap. 7 in Carl Rogers, *Client-Centered Therapy,* Houghton Mifflin, 1951.

ments and practices with normal adult and youth groups. Its aim is to translate a democratic philosophy into action on a group level and to compare the learning and behavioral results of democratic groups with those of nondemocratic groups. An understanding of the dynamics of groups is valuable to teachers. In the concluding section of the chapter, we make applications, and also show why, because of differences in aims and competence of most adult groups involved in experimentation, certain aspects of the management of adult groups are not transferable to classroom situations.

The democratic group-leadership movement is rooted in a democratic social-political philosophy dating in the United States from the Jeffersonian period, and from earlier than that in Europe. The modern concept of group work combines our traditional democratic philosophy with an understanding of group psychology which in human affairs is relatively recent.

In a large sense, the democratic group-leadership movement is a counterpart, for normal groups, of group psychotherapy for the abnormal. Although there is disagreement as to just how directive a leader can be and still remain "democratic," democratic group leadership appears to be an application of some of the principles of nondirective group therapy. It is to be expected, therefore, that among the contributors to our understanding of group process are numerous psychiatrists and psychologists. Haiman suggests that modern methods of group leadership "find their origin in the work of Sigmund Freud and follow the patterns of the psychiatric tradition which has flowered since his time."[11] Because there are significant relationships between the concepts of psychiatric medicine and of leadership of normal groups, psychiatrists have transplanted their philosophy and methods to normal group situations.

Although the contribution of psychologists and psychiatrists to an understanding of group dynamics has been great, it is perhaps no more significant than that of experts in management-worker relations. Of studies along this line, possibly the most notable were those conducted by staff members of the Harvard Graduate School of Business, F. J. Roethlisberger, W. J. Dickson, and colleagues, at the Hawthorne Works (Chicago) of the Western Electric Company between 1927 and 1932.

It was found from these studies that labor contentment and efficiency rose when workers were (1) organized in teams having a sense of common purpose and (2) made participants in an interview system where they could talk freely about whatever they wished.

Among other experiments conducted with self-governing adult groups

---

[11] Franklin S. Haiman, *Group Leadership and Democratic Action*, Houghton Mifflin, 1951, p. 39. This reference is one of the best general treatments of the subject, and the following pages draw heavily from it.

is the famous Peckham Experiment,[12] involving the work of the Pioneer Health Centre of Peckham, England. This health center was established to give family groups a program of mental and physical preventive therapy. In the main, the extensive program is run by members themselves without centralized direction. Marked—sometimes revolutionary— changes in the apparent values and behaviors of many members are noted by skilled observers.

It is from experiences and experiments like these that we have gained much of our knowledge of group dynamics. New concepts have developed as to how a democratic group functions and the role of a leader in it. It has become clear also that the idea of a democratic group, as developed in the democratic group-leadership movement, is very similar to the idea of a therapeutic group, as developed in the field of group psychotherapy.

The Nature of a Democratic Group

Democracy is a philosophic concept. We define democracy as a social arrangement in which all members of a group share equally in determining which freedoms and restraints shall apply. It is presumed that, in general, freedoms and restraints shall apply with the same force to all. But democracy must allow for the granting of special powers for special purposes (as in the case of its executive officers). If we think of democracy as a system of *equally limited* freedom, characterized by shared decisions regarding which specific rules are to prevail, then we have a simple criterion for distinguishing democracy from other social arrangements. A social system may provide *unlimited* freedoms, in which case it is called anarchy. Or it may provide *unequally limited* freedoms, in which case it is called autocracy.

A democratic group is self-governing. But it must provide for situations where disagreement occurs. Ideally, democratic decisions are by consensus, i.e., mutually agreeable decisions reached through discussion and compromise. Then, by common consent, action is taken. If consensus is not possible, a democratic group votes. Each person has an equal vote, and a majority vote wins. Votes are taken to facilitate action, not to enforce belief.

Successful and permanent operation of democracy seems to require that a group maintain certain conditions which, although not a part of the central idea of democracy, contribute to its functioning. For example, if participation is to be full and free, a group must establish an accepting atmosphere—an atmosphere in which every member is considered important and has his opinions guaranteed a hearing. Participation implies rea-

---

[12] See I. H. Pearse and Lucy H. Crocker, *The Peckham Experiment,* Allen & Unwin, 1943.

sonable freedom of communication, and freedom of speech and thought. If any single individual or minority group gains disproportionate control over agencies of communication and opinion, the society has lost equality of participation in decision making.

It would also seem that, if a democratic society is to survive over time, a majority of its members must learn to make reflective decisions where socially important questions are involved. A democratic society assumes competence on the part of its members; any different assumption would lead to distrust and rejection of the principle of equal participation. We assume that without wise leadership no society can solve its problems and endure. In a democracy wise leadership is a function of wise citizenship. If democracy is to survive, its members must take steps to insure that the principle of reflection is employed as widely as possible in making choices of group concern. Among other things, this means that a democracy should always be in the process of reducing the number and extent of its closed areas.

The Role of Democratic Leadership

Behavior of a group is influenced significantly by its leaders. Particularly if a group is immature, its over-all emotional and intellectual climate and its direction and extent of growth depend largely on the conduct of its leadership. As a group matures, it becomes less dependent on particular leaders. It develops capacity to produce leaders from its own ranks and reject and select leaders according to need.

The role of democratic leadership is to *help a group realize its own potentialities for growth*. Such a statement becomes meaningful only when growth is defined in operational terms. One attempt at definition specifies a number of "dimensions" of group growth, including the following:[13]

1. Progress toward fuller intercommunication among members. This includes growing acceptance and understanding by members of mechanics of language, with particular reference to meaning.
2. Progress toward viewing objectively the functioning of the group. This includes ability of all members to make and accept interpretations about member and group functioning and ability to collect and use pertinent information about itself.
3. Progress toward developing shared responsibilities. This includes growth toward a sharing of leadership functions, participation in setting goals, and cooperation in achievement of goals.
4. Progress toward developing group cohesion. Cohesion should be ade-

[13] National Training Laboratory in Group Development, *Report of the Second Summer Laboratory*, Washington, D. C., Department of Adult Education, 1948, pp. 113–114.

quate to permit assimilation of new ideas without group disintegration, assimilation of new members in a way to strengthen rather than disrupt the group, holding to long-range goals when a situation requires, and making constructive use of internal conflicts.

5. Progress toward developing ability to inform itself, to think straight, and to make creative decisions about problems. This includes learning to make full use of the contribution potential of all members, to detect and correct fallacies in group thinking.

What specific functions does a democratic leader perform if a group is to move in these directions? He may execute or administer, serve as judge or arbiter, be an advocate (or shaper of opinion), or render expert advice. He may also play the role of discussion leader. Although a discussion leader may on occasion assume any of the above roles, his function is distinctively different from and more inclusive than any of them. He helps a group to achieve self-growth. Or, as one writer puts it, he tries to "release the creative talents of the members of a group, help them solve their own problems, and reach their own decisions."[14]

Some Significant Experiments with Groups

We have already mentioned the experiments in group climate conducted at the Iowa Child Welfare Research Station by Ronald Lippitt and Ralph K. White. In this study matched groups of 11-year-old boys were subjected to variations in leadership and resulting behavior was noted. Leadership conformed to three contrasting patterns, defined as authoritarian, laissez-faire, and democratic.

Perhaps the greatest significance of these experiments for our purposes rests in the light they throw on insightful outcomes of three possible types of leadership situations. For example, work habits learned under democratic leadership, more than those learned under authoritarian leadership, may have significant carry-over into situations where an adult leader is not present. That is, learning in a democratic group "cuts deeper." However, results of these experiments should not be regarded as conclusive or as suggesting characteristics of "basic human nature." They involved groups having rather special purposes and boys who were products of a culture which prides itself on being democratic. It would have been surprising if these boys had not preferred and functioned better under democratic leadership.

Another group of experiments pertaining to our general theme include those in food use made during World War II, likewise conducted at the Child Welfare Research Station of the University of Iowa. In this case,

[14] Haiman, *op. cit.*, p. 71.

the effects on behavior of lecture and group discussion were compared. Three adult groups of housewives were lectured on nutritional value and contribution to war effort of wider use of beef hearts, sweetbreads, and kidneys. Three other groups *discussed* the problem of getting "housewives in general" to make greater use of these foods and as groups resolved to make use of them in their own families. A resource person who could supply recipes and other information was available to each discussion group.

Of the women listening to the lecture, only 3 percent who had never before served the meats served one of them. Of the women in the discussion groups, 32 percent who had never before served the meats served one of them. Apparently discussion followed by group decision was much more effective than lectures in producing behavioral change. Experiments designed to increase home consumption of milk showed similar results.[15]

Lewin also cites experiments designed to test the relative effectiveness of individual instruction compared with group discussion and decision. In this case, a number of mothers received individual instruction on medically approved practices of feeding infants. Other mothers were formed in groups, received instructions, and then were given an opportunity for discussion and group decision. In this experiment, discussion and group resolve were found to be much more effective than individual instruction in producing behavioral change. We are reminded of experience in group psychotherapy, cited earlier, which indicated that group situations may sometimes be more effective than individual counseling in producing changes in beliefs and behavior.

Lewin concludes that, if group discussion and decision are to produce significant change, leadership must be democratic. It must avoid high-pressure methods and be sensitive to resistance to change. The burden of decision must be placed on group members themselves. Change is likely to be greater, too, if a goal is set on which consensus is possible; majority rule is less effective because minority members who are outvoted sometimes deliberately resist the decision. An object in achieving change is not to apply pressure from outside but to remove counterforces within individuals. Such removal seems to occur best in relatively permissive group situations.

It was also found that less resistance is encountered if subjects are asked to discuss a problem as it relates to other persons, e.g., "How might it be possible to induce the housewives of the nation to use more milk?" Then they do not feel that their own habits are being selected as objects of criticism. This approach reduces resistance to a serious consideration of

15 For a description and interpretation of these experiments and those described below, see Kurt Lewin, "Group Decision and Social Change," in Theodore Newcomb and Eugene Hartley, eds., *Readings in Social Psychology*, Holt, 1947, pp. 330–344.

opposing practices. As is evidenced by their own changed behaviors, group members seldom fail to apply the problem to their own situations.

We shall describe one other experiment which appears significant for teachers. Shaw reports an experiment conducted at Columbia University in which graduate students tackled problems individually and in groups. In each instance, small groups of students, working cooperatively on problems, attained a much higher proportion of correct answers than the same number of students working individually. Also, groups were able to solve problems cooperatively which were too difficult for students working individually to solve. Investigators attributed the results to a tendency of members of a group to criticize and cross-check suggestions raised within the group.[16]

In all the experiments cited, the groups employed were essentially democratic in structure and function, as we have defined this term. The implication is that in our culture a face-to-face group which is democratically structured permits its members to achieve greater ideological and behavioral change, and more permanent change, than any other acceptable organization for learning. Also, if we may generalize from rather scanty data, members of such groups tend to be more productive intellectually and to show more wisdom than individuals working alone. Further, they exhibit better "mental health"—as conventionally defined—than members of either authoritarian or laissez-faire groups.

HOW MAY CLASSROOM TEACHERS FUNCTION AS DEMOCRATIC LEADERS AND CLIMATE MAKERS?

In order to understand the task of teachers as it relates to the problem of creating open-mindedness and willingness to change beliefs and behaviors, we need to examine in detail how emotional blocking can prevent such changes. Only as a teacher understands the process of blocking and how it manifests itself can he take steps for its removal.

Deficiency of Perception as a Cause of "Closed Minds"

In just what way does blocking interfere with reflection? It might be supposed that, no matter how strong one's emotional attachment to a belief, if he is confronted with facts which clearly question it, then question it he must. Any other course would appear highly unreasonable. Yet a normally intelligent and perfectly sane person may seem blind to evidence which others find thoroughly convincing.

Such behavior is not to be interpreted as willful irrationality. We agree

[16] Marjorie Shaw, "A Comparison of Individuals and Small Groups in the Rational Solution of Complex Problems," in *ibid.*, pp. 304–315.

with Wertheimer when he says that human beings usually have a "willingness to face problems straight, a readiness to follow them up courageously and sincerely, a desire for improvement, in contrast with arbitrary, willful, or slavish attitudes."[17] What occurs, as a result of emotional blocking, apparently is *deficiency of perception, which is not understood by the person involved and which without help he cannot prevent or overcome.*

What is deficiency of perception? Answering this question raises complex technical as well as philosophical issues. At any given moment of consciousness a person has a "perceptual field." It is that part of his physical and psychological environment of which he is aware.

There is disagreement as to whether a person can directly perceive the physical, social, and psychological surroundings which are assumed to exist. Philosophical realists assume that he can. The position taken here is essentially that of field theory, which maintains that a person imposes *pattern, order, and meaning*—psychological reality—on the data of sense experience. This imposed pattern is what we mean by insight. Insights are dependent not only on the nature of the environment, or confronting situation, but also on the influence of one's experience and one's purposes at the time. Thus, in a given situation we cannot expect the insights of any two persons to be identical. Nor can we assume that for an individual any reality exists except the insights which he holds.

The literature of psychotherapy usually defines deficiency of perception as "loss of contact with reality." The goal of therapy is the re-establishment of accurate perception, or the re-establishment of contact with reality. What does this terminology mean? In the present book, when we say that perception is accurate, or that a person is in touch with reality, we mean that his insights are accurate guides to action. That is, they have been or can be verified experimentally or experientially. They are consistent with the verified data of past experience (*facts* as we use the term here) or they produce the consequences which a person anticipates when he acts on them. This is what we expect of any scientific theory.

When we say that a person is suffering from a deficiency of perception, we mean either that his insights are inconsistent with one another or that deductions made from them do not check with the data of observation. Now it is true that a person who is out of touch with reality may deduce consequences from a proposition and make observations to see if the anticipated events occur. But he is likely to make faulty deductions and faulty observations; that is, he is likely to claim the occurrence of events which a disinterested public cannot detect, or deny the occurrence of events which, to others, clearly happen.

Ideally, perception brings events of one's physical, social, and psycho-

[17] Max Wertheimer, *Productive Thinking,* Harper, 1945, p. 198.

logical environment into a person's consciousness with a minimum of distortion. But in normal life it is probable that most persons frequently perceive events which others do not and fail to perceive those which others do, or exaggerate or minimize the significance of events which they see. Rationalization, as defined in Chapter 12, is creating or disregarding facts in order to support a foregone conclusion. Most of the time it is quite unverbalized; in fact, when we become conscious that we are reading into a field what we want to see there instead of what might enable us to make more accurate predictions, we tend to become uncomfortable.

A person is especially likely to experience a deficiency of perception when he is under heavy emotional pressure. If he feels insecure or frightened, particularly with respect to the integrity of his own personality, he tries to read into the perceptual field whatever immediately appears most likely to restore his security. In other words, if he feels that a cherished belief is under attack, he will read the facts of perception in such a way as to protect and preserve the belief.

Deficiency in perception is most likely to occur in the closed areas of belief and value. Here a person simply *does not see facts as data.* To him they remain an insignificant—perhaps entirely undifferentiated—part of his perceptual field, bearing no relevance to the issue under consideration. Consequently, the facts do not change his thinking or behavior. We can hardly expect a person to incorporate data into his thinking when he remains unaware of their presence or significance. As Lewin says, "Since action is ruled by perception, a change in conduct presupposes that new facts and values are perceived."[18] Simply telling a person that data are there is often futile. If his perception does not permit him to see them, we must approach the problem in such a way as to remove the distorting factors.

We have not yet distinguished clearly the role of perceptual deficiency in blocking changes in behavior. Deficiency of perception may prevent changes in insight. But very often changes in insight appear to occur, without the accompanying changes in values (and their corresponding behaviors) which we would expect. When this is the case, it would follow from a theory of learning consistent with a cognitive-field view that other, competing insights remain which furnish warrant for the old values. In short, we assume that all values and related behaviors issue logically from insights, and the former will not change unless the latter change also. But a person may hold to competing and contradictory insights (with corresponding contradictory values and attraction toward contradictory behaviors). In this case, the insights, attitudes, and behaviors which seem most attractive at the time remain dominant.

[18] Lewin, *Resolving Social Conflicts,* p. 63.

With the foregoing interpretation we may explain a phenomenon noted earlier in the chapter, namely, that a person may appear to accept a new set of facts, opposed to what he has heretofore accepted, without *observable* changes in behavior (see p. 488). If we understand that an individual in such situations is dominated by one of two competing patterns of insights and corresponding behavioral sets, then clearly he is a victim of inconsistency, either recognized or unrecognized. Deficiency of perception in this case is a failure to recognize the inconsistency.

Once a person is aware of inconsistency, we assume that he will take steps to change one of the two competing outlooks (and its corresponding behavioral pull). But if he has a strong emotional need to follow his old (and, to disinterested observers, perhaps less wise) pattern of behavior, he is likely to try to minimize the conflict, to try to live with it, or to escape through some neurotic response. However this may be, it is apparent that failure to adjust behavior to what seems to be a change in insight indicates a problem of inconsistency and pedagogically it should be treated so. In a democratic school, such incompatibilities are studied reflectively.

What are the conditions under which perception achieves maximum accuracy? How can we set the stage so that a person will most easily adopt new outlooks or see his inconsistencies?

Insofar as experimental evidence allows an answer, it appears that the first requirement is a *nonthreatening* emotional atmosphere. We referred to this need for acceptable nonmenacing atmospheres earlier in the chapter as we discussed experience with psychotherapy and work with normal groups. What are the specific conditions of a nonthreatening climate? A *threat*, as the term is used here, is anything said or done by others which *appears to a learner* to jeopardize his present beliefs. It is the equivalent of an anticipated attack on the self. A normal individual wants to maintain a feeling of consistency and adequacy in his beliefs and values, which feeling is what we mean when we refer to integration or integrity of personality. A person's knowledges and values may be shot through with inconsistency and confusion, but if the person is not aware of this, he may continue to feel integrated. If he feels that someone is trying to destroy his integrity of self, he is likely to resist.

Rogers describes this problem very well: "Experience which, if assimilated, would involve a change in the organization of self tends to be resisted through denial or distortion of symbolization. The structure and organization of self appears to become more rigid under threat; to relax its boundaries when completely free from threat. Experience which is perceived as inconsistent with the self can only be assimilated if the current organization of the self is relaxed and expanded to include it."[19]

[19] Rogers, *Client-Centered Therapy*, p. 390.

For a climate to seem nonthreatening, it is necessary for a subject to feel that no one is trying to judge him. He needs to feel completely accepted. He is particularly likely to resist criticism if it comes from someone he regards as having arbitrary power and authority over him. He needs to feel complete freedom to express his opinions without danger of censure, no matter how ill formed or unorthodox they may be.

The type of climate in which a person feels so secure that he dares entertain evidence contrary to present knowledge and values seems best achieved in a small, face-to-face group in which warmth and considerable permissiveness have been deliberately cultivated. Some techniques which a teacher may use in creating such a situation, and in leading a class to change its views and behavior, are discussed in the following section.

Classroom Techniques for Assisting Conceptual and Behavioral Change

REDUCING THREAT AND PROMOTING OPEN-MINDEDNESS.   We have suggested that a student feels threat to his ego if he regards his beliefs as under fire. The intensity of threat depends on its source, its power, and the valuation placed on beliefs which are in jeopardy. Unless threat can be largely eliminated, a student is not likely to entertain evidence contrary to present beliefs or, when facts warrant, to change his mind. Several techniques are available for keeping a sense of threat to a minimum.

One rule is that a teacher should treat student opinions with respect. This does not necessarily mean that a teacher expresses approval; but he avoids ridicule or sarcasm, or any expressions which might be so interpreted by students. He does not cast aspersions on the intelligence or motives of students who render serious opinions. Opinions offered in good faith are taken for what they are—the best insights which students have been able to achieve up to then.

On occasion, as during relatively undirected discussion preceding serious study of an issue, it may be advisable for a teacher to give students plenty of opportunity to express the very beliefs which he hopes later to bring under question. It may even help for him to express considerable sympathy with these ideas, for the time being to "go along." Lewin, for example, recommends that a group leader may get farther by letting members of a group freely express the very values which he hopes to change because "a feeling of complete freedom and a heightened group identification are frequently more important at a particular stage of re-education than learning not to break specific rules."[20]

When a teacher wishes to challenge an opinion expressed by a student, he should do it in such a way that conflict is internalized. That is, the

[20] Lewin, *Resolving Social Conflicts*, p. 68.

student is made to feel the conflict within his own personality. He may not feel a problem, or at least not the problem which the learning situation demands, if he sees the conflict merely as a contest between him and someone else.

When a teacher wishes to contest the opinion of a student, he may best handle it something like this: "You have an opinion, and I think I understand and appreciate your reasons. But there are contrary opinions which are widely held in this country. I wonder if there is any merit in a point of view such as . . . ?" The student is thus asked to entertain, not an opinion of the teacher or a classmate, but simply an opinion which "some persons" hold. Experiments cited by Lewin and noted earlier in the chapter suggest that, when a group is presented with a problem to discuss, beliefs and behaviors contrary to those accepted by group members are more likely to be seriously entertained and later adopted if the problem is discussed with reference to persons other than themselves, at least in early phases of discussion.

Another means of inducing students to internalize conflict is to arrange the learning situation so that facts "speak for themselves." Other things being equal, facts—especially if impersonal, sharply relevant, and simple enough to be easily grasped—are more likely than expressions of opinion to break through an emotional barrier, particularly if the facts come to students in life situations. It may then only be necessary to remind a student of their relevance and their bearing on a problem. For example, a trip to a slum may speak eloquently against the notion that everyone is adequately housed, or the witnessing of a congressional investigation over TV may show quite convincingly that traditional American principles of fair play are not always employed. Lewin has suggested that "An individual will believe facts he himself has discovered in the same way he believes in himself or in his group."[21]

In most instances it probably pays to minimize, or at least not encourage, emphasis on personal opinion in discussion. Issues may be handled as issues and propositions discussed on their merits. The learning enterprise should focus on raising questions about what will come of acting in accordance with a given proposition or hypothesis. An opinion may be converted to a proposition by saying, "Here is an opinion which is before the class. Let us take it as a proposition to be tested. If it is true, what consequences may we deduce from it?" If propositions are relevant to beliefs of students, then students often make their own connections. Even though beliefs are not studied directly, significant revisions may come. It is necessary, of course, that students *see* connections; if emotional blocking prevents this, steps must be taken to expand perception. Perhaps only

21 *Ibid.*

mentioning the connections will be enough; perhaps patient effort will be needed further to reduce emotional barriers.

ENCOURAGING GROUP DECISION. A student is more likely to drop prejudices, revise his moral values, or make almost any other type of significant change if he is a member of a group *which is making the same change together.* Assuming that a teacher does all he can to produce a nonthreatening climate, what can be done to form a class into a true in-group, a "team," so to speak, and help them, as a team, to change basic outlooks?

Although significant learning may occur in discussion groups formed of strangers, learning in areas of strong prejudice (such as in the closed areas) seems more likely to occur in groups characterized by friendships and some degree of mutual intimacy. There may be sound pedagogical advantages in helping students become well acquainted with each other, whether simply through classroom informality or by deliberately fostering out-of-school contacts.

Cliques, self-contained groupings based on religious or social-class affiliations, racial groupings, or associations based on academic achievement may develop within any school and be reflected in a single classroom. Such groupings may entirely omit certain students, who in turn become social isolates. With development of subgroups of this sort, especially if chauvinistic attitudes are involved, a class may become badly split and team spirit difficult to achieve. If observation or use of sociometric devices suggests to a teacher that an unhealthy social situation exists in his classroom, he should take steps to alleviate it.[22]

In establishing group feeling, there are possible advantages to be gained from group study and group projects. When this sort of thing is attempted, it is usually necessary to divide a class into small groups and to see that the same students do not always work together. A committee system can ordinarily be made to work fairly well for gathering information. Whether it can be made to function in reflective evaluation of data and the productive solution of problems depends on the maturity of students and their familiarity with the rules of reflection. Generally, a teacher must be central to reflective deliberation if it is to be productive.

Encouragement of full and free communication among members will heighten the cohesiveness of a group. If students understand each other, they will almost inevitably work together better as a group. A teacher should urge and help students to state opinions and propositions meaningfully. He should discourage use of emotive language, particularly when students are inclined to direct personal jibes at each other. He should

[22] One of the most useful references on means of analyzing the social structure of groups and techniques to use in establishing greater cohesiveness is Helen Hall Jennings, *Sociometry in Group Relations: A Work Guide for Teachers,* American Council on Education, 1949.

make certain that every member has a chance to be heard and is correctly interpreted.

Although important, these suggestions concerning the development of "groupness" are peripheral to the problem. In a given learning situation, group spirit probably hinges primarily on whether all members of a class feel personally involved in the problem under study. If motivation to study a problem is high, a common interest exists which transcends lack of acquaintance, clique interests, or personal antagonisms. In the final analysis, whether group spirit is achieved at the point where it is needed—where a problem is to be studied and beliefs are to be changed—depends largely on a teacher's skill in focusing effort on a common goal.

No matter how great their internal rapport, groups do not change beliefs automatically. As we have observed, the most effectual situation for producing group change appears to be a democratically led discussion. For purposes of this analysis, probably the most important requirement of discussion (or other modes of study) designed to change basic attitudes is that it have the quality of freely permitting self-learning. (This should not be taken to mean absence of directedness.) We have already noted, in our discussion of threatening situations, that students resist outside pressure to change opinions. As Lewin has indicated the object in achieving change is not to apply pressure from outside but to remove counterforces within the individual.[23]

Although a teacher can and usually must help in eliminating these counterforces, students must perform the actual removal. If they can explore a problem independently, feeling no authoritarian pressure from above to explore it in a particular way or emerge with particular conclusions, they are much more likely than otherwise to undergo real and permanent changes in conceptual patterns. They need to be encouraged to use investigatory techniques of their own, to explore by themselves provocative readings, trips, interviews, radio and TV programs, and the like. A teacher's role here is to suggest possible directions of exploration and to help students evaluate facts which are exposed.

For maximum change, permissive discussion of problems should culminate in group decisions. That is, in addition to discussing and studying a problem, students as a group should consider what conclusions are warranted, what the conclusions mean to them, and what if anything they intend to do about them. Students need to communicate their views to each other, so that intentions of each are known to all. If it is evident to individuals that most members of a group have revised their outlooks and expect to change their behavior in stated ways, then members who are reluctant to change because of long-standing attachment to certain be-

[23] Lewin, "Group Decision and Social Change," in *Readings in Social Psychology*, p. 342.

liefs may find change easier. This should not be interpreted to mean that a group or its leader should pressure individual members to accept conformity. We are referring to changes which individuals see the logic of making but find difficult because of opposing forces. The opposing forces are often social pressures exerted by peer culture, community mores, or parental dictates. These may be combated more successfully if a student feels that others intend to combat them with him.

Ideally, group decision should represent common consensus. Proposed changes in belief should be kept within the bounds of what is possible for all. If a group is in agreement on the rules of reflective methodology, if it confines its learning operations to the testing of propositions which may be defined operationally, and if the threat-removing techniques employed by a teacher are sufficient so that without serious inhibitions all students are able to examine pertinent facts, then at least some degree of consensus is likely. This point of view assumes that for many problems there will be at a given time a "best" answer, in the sense that one hypothesis, more than any other, will adequately harmonize data relevant to it. This is a denial of the common belief that "every problem has two sides" and the further implication that "one opinion is as good as another." Of course, if the perplexity is of such nature that consensus based on reflection is impossible, no attempt should be made by a teacher to force it.

A Teacher's Role in a Democratic Classroom

Within a democratic framework there is room for disagreement as to the amount of centralized direction which is required. According to definitions previously suggested, a democratic group is distinctively different from a laissez-faire or authoritarian group. It would seem as unreasonable to try to establish these as completely hard-and-fast categories as any other differentiated concepts. A democratic group might, under certain circumstances, operate with a minimum of centralized leadership and appear to approach the laissez-faire extreme. On the other hand, it might delegate to particular persons positions of such authority as to appear to approach the authoritarian norm. (The former extreme might be illustrated in a small adult study group, the latter in a democratic nation which, during a war, grants extraordinary powers to its executive branch.)

We would place a nondirective discussion group, as defined by Rogers and others, near the laissez-faire end of our scale. We would hesitate, however, to place such a group outside the democratic framework. Although under certain circumstances it may resemble anarchy (which is not necessarily the same as chaos), a nondirective group may also produce firm leadership from within its own ranks and formulate and pursue purposes with dispatch and efficiency. When nondirection is employed with an immature group, however, such an outcome is doubtful.

We would place an ordinary classroom, as dominated by a textbook-recitation procedure and arbitrary decision making by a teacher, near the authoritarian end of the scale. This is not to suggest that, if a teacher has certain types of authority over students, a teaching-learning situation necessarily violates democratic practice. We shall try to show how such authority may be compatible with democracy. Many classrooms, however, gravitate in structure and pattern of leadership toward the concept of an authoritarian group, as defined in experiments by Lippitt and White.

It is not enough simply to say that in a classroom a democratic pattern is preferable. Democracy in a classroom and democracy in adult discussion or psychotherapeutic groups ordinarily take different forms. In examining the form of democracy in a classroom the following points are pertinent:

1. Although it gives us valuable clues with respect to the dynamics of emotion, experience with therapeutic groups is not fully applicable in classrooms. A typical group of students is composed chiefly of normal persons. The conceptual structure of an ordinary student is often inadequate in the sense that it is a poor guide to behavior, owing to erroneous, incomplete, and contradictory concepts. But concepts of a typical student are certainly not so inaccurate as to be largely unusable, as is the case with psychotic persons or incapacitated neurotics. Conflicts may be troublesome for ordinary high school and college students and emotional disturbance may become conspicuous at times, but we do not expect to find deep neuroses. Basically, then, persons with whom a teacher works are different from those with whom a professional therapist deals.

This difference, between normality and abnormality, immediately suggests some differences in the job of a leader. Emotional blocking which might prevent reflection is probably much easier to remove in a normal group than in an abnormal group. A psychotherapist working with abnormals must usually use extreme and time-consuming methods in order to relieve repression to a point where insights can become reliable predictive tools. Furthermore, a private counseling session or a small discussion group of disturbed adults led by a psychiatrist represents a situation where more drastic means for relieving inhibition may be used. The mores of our culture do not tolerate in school classrooms the freedom of expression which can be permitted in a true therapeutic group. Whenever catharsis requires that a person talk freely about deep personal issues which would seem shocking or embarrassing to others, the case is one not for a teacher but for a trained therapist. One major difference, then, between a class and a therapeutic group is that the former will be less free to delve deeply into personal problems, less free to tolerate extreme and shocking expressions of opinion.

Thus, it is both possible and desirable in a classroom to place more emphasis on intellectual experience and less upon catharsis than is done in a therapeutic group. It seems preferable to think of the expression of emotion—of catharsis—as a *tool* for achieving conceptualization rather than as an end in itself. What we want in a classroom is an increase in amount and an improvement in quality of thinking. Emotional release is to be encouraged only as it helps to achieve reflection.

In the literature of client-centered psychotherapy we find the opinion that, if a patient is placed in a nonthreatening, accepting climate and allowed to talk freely about his problems, he will by himself gain more adequate insights. In a classroom, however, a good psychological climate and free discussion are not usually enough to produce accurate insight *because of the difference in learning goals and type of problems discussed.* In a classroom many of the problems treated involve complex social issues and complicated and extensive evidence. Many of the data required to work with them successfully are unknown to students. Although relatively undirected discussion may be desirable to get issues into the open, to expose data from the prior experience of pupils, and to reduce repression, it is not enough. If students do not know what a tariff is, for example, such discussion will not make them more intelligent about tariff issues. A teacher must be in charge to lead discussion, inject criticism, suggest research, provide basic data, and in general head the learning enterprise.

2. How far can we go in applying to the classroom principles of democratic leadership as developed through experiences of the democratic group-leadership movement? First, a classroom can and should be fully as democratic as any adult group. There are impelling reasons: school may be the only part of a child's environment where he has a chance to experience, by living it, the meaning of democracy. All too often he experiences authoritarian practices in home, church, and part-time employment. Not that a person must necessarily be able to live democratically in order to learn to appreciate democracy; it is conceivable that while in a concentration camp a person could learn to appreciate democracy deeply. But probably a child is more likely to understand and value democracy through direct experience with it than in any other way.

Once having stated the necessity for democracy in classrooms, we must make certain qualifications. In a democratic society every member has an equal share in determining the goals and behavioral rules of the society, an equal share in deciding which freedoms and restraints are to apply. But this democratic principle applies only to the larger group, i.e., the entire society, which may limit the jurisdiction of its own subgroupings in any way it pleases. For example, jurisdiction over certain matters is left to adults, under the assumption that children are not competent to decide some things. Within the limits of their jurisdiction, students should have the same right of equal participation in decision making as adults.

Let us explore further the question of jurisdiction. Adults have seen fit in various ways to limit the overt behavior of children. For example, children are not permitted to destroy property, to flout community mores, or to loaf through school (when it can be helped). The adult community holds teachers responsible for seeing that the actions of children conform to these rules. In this sense a teacher is a representative, or agent, of the larger community. Although a democratic teacher will encourage his students to discuss problems of behavior, independently formulate rules which are reasonably compatible with those of the larger community, and obey them voluntarily, he must retain the right to overrule students if necessary. On some questions a teacher's vote must remain a majority vote—but only where matters of action or overt behavior are concerned. It is presumed that in a democratic school freedom of thought among students is not restricted; students have exactly the same freedom as adult groups. However, even this statement requires qualification.

We have assumed that, if a democratic society is to govern itself wisely, the principle of reflection will be a necessary adjunct of democratic life. We have assumed further that, *if a democratic society is to live into the future,* the principle of reflection must be extended into all problem areas which seriously threaten democracy. Now not all adult members of a democratic society will agree that these needs exist. Many persons may reject reflection and the critical study of certain areas of controversy. But probably a majority of adult Americans do uphold the principle of reflection and the necessity of free and critical thought in all areas of general social concern. If this is the case, then teachers may be regarded as agents of the larger community in acquainting students with the rules of accurate thinking and in encouraging them to think seriously about the most troublesome issues. Even when a local community objects to such practices, a teacher's responsibility to the larger group would seem to obligate him, insofar as he is able, to select methodology and content which are reflective and socially important.

Students in a self-governing classroom might select learning experiences capable of making effective citizens of them; but again they might not. Whether or not students want to think, a teacher must be an instigator of thought. If they want to, the job is easier; if they don't, a teacher has to arouse the desire to think. Whether or not students want to study critical social issues, a teacher must see that, to the best of their ability, they do.

The obligations of leaders in adult democratic groups are no different from the obligations of teachers. But because of their greater competence all members of an adult group presumably are capable to some degree of assuming leadership roles. Although in given cases they may not be, members of adult groups are often somewhat acquainted with reflective problem solving and in a position to decide wisely which problems they should pursue. Student groups, on the other hand, are less mature, less cognizant of the meaning of reflection, less aware of troublesome issues in the culture. By and large, therefore, teachers must play a more dominant role than leaders of adult groups.

BIBLIOGRAPHY

Beukenkamp, Cornelius, Jr., *Fortunate Strangers*, Rinehart, 1958.
A fascinating account of an experiment in group psychotherapy, as told by a psychiatrist. Principles for handling a relatively permissive discussion may be inferred.
Bion, W. R., *Experiences in Groups*, Basic Books, 1961.
Bonner, Hubert, *Group Dynamics*, Ronald, 1959.
One of the best general texts in the field. Covers history of research on groups and present status of group work.
Cartwright, Dorwin, and Alvin Zander, eds., *Group Dynamics*, rev. ed., Row, Peterson, 1960.
A collection of readings, all of which are relevant to this chapter. Readers will detect a strong Lewinian influence. A very useful reference.
Cartwright, Dorwin, ed., *Group Dynamics, Research and Theory*, Row, Peterson, 1956.
An unusually useful collection of readings. Comprehensive.
Fullagar, William A., and others, *Readings for Educational Psychology*, Crowell, 1956.
Cited at end of Chapter 15. Part III bears rather steadily on the foregoing chapter. Good readings.
Haiman, Franklin S., *Group Leadership and Democratic Action*, Houghton Mifflin, 1951.
A superior general treatment of how democratic group leadership can operate.
Krech, David, and Richard S. Crutchfield, *Theory and Problems of Social Psychology*, McGraw-Hill, 1948.
A difficult but rewarding text in social psychology. Reflects a largely consistent field psychology.
Lewin, Kurt, *Resolving Social Conflicts*, Harper, 1948.
A fundamental reference. Lewin's experimental work paved the way for much that is now known about the dynamics of groups.
Miles, Matthew B., *Learning to Work in Groups*, Teachers College, Columbia University, 1959.
The contributions of many experimental and research studies of the nature of group dynamics brought together and focused on the process of helping people to learn to work in groups.

Rogers, Carl, *Client-Centered Therapy*, Houghton Mifflin, 1951.
   A pioneering work which every prospective teacher should read. Chapters 8 and 9 deal specifically with teaching.
Sherif, Muzafer, and Carolyn W. Sherif, *An Outline of Social Psychology*, rev. ed., Harper, 1956.
   A textbook which includes a wealth of material on the dynamics of small groups. One of the best books in this area. See especially Part III, but most of the remainder of the book is relevant to this course.
Slavson, Samuel R., ed., *The Fields of Group Psychotherapy*, International Universities Press, 1956.
   A collection of papers covering a wide range of problem areas. Each author explains how group counseling can be used to treat a specific category of problems.
Warters, Jane, *Group Guidance, Principles and Practices*, McGraw-Hill, 1960.
   Good general textbook which treats the fundamental principles of working with groups.

INDEX OF NAMES

Italicized numbers indicate bibliographical lists.

511

INDEX OF SUBJECTS